Crimes and Trials of
the Century

Crimes and Trials of the Century

VOLUME 1

From the Black Sox Scandal to the Attica Prison Riots

Edited by
Steven Chermak
and
Frankie Y. Bailey

199.95 (2 vols)

GREENWOOD PRESS
Westport, Connecticut · London

Library of Congress Cataloging-in-Publication Data

Crimes and trials of the century / Edited by Steven Chermak and Frankie Y. Bailey.
  p. cm.
Includes bibliographical references and index.
  ISBN: 978–0–313–34109–0 (set: alk. paper)
ISBN: 978–0–313–34110–6 (v. 1 : alk. paper)
ISBN: 978–0–313–34111–3 (v. 2 : alk. paper)
1. Trials (Political crimes and offenses)—United States. 2. Criminal justice, Administration of—United States
—Cases. 3. Criminal justice, Administration of—United States—History. 4. Trials (Murder)—United States.
5. Trials (Kidnapping)—United States. 6. Trials (Espionage)—United States. I. Chermak, Steven M. II. Bailey,
Frankie Y.
KF221.P6C75 2007
345.73'02—dc22   2007030704

British Library Cataloguing in Publication Data is available.

Library of Congress Catalog Card Number: 2007030704
ISBN: 978–0–313–34109–0 (set)
ISBN: 978–0–313–34110–6 (vol. 1)
ISBN: 978–0–313–34111–3 (vol. 2)

First published in 2007

Greenwood Press, 88 Post Road West, Westport, CT 06881
An imprint of Greenwood Publishing Group, Inc.
www.greenwood.com

Printed in the United States of America

♾™

The paper used in this book complies with the
Permanent Paper Standard issued by the National
Information Standards Organization (Z39.48–1984).

10 9 8 7 6 5 4 3 2 1

Contents

Preface to the Set

Crimes and Trials of the Century covers a little over one hundred years of American history, from 1900 to the present. The cases in this two volume set appear in roughly chronological order, based on the starting point of the events described. The reader will note that some cases, such as the 1955 Emmett Till case, are revisited by criminal justice authority years later. The Till case, the Columbine High School shootings case, and many of the other cases that appear in this set had an intense impact on public consciousness at the time of occurrence and remain a part of our "cultural memory." These cases are prone to be referenced during current social and political debates.

In the introductions to the two volumes in this set, we discuss the social and historical contexts in which the cases appearing in the volume occurred. We discuss the evolution of the criminal justice system and the legal issues that were dominant during that time period. We also provide an overview of the popular culture and mass media, examining in brief the nexus between news/entertainment and the criminal justice system. In each introduction, we also identify the common threads weaving through the cases in the volume.

As suggested above, the cases featured in these two volumes provide examples of what Robert Hariman (1990) describes as "popular trials," or "trials that have provided the impetus and the forum for major public debates" (p. 1). As we note elsewhere, cases generally achieve celebrity status because they somehow encapsulate the tensions and the anxieties present in our society; or, at least, this has been the case until the recent past. In the past half-century, the increasing importance of television (and more recently the Internet) in delivering the news to the public, and the voracious appetite of the media for news stories to feed the twenty-four-hour news cycle, has meant that stories—particularly crime stories—move quickly into, and sometimes as quickly out of, the public eye. The cases we have selected for this two-volume set are those that arguably deserve the title of a "crime of the century" because of the social and legal issues that each case embodies.

These cases for one reason or another touched a public nerve at the time when they occurred and continue to resonate with modern readers. We think that readers will agree that the cases included in these two volumes are among the most important of the twentieth and early twentieth-first centuries. Since space was limited, some famous cases had to be excluded. The chapters about the cases that are included cover the crime, the setting, and the participants; the actions taken by law enforcement and the criminal legal system; the actions of the media covering the case; the trial (if there was one); the final resolution of the case; the relevant social, political, and legal issues; and, finally, the significance of the case and its impact on legal and popular culture.

The reader will notice that each contributor has included "sidebars" to accompany his or her case. These sidebars provide additional information that will assist the reader in placing the case in context. The sidebars in the various chapters provide a variety of information, including timelines, additional background on key persons, related cases, key terms and concepts, and "fun facts."

Each contributor also provides a short list of books of "Suggestions for Further Reading" at the end of his or her chapter. These lists are provided for readers who would like to go beyond the overview and discussion of the case provided in the volume. Although each contributor has been thorough, each case could well be the subject of a book and many of them have been. Readers intrigued by a case may enjoy pursuing their interest with the suggested books.

Finally, at the end of Volume 2 in this set, readers will find a "General Bibliography" that provides a longer list of books compiled by the co-editors of this set. These books and articles are provided for readers who have a broader interest in crime history and the media. A comprehensive index completes the set.

REFERENCE

Hariman, R. (1990). *Popular trials: Rhetoric, mass media, and the law.* Tuscaloosa, AL: University of Alabama Press.

Introduction to Volume 1

FRANKIE Y. BAILEY AND STEVEN CHERMAK

On September 14, 1901, Theodore Roosevelt became the twenty-sixth president of the United States. He rose to the presidency not by election but because President William McKinley, with whom he had served as vice president, had died from complications following surgery. McKinley had been the victim of an assassin, a young man named Leon Czolgosz. Czolgosz had shot McKinley twice with a gun concealed in a handkerchief when McKinley reached out to shake hands as he greeted Czolgosz in a receiving line. The attack happened during McKinley's visit to the Pan-American Exposition in Buffalo, New York.

The fallen president was taken to a hospital on the Exposition grounds in an electric ambulance. That he should travel in such a modern invention was in keeping with McKinley's status as the first president of the twentieth century. McKinley was the first president to use the telephone for campaign purposes. He was also the first president to be followed about by newsreel cameramen who recorded his comings and goings. Although he himself had served in the Civil War, McKinley at his death presided over a country that, for better or worse, in the aftermath of the Spanish-American War had become an imperial power with colonial possessions.

The life story of the man who assassinated him reflected the waves of immigration to the United States that occurred in the nineteenth century. Leon Czolgosz's father had arrived from Prussia in 1873, and Leon himself was born in Michigan. Although the family seemed to be pursuing the "American dream," Czolgosz's growing disillusionment with capitalism eventually led him to his encounter with the president (Butler, 2004). McKinley's death and Czolgosz's subsequent trial and execution at Auburn Prison in New York State set the tone for a century of violent crimes that would sometimes shock the nation.

Although the assassination of McKinley plunged the country into mourning and attracted massive media coverage, the first murder case that was widely identified as "the crime of the century" was the Harry Thaw–Stanford White murder case. The heir of a vast Pittsburgh coal and railroad fortune, Thaw shot the famed New York City architect Stanford White to death. Thaw claimed that he had been avenging the lost chastity of his wife, Evelyn Nesbit, the beautiful "Gibson Girl" model and former *Floradora* chorus girl who had been involved with White prior to her marriage to Thaw. Evelyn Nesbit had also grown up in Pittsburgh. After moving with her mother to Philadelphia to begin her career, Nesbit arrived in New York City. The two women hoped that Evelyn's beauty would be the key to their upward mobility. Evelyn married a wealthy man, but with Stanford White's murder, she found herself at the center of a scandalous triangle.

Notoriously unstable, Thaw shot White to death on June 25, 1906, in the rooftop theater at Madison Square Garden (a building that White had designed), in front of a roomful of witnesses. Bringing the wealth of the family fortune to bear, the Thaw family launched a public relations campaign aimed at portraying Thaw, the murder defendant, as a man defending his wife's honor. *The New York Times* observed that Thaw's trial was being reported "to the ends of the civilized globe" (Carlson, 2003).

During the trial, Evelyn Nesbit Thaw took the stand to describe her drugged rape by White and the relationship that had ensued. She provided titillating details of White's fancies that led the press to dub her "the Girl in the Red Velvet Swing." This was a case that was ideal for the "yellow journalism" of the period that thrived on sensation and violence. Readers were offered a peek into the lives of the occupants of the opulent houses that White had designed and in which he and his clients lived. Readers also were presented with a portrait of New York City, a metropolis that even mid-nineteenth century observers had described as a city of both opportunities and dangers.

Twenty years later another New York City murder triangle tantalized the public. This time, there was no hint of wealth or fame. The story in itself was rather mundane; a housewife and her lover had killed her husband. But the Ruth Snyder–Judd Gray murder trial occurred during the "roaring twenties," when "jazz journalism" was the new phrase coined to describe the sensational coverage of sex, violence, and scandal (Emery & Emery, 1984, pp. 387–389). The impact of Freudian psychoanalysis on American culture was evident in the testimony of "alienists" (psychiatrists) as expert witnesses who offered their evaluations of the two murderers who had turned on each other after confessing to the crime and now faced each other in a courtroom (Douglas, 1995, pp. 126–127)

Ruth Snyder was unsuccessful in her attempt to present herself as a loving mother and the wife of a cold, abusive husband. With the increasing importance of photographs, Ruth Snyder was unable to overcome the media images of a woman who was alleged to be "too stylish" and a "brassy blonde." The final photograph of Snyder is the most famous. It is the one that a photographer who had gained admission to the death chamber with press credentials snapped of Snyder at the moment of her death in the electric chair. The photograph gave the public a forbidden glimpse of the executions that in the twentieth century occurred behind prison walls (Bailey & Hale, 2004, pp. 128–133).

Other crimes in the early twentieth century were equally scandalous and attracted as much media coverage. The chapters in this volume cover crimes of the twentieth century that are worthy of note for what they tell us about their eras and about the interaction of media and the criminal justice system. As we note in the Introduction to Volume II, examination of these famous cases reveals certain recurring themes. In these cases from 1900 to 1972, the themes include: (1) the falls of celebrities; (2) national security; (3) notorious gangsters; (4) legal debates; and (5) turbulent social change.

THE FALLS OF CELEBRITIES

The century had begun with a president, Theodore Roosevelt, who epitomized rugged masculinity. Young men and boys were increasingly involved in competitive team sports. For spectators, these team sports were sources of both entertainment and civic pride as they rooted for the "home team" (Chudacoff, 1999, pp. 224–228). In Chapter 1, Jason Ingram recounts the fall from glory of the famed Chicago White Sox baseball team. In 1919, eight players from the team were accused of throwing the World Series against the Cincinnati Reds. With its reputation darkened by the scandal, the team was nicknamed "the Black Sox."

Two years later, in another widely heralded fall from grace, Roscoe "Fatty" Arbuckle, a beloved film comedian, found himself at the center of a scandal following a Labor Day weekend party in his hotel room. In the glare of the media, Fatty Arbuckle stood trial, accused of a sexual attack on one of his female guests that led to her death. As Matthew Pate relates in Chapter 4, the case was cast as symbolic of Hollywood decadence. It came at a time when critics were expressing increasing concern about sex and violence in the budding Hollywood film industry. The case would be linked in the censorship debates to other scandals involving celebrities, including the unsolved murder of film director William Desmond Taylor in 1922.

In another celebrity case, Colonel Charles A. Lindbergh, the man who had become an American hero by flying solo across the Atlantic, became a grieving father when his young son was kidnapped and murdered. Before the tragedy, Lindbergh and his beautiful and accomplished wife, Anne Morrow Lindbergh, had been in the media spotlight as a young couple who seemed to have a charmed life. In Chapter 9, Kelly Wolf discusses the kidnapping/murder and its aftermath, when the accused, Bruno Hauptmann, stood trial. Hauptmann, an illegal immigrant from Germany, faced a hostile public. At the same time, Lindbergh and his wife were dealing with the intense and pervasive media presence that had threatened to hamper the kidnapping investigation as it was underway and now gave them no privacy. The presence of newsreel cameras offered the public who could not be present in the crowded courtroom in New Jersey an opportunity to witness the trial. The carnival atmosphere surrounding the trial became an example of what observers saw as the dangerous impact of the media on the criminal justice process.

NATIONAL SECURITY

In Chapter 2, Lisa Sacco examines the Sacco and Vanzetti case in which two Italian immigrants were accused of a payroll robbery and the murders of the paymaster and his guard. Nicola Sacco and Bartolomeo Vanzetti went to trial in the aftermath of the 1919 "Red Scare." During the "Scare," United States Attorney General A. Mitchell Palmer ordered the roundup of suspected communists and anarchists who he believed were threatening the security of the United States. The fact that Sacco and Vanzetti were Italian immigrants and alleged anarchists worked against them as they stood trial in Massachusetts and as they appealed their death sentences.

In 1948, Alger Hiss also faced doubts about his loyalty to the United States. However, Hiss's circumstances were markedly different from those of immigrants Sacco and Vanzetti. In Chapter 10, Matthew Pate recounts the complex story of Hiss, who had served with distinction in the federal government and found himself accused of being a spy. As the House Un-American Activities Committee conducted its investigation of suspected Communists, Hiss was accused of being an operative who had passed classified government documents to agents of the Soviet Union.

By 1951, Cold War tensions between the United States and the Soviet Union prompted increased concern about the possibility of betrayals by American citizens. Ethel and Julius Rosenberg stood accused of giving secrets to Russian agents that might have aided an enemy of the United States in developing its atom bomb. As Ernest Nickels discusses in Chapter 11, the question of the Rosenbergs' guilt or innocence remains a matter of debate decades after their deaths. The same may be said of Sacco and Vanzetti and Alger Hiss.

NOTORIOUS GANGSTERS

Cultural historians assert that Americans (in common with people of other nations) have always been ambivalent about "outlaws." In the mythology of the American west, the legends of outlaws such as Billy the Kid and Jesse James rivaled those of lawmen such as Wyatt Earp and Bat Masterson. The dime novels and pulp fiction of the nineteenth and early twentieth century featured "good bad men" as heroes. As print tales about lawmen and outlaws became the basis for films about cops and robbers, this fascination with outlaw protagonists remained. Prohibition and the rise of gangsters who supplied the liquor that many Americans were still eager to consume gave impetus to the depiction of gangsters in the news and entertainment media.

In Chicago, Al Capone eliminated his rivals to rise to the top among Prohibition gangsters. In Chapter 3, Joseph Deleeuw examines Capone's involvement in episodes such as the "St. Valentine's Day Massacre," which enhanced Capone's reputation as a ruthless gangster. Capone's exploits inspired both newspaper coverage and radio and film versions of his story. Federal agent Elliot Ness was cast as Capone's arch nemesis and was determined to bring Capone to justice.

The reputation of the Federal Bureau of Investigation (FBI), headed by J. Edgar Hoover, grew as the Bureau pursued urban mobsters such as Capone and rural gangsters such as John Dillinger. In Dillinger's case, his fondness for smiling into a camera enhanced his reputation as a dapper outlaw. In one episode, Dillinger posed for a photo with the female sheriff who had arrested him. This photo became a mocking testament to Dillinger's slipperiness when he later escaped in the sheriff's car (Bailey & Hale, 1998, p. 157).

In similar fashion, Bonnie and Clyde contributed to their own reputation as outlaws by helping to construct their media images. In Chapter 7, Leana Allen Bouffard examines the life and times of Clyde Barrow and Bonnie Parker, Depression-era outlaws who robbed banks. They were immortalized for a modern film audience in *Bonnie and Clyde* (1967), starring Warren Beatty and Faye Dunaway. During her lifetime, the real Bonnie Parker wrote ballads about the Barrow gang's exploits.

LEGAL DEBATES

In the same era that Bonnie and Clyde were engaged in their crime spree, another less likely pair of felons made front-page news. As Diana Proper discusses in Chapter 5, Nathan Leopold and Richard Loeb, two wealthy Chicago teenagers decided to commit the "perfect crime." Influenced by the "Superman" theory of Friedrich Nietzsche, Leopold and Loeb killed a 14-year-old boy in what was described as a "thrill killing." Their attorney, the renowned Clarence Darrow, acknowledged their guilt but made an impassioned plea that they not be put to death for their crime. In his argument, Darrow offered a still-famous denouncement of the death penalty.

Clarence Darrow was also the defense attorney in the Scopes "Monkey Trial." In Chapter 6, Ernest Nickels describes the trial in a small town in Tennessee that pitted the proponents of evolutionary theory against fundamentalist Christians who believed in the biblical account of the Creation. In the courtroom, John Scopes, a schoolteacher who had taught evolutionary theory in his classroom, was defended by Darrow. The prosecutor in the case was William Jennings Bryan, and the encounter between Darrow and Bryan was both dramatic and riveting for spectators.

Six years later, in the midst of the Great Depression, another Southern case attracted international attention. The "Scottsboro Boys," nine young black males, were riding the rails as they looked for work. When the train on which they were illegally riding stopped in Scottsboro, Alabama, the two young white women who were also discovered aboard accused the black youths of gang rape. The actions of a sheriff prevented the youths from being lynched by an angry mob, but the Scottsboro Boys stood trial in a segregated court-room. As the Communist Party entered the case and provided a Jewish defense attorney from New York, the various racial, gender, religious, and regional tensions in the case became even more explicit. As James Acker, Elizabeth Brown, and Christine Englebrecht discuss in Chapter 8, the case became the basis for two major Supreme Court decisions about the rights of the accused.

In the 1954 case involving Dr. Samuel Sheppard, the environment in which the investigation and the trial proceeded was equally hostile. In Sheppard's case, the issue was the hostility of the local media that pushed for his arrest and prosecution. Sheppard was accused of the murder of his wife Marilyn. He claimed that she had been killed by an intruder. In Chapter 12, Kathy Warnes examines Sheppard's case, focusing both on the story itself and the issue raised by the case of the impact of prejudicial pretrial coverage by the media on due process.

TURBULENT SOCIAL CHANGE

A year after the Sheppard case, in 1955, an African American mother in Chicago used the media to bring her son's murder to the attention of the country. Defying the instructions she had received from the Mississippi sheriff who had returned her son's body to her, Mamie Till insisted that her son's coffin be opened for viewing by mourners. In Chapter 13, Marcella Glodek Bush tells the story of Emmett Till, the 14-year-old boy who violated the racial etiquette of the South during a visit to a general store in Money, Mississippi. The *Jet* magazine photo of Till in his coffin helped to galvanize a generation of young people as Civil Rights activists.

The decision by the United States Supreme Court in *Plessy v. Ferguson* (1896) gave the stamp of approval to the Southern system of racial segregation known as "Jim Crow." Reversing itself, the year before the murder of Emmett Till, the Court held in *Brown v. Board of Education* (1954) that racially segregated public accommodations were "inherently unequal." The Court ordered desegregation "with all deliberate speed." In the South, African Americans began what would be a prolonged struggle to implement the Supreme Court ruling. Rosa Parks's refusal to give up her seat on a bus launched a bus boycott in Montgomery, Alabama, and brought a young Black minister, Martin Luther King, Jr., to media attention. As the Civil Rights movement gained momentum, boycotts, sit-ins, marches, and other acts of "non-violent civil disobedience" by African Americans and their white allies would be covered by the media. In a relationship that might well be described as symbiotic, television news brought the Civil Rights movement to America, and the Civil Rights movement helped to build an audience for television news. The violence of water hoses and police dogs unleashed on peaceful marchers and jeering crowds harassing students were images that helped to make viewers aware of what was at stake.

There were casualties in this battle for civil rights. Among them were the four children who were attending a Sunday morning church service. When a bomb exploded, they were killed. The story would later be told in a documentary by director Spike Lee titled *4 Little Girls* (1997). In Chapter 15, Marcella Glodek Bush discusses the impact of this violence against innocent victims on the nation's conscience.

The film *Mississippi Burning* (1998) offered the Hollywood version of the story of the murders of three men who were involved in voting registration in the South. In Chapter 14, Shani Gray presents the story of the murders, the search for the bodies, and the aftermath. The murders of the three men, two white and one black, occurred in an atmosphere in which there was increasing concern among civil rights activists about the safety of those involved in the movement. By the end of the decade of the 1960s, assassins had killed both Martin Luther King, Jr., who had taken his message to the ghettoes of the North and began to discuss the Vietnam War, and Malcolm X, the charismatic Black Muslim leader, who had advocated change "by any means necessary" until a life-altering pilgrimage.

The assassinations of President John Kennedy, Robert Kennedy, Martin Luther King, Jr., and Malcolm X, the war in Vietnam, and the clashes between citizens and police in the streets of Chicago during the Democratic Convention in 1968 were among the events that contributed to the sense of disillusionment among many as the decade of the 1960s ended. Radical political groups, such as the Black Panthers and The Weather Underground (Weathermen), challenged the activities of the government, offered their own social programs, and had violent encounters with the police. The FBI initiated COINTELPRO, a counterintelligence program that targeted individuals and groups identified as "subversives" and "terrorists" and involved infiltration by FBI informants and agents, disinformation, surveillance, and other disruptive tactics.

As Marie Balfour discusses in Chapter 16, the social tensions of the 1960s were reflected in the plot that Charles Manson described as "Helter Skelter" and that allegedly involved starting a race war. The leader of the cult known as the "Manson Family," Manson led his followers in carrying out two brutal murder events. The media coverage of the trials of Manson and his Family offered the public a view of the workings of the mind of a man who many believed insane and/or evil.

The year after the Manson Family murders, students at Kent State University were responding to the Vietnam War with protests. Increasingly unpopular, the war had led Lyndon Johnson not to seek another term as president and inspired resistance by those young enough to face the draft. In Chapter 17, Kathy Warnes discusses the events that led up to the encounter between Kent State students and members of the Ohio National Guard on the university campus.

The next year, 1971, at Attica Correctional Facility in upstate New York, another bloody encounter between Americans occurred in the prison yard. In Chapter 18, Sidney Harring and George Dowdall describe the uprising by prisoners who took correctional officers hostage and demanded improved conditions in the prison. The decision by Governor Nelson Rockefeller to retake the prison by force rather than to continue to negotiate or to wait out the prisoners has continued to be a matter of debate decades after the incident.

The presence of the media at Attica and at the scenes of the other cases discussed in this volume illustrates the importance of the media in informing the public. At the same time, as will become evident in reading these chapters, the presence of the media also raises issues that continue to be relevant about matters such as due process in the context of massive media coverage of criminal cases.

References

Bailey, F.Y., & Hale, D. (Eds.). (1998). *Popular culture, crime, and justice.* Belmont, CA: Wadsworth Publishing.

Bailey, F.Y., & Hale, D.C. (2004). *Blood on her hands: The social construction of women, sexuality, and murder.* Belmont, CA: Wadsworth/Thomson Learning.

Bailey, F.Y., & Green, A.P. (1999). *"Law never here": A social history of African American responses to issues of crime and justice.* Westport, CT: Praeger.

Butler, L. (2004). Dead president and Progressive reform. *Reviews in American History, 32.3,* 399–406.

Carlson, C. (2003 [1995]). *Murder of the century.* PBS American Experience. WGBH Foundation. Transcript at www.pbs.org/wgbh/amex/century/filmmore/pt.html

Chudacoff, H.P. (1999). *The age of the bachelor: Creating an American subculture.* Princeton: Princeton University Press.

Douglas, A. (1995). *Terrible honesty: Mongrel Manhattan in the 1920s.* New York: The Noonday Press.

Emery, E., & Emery, M. (1984). *The press and America: An interpretive history of the mass media* (5th ed.). Englewood Cliffs, NJ: Prentice-Hall.

Mason, F. (2002). *American gangster cinema: From Little Caesar to Pulp Fiction.* New York: Palgrave Macmillan.

Nevins, A., & Commager, H.S. (1992). *Pocket history of the United States* (9th revised ed.). New York: Pocket Books.

Ruth, D.E. (1996). *Inventing the public enemy: The gangster in American culture, 1918–1934.* Chicago: The University of Chicago Press.

Sickels, R. (2004). *The 1940s.* Westport, CT: Greenwood Press.

Trotti, M.A. (2003). Murder made real. *Virginia Magazine of History and Biography, 111*(4), 379–410.

Young, W.H., & Young, N.K. (2004). *The 1950s.* Westport, CT: Greenwood Press.

1

The Black Sox Scandal: More than a Story of "Eight Men Out"

JASON R. INGRAM

On October 26, 2005, the Chicago White Sox swept the Houston Astros to win their first World Series title since 1917. To many who followed the White Sox throughout this 88 year title drought, the 2005 championship team was believed to have finally lifted a curse that had reigned over Chicago's South Side: The curse of the "Black Sox." Perhaps not as well known as other, more famous, baseball curses such as the Red Sox's "Curse of the Bambino" or the Cub's "Curse of the Billy Goat," the origin of the Black Sox curse stemmed from what has been described as the "greatest scandal in the history of sports" (Ginsburg, 1995, p. 100) in which eight members of the White Sox conspired with gamblers to fix the 1919 World Series against the Cincinnati Reds.

Having won the 1917 title and being heavy favorites to win it again in 1919, the White Sox ended up losing the nine game series to the Reds in eight games. Rumors that members of the White Sox had agreed to throw the series surfaced even before the first game. Over time, the eight infamous players—Arnold "Chick" Gandil (first baseman), George "Buck" Weaver (third baseman), Fred McMullin (infielder), Charles "Swede" Risberg (shortstop), Oscar "Happy" Felsch (centerfielder), Eddie Cicotte (pitcher), Claude "Lefty" Williams (pitcher), and "Shoeless" Joe Jackson (leftfielder)—would be indicted for their roles in the scandal by a grand jury, but later acquitted of all charges at trial. Despite their legal innocence, all eight players received a lifetime ban from professional baseball by newly appointed commissioner, Judge Kenesaw Mountain Landis (Asinof, 1963; Gropman, 1979). When one is asked to recall the Black Sox scandal, it is these "eight men out" that likely come to mind. However, by focusing attention on the eight banned ballplayers, one can overlook many of the larger issues embedded within the scandal that has made it such a highly contested and popular topic for over 85 years (Carney, 2006).

Much debate still exists as to what exactly took place during the fall of 1919. It has been noted that "more words have been written about the World Series of 1919 than any other played, yet it still remains the series about which we know the least. From its very beginning the entire affair was characterized by confusion, deception, and lies" (Gropman, 1979, p. 158). As will be seen, the sheer number of people involved, double crosses, and cover-ups make it virtually impossible to determine what actually took place. In addition to the mysteries surrounding the incident, the scandal also raises issues of justice as the appropriateness of banning all eight players for life has remained a highly debated topic as each player's involvement in the fix varied (Carney, 2006). It has also highlighted the importance of the media (e.g., newspapers) to baseball at the time, as they have had a substantial impact on how the scandal has been portrayed. This chapter focuses on these issues and examines the complexities of the Black Sox scandal in terms of the incidents surrounding it as well as the effect it has had on American society. Collectively, these issues are some of the main reasons why the incident has remained a fixture of American popular culture as it has inspired novels, movies, and household phrases to this day. Before this is done, however, it is necessary to discuss the historical context in which the scandal took place to show how it was even possible to successfully pull off something as large as fixing the World Series.

THE SETTING: PROFESSIONAL BASEBALL HEADING INTO THE 1919 WORLD SERIES

By 1919, baseball had been an established, professional sport for only approximately 16 years. Before this time, it had been marked by periods of instability associated with the growing pains that the game had experienced as it evolved from an "exclusive team sport for urban gentleman" to a "commercialized spectacle" where players began to be paid for their services (Voigt, 1976, pp. 4–5). As it moved towards professionalism, a number of different leagues were formed and many were subsequently disbanded as they failed to compete with the dominant National League that had been created in 1876. Control over the game during this time also shifted from the players to club owners with the owners set on profiting from the sport (Voigt, 1970). As a result of these changes, professional baseball was eventually organized into two leagues, the National and American leagues, in 1903 with the winners of each league facing each other in the World Series (Voigt, 1976). As such, it marked the beginning of modern day baseball, and as the sport's popularity increased so did its recognition as America's national pastime by the fans and as big business by the owners.

During this time, fans perceived the sport as "America's greatest game" (Cottrell, 2002, p. 5). Such a perception was due in large part to the belief that baseball characterized traditional American values such as democracy, a strong work ethic, competitiveness, and honesty (Cottrell, 2002; Ginsburg, 1995). The rise of organized baseball took place during the Progressive Era in which the American public grew adamantly opposed to corruptive practices, particularly within government and businesses. Thus, in addition to the fact that the public could readily relate to the game, baseball also benefited from the fact that it had a rather clean reputation and image; something that other popular sports of the time, boxing and horse racing, lost when it was found that gamblers readily fixed these events (Anderson, 2001; Carney, 2006). The state of baseball as the national pastime, then, was appropriately summarized by Boyer (1995) who noted that:

> Baseball, during the Progressive Era, had become more than a game. It had become emblematic of America's social structure. Its teamwork showed democracy in action; its fans were

found among all classes of society; it taught American values to successive waves of immigrants; and it served as an annual ritual which united cities behind their teams. (p. 332)

Baseball's appeal to the fans significantly increased ticket sales and, as a result, also increased the revenue of the owners. By 1917, the sport was the "biggest entertainment business in America" (Asinof, 1988, p. 12). While it was apparent that fans loved baseball, they did not necessarily have the same feelings for club owners, who were often viewed as selfish and profit driven (Voigt, 1976). While a complete discussion of the effect of owners' drive for profit on labor relations within the game is beyond the scope of this chapter, two important events must be mentioned as they bear insight into the reasons behind the 1919 World Series fix: the implementation of the reserve clause and the owners' methods for handling the financial crisis that World War I would have on the game.

The reserve clause was implemented in 1879, three years after the National League had formed. Even then, owners were concerned with profits and the reserve clause served as a way to protect their biggest assets: the players. National League owners encountered problems when their players left their team and signed with another, sometimes even leaving the league for a competing one. To control this, the owners mutually agreed to allow each team to protect five players from signing with other teams. This reserve clause worked so well that eventually it expanded and was included in virtually every player's contract (Asinof, 1963; Calpin, 1996). After merging with the American League, the owners would essentially have complete control over players' salaries because the crux of the clause was that "the club owner would employ the player's services for one year, holding in reserve the right to renew his contract the following year. And so on, in perpetuity" (Asinof, 1963, p. 21). Thus, if the players chose not to accept their contract, they could not play anywhere else and they would be out of Major League Baseball (Carney, 2006, p. 150). The clause allowed the owners to pay the players whatever they wanted and created a monopoly by doing so that was regarded as perfectly legal. Legal challenges of the reserve clause failed as the courts ruled that organized baseball did not violate the Sherman Antitrust Act because baseball was not considered interstate commerce, and therefore not a trust (Carney, 2006; Cottrell, 2002). In other words, baseball was big business to the owners, but to the courts it was a sport. While the reserve clause allowed the owners to continue to reap significant financial rewards from the players' efforts, World War I posed a financial threat to them.

America's involvement in World War I began in April 1917, and it impacted every aspect of society including baseball. Although the government allowed the 1917 season to finish, many players either enlisted in the war or took jobs that qualified as assisting the war effort after the season ended. The 1918 season was the game's worst financial year as attendance figures significantly dropped. Facing similar losses after the war in 1919, the owners agreed to cut players' salaries while extending the season (Asinof, 1963; Voigt, 1976). Attendance in 1919, however, skyrocketed, and it was said that "trouble disappeared and war weary fans returned in droves, bringing unprecedented profits" (Voigt, 1976, p. 124). Even though profits returned for the owners, the players' salaries remained low. While the impact of both the reserve clause and World War I undoubtedly affected all players, they particularly affected the players on the Chicago White Sox due to the management practices of their owner, Charles Comiskey.

Charles Comiskey was one of the most famous owners in baseball history. A former major league player, Comiskey became owner of the White Sox in 1901 and was one of the few who were highly regarded by the public. Unlike other owners of the time, baseball

Figure 1.1 **Charles Comiskey, owner of the White Sox, 1914. Comiskey implemented many policies that made him popular with the fans, but the players held a different view. Courtesy of the Library of Congress.**

was Comiskey's sole source of income, and so he put a lot of time and money into building a winning team and ball park. He implemented many policies that made him popular with the fans, such as letting the public use the ball park for free when there were no games scheduled (Asinof, 1963; Voigt, 1976). While he was highly esteemed by fans, his players did not hold similar views of him.

Much has been written about how Comiskey paid his players. Although he would spend the money to sign the best players, he took full advantage of the reserve clause when re-signing them in subsequent years. For example in 1919, Shoeless Joe Jackson, one of the greatest hitters of the era, was re-signed for $6,000. In comparison, Ed Roush, Cincinnati's best hitter, had a $10,000 contract (Asinof, 1963). It was often noted that "[m]any second-rate ballplayers on second-division clubs made more than the White Sox" (Asinof, 1963, p. 21). As expected, White Sox players were often upset about their salaries. In addition to their salaries, Comiskey's players were also unhappy with his other cost-cutting strategies. He often held back on players' meal allowances for road trips and on laundry services for uniforms. In 1917, he offered a $10,000 bonus to pitcher Eddie Cicotte, one of the players involved in the scandal, if he won 30 games but had him benched when he reached 29 wins. That same year he offered the entire team a bonus if they won the pennant; when they won, they received only a case of champagne in the locker room (Asinof, 1963). Although the players were often upset with their salaries, they were still one of the best teams in baseball. They won the 1917 championship and played again in the 1919 series.

Comiskey's stringent use of the reserve clause combined with the lower salaries caused by the effects of World War I have generally been described as important motivating factors for the eight players' attempt to throw the 1919 World Series (Asinof, 1963; Carney, 2006; Ginsburg, 1995). While the players had money in mind when agreeing to fix the series, they still needed the means by which to do so. Professional gamblers who were secretly invading the inner dealings of the game provided these means. Gambling and baseball have been connected since the game's inception (Asinof, 1963). Before the 1919 series, there were many documented instances of players working with gamblers to throw games, and there would be many more following the scandal (Ginsburg, 1995). Still, in order for something as sophisticated as a nine game World Series to be thrown, it would take a number of major players on the team to be involved, as "the game's uncertainty . . . would hardly guarantee the desired outcome" (Cottrell, 2002, p. 10). When the White Sox won the 1919 American League pennant sending them to the World Series to face the Cincinnati Reds, this is precisely what happened.

HOW THE 1919 WORLD SERIES WAS FIXED[1]

The idea for throwing the series was first conceived by Sox first baseman, Chick Gandil, and his acquaintance, professional gambler Joseph "Sport" Sullivan, in Boston three weeks before the start of the series. From this conversation, it was proposed that Gandil would recruit other team members to throw the series in exchange for $80,000. While nothing had been finalized, the fix had been set in motion as Sullivan left to try and obtain financial backing for the players' payment, and Gandil tried to recruit other Sox players to join him.

Gandil is often credited as the organizer of the scandal, and the first person he sought to join him was the Sox's star pitcher,

Figure 1.2 White Sox first baseman, Chick Gandil, 1913. The idea for throwing the series was first conceived by Gandil and his acquaintance, professional gambler Joseph "Sport" Sullivan. Courtesy of the Library of the Congress.

Cicotte, who was in financial trouble. Cicotte reluctantly agreed to take part for $10,000 cash to be paid before the series started (Linder, 2001). With Cicotte on board, Gandil used the team's shared dislike of Comiskey's ownership practices to recruit the remaining six players: Risberg, Felsch, McMullin, Williams, Weaver, and Jackson. On September 21, 1919, all eight players met in Gandil's hotel room during the team's stay in New York. While the result of the meeting had the players agreeing in principal to participating in the fix, it is at this point where things become more complicated (Linder, 2001).

Shortly after the players' meeting in New York, Cicotte ran into a former major league pitcher, "Sleepy" Bill Burns. Burns had heard rumors of the fix and wanted a part in it. After some questioning, Cicotte told Burns of the plan, but that the money for the players' payment had yet to be raised. Burns told Cicotte that he could get the players $100,000 and would find a way to raise the money. Burns employed the services of another small-time gambler, Billy Maharg. Although two sets of gamblers were working to raise money (e.g., Sullivan and Burns/Maharg), both ended up proposing the scheme to the same man: Arnold Rothstein.

Rothstein was a prominent figure in America's underworld. He was nicknamed "the Big Bankroll" and was regarded as the "first great financier of organized crime" (Boyer, 1995, p. 437). He owned a number of gambling establishments and was the only one with access to the amount of money needed to fund the players' request. Burns and Maharg were the first to propose the fix to Rothstein, who had his associate, Abe Attell, speak with the two. When Attell told Rothstein of the two gamblers' plan, Rothstein declined to become involved, noting that throwing the series could not be done. Attell, on the other hand, wanted in on the fix, and, after initially relaying Rothstein's decline to the two, he told Burns that Rothstein had changed his mind. In essence, Attell deceptively

Figure 1.3 One of the eight infamous players, Eddie Cicotte (pitcher), 1917. He would be indicted, along with the others, for his role in the scandal by a grand jury. All eight, however, would later be acquitted of all charges at trial. Courtesy of the Library of Congress.

Figure 1.4 Undated photo of Arnold Rothstein, aka "the Big Bankroll," a reluctant participant of the scandal. Courtesy of the Library of Congress.

used Rothstein's name to lead Burns and Maharg to believe that Rothstein had agreed to the fix.

On September 26, Sullivan contacted Rothstein with his proposal. Having heard of Sullivan's name before within gambling circles, Rothstein became optimistic and agreed to fund $40,000 to the players up front and the remaining $40,000 after they lost the series. Rothstein sent the cash and his partner, Nat Evans, to Chicago to meet with Sullivan and the players. When the details had been agreed upon, Evans left the $40,000 with Sullivan to be paid to the players. While it would seem that the fix had been set, greed and double crosses between the two sets of gamblers and the players would lead to anger and confusion throughout the series.

Instead of giving the players their share, Sullivan bet approximately $30,000 of it on the series and gave the other $10,000 to Gandil two days before the start of the series. While Gandil was angry, there was not much he could do at this point. He took the money and gave it to Cicotte who had agreed to take part in the scandal only if he was given $10,000 up front. The day before the series, Gandil ran into more problems securing the players' money as Attell entered back into the picture and met with those involved (except Jackson who did not attend the meeting) at the players' hotel in Cincinnati. Attell told the players (falsely) that Rothstein would back the fix for $100,000, but that it would be paid in $20,000 increments for each loss. Again, the players reluctantly agreed and to show the gamblers that they would hold up their end, the Sox were to intentionally lose the first three games; Cicotte was to hit the first batter of Game 1 to signal that the fix was on.

On October 1, 1919, Maurice Rath, lead hitter for the Cincinnati Reds, took a Cicotte curve ball "squarely in the back" in the first game of the series (Asinof, 1963, p. 64). The fix was officially underway and the Sox lost the first two games by a combined score of 13 to 3. While the players were holding up their end of the bargain, the gamblers were not, as Gandil only received another $10,000 for the two losses. Frustrated, the Sox went against their word, won Game 3, and threatened to call off the fix if they did not receive their money. Sullivan resurfaced and managed to raise $20,000 to give Gandil before Game 4 to keep the fix alive, but Gandil was adamant about receiving another $20,000 before Game 5. This was a problem for Sullivan as the money originally reserved for the players was still out on bets, and he had to pull every string he had to raise the $20,000 he had already given to Gandil. The Sox lost both Games 4 and 5, but when they did not receive any more money, Gandil called off the fix and the team ended up winning the next two games.

With the Reds up 4 games to 3 and the White Sox threatening to come back and take the series, Rothstein had seen enough. He made it clear to Sullivan that the Sox were to lose Game 8. Sullivan knew what this meant, so he hired a gangster to threaten Lefty Williams, the starting pitcher in Game 8. The threat worked as Williams gave up four runs in the first inning and the Sox lost both the game and the series. After the series, Gandil received the other $40,000 from Sullivan. The final distribution of the money to the players went as follows: Gandil ($35,000), Risberg ($15,000), Cicotte ($10,000), and Jackson, Williams, Felsch, and McMullin ($5,000 each) (Anderson, 2004). Gandil refused to give Weaver any of the money because he had done nothing to aid in the fix besides attending the initial meetings. With the exception of Burns and Maharg, who lost a large amount of money on Game 3, the major gamblers involved also pocketed significant amounts of money. This is how the 1919 World Series was thrown.

THE (IN)ACTION OF MAJOR LEAGUE BASEBALL

After the World Series, it seemed that both the players and the gamblers involved would get away with fixing the games. This was not, however, due to the fact that the scandal had been kept a secret. Rumors of the fix had circulated throughout the country before the series had even started. Such rumors had affected gambling circles because when Sullivan initially bet the players' half of the money, the odds on the series had already dropped from favoring the Sox 7–5 to even money (Asinof, 1963). Because gambling and baseball were so closely tied, it was almost certain that people in baseball, particularly Comiskey, had heard the rumors as well.

Indeed, reports indicated that Comiskey had learned of the rumors either just before or after Game 1. There would be additional evidence that Comiskey knew that some of his players had thrown the series, the most notable being Jackson's attempt to meet with Comiskey after the series to discuss his involvement. For whatever reason, Comiskey chose not to hear Jackson's story. Besides Jackson's attempt, sources have noted that the team's manager, Kid Gleason, confronted the players during the series. Also, after the series Comiskey held the paychecks of the eight suspected players for weeks before his lawyer advised him to pay them, and he was also hesitant to offer the eight players their 1920 contracts (Asinof, 1963; Carney, 2006). If Comiskey knew that his players threw the series and cost him money in doing it, he did nothing to expose them. The question then becomes: Why?

The answer arises out of the state of baseball at this time. In order for baseball to remain big business, the fans had to believe that the game was being played honestly. If the scandal was exposed and the extent of gambling in baseball surfaced, significant

TIMELINE

9-18-1919	White Sox first baseman Chick Gandil meets with gambler Sport Sullivan to discuss throwing the World Series.
9-21-1919	The eight Sox players involved meet in Gandil's hotel room in New York City to discuss fixing the series against the Reds.
10-1-1919	White Sox pitcher Eddie Cicotte hits Cincinnati Red's lead-off hitter, Maurice Roth, signifying that the fix was on.
10-9-1919	The White Sox lose Game 8 and the series.
12-15-1919	Sportswriter Hugh Fullerton publishes the article, ''Is Big League Baseball Being Run for Gamblers, with Players in the Deal?'' in the *New York Evening World,* which called for baseball to take a stance against gambling.
9-22-1920	A Cook County Illinois grand jury convenes to examine gambling issues in baseball and leads to investigations into the 1919 World Series.
9-28-1920	Cicotte confesses to the grand jury about the fix. A few days later, both Shoeless Joe Jackson and Lefty Williams would also confess.
10-22-1920	The grand jury indicts the eight players and four gamblers on charges of defrauding the public and White Sox owner Charles Comiskey.
11-11-1920	In response to public exposure of the fix, Major League Baseball appoints Federal Judge Kenesaw Mountain Landis as the game's first commissioner.
6-27-1921	The trial begins for the players and gamblers.
8-2-1921	All players and gamblers are acquitted of the charges. The next day Commissioner Landis rules that despite the verdict all eight players would be banned from professional baseball for life.

damage would be done to the game. Furthermore, Comiskey had a lot at stake as he had large sums of money invested in his players (Ginsburg, 1995). Ultimately, Comiskey decided he needed to protect his team and his income, while at the same time making it seem that he was investigating the matter. He publicly supported his players and offered a $10,000 reward for information concerning the scandal. Thus, he started his own investigation, but not for exposure as it would be pointed out that ''[i]f there was evidence, Comiskey wanted it. And as soon as it started coming his way, he buried it'' (Carney, 2006, p. 48).

Besides Comiskey, others within baseball also started their own investigations. Ban Johnson, a member of the National Commission, which was baseball's governing body at the time, started his own investigation, as did some of the other team owners as well. At this point, nothing ever came out of these investigations, and rumors of the fix had dwindled by the start of the 1920 season. The way that investigations into the scandal were handled screamed cover-up. As the 1920 season started, it was said that the owners ''had dodged an enormous bullet that might have shattered baseball's image and sharply reduced the value of their teams'' (Carney, 2006, p. 60). For the moment the extent of gambling in baseball remained hidden, but as the 1920 season moved along another incident of gambling would take place that would reopen investigations into the 1919 World Series and this time bring actions by the legal system.

A GRAND JURY CONVENES

On August 31, 1920, suspicions arose that players on the Chicago Cubs were set to throw a game against the Philadelphia Phillies. Circumstances were peculiar because large amounts of money were being bet on a rather unimportant game. This was not the first time during the season that games were rumored to have been thrown, and some of these rumors again involved the White Sox (Asinof, 1963). As a result of the increased problems with gambling in baseball, Ban Johnson of the National Commission convinced Judge Charles McDonald to form a grand jury in Cook County, Illinois, to look into the matter. While the initial aim of the grand jury was to look into the Cubs-Phillies game, many believe that Johnson's real ambition was to look into the 1919 World Series (Carney, 2006).

The grand jury convened on September 22, and through the testimony of other major league players who had heard of the fix, evidence was mounting against those involved in the Black Sox scandal. A breaking point in the case came when Cicotte, feeling his own guilt and pressure from the state attorney's office, confessed to his involvement in the fix to Comiskey's lawyer, Alfred Austrian. Austrian had Cicotte appear before the grand jury and also had him sign a waiver of immunity, which would allow his grand jury statements to be admissible in any further legal proceedings. After Cicotte confessed and gave the names of the other players and gamblers, Jackson and Williams followed Cicotte's lead and voluntarily went before the grand jury, also signing waivers of immunity. As a result of the confessions and implications, Comiskey had no choice but to suspend the eight players indefinitely (Carney, 2006).

The testimony and players' confessions presented to the grand jury also began to implicate Rothstein, Attell, and Burns. Rothstein's attorney felt it would be best if Attell and Burns left the country. Rothstein then volunteered to testify before the grand jury "to set the record straight" and implicated Attell, who he said had unknowingly used his name to start the proceedings that led to the fix (Asinof, 1963, p. 219). The grand jury believed Rothstein, and he was cleared of any involvement.

The grand jury concluded in late October and, based upon the hearings, indicted the eight White Sox players and the gamblers, Attell, Burns, Sullivan, and Nat Evans. Among other things, those indicted were charged with conspiring to defraud the public and conspiring to injure the business of Comiskey (Linder, 2001). Despite the fact that it had been almost a year since the 1919 World Series was thrown and despite considerable efforts by those within baseball to keep the rumors quiet, the case against the players and gamblers was set to go to trial.

BASEBALL FORCED TO RESPOND

The grand jury hearings, confessions, and indictments were a significant blow to baseball as both the media and the public denounced the sport. The owners had to do something to save the image of the game, and the current structure of organized baseball was inadequate. As Ginsburg (1995) noted, the owners' stance was that the National Commission had failed and "[w]ithout strong central leadership, baseball had floundered, providing an opening to evil gamblers and crooked ball players" (p. 141). Before the trial took place, baseball made drastic efforts to clean up its image by forcing the head of the National Commission to resign and putting the governance of baseball into the hands of an outside party (Anderson, 2001). The two leagues essentially remained intact, but they needed to appoint a commissioner. On November 11, 1920, the baseball team owners gave the job to Kenesaw Mountain Landis, a Federal Judge who had knowledge of baseball and would prove to rule with a heavy hand (Asinof, 1963). While his appointment gave the impression to the fans that baseball was working to curb corruption within the game, it also soon had a dramatic impact on the now uncertain careers of the indicted ball players.

THE TRIAL: *PEOPLE OF THE STATE OF ILLINOIS V. EDWARD V. CICOTTE ET AL.*[2]

Although both the players and the gamblers had been indicted, it was unknown if an actual criminal trial would take place. First, even though gambling was now exposed as rampant in baseball, "cases involving bribery to influence the outcome of games had not been routinely brought into the court system" (Carney, 2006, p. 138). Furthermore, because conspiring to fix baseball games was not a crime, it was not even probable that the burden of proof could be met for charges of defrauding the public and Comiskey. There were also some mysterious proceedings that took place after the grand jury hearings. Most notable was the disappearance of the signed confessions of Cicotte, Jackson, and Williams. Many believed that the disappearance of the papers was due to the combined efforts of Rothstein and Comiskey, as this would be a significant advantage for both of them. Getting rid of the confessions would further distance Rothstein from the scandal as the players had implicated him in the fix, and it would allow the players to refute their statements, giving Comiskey the hope that his players would be reinstated.

This was not the only aspect of the legal proceedings that Comiskey was peculiarly involved in. It was also said that he had hired the best lawyers in Chicago to defend the players, some of whom were originally slated to work on the prosecution's side. If the players were charged with injuring his business, why would he provide the assistance to defend them? To many this was further evidence that "Comiskey held out hope that some or all of the players would be reinstated after they were acquitted, perhaps after paying fines or serving suspensions" (Carney, 2006, p. 146).

Because of these circumstances, an actual trial was still in doubt until Ban Johnson once again intervened. He tracked down gamblers Burns and Maharg and gave them to the prosecutors, who in exchange gave them immunity. While preparations for the trial were still slowly moving along, it eventually began on June 27, 1921. After two weeks of jury selection, opening statements finally began on July 18.

The prosecution made a strong case with their witness Sleepy Bill Burns. Burns recounted his involvement with the players and the other gamblers. It was said later that "Burns was a convincing witness on the stand, and his confidence seemed to grow the longer he testified. This was even more evident when he was cross-examined" (Anderson, 2004, p. 43). He became the prosecution's star witness. The prosecution also benefited from the fact that copies of Cicotte, Jackson, and Williams's confessions were in existence even though the signed originals were missing. A battle took place over the admissibility of these papers, but because the players all admitted to the judge that they had initially signed the immunity waivers, the copies of the confessions were admitted into court. While this was a break for the prosecution, the confessions could only be used as evidence against the three players, not the other five (Asinof, 1963).

The defense focused on Comiskey's wealth and Ban Johnson's role in the trial. They showed through the records of Comiskey's secretary that Comiskey had significantly increased his profits in 1920, and so the players could not possibly have injured his business (Anderson, 2004). The defense also questioned Johnson's intentions as it was clear the focus of the trial was on Comiskey's players and not the gamblers. They argued that a growing feud between Comiskey and Johnson gave Johnson incentive to seek legal action against the players in order to ruin Comiskey's team. Finally, the defense also benefited from the fact that there was virtually no hard evidence against the players. Other than the testimony of gamblers and the copies of the confessions, hardly anything connected those involved directly to the charges against them. The presiding judge even noted that he would not be able to let a conviction against Weaver or Felsch stand.

As the trial came to an end, the chances that there would be any convictions decreased as the judge specifically instructed the jury to decide only on whether there was proof that the players and gamblers had committed fraud and had not just conspired to throw baseball games (Asinof, 1963). Thus, on August 2, 1921, the players and gamblers were acquitted of all charges. To many the trial was described as "superficial" and "farcical" (Carney, 2006, p. 148). This became more apparent as the players celebrated their victory in the company of the jury at a nearby restaurant after the trial (Asinof, 1963).

EIGHT MEN OUT

Despite their acquittal and much to the dismay of Comiskey, the players still paid severely for their roles in the 1919 World Series fix. The newly appointed commissioner of baseball, Judge Landis, placed a lifetime ban on the players the day after the trial had ended to ensure that baseball's image would remain clean and to show that it would no longer allow corruption to occur (Carney, 2006). None of them would ever play professional baseball again, and none of them have ever been reinstated. Landis's ruling impacted the players in different ways.

Jackson, Cicotte, and Risberg tried to continue to play semiprofessional baseball under aliases. Each time their real identity was discovered, and they were often removed from the

THE "SYNTHETIC CHAMPIONS"

Much of what we know about the 1919 World Series has come from accounts that have focused heavily on the roles of the Black Sox and how the scandal affected them. Less emphasis has been placed on the effect that the scandal had on those who took the field against the Sox: the Cincinnati Reds. After the series ended, the Reds were in a celebratory state after winning their first ever title by upsetting the heavily favored White Sox. The players returned home to a hero's welcome by the fans. Less than a year later though, the scandal was exposed and the "what ifs" surrounding the series followed the Reds players throughout the rest of their lives. Their once heroic feat was forever questioned as critics stated that the only way the Reds could have won was because the eight Sox players chose to lose. The scandal particularly affected Reds' star outfielder, Ed Roush. He claimed until his death that the Reds were better than the White Sox and that the best team did win the series. It is important to remember that there is more than one side to every story, and Roush's granddaughter, Susan Dellinger, offers interesting insight into how the Black Sox scandal was perceived by Roush and the other Reds' players in her book *Red Legs and Black Sox*. In it she describes how the players dealt with their treatment as "synthetic champions" after the scandal broke.

teams as fans protested. After their playing days were over, many of the banned players moved out west and almost all of them worked odd jobs. Lefty Williams, for instance, moved to Laguna Beach, California, and operated a garden nursery. Gandil, who actually retired from baseball after the 1919 season, became a plumber in California. Cicotte moved to Detroit and became a game warden. Happy Felsch became a bartender in Milwaukee. Jackson moved back to Greenville, South Carolina, and owned a dry cleaning service, restaurant, and liquor store before his death at the age of 62. Swede Risberg became a dairy farmer in California and was the last living member of the eight men out until his death in 1975. Of the eight, only Buck Weaver remained near Chicago. As will be discussed later, his minute role in the fix has led to the belief that he was an innocent victim. As such, he petitioned for reinstatement a number of times before his death in 1956, being denied each time (Chicago Historical Society, 1999; Cottrell, 2002).

THE ROLE OF THE MEDIA

The incidents surrounding the Black Sox scandal have focused here largely on the people involved, baseball's response, and the subsequent legal proceedings in order to describe the case. While such a focus provides adequate insight into the scandal, it gives only a partial outlook on the case. The media also played a significant role in how it handled the information on the 1919 World Series fix as it surfaced. The media's treatment of the case also has had a dramatic impact on how the Black Sox scandal has been portrayed and affects how we understand the case today. Although considerable growth in the use of different media outlets occurred during the time of the Black Sox scandal, such as the rise of the cinema and magazines, newspapers were still the primary news source in the country. Around the time of the scandal, circulation of newspapers rose substantially, making them "preeminent cultural institutions" (Nathan, 2003, p. 14). Thus, they were the primary way in which Americans came to view and interpret important events. The years preceding the scandal also saw an increase in the importance of sports journalism to the papers. As such, sportswriters became the agents by which sporting news was relayed to the public and, as a result, had significant influence on how the game was perceived by fans (Nathan, 2003).

Recall that a major benefit for owners was the portrayal of baseball as the national pastime. The relationship between owners and the press was a major reason why fans perceived the game to be so as this was how the game was portrayed in newspaper articles. During this time, sportswriters had developed close relationships with baseball owners and players. This was due to the fact that such relationships were mutually advantageous because it created a profitable partnership. It was noted that "sportswriters increased the amount of baseball coverage, which helped increase attendance at baseball games, which boosted newspaper circulations" (Anderson, 2001, p. 107). In other words, organized baseball and newspapers were allies as baseball could count on the sportswriters' support and the newspapers could count on baseball selling papers.

This alliance initially caused members of the news world to ignore gambling allegations made prior to the 1919 World Series. Even after rumors of the Black Sox scandal began during the series, newspapers were hesitant to publish articles on it. In addition to the close relationship between the media and baseball, rumors of the scandal were ignored due to the fact that many sportswriters refused to believe that it was possible to throw even a single game, let alone a World Series. This, coupled with the news media's fear of libel suits for publishing what was at this point still speculation, led to little coverage of the scandal until much later (Anderson, 2001).

This does not mean, however, that members of the media did not work to uncover and expose the scandal. One sportswriter in particular, Hugh Fullerton, is often given just as much credit for attempting to expose the fix as the events surrounding the 1920 Cubs-Phillies game that eventually placed the scandal in the national spotlight. Fullerton, who wrote for the *Chicago Herald and Examiner,* was a famous baseball writer of the time and, like many others, had heard rumors of the fix before the series had started. During the series, he asked for the assistance of former pitcher, Christy Mathewson, who was also covering the series for another paper. Together, the two documented every questionable play during the games that may have suggested that the players were not playing to the best of their ability and possibly throwing ball games (Carney, 2004). Fullerton's findings were not well received, but his journalistic efforts played a significant role in shedding light into the scandal.

Fullerton wrote about seven questionable plays made by Sox players during the series and tried to expose the players involved. The newspaper, however, severely edited his work out of fear of a libel suit. In another column on October 10, 1919, Fullerton made a foreboding proclamation when he wrote that seven Sox players would likely not return to baseball the following year.[3] One of his most significant contributions came on December 15, 1919, when his article entitled "Is Big League Baseball Being Run for Gamblers, with Players in the Deal?" appeared in the *New York Evening World* and called for baseball to take a stance against gambling. His subsequent writings named many of the gamblers who were eventually indicted. For his work, Fullerton was no longer well received as the rest of the media criticized him, and the reactions of the public were so harsh that an attempt was made on his life (Carney, 2004). Even though his work to publicly expose the fix had largely failed, Fullerton deserves credit as others have noted that he "at least brought to national attention the very real problem of baseball being strangled by gamblers" (Carney, 2004, p. 48).

After the grand jury hearings began and the players confessed, the media's stance on the scandal changed from support of baseball to attacking the profession. As a result, the scandal broke publicly and the newspapers extensively covered the scandal so much that it was now on the front page of every newspaper across the country for months afterwards (Nathan, 2003). The subject now became the hot topic to write about, and many tried to uncover the plot themselves. Jimmy Isaminger, reporter for the Philadelphia *North American,* procured gambler Billy Maharg for an exclusive interview where he told his side of the story. The title of the article ran as "The Most Gigantic Sporting Swindle in the History of America!" Furthermore, Harry Reutlinger of the Chicago *American* tracked down Happy Felsch and was able to get him to confess to the press (Asinof, 1963). Thus, in addition to the legal proceedings, the media now also played a significant role in uncovering the scandal, and much of what was written at the time impacts how we presently understand the case.

For starters, the referral of the players involved and the subsequent scandal as *Black Sox,* was first coined in the headline of the October 1, 1920, issue of the *Chicago Herald and Examiner,* which read "Here's hope for Black Sox, Let 'Em Grow Beards and Change Names." The phrase caught on, and by the middle of 1921 it was the primary way in which the players and scandal would be referred to (Nathan, 2003, p. 23). The media, however, not only influenced what the scandal was called but also how the players and gamblers were portrayed.

The players, for example, fell hard from their celebrity status because of how they were subsequently described in the newspapers. In the course of a little over a year the players went from "heroic athletes" to "loutish, distasteful dolts" as they were condemned by the media (Nathan, 2003, p. 39). Although still largely despised by the media, the players also eventually came to be treated in a sympathetic light. Many reports highlighted the fact that the players were unrefined, poorly educated dupes, which made them in some sense victims of the situation (Nathan, 2003). They were believed to have been taken advantage of by both the gamblers during the fix as well as organized baseball due to the current labor relations between the owners and players.

The gamblers, however, fared much worse in print. This stemmed from their portrayal as the scapegoats for the underlying problems of gambling in baseball and their religious backgrounds. Nathan (2003) aptly summarizes this when he stated that "given the nation's nativist temperament during the early twentieth century and the conspicuous presence of professional gamblers from Jewish backgrounds at the 1919 World Series, it is not surprising that an undercurrent of anti-Semitism is detectable in the media's Black Sox scandal coverage" (p. 33). Some media outlets, then, decided to portray the Black Sox scandal as a "Jewish conspiracy to corrupt Anglo-Saxon institutions" and identified them as not only the underlying cause for the fix but also for the problems of gambling in base-ball as a whole (Nathan, 2003, pp. 35–36). This was obviously an incorrect assessment as not all the indicted gamblers were Jewish and gamblers were not the sole cause for the extent of corruption in baseball. These were not the only inaccurate facts reported by the media that would affect the public's later understanding of the events surrounding the scandal.

Even those unfamiliar with the Black Sox scandal have likely heard the phrase, "Say it ain't so, Joe." The popular phrase originated from a widely held exchange between Shoe-less Joe Jackson and a boy on the street who went up to him as he exited the courthouse after his grand jury confession. Jackson's response to the boy's inquiry was "Yes, kid, I'm afraid it is." The exchange was included in every major newspaper and seemingly con-firmed the occurrence of the scandal to the public. Much debate now exists on the extent to which the encounter ever took place. While some argue that the exchange did indeed take place, others believe that the news story was at best embellished and at worst com-pletely made up (Carney, 2006, pp. 128–129). This is perhaps one of the most notable debates in the media's portrayal of the Black Sox scandal that has influenced how it has been perceived until this day. The media, however, are not the only institution from which debates over the scandal have arisen.

THE DEBATE ON THE LIFETIME BANS

The Black Sox trial is unique in the sense that all the indicted players and gamblers were treated the same by the court system, even though each individual's involvement in the scandal varied. The same can be said about Judge Landis's lifetime banishments for the eight acquitted players. While the ban was implemented as a way for baseball to clean up its image for the American public, Landis's harsh ruling has often been criticized on the grounds that "by failing to give consideration to the different degrees of participation in the fix, and by pretending that banning eight ball players solved the whole problem, baseball officialdom has perpetuated a cover-up" (Carney, 2006, p. xiv). Others have argued that the lifetime bans for all the players is "preposterous" (Voigt, 1976, p. 130). Such criticisms have particularly been made for two of the eight players: Jackson and Weaver.

Throughout the time when the scandal unfolded up until his death, Joe Jackson maintained his innocence. He contended that he had played every game to win, and his statistics during the series seemingly indicate this as he had a .375 batting average, a series record 12 hits, the series' only home run, and no fielding errors (Kindred, 1999). He also took other actions to show that he had tried to distance himself from the fix. For instance, he attempted to get Sox manager, Kid Gleason, to bench him before the first game of the series, and after the series he had tried to meet with Comiskey to tell his side of the story and to give him the $5,000 he had received (Asinof, 1963). Although his actions indicate that he must have known of the fix, many would argue that his actions and his role during the series do not fit the punishment that he received.

Weaver, on the other hand, is generally considered innocent by most accounts. In addition to the fact that the judge in the trial explicitly acknowledged that there was virtually no evidence against him that would uphold a conviction, his only documented connection to the scandal was his presence at the players' initial meetings to plan the fix. Despite this, Landis would uphold Weaver's ban based on the fact that he had "guilty knowledge" of the scandal (Cottrell, 2002). Despite attempts by both the players, and even in some cases members of the U.S. Congress, to petition for their reinstatement to baseball and make them eligible for the Hall of Fame, neither Landis nor any of the subsequent baseball commissioners have overturned their bans.

THE SCANDAL'S IMPACT ON AMERICAN POPULAR CULTURE

The Black Sox scandal has permeated throughout American popular culture. Aspects of the scandal, for example, have appeared in popular literary works. In F. Scott Fitzgerald's novel, *The Great Gatsby,* the character Meyer Wolfsheim is said to represent the gambler Arnold Rothstein. When Gatsby speaks of Wolfsheim to character Nick Carraway he describes him as the gambler who fixed the 1919 World Series. References to the scandal were also made in Bernard Malamud's novel, *The Natural,* where Malamud tells the story of Roy Hobbs, a ballplayer who is pressured to throw a playoff game. Although fictional, many of the events that occurred in the book closely parallel the events of the Black Sox scandal. The book was later made into a movie of the same name starring Robert Redford as Hobbs.

This was not the only reference to the Black Sox scandal that would hit the big screen. In 1988, *Eight Men Out* was adapted from Eliot Asinof's popular account of the scandal of the same name. The movie is often credited for "its stark realism and historical veracity" in documenting the scandal and the events leading up to it (Nathan, 2003, p. 179). The movie also proved to be a big break for actors John Cusack and Charlie Sheen who portrayed Buck Weaver and Happy Felsch, respectively, in the film. A year later, *Field of Dreams* was released starring Kevin Costner. From this movie the often cited phrase, "if you build it, he will come," was born, which referred to the mysterious voice that Costner's character heard urging him to build a baseball field in his cornfield. After the field was constructed, the ghosts of Shoeless Joe Jackson and the other banned players emerged to play ball once again. Hugely popular, the film was nominated for three Academy

Awards. In addition to novels and movies, aspects of the incident have also been incorporated into plays and musicals (e.g., *Out!* and *1919: A Baseball Opera*) as well as numerous biographies of individuals involved in the scandal from Arnold Rothstein to Shoeless Joe Jackson. It is undoubtedly Jackson who has received the most notoriety of any of the individuals involved, and as such has received a substantial following. The Shoeless Joe Jackson Society, for example, was formed to petition for Jackson's removal from baseball's ineligible list to make him eligible for induction into the Hall of Fame and currently maintains a virtual Hall of Fame Web page dedicated to Jackson that takes the name of his now mythical bat, blackbetsy.com. While the scandal has become a popular story to portray and maintain in popular cultural mediums such as books, movies, and the Internet, these are not the only ways by which the incident has become ingrained into America's "collective memory" (Nathan, 2003, p. 60) as subsequent real-life events have also made it a permanent fixture in American history.

The historical impact of the Black Sox scandal is most notable within the realm in which it occurred: professional baseball. It has not been the only incident of gambling in baseball, and on August 23, 1989, it was another such incident that conjured up past memories of the Black Sox. On this date Pete Rose, baseball's all-time hits leader, was banned for betting on baseball. The Pete Rose scandal was almost automatically christened as the "biggest and most controversial since the 1919 Black Sox scandal" (Ginsburg, 1995, p. 239). Rose's actions have precluded his induction into the Hall of Fame, a sanction that others have noted forever ties him to Shoeless Joe Jackson (Nathan, 2003).

References to the Black Sox scandal have also resurfaced in light of baseball's recent steroids scandal. Those who have investigated the steroids scandal have noted its similarities to the Black Sox scandal, especially the fact that initial evidence of the presence of steroids in baseball was ignored in much the same way as evidence concerning the 1919 World Series was. They have also used the actions of baseball to compare how the two commissioners, Landis and Bud Selig, have handled the two incidents (Wada & Williams, 2006).

Historical references to the Black Sox scandal, however, are not limited to professional baseball. Interestingly, such references have also been made in American politics. When Watergate unfolded in the 1970s, journalists of the time compared the scandal to that of the Black Sox (Nathan, 2003). More recently, the incident has been compared to the 109th Congress as one journalist wrote that "[i]n its waning months, the 109th Congress has finally achieved a status in politics that the 1919 Black Sox achieved in sports: It is a symbol of utter corruption" (Turley, 2006, p. 13A). The significance of the scandal, then, is the fact that it serves as a reference point for almost every major corrupt act that has taken place since. As Nathan (2003) points out, "acts of corruption remind people of previous acts of corruption" (p. 139), and, as a result, the Black Sox scandal has become an important aspect of American history.

When the 2005 White Sox team won the World Series, journalists were again quick to reference the scandal, but this time to finally lay to rest the curse associated with it. Although the curse may have been lifted, it is highly unlikely that memory of the scandal will ever fade away because of its historical significance. To be sure, at the time this chapter was written, Mark McGwire had just fallen well short on his first attempt to be inducted into the Hall of Fame due in large part to his perceived role in the current steroids scandal. Members of the media again mentioned the Black Sox incident as a reference point for the corruption associated with baseball's newest scandal. At this point, only time will tell if McGwire becomes tied to Jackson much in the same way that Rose has over the past 18 years.

SUGGESTIONS FOR FURTHER READING

Accounts of the Scandal

Asinof, E. (1963). *Eight men out: The Black Sox and the 1919 World Series.* New York: Henry Holt and Company.

Carney, G. (2006). *Burying the Black Sox: How baseball's cover-up of the 1919 World Series fix almost succeeded.* Washington, DC: Potomac Books.

Additional Perspectives

Dellinger, S. (2006). *Red legs and Black Sox: Edd Roush and the untold story of the 1919 World Series.* Cincinnati: Emmis Books.

Ginsburg, D.E. (1995). *The fix is in: A history of baseball gambling and game fixing scandals.* Jefferson, NC: McFarland & Company.

Nathan, D.A. (2003). *Saying it's so: A cultural history of the Black Sox scandal.* Chicago: University of Illinois Press.

NOTES

1. Unless otherwise cited, information provided in this section is based on Eliot Asinof's (1963) book, *Eight Men Out: The Black Sox and the 1919 World Series.*
2. Information provided on the trial is based on Gene Carney's (2006) book, *Burying the Black Sox: How baseball's cover-up of the 1919 World Series fix almost succeeded,* unless otherwise cited.
3. It should be noted that while Fullerton's statement did foretell of the fact that players would eventually be suspended, it is not 100 percent accurate as Carney (2006) points out that technically only Gandil did not return to baseball at the start of the 1920 season.

REFERENCES

Anderson, W.B. (2004). *The Chicago Black Sox trial: A primary source account.* New York: Rosen Publishing.

Anderson, W.B. (2001). Saving the national pastime's image: Crisis management during the 1919 Black Sox scandal. *Journalism History, 27*(3), 105–111.

Asinof, E. (1963). *Eight men out: The Black Sox and the 1919 World Series.* New York: Holt, Reinhart, & Winston.

Asinof, E. (1988). *Eight men out: The Black Sox and the 1919 World Series.* New York: Henry Holt and Company.

Boyer, A. (1995). *The Great Gatsby,* the Black Sox, high finance, and the American law. In S. W. Waller, N. B. Cohen, and P. Finkelman (Eds.), *Baseball and the American legal mind* (pp. 436–450). New York: Garland Publishing.

Calpin, M. (1996). It ain't over 'til it's over: The century long conflict between the owners and the players in Major League Baseball. *Albany Law Review, 60,* 205–238.

Carney, G. (2006). *Burying the Black Sox: How baseball's cover-up of the 1919 World Series fix almost succeeded.* Washington, DC: Potomac Books.

Carney, G. (2004). Uncovering the fix of the 1919 World Series: The role of Hugh Fullerton. *Nine, 13* (1), 39–49.

Chicago Historical Society. (1999). The Black Sox. Retrieved August 27, 2006, from http://www.chicagohs.org/history/blacksox.html

Cottrell, R. (2002). *Blackball, the Black Sox and the Babe: Baseball's crucial 1920 season.* Jefferson, NC: McFarland & Company.

Ginsburg, D.E. (1995). *The fix is in: A history of baseball gambling and game fixing scandals.* Jefferson, NC: McFarland & Company.

Gropman, D. (1979). *Say it ain't so, Joe! The story of Shoeless Joe Jackson.* Boston: Little, Brown and Company.

Kindred, D. (1999, April 12). A shoeless, clueless schmo. *Sporting News,* p. 95.

Linder, D.O. (2001). The Black Sox trial: An account. Retrieved June 12, 2006, from http://www.law.umkc.edu/faculty/projects/ftrials/blacksox/blacksox.html

Nathan, D.A. (2003). *Saying it's so: A cultural history of the Black Sox scandal.* Chicago: University of Illinois Press.

Turley, J. (2006, October 19). 109th Congress just can't resist. *USA Today,* p. 13A.

Voigt, D.Q. (1976). *America through baseball.* Chicago: Nelson-Hall.

Voigt, D.Q. (1970). *American baseball volume II: From the commissioners to continental expansion.* Norman: University of Oklahoma Press.

Wada, M.F., & Williams, L. (2006). *Game of shadows: Barry Bonds, BALCO, and the steroids scandal that rocked professional sports.* New York: Gotham Books.

2

The Sacco-Vanzetti Trial: Judging Anarchy

LISA N. SACCO

On April 15, 1920, a paymaster and his guard were carrying payroll boxes from one building to another when they were shot dead by two men. The two murderers picked up the payroll boxes and fled the scene with a third man to a getaway car, where an additional two men were waiting for them. Five men were involved in this shocking crime, but ultimately only two men would be executed for it—Nicola Sacco and Bartolomeo Vanzetti. The incident took place in South Braintree, a small suburb south of Boston, Massachusetts, but the entire world would come to know the story of Sacco and Vanzetti. History would remember the case as a gross miscarriage of justice and a tragic example of prejudice and intolerance, and the Commonwealth of Massachusetts would continue to make amends for this apparent injustice even 70 years after Sacco and Vanzetti were electrocuted under its authority.

THE POLITICAL CLIMATE OF THE EARLY 1920S

At the time the South Braintree murders took place, America was recovering from the aftermath of World War I, which had officially ended in 1918. Patriotism was strongly emphasized throughout the war period, and most of the world seemed to be in political turmoil as communist, fascist, socialist, and anarchist movements were spreading quickly, especially in Europe. The Russian Revolution of the Bolsheviks, a socialist party, occurred in 1917, and the subsequent civil war in Russia between the Bolsheviks and the anti-Bolsheviks did not end until 1920 (Karpovich, 1930). This political unrest did not go unnoticed by the United States, and President Woodrow Wilson, a leading pioneer for worldwide democracy, was keenly aware of what was transpiring in the rest of the world.

Wilson's resolve to create democracy throughout the world was not supported by all Americans and, importantly, not by all foreign immigrants who were entering the United States in record numbers at the time. Those who had views that were alternative to democracy were labeled radical, unpatriotic, and dangerous. This generated fear among the American public and in many cases resulted in the display of hatred and bigotry.

THE RED SCARE

After World War I, the United States experienced an economic depression. Many workers joined unions, and, as working conditions worsened with the poor economy, workers went on strike. Strikers were immediately labeled "Reds," and many were arrested and denied their civil liberties. These strikes were viewed as conspiracies against the government. In January 1912 one of the more infamous strikes took place at the Lawrence textile mill in eastern Massachusetts, not far from where Sacco and Vanzetti were arrested and tried. Earning extremely low wages and facing starvation and poor living conditions, the strike was led by Italian workers and the Industrial Workers of the World, a radical union that had strong socialist support (Morreale and Carola, 2006). The Bureau of Investigation (later the Federal Bureau of Investigation), under the direction of William J. Flynn, compiled over 200,000 files on radicals living in the United States. Thousands were arrested or deported, and on just one day, January 20, 1920,[1] 4,000 alleged radicals were arrested all over the United States. Many state and local governments, including Massachusetts, passed laws against radical activity (Burnett, 2000b). The Red Scare lost momentum by the summer of 1920, but Sacco and Vanzetti had been arrested in May of that year, and their case would forever be tainted by the fear and hatred that plagued the justice system during this time period.

The Sacco-Vanzetti case fell during a hostile period for those in America who did not believe in democracy. This period would later be termed the "Red Scare."

THE ACCUSED

Nicola Sacco[2] was born in a small village in southern Italy; and Vanzetti, also from a remote village, was from the northern part of Italy. Both men came from large conservative Catholic families. While living in Italy, neither strayed from his family's traditional republican political views at a time when many of their fellow countrymen turned to radical politics and religion. Although one day Sacco and Vanzetti would both call themselves atheists and anarchists, they left Italy as traditional conservative men with no controversy surrounding their soon-to-be famous names (Avrich, 1991).

Sacco and Vanzetti both left Italy in 1908 but did not meet until 1917. Like many at that time, they were drawn to America by promises of freedom and opportunity. Sacco was the lesser educated but more excited of the two. He was later quoted while in prison as saying he was "crazy to come to this country," because it was a free country—"the country that was always in my dreams" (Sacco and Vanzetti, 1997, p. 10). This notion of freedom is, ironically, what attracted them to anarchism.

Italian anarchist groups had existed in the United States for nearly 30 years when Sacco and Vanzetti arrived in America. They adhered to a branch of anarchism that was the most radical of all, and they advocated for a violent retaliation against an oppressive government. The use of dynamite and assassination was an approved method of action for this group, justified by its belief that its actions were in response to an even more violent state (Avrich, 1991).

A well-known Italian anarchist, Luigi Galleani, was living in Lynn, Massachusetts, in the early 1900s, and was the publisher of an Italian anarchist newspaper called *Cronaca Sovversiva* (Subversive Chronicle). Galleani was the mentor of many anarchists in the area, and Sacco and Vanzetti were close followers of his ideals and principles. They not only subscribed to his periodical but also contributed articles and aided in its distribution (Avrich, 1991). Galleani attracted attention from federal investigators when he wrote in a May 1917 issue about whether immigrants should register for the draft for World War I.

In this piece he stated that anarchists who did register would most likely not be sent into the military anyway because they would not be trusted. The Bureau of Investigation launched a serious investigation into Galleani, and this is how the government came to know of Sacco and Vanzetti, who were subscribers to the *Cronaca Sovversiva* (Young and Kaiser, 1985).

In 1917, during the height of the Red Scare, both Sacco and Vanzetti moved to Mexico along with several anarchist friends for a short time to escape the draft for World War I. Sacco had already begun a family with his wife, Rosina, whom he had married in 1912. They had a son, Dante, and Rosina later gave birth to a daughter, Ines, only months after Sacco's arrest. Vanzetti never married. When they left for Mexico, they both assumed different names. Vanzetti did not keep his pseudonym upon returning to the United States, but Sacco would forever be known as Nicola, rather than his true name, Ferdinando Sacco. After living in Mexico for several months, Sacco returned to his family in Stoughton, Massachusetts. Vanzetti moved around the United States and eventually settled in Plymouth, Massachusetts, where he became a fish peddler (Burnett, 2000a). During the three-year period preceding their arrest in 1920, many of their friends, who also subscribed to Galleani's periodical, were arrested and deported back to Italy. The clear message from the government was that radicalism would not be tolerated.

However, Sacco and Vanzetti held steadfastly to their radical beliefs until their deaths in 1927. From Dedham Prison they continued to write for anarchist newspapers and sent hundreds of anarchist-themed letters and pamphlets to those outside the prison. In one letter to Sarah Adams, Vanzetti wrote this of Sacco and himself:

> Both Nick and I are anarchists—the radical of the radical—the black cats, the terrors of many, of all the bigots, exploitators, charlatans, and oppressors. Consequently, we are also the more slandered, misrepresented, misunderstood, and persecuted of all. After all we are socialists as the social-democrats, the socialists, the communists....The difference...between us and all the other is that they are authoritarian while we are libertarian; they believe in a State or Government of their own; we believe in no State or Government. (Sacco and Vanzetti, 1997, pp. 274–275)

Further on in this letter, Vanzetti stated that he and Sacco did not believe in religion. He told Adams that he and Sacco could have stayed in Italy and grown rich off the poor but they chose freedom instead and denounced that other way of life. Many scholars feel that because they chose anarchism, they were targeted by the government and subsequently eliminated for a horrible crime that they may or may not have committed.

THE CRIME

The robbery and murders took place at the Slater and Morrill shoe factory in South Braintree, Massachusetts, at approximately 3 p.m. on April 15, 1920. Several people witnessed the crime, and these people later provided the crucial testimony that helped to convict Sacco and Vanzetti. The shoe factory had two buildings, and between the two buildings was a railway station. At around 9:30 in the morning, a train arrived at the station and an employee of the American Railway Express delivered money from the train to the factory. This money was intended for distribution to the Slater and Morrill workers. The railway employee later testified that he had seen two strangers in a car, and he claimed that this was the car the murderers used that day. Other people around town had seen the car in various places that day as well and were able to give general descriptions of the men in the car. The railway employee described one of the men as thin and blonde. Other witnesses gave this description, and later in court the prosecution claimed that this description fit Sacco. Just prior to the shooting, these same two men from the car were seen standing against a fence on the shoe factory grounds on Pearl Street. What people did not know was that these two men were waiting for a scheduled delivery of the factory's payroll that had just arrived on the morning train (Fraenkel, 1969).

The money had been separated into pay envelopes and was parted into two separate metal boxes, and these boxes were given to the shoe factory's paymaster, Frederick Parmenter, and his guard, Allesandro Berardelli, to bring to the other factory building. They left the building together with the two metal boxes filled with $15,776.51 in cash. As they approached the next factory building on Pearl Street, the two men who had been standing against the fence jumped from their positions and confronted Parmenter and Berardelli. Berardelli struggled with one of the men, who then shot him three times. This same armed man shot Parmenter twice. The other man picked up the cashboxes that had been dropped and waited for the getaway car as it was driven up the hill toward them. Berardelli, still struggling, tried to get up from the ground when a third man sprang from the car and shot him point blank in the chest. The first two robbers were already in the car, the third bandit joined them, and as they drove away they fired several more shots at the factory windows (Russell, 1971).

One witness, Jimmy Bostock, saw Berardelli and Parmenter fall to the ground from a distance and was even shot at when he tried to approach the scene. Witnesses inside the factory buildings had heard the shots even though the windows were closed, and some had peered through a slit in a jammed window to see the final part of the crime take place. As the car drove away, a barrier blocked its path before the train tracks because a train was nearing the station. After being threatened with a pistol by one of the men in the car, Mike Levangie raised the barrier to let them pass. Other witnesses were able to generally describe the bandits, but few could give specific details. The length of the incident was less than a minute from the time the first shots rang out to when the car disappeared from the scene (Russell, 1971).

There were more than 50 witnesses to the crime, and there were many differing accounts of what took place that afternoon as "the actuality faded and the myth took over" (Russell, 1971, p. 41). Many believe that none of the eyewitness accounts can be taken seriously, because there were so many different stories told to the police:

> The car was black, it was green, it was shiny, it was mud-streaked. There were two cars. The men who did the shooting were dark, were pale, had blue suits, had brown suits, had gray suits, wore felt hats, wore caps, were bareheaded. Only one had a gun, both had guns. The third man had been behind the brick pile with a shotgun the whole time. Anywhere between eight and thirty shots had been fired. (Russell, 1971, p. 42)

The witnesses agreed upon some details. There had been five men inside the car, which they identified as a touring car, and the driver was fair-skinned. The two bandits who had initiated the shooting were short and clean-shaven. Three witnesses, including Bostock, identified the man who had been hanging outside the getaway car from a picture that police showed them, but as it turned out that man was in jail in western New York State at the time the crime took place (Russell, 1971). The case was primed to become one of the most controversial in history, because, despite conflicting eyewitness accounts and

22

ITALIAN IMMIGRANTS IN AMERICA

The large wave of Italian immigration to the United States began in 1880. Around 80 percent of these immigrants were from southern Italy, an area stricken by poverty, shortage of food, droughts and floods that worsened the already imperfect farming terrain, and cholera epidemics. Facing this devastation and prejudice as well as unfair taxes from their government, thousands of southern Italians left their homes for Western countries. Those who chose the United States were welcomed by the Statue of Liberty and the promise of a new life, but prejudice and scorn awaited them as well. As nationalists pushed for severe restrictions on immigration, Congress failed many attempts to mandate literacy tests for immigrants, but eventually succeeded in 1917. President Woodrow Wilson stated that southern Italians came from the lowest class of Italians, and they lacked both skill and intelligence. President Wilson, who was in office when Sacco and Vanzetti were arrested, made many derogatory comments about Italians. He once said, "hyphenates have poured the poison of disloyalty into the very arteries of our national life...Such creatures of passion, disloyalty, and anarchy must be crushed out" (as quoted in Morreale and Carola, 2000). Despite Wilson's charge of disloyalty, Italian Americans strongly supported the American cause in both World Wars, and most embraced the democratic way of life in America (Morreale and Carola, 2000).

lack of evidence, the Massachusetts authorities were, nonetheless, able to arrest, convict, and execute two men for this heinous crime.

EVENTS LEADING TO THEIR ARREST

Sacco and Vanzetti were well known by Massachusetts law enforcement officials by the time of their arrest in 1920 because they were Galleanistis.[3] Galleani had been deported in 1919, but he continued to publish the *Cronaca Sovversiva* from Italy with monetary support from Massachusetts anarchists (Young and Kaiser, 1985). All Galleanistis were under heavy scrutiny because of a series of bombings that had occurred in the Massachusetts area in 1919 and 1920. This group was suspected of having set off these bombs. Andrea Salsedo, a Galleanisti and close friend of Sacco and Vanzetti, had been arrested by federal authorities in March 1920 on suspicion that he was one of the men behind the explosions. Two months after his arrest and while being detained, Salsedo committed suicide[4] by throwing himself out of a window in New York. The newspapers reported his death and the news that Salsedo had supposedly given the names of all those involved in the bombings before leaping to his death. The *Boston Herald* headline read: "Salsedo Gave Names of All Terrorist Plotters Before Taking a Death Leap" (Avrich, 1991, p. 198). Many Galleanistis fled the country in the two months following his arrest. Sacco was planning to return to Italy but was arrested before he could do so.

In March, Sacco learned of the death of his mother in Italy. When that was coupled with the arrest and deportation of many friends, he decided it was time to move back to Italy with his family. He had made the necessary arrangements with the Italian consulate, he had quit his job at the 3-K Shoe Factory, and he and his family were to leave the weekend following his arrest. Many suspect that Sacco and Vanzetti believed their names had been given to the authorities by Salsedo before he died, and this is why they were "acting guilty" the night of their arrest. Many also believed that they were plotters of the 1919 and 1920 bombings in Massachusetts. Although police believed that Sacco and Vanzetti were involved in these bombings,[5] this belief is not why they were arrested on May 5, 1920.

On December 24, 1919, several months prior to the shoe factory murders, there had been an attempted robbery at the L.Q. White Shoe Factory in Bridgewater, Massachusetts. In this case, no one was injured, and the four men involved managed to escape but without the $30,000 payroll they were seeking (Avrich, 1991). Chief Michael Stewart of the Bridgewater police believed he knew two men who were guilty of both holdups: Feruccio Coacci, a Galleanisti and a shoe worker who had worked at both the L.Q. White and Slater and Morrill shoe factories; and Mario Boda, a man who was sharing a home with Coacci and his family.

Coacci had been arrested in 1918 and was marked for deportation, but was temporarily released on bond while awaiting a deportation date. He had received notice to report for deportation on April 15, 1920, the day of the South Braintree holdup and murders, but he failed to appear at the immigration station in East Boston. He had telephoned saying that his wife was ill, and as it turned out this alibi was false. When officers arrived at his house, they offered to allow him to postpone his deportation for an additional week, but Coacci refused and left the country on April 18. Stewart heard of this case and immediately suspected Coacci of having committed the South Braintree crime. Stewart also heard an informant's story that a group of Italian anarchists had committed the Bridgewater holdup and believed that both crimes were committed by the same men; Coacci was one of them (Avrich, 1991).

Coacci had already left the country, but Stewart searched his home and found Boda. Stewart questioned him and learned that Boda's car was being repaired at a local shop and that he owned a gun. That Boda owned a car and that he was an associate of Coacci placed him under suspicion (Fraenkel, 1969). Stewart suspected that Boda had hidden the Buick used in the South Braintree crimes in a shack behind the house before it was abandoned. When Stewart returned to question Boda again, he had already escaped through the back door. Stewart located Boda's car at the shop he had specified earlier and told the shop owner, Simon Johnson, to call him if someone came to retrieve Boda's car.

So it came to be that police in southeastern Massachusetts[6] were searching for the perpetrators of both holdups. Since Chief Stewart believed that the perpetrators were the same for both incidents and that they were Italian anarchists, police of the area were on the lookout for Italians who were acting suspiciously and who were looking for a car. Stewart's theory was supported by the Norfolk district attorney's office. However, the Massachusetts state police believed that the South Braintree holdup was the work of professionals. Nevertheless, on the evening of May 5, 1920, when Boda arrived at Johnson's repair shop with three other men—Sacco, Vanzetti, and Riccardo Orciani—to retrieve Boda's car, Johnson's wife called the police. Johnson did not greet them, and because they were unable to retrieve the car, they left. Sacco and Vanzetti boarded a streetcar while Orciani and Boda left separately. Shortly after, Sacco, Vanzetti, and Orciani were arrested by police in Brockton, Massachusetts. Boda was never caught by the police and escaped to Italy later that year (Avrich, 1991).

When they were arrested, Sacco had a loaded Colt automatic with 23 extra cartridges in his pocket and Vanzetti had a .38-caliber Harrington & Richardson revolver and shotgun shells in his pocket. Sacco was marked as one of the shooters in the South Braintree robbery, and Vanzetti was pegged as the "shotgun bandit"[7] from the Bridgewater attempted robbery (Avrich, 1991). They were brought to the police station for questioning but were not told why they were being held. Stewart asked Sacco and Vanzetti why they were out on the streets so late at night; they replied that they had been visiting a friend and were on their way home. They both denied knowing Boda or Coacci, and before the guns were found on them they had denied having guns. They were asked whether they were anarchists and whether they supported the government. Vanzetti simply replied that he was different and that he liked things different. When asked why he carried a gun, Vanzetti replied that he needed it for protection because he was in business.[8] Sacco denied being an anarchist and said he needed a gun because there were many bad men around (Russell, 1971). After this questioning, they were locked up at the Brockton police station. The next day Frederick Gunn Katzmann, the district attorney for Norfolk and Plymouth counties, questioned them again, and they repeated the same answers they had given to Chief Stewart. They were brought to Brockton police court, where they pled guilty to carrying concealed weapons, and the judge ordered that they be held without bail.[9]

Over the next several days, many witnesses were brought to Brockton to view the three men. They were not placed in a lineup but rather brought into a viewing room and told to position themselves in various ways. They were told to pretend that they were holding a gun and to crouch in firing position. One witness identified Orciani as one of the men in the South Braintree holdups and another identified him as a gunman in the Bridgewater holdup (Russell, 1971), but the police released him because he had a substantiated alibi for both dates. He had been at work on April 15 and on December 24 and could not have been involved in the crimes (Young and Kaiser, 1985). Sacco and Vanzetti were not so fortunate.

Most of the witnesses could not identify Sacco or Vanzetti as perpetrators in the South Braintree incident. Bostock, one of the witnesses who had been closest in distance to the crime, could not identify either man. One witness thought Sacco resembled the man he saw shoot the guard, Berardelli, and two other witnesses thought Sacco resembled a man they had seen in the getaway car. One witness identified Vanzetti as the driver of the getaway car, but the most common reply from the South Braintree witnesses was that they did not recognize either Sacco or Vanzetti. One of the three eyewitnesses from the Bridgewater holdup who came to the station believed Vanzetti was the man carrying the shotgun, although he had previously given a description different from that of Vanzetti. Of the other two witnesses, one was not sure that Vanzetti was the "shotgun bandit," and the other did not believe Vanzetti was the one he had seen (Russell, 1971). Vanzetti was first prosecuted for the Bridgewater holdup in Plymouth but will forever be known because of the trial held in Dedham a year later.

THE PLYMOUTH TRIAL

On June 11, 1920, Vanzetti was indicted for assault with intent to rob and assault with intent to murder for the attempted holdup in Bridgewater. The trial commenced in Plymouth on June 23 with Katzmann and Assistant District Attorney William Kane representing the Commonwealth of Massachusetts (Joughin and Morgan, 1948). Sacco and Vanzetti's comrades aided the two men by locating lawyers for them. Vanzetti's friends chose Judge John Vahey of the local district court, and Sacco's associates selected James Graham, who was known for getting along well with politicians and helping to exonerate Italians in trouble with the law (Russell, 1971). Both men defended Vanzetti in Plymouth.

The presiding judge was Judge Webster Thayer, who had a reputation for disliking foreigners but nonetheless was considered a fair judge (Russell, 1971).

The prosecution built a case around the eyewitnesses to the crime, and they succeeded in discrediting Vanzetti's alibi. Several witnesses testified in court that they believed Vanzetti was involved in the attempted holdup. When Vanzetti was arrested, he was carrying shotgun shells in his pocket, and this was additional circumstantial evidence used against him, since there was a similar exploded shell found at the scene of the crime. Later, in the Dedham trial, Vanzetti stated that he had taken the shells from the Sacco home on May 5 so he could sell them to fund propaganda. In a separate room, the jury opened the shells that were used as evidence against Vanzetti, thereby violating his right to be tried on evidence in an open court. But Judge Thayer never declared the incident, and Vanzetti's lawyers discovered the violation only after the trial was over (Ehrmann, 1969).

The defense had 21 witnesses testify on Vanzetti's behalf. Most of these witnesses were Italian, and some of them required an interpreter. Vanzetti was a fish peddler in Plymouth, and the Italian witnesses testified in court that Vanzetti had sold them eels on December 24. The date is important because, in Italian Catholic tradition, eel is the essential part of the feast that is celebrated to end fasting on December 24, Christmas Eve. The prosecution attacked these testimonies as substantial alibis for Vanzetti, asserting that they could not possibly remember specific times from so long ago. Other witnesses for Vanzetti testified that he never kept his mustache short and "cropped" as the prosecution witnesses had described the "shotgun bandit" (Joughin and Morgan, 1948).

Vanzetti did not testify on his own behalf, and he later harshly criticized his Plymouth lawyers for not having allowed him to do so. Some believe this influenced the jury in convicting Vanzetti. He was found guilty on July 1, 1920, and Judge Thayer sentenced him to 12 to 15 years in prison. This trial did not receive much publicity. There was only brief mention of it in the newspapers, and very few people attended the trial itself. The case seemed inconsequential to the public, but it was a significant strike against Vanzetti in his upcoming trial with Sacco. In 1927, the year of the executions, Governor Alvan Fuller was presented with new evidence that substantiated Vanzetti's alibi for December 24. A record of an eel delivery for Vanzetti surfaced from an old box of American Express delivery receipts, thus proving that Vanzetti was selling eels that day as witnesses had testified. Fuller did not exonerate Vanzetti, however. He said it was possible that Vanzetti could have sold eels in Plymouth and committed the crime in Bridgewater that same morning, since Bridgewater and Plymouth were only 20 miles apart (Ehrmann, 1969). Vanzetti's lawyers thought the governor's theory was ludicrous. Many people believe that Vanzetti was wrongly convicted of both crimes and that the only conclusion that can be drawn today is that both trials proceeded in a biased and prejudicial manner.

THE TRIAL IN DEDHAM

Sacco and Vanzetti were indicted for the South Braintree murders on September 14, 1920. Their trial began on May 21, 1921, at the Norfolk County Courthouse in Dedham, Massachusetts. The presiding judge was once again Webster Thayer. Defense counsel had changed since Sacco and Vanzetti were arrested. The lawyers representing Sacco were Fred H. Moore and William J. Callahan. Moore was from California and was well known for his defense of radicals and workers. Callahan had represented Sacco at a preliminary hearing in Quincy. Jeremiah and Thomas McAnarney, two brothers and well-known

Figure 2.1 **Bartolomeo Vanzetti (left) and Nicola Sacco, about to enter the courthouse at Dedham, Massachusetts, where they received the death sentence for murder. Courtesy of the Library of Congress.**

lawyers from Norfolk County, represented Vanzetti. Prosecuting for the Commonwealth again was District Attorney Frederick Gunn Katzmann.

The prosecution went forward with Chief Stewart's theory that the same group of men committed the crimes in both Bridgewater and South Braintree. Holes in the theory were ignored, and this is partly why the case became extremely controversial. The money taken from the Slater and Morrill shoe factory was never recovered. Stewart assumed that Coacci had taken it back to Italy with him, but it was learned that the Italian police had stopped Coacci upon his return to Italy, searched his belongings, and found nothing. Sacco was able to prove that he had been at work on December 24 and therefore could not have been involved in the Bridgewater crime. However, records showed that he was not at work on April 15, which bolstered the prosecution's argument that he was in South Braintree that day committing robbery and murder with four other men (Avrich, 1991).

This theory was not supported by all officials involved in the case. The state police never backed down from their theory that professionals had committed the South Braintree crime. Nevertheless, the prosecution continued with Stewart's theory and brought evidence before the court against Sacco and Vanzetti. The jurors were brought to the scene of the crime, and on the sixth day of the trial they began to hear evidence against the defendants. The state presented 16 witnesses to identify Sacco. Three of the witnesses placed him at the shoe factory before the crime took place. Of these three witnesses, the defense, upon cross-examination, discovered that one of them had previously failed to

27

identify Sacco's photograph. Another witness put it this way: "While I wouldn't be positive, I would say that to the best of my recollection, that was the man" (W.S. Tracy as quoted in Joughin and Morgan, 1948). The third witness was "pretty sure" that Sacco was the man he saw. Of those who witnessed the shooting, none could positively say that Sacco was the man they saw. Bostock was unable to identify either man at the police station or at the trial. Lewis Wade, who had positively identified Sacco at the police station, expressed his doubts at the trial. Most of the witnesses could only generally describe the men they saw. Some called them short, stout, or dark-skinned, and some said that two of the men were wearing dark hats (Joughin and Morgan, 1948).

A cap found near Berardelli's body was used as additional evidence against Sacco. Sacco's employer and friend George Kelley was asked in court if the cap was Sacco's. He could not say either way. Kelley knew that Sacco's cap was dark and that he hung it on a nail at work every day (Russell, 1971). The cap that had been admitted into evidence was torn in the back, and Judge Thayer concluded that this was a result of Sacco hanging it on a nail. However, it was later learned after the trial's conclusion that a police officer had torn the hat while searching for an identifying mark. When Sacco tried the cap on in court, it appeared to be too small, and this aspect of the case was made famous by cartoonists from the *Boston Post* and the *Boston Herald* (Ehrmann, 1969). Some newspapers mocked the lack of evidence against Sacco and Vanzetti, and cartoons were a popular way to do so.

A bullet found in Berardelli's body was further evidence provided by the prosecution to prove Sacco's guilt. Captain William H. Proctor of the state police was unsure but said it was possible that the fatal shot could have originated from a gun such as the one Sacco carried (Joughin and Morgan, 1948). The defense presented expert witnesses who claimed that the fatal bullet found in Berardelli could not have been fired from Sacco's gun. The ballistics evidence became one of the most controversial issues surrounding the Sacco and Vanzetti case.

The final evidence used against Sacco and Vanzetti involved their actions on the night of their arrest. Evidence of lies and an apparent guilty manner on that night was presented to the jury. Katzmann and Chief Stewart had questioned them and were witness to their deliberate deceit. Later, author Paul Avrich argued that this elusive behavior was logical, considering that Sacco and Vanzetti most likely believed that they were being arrested for anarchy. Only two days before their arrest, they learned that Andrea Salsedo had given up the names of his anarchist comrades who were part of the 1919 and 1920 bomb plots in Massachusetts. Fear that their names had been given to officials may have caused them to lie about their political beliefs and their weapons (Avrich, 1991).

Overall, there was less evidence presented against Vanzetti. The prosecution connected Vanzetti to the crime by stressing his association with Sacco, presenting eyewitnesses who believed that one of the men in the car looked like Vanzetti, and claiming that the gun found on Vanzetti the night of his arrest had originally belonged to Berardelli. Those witnesses who identified Vanzetti were unable to describe anyone else with Vanzetti. The testimony of one of the witnesses, Mike Levangie, was impeached because he had previously given different testimony. He had claimed in court that Vanzetti was the driver of the getaway car, but had previously said that he was a passenger. The prosecution then admitted that Vanzetti was not driving the car but perhaps Levangie was confused as to Vanzetti's location in the car. The eyewitness testimony against Vanzetti was not strong (Joughin and Morgan, 1948).

The defense and prosecution presented conflicting testimony as to whether Berardelli had been armed at the time of the robbery. It was known that he had left his gun at a shop a few weeks prior to the incident so that the broken hammer could be replaced. Testimony was given that Berardelli's gun was similar to Vanzetti's gun, which had been presented as evidence. Vanzetti, however, was able to show when and where he had purchased his gun, and expert testimony showed that Vanzetti's gun did not have a new hammer (Joughin and Morgan, 1948). The final evidence presented against Vanzetti was his display of guilt on the night of his arrest.

Vanzetti's alibi was deemed "overwhelming" by Felix Frankfurter, a lawyer and future Supreme Court justice who had been following and assisting with the case. Thirty-one eyewitnesses testified in court that Vanzetti was not one of the men they saw in the get-away car. There were 13 witnesses who testified that they had seen Vanzetti selling fish in Plymouth on the day in question (Frankfurter, 1954). Sacco claimed to have been in Boston. Several witnesses supported this claim and remembered the day because it was the day of an Italian feast in the predominantly Italian north end of Boston. Sacco had met with an Italian consulate to discuss the paperwork necessary for his upcoming return trip to Italy with his family. The consulate also testified on Sacco's behalf. Katzmann, as he had done with previous defense witnesses, asked the alibi witnesses to recall other events and people from that day and they could not (Ehrmann, 1969). The trial, which lasted nearly seven weeks, did not go well for Sacco and Vanzetti. On July 21, 1921, they were convicted of murder in the first degree.

THE APPEALS PROCESS AND THE WORLD'S REACTION

Two men who came to America to realize a dream unintentionally divided a nation and mobilized the world around them. While many spoke out against Sacco and Vanzetti, millions rallied to their side. After their conviction in 1921, most of the country still had not heard of Sacco and Vanzetti. The *New York Times* only briefly mentioned the conviction in a small piece several pages into the newspaper (Trasciatti, 2003). It was only after six years of appeals and extraordinary defense strategy that international fame came upon these two men. Their plight attracted widespread media attention and their names appeared in headlines all over the world. But newspapers were not the only venue through which their story was told. One of the chief defense attorneys to serve for Sacco and Vanzetti, Fred H. Moore, transformed the traditional means of defending murder suspects by not solely disputing the facts surrounding the crime. Moore heavily politicized the case by openly discussing Sacco and Vanzetti's anarchist beliefs in court, and he tried to establish that his clients were prosecuted solely because of their radical beliefs. The prosecution, of course, denied these accusations, but Moore went further and claimed that this was all part of a government plan to halt the anarchist movement in the United States (D'Attilio, 1999).

Moore's efforts involved contacting unions around the world, distributing many thousands of defense pamphlets throughout several countries, and organizing public meetings. Moore also managed to gain the aid of the Italian government despite the defendants' anarchist background. Italian dictator Benito Mussolini had taken office in 1922 and was well known for his repression of anarchists in Italy. Surprisingly, he was more than eager to defend Sacco and Vanzetti. He recognized the importance of Sacco and Vanzetti's case and witnessed the insurrections among the Italian people after they had read about the fate of their comrades in the Italian newspapers (Cannistraro, 1996).

Moore had sent a young liberal journalist, Eugene Lyons, to Italy hoping to stir up emotions in favor of Sacco and Vanzetti. Lyons helped set up organizations to gather support and sent countless numbers of articles to leftist newspapers in Italy. The Sacco-Vanzetti Defense Committee, which had been formed in Boston shortly after their arrest, coordinated efforts with those of Lyons in Italy and sent letters and leaflets to Italy declaring that Sacco and Vanzetti had been arrested as a result of their political beliefs. Lyons was later expelled by Mussolini after anarchists, in an unrelated matter, detonated a bomb that killed 21 people. The Italian protests nevertheless continued, as did the Italian government's support for Sacco and Vanzetti, even after their executions in 1927 (Cannistraro, 1996).

The Italian government's involvement did not please many anarchist comrades, but it became very apparent that the cause was backed by more than just radical left-wing groups such as socialists and anarchists. Moore's tactics had transformed a small-town case into an international affair, gathering support from every corner of the world. This outreach did not come without costs, however, and Moore's unprecedented methods of defending this case eventually led to his dismissal:

> His manner of utilizing mass media was quite modern and effective, but it required enormous sums of money, which he spent too freely in the eyes of many of the anarchist comrades of Sacco and Vanzetti, who had to raise most of it painstakingly from working people, twenty-five and fifty cents at a time. Moore's efforts came to be questioned even by the two defendants, when he, contrary to anarchist ideals, offered a large reward to find the real criminals. (D'Attilio, 1999, p. 11)

By the time of his dismissal, however, his goal had been accomplished, and Sacco and Vanzetti were international celebrities.

William Thompson and Herbert Ehrmann succeeded Moore and continued the attempts to receive a new trial. During the six years after the conviction, many new issues came to light and were raised in appeals. These issues further enraged the public and reinforced the notion that these men had not received a fair trial. Judge Thayer was undoubtedly a prejudiced man, although he did not reveal this prejudice in court records. Before the trial commenced, Thayer, while in the company of several newspaper reporters, learned of the leaflets being distributed in support of Sacco and Vanzetti. In his anger over this public support, he declared before several witnesses, "You wait till I give my charge to the jury. I'll show 'em!" (as cited in Ehrmann, 1969, p. 462). The foreman of the jury, Walter Ripley, had spoken candidly with a friend who had expressed his belief in their innocence, and to this Ripley replied, "Damn them, they ought to hang anyway!" (as cited in Feuerlicht, 1977, p. 202). While Governor Fuller was considering the clemency appeal, he received a letter from a conservative Dartmouth professor, James Richardson, who had spoken with Thayer after the trial ended. Richardson revealed Thayer's comment: "Did you see what I did to those anarchistic bastards the other day? . . . They wouldn't get very far in my court" (as cited in Feuerlicht, 1977, p. 349).

The most intriguing new evidence that was brought before Judge Thayer, and later before an advisory committee, was the confession of a prisoner by the name of Celestino Madeiros. In 1925, while in Dedham Jail with Sacco, he confessed in a note to Sacco that he had taken part in the South Braintree robbery and murders with the four other members of the Morelli Gang. The Morelli Gang was a well-known professional group of robbers from the area. It is important to note that the state police believed that the crime had been committed by professionals. This gang was known for stealing shoes and textiles from freight trains, and many of these crimes had occurred in South Braintree. They spoke English without accents because they were American-born Italians. Some of the witnesses had testified in court that the bandits had spoken perfect English without a trace of an Italian accent. Both Sacco and Vanzetti spoke broken English. Joseph Morelli, the leader of the gang, bore a striking facial resemblance to Sacco. All of the gang members were out of jail at the time of the crime, and two of them had just been released a few weeks before April 15, 1920. One of the Morelli brothers drove a Buick, and the getaway car was determined to be a Buick. Another brother owned a 32 Colt revolver, and it was this type of gun that was used to kill the two men from the factory (Ehrmann, 1969).

Thompson and Ehrmann spent a great deal of time interviewing Madeiros. One startling discovery they made was that Madeiros's account of the incident differed from the trial account in that he spoke of two separate getaway cars. He claimed they switched cars after the robbery, but the trial record shows that there was only one car. It was discovered a few months later that Madeiros was correct in his version of what happened, and the trial record was wrong (Ehrmann, 1969). Finally, Thompson and Ehrmann learned that Madeiros had $2,800 after he was released from jail in 1921. This was just under one-fifth of the money stolen from the shoe factory. In Thompson and Ehrmann's view, the case seemed very strong against the Morelli Gang. They presented this evidence on appeal for a new trial, but Thayer denied the motion (Ehrmann, 1969).

Six appeals for a new trial were made to Thayer, and he denied all of them. This system in which the trial judge ruled on appeals seemed absurd to many people at the time. Judge Thayer ruled on accusations of prejudice made against him. It was because of the Sacco-Vanzetti case that the appeals system was changed following their executions. However, on April 5, 1927, the Supreme Judicial Court of Massachusetts overruled all objections to Thayer's denials. On April 9, Thayer condemned Sacco and Vanzetti to death by electrocution.

An application for clemency was filed with Governor Alvan Fuller on May 4, 1927. In response to this and growing social pressure, Fuller appointed an advisory committee to review the case. The committee consisted of Abbott Lawrence Lowell, the president of Harvard University; Robert Grant, a former judge; and Samuel Stratton, president of the Massachusetts Institute of Technology. This committee became known as the Lowell Committee. Ehrmann and Thompson were dismayed at the Lowell Committee's reaction to evidence of prejudice by Judge Thayer. The committee condemned Thayer's prejudicial conduct, calling it a "grave breech of official decorum" (Lowell as quoted in Ehrmann, 1969, p. 501). However, they did not judge that it justified an order for a new trial. The Lowell Committee dismissed all issues raised before them, and they advised Governor Fuller that Sacco and Vanzetti were guilty. Upon this advice, Fuller denied the appeal for clemency.

After the Lowell report was made public, many newspapers, including the *New York Times*, applauded the decision, while many writers did not agree. Heywood Broun, a reporter for the *New York World*, referred to Harvard University as "Hangman's House" in criticism of its president and added, "What more can these immigrants from Italy expect? It is not every prisoner who has the president of Harvard University throw on the switch for him" (as quoted in Feuerlicht, 1977, p. 381).

THE EXECUTIONS

Many last-minute attempts were made to save Sacco and Vanzetti. An appeal made to the Supreme Judicial Court of Massachusetts was denied, and August 1927 became a tense month for most of the world. Newspapers reported their surprise at the growing international concern for the two anarchists. The Sacco-Vanzetti Defense Committee made a plea to liberals and intellectuals for support. Dorothy Parker, Jane Addams, John Dewey, Edna St. Vincent Millay, and Katherine Porter were among the hundreds of well-known figures of the time to rally to the cause. Letters were sent, petitions were signed and sent to the newspapers, thousands picketed the streets of Boston and other cities, and there were countless strikes and demonstrations for Sacco and Vanzetti (Feuerlicht, 1977). Governor Fuller granted a stay of execution for 12 days while final deliberations were made, but ultimately Sacco and Vanzetti were executed just after midnight on August 23, 1927. The streets of Boston were empty at the time due to strict city orders, but thousands turned out in New York City to protest their executions. After the executions, thousands rioted on the streets of cities all over the world, including Boston, Paris, New York, and Buenos Aires (Selmi, 2001). Thousands of supporters also marched with the funeral procession in Boston, and as the coffins passed, they strew flowers in the coffins' direction. In Massachusetts, however, the population seemed divided. The lower class was sympathetic to Sacco and Vanzetti, but the upper and middle classes were hostile toward them (Feuerlicht, 1977). To the dismay of millions all over the world, Sacco and Vanzetti were not saved, but this is not the end of their story.

THE AFTERMATH AND THE LEGACY OF SACCO AND VANZETTI

Many famous people at the time were convinced that Sacco and Vanzetti were two innocent men who were wrongly executed. Upton Sinclair was one such famous person. Four years after the executions, Sinclair traveled to Boston to gather facts surrounding Sacco and Vanzetti. He came to Boston under the impression that these were peaceful men and that they were merely "philosophical anarchists" (Sinclair as quoted in Avrich, 1991, p. 161). After learning a great deal from those who worked closely on the case, he concluded just the opposite: they were militant anarchists who believed in and preached the use of violence. Paul Avrich, author of *Sacco and Vanzetti: The Anarchist Background,* concluded that Sacco and Vanzetti were undoubtedly involved in the 1919 bombings in Massachusetts. He was uncertain of their roles in the crime, but their involvement was a "virtual certainty" (Avrich, 1991, p. 162).

Many books were written about the Sacco-Vanzetti case. Some authors believed they were guilty, but most firmly believed in their innocence. In 1969, Herbert Ehrmann published *The Case That Will Not Die,* and he shed new light on the ballistics evidence used against Sacco. He included photos of the bullets admitted into evidence, and he showed that bullets had been tampered with and possibly replaced before the trial began. Many academics and intellectuals have gathered at conferences to discuss the Sacco-Vanzetti case. The injustice that occurred has even stirred much discussion about the fairness and validity of the death penalty in the United States.

The media world has continued to cover the story even as it grows more distant in history. This is partly because of the lasting political and legal effects of the case. The Massachusetts appeals laws were rewritten so that trial judges could not rule on appeals. In 1977, fifty years after the executions, Governor Michael S. Dukakis declared August 23

"Nicola Sacco and Bartolomeo Vanzetti Memorial Day" in Massachusetts. He did not officially pardon them, but he declared that they had received an unfair trial and stated that any stigma attached to their names was removed that day (Young and Kaiser, 1985). In 1997, the first Italian American mayor of Boston, Thomas Menino, dedicated a bronze sculpture of Sacco and Vanzetti and ordered it placed in a public area of Boston. Gutzon Borglum, the creator of Mount Rushmore, had created this sculpture many years ago, but previous Massachusetts governors and Boston mayors had refused to display it (Gelastopoulos, 1997).

In the arts, many writers and directors have honored the memory of Sacco and Vanzetti. There were numerous plays written and acted out on television and in the theater. An opera, *The Passion of Sacco and Vanzetti,* was performed in New York City and other major venues. Several songs were inspired by their story. Documentaries, speeches, and newspaper articles have appeared in the media every year since their death. It is likely that the majority of Americans are still somewhat familiar with the story of the two men because of the attention it has received from the media.

The Sacco and Vanzetti saga will continue to be told in books, plays, periodicals, and television productions. No one can ever be truly positive about whether these men were guilty or innocent, but the majority support the latter. It is undeniable that Sacco and Vanzetti received an unfair trial, and this injustice stirred universal emotions and caused many to criticize the American criminal justice system. They could not possibly have realized in 1927 what their legacy would be, but perhaps Vanzetti had some hint. He found solace in knowing that their deaths would not be in vain, and three months before his execution, he declared in a letter to the *New York World:*

> If it had not been for these thing, I might have live out my life talking at street corners to scorning men. I might have die, unmarked, unknown, a failure. This is our career and our triumph. Never in our full life could we hope to do such work for tolerance, for joostice [*sic*], for man's understanding of man as now we do by accident. Our words—our lives—our pains—nothing! The taking of our lives—lives of a good shoemaker and a poor fish peddler—all! That last moment belongs to us—that agony is our triumph. (Vanzetti in Sacco and Vanzetti, 1997, p. lvi)

Their triumph was realized even before their deaths. The power and influence of these two men have been far greater than those of many other foreigners who moved to America to realize a dream.

SUGGESTIONS FOR FURTHER READING

Morreale, B., and Carola, R. (2006). *Italian Americans: The immigrant experience.* New York: Barnes & Noble.

Rappaport, D. (1992). *The Sacco-Vanzetti trial,* part of the *Be the judge–Be the jury series.* New York: Harper-Collins Publishers.

Sacco, N., and Vanzetti, B. (1997). In M.D. Frankfurter and G. Jackson (Eds.), *The letters of Sacco and Vanzetti.* New York: Penguin Books.

NOTES

1. Three months prior to the arrest of Sacco and Vanzetti.
2. His name given at birth and as he was known to his family is Ferdinando Sacco, but later while living in Mexico, he assumed the name of his older brother, Nicola, who was then deceased (Avrich, 1991).

3. A Galleanisti is a follower of Galleani's anarchist belief system.

4. Salsedo's death while being detained was considered highly suspicious, but was labeled a suicide by authorities.

5. After the deportation of Galleani, the police recovered a list that contained all subscribers to the *Cronaca Sovversiva,* and Sacco and Vanzetti were among the names they found.

6. Both South Braintree and Bridgewater are located in southeastern Massachusetts.

7. In the Bridgewater robbery attempt, one of the four men involved in the crime had been firing a shotgun at the truck carrying the $30,000 payroll.

8. Vanzetti was a fish peddler but worked for himself.

9. The Brockton judge had the power to do this because of a wartime act still in place. This act stated that men who were suspected of major crimes could be held in jail without bail (Russell, 1971).

REFERENCES

Avrich, P. (1991). *Sacco and Vanzetti: The anarchist background.* Princeton, NJ: Princeton University Press.

Burnett, P. (2000a). The Sacco and Vanzetti trial: Key figures. Retrieved February 10, 2004, from http://www.law.umkc.edu/faculty/projects/ftrials/SaccoV/SaccoV.html

Burnett, P. (2000b). The red scare. Retrieved February 10, 2004, from http://www.law.umkc.edu/faculty/projects/ftrials/SaccoV/redscare.html

Cannistraro, P.V. (1996). Mussolini, Sacco-Vanzetti, and the anarchists: The transatlantic context. *The Journal of Modern History, 68,* 31–62.

D'Attilio, R. (1999). Sacco-Vanzetti case. Retrieved February 11, 2004, from http://www.english.upenn.edu/8afilreis/88/sacvan.html

Ehrmann, H.B. (1969). *The case that will not die: Commonwealth v. Sacco and Vanzetti.* Boston: Little, Brown and Company.

Feuerlicht, R.S. (1977). *Justice crucified: The story of Sacco and Vanzetti.* New York: McGraw-Hill.

Fraenkel, O. (1969). *The Sacco-Vanzetti case.* New York: Russell and Russell.

Frankfurter, F. (1954). *The case of Sacco and Vanzetti: A critical analysis for lawyers and laymen.* Stanford, CA: Academic reprints.

Gelastopoulos, E. (1997, August 24). Sacco, Vanzetti memorial unveiled. *Boston Herald.* Retrieved February 20, 2004, from http://web.lexis-nexis.com/

Joughin, L., and Morgan, E.M. (1948). *The legacy of Sacco and Vanzetti.* Chicago: Quadrangle Books.

Karpovich, M. (1930). The Russian Revolution of 1917. *The Journal of Modern History, 2*(2), 258–280.

Library of Congress. (2002). Celtic roots: Stories, songs, and traditions from across the sea. Retrieved November 1, 2006, from http://www.loc.gov/loc/kidslc/live-celticroots.html

Morreale, B., and Carola, R. (2006). *Italian Americans: The immigrant experience.* New York: Barnes & Noble.

Rappaport, D. (1992). *The Sacco-Vanzetti Trial.* New York: Harper-Collins Publishers.

Russell, F. (1971). *Tragedy in Dedham: The story of the Sacco-Vanzetti case.* New York: McGraw-Hill.

Sacco, N., and Vanzetti, B. (1997). In M.D. Frankfurter and G. Jackson (Eds.), *The letters of Sacco and Vanzetti.* New York: Penguin Books.

Selmi, P. (2001). Social work and the campaign to save Sacco and Vanzetti. *Social Science Review, 75* (1), 115–134.

Trasciatti, M.A. (2003). Framing the Sacco-Vanzetti executions in the Italian American press. *Critical Studies in Media Communication, 20*(4), 407–430.

Young, W., and Kaiser, D.E. (1985). *Postmortem: New evidence in the case of Sacco and Vanzetti.* Amherst, MA: The University of Massachusetts Press.

3

Alphonse Capone: The Man Behind the Legend

JOSEPH GREGORY DELEEUW

Throughout history there are few individuals who have become so closely tied to an event or period of time that the two become synonymous. The mention of Prohibition or 1920s Chicago is often followed by thoughts of Al Capone and his work as a bootlegger, a violent criminal, and the man who provided vices demanded by the people. Though his most widely acknowledged crimes included violations of Prohibition laws and the violence associated with organized crime during the 1920s, it was his violations of federal tax laws that would lead to his incarceration. Over 50 years after his death Al Capone remains a prominent criminal figure in the history of American crime.

EARLY LIFE

Gabriele Capone left the village of Castellmarre di Stabia, just south of Naples, and arrived in the United States in 1894. A barber by trade, Gabriele was unique among immigrants who arrived at the same time because he possessed the ability to both read and write in his native language. Along with his 27-year-old wife Teresina, 30-year-old Gabriele also brought his sons, two-year-old Vincenzo and the infant Raffaele, to America (Bergreen, 1994, pp. 24–31).

When the family arrived in the United States they established a residence in Brooklyn, New York. Initially unable to finance his own barbershop, Gabriele used his ability to read and write to gain employment in a local grocery store. In 1895 the family welcomed a third son, Salvatore, whom a pregnant Teresina carried during the family's voyage to America. Although the family would ultimately reach nine children, the next addition would leave a lasting mark on the early twentieth century and beyond. On January 17, 1899, Alphonse Capone was born (Kobler, 1971, p. 23).

35

The Capone family moved after Al was born, relocating to an apartment upstairs from a barbershop that Gabriele had recently opened. This move would have a major impact on Al later in life, as it exposed him to a diverse collection of cultures. With the move the Capones left their predominately Italian neighborhood to live in a culturally diverse area that mixed German, Irish, and Chinese cultures. Exposure to these different cultures at a young age helped Al avoid the prejudice and cultural divides that would fuel conflicts among the criminal organizations of Chicago two decades later (Kobler, 1971).

By all accounts the Capone family was a normal Italian family, average in every way. There were no indications that their son would one day rule a powerful criminal organization. Although the Capone family showed no signs of what might influence Al's behavior later in life, his childhood was not free of conflict.

As a boy Al had an average to above average intelligence. He met expectations in school and was generally a problem-free child until he reached the sixth grade. Fourteen-year-old Al was expelled from school after a confrontation with his teacher in which blows were exchanged. When his teacher struck him, Al returned the favor and hit her back (Schoenberg, 1992).

Following Al's expulsion from school, the Capone family moved again, this time to a new neighborhood that would introduce Al to two individuals who would change his life. The first was a young woman two years his senior named Mae Coughlin. The second was the businessman who would give Al an opportunity to begin his career in organized crime.

It was here that Al met Johnny Torrio. Known as a businessman's criminal, he was highly organized and used his savvy sense of business to create structure along with corporate leadership in his ventures. In a profession where violence often prevailed, the physically small Torrio used his intelligence rather than physical force to gain power and influence (Schoenberg, 1992, pp. 2–24). Torrio would become Al's mentor and, in the process, teach him a lesson that when violated would cause great problems for Al. Torrio believed that keeping a low profile was the key to survival in organized crime. Later in life Al's desire for public acknowledgement and social status would lead him to violate Torrio's simple rule.

Like many young men in the community Al began working for Torrio at a young age. He served as a runner, delivering packages and messages for Torrio's criminal organization. Al's desire for knowledge led him to observe his surroundings at all times. By watching closely Al learned from the day-to-day operations of the organization, an experience that would help to shape him as a future leader (Schoenberg, 1992, p. 27).

Torrio, the constant businessman, recognized the high level of competition in New York and what it meant for business. It was in 1909 that Torrio decided to pursue opportunities in Chicago, a town yet to be significantly divided by criminal organizations (Kobler, 1971, p. 52). The move would not mark the end of his relationship with Capone.

Without Torrio in New York to guide him, Al found a place among a string of several street gangs. Unlike gangs today, these were similar to social clubs where boys would gather to occupy their time. Minor offenses such as smoking and the occasional fistfight were common between rival gangs, but the structure they provided was vital in preventing the young men from moving on to more serious crimes. Al spent time with several street gangs including the South Brooklyn Rippers, the Forty Thieves Juniors, and the Five Point Juniors (Kobler, 1971, pp. 28–31). During this time Al still lived at home with his family and worked legitimate jobs in order to help support his siblings. For six years he held various jobs including positions in a munitions factory and as a paper cutter.

On the advice of Johnny Torrio, a rising criminal presence in New York by the name of Frankie Yale hired Al as a bartender at his newly opened establishment, the Harvard Inn. Al served as a bartender and bouncer at the club (Bergreen, 1994, p. 49). It was during his time as an employee of the Harvard Inn that Al earned the nickname that he would become known by for the rest of his life.

One evening at the Harvard Inn, an 18-year-old Capone approached an attractive young woman and her party. Attempting to get the attention of the woman, Al leaned close to her and said, "You got a nice ass, honey, and I mean it as a compliment. Believe me." The woman's brother Frank Gallucio, a local thug, overheard the comment and demanded an apology from Capone. When he refused, Gallucio lunged at him, knife in hand. The smaller Gallucio landed a series of clean blows, slicing Capone's left cheek twice and his neck once. The cuts on his face measured four inches and two and a half inches. After nearly 30 stitches the wounds healed well, but the scars remained. It was these scars that would forever mark Capone with the nickname "Scarface" (Schoenberg, 1992, pp. 33–34).

MARRIAGE

A 19-year-old Capone met the young Irish woman named Mae Coughlin, who was two years older than Al, and quickly began a relationship. Their marriage took place shortly after the birth of their son Albert Capone, who was born on December 4, 1918 (Bergreen, 1994, pp. 52–53). Sonny, as the boy was called, found his godfather to be none other than Johnny Torrio.

In his new role as a family man and father, Al was compelled to pursue a legitimate career. Al and the family moved to Baltimore where he was employed as a bookkeeper for a construction firm (Bergreen, 1994, p. 56). Although the life-style of a legitimate bookkeeper worked for Al, it ended quickly in 1920 when tragedy called him back to New York. On November 14, 1920, Gabriele Capone died of a heart attack at age 55. This loss of his father signaled the beginning of several changes for Al.

While in New York to address the death of his father, Capone made a mistake that changed the course of his life. After severely injuring a man in a fight, it was discovered that Al's victim was a protected member of a local crime family. As the search began for the man with scars on his face, Frankie Yale devised a plan to save Capone's life. In order to protect him from the wrath of his victim's friends, Al and his family would have to leave New York. An arrangement was made with Johnny Torrio, who was eager to have the hardworking Capone join him in Chicago (Kobler, 1971, pp. 35–36).

In 1919, Al joined Torrio in Chicago. Torrio's operation was growing quickly thanks to the reduced level of competition in Chicago. With unchecked growth at hand, Al would have the opportunity to become a valuable member of the organization.

CHICAGO

In Chicago Johnny Torrio worked for a man named "Big Jim" Colosimo, who ran a large number of brothels. Big Jim and his wife were highly successful in the brothel business, but relied on Torrio to provide them with the organization skills and leadership necessary to operate their collection of "businesses" efficiently. Despite Big Jim Colosimo's success as a brothel owner, his death would become his most important contribution in shaping the future of Chicago's criminal organizations.

THE 18TH AMENDMENT

After receiving approval from 36 states, the 18th Amendment went into effect on January 16, 1920, making it illegal to manufacture, sell, or transport intoxicating liquors within the United States. In order to enforce this new amendment, the National Prohibition Act of 1919, also known as the Volstead Act, was passed and went into effect along with the amendment despite President Woodrow Wilson's veto (Allsop, 1961, p. 29). Nearly 14 years after the 18th Amendment went into effect it was repealed. On December 5, 1933, the 21st Amendment was passed, repealing the 18th Amendment and the Volstead Act as well as effectively ending prohibition (Coffey, 1975, p. 317).

When Big Jim left his wife and business partner for a young singer, a familiar face to both Johnny Torrio and Capone saw an opportunity to remove Colosimo from power. The weakness demonstrated by Colosimo's lack of focus on business provided the opening needed for Frankie Yale to make a move and establish himself in Chicago. Frankie Yale murdered Big Jim in his own nightclub in May 1920. A lack of witnesses prevented Yale from being prosecuted, and his attempt to move into Chicago was unsuccessful (Schoenberg, 1992, pp. 63–64). What had once been a working relationship between Yale and Torrio began to strain as Torrio himself took control of Colosimo's empire. Preventing Yale's effort to move into Chicago also forced Al to choose a side. He aligned with Torrio in a move that would foreshadow the future of his relationship with Yale (Coffey, 1975, pp. 34–35).

Now running Colosimo's empire alone, Torrio promoted Capone to partner. Capone's intelligence and experiences in New York helped him to adapt quickly to his new leadership roll. It was not long before Al was running Torrio's headquarters, a speakeasy named The Four Deuces. Al met a man named Jack Guzik while running the speakeasy, and they eventually became best friends. Although the men were different in many ways—Guzik came from an Orthodox Jewish family—they found common ground in the businesses they ran. Guzik's family made their living through prostitution, a business Al knew very well (Bergreen, 1994, p. 90).

Shortly after the death of his father, Al moved the remainder of his family from New York to his home in Chicago (Bergreen, 1994, p. 58). Although his family was aware of his business ventures and the company that he kept, Al was still concerned about the way he was perceived by the community. In order to maintain an image of respectability, Al posed as a secondhand furniture dealer to his neighbors. Not until later in life would Al be comfortable enough with his own profession to openly admit his role in the criminal world.

AN ELECTION VICTORY: AT WHAT COST?

An unfavorable mayoral election for the Torrio and Capone organization's preferred candidate in Chicago forced the two leaders to reconsider their base of operations. A new reform-minded mayor, focused on targeting their organization, and the lack of high-ranking political figures who could be influenced by their wealth was bad for business. The two men decided that a large portion of their operations would be moved out of the reach of the new leadership in Chicago.

The suburb of Cicero offered the perfect setting for their new center of operations. Moving to Cicero was viewed as a cost effective way of operating, as they would be able to influence the entire city government with far less financial burden than what it had cost to influence a small number of officials in Chicago (Bergreen, 1994).

In 1924, with Torrio on an extended trip to Italy, Capone was left to run the organization, and he quickly moved to influence the upcoming elections in Cicero. Capone's men kidnapped election workers, threatened individual voters, and disrupted polling stations on election day in an effort to influence the vote. By midday word of the "Cicero Takeover" had reached Chicago, infuriating local authorities. The police department quickly sent a force of heavily armed plainclothes officers to Cicero in response. Although the group of out-of-town enforcers sent to target Capone's men were outside of their normal jurisdiction, they were about to cost Capone more than he could have imagined when the day began (Schoenberg, 1992, p. 98).

It was Al's brother Frank who would pay the ultimate price in the effort to win the election that day. When Frank Capone was spotted walking down the street, a number of the plainclothes officers approached him with their guns drawn. Possibly confused by the situation or as a reflex, Frank reached for his own weapon and was quickly killed (Schoenberg, 1992, p. 98).

When word of his brother's death reached Capone, he ordered a series of kidnappings that targeted election officials and the theft of ballot boxes. Although Al's candidates were successful in the election, Frank Capone's death would forever haunt Capone as his election day victories came at the cost of his brother's life. The often short-tempered Capone remained relatively calm and collected following the election as he refrained from engaging in counterattacks against the police.

The aggression that Capone had controlled following his brother's death could not be contained forever. Capone's anger got the best of him only a few weeks after the election when a local thug attacked his best friend, Jack Guzik. When Al confronted his friend's attacker, the man responded with a string of insults. What Al's response lacked in proportionality was made up for in raw violence. The man was swiftly shot in the head by an enraged Capone (Kobler, 1971, p. 120).

The murder of the street thug who assaulted Guzik did not go unnoticed. "The Hanging Prosecutor," William H. McSwiggin, attempted to prosecute Capone for the murder but found that several eyewitnesses could not recall the event. This epidemic of "faulty" memories would plague witnesses of numerous crimes committed by Capone during his criminal career (Kobler, 1971, p. 120). Publicly, the 25-year-old Capone seemed to have succeeded in getting away with murder, but the publicity surrounding the case would permanently deny Al the anonymity that had protected him so far. The publicity that now surrounded Capone brought the attention of law enforcement as well as rival gangs. Capone's status in the public eye would force him to use all of his assets including his wealth, power, and intelligence to face the violent future that was ahead.

HIGH PROFILE MURDER

Dion O'Banion was a rising bootlegger and florist who was prone to erratic behavior. Initially, he was an associate of Torrio and Capone, but eventually began his own operations. After leaving the organization, it became clear that O'Banion lacked the self-control demonstrated by Torrio. His lack of self-control was bad for business, and there was little doubt between Capone and Torrio that O'Banion was capable of murdering a man over the smallest insult or disagreement (Schoenberg, 1992, p. 109).

Their fears were realized in February 1924 when O'Banion's uncontrolled behavior became a problem for Capone. Al was brought into a murder investigation after O'Banion killed a man he had met at The Four Deuces. The murder was brutal and the body was dumped on the side of the road, leading to a flurry of attention from police and the media. When police began to interview witnesses and suspects, Capone's club was mentioned. After turning himself over to police, Capone was released without being charged, but the danger of O'Banion and his temper had been made perfectly clear (Schoenberg, 1992, p. 109). O'Banion continued to be a growing problem as he engaged in feuds with other local bootleggers that included highjacking each other's alcohol trucks. Torrio had seen enough and offered to buy O'Banion's share of The Sieben brewery in order to create peace.

On the day that the deal was to be closed, O'Banion was nowhere to be found. While Torrio was at the brewery waiting to complete the deal, the location was raided and Torrio was arrested. Not only did O'Banion know about the raid beforehand, there was speculation that he had set it up. He later refused to return the money Torrio had paid him for the brewery that was now closed and openly bragged about the new owner's arrest (Allsop, 1961, p. 74).

A local union leader died in November 1924, and the funeral was a highly anticipated social event. When a man of great stature died, there was sure to be a long list of local celebrities, politicians, and criminals at the funeral. Funerals for fallen gangsters became more like high profile parties than opportunities for mourning.

On the day of the funeral three men arrived at Dion O'Banion flower shop under the guise of picking up flowers for the event. An employee overheard the men discussing business and then heard six gunshots. By the time the employee reached him, O'Banion laid dead on the floor of his own flower shop (Schoenberg, 1992, p. 108). A search for the three gunmen proved to be futile as none of the killers were ever captured. Shortly after the murders occurred, a familiar name was mentioned in connection with the crime. Speculation began to circulate regarding the whereabouts of Frankie Yale. It was believed that Yale, who was in town for the funeral, had been one of the three shooters.

Following Dion O'Banion's funeral, Torrio and Capone took over his lucrative bootlegging business, furthering their control of the industry in Chicago. The death of O'Banion seemed to solve several problems for Torrio and Capone including O'Banion's constant creation of conflict with rival gang members and business associates. What they did not realize was that O'Banion's close friend Earl Wajciechowski, better known as "Hymie" Weiss, would seek revenge for his friend's death.

Capone and Torrio became aware of Hymie Weiss very quickly and lived their lives accordingly. Weiss found a likely ally in George "Bugs" Moran, a man who got his nickname because of his "buggy" behavior (Asbury, 1940, p. 352). Both men were friends of Dion O'Banion, and both men had an interest in regaining the territory that was lost to Torrio and Capone following their friend's death.

The constant threat of retaliation from Weiss and Moran eventually got to Torrio, and the powerful gang leader decided that it might be time to leave Chicago for a bit. Torrio left the organization in the hands of Capone as he traveled to Arkansas (Bergreen, 1994, p. 139). Capone understood the concerns of Torrio and took every precaution to protect himself from his enemies. During the two years following the death of Dion O'Banion, his friends and associates made over ten attempts on Capone's life. Capone was able to survive the multiple assassination attempts by never traveling without at least two bodyguards. Al also traveled in only his own vehicles, whenever possible at night, where he would sit between his two bodyguards.

THE FALL OF JOHNNY TORRIO

Torrio returned from his vacation in January 1925, shortly after another attempt on Capone's life. As Torrio was returning to his apartment building from a day of shopping with his wife, gunshots rang out. Hymie Weiss and Bugs Moran opened fire on Torrio's vehicle first and then on the man as he escaped. Torrio was wounded four times but survived when Moran's gun went dry as he attempted to finish the job. With an empty gun placed to his head and four bullets inside of him, Torrio began to consider his future, if he were to have one (Bergreen, 1994, pp. 144–145).

Torrio recovered from his numerous wounds in short order. His recovery went so well that he arrived at court, four weeks after the murder attempt, to stand trial for his arrest at the Sieben Brewery. Still recovering from his wounds, he pleaded guilty to the charges and was sentenced to nine months in jail. While serving his sentence, Torrio was treated well and afforded privileges not given to the average prisoner (Kobler, 1971).

During his nine month stay in jail, Torrio reevaluated his position in Chicago. In March 1925, while still in jail, Torrio contacted Capone to let him know of his intentions to leave Chicago. The entire organization would be turned over to Al, making him the most powerful man in the city. Sole ownership of the breweries, speakeasies, brothels, and other ventures around the city would forever change Al's role in Chicago (Schoenberg, 1992, p. 127).

After taking control of the entire criminal empire he once shared with his longtime mentor, Capone adopted an openness and position in the public eye that would have been frowned upon by his former partner. Again violating his mentor's single rule of avoiding actions that draw attention, he sprung into the spotlight. Capone moved the headquarters of his operation to the Lexington Hotel. His operations were housed in a five-room luxury suite. Along with his new luxury headquarters, Al began to frequent social functions, sporting events, and the opera in an attempt to legitimize his status in the community.

From a young age Al had desired the approval of others, and now he sought the approval of the public. Al saw himself as a public figure who need not hide because of his business practices. In his mind he was the provider of services that the adult population desired. Providing alcohol, prostitution, and gambling to a consumer who wanted it was no different from supplying bread to a family in need.

NEW YORK, NEW YORK

On a trip to New York in December 1925 Capone began a new business partnership with his former associate Frankie Yale. Despite the conflicts that may have arisen in the past and the violence demonstrated recently in Chicago by Yale, he was capable of importing whiskey from Canada, something that was difficult for Al to accomplish in Chicago. The partnership called for Yale to import the whiskey to New York, where Al would then transport it to Chicago (Bergreen, 1994, pp. 155–160).

During his trip to New York, Al left a permanent mark on the city. When an invitation to Yale's Christmas party was put in doubt after threats from a rival gang to disrupt the celebration, Al took action. He assured Yale that he would handle any situation that arose during the celebration at the Adonis Social and Athletic Club. When the rival gang arrived late in the evening, Capone initiated an attack on the men before they had the opportunity to assess their surroundings. The attack was brutal and demonstrated Capone's ability to exert his power outside of Chicago (Bergreen, 1994, pp. 155–160). This show of force was covered by the national media and seen as a declaration of superiority by Chicago's gangs.

After returning from New York, Al spent the first months of 1926 enjoying his recent successes and rise to self-perceived legitimacy in the public eye. Al continued to engage in the behaviors he enjoyed prior to going to New York, but the Christmas party and recent murders in Chicago were starting to catch up to him. There was a cost for the public notoriety, and Al was about to find out how quickly the tides of public opinion could change.

DEATH OF THE HANGING PROSECUTOR

On April 27, 1926, Capone's fragile public image was about to be dealt a severe blow. The man known as the "Hanging Prosecutor," who had unsuccessfully tried to prosecute Capone for a previous murder, was at a bar just blocks from the Hawthorne Inn where Al was dining. McSwiggin, the Hanging Prosecutor, was at the bar with the O'Donnell brothers, two sworn enemies of Capone (Bergreen, 1994, pp. 162–165).

When Al learned that the O'Donnell brothers were in his neighborhood, he took it as a direct threat to his territory. Not one to accept a blatant disregard for his authority Al and his men waited outside the bar for the brothers to emerge. As the men exited the bar, Al's men opened fire, killing the O'Donnell brothers and their associates, including McSwiggin (Bergreen, 1994, pp. 162–165).

The responsibility for the murder of the respected prosecutor fell on Capone. Although McSwiggin's death was not intended and the man was in the company of criminals, the public's response was unwavering: Capone was responsible. In the weeks that followed the murder of McSwiggin, the public demanded justice and a response to the violence that came with the gang culture of Chicago. Law enforcement, frustrated by an inability to prosecute Capone for the murders, conducted several raids on Al's businesses. These raids, which would unknowingly produce vital evidence in the eventual prosecution of Capone and the public backlash over the murder, were costly for Capone and his attempts to establish a legitimate public image.

In the summer of 1926, Capone left Chicago to withdraw himself from the hostile situation caused by increased attention from law enforcement and negative public perception. Al spent most of the summer in Lansing, Michigan, struggling with his future. Detectives were still investigating him in relation to the murder of McSwiggin, and he had recently seen his mentor effectively retire in order to save his own life. During this period, Al also struggled with a desire to be viewed as a positive public figure. It was this desire that would ultimately draw him back to Chicago.

When Capone finally returned to Chicago at the end of the summer he found that authorities were still unable to charge him with the murders. Having avoided prosecution once again Al moved to create a level of peace between himself and his enemies. If he was going to continue to be a criminal figure in Chicago, it would be done with the smallest amount of bloodshed possible, at least that was Capone's original plan.

In an attempt at peace, Capone offered Hymie Weiss an opportunity to end their conflict without violence. When Weiss rejected Al's proposed business deal, he was found dead the next day (Schoenberg, 1992, pp. 162–165). Still hoping for peace, Capone called together a collection of criminals from around the city to participate in a "Peace Conference." This meeting was well publicized and resulted in an agreement that there would be an end to the violence. Also, prior acts of aggression would not be used to justify retaliation. The peace agreement lasted for over two months before one of Capone's friends was found murdered.

MANLEY SULLIVAN

The tide was slowly turning against Capone in May 1927. While Al continued to operate as usual, the Supreme Court was in the process of opening the door that would eventually allow law enforcement to pursue a case against him. The Supreme Court ruled against a bootlegger named Manley Sullivan, deciding that although the requirement to pay taxes on money earned from bootlegging was self-incriminating, it was not a violation of an individual's constitutional rights. The Supreme Court effectively said that all income, even that earned illegally, was subject to taxation. This ruling would give the IRS the opening it needed to begin an investigation into Capone's obvious wealth that had not been taxed (Kobler, 1971, p. 271; Schoenberg, 1992, p. 230).

THE WINTER OF 1928

Al spent the winter of 1928 in Miami, Florida. The community was not excited about the presence of the famous bootlegger from Chicago. The cold reception he received did not deter Al as he enjoyed the weather and the change of pace from Chicago. During his time in Miami, Al bought a 14-room estate that came to be known as "Palm Island." During the winter Al and his wife, Mae, spent time adding their own personal touches to their new home. Mae decorated the entire estate with the finest items she could find, while Al fortified doors and focused on creating a secure compound (Schoenberg, 1992, pp. 194–195).

The estate in Miami drew the attention of treasury agent Elmer Irey and the IRS Intelligence Unit. Irey began the investigation against Capone by assigning Frank Wilson to investigate his financial transactions. Capone was a wise man who was careful about conducting his business. A standard practice in his operation was to have all financial transactions conducted in cash and through a third party to avoid liability. Although Capone was careful about maintaining separation from his financial assets, the purchase of a major estate in Miami demonstrated his control of, and access to, a large amount of financial resources.

Throughout his time in Miami Al tried to establish himself as a respectable member of the community, just as he did in Chicago. Al worked throughout his first stay in Miami to establish a working relationship with the politicians and law enforcement of the area. He made himself available for questioning by authorities and continued to demonstrate nothing but good intentions. Although Al enjoyed Miami, he made his return to Chicago in April 1928 as business called. The primary elections of 1928 had begun, and it was Al's intention to assist his candidate in person.

After a victory for his candidate in the election, Al returned to Miami to address a growing problem on the East Coast. A continuous string of hijackings involving the whiskey shipments from Frankie Yale in New York raised Al's suspicions. After having a friend investigate the string of costly strikes on Al's shipments, he determined that Yale himself was behind the hijackings. It seemed as though Yale was looking to cover losses in his own business ventures. The hijackings continued for over a year until Al found time to plan a suitable response (Bergreen, 1994, pp. 286–290).

In June 1928 Capone met with a collection of friends at his Miami estate. Jack Guzik and Jack "Machine Gun" McGurn were present along with several trusted killers whom Al had used in the past (Coffey, 1975, p. 255). Once a plan was completed, the men adjourned to return home. On July 1, 1928, on the orders of Al Capone himself, several men present at the meeting in Miami addressed the situation with Frankie Yale. Frightened by a phone call he received while drinking at his own club, Yale rushed to his car, without his driver, to return home. On his way home a vehicle approached his and opened fire. Riddled with bullets, Yale's car ran into a curb at which point it was approached by a single gunman from the other vehicle. Trapped inside his vehicle, severely wounded, Yale was no match for the killer. One well-placed shot to the head marked the end of the 20-year relationship between Capone and Yale (Bergreen, 1994, pp. 286–290).

ST. VALENTINE'S DAY MASSACRE

Al had begun to enjoy spending the winter months removed from the cold of Chicago at his new home in Miami. Jack McGurn, one of Capone's top hit men, visited Al in the winter of 1929 at the Palm Island estate to discuss an issue involving a rival gang member. It is here that the plan for the famous St. Valentine's Day Massacre began. McGurn continued to be the victim of assassination attempts by Bugs Moran, and sought Capone's help in finding a solution.

Although Moran posed little threat to Capone while he was in Florida, he knew it was in his best interest to help Jack McGurn handle what had become a mutual threat to their safety and the safety of their businesses. The plan centered on offering Moran an opportunity to buy high quality whiskey at a low price. Using a trustworthy and respectable bootlegger, Moran would be offered the deal, which was to be completed at a local garage. The goal was to catch Moran inside the garage and convince him to surrender to McGurn's team of killers who would be disguised as police officers. Upon his surrender to what appeared to be a bootlegging charge he was to be executed before an "arrest" could be made (Schoenberg, 1992).

On the morning of February 14, 1929, McGurn's killers believed they saw Bugs enter the garage where the setup was going to take place. This prompted them to spring their trap, storming the garage as though they were police officers conducting a surprise raid. Once inside the killers ordered Moran's men to lay down their weapons and face the wall. After Moran's men complied, the killers opened fire, killing six men and leaving one barely alive. The killers exited the building, two in trench coats with their hands raised in an attempt to portray the arrested criminals and two in police uniforms walking them to the car (Schoenberg, 1992, pp. 210–215).

The execution lasted two minutes and 150 rounds of ammunition were fired. Only one thing was missing, Bugs Moran. As Moran approached the building where the deal was to take place, he saw the assassination squad dressed as police officers outside and assumed a raid was about to take place. Hoping to avoid an arrest, Moran escaped and never made it to his own execution that morning (Schoenberg, 1992, p. 210–215).

The man left alive, Frank Gusenberg, the one-half of the Gusenberg brothers not killed during the initial "raid," had been responsible for one of the attempts on McGurn's life.

He survived long enough for the real police to arrive. When asked who had shot him, he refused to answer and died shortly thereafter (Kobler, 1971, p. 246).

The plan was perfect, but the execution was not. It was not long before the press, the public, and law enforcement began to blame Capone for the killings. Although Al was in Florida and Jack McGurn had created a strong alibi by checking into a local hotel before the murders, there was no denying who would receive the greatest benefit from the death of Moran (Bergreen, 1994).

No one was ever convicted of the murders that took place on that bloody St. Valentine's Day, but the killings became national news and the spotlight was now permanently fixed on Chicago and its criminal element. What had been planned as a simple murder, much like numerous killings that had taken place in the years before, had become the event needed to force action against the crime organizations of Chicago. Al Capone was about to get the public attention he coveted so much, but he had no idea how quickly the media would turn on him.

CAPONE: THE CHARACTER

In life and death Al Capone has became the standard by which the media and entertainment industries measures its criminal leaders. Since the height of his power there have been several stage performances, television shows, and movies based on his life. In many cases fictional characters have been modeled after him, drawing from his most dominant characteristics. His rise from immigrant to organized crime leader and his physical appearance including his short height, bulky build, predominate scar, and manner of dress have all been used in varying combinations in the creation of fictional characters intended to convey power and dominance. Popular films and television shows such as *Scarface, The Godfather,* and *The Sopranos* have drawn directly from his life in order to create intriguing and deep characters that are capable of drawing the same reaction from viewers that Al received.

PUBLIC ENEMY NO. 1

The St. Valentine's Day Massacre was the latest in a string of increasingly high profile crimes that were attributed to Capone. Ultimately, it was his attachment to these crimes in the public eye that would lead to another nickname that Al would learn to dread, Public Enemy Number One.

Within days of taking office, President Herbert Hoover insisted that then Secretary of Treasury Andrew Mellon take control of the government's initiative against Capone. Mellon's plan involved two separate approaches to ensure the greatest probability of successfully convicting Capone (Schoenberg, 1992, p. 242). First there would be an effort to gather evidence of tax evasion and violations of federal tax laws. The man given the responsibility for investigating Capone's tax violations was Elmer Irey of the IRS Special Intelligence Unit. Irey, who had in the past investigated Capone as well as his brother Ralph, again chose the leader of his investigations unit, Frank J. Wilson, to assist him (Schoenberg, 1992). The investigation was aided by the Supreme Court ruling that found it was not unconstitutional to require the payment of taxes on illegal income.

The second approach involved the violations of Prohibition laws. Assigned to investigate Capone's bootlegging and other crimes associated with Prohibition was Treasury agent Eliot Ness. The efforts of Eliot Ness and his team of "Untouchables," named for their unwillingness to accept bribes and influences from Capone, were vital in the

Figure 3.1 Two "mug shots" of Al Capone, ca. 1931. Courtesy of the Library of Congress.

construction of the government's case on the Prohibition violations. Their contributions are often presented out of context as their efforts served more to disrupt the operations of Capone's organizations than to lead to a conviction. At the time it was believed that if Capone was to be convicted the most likely approach involved his violations of federal tax laws (Heimel, 2000).

Capone left Chicago again in May 1929, this time to attend a "gangster's conference" in Atlantic City. Al made the trip not knowing the magnitude of the investigation set in motion by President Hoover. Shortly after the conference ended, Capone went to Philadelphia to see a movie. As he was leaving the theater, he was arrested by local detectives for carrying a concealed weapon. What started as a short trip to the East Coast ended in March 1930, almost a year later, when Capone was released from jail after serving his sentence for carrying a concealed weapon (Schoenberg, 1992, pp. 239–240).

While Capone was in jail on the East Coast, Elliot Ness and his team of Untouchables carried out a series of high profile raids on Capone's breweries in Chicago. Although these raids did not produce enough evidence for a conviction, their adverse impacts on the profits of the organization as well as morale were widespread. In the absence of their leader, members of the Capone organization faced a legitimate threat from law enforcement (Heimel, 2000, pp. 279–280). One week after his release from prison Capone was faced with his greatest public humiliation yet. Frank Loesch, head of the Chicago Crime Commission, released a list of "Public Enemies." This list of the top criminals in Chicago was headlined by none other than Al Capone himself (Asbury, 1940, p. 352). As a man who desperately tried to maintain a positive public image, Capone was crushed.

In December 1930, Capone opened a soup kitchen to improve his public image. The soup kitchen was representative of several gestures that Capone used to try and win back the favor of those who blamed him for the violence and crime in the city (Bergreen, 1994, pp. 400–403). Even at his lowest point, following the announcement of his new status as "public enemy number one," Capone still saw himself as a man of the people, capable of helping those in need in return for the absolution of his crimes.

TRIAL

Al, unlike his brother Ralph who was indicted on tax violations in October 1930 along with various other member of his organization, was careful to avoid detection by the IRS. All of Capone's financial transactions occurred through third parties and could not be linked back to him. Capone had done such a good job of disconnecting himself from finances it was by pure luck the evidence needed to bring him before a grand jury was found.

Frank J. Wilson, leader of the investigation into Capone's tax violations, spent the summer of 1930 searching through the documents and materials that had been seized in raids of Capone's establishments since 1924. Late one evening as Wilson prepared to leave, he began to organize his materials and noticed a brown package in a file cabinet. When he opened the package, he found a set of bookkeepers' ledgers dated 1924–1926 (Schoenberg, 1992, pp. 298–230).

The ledgers had been part of a large collection of information turned over to the investigation and had never been examined. The government had seized the financial ledgers from the Hawthorne Hotel during a raid in 1926, shortly after the murder of the Hanging Prosecutor. The ledgers were written in code but contained detailed payments to three parties, "A," "R," and "J." Wilson determined that these abbreviations likely represented Al Capone, Ralph Capone, and Jack Guzik. If these ledgers could be validated, they would provide direct evidence that Capone did, indeed, have a taxable income. The next step was to identify the handwriting of the bookkeepers who had written in the ledgers (Schoenberg, 1992, pp. 298–230).

After an intensive investigation, Wilson and his team were able to identify the handwriting of one bookkeeper, Leslie Shumway, which led to the identification of an additional bookkeeper, Fred Reis. A massive search began for the two men (Schoenberg, 1992, pp. 298–230). The men who had been responsible for organizing the books had disappeared following the raid. It was believed that they had been killed in order to protect Capone from being connected to the seized ledgers.

In the beginning of 1931, the team investigating Capone's tax violations found Leslie Shumway working in Miami, Florida, at a racetrack Al frequented. Less than an hour before Capone's men arrived to capture and presumably kill Shumway, Irey and Wilson's agents were able to reach the bookkeeper and convince him to testify. The second bookkeeper, Fred Reis, was found hiding in Illinois and took very little convincing to testify against Capone.

With the help of the ledgers and information collected through the years of investigations, the case was brought before a grand jury. On June 5, 1931, Capone was indicted on 22 counts related to tax law violations between 1925 and 1929. It was estimated that Capone had an income of over $1 million between 1924 and 1929 and that he had failed to pay just over $200,000 in taxes. Capone's estimated income was not complete but was based on the evidence collected by investigators and could be proven in court. Capone was indicted one week later on charges that he violated Prohibition related laws. This indictment was one of many that were handed out to various bootleggers as a result of Eliot Ness's work (Schoenberg, 1992, 309–310).

Entering court to face the charges against him, Capone was under the impression that there were forces working in his favor. Earlier he had agreed to a plea bargain with prosecutors that would assure him a relatively light sentence in return for a guilty plea. Prosecutors were willing to bargain with Capone for several reasons. First, there were doubts that the statute of limitations on the tax evasion charges would be upheld by the court for the earliest charges against Capone. In a previous case, an appeals court ruled against a six-year statute of limitations on tax evasion, settling on a three-year statute. They also understood the potential for Capone and his men to influence perspective jurors. Finally, there was concern over the safety of their star witnesses, the bookkeepers, thanks to a $50,000 bounty offered by Capone for their death. Once a plea was agreed upon, it was not made public for fear that it would jeopardize the images of the prosecutor's office and Capone.

After entering a guilty plea, Capone was shocked at the judge's response. Judge James Wilkerson made it very clear that his plea would not have an impact on sentence length. Capone had believed that in return for his plea the judge would grant the sentence length of two and a half years that he had agreed upon with the prosecutor. Before Judge Wilkerson accepted the plea he said, "It is time that somebody impress upon this defendant that it is utterly impossible to bargain with a federal court" (Schoenberg, 1992, p. 315). Understanding that his light sentence was no longer available, Capone withdrew his guilty plea with the permission of Judge Wilkerson and a trial date was set for October 6, 1931.

Prior to the start of his trial Capone tried desperately to influence the outcome. A bribe of $1.5 million was offered to a high-ranking treasury official if Capone could be guaranteed not to serve any time in jail. The second approach involved an unreleased list of ten jurors that even the judge had not received. These individuals were offered a variety of financial rewards, physical gifts, and threats to influence their verdict during the trial. When Judge Wilkerson was made aware of this secret list of jurors, he ordered the case to be brought before his courtroom without change. When Capone arrived for the beginning of his trial, he believed that he had achieved the upper hand and had planned to graciously accept the not guilty verdict his hired jurors would return. Al was prepared to thank the jury and the prosecution for their efforts and offer his understanding that they were simply doing their jobs.

Before the jurors could enter the courtroom, Judge Wilkerson ordered that the jury pool be switched with another nearby courtroom that was also scheduled to begin a trial that day. A stunned Capone could do nothing as his last hope for a guaranteed acquittal vanished. The new jury pool consisted of mostly farmers and men unlike Capone. They could not be influenced by his public image and were not likely to sympathize with the wealthy gang leader. The new jury pool was also sequestered at night so that they would be protected from the influence of Capone and his men. There were now 60 potential jurors that could not be influenced by Capone (Schoenberg, 1992, p. 316). What had begun as show, a trial with a predetermined conclusion in Capone's mind, had become a real trial. For once Capone began to feel uncertain about the future.

The trial ended 11 days after it began, and throughout that time the prosecution presented numerous witnesses and suggestive evidence in an attempt to prove that Capone received an income from his criminal activity. Witnesses testified to receiving payments, in cash, for services and goods provided to Capone and his family. The prosecution continually pointed to Capone's luxurious life-style as a demonstration of his wealth. How

Figure 3.2 Aerial view of Al Capone's Florida estate, 1937. Courtesy of the Library of Congress.

could a man with an estate in Florida, diamond belt buckles, and expensive suits have no income? It was easy to see that the prosecution was doing its best to highlight the extreme differences that existed between Capone and the jury of his "peers."

Despite the information provided about Capone's life-style, the prosecution knew that their case would succeed or fail based on the testimony of two key witnesses, the book-keepers. Their testimony, along with the ledgers found by Wilson that had been seized by authorities in their raid on the Hawthorne Hotel in 1926, was the key to linking Capone to the taxable income. The bookkeepers testified that Al Capone was in charge of the entire criminal operation and the ultimate benefactor of payments made to other individuals in the organization (Schoenberg, 1992, pp. 318–324).

Capone's defense was surprisingly weak. The prosecution presented 23 witnesses during the trial, each offering testimony to Capone's wealth and lavish life-style. The defense called to the stand a collection of bookies who testified that Capone was not a successful gambler (Schoenberg, 1992, pp. 318–324). The defense failed to answer the challenge of the prosecution to disprove the wealth of Capone. The witnesses called by the defense did nothing to explain or disprove the testimony provided by the prosecution's witnesses and in several cases supported the prosecution's case by demonstrating Capone's wealth through his ability to finance his gambling.

The failure of the defense to offer even the slightest bit of resistance to the prosecution only strengthened the magnitude of the information presented against Capone. Following

Figure 3.3 Chicago Cubs player Gabby Hartnett autographing a baseball for Sonny Capone, who is sitting with his father Al Capone and other gangsters at a charity baseball game, 1931. Courtesy of the Library of Congress.

the closing arguments, Judge Wilkerson gave the jury their final instructions before deliberation. In a speech that lasted more than an hour, Wilkerson explained to the jury the role of circumstantial evidence and that the money Capone had spent in Chicago and Miami could be considered a demonstration of income (Bergreen, 1994, p. 483). On October 17, 1931, the case was sent to the jury for a decision. In eight hours the deliberation was complete and a verdict delivered. Capone was found guilty on five of the 23 charges. He was found guilty of three counts of federal tax evasion for the years 1925, 1926, and 1927. He was found not guilty on three additional charges for each year; these charges closely mirrored the charges on which he was convicted. Al was also found guilty of two misdemeanor counts of willing failure to file a tax return for 1928 and 1929 (Schoenberg, 1992, p. 324).

On October 24, 1931, Capone returned to court for sentencing where he was given the sentence and fine for each of the convictions. Judge Wilkerson decided to allow the first two felony tax evasion charges to be served concurrently followed by the third felony conviction, in what essentially became two five-year sentences. The misdemeanor charges were to be served with one running concurrent to the first felony conviction and the second to run consecutive to the federal charges. There was also a contempt of court judgment against Capone for missing court that resulted in an additional six-month sentence to be served consecutively with the other sentences. Capone's fines reached $50,000, and he was ordered to pay the court costs of $30,000. If Capone failed to succeed in an appeal, he would serve a maximum of ten years in federal prison followed by one year in a county prison in addition to his fines (Schoenberg, 1992, p. 325).

PRISON (1932–1939)

Al began the first part of his sentence in the Cook County Jail. His lawyers had arranged with the courts for him to stay there until his appeals had been concluded. During his stay in county jail, Al was able to remain in control of his organization and its operations. Capone met with his associates and presided over matters as though things had not changed. The appeals process was unsuccessful, and, once concluded, Capone could no longer avoid the inevitable, a trip to federal prison.

On May 4, 1932, Al made his first stop in Atlanta at the toughest penitentiary in the country. Capone's stay there was short, as his criminal connections were able to provide him with resources that allowed him the comforts normally denied to the average prisoner. While in the Atlanta prison, Al was able to bribe prison guards and still influence the operation of his organization in Chicago through special business correspondence (Bergreen, 1994, pp. 520–521). When it became apparent that Al had found a way around the system again, he was transferred to a facility considered to be the most secure in the world, Alcatraz (Schoenberg, 1992, pp. 330–333).

Capone's journey to Alcatraz began on August 18, 1934. He was transferred using a secure train to the San Francisco waterfront. The train car he was traveling in was loaded directly onto a barge and sent to the island prison (Kobler, 1971, p. 357). Once unloaded, Capone was assigned a number and a cell like every other prisoner, an indication that he would not receive special treatment. From this day forward the greatest criminal leader the world had known would be referred to as prisoner number 85, with his residence, cell 181 (Schoenberg, 1992, p. 335).

Alcatraz was a federal prison unlike any other in the country. It was housed on an island in the San Francisco bay and was considered inescapable. When Al arrived there, it was with the intention of removing all of the influence and power that he demonstrated in Atlanta. Here Capone, like the other "residents," was denied contact with the outside world and thus lost his ability to buy the comforts and privileges he once enjoyed in Atlanta. Capone saw his influence in prison life diminish as the guards at Alcatraz worked to eliminate any potential currency that could be exchanged between prisoners. Cigarettes were readily available, and with no outside contact luxury items could not be smuggled in. In a prison designed for the worst possible prisoners, Al had lost his greatest asset, his ability to influence other people (Schoenberg, 1992, pp. 337–347).

Isolation was not the worst part of Al's stay at Alcatraz. During his time at the island prison, Capone became increasingly sick as the syphilis he had carried since his youth progressed towards neurosyphilis. This late stage of syphilis caused Al to suffer a great deal of confusion and deterioration of his mental capacity. When he reached his final year of incarceration at Alcatraz, Al was forced to spend his remaining days in the hospital wing of the prison. Upon his release in November 1939, after serving just six years and five months, Capone entered the Baltimore State Mental Institution, where he stayed until March 19, 1940 (Schoenberg, 1992, pp. 348–349).

THE FINAL DAYS OF AL CAPONE

Declining health prevented Capone from returning to a leadership role in his organization. No longer a leader in Chicago, Capone moved to Miami following his release from the Baltimore State Mental Institution. Al found comfort with his wife at the Palm Island estate. Removed from the criminal organizations and confines of prison that had dominated his life for more than 25 years, Capone lived in peace. As the advanced stages of syphilis continued to take their toll on his body, Al's health began to fail and he suffered an apoplectic stroke that was followed by the onset of pneumonia. On January 25, 1947, just eight days after his birthday, Capone died of cardiac arrest. Al Capone had lived to age 48, a feat reserved for only a select few in his profession (Kobler, 1971, pp. 375–378).

THE LASTING IMAGES OF AL CAPONE

Once the favorite subject of reporters and the media throughout the country, Al remained an intriguing story even after his release from prison. In Chicago particularly, Al was often portrayed as a hero and a villain. In his early years the media helped to fuel the creation of his image by presenting stories that exaggerated his everyday activities. When the public opposition to prohibition began to grow, the media would present Capone as a champion of the people defying the oppressive laws. When they became enraged by the violence and crime that accompanied Capone's operation, the media were more than willing to present him as a menace to the city who needed to be removed. On one page of the local newspapers Al might be labeled in headlines as "Public Enemy Number One" and yet on another page cited for his donations to needy children. While Al was in prison, other criminals grabbed the attention of the national media, but he was never forgotten. Seldom would an extended period of time go by without coverage of his exploits in prison or his family's activities following his incarceration. As his health began to fail, reporters camped outside of his Miami estate in hopes of catching a last glimpse of Capone. At the time of his death, the entrance gates to the Palm Island estate were lined with news reporters from around the country.

Since his death in 1947, Al Capone's celebrity status has grown. In death, Capone's life has been portrayed in literature, television, and movies. Countless books have been written about his life; the most complete and thorough biographies have been written by Schoenberg, Bergreen, and Kobler. The pursuit of Capone has become the source of material for numerous movies, TV shows, and

ALCATRAZ

Located in the San Francisco Bay, the prison known as Alcatraz was designed with isolation in mind. When the Department of Justice opened the prison in August 1934, the facility was intended to house the worst prisoners in the country and was ironically located within a mile of downtown San Francisco. Although the island prison was never filled to capacity, it was home to, on average, over 250 prisoners at any given time. At the time of Al Capone's stay, the island consisted of a military garrison, loading dock, lighthouse, and prisoner housing (Bergreen, 1994, p. 536).

Alcatraz closed in 1964. During its 29 years of operation, Alcatraz was considered inescapable. Although no successful escapes were ever officially recognized, there were several escape attempts in which neither the prisoner nor a body were recovered. When investigated by the FBI, these cases were ruled to have ended when the prisoners likely drowned in the cold water surrounding the prison. Today, the prison known as Alcatraz still exists as a tourist attraction under the control of the National Park Service. It has often been used in television and films for its powerful image as a landmark and its historical status.

fictional literary works. These representations of Capone's organization are often accompanied by images of Eliot Ness and his Untouchables (Heimel, 2000, pp. 279–280). Although the work of Eliot Ness had little to do with Capone's eventual incarceration, the idea of an incorruptible lawman bringing down the organized crime leader has proven to be financially successful.

Interest in Capone after his death has also increased demand for artifacts from his life. Everyday items like shaving razors and household goods that have had their origins traced to Capone have become highly sought after collectibles. Since his burial, two headstones have been stolen from his grave and are now likely in the hands of private collectors.

It is a combination of his life and the ways in which he is represented in death that will ultimately determine the legacy of Al Capone. He was a man who did not hesitate to use violence in pursuit of his business and political goals, but was willing to help those in need. In a time when many Americans were willing to violate the law in pursuit of alcohol, he supplied the product and opportunity to satisfy their thirst. Alphonse Capone will be remembered as one of the most dynamic characters in American history, forever attached to Prohibition and 1920s Chicago.

SUGGESTIONS FOR FURTHER READING

Allsop, K. (1961). *The bootleggers.* New York: Hutchinson & Co.

Bergreen, L. (1994). *Capone: The man and the era.* New York: Touchtone.

Heimel, P.W. (2000). *Eliot Ness: The real story.* Nashville, TN: Cumberland House Publishing, Inc.

Kobler, J. (1971). *Capone: The life and world of Al Capone.* Cambridge, MA: Da Capo Press.

Ruth, D. (1996). *Inventing the public enemy: The gangster in American culture.* Chicago, IL: University of Chicago Press.

Schoenberg, R.J. (1992). *Mr. Capone: The real and complete story of Al Capone.* New York: HarperCollins.

Woodiwiss, M. (2001). *Organized crime and American power: A history.* Toronto: University of Toronto Press.

REFERENCES

Allsop, K. (1961). *The bootleggers.* New York: Hutchinson & Co.

Asbury, H. (1940). *The gangs of Chicago: An informal history of the Chicago underworld.* New York: Thunder's Mouth Press.

Bergreen, L. (1994). *Capone: The man and the era.* New York: Touchtone.

Coffey, T.M. (1975). *The long thirst: Prohibition in America: 1920–1933.* New York: W.W. Norton & Company, Inc.

Heimel, P.W. (2000). *Eliot Ness: The real story.* Nashville, TN: Cumberland House Publishing, Inc.

Kobler, J. (1971). *Capone: The life and world of Al Capone.* Cambridge, MA: Da Capo Press.

Schoenberg, R.J. (1992). *Mr. Capone: The real and complete story of Al Capone.* New York: HarperCollins.

4

The Tragedy of Arbuckle, "Prince of Whales"

MATTHEW PATE

By the time Roscoe "Fatty" Arbuckle was acquitted for the manslaughter of Virginia Rappé in 1922, his movie idol status had been supplanted by that of a pariah. In the early days of American movie-making Roscoe Arbuckle had a meteoric rise. His stage and film comedies brought delight to millions of fans, but this amusement proved insufficient in the wake of a young starlet's untimely death.

Arbuckle's early years were marked by rejection and bad fortune. Born on March 24, 1887, in Smith Center, Kansas, Arbuckle moved with his family to Santa Ana, California, by his first birthday. The boy's father, William G. Arbuckle, left the family soon thereafter to open a business in Watsonville, California. Around the time of Arbuckle's twelfth birthday, his mother, Mary Arbuckle died, leaving him ostensibly alone.

While in Santa Ana, Arbuckle began performing at local theater amateur nights. Arbuckle quickly showed himself to possess many marketable talents. The minor celebrity he gained as a traveling vaudevillian translated into terrific fame as the star, director, and writer of numerous silent films. Despite his portly form, Arbuckle was an expert tumbler and adept dancer. These skills evolved into now legendary physical comedy alongside the likes of Buster Keaton and Charlie Chaplin. Arbuckle also holds the notable distinction of garnering the first million-dollars-a-year contract in cinema history (Yallop, 1976, p. 62). Yet, by the end of 1921 he had been vilified in the press, and his films had been banned in theaters across the country.

The scandal and trials surrounding the suspicious death of Virginia Rappé, a 25-year-old aspiring actress, might not have been so sensational had the accused been other than Roscoe "Fatty" Arbuckle. Arbuckle was one of America's first "mass" celebrities (Henry, 1994). The novelty of the expanding film industry made possible the spread of performers' images in ways that live shows could not. Just as Arbuckle had benefited by innovations in entertainment technology, he fell victim to another more traditional information medium. When he stood accused of rape and manslaughter, Arbuckle unwittingly faced two parallel sets of trials: one in the California court system, and one carefully managed in newspapers owned by William Randolph Hearst and the motion picture standards office of Will Hays.

The set of events leading to the death of Virginia Rappé were in many respects tailor-made for exploitation in the press. The principals were all Hollywood notables. In the middle of Prohibition, the alleged crime took place at a drunken party set in a San Francisco luxury hotel. Sexual promiscuity, predatory guile, and unscrupulous motives enveloped and obscured many of the details. Wealthy newspaper publisher Hearst recognized the unique opportunity before him and crafted a version of Arbuckle's predicament engineered more to sell newspapers than to present balanced accounting of the facts at hand. After weathering two mistrials in the winter of 1921–1922, Arbuckle was acquitted by a third jury with only a few minutes of deliberation, but by that point the damage to his reputation and career was largely insurmountable.

THE LABOR DAY PARTY

By mid-August 1921, Arbuckle was at the top of his career. He had been given a contract by Paramount studios that included the formation of the *Comique Film Corporation* for his productions and complete artistic control over his films. He had a deal from Paramount that only one other filmmaker has ever garnered and then only once: Orson Welles for *Citizen Kane* (Yallop, 1994, pp. 61–62). Arbuckle had finished simultaneous filming of three features: *Gasoline Gus, Crazy to Marry,* and *Freight Prepaid* (Oderman, 1994, p. 43). This was a cap to a year in which he had filmed a total of 9 seven-reel feature films. As a respite from the hectic schedule, Arbuckle, along with director Fred Fischbach and actor Lowell Sherman, took his Pierce-Arrow automobile to San Francisco to spend the Labor Day weekend (Young, 1994, p. 64). The trio checked into a twelfth floor luxury suite at the St. Francis hotel. The hotel was one of Arbuckle's favorites and listed him along with General John Pershing and Billy Sunday as honored guests.

By many accounts, Arbuckle was a man who partied as hard as he worked (Oderman, 1994, p. 152). He allegedly arranged to have a Victrola, several phonograph records, and a quantity of illegal gin and whiskey delivered to his suite at the St. Francis. As this was 1921, the latter delivery was in violation of Prohibition and the Volstead Act.

Almost every detail of the weekend in San Francisco has since fallen under dispute. To begin with, sources differ on exactly how Rappé came to be in Arbuckle's suite at the St. Francis. One account (Young, 1994, p. 65) suggests that on Monday, September 5, Fischbach met Ira Fortlouis, a friend and clothing salesman at the Palace Hotel. At the Palace he also chanced to meet struggling actress, Virginia Rappé, her manager, Al Semnacher, and another of Rappé's friend's, Bambina Maude Delmont. Fortlouis, Rappé, and Delmont were invited by Fischbach to join him, Arbuckle, and Sherman back at the St. Francis. According to this version, that afternoon Rappé, along with Delmont, went to the St. Francis. Shortly thereafter, Alice Blake, a showgirl friend of Sherman's along with her friend, Zey Prevon, also joined the party.

Another account has Arbuckle calling Rappé (or possibly calling Semnacher or Delmont in order to reach Rappé) out of a long-held infatuation with her. Arbuckle had come to know Rappé through her fiancé, director Henry "Pathé" Lehrman, when he and Lehrman worked at Keystone studios together (Oderman, 1994, p. 153). Some have

MORE THAN JUST A KEYSTONE KOP

Roscoe Arbuckle achieved many notable "firsts" in cinema. As stated above, he was the first entertainer to be given a million dollar contract by a studio. Arbuckle was the first comedy star to direct his own films. Arbuckle was the first comedian to take a pie in the face on film. He was the first filmmaker to use preview audiences as a way of fine-tuning a movie before release. Arbuckle was also the first Hollywood star to be "blacklisted" by the industry. That occurrence notwithstanding, Arbuckle's influence was important to many rising stars. He is the only entertainer to have had Buster Keaton, Charlie Chaplin, and Harold Lloyd all appear as supporting players in his films. Arbuckle is also regarded as having given comedian Bob Hope his first big break in show business. Add to this list Arbuckle's pioneering use of many camera tricks and other special effects, and one quickly sees that Arbuckle was not only a famous silent film star, but an innovator and visionary for early cinema.

also advanced the less probable theory that Rappé, Delmont, and Fortlouis traveled to San Francisco with Arbuckle and company in his automobile (Anger, 1975, p. 33).

The various versions of subsequent events are no less divided. Henry (1994) contends that a parade of guests came and went from the Arbuckle suite and that Arbuckle received his guests wearing only a pair of pajama bottoms. Henry also states that large amounts of alcohol were consumed by the many guests and that this detail would later complicate the prosecution's case against Arbuckle. The vigorous consumption of alcohol appears consistent across all descriptions of the party.

In an account somewhat more sympathetic to Arbuckle (Young, 1994, p. 65), the actor receives Rappé with a surprised, "My God! Virginia! Long time no see!" Young's version also has Arbuckle quickly cornered by Rappé who proceeded to tell him that she was pregnant and that Lerhman would leave her if he found out about it. There also appears some unanimity about the fact that Rappé was quickly drunk and may have passed out.

At some point, possibly Monday afternoon, a drunk Rappé stumbled into the bathroom of Room 1221. It is at this point that the prosecution alleged Arbuckle to have said, "I've been trying to get you for five years" (Oderman, 1994, p. 153). The prosecution further alleged that Arbuckle followed Rappé into the bathroom, shut the door, and raped her.

Arbuckle's version of events contends that he went in the bathroom only to discover Rappé draped over the toilet vomiting and in pain. He helped her over to his bed, thinking that she was just suffering the ill effects of too much alcohol. He then changed out of his pajama pants and rejoined the party (Oderman, 1994, p. 154; Yallop, 1976, p. 113–114).

Not long afterward, a crowd gathered around Rappé as she lay on Arbuckle's bed. Her condition was not improving, and at some point she became hysterical. She tore off her clothes and began screaming that she was hurt or dying (Yallop, 1976, p. 114). According to Young (1994, p. 114), this scene was reminiscent of a 1917 party hosted by Keystone studio head, Mack Sennett, in which Rappé had also gotten drunk and passed out. There is some consensus that an argument broke out among the inebriated guests as to the best way to treat Rappé (Yallop, 1976, p. 113–115; Oderman, 1994, p. 154). Allegedly a number of bizarre things were tried, including submersion of the girl in a bath of ice water. One version also has Arbuckle placing a piece of ice on the girl's thigh (or vulva). It is generally thought that this detail is the origin of a rumor that Arbuckle tried to rape Rappé with a shard of ice.[1]

Eventually Arbuckle summoned the hotel management and had Rappé taken to another room where she could recuperate. Her condition persisted even after visits from multiple physicians, who apparently took her malaise as merely an acute hangover (Oderman, 1994, pp. 154–155; Yallop, 1976, p. 116). Though unimproved, Rappé was not taken to a hospital until approximately three days after the illness began. When she was finally admitted to the Wakefield Sanatorium, her situation did not improve. Wakefield was not a hospital in the conventional sense. Rather, it was "a maternity hospital and a well-known haven for well-to-do women seeking semi-legal abortions" (Henry, 1994). Oderman (1994, p. 175) suggests that Rappé's injuries were the result of a botched abortion that Rappé underwent not long before the Arbuckle party. A contrasting account (Young, 1994, p. 65; also Yallop, 1976, p. 124) states that doctors [at Wakefield] confirmed the pregnancy. These accounts also report the existence of a venereal disease and "a running abscess in her vagina for upwards of six weeks" (Young, 1994, p. 65).

Virginia Rappé died at Wakefield Sanatorium on Friday, September 9, 1921. According to Oderman (1994, p. 175) the cause of death was listed as peritonitis brought on by a rupture of the bladder...caused by an extreme amount of external force. Again, this detail, the "external force," would fuel rumors of rape at Arbuckle's hand.

Ironically, by the time Rappé died, Arbuckle with his companions, Fischbach and Sherman, had long since departed San Francisco. Having loaded Arbuckle's Pierce-Arrow automobile aboard a ship named *Harvard,* the trio set sail back to Los Angeles. As they journeyed south, Rappé's condition worsened, but, according to Young (1994, p. 66), "At no time during her illness did [Rappé] accuse Arbuckle of any misconduct, and she loudly denied he had injured her in any way when others tried to get her to do so." Whether this accurately reflects Rappé's perspective is unclear. What is certain, however, is that the version of events told by Bambina Maude Delmont was entirely different.

Delmont told police and the press that Arbuckle had taken Rappé into his room, where he beat and raped her. She demanded that he be arrested and prosecuted for murder (Young, 1994, p. 66). According to Delmont, Rappé's last words were, "Maude, Roscoe should be at my side every minute and see how I am suffering from what he did to me" (Yallop, 1994, p. 123). As Young (1994, p. 66) points out, Delmont was not actually present at the time of Rappé's death. Nonetheless, the tide of public curiosity rolled forward.

Instead of a jubilant homecoming to celebrate the hit *Gasoline Gus* had become, Arbuckle was greeted in Los Angeles by a throng of hungry reporters. The headline of the *San Francisco Call,* a Hearst newspaper, read, "Grill for Arbuckle: Actress Death Quiz" (Young, 1994). By the end of the day on Monday, September 10, Arbuckle had returned to San Francisco whereupon he was arrested and, after a coroner's inquest, charged with manslaughter in the death of Rappé. Bail was denied. Back in Hollywood, *Gasoline Gus* was removed from theaters.

THE THREE TRIALS

It appears immutably certain that Roscoe Arbuckle liked to drink, that he enjoyed the trappings of a Hollywood movie star's life-style, and that he condoned a certain amount of excessive behavior on the part of his associates. What is less certain, however, is that he had any causal part in the death of Virginia Rappé. In the course of establishing this point, Roscoe Arbuckle would lose his career, his reputation, and almost everything he owned.

There were a number of individuals who stood to gain at Arbuckle's misfortune. San Francisco District Attorney Matthew Brady clearly saw the groundswell of public attention as an opportunity to advance his political fortunes. Brady, a former judge, wanted to be governor of California. The lure of publicity attached to prosecution of a famous film star was apparent in his zealousness (Young, 1994, p. 68).

Some have also made the case that Brady had direct financial motives for an aggressive treatment of Arbuckle (Edmonds, 1991). In a twist reading more like a Hollywood script than reality, Adolph Zukor, founder of Paramount Pictures, gave Brady a check in the amount of $10,000 on at least two occasions (Edmonds, 1991, p. 215). While a clear intent has never been established for these payments, Edmonds tentatively contends that Zukor, long angered over Arbuckle's cost to the studio and his rebelliousness was possibly using the trial as a means either to get back at Arbuckle or to cover his own involvement in Arbuckle's predicament. In particular, Edmonds (1991, pp. 252–253) asserts that Fred Fischbach may have had a hand in setting up Arbuckle at the behest of Zukor.

Zukor allegedly had a number of reasons to want the proverbial pound of Arbuckle's flesh. He had been forced into a bidding war over Arbuckle, which resulted in Arbuckle's salary quadrupling. Arbuckle refused to make public appearances as Zukor had instructed. Arbuckle purportedly engaged in pranks that irritated Zukor. As testament to this position, Zukor is quoted as having stated that Arbuckle needed "knocking down a few pegs" (Edmonds, 1991, p. 253).

As the theory goes, Fischbach was to orchestrate a wild weekend of drinking, loose women, and tawdry behavior in which Arbuckle could be swept up and then extorted into a more manageable position for the studio. As Edmond (1991) states, "There also needed to be someone who was Zukor's eyes and ears at the party but who would not be implicated. Fischbach seems the likely candidate...." Unfortunately for all involved, Virginia Rappé not only brought her soiled reputation with her, but also a life threatening health condition and bad timing.

As for Rappé's motives or intent in the scheme, no source has offered much in the way of definitive explanation. It is reasonable to assume that she hoped the affair might stimulate her unremarkable acting career, but this is admittedly just informed speculation. However, the motives of her counterpart, Bambina Maude Delmont, have been widely explored and are substantially clearer. Without dissent, all accounts of the Arbuckle trials and scandal paint Maude Delmont as an inveterate liar and con artist. Young (1994, p. 65) states that she was, "a woman of few scruples whose sordid past included prostitution, swindling and blackmail." Fussell (1982, p. 65) documents a Delmont telegram to associates in Los Angeles and San Diego, "We have Roscoe Arbuckle in a hole here. Chance to make some money out of him."

Immediately upon Rappé's death, Delmont set off telling the press and authorities that Arbuckle was behind it. To the chagrin of District Attorney Brady, the essential facts of Delmont's story changed with each telling (Edmonds, 1991, pp. 185–186). Even though she was the most vocal Arbuckle accuser and was poised to be the state's star witness, the prosecutors were so dubious of her veracity she was never allowed to testify in any of the three trials. Brady knew that her testimony would not stand under defense scrutiny. As a matter of convenience and preservation of his own reputation, he had Delmont locked up on a charge of bigamy and in so doing made her unavailable to testify.

Just as many individuals had a stake in Arbuckle's undoing, there were many others who remained steadfast on the matter of his innocence. Arbuckle's wife, Minta Durfee, stated, "The only thing he's guilty of is being too good-natured to throw out a lot of those no-goods who come hanging around a movie star and cage free drinks" (St. Johns, 1978, p. 61). Former boss, Mack Sennett, told the press, "Fatty wouldn't hurt a fly.... He was a good-natured fat man and a good comic" (St. John, 1978). Buster Keaton, along with several other Hollywood associates, would eventually loan Arbuckle money to pay his legal bills.

Even Zukor, in what was probably a move of obligation (or hedging his bets) more than loyalty, retained attorney Frank Dominguez to represent Arbuckle. Zukor was initially opposed to assisting in Arbuckle's defense, but Joe Schenck, a Paramount executive, convinced Zukor that it was in the studio's financial interest to do so. Zukor had originally hoped to enlist the aide of Clarence Darrow, but Darrow, who was in the midst of his own legal problems, had to decline. Paramount also tried to retain famed defense attorney Earl Rogers, but Rogers's ill health precluded his service. As such, Zukor settled on Paramount's third choice: Dominguez. Dominguez was an able attorney from an old and respected California family (Young, 1994, p. 67). Zukor pressed Dominguez to get the charges against Arbuckle dismissed. When the grand jury instead returned a manslaughter indictment against Arbuckle, an angry Zukor had Dominguez dismissed (Young, 1994, p. 69).

Zukor replaced Dominguez with a team of five attorneys headed by Gavin McNab. McNab was a prominent San Francisco attorney whose familiarity with the local court was thought to be advantageous. McNab proved to be a formidable adversary for District Attorney Brady. McNab's first action as Arbuckle's attorney was to order a background investigation of Rappé (Edmonds, 1991, pp. 213–214).

This investigation turned up numerous licentious details about the woman whom Brady et al. portrayed as "sweet and innocent." McNab's Chicago investigators produced reports that Rappé had been in ill health for a number of years. She had undergone several abortions, had possibly borne a child out of wedlock, and had received repeated treatment for venereal disease all by the time she was 16. A physician, Maurice Rosenberg, said that Rappé had been treated for chronic cystitis, a condition that could have started the infection and inflammation that ultimately led to her death (Edmonds, 1991, p. 214).

While the news about Rappé's past would prove helpful, the defense team's joy was short-lived. Before jury selection had begun in Arbuckle's manslaughter trial, federal agents filed charges against the actor on violation of the Volstead Act stemming from the liquor present at the Labor Day party. While the case was eventually dropped, the timing of it was distracting for the defense.

Meanwhile, the prosecution was dealing with problems of its own. Fellow party guests Zey Prevon and Alice Blake were kept "in protective custody" by the prosecution to make certain that their testimony would hold up under cross-examination (Edmonds, 1991). Nevertheless, Blake managed to slip away to Alameda County and the home of a friend. Once located, Brady placed her under a subpoena to ensure further compliance.

Jury selection in what would be the first of three trials began on Monday, November 14, 1921. Superior Court Judge Howard Louderback presided. A list of 207 potential jurors had been drawn. The process was almost instantly heated and volatile. Much of the drama stemmed from McNab's accusation that the prosecution had intimidated witnesses, Blake and Prevon, in particular. At one point, McNab stated, "...I will bring seven

Figure 4.1   T.M. Smalevitch, Milton Cohen, Gavin McNab, Charles Brennan, Roscoe "Fatty" Arbuckle, and Arbuckle's brother at the manslaughter trial of Arbuckle, 1921. Courtesy of the Library of Congress.

witnesses into this court to prove that this is more than an allegation, this is a charge. You have tampered with, threatened and intimidated witnesses into lying. You know this is true and I know this is true..." (Edmonds, 1991, p. 218).[2] This typified the scene that continued for five days.

Finally, both sides agreed upon seven men and five women. Fatefully for Arbuckle, one of the women was Helen Hubbard, the wife of a prominent San Francisco attorney and self-admitted fan of Brady, who while stating that she was a movie fan (Edmonds, 1991, pp. 219–220) later confessed that she had made up her mind that Arbuckle was guilty the "moment [she] heard he was arrested" (Young, 1994, p. 69; Noe, 2007).

The prosecution's first witness was a nurse from the Wakefield Sanatorium named Grace Halston (Edmonds, 1991, pp. 220–221). Halston glared at the defendant and through her tone showed an obvious contempt for Arbuckle. She testified that Rappé's body was "riddled with bruises, that she found numerous organ ruptures, and that both had most likely been caused by force—from a man." Under cross-examination, McNab got Halston to admit that the ruptured bladder could have been caused by cancer and that the bruises might have been caused by Rappé's heavy jewelry. McNab also called Halston's credibility into question, You claim you saw several lesions on the bladder during your examination. I would like to know what qualified you to examine the body because you are neither a physician nor a graduate nurse" (Edmonds, 1991, p. 221).

Brady's next witness, Dr. Arthur Beardslee, testified that the bladder seemed to be injured from external force. On cross-examination, he admitted that Rappé had said nothing to him indicating she had been assaulted by the accused. Inadvertently opening himself up to criticism, Beardslee also stated that Rappé might have benefited from surgery, "It was evident that I was dealing with an operative case" (Edmonds, 1991, p. 222).

McNab attacked, "Then, Dr. Beardslee, let me ask you this. If you saw evidence that Miss Rappé would benefit from surgery, why was no surgery ordered at that time?"

"I have no answer for that," Beardslee replied.

"You have no answer," McNab observed. "I wonder if Miss Rappé might be alive today if you had."

On Monday, November 21, Brady called model and party guest, Betty Campbell, to the stand. Campbell testified that she arrived about an hour after the alleged rape to find Arbuckle, Sherman, Fischbach, Semnacher, and Prevon sitting around the hotel room relaxed. Edmonds (1991, p. 222) contends, "Brady tried to use this in an attempt to show Arbuckle had neither remorse nor concern for the condition of Virginia Rappé." Under cross-examination, Campbell said the comedian showed "no signs of intoxication."

Under cross-examination McNab elicited a bombshell from Campbell. She testified that the prosecutor had threatened to have her imprisoned if she didn't testify against Arbuckle. Predictably, this sent Brady into a storm of objections.

McNab presented the judge with affidavits from Alice Blake and Zey Prevon reasserting the defense's claim of intimidation on the part of the prosecution. Prevon testified that she had been under duress when she signed the statement that Rappé had claimed, "He killed me." Alice Blake provided similar testimony. According to Edmonds (1991, p. 224), Blake was "visibly frightened" while under prosecution questioning and "obviously relieved when McNab stepped in."

The prosecution's next witness was a security guard who had worked at Lehrman's Culver City studio. Former guard Jesse Norgard testified that Arbuckle had once approached him with an offer of cash in exchange for the key to Rappé's dressing room. According to Norgard's testimony, Arbuckle wanted it to play a joke on the actress. Norgard said he refused to give Arbuckle the key.

Dr. Edward Heinrich, a criminologist who was especially expert in fingerprints, testified that partial prints of Rappé were found on the inside of the door to 1219 with Arbuckle's superimposed over them. To Heinrich this indicated that Arbuckle and Rappé had struggled over the door with Arbuckle preventing her exit. Heinrich also testified that he had sealed the Arbuckle suite 11 days after the party took place.

In rebuttal, McNab called former federal investigator Ignatius McCarthy. McCarthy said he could prove the fingerprints were faked and made a strong implication that Brady was behind the act. McNab also summoned the testimony of a hotel maid who stated she had dusted the door "with a feather duster" several times before it was sealed by Heinrich.

After making an opening statement that drew heated objection from Assistant District Attorney Friedman, the defense began by calling several witnesses with information about Rappé's medical and personal history. The first of these was Dr. Melville Rumwell, who had been one of the attending physicians at Wakefield.

Among Rumwell's testimony were observations that Rappé had gonorrhea and that she was not a virgin. Rumwell's position in the course of events is also suspect because he performed what the coroner's office termed "an illegal autopsy" (Edmonds, 1991, p. 170). It is widely suspected that Rumwell's primary motivation to perform a hasty post-mortem examination was an effort to conceal that he had also performed an illegal abortion on Rappé. Most importantly for the defense, however, was Rumwell's testimony that Rappé never accused Arbuckle of injuring her.

Nurse/masseuse Irene Morgan testified that she had treated Rappé at the home of Henry Lehrman in Hollywood. Morgan said that Rappé suffered from abdominal cramps and had been catheterized on several occasions due to trouble urinating (Edmonds, 1991, p. 227). Morgan also testified that Rappé was known to tear off her clothes and run through the streets naked after a few drinks. Perhaps coincidentally, two days after she testified, Morgan was found poisoned in her hotel. She claimed that she had been threatened by anonymous phone calls, that she would be killed if she testified (Edmonds, 1991, pp. 227–228).

Fred Fischbach also took the stand for the defense. He admitted that he invited Rappé to the party. He also stated that he had heard Rappé "moaning or screaming" and that he had been the one to dunk her in a cold bath as a means to calm her. He also disavowed any knowledge as to why Rappé was hysterical in the first place, because he was, "gone for a few hours in the automobile . . . out of the room" (Edmonds, 1991, p. 228).

In a telling moment of character, Arbuckle asked McNab to deliberately stay away from the issue of the alcohol and the Victrola with Fischbach. Arbuckle knew that Fischbach was responsible for bringing the items as well as the party guests to the room, "I'm on trial here, not Freddy" (Edmonds, 1991).

After a recess for Thanksgiving, on Monday, November 28, Roscoe Arbuckle took the stand (Edmonds, 1991, pp. 230–233). He stood accused of horrible crimes

Figure 4.2 Undated photo of Roscoe "Fatty" Arbuckle. Courtesy of the Library of Congress.

and was apparently relieved at the opportunity for refutation of the charges. Arbuckle's testimony lasted for a little over four hours.

"Mr. Arbuckle," Gavin McNab began, "where were you on September 5, 1921?"

"At the St. Francis Hotel occupying rooms 1219, 1220, and 1221," the entertainer answered.

"Did you see Miss Virginia Rappé on that day?"

"Yes, sir."

"At what time and where did you see her?"

"She came into room 1220 at about 12:00 noon."

Arbuckle described many details about the party, but mention of the excessive drinking was carefully avoided. He told how he had planned to take a friend, Mae Taub, riding in the Pierce-Arrow and that he was going into the bathroom to get dressed when he discovered Virginia in pain.

"When I walked into 1219, I closed and locked the door, and I went straight to the bathroom and found Miss Rappé on the floor in front of the toilet. She'd been vomiting."

"What did you do?"

"When I opened the door, the door struck her, and I had to slide in this way to get in, to get by her and get hold of her. Then I closed the door and picked her up. When I picked her up...she vomited again. I held her under the waist...and the forehead, to keep her hair back off her face so she could vomit. When she finished, I put the seat down, then I sat her down on it.

"'Can I do anything for you?' I asked her. She said she wanted to lie down. I carried her into 1219 and put her on the bed. I lifted her feet off the floor. I went to the bathroom again and came back in two or three minutes. I found her rolling on the floor between two beds holding her stomach. I tried to pick her up but I couldn't. I immediately went out of 1219 to 1220 and asked Mrs. Delmont and Miss Prevon to come in. I told them Miss Rappé was sick."

Arbuckle vehemently disputed Heinrich's conclusions about the door. He also described how Rappé had torn at her clothes including an instance where he helped her remove her shredded dress when Fischbach came into the room. Arbuckle also corroborated Fischbach's version of having put Rappé into a tub of cold water. When Rappé was carried back to the bed, Maude Delmont rubbed her nude body with ice. Arbuckle stated he tried to cover the girl with the bedspread and an outraged Delmont rebuked him. Arbuckle's reply to Delmont, "If you don't shut up, I'll throw you out the window."

Assistant District Attorney Leo Friedman conducted the state's cross-examination, "What time did you say Miss Rappé entered your rooms?"

"Around 12:00," Arbuckle said.

"You had known her before?" Friedman asked.

"Uh-huh. About five or six years."

Friedman returned to individual details several times. He tried to shake inconsistencies out of Arbuckle, but the comic remained focused.

Just after a recess in the middle of Arbuckle's testimony, the prosecution did a curious thing. In an act that McNab characterized as "disgusting and obscene," prosecutors brought Rappé's ruptured bladder into the courtroom. Other than for the presumed shock value, the utility of the introduction at that particular point is unknown.

In a continuing series of questions, Friedman tried to get Arbuckle to admit he had deliberately followed Rappé into room 1219. This failing, Friedman tried to depict Arbuckle as indifferent to Rappé's condition.

"Did you tell the hotel manager what had caused Miss Rappé's sickness?"

"No. How should I know what caused her sickness?"

"You didn't tell anybody you found her in the bathroom?" Friedman continued.

"Nobody asked me."

"You didn't tell anyone you found her between the beds?"

"Nobody asked me. I'm telling you."

"You never said anything to anybody except that Miss Rappe was sick?"

"Nope."

"Not even the doctor?"

"Nope," Arbuckle again replied.

By the time Arbuckle was finished on the stand, most accounts contend he had done well in defending himself and maintaining composure despite the prosecution's best

TIMELINE

March 24, 1887	Roscoe Conkling Arbuckle born Smith Center, KS.
1888	Arbuckle family moves to California.
1899	Roscoe's mother, Mollie Arbuckle, dies. Arbuckle is given first vaudeville opportunity.
1909	Appears in the movie, *Ben's Kid,* produced by Bud Selig.
1909	Marries Minta Durfee.
1913	Begins career with Mack Sennett at the Keystone film company.
1916	Leaves failing Keystone studio for contract with Comique film company.
1917	Separates from wife, Minta Durfee.
1917	Joined in Comique films by young comedian Buster Keaton.
1919	Adolph Zukor of Paramount studios offers Arbuckle a million-dollars-per-year contract to star in feature-length films.
September 5, 1921	Arbuckle hosts a vacation party at the St. Francis hotel in San Francisco. During the party, the actress Virginia Rappé becomes very ill.
September 9, 1921	Virginia Rappé dies from peritonitis.
Mid-September 1921	Arbuckle accused of Virginia Rappé's rape and murder.
November 14, 1921	The first of three trials begins.
December 4, 1921	After 22 ballots, jury announces its deadlock: 10 to 2 in favor of acquittal.
1922	The second trial produces the same result, in reverse: deadlock, 10 to 2 in favor of conviction.
April 12, 1922	The third trial jury votes to acquit and reads a formal apology to Arbuckle.
April 18, 1922	Arbuckle is blacklisted by the motion picture industry.
December 20, 1922	Ban is lifted, but Arbuckle would not work on screen for ten years.
1924	Arbuckle returns to film as the director of the Buster Keaton picture, *Sherlock, Jr.*
1925	Arbuckle, as "William Goodrich," directs several more films. Arbuckle marries Doris Deane. The couple would divorce in 1928.
1932	Warner Brothers Studios signs Arbuckle to a six picture deal. Arbuckle marries fourth wife, Addie McPhail.
June 28, 1933	Arbuckle finishes last of the Warner contract pictures and is signed to a new, long-term contract.
June 29, 1933	Arbuckle and friends celebrate the new contract. Arbuckle retires for the evening and dies in his sleep. The listed cause of death was heart failure.

efforts to break him. What followed next were an odd set of rebuttal witnesses, whose testimony focused on the aforementioned bladder.

Dr. William Ophuls (who attended Rappé with Dr. Rumwell) was called by the prosecution and Dr. G. Rusk by the defense. Edmonds (1991, p. 236) summarizes the findings,

> The experts agreed on four points: that the bladder was ruptured, that there was evidence of chronic inflammation, that there were signs of acute peritonitis, and that the examination failed to reveal any pathological change in the vicinity of the tear preceding the rupture. In short—the rupture was not caused by external force.

Going into summation, both sides felt confident in the case they had made. District Attorney Friedman's summation continued to portray Arbuckle as a callous villain,

> This big, kindhearted comedian who has made the whole world laugh; did he say "Get a doctor for this suffering girl?" No. He said, "Shut up or I'll throw you out the window."
> He was not content to stop at throwing her out the window. He attempted to make a sport with her by placing ice on her body. This man then and there proved himself guilty of this offense. This act shows you the mental makeup of Roscoe Arbuckle.

In his closing, McNab forcefully argued that Arbuckle was the victim of overzealous prosecution, "It was a deliberate conspiracy against Arbuckle! It was the shame of San Francisco. Perjured wretches tried, from the stand, to deprive this defendant, this stranger within our gates, of his liberty."

McNab also cast aspersions against the prosecution's case and its tactics, particularly where Blake, Prevon, and Delmont were concerned. Finally, he made a final dig at Rappé, "The evidence presented on both sides has proven that Virginia Rappé was not a girl in excellent health but a sickly, broken down woman...lying there writhing and vomiting would not have excited the passions of the lowest beast that was ever called man."

The first trial ended on December 4, 1921. After 43 hours of deliberation and 22 ballots, the jury sent word that it was hopelessly deadlocked. The final count was 10 to 2, in favor of acquittal. One of the two holdouts was Helen Hubbard, the self-admitted fan of District Attorney Brady.

The state decided to retry Arbuckle on the manslaughter charges, and a date of January 11, 1922, was set in San Francisco Superior Court. Jury selection took six days, nearly twice as long as before (Edmonds, 1991, p. 245). Eighty people were interviewed, and some difficulty was experienced in finding prospective jurors who had not heard details of the previous trial and scandal.

The trial went poorly for both sides. Both Prevon and Blake were recalled for the second trial. Neither produced compelling testimony and again, McNab alleged witness tampering. Heinrich reversed his position from the first trial, stating that it was possible that the doorway fingerprints had been forged.

The defense took a different strategy with regard to Rappé's virtue. It became a centerpiece of their case. McNab portrayed her as a woman of loose morals who drank to excess and slept her way around town (Edmonds, 1991, p. 246). The defense called numerous witnesses who each told of Rappé's questionable behavior.

Again, the prosecution failed to bring Maude Delmont to the stand, eschewing her testimony for the testimony of Dr. Beardslee. Beardslee relayed to the court stories about Rappé that Delmont had told him.

The defense made two critical errors in the second trial: they did not put Arbuckle himself on the stand, and they did not offer a closing argument. McNab later admitted that both decisions were a mistake.

On February 2, the jury retired to consider Arbuckle's fate. The jurors deliberated for 44 hours, held 13 ballots, and again returned with a deadlock. This time the jury voted 10 to 2 for conviction. One juror later admitted that he was wavering in his decision to acquit Arbuckle and that if the other holdout had voted for conviction, so would he (Edmonds, 1991, p. 246).

The third trial commenced on March 6. It was very different from either of the other two trials. McNab would not make the same mistakes as before. He provided a very explicit description of Virginia Rappé, her life, lovers, and faults. Whatever delicacy or euphemistic treatment given the matter in the first two trials was set aside in trial three. As Edmonds (1991, p. 247) observes, "Though women in the courtroom gasped, fainted and stamped their feet to drown out the 'vulgarity,' McNab got his point across." McNab also let Arbuckle testify.

The trial was, by comparison, very brief. The prosecution presented only six witnesses. The jury began deliberations on April 12. The jurors were out for less than five minutes. During that time the jury prepared the following note for the court:

> Acquittal is not enough for Roscoe Arbuckle. We feel that a great injustice has been done him. We feel also that it was only our plain duty to give him this exoneration, under the evidence, for there was not the slightest proof adduced to connect him in any way with the commission of a crime.
>
> He was manly throughout the case, and told a straightforward story on the witness stand, which we all believed.
>
> The happening at the hotel was an unfortunate affair for which Arbuckle, so the evidence shows, was in no way responsible.
>
> We wish him success, and hope that the American people will take the judgment of fourteen men and woman who have sat listening for thirty-one days to evidence, that Roscoe Arbuckle is entirely innocent and free from all blame.

Arbuckle was finally free from the clutches of Brady and the Superior Court of California, but his ordeal had scarcely begun. The trial cost nearly $750,000, which left him nearly bankrupt, and no one in Hollywood would touch an Arbuckle picture. As if this were not enough, Arbuckle was soon contacted by the Internal Revenue Service. The IRS found that he owed nearly $100,000 in back taxes (Edmonds, 1991, p. 248). The IRS attached what was left of his estate and garnered a court order for any earnings until the debt was settled. Ironically, the worst was yet to come.

A PUBLIC SACRIFICE

In the days following the death of Virginia Rappé, Arbuckle was besieged by the press. They clamored around him upon his return to Los Angeles and continued to dog him throughout the trials. Most of the scholarship on Arbuckle indicates that the coverage was generally balanced, except in the newspapers owned by William Randolph Hearst. The Hearst newspapers vilified Arbuckle with exaggerated headlines. The *San Francisco Examiner* reported that Arbuckle had been stoned by the crowd when he returned from

San Francisco (Edmonds, 1991, p. 208), when, in point of fact, the reception was, if anything, mixed.

Shortly after his arrest, theaters nationwide began pulling Arbuckle films. On September 12, 1921, the Theater Owners Chamber of Commerce in New York banned exposition of Arbuckle films in any of its 300 member venues (Young, 1994, p. 111). Similar bans were enacted by theater owners in Philadelphia, Chicago, Memphis, Buffalo, and several other large cities. By December 1922 even New York's Sing Sing Prison had banned Arbuckle films (Young, 1994, p. 114). This left Arbuckle and the production studios in a tight spot. Famous Players-Lasky had three completed Arbuckle films in the can and no place to show them (Edmonds, 1991, p. 209).

Arbuckle was also the victim of unlucky timing. On the same day that the jury retired during Arbuckle's second trial, Paramount film director, William Desmond Taylor, was found murdered in his home. Among the prime suspects were Arbuckle costar, Mabel Normand, Paramount star Mary Miles Minter, and her mother, Charlotte Shelby. The murder generated nasty rumors of homosexuality, a love triangle, and even a drug deal having gone bad (Edmonds, 1991; Young, 1994).

As if this were not enough, by March another scandal, this time focused on the drug addiction of actor Wallace Reid, was made public. Reid's hasty withdrawal from his narcotics habit nearly drove the actor insane, forcing him into a sanitarium where he died the following year (Edmonds, 1991; Young, 1994).

The three scandals taken together were enough of a warning signal that the Hollywood establishment felt it had to act. Former United States Postmaster General Will Hays was brought in by studio executives (Zukor, Joseph Schenck, and Jesse Lasky among them) to head the newly formed Motion Picture Producers and Distributors Association (MPPDA), an organization designed to regulate film morals and self-censorship (Young, 1991, p. 71). The Hays Office, as it became known, spent the next 23 years enforcing a very tight code of behavior for individuals both on and off screen. So-called "morals clauses" were written into studio contracts and as Young (1991) reports, "[M]inisters nationwide, the powerful Federation of Women's Clubs and bigoted moralists who had deplored films since their beginnings, felt their day had finally arrived."

For whatever reason, the blanket self-censure of Hollywood was deemed insufficient. The movement against the perceived debauchery of the film community needed an obvious sacrifice. Arbuckle provided an easy target. On April 18, 1922, the Hays Office issued the following statement:

> After consulting at length with Mr. Nicholas Schenck, representing Mr. Joseph Schenck, the producers, and Mr. Adolph Zukor and Mr. Jessy Lasky of the Famous Players-Lasky Corporation, the distributors, I will state that at my request they have cancelled all showings and all bookings of the Arbuckle films. They do this that the whole matter may have the consideration that its importance warrants, and the action is taken notwithstanding the fact that they had nearly ten thousand contracts in force for the Arbuckle pictures.

Arbuckle, whose film career boasted many "firsts" for the industry, now added the mantle of being the first performer ever blacklisted by Hollywood. While the formal ban was lifted only nine months later, the damage to Arbuckle's career had been solidified.

The year 1923 brought a mixed bag of circumstances for Arbuckle. The MPPDA ban was lifted on January 20, but public opposition was still pervasive. On January 30, papers of incorporation were filed for Reel Comedies in Trenton, New Jersey (Young, 1994,

CONTROVERSY EVEN IN DEATH

Just as Arbuckle's relationship to events at the St. Francis hotel sparked decades of heated debate, so too did the matter of his final resting place. While Young (1994) correctly states that Arbuckle was cremated, numerous alternate accounts persist. Bent and Cross (1991) have Arbuckle buried in New York's Woodlawn Cemetery. Oderman (1994) not only states that Arbuckle was buried in Hollywood's famous Forest Lawn but also presents an account of first wife, Minta Durfee, visiting the grave. Pearson (2006) confirms Young's version with records from the Frank E. Campbell Funeral Service of New York, who verified the cremation on July 1, 1933. Further, Pearson cites his direct conversations with Addie McPhail regarding the final disposition of Arbuckle's ashes.

p. 115). The company was formed by Nicholas and Joseph Schenck for the purpose of giving Arbuckle employment and income. Six of Hollywood's largest studios secretly put up a total of $200,000 funding for the new company. A day later Arbuckle issued a statement in which he said he was "through with acting" and that he was joining Reel Comedies to produce and direct. During the next three years, Arbuckle went on to make 13 two-reel comedies, but received no screen credit for the work. Throughout the rest of 1923, Arbuckle gave numerous live performances in Chicago and Atlantic City.

While his star was on apparent reascension, Arbuckle's personal life again found trouble. In October, Minta Durfee Arbuckle sued for divorce. The pair briefly reconciled, but Arbuckle began a romance with Doris Deane, whom he married shortly after divorcing Durfee.

POSTSCRIPT: A FILM HISTORIAN GIVES PERSPECTIVE

Noted Arbuckle researcher David Pearson was contacted in preparation for this chapter. Pearson was asked to say what he thought was important for the public to know about Arbuckle. The following is an excerpt from his answer (Pearson, 2006).

Because of [the] trials, [Arbuckle] lost his stardom, his film contract, his business interests, his home, his cars, and every penny he had—winding up deeply in debt to friends who stepped forward to pay his legal fees. And despite being found innocent, he was also considered to be an "immoral" person by much of the American public. Most people would have been crushed by all this. Not Roscoe Arbuckle. Roscoe worked his tail off for the next decade, first to completely repay all his friends, and then to rebuild his film career. He directed dozens of film comedies for other comics. He also repeatedly went on theatrical tours to rebuild his fan base—which often included visits to various city council meetings to disarm "moralists" trying to ban him. After ten years, he was finally allowed to make movies again. And after six well received short comedies made in 1932–33, he died. Some people claim, after the trials, Arbuckle climbed into a whiskey bottle until he died, forgotten in self-pity. Of all the outrageous lies said about Roscoe Conkling Arbuckle, that may have been the biggest lie of them all.

By August 1925, a poll of *Photoplay Magazine* readers indicated that the majority of the public was still against Arbuckle's full return to the screen (Young, 1991, p. 117). Nonetheless, Arbuckle continued to work with old friends like Buster Keaton and Lew Cody. Oddly enough, in the summer of 1925, Arbuckle and new wife, Deane, vacationed at the San Simeon home of William Randolph Hearst. Hearst's girlfriend, actress Marion Davies, was set to star in a new film, and Hearst hired Arbuckle[3] to direct it. Of his involvement in the smear of Arbuckle's reputation, Hearst purportedly told Arbuckle, "I never knew anything more about your case, Roscoe, than I read in the newspapers" (Yallop, 1976, p. 285). Arbuckle is said to have not replied.

Arbuckle continued to work in the entertainment industry over the next few years. He was involved in several film projects, a number of stage productions, and various side investments. His marriage to Doris Deane ended in 1928 over allegations of desertion. By late 1931, a readers' poll in *Motion Picture Magazine* indicated that the public was ready for a return of Arbuckle to the screen (Young, 1991, p. 119). In January 1932 Jack Warner, head of Warner Brothers Studios, offered Arbuckle a contract for a two-reel comedy at the company's Vitaphone Studios in New York.

While in New York, Arbuckle began a romance with Addie McPhail. The couple married in June 1932. She was 26; he was 45. Not long after the marriage, filming was completed on *Hey, Pop* at Vitaphone. The trade publication, *Film Daily,* touted the comedy as an overwhelming success. Arbuckle was immediately signed to make five more films for Warner Brothers.

On June 21, 1933, Arbuckle and McPhail celebrated their first wedding anniversary. A week later Arbuckle finished filming *In the Dough,* the second of his "comeback" films for Warner Brothers. On June 28, the couple held a party (a belated anniversary celebration) at Billy LaHiff's Tavern in Manhattan. After the party, the couple returned to their suite in the Park Central Hotel on Manhattan's West Side. Tired from the party and a tough film schedule, Arbuckle retired for the evening. At approximately 2:30 a.m. the comedian's heart gave out. Arbuckle died in his sleep. Long time friend Buster Keaton would often remark that Arbuckle had "died of a broken heart."

While most newspapers made a gentle report of Arbuckle's demise, Hearst's newspaper, *New York American,* ran the headline, "Fatty Arbuckle Lies Dead in the Chapel, But No Eager Crowd Comes to Look" (Young, 1994, p. 85). Even in death, Arbuckle made for scandalous Hearst copy. Arbuckle's body was placed for viewing in the Gold Room of Frank E. Campbell's Funeral Church on Broadway in Manhattan. This was the same chamber in which Rudolph Valentino's funeral viewing had taken place eight years earlier. Despite the Hearst reports, a crowd estimated between 800 and 1,000 mourners came to see Arbuckle. The funeral itself was attended by more than 250 of his friends and associates. Among the mourners were noted director Ray McCarey and comedian Bert Lahr. The famed humorist Will Rogers delivered the eulogy. At Arbuckle's request, his body was cremated. On September 6, 1934, his widow, Addie McPhail Arbuckle, spread the ashes out over the Pacific Ocean near Santa Monica (Young, 1994).

SUMMARY

Roscoe Arbuckle was an important force in determining the shape of early American comedic cinema. He was one of Mack Sennett's *Keystone Kops.* He was a mentor to Buster Keaton and a peer of Charlie Chaplin. He was among the first, if not the first person, to throw a pie in someone's face on film. He was the first performer to be given complete creative control over his movies. Yet, for all his impact as a pioneering filmmaker, "Fatty" Arbuckle became instead a synonym for disrepute and reputations destroyed.

As the first film star to be blacklisted by Hollywood, Arbuckle fell victim to a reactionary climate of oppression that typified studios of the era. In so doing, he became something of an iconic reference point, a touchstone, for almost every celebrity who has since stood accused of foul crimes. Popular culture references to Arbuckle have even surfaced in current film. In *Death to Smoochy* (2000), actor Robin Williams as the disgraced children's character, "Rainbow Randolph," utters the line, "Welcome to Fatty Arbuckle-land," while plotting the ruination of another character.

It is arguable that Arbuckle's trials were perhaps the most important celebrity trials of the twentieth century, at least until the murder trial of football star, turned actor, O.J. Simpson. Even in the shadow of the more recent Simpson trial(s), the Arbuckle case is perennially invoked by the media as a point of historical context.

That Arbuckle's predicament became fodder for the yellow journalism of the Hearst newspaper empire was also a harbinger of things to come. While fan magazines such as *Photoplay, Motography,* and *Movie Weekly* were popular during Arbuckle's career, their circulation did not reflect the same magnitude of apparent public interest evidenced by current television programs such as *Celebrity Justice* or tabloids like *The Star* or *The National Enquirer.*

Apart from the media-driven frenzy, the Arbuckle trials and associated scandals were the locus of a broad reconsideration of Hollywood, its products, and personalities. When Hollywood studios sought the aid of Will Hays and the MPPDA in fear of government-mandated censorship, Roscoe Arbuckle's fate was essentially sealed. Even though his formal blacklisting lasted only about nine months, the damage was done. Images of Arbuckle's cherubic slapstick were forever replaced in the public memory by unsubstantiated acts of drunken excess, rape, and murder. Whether he had actually done the things of which he was accused (and acquitted) was largely irrelevant. Regrettably for the waning star, the popular press along with the film industry had reached an equally damning verdict: Roscoe Arbuckle was no longer wanted. That he had begun to regain public favor just before his death was meager compensation for the needless hardship.

SUGGESTIONS FOR FURTHER READING

A note on the sources: Just as the Arbuckle trials produced myriad versions of what "really" took place in the St. Francis Hotel on Labor Day 1921, so too are there many subsequent historical accounts, some quite scholarly and well prepared, some not. That being said, there appears little consensus on many details, conversations, and other aspects of Arbuckle's life, career, and role in the Labor Day party. Anyone with a further interest in this topic is advised to begin with those titles listed below, but be aware that there are many, often conflicting perspectives.

Anger, K. (1975). *Hollywood Babylon.* San Francisco: Straight Arrow Books.

Edmonds, A. (1991). *Frame up! The untold story of Roscoe "Fatty" Arbuckle.* New York: William Morrow.

Fussell, B.H. (1982). *Mabel: Hollywood's first I don't care girl.* New York: Ticknor & Fields.

Oderman, S. (1994). *Roscoe "Fatty" Arbuckle: A Biography of the silent film comedian, 1887–1933.* Jefferson, NC: McFarland & Company.

Pearson, D. (2006, May–June). Personal correspondence with author.

Yallop, D.A. (1976). *The day the laughter stopped: The true story of Fatty Arbuckle*. New York: St. Martin's.

Young, R., Jr. (1994). *Roscoe "Fatty" Arbuckle: A bio-bibliography*. Westport, CT: Greenwood Press.

NOTES

1. The rumor that Arbuckle used a shard of ice to violate Rappé is one of several stories popularized by the Hearst newspapers (Edmonds, 1991, p. 243). Equally violent is the rumor that Arbuckle, frustrated from having been made impotent from too much liquor, may have used either a Coca-Cola or a champagne bottle against Rappé. Neither story has ever been substantiated.

2. It should be noted that the vast majority of courtroom dialog presented in this account of the Arbuckle trials comes from the work of Andy Edmonds. Edmonds notes in his forward to *Frame Up!* that "someone connected to the case" provided him with "fairly complete" court transcripts (which were presumed destroyed) and for this reason his accounts should be credited as the most authoritative source on the matter of the trials. If there are points that to the more critical of readers appear to need additional documentation with regard to who said what to whom, let this note serve as a blanket acknowledgement that Edmonds is, unless otherwise noted, the source for exact courtroom dialogue.

   Young (1994, p. 247) takes issue with some of the dialog in the Edmonds work. Specifically, Young states, "It [Edmonds] contains considerable invented dialog." However, Young gives no indication of which instances in particular are of concern. Whether the courtroom dialog fits that category is unknown.

3. Arbuckle began working under the name William B. Goodrich (sic. "Will B. Good"), and it was under this name that he directed Davies in the MGM adaptation of *The Red Mill*. The film had a number of other directors and was a failure at the box office.

REFERENCES

Anger, K. (1975). *Hollywood Babylon*. San Francisco: Straight Arrow Books.

Bent, R., & Cross, D. (1991). *Dead ends: An irreverent field guide to the graves of the famous*. New York: Plume.

Edmonds, A. (1991). *Frame up! The untold story of Roscoe "Fatty" Arbuckle*. New York: William Morrow.

Fussell, B.H. (1982). *Mabel: Hollywood's first I don't care girl*. New York: Ticknor & Fields.

Henry, P.H. (1994, April 4). *Roscoe "Fatty" Arbuckle: Profile of an American scandal*. http://www.phenry.org/text/arbuckle.txt

Noe, D. (2007). Who killed William Desmond Taylor? http://www.crimelibrary.com/notorious_-murders/classics/william_taylor/2.html

Oderman, S. (1994). *Roscoe "Fatty" Arbuckle: A biography of the silent film comedian, 1887–1933*. Jefferson, NC: McFarland & Company.

Pearson, D. (2006). Arbucklemania: The Roscoe "Fatty" Arbuckle Web site. http://silent-movies.com/Arbucklemania/home.html

Pearson, D. (2006, May–June). Personal correspondence with author.

St. Johns, A.R. (1978). *Love, laughter and tears: My Hollywood story*. Garden City, NY: Doubleday.

Yallop, D.A. (1976). *The day the laughter stopped: The true story of Fatty Arbuckle*. New York: St. Martin's.

Young, R., Jr. (1994). *Roscoe "Fatty" Arbuckle: A bio-bibliography*. Westport, CT: Greenwood Press.

5

The Incomprehensible Crime of Leopold and Loeb: "Just an Experiment"

DIANA PROPER

On May 21, 1924, two young men, 19-year-old Nathan Leopold and 18-year-old Richard Loeb, set out to commit the "perfect crime." Partially inspired by an inaccurate, self-absorbed reading of the philosophy of Friedrich Nietzsche (Higdon, 1975), the two teens wanted to prove that they were Nietzschean "Supermen" by committing and getting away with the perfect crime. The teens were obsessed with the Superman theory, which states, in part, that there exist in society some supermen (the "übermensch") whose talents and intellectual superiority mean that they are above human-made law and, therefore, not subject to punishment for violation of such laws. For Leopold and Loeb (and the very embodiment of evil, Adolf Hitler), the theory allowed them to play with the idea that, as Supermen, they should be able to commit the perfect crime and get away with it. However, if caught, they felt that their superior status should exempt them from legal punishment (Higdon, 1975, p. 210). Many scholars of Nietzsche argue that the boys misread the Superman theory. These experts maintain that Nietzsche's Superman is a person so superior that (s)he would never consider committing evil acts and, therefore, would never be subject to punishment. In this reading, the Superman is not above the law but rather is so superior in nature that violation of any form of human or natural law would simply never occur.[1]

Both Leopold and Loeb were from prominent Jewish families in Chicago, well educated, and considered brilliant. Loeb's IQ was measured at 160, Leopold's at 210 (Higdon, p. 200). However, Leopold and Loeb would quickly learn that they were not their idea of Nietzschean Supermen who were above the law. They were flawed and ultimately "abnormal" boys, subject to law in the same way as the "ordinary people" around them.

FORCES UNITING LEOPOLD AND LOEB IN CRIME

Earlier in 1924, Leopold and Loeb had burglarized two fraternity houses at the University of Michigan. Their most successful burglary was of Zeta Beta Tau. There they stole many items, including a portable Underwood typewriter (Higdon, 1975). But this was small-time crime. For months after the burglaries, the teens planned to commit a perfect crime. Their goal was to commit this crime, and then end their criminal careers altogether.

Why were Leopold and Loeb interested in committing such a crime? While both were from very wealthy families, and were provided generous allowances, both teens also considered themselves intellectually superior to others. Their feelings of superiority were reinforced by the philosophy of Nietzsche and his concept of the Superman. To Leopold, Loeb represented the Superman. He was handsome, well built, and charming (Leopold, 1958). Each saw the other as superior to himself. However, each was often frustrated by the other. Both, at times, contemplated killing the other, and both had considered committing suicide (Hulbert-Bowman report, in Higdon, 1975). Their relationship was intense and intertwined. Thus, unable to successfully commit a perfect crime alone, they believed it must be planned and carried out together.

THE KILLERS' MASTER PLAN

Leopold and Loeb planned to kidnap and murder the child of a wealthy family. Neither boy relished the idea of killing, but both thought murder a necessary ingredient of the perfect crime (Higdon, 1975, p. 97). Their obsession was with the successful completion of a masterful crime and subsequent escape from detection. After the murder, they would dispose of the child in a culvert by the Wolf Lake area south of Chicago, an area with which Leopold was familiar, because that was the desolate area where he often conducted his ornithological studies. Leopold was well known in the ornithological community. At age 19, he published a paper and lectured locally on the subject (Linder, 2003).

After hiding the body, the two men would call the murder victim's family and send them a letter with precise instructions detailing the method by which a ransom should be delivered in exchange for the safe return of their child. The family would then be told to await a telephone call that would direct the father to wait for a Yellow Cab that would be sent to the family home (*New York Times,* May 23, 1924). The father was to take the cab to a nearby drugstore and wait for further instructions. Leopold and Loeb would call the father at this phone and direct him to go to a nearby railway station and purchase a ticket to Michigan City, Indiana (*New York Times,* June 1, 1924). They chose this train because, by the time the father arrived at the station, he would have little time to purchase a ticket and make the train. Therefore, he would be unable to contact police.

On the train, the father was to proceed to the last Pullman car and open the telegraph box (*New York Times,* June 1, 1924). There, he would find a letter from the kidnappers explaining exactly how the money was to be delivered. The father was to wait until he passed a brick building, the Champion Manufacturing Company, then to quickly count *one, two, three,* and throw the package containing the money from the end of the train (Linder, 2003).

After retrieving the money, Leopold and Loeb would go back to their normal lives, attending law school in the fall. Once they had proven to themselves that they could commit the perfect crime, they would have confirmed their superior Supermen status. But as the saying goes, the best-laid plans of Supermen often go awry, as Leopold and Loeb soon discovered.

Criminal Mistakes

Several weeks prior to the kidnapping, Leopold and Loeb set their plan in motion, acquiring items needed to commit their crime. Most were easily purchased: rope, a chisel, and tape to wrap around it (Higdon, 1975). But the matter of transportation to use during the crime proved more challenging. They could not use Leopold's car because its bright red color was too noticeable. Loeb's car needed repair. Furthermore, neither wanted his own car traced back to him. So they devised an elaborate scheme to rent a car without revealing their identities (Rackliffe, 2000–2003).

First, Loeb established a temporary address by renting a room at the Morrison Hotel under an assumed name, Morton D. Ballard (Rackliffe, 2000–2003). He brought a suitcase (which he had filled with library books) with him to the room, and then met Leopold outside. The two then went to a local bank where Leopold opened an account as Ballard and deposited $100, which Loeb had taken from his own account earlier that day (Rackliffe, 2000–2003). Leopold used the Morrison Hotel as his address.

Armed with the hotel address, the bank account, and a list of phony references, Leopold posed as the fictitious Mr. Ballard, a traveling salesperson, in order to secure a rental car from the Rent-A-Car Company. His main reference was a "Mr. Louis Mason," who was actually Loeb, waiting across the street, ready for a possible reference call. Apparently suspicious of Ballard, the company boss called the reference, "Mason," who vouched for Ballard's authenticity. As Ballard, Leopold rented a gray Willys-Knight automobile. The teens kept the car for several hours and then returned it to the car company. Leopold (Ballard) asked the company to send an identification card to his hotel address. This was to ensure that he would have no problem renting a car on the day of the crime.

The next day, Loeb went to the Morrison Hotel to collect the car rental identification (Rackliffe, 2000–2003). When he arrived, he found no mail awaiting Ballard, and his suitcase was missing. He fled the hotel. Now in need of a new address for the rental identification, the teens drove to the Trenier Hotel, where Leopold explained that he, Ballard, planned to stay at the hotel, but had a change of plans (Rackliffe, 2000–2003). He asked the hotel to hold his mail; the staff agreed. "Ballard" then called Rent-A-Car and asked that the identification card be sent to the new Trenier Hotel address (Leopold confession, 1924). Finally, the plan for the car was ready.

Prior to committing the crime, Leopold and Loeb wrote two ransom letters to be addressed once they decided upon a victim. The first letter read:

A. Dear Sir: As you no doubt know by this time, your son has been kidnapped. Allow us to assure you that he is at present well and safe. You need fear no physical harm for him, provided you live up carefully to the following instructions and to such others as you will receive by future communications. Should you, however, disobey any of our instructions, even slightly, his death will be the penalty.

B. 1. For obvious reasons make absolutely no attempt to communicate with either police authorities or any private agency. Should you already have communicated with the police, allow them to continue their investigations, but do not mention this letter.

C. 2. Secure before noon today $10,000. This money must be composed entirely of old bills of the following denominations: $2,000 in $20 bills, $8,000 in $50 bills. The money must be old. Any attempt to include new or marked bills will render the entire venture futile.

D. 3. The money should be placed in a large cigar box, or if this is impossible, in a heavy cardboard box, securely closed and wrapped in white paper. The wrapping paper should be sealed at all openings with sealing wax.

E. 4. Have the money with you, prepared as directed above, and remain at home after one o'clock. See that the telephone is not in use.

F. You will receive a further communication instructing you as to your final course.

G. As a final word of warning, this is an extremely commercial proposition and we are prepared to put our threat into execution should we have reasonable grounds to believe that you have committed an infraction of the above instructions.

H. However, should you carefully follow out our instructions to the letter, we can assure you that your son will be safely returned to you within six hours of our receipt of the money.

I. Yours truly,

J. George Johnson (Ransom letter, reprinted in Higdon, 1975, pp. 41–42)

The kidnappers collectively called themselves George Johnson.

The next note supplied the instructions for the victim's family to be placed in the Pullman car. The notes and the plan were ready. All they needed was a victim.

May 21, 1924

On May 21, the day of the planned kidnapping, Leopold and Loeb went to the Rent-A-Car Company and rented a Willys-Knight. They drove until approximately 5 p.m. before they found a suitable victim. He was a young boy from a wealthy family who was walking alone.

Bobby Franks, age 14, lived near both kidnappers' homes and often played tennis at the Loeb family's tennis court (Higdon, 1975). Since he knew Loeb, he was not afraid to approach the kidnappers. Loeb called to the boy and, as a pretense, asked him about a tennis racket. Loeb asked Bobby if he would ride around the block (Higdon, 1975). Bobby agreed. One kidnapper was driving; the other was in the backseat. The driver (whether Leopold or Loeb remains unknown) opened the front passenger door so that Bobby would sit in the car's front passenger seat with one kidnapper sitting behind him (Higdon, 1975).

As the car turned the corner, the kidnapper in the backseat began to bludgeon Bobby Franks over the head with the chisel. Franks was severely injured and bleeding heavily from the attack, but he was not dead. The kidnapper in back pulled Franks into the car's backseat and stuffed a gag into his mouth. Franks suffocated to death, while Leopold and Loeb continued to drive (Loeb confession, in Higdon, 1975).

The brutal murder was complete. Leopold and Loeb drove through Chicago toward Indiana. In Indiana, they deliberately discarded the items of Franks's clothing that they did not think would burn, including the boy's shoes, class pin, and belt. The pair went back to Chicago and waited until dark. With Bobby's dead body still in the car, the kidnappers stopped for food (Higdon, 1975).

When night fell, the two drove to remote Wolf Lake (*New York Times*, May 24, 1924). As planned, they took Franks's body to the culvert underneath the railroad tracks, where they placed him in an automobile robe, stripped him of the rest of his clothes, and poured hydrochloric acid on his face, body, and genitals to prevent identification. They pushed the body into the culvert. Unwittingly, Leopold dropped his eyeglasses near the culvert. The kidnappers collected Franks's clothes and wrapped them in the robe. On the way to the car, one of the boy's socks fell from the robe (Leopold confession, 1924). Neither kidnapper noticed.

Upon returning from Wolf Lake, the young kidnappers made two phone calls. The first was to Leopold's parents. He explained that he would be late returning home and that, yes, he would drive his aunt and uncle home when he returned to the house (Leopold confession, 1924). They then stopped at a drugstore to call the Franks' home, but became nervous when the operator took awhile to connect. They left the store, addressed the previously written kidnap letter, marked it "special delivery," and deposited it into a nearby mailbox (Higdon, 1975, p. 106). They stopped again to call the Franks' home. This time the phone was answered, and Mrs. Flora Franks was told that her son had been kidnapped and that she should await further instructions to ensure the safe return of her son. She hung up and fainted (Testimony Flora Franks, July 23, 1924, in Higdon, 1975).

The teens then went to Loeb's house, where they burned most of Franks's clothes. Since they feared the smell of the much heavier automobile robe, they hid it behind some bushes. Then they went to Leopold's home. Leopold drove his aunt and uncle to their home, then returned home, where he and Loeb had a drink with Leopold's father, and then played cards (Leopold confession, 1924). Leopold and Loeb then left the house in the rental car. While driving, one kidnapper threw the chisel from the car. A passing police officer saw this, retrieved the chisel, and brought it to the police station (Testimony Officer Hunt, July 24, 1924, in Higdon, 1975). (According to some accounts, the teens met later that evening with two dates and a friend for a meal. They then dropped off the group and returned home.) The next day, the two met on the street where they had parked the rental car and drove it to Leopold's driveway, where they attempted to clean bloodstains from the backseat (Leopold confession, 1924). The Leopold family chauffeur, Sven Englund, offered to help, but the boys said that they had merely spilled some red wine in the backseat and could clean it themselves (Higdon, 1975, p. 109).

The Franks Family

Meanwhile, the Franks, also a wealthy family of Jewish descent, had been worried for some time about their missing son. Prior to receiving the call from the kidnappers, Bobby's father called the boy's friends and teachers, as well as a family friend, Attorney Samuel Ettelson (Higdon, 1975, p. 109). Franks, Ettelson, and a teacher searched the school, but Bobby was not there. When they returned to the Franks' home, they found Flora, delirious from the call she received while the men were at the school. Franks and Ettelson went to the police that night, briefly explained to officers on duty what had happened, and decided to wait until the next day to speak to lead officers with whom they were acquaintances (*New York Times*, May 23, 1924).

The Immigrant

Early on May 22, Polish immigrant Tony Mankowski (Manke) was walking near Wolf Lake on his way to work when he noticed something odd protruding from a culvert under the Pennsylvania Railroad. It was a human foot. He looked further and found a dead young boy. He flagged down several railroad workers riding toward the scene on a handcar (Higdon, 1975, pp. 39–40). Manke spoke little English, but communicated that there was a body in the culvert. Immediately, the men removed the body to bring it to the police. One railroad worker noticed a pair of eyeglasses near the culvert. He decided to keep them (Higdon, pp. 40–41).

The men placed the body on the handcar, rode to a nearby train station, and called Chicago police. The police asked if the men had noticed anything at the crime scene. One railroad worker mentioned the eyeglasses. The body and the eyeglasses were confiscated and taken to a nearby funeral home (Higdon, 1975, p. 43).

The Investigating Journalists

Meanwhile, the *Chicago Daily News* received an anonymous tip that Attorney Ettelson could provide information on a young male kidnapping victim (*The Chicago Daily News*, 1924, May 31). Reporter James Mulroy located Ettelson at the Franks' home, where Ettelson explained what had occurred and asked Mulroy to remain silent for the time being (Higdon, 1975, p. 44). Back at the newspaper, the city editor discovered that police had brought the body of a young boy to a local funeral home. The paper's editors became suspicious that the two cases were related: Was the body at the funeral home that of the kidnapped boy? The editor sent reporter Alvin Goldstein to the funeral home; an *Evening American* reporter had also been sent (Higdon, p. 44). Back at the Franks' home, Mulroy told the family that a boy's body had been recovered from a nearby culvert. He suggested that someone go to the funeral home where the body was being held so as to ensure it was not that of young Bobby. Jacob Franks's brother-in-law went to identify the body (*The Chicago Daily News*, 1924, May 23).

By now, the Franks had received the kidnap letter promised the night before by "George Johnson." Jacob Franks secured the money requested and awaited the phone call promised in the kidnap letter for further instructions. In mid-afternoon, the phone rang. The caller identified himself as Johnson, and he told Franks to expect a Yellow Cab at his house soon (*New York Times*, 1924, May 24). The caller then provided a drugstore address where Franks was to direct the driver. There, Franks was to wait by the phone for further instructions. Ettelson took the phone and was also given the address. The phone rang again. It was the brother-in-law. The body at the morgue was that of Bobby Franks (*New York Times*, 1924, June 1).

Soon, the Yellow Cab driver appeared at the Franks' door. He explained that a man identifying himself as "Mr. Franks" called for a cab at their address, but provided no destination address (Higdon, 1975). Franks and Ettelson immediately phoned the police.

Meanwhile, Leopold and Loeb called the drugstore where they had instructed Mr. Franks to go. A store employee informed them that no such person was there. The teens hung up, left the first drugstore, and drove one block to another drugstore, where they again called the drugstore to which they had directed Mr. Franks. Again, no one matching Mr. Franks' description was at the store. The teens hung up the phone and then saw the afternoon newspaper's headlines. The body of Bobby Franks, kidnapping victim, had been found and identified. The young men aborted their plans, knowing that if they continued to try to contact Franks, they would be caught. Leopold and Loeb had failed in their attempt to commit the perfect crime.

THE CRIMINAL JUSTICE PROCESS

The Investigation

The police were called after the Franks family learned that the body at the funeral home belonged to Bobby Franks. Police had little information, so they first directed their attention to three teachers at the Harvard School, where Bobby was a student, but there was no evidence to link any of the schoolteachers to the crime (Higdon, 1975).

The main evidence was the eyeglasses found near the dead boy by the railroad workers (Higdon, 1975). The glasses were a common frame and prescription. However, investigators learned that a specific company made the hinges on the glasses, and these were sold only at Albert Coe & Company. A store salesman examined approximately 54,000 records before compiling a list of three possible owners. One pair belonged to a woman, another to an attorney, and the third to Nathan Leopold (Higdon, 1975). At this point, the state's attorney, Robert E. Crowe, called police to bring Leopold in for questioning. When they arrived at the Leopold home, they asked Leopold if he wore glasses. He replied that he did, but only for reading. When asked if the glasses were in the house, Leopold was evasive (Higdon, 1975).

The Polite Interrogation

The police asked Leopold to go with them for questioning by State's Attorney Crowe. To avoid publicity, Crowe met the teen at a hotel rather than at his offices (Higdon, 1975, p. 78). Crowe showed Leopold the glasses and asked whether they looked like the ones he owned. Nathan said they did, but his were at home. After a second fruitless search of the Leopold home for the glasses, Leopold was brought back to the hotel, where he eventually admitted that the glasses belonged to him (Leopold confession, 1924). He suggested that the glasses must have fallen from his pocket while he was birding that prior weekend. Leopold attempted to demonstrate this possibility to investigators by placing the glasses into his coat pocket and falling to the floor. The glasses did not fall out (Linder, 2003). Investigators continued to question Leopold, during which time he acknowledged his friendship with Richard Loeb (Higdon, 1975).

Later that day, Loeb was brought to the hotel for questioning (Higdon, 1975, p. 86). The teens told conflicting stories of their whereabouts on the evening of May 21. Both admitted driving in Nathan's car that day, but then their stories diverged. Nathan said the two remained together; Loeb said they parted in the afternoon (*New York Times*, June 1, 1924).

While state officials questioned the teens, Mulroy and Goldstein of the *Chicago Daily News* continued their own investigation into the Franks murder. They learned that Leopold was part of a law school study group. Each week, he typed the session's notes. Goldstein visited a group member and asked to see his notes. Some looked different from others (Higdon, 1975). Goldstein took some sample notes back to the newspaper (*The Chicago Daily News*, May 31, 1924), where a typewriter expert examined the notes and compared them with the kidnap letter. The expert concluded that the notes and the letter were typed using the same machine.

The *Chicago Daily News* handed the evidence to the state's attorney. Although all members of the study group remembered Leopold using a portable typewriter, he denied owning one. No portable was found at his home (Higdon, 1975, p. 90). Leopold and Loeb both maintained their innocence.

State's Attorney Crowe knew he could not hold the teens very long without further evidence. Eventually, an assistant decided that before releasing the youths, he wanted to speak with the Leopold family chauffeur (Higdon, 1975, p. 91). Sven Englund was brought to the hotel and asked about Nathan's use of his car on the night of the murder. Thinking he was helping the boy (Linder, 2003), Englund stated that Leopold drove home that afternoon and asked Englund to fix the car's brakes. According to Englund, the car remained there all day. This directly conflicted with the statements of Leopold and Loeb, in which they both now agreed that they had used Leopold's car to pick up two girls (*New York Times*, June 1, 1924).

Figure 5.1   Police investigate the discovery of the body of Bobby Franks, 1924. © Bettmann/
CORBIS.

The Confessions

Armed with this new evidence, questioning became more intense. Investigators told Loeb that they knew the teens were lying about their use of Leopold's car. Their alibi had been broken. Loeb confessed at 1:40 a.m. on May 31 (Higdon, 1975, p. 93).

Crowe then went to see Leopold. He told Leopold that Loeb had confessed, and bombarded him with evidence provided by Loeb, including information about the rented car and the false identities. He then said that Loeb testified that Leopold alone planned the crime and struck the blow that killed Franks (Higdon, 1975, p. 93). Provided this information, Leopold knew Loeb had confessed. Only Loeb knew these details, and Leopold was angry that Loeb had identified him as the killer. At 4:20 a.m., Leopold also confessed (Higdon, 1975, p. 94).

The kidnappers were eventually questioned together. They confessed to everything, agreeing on most points regarding commission of the crime. However, there were some points of contention, the most important one being who struck the deathblow. Both pointed the finger at the other (*New York Times*, June 6, 1924).

After confessing, the teens took an odd pride in parading investigators and the press on a two-day hunt to the areas where they had hidden physical evidence. Loeb fainted from stress early in the process, but Leopold continued to take investigators on a step-by-step trip to retrieve evidence. He provided rubber boots used to wade in the mud when disposing of Franks's body. He identified the chisel, found by the police officer when it was thrown from the rental car, as the murder weapon. At the culvert, they found Bobby's stocking. Later, Leopold took the group to a bridge. There, he showed police where to find remnants of the typewriter used to write the kidnap notes (*New York Times,* June 1, 1924).

At the end of the day, Leopold was taken to the hotel where Loeb had been resting (*New York Times,* June 1, 1924). As long as they were providing information, Leopold and Loeb were treated well. They were taken for a lavish dinner and provided changes of clothing from home.

The next day, the macabre evidence-gathering field trip continued. At one point, talking proudly of their research into and commission of the crime, Leopold made his famous statement about killing Franks: "It was just an experiment. It is as easy for us to justify as an entomologist in impaling a beetle on a pin" (*The Chicago Daily Tribune,* June 2, 1924). The teens showed no remorse.

The Defense

Throughout this period, Mike Leopold desperately tried to see his brother. During the first day of evidence gathering, Mike, Loeb's uncle Jacob, and family cousin/attorney Benjamin C. Bachrach, went to see Crowe. They asked to see the teens, but were denied access.

Frantic, Jacob Loeb knew there was one person who could save his nephew from death. He went to attorney Clarence Darrow, begging him to take the case (*The Chicago Daily*

CLARENCE SEWARD DARROW (1857–1938): A STEADFAST DEFENDER

Almost 70 years after his death, Clarence Seward Darrow (1857–1938) remains one of the most renowned defense attorneys in American history. Darrow was a leader in the American Civil Liberties Union and an ardent opponent of the death penalty. Among his clients who faced execution, none ever received the ultimate punishment.

During the late 1800s and early 1900s, Darrow was a central figure in many historic legal battles that resonate to this day. In addition to his passionate defense of Leopold and Loeb against the death penalty, Darrow was also a civil rights crusader who defended an African American doctor, Ossian Sweet, and his family after they were charged with murder of a member of a mob that had formed outside their home to intimidate them into moving from an all-white Detroit neighborhood. Darrow also defended trade union members, including Chicago American Railway Union leader Eugene Debs (later a prominent American Socialist) against charges of contempt of court during the 1894 Pullman Strike. He was later successful in securing an acquittal for Bill Haywood, a leader of the Industrial Workers of the World and the Western Federation of Miners, who was charged with the murder of the former governor of Idaho, Frank Steunenberg. And in a trial that dealt with issues still controversial and unresolved today, Darrow defended a science teacher accused of violating a Tennessee law that forbids teaching the theory of evolution in the state's public schools.

Darrow is remembered as a tireless opponent of the death penalty, an advocate for the rights of minorities and organized labor, and a dogged pursuer of fairness in an American criminal justice system he believed was skewed in favor of the wealthy. He often took cases defending unpopular clients or contentious issues. In all cases, he became a modern icon of criminal defense, defending his beliefs and upholding his clients' Constitutional right to the best possible defense, regardless of race, economic status, or popularity.

Figure 5.2   Nathan Leopold, 19, far right, and Richard Loeb, 18, second from right, during their arraignment in a Cook County courtroom with attorney Clarence Darrow, left, 1924. © AP Photo.

Tribune, June 3, 1924). By the 1920s, Clarence Darrow had become well known as the "champion of the poor and the oppressed" (Higdon, 1975, p. 123). He had defended everyone from murder suspects to union leaders. Though in poor health, he was still a great orator and speechwriter and was known for excellent cross-examinations and an ability to remember facts without use of written notes (Higdon, p. 123). Darrow took the case because he saw in it the perfect opportunity to speak out against capital punishment, a practice he had fought throughout his life (Linder, 2003).

Following the second day of evidence gathering, Leopold and Loeb were taken back to Crowe's office. During that Sunday morning, Crowe assembled the area's best-known alienists (as psychiatrists were then known) so the defense would be unable to use them in an attempted insanity plea. Prior to the teens' individual examinations, defense attorneys Bachrach and Darrow, along with Jacob Loeb, requested to see their clients. Crowe again denied their request (Higdon, 1975, p. 128). The attorneys would have to wait until Monday to bring the matter before a judge.

Crowe had Leopold and Loeb examined by his expert psychiatrists. All were "traditionalists," who were concerned with elements of the conscious mind. The teens were tested and retested. Afterward, Crowe took them to identify the Willys-Knight they had rented on the night of the murder. That night, Crowe took the teens for another lavish meal (Higdon, 1975, p. 128).

On June 2, Darrow and Bachrach returned to Crowe's office, demanding to see their clients. Again, Crowe denied them access by refusing to send the teens to the county jail

(Higdon, 1975, p. 130). In response, the defense brought a writ of *habeas corpus* against Crowe, and was granted a hearing in front of Judge John R. Caverly, then chief justice of the criminal court.

Eventually agreeing that the minors were being denied their constitutional rights, Caverly ordered Crowe to move the teens to the county jail, where they could meet with their attorneys. Upon seeing his clients, Darrow told them to stop providing evidence, because by doing so they were helping the state to make its case (Higdon, 1975, p. 131). After their meeting, the teens took the Fifth Amendment when asked further questions. In response, Crowe held them in jail (Higdon, 1975, p. 132).

The Defense Strategy

With the most famous alienists in the region already employed by Crowe, Darrow and Bachrach sent Bachrach's younger brother, attorney Walter Bachrach, to the annual American Psychiatric Association meeting to find the era's top alienists to analyze Leopold and Loeb (Higdon, 1975, p. 137). Unlike Crowe's alienists, Bachrach chose doctors who were part of the new school of psychiatry, which was more concerned with subconscious rather than conscious motives. Sigmund Freud heavily influenced this new school. In addition to the alienists brought to Chicago, Darrow hired two local doctors, Harold Hulbert and Karl Bowman, to conduct extensive evaluations of the teens. Their 300-page report would be entered into evidence and play a huge role in the youths' defense.

Crowe was prepared to go to trial. He was convinced that Darrow was going to plead Leopold and Loeb not guilty by reason of insanity (*The Chicago Daily News,* June 7,

WHAT IS A WRIT OF HABEAS CORPUS?

Habeas corpus (Latin for "you have the body") is a writ issued by a judge ordering that a detained person be released from custody. The writ is designed as a check against unlawful imprisonment. Today, a petition for a writ of habeas corpus is usually filed by an individual seeking federal court review of the constitutionality of his/her imprisonment by the state. A writ succeeds and the person is freed if the reviewing court finds that a lower court has erred in its interpretation of the Constitution when it imprisoned the person.

The right *to file* a writ of habeas corpus is guaranteed by the U.S. Constitution (Article I, Section 9). However, this did not stop President Lincoln from suspending the writ during the Civil War, leaving those jailed upon suspicion of collaboration with the Confederacy no recourse to challenge their confinement. In 2006, President George W. Bush signed into law the Military Commissions Act, which suspends the availability of habeas corpus to non-U.S. citizens (including those living in the United States) detained as potential enemy combatants by the U.S. government (DeYoung, 2006). While the Act was designed to facilitate prosecutions against terror suspects after 9/11, many argue that it represents a violation of the Constitution's habeas corpus guarantee. The law's constitutionality is currently under review by federal courts.

Source: DeYoung, K. (2006, October 20). Court Told It Lacks Power in Detainee Cases. *Washington Post,* p. A18.

1924). However, Crowe was armed with his alienists' evidence that the teens knew that their actions were wrong.[2] With all of the physical evidence provided by the teens, Crowe announced that he had a "hanging case" (*New York Times*, June 1, 1924).

Darrow also knew the prosecution had a strong case. He had to rethink the insanity plea strategy. In a move that shocked the state's attorney, Darrow had Leopold and Loeb plead guilty to the kidnap and murder. Darrow explained to the defendants and their families that the plea would do two things: first, it would prevent the defense from being able to seek death on two separate charges: murder and kidnapping. As it stood, the state could ask a jury to seek death on one charge, and if it lost, it could impanel another jury to seek death on the other charge. The only way to prevent Crowe from getting two bites at the apple was to have the teens plead guilty to both charges (Higdon, 1975, p. 64).

Second, and perhaps more importantly, Darrow knew that a not-guilty-by-reason-of-insanity plea meant that a jury would decide the teens' ultimate fate, but a guilty plea would require a judge to make the death decision. It seemed much easier for a jury of 12 persons to sentence the teens to death since they could always argue that it was not themselves, but others on the jury, who pushed for the ultimate sentence. By pleading guilty, the decision whether to take the teens' lives would rest with one person, the judge. Thus, what was to be the trial of the century became a sentencing hearing during which the judge would hear mitigating and aggravating circumstances that he would then weigh in deciding whether the teens should live or die.

The Sentencing Hearing

State's Attorney Crowe was outraged that there would be no trial. Although the young men pled guilty, making moot the need to provide evidence of guilt, Crowe was determined to put all evidence before the court to prove their utter guilt and lack of remorse. During his evidence presentation, he portrayed Leopold and Loeb as evil monsters, suggesting that the boys had sexually molested Franks before killing him, a charge that was unfounded (*New York Times*, May 24, 1924). However, he was careful to maintain that, while their deeds were evil, the teens were not insane.

Darrow and Bachrach's strategy was to show that due to their mental condition and youth, the boys' lives should be spared. Darrow used psychiatric testimony as the primary mitigating factor. Crowe objected. If the defense were to argue that the boys were mentally unbalanced and therefore insane, the hearing should be concluded and a jury impaneled to hear a not-guilty-by-reason-of-insanity case (Higdon, 1975). In response, Darrow maintained that he would prove that the boys were not insane, but instead were mentally "abnormal," and that he would show the distinction between the two and the number of ways in which the teens' abnormalities were shaped and intertwined to produce the crime (Higdon, 1975).

There had been psychiatric testimony in previous trials (Fass, 1993), but there was no real precedent about the use of psychiatric testimony as mitigation in a death sentencing hearing. According to Higdon (1975), the Franks case set this precedent (p. 190). Judge Caverly agreed to hear defense testimony about the psychiatric state of Leopold and Loeb to determine whether such testimony should be allowed in court as official mitigation.

The defense turned to the findings in the Hulbert-Bowman report. In the report, and in all testimony by defense alienists, Darrow insisted that they refer to the teens by their nicknames, "Babe" (Leopold) and "Dickie" (Loeb). He believed that reference to their childlike nicknames would reiterate the boys' youth (Higdon, 1975, p. 206). The Hulbert-Bowman report stated that Babe had been an outcast youth who turned to education and his superior intellect for solace. Babe's life philosophy had been altered by two events. The first was the loss of his mother at age 14 (Fass, 1993, p. 934). Babe reasoned that if a good person could be taken away at an early age, there must be no God. He decided to avoid emotions and to follow only "cold-blooded intellect" (Higdon, 1975, p. 201). The second experience involved Leopold's sex life. Though never really sexually attracted to women, he was sexually attracted to his friend, Dickie Loeb.

The report next turned to the boys' childhood and fantasies. During his youth, Dickie was provided an extremely strict governess who refused to allow Dickie to play with friends or to read books for fun (Higdon, 1975, p. 201). He was only to study. She wanted to mold him into a great man. In response to this pushing, Dickie began reading his favorite books, detective novels, in secret. He read them whenever he got the chance. Eventually, he became obsessed with, and fantasized about, crime (Hulbert-Bowman report, 1924, in Higdon, 1975).

The alienists reported that Babe's governess had sexually abused him (Higdon, 1975, p. 198). Perhaps as a result, he maintained a rich fantasy life, which usually involved himself as a slave to a king. In this fantasy, he, the slave, saved the king's life and was offered his freedom. But he refused and remained an anointed slave to the king (Higdon, 1975, p. 198).

The boys' fantasies merged when they met. According to the report, in Babe's mind, he became the slave to what he considered to be the superior Dickie (Higdon, 1975, p. 205). He wanted to please Dickie, whom he believed to be a Nietzschean Superman. Dickie wanted a partner in crime and believed Babe was superior in intelligence and capable of committing crimes. Through the intertwining of these fantasies, the forces united to result in the death of Bobby Franks.

After hearing this preliminary testimony, Judge Caverly decided that the defense's psychiatric evidence was not the same as evidence of insanity and, therefore, could be used as mitigating evidence of abnormality (Fass, 1993).

Once allowed to testify, defense alienists reiterated much of what they had previously stated. Babe had fears of inferiority. Alienists testified about his obsession with Nietzsche's Superman theory. On the subject of homosexuality, Dickie admitted to allowing Babe some sexual interactions, but solely in exchange for Babe's help in committing crimes (Fass, 1993).

At points during the hearing, Babe was labeled a "paranoid personality" (Higdon, 1975, p. 216), while Dickie was considered to be "abnormal mentally" and to have a "split personality" (Higdon, 1975, p. 217). Alienists suggested that Loeb suffered from disorders of the endocrine glands and the sympathetic nervous system, which could partially account for his abnormal behavior (Fass, 1993, p. 933). In effect, he was both mentally and physically abnormal. All of the alienists agreed that the crime never could have happened but for the intertwining of the disordered needs and personalities of the pair (Higdon, 1975).

In response to recasting the boys as victims of their abnormalities, Crowe offered rebuttal evidence. He called a prosecution alienist who testified that he could find in the teens "no evidence of any mental disease" (Testimony, Dr. Church, August 13, 1924, in Higdon, 1975).

The state rested.

Closing Arguments

Darrow was the first to close. This was his opportunity not only to convince the judge to spare the boys' lives but also to convince the nation of the evils of capital punishment. It would become his most widely renowned speech and is considered one of history's most impassioned and moving pleas against the death penalty.

First, however, he began his closing argument by denouncing the continual publicity surrounding the case and the unfairness of newspapers' widespread calls for death. Darrow believed public opinion was the greatest enemy to justice (Higdon, 1975, p. 124). He maintained that because the press had devoted such unprecedented time to the case, everyone in Chicago must have already decided whether the defendants should be put to death (Darrow summation, 1924).

Darrow next argued that the state would be out of touch with prior cases if it put to death youth of ages 18 and 19. No one in Illinois under age 23 at that time had ever been put to death. He argued that boys of such ages were still children in need of direction. The very act of snatching and killing a child for no reason, and ultimately sacrificing their own lives, could only be the work of "a couple of immature lads" (Darrow summation, 1924). Darrow also argued that the defense alienists' testimony proved that the boys were abnormal. The boys lacked the ability to reason. They killed for the experience of it. Clearly, this was not the behavior of normal boys.

Darrow then tried to persuade the court to understand and accept his theory of determinism. He believed a person's life was set at birth, that there was really no free will, but that actions were predetermined by heredity, upbringing, and mental capacity (see Shattuck, 1999). Therefore, these boys should not be held responsible for traits they displayed that had been passed down to them by distant relatives. It was the hand they had been dealt (Darrow summation, 1924).

Finally, Darrow turned to his famous argument against the death penalty. He argued that justice should be tempered with mercy, and reiterated that the boys would be imprisoned for life if allowed to live. This case was horrible, he agreed, but not as serious as some others that had previously been before the court. Yet, because the boys came from wealth, they were treated with severe public scrutiny and outcries for death (Darrow summation, 1924).

Darrow acknowledged laying the death decision at Judge Caverly's feet, arguing that the judge must live forever with his ultimate decision. It would be easy to sentence the boys to death, thereby caving to "popular" desire. But Darrow pled with the judge to recognize that such a sentence would be looking to the past:

> I know your Honor stands between the future and the past. I know the future is with me, and what I stand for here;...I am pleading for life, understanding, charity, kindness, and the infinite mercy that considers all...that we overcome cruelty with kindness and hatred with love....You may hang these boys...by the neck until they are dead. But in doing it you will turn your face toward the past....I am pleading for the future; I am pleading for a time when hatred and cruelty will not control the hearts of men. When we can learn by reason and judgement and understanding and faith that all life is worth saving, and that mercy is the highest attribute of man. (Darrow summation, 1924)

By the end of the twelve-hour closing, Judge Caverly was in tears (Linder, 2003).

Next, it was Crowe's turn to convince Judge Caverly to sentence the boys to death. He asked Leopold whether he now believed in God—had it been an accident by the Nietzsche disciple that led to his capture, or "an act of Divine Providence to visit upon your miserable carcasses the wrath of God in the enforcement of the laws of the State of Illinois" (Crowe summation, 1924). Crowe implied that the youths' capture was an act of God.

Crowe attacked Darrow's emotional closing. He suggested that Darrow relied too heavily on oratory and ignored facts, the only material the court should consider (Crowe summation, 1924). He criticized the determinism defense. Heredity could not be blamed for the boys' behavior. Even the defense's alienists admitted that there was no evidence of hereditary imbalance in the boys known to pass from one generation to another. Crowe called the teens "two perverts" and maintained that they should pay the ultimate penalty.

Crowe further claimed that the wealthy "spoiled" killers could not rely on the age defense, since the Illinois statute under which the case was being tried held that when an individual reached age 14, "the law presumes that he has the capacity to commit a crime and is entirely and thoroughly responsible for it" (Crowe summation, 1924). In addition, he argued, if American boys were old enough at age 18 to die to protect the laws of their country in WWI, then these boys, now both 19, were old enough to die when they violated such laws.

Finally, Crowe attacked Darrow's blame of Nietzsche for the crime. Students had been reading the philosopher for years, and yet no one had used it as a defense in committing a crime (Crowe summation, 1924).

Crowe concluded by reiterating that the case facts proved Leopold and Loeb's guilt, that the young men represented evil incarnate, and that they should be put to death for their actions (Crowe summation, 1924).

The fate of Leopold and Loeb now lay with Judge Caverly.

Sentencing

On September 10, in a packed courtroom, Caverly announced his long-awaited ruling (Higdon, 1975). He stated that, although the defense testimony about mental abnormality was strong, it was more important to the study of criminology than to this case. Indeed, Caverly maintained that he was not swayed at all by the defense's psychiatric evidence in making his decision. The crime, he held, was one of "singular atrocity" (Caverly decision, 1924).

Caverly sentenced the youths to life for the murder, plus 99 years for the kidnapping and ransom of Bobby Franks. Caverly chose life over death based solely on the teens' youth. This decision, he proclaimed, was in keeping with enlightened changes in criminal law occurring around the world, and with Illinois's own precedents (Caverly decision, 1924). Caverly stressed that life imprisonment seemed the worse punishment, as the teens would suffer years of confinement, unable to use the intellectual talents with which they had been so gifted and, ultimately, cursed.

Prison and Beyond

Leopold and Loeb were eventually placed in Stateville Prison after a period of separation (Higdon, 1975, p. 288). There, they began a correspondence school so that inmates could advance their educations, and they reorganized the prison library (Leopold, 1958).

On January 28, 1936, a former cell mate murdered Loeb in the shower. Though the death was ruled self-defense, state prison officials believed that Loeb had been murdered over a dispute about money (Higdon, 1975).

Leopold maintained the correspondence school after Loeb's death (Leopold, 1958). During World War II, he volunteered with other inmates as a test subject for a new malaria vaccine (Higdon, 1975, p. 304). In 1947, the governor decided to review the cases of all men who had volunteered for the malaria project. In 1949, Leopold's sentence was commuted from life plus 99 years to 85 years, thus reducing the period he would have to serve before being eligible for parole (Higdon, 1975, p. 311).

When parole became a possibility, Leopold spoke with Meyer Levin, a journalist who had originally been assigned to cover the case when it was heard in 1924. They discussed collaboration on a book about Leopold's life. But Leopold wanted to concentrate on his prison years and refused to discuss the crime (except to maintain that he was led by Loeb). This was unacceptable to Levin, who wanted to write about the crime itself (Levin, 1956). The men went their separate ways, each deciding to write a book. Levin went on to write *Compulsion* (1956), a fact-and-fiction account of the crime. Leopold wrote *Life Plus 99 Years* (1958), in which he focused on his accomplishments in prison. He also discussed his relationship with Loeb. He claimed that he loved Loeb, but also hated him for involving him in the crime that had forever changed his life.

In 1957, after turning down his first request, the parole board again reviewed Leopold's case. This time the board had read Leopold's book, and Leopold had retained Elmer Gertz, a famous civil rights attorney, to represent him (Gertz, 1965). Gertz also represented Leopold in a lawsuit against Levin's *Compulsion* and became his lifelong friend (Gertz, 1965). Gertz stressed that Leopold must provide a reason for his crime to be paroled (Higdon, 1978, p. 318). In his prior hearing, Leopold would give no reason. Finally, in 1957, he gave the parole board what they wanted to hear. He stated that he had committed the crime to please Richard Loeb (Leopold, 1958).

Leopold was granted parole in 1958. He moved to Puerto Rico, where he wrote about ornithology. He married and taught mathematics at the University of Puerto Rico. He died in 1971.

THE PRESS: HELPING READERS TO REIMAGINE THE CRIME

Chicago in the 1920s witnessed two simultaneous conflicts: the first concerned Prohibition, and the second involved the city's newspapers (Higdon, 1975, p. 28). The latter provided much space for the former. By 1923, there were over 400 deaths per year in Chicago. Most were gangland murders. Life seemed cheap (Higdon, 1975, p. 20). In contrast stood the death of Bobby Franks. He was an innocent young victim, and his murder had no connection with the criminal underworld. If Bobby Franks could be murdered, so could any child. Newspapers pounced on this different murder, spreading the word quickly and vying for readers (Higdon, 1975, p. 20).

Though *Chicago Daily News* journalists Mulroy and Goldstein were responsible for some important case breaks, these were overshadowed by the sensationalism surrounding the crime. Editorials demanded Leopold and Loeb be hanged, asserting that mothers were afraid to let their children out for fear that strangers would murder them. William Randolph Hearst, who owned two Chicago newspapers, offered Sigmund Freud any amount of money to come to Chicago and comment on the hearing. [Freud declined due to ill health and his concern that all he knew of the case was what was printed in newspapers, and he was unprepared to comment on evidence related by them (Higdon, 1975).] The *Chicago Daily Tribune* (July 17, 1924) argued that courtroom events should be broadcast on its affiliate radio station WGN and hosted an opinion poll to determine whether the public would support such a broadcast. Readers voted against it.

News of each day's court events could be found in each newspaper's next edition. The press published the boys' confessions (for example, *New York Times*, June 6, 1924), conducted interviews with families and friends of the victim and the accused boys, "and speculated about the nature of the 'million-dollar defense' to be mounted by Clarence Darrow and his expensive psychiatric witnesses" (Fass, 1993, p. 923). In his turn, Darrow maintained that newspapers were purveyors of lies and misrepresentations that ultimately shaped public opinion (Darrow summation, 1924).

Along with the victim's family and police, two newspapers had each offered a $5,000 reward for information relating to the crime. But at the same time, newspapers published inaccurate stories, including one from the *New York Times* (July 19, 1924) stating that Loeb confessed to striking the fatal blow after learning that the crime's penalty would be the same regardless of who actually committed the physical murder. This was untrue; Loeb never confessed to carrying out the killing.

WHAT IS PHRENOLOGY?

The theory of phrenology was first developed in the late eighteenth and early nineteenth centuries. Phrenologists believed that examination of the human head could reveal much about a person's personality and character traits, including whether that person was likely to commit crime. While phrenology was used by some scientists to suggest that individuals were not responsible for criminal behavior (since it was predetermined by biological traits), it was also used by racist groups (such as the Nazis) to argue that the physical traits of some races revealed their general superiority. Phrenology has been completely discredited; however, those who developed the theory contributed to the more modern concept that different thoughts and actions may be attributed to different parts of the brain (van Wyhe, 2004).

For more information about phrenology on the Internet, see John van Wyhe, *The History of Phrenology on the Web* (http://pages.britishlibrary.net/phrenology/), [November 20], 2004.

Press stories covered every sensational case detail (Fass, 1993). Rumors that Franks had been sexually abused intensified when the press became aware of the implied homosexual liaisons between Leopold and Loeb. However, there was no evidence to suggest that such abuse occurred (*The Chicago Daily Tribune*, May 24, 1924).

The press also dissected the teens' behavior by examining their facial features using the now-debunked science of phrenology (*The Chicago Daily Tribune*, June 1, 1924; *The Chicago Herald and Examiner*, June 1, 1924).

Leopold was portrayed as a coldhearted scientist who brutally took part in the murder as an experiment. In contrast, Loeb was seen as popular, and he was at first, as well as friendly with the press.

Prior to the guilty pleas of Leopold and Loeb, newspapers provided intensive tutorials for readers on the insanity defense (Fass, 1993, p. 931). But once the case became a sentencing hearing, coverage of psychiatry changed. As the hearing progressed, the public became familiar with new ideas, specifically those coming from the new school of psychiatry called psychoanalysis. The term "abnormal" became part of the social understanding of the apparently senseless crime that had been committed (Fass, 1993, p. 931). As the alienists described, the press reconstructed Leopold from a coldhearted killer to an abnormal, insecure boy.

As defense testimony about the teens' lives was given, some newspapers' sympathy toward the youths increased. The *Chicago Daily News* (June 3, 1924) wrote that Loeb, while in jail, was seen teaching a young African American inmate to read. The same article detailed the harsh conditions the wealthy teens faced in jail. One column asked Chicago families to think about how they would feel if one of their children were on trial for murder (Fass, 1993, pp. 928–929). By the end of the hearing, the perception of the boys would change completely, mainly due to the defense's psychiatric testimony. The wealthy monsters became mere boys who had committed a heinous crime (Fass, 1993, p. 929). These boys were now written about as abnormal in the psychiatric sense, and this abnormality helped to explain the seemingly random and horrific nature of their crime.

The press reconstruction of the boys from monsters to misguided youth helped the public to reimagine the crime in understandable terms—it was the work of severely "abnormal" and "disordered" boys (Fass, 1993, p. 938). In the process, understanding of psychological concepts, though both criticized and accepted, became more widespread.

THE LEGACY

The Leopold and Loeb case forever altered perceptions of youth, public knowledge of psychiatry, and problems involved with the interaction between psychiatry and law. In addition, it framed the debate over capital punishment for the rest of the century.

One of the many concerns after the hearing was the fear that the crime represented changes occurring among youth. Young people were becoming uncontrollable, a result of the new parenting culture that allowed too much freedom. While this was not the first time that writers disparaged the waywardness of youth, the reconstruction of Leopold and Loeb as abnormal boys struck fear in the hearts of many Chicagoans (Higdon, 1975; Fass, 1993). Crime and juvenile delinquency became not just the realm of the poor, but of the wealthy as well (Fass, 1993, p. 939). The public was concerned, not only that their children might be victims of "abnormal" others, but that their children might actually *be* "abnormal" (Fass, 1993, p. 939).

In the realm of criminal justice, appropriate use of expert psychiatric testimony became an issue. While psychiatric testimony had been introduced in trials long before the Leopold and Loeb case, Darrow was the first to use it as mitigating evidence to a crime, and the case brought expert testimony problems into public discourse (Fass, 1993, p. 930). Darrow used it to prevent an ultimate death sentence. But in doing so, he raised troubling questions concerning the appropriate scope and utility of psychiatric testimony that continue to persist.

Even before the expert psychiatric testimony was introduced, a battle waged over its appropriate use in the courtroom. Defense psychiatrists were concerned that the hearing would result in a war between opposing psychiatrists (Fass, 1993, p. 930). The judge would be left with two opposing points of view given by doctors paid by each side to support their positions. But, psychiatry was regarded as a science, and though reasonable doctors could disagree about diagnosis, defense psychiatrists suggested that doctors for both sides meet and agree to an ultimate diagnosis of the boys (Higdon, 1975, p. 166). But Crowe rejected this idea. He planned for a trial in which insanity would be the question. A consensus among psychiatrists about the teens' states of mind would not help his case, and might very well hurt it.

Years later, one defense alienist who had been involved in the case wrote about the problem of retaining experts to provide findings sympathetic to a client (Fass, 1993). He maintained that the only way to fairly analyze a state of mind in a court setting required that the court itself appoint experts to make diagnoses independent of those argued by prosecutors or by defense attorneys.

Such ideas have been repeatedly voiced as the criminal justice system continues to struggle with often-confusing evidence by dueling experts, but reforms have not been implemented. Perhaps this lack of implementation reflects both the realities of the adversarial setting of the courtroom and the court's unwillingness to take on the additional responsibility of providing oversight of experts.

Continuing Fascination

Publicity played a huge role in shaping public opinion about Leopold and Loeb. They started as Nietzsche-trained monsters and ended up as victims of determinism, self-doubt, and each other's fantasies. But unlike many other trials in American history, the question of Leopold and Loeb's guilt was never an issue (Steinberg, May 16, 1999). The primary concern was always, why would two wealthy boys of strong intelligence commit such an atrocious act? The teens' response, that they killed Bobby Franks to see if they could get away with the perfect crime, was never accepted as sufficient. Where did ultimate responsibility rest?

No answer to the boys' behavior has been deemed adequate, and so fascination with the case continues. No current theories of criminal behavior appear to be able to explain the apparent thrill killing (Entin, 1999). At the time, most psychiatric experts who examined the boys thought that Loeb was a psychopath (Higdon, 1975, p. 217) and Leopold a paranoid schizophrenic (Higdon, p. 339).

Scholarly publications still dissect the case, and it continues to be the subject of plays, books, and films. Although the film adaptation of Meyer Levin's novel *Compulsion* (1958) confuses the actual nature of events, blending fact and fiction, both the book and the film remain popular accounts of the pair's crime and sentencing. Inspired by the pair's alleged motivation, Alfred Hitchcock's *Rope* (1948) examines the cold Nietzschean philosophy that led two young men to kill a college-age peer—and then entertain dinner guests over his dead body. More recently, *Swoon* (1992) explores the nature of the homosexual and intertwined relationship between Leopold and Loeb. A decade later, *Murder by Numbers* (2002) provided another loosely based account of the Leopold and Loeb case.

Such long-lasting media attention reflects continued interest in the nature of "good" and "evil," and in the intense shades of gray represented by the Leopold and Loeb case. Perhaps more interesting today is Darrow's plea for the future and humanity. He believed himself on the side of history—that state-approved death sentences would soon be abolished. Darrow envisioned a moral society capable of learning from past mistakes. Perhaps mercifully, Darrow died only one year before his faith in a world moving toward a more moral path would be shattered: in 1939, the world was dragged down into the bloodiest war in history, and any hope for a more tolerant and peaceful civilization was eclipsed by one of the darkest eras of humankind.

But in 1924 Chicago, Darrow's beliefs in the future seemed possible, even as society struggled to understand his clients. Leopold and Loeb killed young Bobby Franks and left the world with their disturbing and incomprehensible vision of "the perfect crime." It is this incomprehensibility that has led to fascination with the strange and frightening behavior of the two young men and ensures their immortality in the annals of American crime.

SUGGESTIONS FOR FURTHER READING

Fass, P.S. (1993). Making and remaking an event: The Leopold and Loeb case in American culture. *The Journal of American History, 80*(3), 919–951.
Higdon, H. (1975). *The crime of the century: The Leopold and Loeb case.* New York: G.P. Putnam's Sons.
Leopold, N. (1958). *Life plus 99 years.* New York: Doubleday.
Levin, M. (1956). *The obsession.* New York: Simon and Schuster.

NOTES

1. For Nietzsche's "übermensch" theory, see *Thus Spake Zarathustra* (Nietzsche, 1891/1966).
2. Illinois used the M'Naghten Test at that time, which required that, in order to prove insanity, the perpetrator not have known the difference between right and wrong at the time of the crime (Fass, 1993).

REFERENCES

The Chicago Daily News. (1924, May 23; 1924, May 31; 1924, June 3; 1924, June 7).
The Chicago Daily Tribune. (1924, May 24; 1924, June 1; 1924, June 2; 1924, June 3; 1924, July 17).
The Chicago Herald and Examiner. (1924, June 1).
Clarence Darrow: A plea for mercy. (1924). Retrieved July 1, 2004, from http://www.americanrhetoric.com/speeches/cdarrowpleaformercy.htm
Crowe summation for the state. (1924). Retrieved September 30, 2003, from http://www.law.umkc.edu/faculty/projects/ftrials/leoploeb/LEO_SUMP.HTM
Entin, J. (1999). Using great cases to think about the criminal justice system [Book review]. *The Journal of Criminal Law and Criminology, 89*(3), 1141–1156.
Fass, P.S. (1993). Making and remaking an event: The Leopold and Loeb case in American culture. *The Journal of American History, 80*(3), 919–951.
Gertz, E. (1965). *A handful of clients.* New York: Follett.
Higdon, H. (1975). *The crime of the century: The Leopold and Loeb case.* New York: G.P. Putnam';s Sons.
Judge Caverly's decision. (1924). 29 Dick. L. Rev. 1. Retrieved September 30, 2003, from http://www.law.umkc.edu/faculty/projects/ftrials/leoploeb/LEO_DEC.HTM
Leopold, N. (1958). *Life plus 99 years.* New York: Doubleday.
Leopold, N. (2003). Full confession as found at Linder, D., *Famous American trials: Illinois v. Nathan Leopold and Richard Loeb.* Retrieved September 30, 2003, from http://www.law.umkc.edu/faculty/projects/ftrials/leoploeb/leopold.htm
Leopold confession. (1924). Retrieved September 30, 2003, from http://www.law.umkc.edu/faculty/projects/ftrials/leoploeb/LEO_CONF.HTM
Levin, M. (1956). *The obsession.* New York: Simon and Schuster.
Linder, D. (2003). *Famous American trials: Illinois v. Nathan Leopold and Richard Loeb.* Retrieved September 30, 2003, from http://www.law.umkc.edu/faculty/projects/ftrials/leoploeb/leopold.htm
New York Times. (1924, May 23; 1924, May 24; 1924, June 1; 1924, June 6; 1924, July 19).

Nietzsche, F. (1966). *Thus spoke Zarathustra: A book for none and all* (W. Kaufmann, Trans.). New York: Viking Penguin, Inc. (Original work published 1891.)

Rackliffe, M. (2000–2003). I teach you the overman. Retrieved September 30, 2003, from http://www.leopoldandloeb.com

Shattuck, R. (1999, January). When evil is "cool." *The Atlantic Monthly, 283*(1), 73–78.

Steinberg, N. (1999, May 16). Leopold and Loeb case still haunts after 75 years. *The Chicago Sun Times.*

6

Fundamental Divides: The Trial of John Scopes

ERNEST L. NICKELS

The trial of John T. Scopes was brought to session on the morning of July 10, 1925, in the Rhea County Courthouse of Dayton, Tennessee. On its face, the case is hardly noteworthy. It was a misdemeanor criminal trial of a small-town schoolteacher on charges he readily admitted to and—surprising no one—would ultimately be convicted of. As a question of law, however, the case probed the profound frictions in the history of American jurisprudence among academic freedom of public educators, protections against state establishment of religion, and the right of the people to legislative control of the form and operation of public agencies. Further, the case of *Tennessee v. Scopes* served as a spectacular finale to the end of an era, one marked by rapid change in the social, cultural, and intellectual institutions of American life—transformations to which a single trial could no more than bear witness. As narrated by an attentive press, these mere eight days of trial, squaring off the towering figures of William Jennings Bryan and Clarence Darrow, reflected back to a transfixed public all the aspirations and anxieties of a people finding themselves at the dawn of a new age. These were a people diversely, if uneasily, invested both in progress and in tradition, in reason and in faith, in science and in religion.

RECEPTION OF DARWINIAN EVOLUTION

Evolution had the attention of philosophers and scientists alike well before Charles Darwin's *Origin of Species* in 1859. It was Darwin's thoroughly naturalistic rendering of an evolutionary account, his contribution of such concepts as "natural selection," and his 1871 attempt in *The Descent of Man* to place the human species within this framework that placed him (if belatedly) at the forefront of a scientific revolution.

Religious antagonism to Darwinism fluctuated in proportion to its acceptance in the field. Mildly condemned for contradicting Biblical teachings on the special creation[1] of life and allowing no explicit role for God in its development, initial scientific resistance to Darwin calmed critics in the religious community temporarily. Until advancements in genetics breathed new and certain life into the Darwinian paradigm after the turn of the century, his works held an uncertain place in the budding sciences. Special creationism (particularly in the United States) and pre-Darwinian evolutionary theories continued to thrive in the meantime. Only with the onslaught of a younger generation of post-*Origin* researchers, rapidly filling the expanding institutions of professional science, were such views eventually displaced.

Dissemination of this growing scientific consensus into the public sphere through high school science curricula lagged behind the field for some time.[2] Revisions of established textbooks, then dominated by creationist views, were not affected by the sweeping changes in the field at the close of the nineteenth century. Newer texts began to appear in the 1880s. However, only after the exponential growth of the public education system at the turn of the century, and the merging of zoology and botany into a single course called biology, did the intellectual monopoly held by older texts loosen. These forces required that the industry produce more, as well as original, materials to meet novel institutional demands—an opportunity for younger scientists. Over the next 30 years, these texts adopted an increasingly evolutionist and explicitly Darwinian stance, one progressively hostile to creationist concepts. In 1914, George Hunter published the hugely successful *Civic Biology*. It included a section on evolution as well as a biographical sketch of Darwin himself. It was Scopes's use of this text that led to his arrest and trial.

It is difficult to discern how the public initially received such ideas. Evidence suggests, however, that Americans today are generally more inclined to view science and religion as competitive realms of knowledge and to be antagonistic toward evolutionary ideas than at the turn of the century. Current views on evolution in the classroom are certainly more defined and polarized now. Far from predetermined, antievolutionism in the United States emerged from specific forces at work in religion in Progressive America. One man, a force in himself, was particularly instrumental in how history would unfold: William Jennings Bryan.

THE GREAT COMMONER

A gifted orator, scholar, lawyer, and journalist for popular and religious publications, the Great Commoner (as Bryan was known) had served as secretary of state under President Wilson, and three times ran as the Democratic candidate for the presidency. Committed to populist reform, world peace, welfare, and organized labor, Bryan's politics were emblematic of the Progressive Era. Like many progressives, he was devoutly religious, actively involved in the Social Gospel movement[3] and dedicated to the advancement of society through institutional reform and personal salvation—and, failing that, state intervention. Socially progressive and religiously conservative, Bryan and his fellow travelers constituted an enigmatic but effective force of change.

Darwinism initially commanded little attention from American Protestantism. It would, however, become the incidental enemy to a development movement in these congregations. At the dawn of the twentieth century, substantial numbers came to staunchly oppose "modernism" in the church—a trend toward liberal, nonliteral interpretations of Scripture informed by (among other things) scientific discovery. This oppositional offshoot, called fundamentalism, was more socially pessimistic and doctrinally conservative than the Social Gospel movement before it. Fundamentalists yearned for a return to "old time religion" premised on unchanging, universal principles (fundamentals) derived from Scriptural literalism. As the movement grew, absorbing the energies and political clout of its forbearers, fundamentalism became a powerful force in the interwar political landscape. Unsettled by the expanding influence science held in shaping the minds of the nation's youth through the public education system, fundamentalists particularly resented what they viewed as indoctrination to evolutionary ideas in the classroom. Bryan's activism helped galvanize these vague sentiments into a full-scale cause.

Though a self-professed "fundamentalist," Bryan's relationship to the anti-evolutionist movement was complex. Not sharing fundamentalism's cornerstone doctrine of Scriptural literalism, Bryan's own motivations were varied. Aware of early scientific criticism of Darwin, Bryan had been initially dismissive of Darwin's theory and continued to insist it was simply flawed science. However, while publicly categorical in rejecting evolution, privately he recognized that future science might demonstrate its factuality (De Camp, 1968, p. 45). Bryan's open objections to teaching human evolution were limited to its presentation as *fact* (rather than hypothesis) and pertained only to public (rather than private) schools. A progressive reformer, Darwinism troubled Bryan more in its application than its idea.

He viewed concepts like "survival of the fittest" as legitimating a *social* Darwinism, an ethic of might-makes-right that he believed alienated people from their moral obligations to care for the most vulnerable members of a society. Further inflaming these apprehensions was the popularization of eugenic social policy in interwar America—a movement pioneered by Sir Francis Galton (Darwin's cousin) to apply hereditary knowledge to the cultivation of a genetically

THE FUNDAMENTALS

"Fundamentalism" today is often used to refer to any strict or intolerant ideology (religious or otherwise), and its connotations are almost uniformly negative. Originally, however, fundamentalism was the proper and self-selected name for a religious movement that peaked in the United States during and shortly after World War I. Intellectually, this movement was a blend of the teachings of the Princeton Theological Seminary and Darbyite dispensationalism (see Sandeen, 1970). Princeton led the charge against modernism, eschewing higher criticism of the Bible, the incorporation of scientific knowledge into theology, the idea that there might be multiple valid paths to God, and the evaluations of good works over faith and convictions over doctrines. Dispensationalism, as taught by Darby and imported from the United Kingdom, taught a premillennialist theology that viewed the historical relationship between mankind and God as existing in a series of periods governed by different laws (i.e., dispensations). At the end of history, which dispensationalists believed was upon them, an apocalypse would precede a second, millennial reign of Christ on earth.

Spread primarily among Presbyterian, Baptist, and Methodist congregations, this movement flourished amidst revival circuits, Bible retreats, and dispensationalist conventions at the start of the twentieth century. The most complete statement of doctrine was put forth in a series of pamphlets published between 1910 and 1915, titled *The Fundamentals*. Among the cornerstones of faith most commonly identified by fundamentalist organizations and literatures are belief in biblical literalism and inerrancy, the bodily resurrection and deity of Christ, the total depravity of mankind, original sin, and the imminence of a second coming, which would begin with the rapture. Fundamentalism saw social improvement as futile, and thus emphasized faith as the sole path to personal salvation. The Social Gospel movement had instead believed that the second coming would not occur until mankind, through good works, brought the kingdom of God to earth.

"fitter" population through methods perceived un-Christian to many. Likewise, Bryan recognized Darwin's influence on the work of nineteenth-century German moral philosopher Friedrich Nietzsche,[4] a self-proclaimed immoralist many blamed for inspiring

German militancy that resulted in World War I. Furthermore, though helping to define the movement, Bryan clearly believed that his activism merely gave voice to the people's will. Dedicated to the populist creed that the people are the ultimate authority on all things public, including public science and its instruction, Bryan believed it was within their rights to banish Darwin from their schools. Likewise an advocate of free speech and an opponent of state establishment of religion, Bryan differed intellectually with measures sought by some fundamentalists to criminalize the teaching of evolution and institutionalize creationism. However, he was not one to highlight such ideological differences. His activism did much to produce antievolutionist legislation he could not fully endorse, but would defend nonetheless on principle.

THE MAKING OF A TRIAL

With the backing of groups including the World's Christian Fundamentals Association (WCFA), antievolutionism bills found their way first into the legislatures of Kentucky and South Carolina in 1922. Each bill met narrow defeat. Much to Bryan's credit, 1923 brought success in Oklahoma, with the passage of an antievolutionist textbook bill. Shortly thereafter, Florida approved a resolution he authored that prohibited the teaching of evolution as fact. Tennessee went further, in 1925, with the passage of the Butler Act, which read,

> Chapter 17, House Bill 185 (By Mr. Butler) Public Acts of Tennessee for 1925.
> AN ACT prohibiting the teaching of the Evolutionary Theory in all the Universities, Normals and all other public schools of Tennessee, which are supported in whole or in part by the public school funds of the State, and to provide penalties for the violations thereof.
> *Section 1.* BE IT ENACTED BY THE GENERAL ASSEMBLY OF THE STATE OF TENNESSEE, That it shall be unlawful for any teacher in any of the Universities, Normals and all other public schools of the State which are supported in whole or in part by the public school funds of the State, to teach any theory that denies the story of the Divine Creation of man as taught in the Bible, and to teach instead that man has descended from a lower order of animals.
> *Section 2:* BE IT FURTHER ENACTED, That any teacher found guilty of the violation of this Act, shall be guilty of a misdemeanor and upon conviction, shall be fined not less than One Hundred ($100.00) Dollars nor more than Five Hundred ($500.00) Dollars for each offense.
> *Section 3:* BE IT FURTHER ENACTED, That this Act take effect from and after its passage, the public welfare requiring it.

After it passed both state houses, Governor Austin Peay signed the bill into law in March of that year. Many, Peay included, saw the Butler Act as merely symbolic legislation. Plans for enforcement were never publicly entertained (Ginger, 1958, p. 7). Nevertheless, it quickly found application in the arrest of John Scopes.

The American Civil Liberties Union (ACLU),[5] having watched antievolutionist initiatives grow bolder, responded decisively to the Butler Act. It issued a press release, quoted in the May 4 edition of the *Chattanooga Daily Times,* announcing that the organization was "looking for a Tennessee teacher who is willing to accept our services in testing this law in the courts" ("Plan," 1925). In Dayton, a small mountain town outside Chattanooga boasting a population of less than 3,000, the ACLU's volunteer was found.

George Rappelyea, an employee of the Tennessee Coal and Iron Company who managed mining properties around Dayton (Scopes and Presley, 1967, p. 36), apparently saw in the ACLU release an opportunity for civic promotion—an event that could put Dayton on the map and bring in new sources of revenue, even if only through tourism during the event. Together with area locals and business leaders, Rappelyea set about enlisting John Scopes, a Rhea County Central High School science teacher and sports coach, in bringing a test case of the Butler Act.

At a local drugstore, the pitch was made. Initially reluctant, Scopes was unsure whether he had even broken the law.[6] Although Scopes did not normally teach biology, the drugstore meeting did uncover that he had substituted for the regular instructor and had used *Civic Biology* to help students review for the final exam. Eventually, Scopes was talked into volunteering for his own arrest. Once agreeable, Rappelyea swore out a warrant against Scopes and sent word to the ACLU, who responded promptly with a promise of *pro bono* representation, financial help, and publicity for his cause. The arrest came May 7, with formal charges three days later accusing Scopes of having taught evolution in April of that year.

Speaking before the annual convention of the WCFA in Memphis on the May 11,

Figure 6.1 Unassuming schoolteacher John Scopes. The case of *Tennessee v. Scopes* served as a spectacular finale to the end of an era, one marked by rapid change in the social, cultural, and intellectual institutions of American life. Courtesy of the Library of Congress.

where the impending Dayton trial was much discussed, Bryan noted in his address his hope that the statute would be upheld. Promptly, the WCFA leadership approached him for assistance in the prosecution. Sue Hicks, a Dayton merchant who helped instigate the case, had also been attempting (without luck) to contact Bryan to elicit aid with the prosecution (Ginger, 1958, p. 21). Two days later, in Pittsburgh, Bryan announced his willingness to aid the state, and he was appointed shortly thereafter as special prosecutor —an unusual occurrence for a misdemeanor trial (Larson, 2003, p. 61). Bryan and his son joined District Attorney General Thomas Stewart and District Attorney Ben McKenzie and his son, Judge J.G. McKenzie, on the prosecution.

On defense, Scopes's Dayton attorney, John Neal, was joined by ACLU trial lawyer Arthur Hays. On learning that Bryan would aid the prosecution, Clarence Darrow and Dudley Malone jointly volunteered their services directly to Neal.

Darrow was a prominent defense attorney and, like Bryan, a social progressive, a friend of labor, and a Democrat. Originally friendly acquaintances, Darrow had even supported

Bryan's early political careers. However, Darrow did not share Bryan's populism, tending instead toward libertarian values with pronounced intellectualist overtones. A skeptic, rationalist, and fervent individualist, Darrow was viewed by many as a radical for aiding in the defense of clients who were anarchists, socialists, and communists (De Camp, 1968, pp. 74–79). The Federal Bureau of Investigation (FBI) even maintained a file on him.[7] Particularly on matters of religion and evolution, the two men stood in stark opposition. Their relationship grew publicly antagonistic as a result. In 1923, Darrow challenged Bryan in an open letter to the *Chicago Tribune* to answer 50 questions about human history, attacking Bryan's (inferred) Scriptural literalism. Bryan indignantly declined (De Camp, 1968, pp. 74–79).

For his zealous agnosticism[8] and personal antipathies toward Bryan, Darrow rightfully anticipated that the ACLU would wish to avoid his involvement for fear of "transform [ing] the trial from a narrow appeal for academic freedom to a broad assault on religion" (Larson, 1997, p. 100). John Neal had no such reservations. Renowned and experienced in high-profile cases, Darrow had a reputation for winning seemingly unwinnable cases. In the year prior, he had successfully defended Richard Loeb and Nathan Leopold, two wealthy teenagers accused in a thrill-kill murder of a 14-year-old boy, against a death penalty verdict by arguing that the defendants were pitiable victims of (among other things) exposure to Nietzschean philosophy. Ironically, Bryan later drew upon Darrow's defense of Leopold and Loeb to illustrate the need to prohibit evolutionism in schools (Larson, 1997, p. 100).

All involved in the making of the trial had aspirations for a show of sensational proportions, with various hopes for personal, economic, and ideological gains. The ACLU sought to rigorously defend Scopes. However, expecting defeat, they aimed to win on appeal at the state supreme court and have the law ruled unconstitutional—and, if not there, at the U.S. Supreme Court, where the impact would be national. Further, they hoped to use the trial's publicity to demystify evolution to a national audience, and then rouse popular disfavor for the Butler Act to put the antievolutionist movement in check, if not reverse it. Rappelyea and the business interests of Dayton were eager to attract attention and visitors to their town in the hope of spurring the community's economic growth. The WCFA sought a symbolic victory over the forces of modernism, as did Bryan, who further believed that the American public simply lacked understanding of the true fallacies and imminent dangers Darwinism posed for the moral fabric of the nation. Darrow aimed to take a well-publicized shot at fundamentalism by publicly defeating its most visible proponent, and his personal antagonist, Bryan. As these interests converged piece by piece, the stage was set for an event with far greater cultural than legal significance. With Darrow and Bryan now commanding the spotlight, the spectacle was set to begin. Arriving in Dayton, Bryan set the tone:

> The contest between evolution and Christianity is a duel to the death....If evolution wins in Dayton, Christianity goes—not suddenly of course, but gradually—for the two cannot stand together. They are as antagonistic as light and darkness, as good and evil. ("Bryan," 1925, p. 6)

THE MONKEY TRIAL

The defense's trial strategy was simple enough: challenge the law on constitutional grounds. Failing that, attack the substance of the statute as incoherent and an unreasonable restriction on public educators by demonstrating the factuality of evolution and its compatibility with (modernist) Biblical interpretation. Waiting in the wing were a number of scientific and religious authorities to provide expert testimony to that effect. A victory at Dayton was unlikely, so they would seek to produce a record of the trial favorable to a case for appeal (Scopes and Presley, 1967, p. 158). The prosecution would move to exclude expert testimony and would likely succeed. Any opportunity to enter even a sample of that testimony into the record, however, would be a partial victory.

The prosecution's strategy was simpler: fend off constitutional challenges and argue the case purely on the factual question of whether or not Scopes had taught human descent in violation of the law's letter and intent. They would try to suppress expert testimony to avoid debate on evolution's scientific merits and compatibility with Scripture—they simply would not win a contest of credentials with the expert witnesses available to the prosecution (Larson, 2003, p. 66).

John Raulston, an elected circuit court judge for east-central Tennessee and a lay minister, presided. Sharing the town's enthusiasm for its newfound fame, he likewise enjoyed his own. Aside from the throngs of journalists from the national media, Scopes is also a landmark trial in criminal justice history in the media for its pioneering use of live radio broadcasts and its continuous feed by cable of the unfolding events to Europe and Australia. Raulston himself was heard to remark, "[m]y gavel will be heard around the world" (Ginger, 1958, p. 103). He was, no doubt, correct.

When proceedings[9] opened on Friday morning of July 10, the first issue was the securing of a new grand jury indictment. The original had been invalidated by a procedural error. Jury selection dominated the afternoon. Darrow was known to engage this process

Figure 6.2   Clarence Darrow (left) seated with Judge John F. Raulston, 1925. Courtesy of the Library of Congress.

101

meticulously. So convinced of its importance in determining the outcome of a trial, he had once spent six months in selecting whom to seat. Regional custom in misdemeanor cases, however, was rather informal. A small, initial pool of potential jury members, if insufficient, could be enlarged by having the sheriff round up willing bodies from the available bystanders. Although concessions were made, Darrow was further dismayed to find himself limited to only three preemptory challenges (the ability to dismiss a potential juror without stating cause). Further, these challenges had to be exercised while the person was under questioning or not at all, meaning that he was forbidden to question them all before selecting out those he predicted to be least sympathetic to the defense (Ginger, 1958, pp. 96–97). In short order, then, the 12 jurors were settled upon.

Mostly farmers and primarily Baptists and Methodists, the jury displayed a diversity of viewpoints on faith and evolution largely unappreciated by a national media that lumped the lot of them as "fundamentalists" (Conkin, 1998, p. 87). It mattered little, however, as the jury would spend the vast majority of the trial excused from the courtroom as the prosecution and defense wrangled over legal questions of statutory interpretation and the relevance of expert testimony—matters to which the jury was not permitted to be an audience. Instead, the jury followed events as many in the town did, listening to the broadcast of the proceedings over a pair of large speakers on the courthouse lawn. At the close of the day, the defense requested that the jury be sworn before the weekend, to limit their permission to discuss the substance of the case. Local custom held that jurors not be sworn until the first day of trial, in case one should fall ill in the meantime. In keeping with that, Raulston ordered the swearing-in postponed until after opening statements on Monday.

Monday morning, then, with the jury excused, the defense raised its motions to quash the indictment. The law, they argued, was unreasonable in its limitations, it violated protections of due process and free speech as articulated in the state and federal constitutions, and it ran afoul of the state's own constitutional guarantees against the separation of church and state and its expressed mandate in support of the sciences. Attorney General Stewart, for the prosecution, countered. The language of the statute was clear enough. It in no way infringed upon religious freedom to limit the subjects public educators were permitted to speak on in the course of their duties. Further, as the state supreme court had ruled, control of the public schools fell to the discretion of the legislature.

The day concluded with Darrow's first speech to the court, arguing to quash. The speech oscillated between a folksy, good-natured appeal to reason and a terse rebuff of religiously inspired bigotry. On one hand, Darrow attempted to shame the religious sentiments of those in the audience for zealous persecutory practices of the Christian past (alluding to sixteenth-century witch hunts targeting intellectuals). On the other, he largely absolved his audience of responsibility for the Butler Act, casting blame instead onto out-of-state fundamentalist demagogues—those such as Bryan—and appealed to the jury's higher mindedness to put this bad law to rest. By most accounts, it was a brilliant speech, lionized by those in attendance and the press alike. H.L. Mencken, a widely read and influential syndicated editorialist for the *Baltimore Sun* who, as a friend, had encouraged Darrow to take the case (Larson, 1997, p. 100), was particularly generous in his praise. Likewise, as would be typical of his coverage, he was generously contemptuous of the fundamentalist "yokels" and "morons" in the audience.

Figure 6.3 Clarence Darrow defending John Scopes at the Scopes evolution trial, 1925. Courtesy of the Library of Congress.

Tuesday morning found the court in conflict, once more, over customary procedure. With the jury excused, Darrow objected to the practice of opening prayer at the start of each day. Raulston was unmoved. Noting his own reliance on divine guidance on the bench, he hardly saw impropriety in encouraging the same of jurors. He would concede only to allowing the local ministerial association to provide representatives of other faiths to lead opening prayer. The out-of-town press, believing Dayton was exclusively fundamentalist, interpreted Raulston's attempt at compromise as sarcasm. Of the remaining days of trial, prayer was conducted once by a Jewish rabbi and once by a Unitarian preacher. This also largely escaped the notice of a press selectively attending to its misperceptions of Dayton's residents (Conkin, 1998, p. 89).

After a recess, and a photo opportunity for the press (Ginger, 1958, p. 131), Raulston spent the remainder of the morning dictating his decision on the constitutional issues raised by the defense in private to a court stenographer. Somehow the ruling was leaked to the press. Raulston deferred his ruling until morning, until the culprit was identified and publicly scolded in court. Summarily, then, Raulston dismissed the defense's arguments as without merit. The trial continued. With the jurors now in attendance, the defense entered its plea: not guilty.

The prosecution succinctly stated the charge. Attempting to strengthen its case on appeal, the defense moved for dismissal. Unsuccessful, the defense then stated what would be its two-pronged theory of the case. By the wording of the statute, it argued, the state must first prove that Scopes had taught evolution. The defense conceded Scopes had.

ILLUSTRATING THE TRIAL

Historians regularly debate whether and how history might be usefully divided into periods that can be understood as backdropping the more localized events that comprise them. Still, there is broad consensus that the years between the end of World War I and the start of the Great Depression were a distinct time in American history. Culturally, it was a period of great turmoil. First, progressivism, a fragile (if not illusory) constellation of principles collapsed amidst a conservative turn and factional infighting. Second, divides between generations and geographies grew and spurred cultural conflicts. In both respects, the face-off between Bryan and Darrow are emblematic. More so, however, it is a bipolar character to the culture of the 1920s that seems to have given it such distinctive flavor. At one level, it was dominated by a vibrant and often garish pop culture, a celebration of the superficial, the momentary, and the *avant-garde*. Bubbling beneath, however, was a pervasive melancholy—a *weltschmerz*, roughly meaning "world-historical sadness," most clearly illustrated in the literature of the Lost Generation or the art of the Dadaists.

Editorials of the Scopes trial invoked a number of recurrent themes. Among them is the portrayal of Bryan and antievolutionists as, alternately, quixotic figures and zealous bigots. Darrow and evolutionists, in turn, are mocked as befuddled intellectuals deeply confused about their genealogy, mistaking monkeys for their ancestors. A third position is marked out in another common device. Here, the debate is satirized by using the antievolutionist premise, that Darwinism teaches humans are descendants of monkeys, to suggest that the idea might be offensive to monkeys. In this way, commentators used the Scopes trial to criticize American culture at the time as unserious precisely by trivializing this event, and themselves, by contrasting the importance attached to it relative to the vast inhumanity they saw around them. As such, they reinforce despair for human nature and the prospect of progress. "I say, Genevieve, in this evolution trial—are they trying to class men with monkeys or monkeys with men?"

See, also, Moran (2003) for an excellent analysis of the use of this and other framings of the Scopes trial in the African American press to renegotiate the place of black intellectuals in American society at the time.

Second, however, the state must prove that in so doing he had contradicted the Biblical account of creation. The defense contended that there was nothing inherent to evolution that contradicted anything other than a literalist interpretation of Genesis, and they were prepared to offer expert testimony to that effect.

With the jury finally sworn, the state called its witnesses. First came the superintendent of the Rhea County schools, who had signed the complaint against Scopes. Following that, the state called two students from Scopes's class to testify to Scopes's use of *Civic Biology,* and concluded with F.E. Robinson, a party to the drugstore conspiracy. The defense again moved for dismissal and, again unsuccessful, called its own first witness—Maynard Metcalf, an eminent zoologist from Johns Hopkins University.

The prosecution interjected. If Scopes was to testify, he must, under the rules of Tennessee process, be called as first witness. The defense responded that Scopes could provide nothing useful to his defense, as the use of the text was already conceded. Darrow returned to his examination of Metcalf, who had testified to being both an evolutionist and a Congregationalist. When Darrow asked whether he was aware of any scientist who was not an evolutionist, Stewart objected. Raulston concurred. Under the rules of hearsay, one cannot testify on the content of opinions held by anyone other than one's own self. Raulston would, however, allow Darrow to proceed with his examination as a matter of record while deferring judgment on the admissibility of testimony overall. Though clearly predisposed to exclude the testimony, Raulston was reluctant to rule so early on the matter, perhaps thinking of interests at stake for the community (Conkin, 1998, p. 90) and perhaps out of reluctance to let go his own place in the spotlight. In any case, the ruling surely would have brought the trial to a premature close. After instructing court reporters that the testimony to follow was not to be released to the press, the judge permitted examination to resume. Metcalf testified that, familiar with the leading authorities in the zoological, geological, and botanical sciences, he was confident that each took evolution to be a fact. They might, however, differ on the particulars of its theory.

Stewart now raised the first of repeated objections insisting that, whatever the factuality of evolution, the sovereign people of Tennessee had decided that the teaching of human descent was inconsistent with Biblical scripture. Therefore, the jury, as the people's representatives, needed no further interpretation by experts of any sort on either the wording or intent of the legislature in putting the act to law. The only pertinent questions were those of the factual circumstances surrounding Scopes's use of the offending text. All other testimony was irrelevant.

Raulston, again excusing the jury, allowed Darrow to proceed. Metcalf testified to his belief that all life began as unicellular plants in the sea, and offered his estimation of this Cambrian period to have occurred more than 600 million years ago—a stark contrast to literalists' estimations that placed the earth's age at a mere 6,000 years. At the close of the session, Raulston announced that the question of admissibility would be settled the following day.

When the trial resumed Thursday, and before Metcalf was allowed to continue, the prosecution called for Raulston's ruling on the testimony. Darrow insisted that "evolution" and "creation," key terms in the statute under which their defendant was charged, were not adequately clear and that expert testimony was necessary to demonstrate that Scopes taught the former and contradicted the latter. Raulston ruled that formal arguments on admissibility would be opened by the state, though Darrow argued that that privilege fell to the defense.

Bryan's son presented the prosecution's initial points. Offering a rigorous, if dry, account of the case precedent bearing upon the use of expert testimony, he argued that any experts presented by the defense could only testify to their own opinions on whether they *personally* saw conflict between the account of evolution and the story of creation as they understood it. Further, as a question of fact, it fell upon the jury alone to determine whether Scopes's use of the materials in question had violated the law. Hays responded for the defense. Interpretation of the statute was necessary, and the *factuality* of evolution—which only expert testimony could establish—was certainly relevant to the case before them. The debate carried on fruitlessly for some time, and Darrow moved for its immediate resolution, out of consideration for the witnesses left waiting in the wing. Showing hesitancy once more, Raulston postponed his decision until after the noon recess.

When the trial resumed, William Jennings Bryan took the floor. Up to this point, he had scarcely said a word, passively observing the proceedings. The expectant audience awaited the Commoner's speech. Though evaluations varied, he was mostly in classic form. Animated, he directed his impassioned speech directly to the attentive crowd, rather than the bench—which should have elicited a reprimand from Raulston, but did not. He was, however, an older man now and in declining health, and largely drew upon an arsenal of rhetorical arrows crafted for antievolutionist lectures he delivered on circuits around the country. Nonetheless, he ruthlessly lampooned evolutionary thought and strung together Darwin with Nietzsche and German aggression. He attacked a diagram of speciation included in *Civic Biology* that placed the human race indistinctly amid branches representing other life forms in the animal kingdom, all sharing a single genealogical trunk. "Talk about putting Daniel in the lion's den?" he exclaimed (*Trial,* 1997, p. 175).

He mocked the notion of reconciling evolution with Genesis, and stressed the caustic effects of Darwinism on a social morality. He accused science of fostering atheism, and proclaimed the jury better qualified for Biblical interpretation than any supposed expert the defense could produce. He attacked Darrow personally, quoting from the record of the Loeb-Leopold case to accuse him of propagating an amoral worldview. Darrow objected, reproaching Bryan for misrepresenting the context of his statements. Bryan concluded by reiterating the prosecution's contention that it was for Tennesseans alone to decide what belonged in their own public classrooms. The jury, as their representatives, should alone determine whether Scopes stood in violation of their law, in its wording and its intent. When he finished, the courtroom burst into applause. Raulston simply looked on.

Malone, who had served under Bryan in the state department and harbored no small amount of resentment toward his old boss, responded for the defense. He reiterated its two-pronged interpretation of the Butler Act and its contention that the state had yet to satisfy both standards. Only the inclusion of expert testimony, he argued, could establish that evolution did not contradict Biblical teachings on divine origin. He appealed to a sense of fairness. To exclude such testimony would leave Scopes without defense, and the prosecution alone would be free to define the issues of the case such that his guilt was predetermined. The defense, he insisted, had a right to use the means necessary to establish its theory of the case. To limit the interpretation of Genesis to fundamentalist viewpoints advanced by the prosecution, and to use that interpretation as the standard of reasonableness in evaluating the law and its application in this case, was to establish an uneven playing field. To punctuate his appeal, Malone summoned a shameful portrait of zealous dogmatism, analogizing Scopes's prosecution under such conditions to the Roman Catholic Church's persecution of Galileo. He criticized the state team for seeking to exclude knowledge that would enable the jury to reach a fair and informed judgment on the merits of the case.

The crowd again responded favorably—but more so than with Bryan. Malone had won the match. Raulston called for order, but unsuccessfully, as even the bailiff himself pounded the table with his club in cheer. After the crowd calmed, Raulston inquisitively prompted the defense to elaborate its views on compatibility between Scripture and evolution, particularly regarding the ultimate origin of humankind and the immortality of the soul. Darrow skillfully replied that such matters lay beyond the scope of material science, which dealt only with physical processes. As distinct realms of knowledge, science and religion could never be in contradiction. Stewart, concluding for the state, called for a "purely legal discussion" of the principles of construing statutory law, attempting to stymie the defense's two-pronged interpretation. Quickly, however, discussion disintegrated into contentious bickering. Little else more was accomplished that day. The courtroom cleared. Bryan himself gave the starkest evidence that the defense team had taken the day. He complimented Malone on what he claimed to be the greatest speech he had ever heard (Scopes and Presley, 1967, pp. 154–155).

Friday morning, Raulston finally ruled on expert testimony as inadmissible. Defense experts could, however, enter their testimony into the record: a small victory, but nonetheless the most profound blow the defense had sustained thus far. Stewart sought tight constraints on the testimony, suggesting a limitation to written affidavits. Bryan rose to inquire about the prosecution's right to cross-examine. Raulston consented, should those witnesses take the stand. Darrow, facing yet another unfavorable ruling, objected. Witnesses served only to state what the defense intended to prove—and at a higher court, to boot. Cross-examination would do nothing to inform this court's decision.

Failing to move Raulston on the point, Darrow's frustration turned to hostility. "We want to make statements here of what we expect to prove. I do not understand why every request of the state and every suggestion of the prosecution should meet with an endless amount of time and a bare suggestion of anything that is perfectly competent on our part should be immediately overruled," Darrow complained.

"I hope you do not mean to reflect upon the court," Raulston replied.

"Well," Darrow quipped, his back to the bench, "your Honor has the right to hope!" The laughter of the audience turned to a quiet tension. Raulston ominously suggested that he had the "right to do something else, perhaps" (*Trial*, 1997, p. 207).

Darrow desisted, and court was adjourned early to allow the defense to prepare its statements over the weekend. With expert testimony excluded, popular opinion believed the case was over. As rapidly as they had descended on Dayton in anticipation of the trial, the swarm of reporters seemingly evaporated—including Mencken. Over the weekend, the conflict spilled out of the courtroom and into the press, with Darrow and Bryan each issuing statements, baiting one another on the issues of constitutionality and the integrity of evolutionary theory (Scopes and Presley, 1967, p. 161).

In belated response to Darrow's outburst Friday, Raulston opened Monday's proceeding by citing him in contempt of court, to be held on $5,000 bail. After another brief spat on their relevance, Hays proceeded to read the defense affidavits into the record. Just prior, the defense had outlined the purpose with which the testimonies were submitted. Scientific experts, the majority of the witnesses, would speak regarding the factuality of evolution. Biblical scholars, then, would lend support to the defense's two-realms-of-knowledge claim outlined earlier. Evolutionary science could not contradict divine creation, they contended, because the teaching that God made man in His own image refers to man's *soul* rather than his body. The soul is the domain of religious knowledge, whereas the body is properly known through material science. The court recessed at noon.

After reconvening, Darrow publicly apologized to Raulston and was relieved of the contempt charge. Nothing seemingly remained but a few affidavits, finding Scopes guilty, and his sentencing. Citing a fear that the large crowds from the prior week had threatened the architectural integrity of the building, but perhaps moved instead by the relentless heat of the courtroom, Raulston adjourned proceedings to the courthouse lawn (Scopes and Presley, 1967, p. 164). Court resumed under the shade of the maple trees.

Hays finished reading the statements into the record. Raulston was prepared to call the jury to return when Darrow demanded the removal of a sign stating, "Read Your Bible," affixed to the wall of the courthouse, in plain view of the makeshift jury box.

Unsympathetic, but sensing that all was winding down, Raulston consented. Hays unceremoniously entered two versions of the Bible, Roman Catholic and Jewish, as evidence that, contrary to the wording of the statute, more than one Bible existed. Though surprising to many onlookers, the fact that both texts in question told the same creation story escaped the notice of all involved. The court again prepared to summon the jury when the defense played its last, and most famous, hand. Hays requested to call one final witness—Bryan himself. Though recognizing that his testimony could be given no more weight than those entered thus far into the record, the defense wished to have Bryan testify on "other questions involved" (*Trial,* 1997, p. 284).

"Other Questions Involved"—Bryan Testifies

Expectedly, the prosecution objected. Bryan, unexpectedly, did not. A bewitched Raulston indicated no resistance to this wildly unorthodox request. Whether welcoming the opportunity or not, Bryan could scarcely refuse. As one who, time and again, proffered himself as a Biblical authority, refusing to testify as an expert student of Scripture was unthinkable. After requesting an equal opportunity to question the defense, Bryan took the stand. Darrow directed.

"You have given considerable study to the Bible, haven't you, Mr. Bryan?" Bryan responded that he had tried, more so now than when he was younger. Over Stewart's repeated objections and pleas to the bench to end this examination, Darrow proceeded to interrogate Bryan on issue after issue regarding internal inconsistencies in Biblical accounts and problems for literal interpretation in the face of modern scientific knowledge. In 1923, Bryan had dismissed Darrow's challenge in the *Chicago Tribune.* Now, as Darrow resurrected much of that list in serial fashion under the scrutiny of the crowd and remaining reporters, Bryan was forced to engage Darrow's assault.

The questions themselves were scarcely profound and were rather unoriginal observations. Clearly provoked and frustrated, Bryan responded tersely (if not evasively) to Darrow's questions. At times displaying the subtle wit of his earlier years as an orator, Bryan's answers were largely guarded, murky, and often meandering. Darrow sprinkled the strained façade of an offhanded demeanor with bitter tirade, revealing his own frustration with the exchange.

Was it a fish or a whale that swallowed Jonah? Bryan recalled no mention of a whale. *What of the story of Joshua commanding the sun to stand still, in order to lengthen the day —is it not the Sun, which is fixed, and the earth that revolves?* "Well, it is relatively so, as Mr. Einstein would say," Bryan retorted, before conceding the point that if Joshua lengthened the day, he did so by halting the earth, rather than the sun. *What would happen if the earth were to suddenly come to a standstill in its orbital path?* Bryan said he had not considered the question before. *Isn't it true the earth would have converted into a molten mass of matter?* "You testify to that when you get on the stand, I will give you a chance." *Is the Noachian flood to be taken as a literal event?* Yes, Bryan replied, though he would not testify to the accuracy of the date of 2348 BC, as calculated by Bishop James Ussher and included in the marginalia of some Bibles. *How exactly was that estimate arrived at?* "I do not think about things I don't think about," Bryan replied. "Do you think about things you do think about?" Darrow shot back in frustration. "Well," Bryan responded slyly, "sometimes" (World's Most Famous Court Trial, 1997, p. 287).

Darrow moved to questions that were focused squarely on Biblical chronology and genealogy. How could Bryan defend literalist calculations of the age of humankind in the face of modern anthropological knowledge of ancient religions and civilizations, including those of the Chinese and Egyptians? How could he believe that the Tower of Babel was the origin of language types in the face of discoveries in philology? Bryan confessed to having neither an awareness of modern scholarship nor an interest in these questions. Shocking, however, was Bryan's admission that he believed the earth to be "much older" than the 6,000-year estimate offered by literalists, followed by his stated rejection of the idea that the earth was created in six days of 24 hours.

To those who failed to appreciate Bryan's ideological differences between himself and the fundamentalist movement with which he had aligned (and Bryan, of course, was loathe to call attention to such disagreements), his answers were a shocking revelation (Conkin, 1998, p. 97). To his fundamentalist supporters, it was a disgraceful concession to modernism and evolutionist heresy. To the prosecution, it was a symbolic regicide of the antievolutionist movement. As reported in the press, it was the *coup de grace* in Darrow's thorough and crushing defeat of Bryan on the stand. It was this account of a humiliated and demoralized Bryan having been dressed down by the coolly rational Darrow, hastening Bryan's death, that would dominate headlines and work its way into mythology of the "monkey trial," memorialized in the 1950 stage production and its film adaptation (1955) of *Inherit the Wind*.[10]

Bryan died shortly after the trial, but from years of poor diet and diabetes. Hardly a broken spirit, Bryan had planned to mount a full-scale campaign to reverse the tide, recover face, and renew his antievolutionist efforts. Bryan was well aware that Darrow had bested him, but the victory was less than complete and, in the views of many, dishonorably won. Many found Bryan the sympathetic figure and perceived Darrow's attacks as cruel taunts of a respected man of the people and his faith—and, by proxy, their own. The ACLU itself attempted to drop Darrow from the appellate team in light of his conduct (Conkin, 1998, p. 96).

Amid the fray, Bryan was able to carve out a minor martyrdom. To Stewart's demand that Raulston explain the purpose of the examination, Bryan responded, "[t]he purpose is to cast ridicule on everyone who believes in the Bible..." Darrow unwittingly took the bait, putting his own intolerance on bold display, retorting, "[w]e have the purpose of preventing bigots and ignoramuses from controlling the education of the United States and you know it, and that is all." This was just the opening the Commoner required to recover some lost ground: "I am simply trying to protect the word of God against the greatest atheist or agnostic in the United States. I want the papers to know that I am not afraid to get on the stand in front of him and let him do his worst. I want the world to know" (*Trial*, 1997, p. 299). The crowd erupted in cheer.

Darrow did not have the opportunity to finish his examination of Bryan, nor did Bryan have the opportunity to turn the tables. Neither had the chance for closing arguments. Reminiscent of Darrow's 1923 challenge to Bryan in the *Chicago Tribune*, Bryan would, however, issue a release to the press posing nine questions for Darrow. Darrow, in turn, issued his response to each—usually with the agnostic creed, "I don't know" ("Evolution," 1925). Following his death, Bryan's widow released a copy of his closing speech to the press.

When court reconvened on Tuesday, Bryan's testimony and the entire account of the exchange were stricken from the record at Raulston's direction. Dismissing the defense's two-pronged theory, at last, the judge stated that the only thing left to be decided was whether or not Scopes had, in fact, taught the evolutionary descent of humans. With that, little else remained but to find Scopes guilty and close the trial. The defense agreed that the jury should be instructed to reach a finding of guilt. After arrangements to file the appeal were made, Raulston called the jury and charged them. Raulston informed them that if they found Scopes guilty, and were content with the minimum penalty, the bench could set the fine. Stewart interjected to note that under the state constitution, the *jury* must formally set any fine in excess of $50. Here, once more, customary norms prevailed. Defense stated that it had no objection. After nine minutes deliberating, the jury returned a verdict of guilty.

At last, Scopes rose to address the court on his own behalf, to explain why the penalty should not be imposed. Denouncing the law as unjust, Scopes swore he would continue to oppose it however he could. "Any other action would be in violation of my ideal of academic freedom—that is, to teach the truth as guaranteed in our constitution, of personal and religious freedom. I think the fine is unjust" (*Trial,* 1997, p. 313). Scopes was then fined $100, which Bryan himself had offered to pay. The defense filed notice of appeal to the state supreme court. Bond was set at $500, a cost assumed by Mencken's paper, the *Baltimore Sun,* which had provided material support for the defense.

The various parties all made their final addresses to the court. Bryan struck an optimistic tone. He claimed faith that the case would ultimately be decided correctly, whatever the outcome, by the people. Darrow concurred, but once more expressed his apprehension with what he feared to be a return to the days of pious witch-hunts. Raulston thanked the visiting attorneys. With that, the "monkey trial" closed.

THE EVOLVING AFTERMATH

As circulated popularly and in the press, the term "monkey trial" cut both ways. For antievolutionists, it lampooned the absurd (though misunderstood) proposition that humans evolved from primates. Conversely, modernists used it as a rebuke of a proceeding (wrongly) attributed to religious bigotry run amok in the "backward" culture and institutions of the South. Generally, it suggested the surreal, circus-like atmosphere surrounding the trial as chronicled by swarms of (mainly northern) reporters who had infested Dayton for the event. Packaged as a showdown of religion versus science, Bryan versus Darrow, the subtext of these accounts revealed the deeper cultural tension between an urban and progressive North and the rural and traditional South—another chapter in an age-old conflict between populism and elitism in the contest for Truth. Who won or lost are matters of perspective, as well as time frame.

Scopes was found guilty, but none expected otherwise. Dayton enjoyed notoriety, if not infamy, for its moment in the spotlight, much to the chagrin of Tennesseans who wished that the embarrassing affair had never occurred. Far less economic gain resulted than anticipated, perhaps even resulting in net loss. The ACLU claimed victory in having both stirred a national backlash against antievolutionism and in securing the appeal as a stepping-stone to the U.S. Supreme Court. National press coverage of the trial, at all stages, would support the first claim (Larson, 2003, p. 72). Scopes lost his appeal before the Tennessee Supreme Court, but few followed the story. In ruling against Scopes, the Court also saw fit to overturn his conviction on a technical error. Stewart was correct to insist that the jury, not the bench, set Scopes's fine (*Scopes v. State,* 1927). The Court instructed that the case should not be retried, in the interest of preserving the dignity of

CREATIONISM ADAPTS

Christian conservatives reemerged as a political force in national politics in the United States during another period of rapid social change and profound pessimism beginning in the 1970s. Industrial economies were quickly giving way to service economies. Women were entering the workforce in numbers unprecedented in peacetime. Crime was on the rise. Population centers were shifting from the North toward the Sun Belt. Galvanizing this movement was fierce opposition to the Equal Rights Amendment and the Supreme Court's decision in *Roe v. Wade,* which had legalized abortion. Pursuing prayer in schools and abstinence-only sex education, this movement also sought to reintroduce creationism into the science classroom. Unlike their fundamentalist forbearers, however, this antievolutionist cause did not (at least overtly) seek a ban on the teaching of evolution. Instead, the strategy was to revive Bryan's position that evolution is a hypothesis rather than a fact. Rather than using this premise to denigrate science as inferior to biblical scripture, however, the purpose was to put creationism on the same footing as evolutionary theory. "Creation theory" was posed as an equally valid, equally scientific account of human origins. Over time, however, this message mutated into something far stranger—the idea that creationism is science, and science is religion.

In 1969, California adopted a statement into its science curriculum guidelines suggesting that "creation theory" may better account for certain scientific data than evolutionary theories. Although eventually defeated, creationism activists used this model to formulate similar policy statements picked up for consideration around the country. In 1973, Tennessee introduced new legislation requiring creationism to receive equal time in any biology textbook dealing with human origins adopted by the public schools. Struck down two years later, legal challenges for equal time in Colorado and later California, though likewise unsuccessful, served to publicize and popularize the antievolutionist cause. Subsequent legislative efforts introduced around the country adapted to court rulings by modifying "creationism" and "creation theory" into "creation science." "Equal time" and "balanced education" were replaced with language referring to the "unbiased" presentation of evolution and creation sciences. Challenges conflated evolutionary thought with the "religion" of secular humanism, and accused the "biased" presentation of evolution "dogma" as violating the Establishment clause (see Nelkin, 1982). As "creation science" morphed into the presently more popular "intelligent design," states began experimenting with stickers and inserts for biology books warning that evolutionary theory remains a controversial, incomplete, and flawed account and that it must therefore be read skeptically or with an "open mind." Although also largely unsuccessful, these events suggest a broader trend with some history still ahead of it.

the state. It was clearly a dead end and, as Malone charged, a well-crafted "subterfuge" ("Malone," 1927).

Until the Scopes trial, "fundamentalism" was primarily a pejorative only among intellectuals, such as Mencken and Darrow. Now it held strong negative connotations for large swaths of the American public, particularly in the North. Press coverage indelibly linked "antievolutionism" with "bigotry" and "ignorance." Its adherents were termed "cranks" and "freaks" ("Cranks," 1925). In Bryan's purported defeat, punctuated by his subsequent death, the movement organized behind the Commoner lost significant momentum nationally. Mississippi passed an antievolutionist bill in 1927, as did Arkansas in 1928, but these statutes remained inactive—as had the Butler Act before and after Scopes. A year after the repeal of the Butler Act in 1967, in *Epperson v. Arkansas,* the U.S. Supreme Court finally ruled such laws an unconstitutional endorsement of religion.

Disenfranchised in the North and significantly marginalized in the South, fundamentalism and its antievolutionist cause were down, but not out. As the nation moved on to the tribulations of the Depression and World War II, and oppositional voices diminished under the illusion of an end-all victory at Dayton, fundamentalism faded from the public conscience. However, closed off behind institutional structures tailored to their own specifications, buffered from trends in the broader culture (Larson, 2003, p. 233), fundamentalists thrived. Their numbers swelled, convictions polarized, and influence grew; and their tactics changed.

Through localized efforts, fundamentalists sought district-by-district democratic control over public education administration in their communities. They also targeted state agencies responsible for approving classroom texts. Both strategies were unlikely to be met with judicial review, cutting out the problem at its source. It was wildly successful. In order to stay viable, the textbook industry was forced to produce editions marketable in all regions. This meant vetting evolutionary content, and even explicitly catering to creationist demands. Teachers were left to their own resources (and, in fundamentalist-controlled districts, their own peril) to introduce evolution in the classroom. In the end, subtle political pressures and the logic of markets did what even a vigorously enforced Butler Act could never have achieved. In subsequent decades, upwards of 70 percent of public high schools dropped evolution from their curriculum. It was all but eclipsed in portions of the South and West (Larson, 2003, p. 231). Effectively stifling the main conduit of scientific knowledge of evolution to the public consciousness, for three decades antievolutionist ideas ran largely unopposed. Their influence expanded even to mainstream sectarians.

While the agents of science pushed back beginning in the 1960s (Larson, 2003, p. 86), recovering lost ground in public school curricula, the intellectual commitments and ideological trenches had, by then, grown unfathomably deep.[11] By this point, the conflict of "science versus religion," a conflict few Americans even perceived at the dawn of the twentieth century, had gathered a lengthy and profound history—one complete with heroes and villains, insurgents and martyrs, battles won and battles lost. Always and unerringly, this folklore draws us back to the day Darrow met Bryan in Dayton.

SUGGESTIONS FOR FURTHER READING

Conkin, P.K. (1998). *When all the gods trembled: Darwinism, Scopes, and American intellectuals.* New York: Rowman and Littlefield Publishers, Inc.

De Camp, L.S. (1968). *The great monkey trial.* Garden City, NY: Doubleday and Company, Inc.

Ginger, R. (1958). *Six days or forever?: Tennessee v. John Thomas Scopes.* Boston: Beacon Press.

Larson, E.J. (1997). *Summer of the gods: The Scopes trial and America's continuing debate over science and religion.* New York: Basic Books.

NOTES

1. The belief that God created all species uniquely, and that their forms exist unchanged to this day. Some adherents accept evolution among nonhuman animals.
2. See, generally, Larson (2003).
3. The Social Gospel movement primarily consisted of mainstream denominational Protestants who dedicated themselves to social reform by living and proselytizing their faith through good works—what Bryan termed "applied Christianity." As the religious force of progressivism, this movement agitated for racial equality, women's suffrage, prohibition, labor reform, welfare, and universal public education.
4. Bryan (1924) noted, "Nietzsche carried Darwinism to its logical conclusion and denied the existence of God, denounced Christianity as the doctrine of the degenerate, and democracy as the refuge of the weakling; he overthrew all standards of morality and eulogized war as necessary to man's development" (p. 146).
5. Originally, the Civil Liberties Bureau—a collection of activists and lawyers who organized during World War I to protect the rights of conscientious objectors. Afterward, the ACLU adopted a broader mission of defending civil rights, particularly those of organized labor, minorities, free speech, and academic freedom.
6. Under Tennessee's declaratory judgment act, the mere fact that Scopes was a state-employed teacher with a vested interest in the law gave him standing to challenge its constitutionality—a criminal indictment was unnecessary (Larson, 2003, p. 60).
7. Surviving documents are now available through the Freedom of Information Act, and online from the FBI's Freedom of Information Act Web site at http://foia.fbi.gov/foiaindex/darrow.htm
8. Agnosticism is a position of principled skepticism on questions of theology, such as the existence of divine entities, a creed captured as "I don't know." Darrow's agnosticism was rather militant, closer to "I don't know, *and neither do you!*"
9. The account to the proceedings, unless otherwise specified, is taken from the stenographic record of the case trial, as published in *The World's Most Famous Court Trial* (1997), hereafter referred to as *Trial*.
10. Which were, in fact, fictionalized accounts written as commentaries on the politics of McCarthyism.
11. Gallup polls conducted during the 1980s and 1990s on attitudes toward creationism and evolutionism show a remarkable stability in responses. Consistently, 35–40 percent believe humans developed over millions of years from less-advanced forms of life with God guiding the process. Approximately 45 percent believe God created humans essentially as they exist today within the past 10,000 years. About 10 percent of respondents reliably respond that human evolution occurred with God having no part in the process.

REFERENCES

Bryan in Dayton, calls Scopes trial duel to the death. (1925, July 8). *New York Times*, p. 1.

Bryan, W. J. (1924). *Seven questions in dispute.* New York: Flemming H. Revell.

Cranks and freaks flock to Dayton. (1925, July 11). *New York Times*, p. 1.

Conkin, P. K. (1998). *When all the gods trembled: Darwinism, Scopes, and American intellectuals.* New York: Rowman and Littlefield Publishers, Inc.

De Camp, L. S. (1968). *The great monkey trial.* Garden City, NY: Doubleday and Company, Inc.

Evolution battle rages out of court. (1925, July 22). *New York Times*, p. 2.

Ginger, R. (1958). *Six days or forever?: Tennessee v. John Thomas Scopes.* Boston: Beacon Press.

Larson, E. J. (1997). *Summer of the gods: The Scopes trial and America's continuing debate over science and religion.* New York: Basic Books.

Larson, E.J. (2003). *Trial and error: The American controversy over creation and evolution* (3rd ed.). Oxford: Oxford University Press.

Malone criticizes decision. (1927, January 16). *New York Times,* p. 28.

Moran, J.P. (2003). Reading race into the Scopes trial: African American elites, science, and fundamentalism. *The Journal of American History, 90*(3), 891–911.

Nelkin, D. (1982). From Dayton to Little Rock: Creationism evolves. *Science, Technology, & Human Values, 7*(40), 47–53.

Plan assault on state law on evolution. (1925, May 4). *The Chattanooga Times,* p. 5.

Sandeen, E.R. (1970). *The roots of fundamentalism: British and American millenarianism, 1800–1930.* Chicago: University of Chicago Press.

Scopes v. State, 154 Tenn. 105, 289 SW 363 (1927).

Scopes, J.T., and Presley, J. (1967). *Center of the storm: Memoirs of John T. Scopes.* New York: Holt, Reinhart and Winston.

The world's most famous court trial: Tennessee evolution case, a complete stenographic report of the famous court test of the Tennessee anti-evolution act, at Dayton, July 10 to 21, 1925, including speeches and arguments of attorneys. (1997). Union, NJ: The Lawbook Exchange, Ltd.

7

Bonnie and Clyde: A "Mad, Dizzy Whirl"

LEANA ALLEN BOUFFARD

You've read the story of Jesse James
Of how he lived and died
If you're still in need for something to read
Here's the story of Bonnie and Clyde.

—"The Story of Bonnie and Clyde,"
by Bonnie Parker (Milner, 1996)

In January 1930, to help out with housework, Bonnie Parker agreed to temporarily move in with a neighbor who had broken her arm in a fall. During her stay, another friend of the neighbor, convicted car thief Clyde Barrow, also paid a visit. Clyde's mother claims that over a shared pot of hot chocolate, he instantly fell in love with Bonnie. For Bonnie, it was also love at first sight. This chance encounter set off a two-year violent crime spree and an enduring nationwide fascination with the gangster couple Bonnie and Clyde.

Clyde Chestnut Barrow was born in March 1909 to Henry and Cumie Barrow, tenant farmers in Texas. Clyde was the fifth of eight children. Because his parents often had trouble with money, the children were frequently shuffled among the homes of various relatives. Finally, they gave up farming and moved to a poor part of Dallas. Clyde was a fan of Western outlaw movies, idolizing Jesse James. He often skipped school, and he dropped out at 16 to begin working. Clyde's earliest criminal activity involved stealing a flock of chickens with his older brother, Buck. After that, he continued getting into trouble with the law.

Bonnie Parker was born in October 1910 to Charles and Emma Parker. She was the middle child, with an older brother and younger sister. Bonnie's family was somewhat better off than the Barrow family. Her father was a brick mason, and the family lived a quiet and comfortable life in a small town near Dallas. When Bonnie was five years old, her father died suddenly, and her mother was forced to move to one of the toughest parts of Dallas to live with her parents (Bonnie's grandparents). Bonnie was described as a good student in school, high-spirited and tenderhearted. She won awards for her essays and poetry. At 15, Bonnie began spending time with a classmate, Roy Thornton. By the next

115

year, they were married, and eventually the couple moved in with Bonnie's mother. Bonnie was deeply infatuated with Thornton and had their names tattooed above her right knee. Despite this infatuation, Thornton was not the most loyal and attentive of husbands. He frequently left. In January 1929, he reappeared after an absence of nearly a year, and Bonnie refused to take him back. Thornton was later arrested during a robbery and sentenced to five years in prison. Bonnie stayed married to him, believing that it would be inappropriate to divorce him while he was in prison, but that did not prevent her from seeing Clyde.

BONNIE'S FIRST CRIME

> Then I left my old home for the city
> To play in its mad dizzy whirl,
> Not knowing how little of pity
> It holds for a country girl.

—"The Story of Suicide Sal,"
by Bonnie Parker (Milner, 1996)

During the first few weeks that Bonnie and Clyde were seeing each other, police found him at the Parker home and arrested him on suspicion of burglary. While he was in jail, Bonnie sent him letters urging him to go straight and get a job when he got out. In March 1930, Bonnie traveled with Clyde's mother to Waco, Texas, to see him. She stayed with her cousin and visited Clyde in jail. During one visit, Clyde and one of his cell mates, William Turner, convinced Bonnie that she could help them escape by smuggling a gun into the jail. Turner drew a map of his parents' home and told her where she could find the key and the gun. Taking her cousin with her, Bonnie went to the Turner home, found the key, and began looking for the gun. It was not where Turner said it would be, and the two girls left the house in considerable disarray. But they had found the gun, and Bonnie smuggled it into the jail. This was Bonnie's first foray into criminal activity.

The next night, Turner pretended to be sick. When the jailer opened the cell door, another inmate, Emery Abernathy, pulled the gun and placed the jailer in the cell. Clyde, Abernathy, Turner, and another inmate strong-armed the keys away from the jailer and escaped into the night, stealing a car and driving through Texas, Missouri, and into Illinois. When they reached Illinois, Clyde sent Bonnie a telegram to let her know that he was safe. With Clyde on the run, Bonnie returned home to wait for him. However, Mrs. Parker suspected Bonnie's involvement in the escape. She believed that Bonnie enjoyed being the center of attention and viewed the whole incident as exciting and romantic.

Meanwhile, Clyde and the other escapees committed several robberies, burglaries, and car thefts. During one of their burglaries, a witness noted their license plate number, and police caught up with the group. Though Clyde used an alias, police eventually learned that the three were the Waco escapees. In April 1930, Clyde was transferred to Huntsville Prison. On intake, he claimed that his middle name was "Champion" and that Bonnie was his wife. From Huntsville, Clyde was assigned to the Eastham Prison Farm. During his imprisonment, Bonnie went back to work, started dating, and for a while stopped corresponding with Clyde.

Clyde's mother lobbied authorities to shorten his sentence from 14 years to only two years. But Clyde, depressed by the slow progress of the appeal, persuaded another inmate to cut off two of his toes so that he would be transferred back to the prison hospital at Huntsville. Soon after, the governor agreed to parole Clyde. He returned to Dallas and immediately went to see Bonnie. Reunited with Clyde, she dropped her current boyfriend and the two resumed their relationship. When Clyde's sister arranged for him to have a construction job in Massachusetts, Bonnie was pleased that he seemed to be going straight. Two weeks after starting the job, Clyde returned to Dallas because he was homesick. Soon Bonnie told her mother she was moving to Houston for a job selling cosmetics. In reality, she was joining Clyde and his new associates.

THE BARROW GANG

> Now Bonnie and Clyde are the Barrow gang,
> I'm sure you all have read
> How they rob and steal
> And those who squeal are usually found dying or dead.
> —"The Story of Bonnie and Clyde,"
> by Bonnie Parker (Milner, 1996)

Upon his return to Dallas, Clyde hooked up with Raymond Hamilton and Ralph Fults, two petty criminals. In March 1932, the three attempted to rob a hardware store, with Bonnie acting as lookout. A night watchman spotted them and alerted police, who gave chase. The gang's car became stuck in the mud, and the four tried to escape by running through nearby fields. Fults was captured, Hamilton and Clyde escaped, and Bonnie hid in the field until the next day. She began hitchhiking home but was stopped and taken in for questioning. While in jail waiting for the grand jury to convene, Bonnie wrote a poem, "Suicide Sal," about a

TIMELINE

March 1909	Clyde Barrow is born.
October 1910	Bonnie Parker is born.
January 1930	Bonnie and Clyde first meet at the home of a mutual friend.
March 1930	Bonnie commits her first crime in helping Clyde escape from jail.
March 1932	A failed bank robbery attempt results in Bonnie being captured by law enforcement. Clyde escapes.
April 1932	While Bonnie sits in jail, Clyde and others rob a service station, murdering the owner.
June 1932	Bonnie is released from jail and rejoins Clyde. The gang is involved in a series of robberies, car thefts, and murders over the next several months.
April 1933	Police attempt to ambush the gang multiple times in Missouri, Arkansas, and Iowa. Some gang members are captured, but Bonnie and Clyde escape.
November 1933	Bonnie and Clyde conduct a violent raid on Eastham Prison Farm, helping fellow gang members to escape and killing a prison guard. The Texas Prison System names former Texas Ranger Frank Hamer as special investigator responsible for hunting down Bonnie and Clyde.
April 1934	Bonnie and Clyde steal the car in which they would eventually be killed and meet with their families for the last time. Bonnie gives her mother a poem she had written, "The Story of Bonnie and Clyde."
May 23, 1934	Hamer and other law enforcement officers ambush Bonnie and Clyde near Arcadia, Louisiana, killing them.

117

Figure 7.1   **Bonnie Parker mockingly points a shotgun at Clyde Barrow, 1933. Courtesy of the Library of Congress.**

woman who fell for a criminal and eventually took the blame for his crimes. This appears to have been a period of disenchantment with Clyde.

While Bonnie languished in jail, Clyde and Hamilton met up with Frank Clause, who had recently been released from prison. The group committed several crimes, but the most serious occurred in April 1932 when they robbed a small service station owned by John and Martha Bucher in Hillsboro, Texas. The three scoped out the store and returned at midnight, requesting entry to purchase guitar strings. As the Buchers opened the safe, Hamilton fired his gun, killing John Bucher. He later claimed that the shooting was an accident. Martha called the police after the three robbers left, and a few days later, she identified Clyde and Hamilton from police photographs. Clyde hid out temporarily at his family's home, and a few days later, he joined Clause in another robbery. This time they held up two service stations, kidnapping the attendants at gunpoint. Both men were later released unharmed.

After Bonnie's grand jury hearing in June 1932, she was released due to lack of evidence. She returned home to her mother, claiming she would have nothing more to do with Clyde. Toward the end of June, Bonnie went to Wichita Falls, telling her mother she would be applying for a job. In reality, she, Clyde, and Hamilton had rented a house there. In August 1932, the group returned to Dallas and picked up another gangster, Everett Milligan. With Milligan serving as the getaway driver, Clyde and Hamilton robbed a packing company at gunpoint. The police gave chase, but Clyde's speedy and reckless driving left them in the dust. Leaving Bonnie at her mother's, the men headed out of state to Oklahoma.

In Oklahoma, Hamilton wanted to stop at an open-air dance floor. Despite feeling that it was too dangerous, Clyde stopped. They danced and tried to relax, drinking whiskey from fruit jars, which caught the notice of a local sheriff, C.G. Maxwell, and deputy, E.C. Moore. The Prohibition laws were strictly enforced in Oklahoma, and the officers told the men that they were under arrest. Clyde and Hamilton both began firing their pistols, shooting Moore in the head and wounding Maxwell. The two men then sped away, heading back to Texas along back roads. Milligan, who had been dancing at the time of the shooting, tried to blend into the crowd. He asked a new friend for a ride into town, where he left for Texas by bus. Hearing from witnesses about a third member of the group, police tracked Milligan to Texas and captured him there. Between Milligan's confession and Clyde's fingerprints on one of the abandoned vehicles, police were able to put names to the suspects.

Hamilton retrieved Bonnie from her mother's house, and they met up with Clyde. With search parties looking for them, the gang decided they should move to a place where they were not known. They decided to go to New Mexico. A sheriff's deputy in New Mexico became suspicious of their out-of-state license plates. Upon learning that their car was stolen, Deputy Joe Johns followed the gang to their hideout and asked to speak to the car's owner. With a shotgun, Clyde confronted the deputy, taking him hostage, and the three began another flight from the law. Police throughout New Mexico and Texas began an intense manhunt. Deputy Johns was released

PROHIBITION

The 18th Amendment, prohibiting the importing, exporting, selling, and manufacturing of intoxicating liquor, was enacted January 16, 1920. Though illegal, consumption of alcohol continued, creating a profitable black market. Prohibition has been credited with the growth of organized crime and the emergence of high-profile gangsters, like Al Capone, as well as with increasing levels of violent crime during this period. Prohibition ended in December 1933 with the passage of the 21st Amendment, which repealed the 18th Amendment and allowed states to regulate the production and consumption of alcohol.

unharmed several hours and several hundred miles later. On their flight, the gang continued to steal various cars. One of the victims reported the theft immediately, giving police the information they needed to set up an ambush. Clyde, however, noticed the trap and quickly turned the car around, firing his pistol and wounding one officer in the process. Despite a large posse with heavy firepower, the gang was again able to evade police.

Until September, the gang robbed various businesses in Texas—but did not kill or kidnap any of their victims. Hamilton left the gang, and in October, Clyde met up with two other men, Frank Hardy and Hollis Hale, to rob a small grocery store. As Clyde held the salesclerk at gunpoint and collected the money, the meat market manager, Howard Hall, appeared and offered some resistance. Clyde punched the man once, and Hall grabbed at his arm to prevent a second blow. In a rage, Clyde fatally shot Hall. He attempted to shoot the clerk as well, but the gun misfired. Police broadcast a description of the gunmen to agencies in the surrounding area. Another manhunt ensued, but Clyde evaded capture, picking up Bonnie around midnight, then driving into Oklahoma. Two individuals later positively identified Clyde Barrow as the person who committed the robbery and murder.

Throughout November, Clyde, Hardy, and Hale committed various robberies in Missouri. At the end of the month, they decided to rob a bank. Bonnie scoped out the bank but was not allowed to participate in the actual robbery. When the men entered the bank with guns drawn, the guards began firing. Hardy grabbed as much money as he could while Clyde fired back, and they ran to the getaway car. Hardy and Hale took all of the money, hitchhiked into town, and disappeared. Short on cash, Clyde decided to rob another bank using Bonnie as a lookout. Unfortunately, it had gone bankrupt, and there was nothing to steal. After those failures, the couple decided to return to Texas. During December, Bonnie and Clyde stayed with family and added another member to their gang, 16-year-old W.D. Jones, who had known the Barrow family for nearly ten years.

On Christmas Day, 1932, Clyde decided to steal another car. Jones found a car with the keys inside and attempted to start it. Neighbors noticed the attempted theft and ran out to stop him. With three people standing on the sidewalk yelling, Clyde became agitated, and he and Jones began pushing the car to get it started. After it got rolling, Clyde jumped into the driver's seat, and Jones stood on the running board waving his gun. Doyle Johnson, the owner, ran after the car and jumped on the driver's side running board, grabbing Clyde's arm to prevent him from getting away. Clyde fired his gun, hitting the front fender of the car, and Jones reacted to the shot by firing his own pistol. Johnson was hit in the neck, and he fell to the street and later died. The two men fled in the stolen car. Meanwhile, Bonnie had remained in Clyde's car, so she slid behind the wheel and left the scene, unnoticed. Also in December, Raymond Hamilton was captured by police and awaited trial for his part in the Bucher murder.

In January, the Barrow gang returned to Dallas. Bonnie spent a few minutes with her mother while Clyde visited Hamilton's sister, Lillie McBride. He gave her a radio with a hidden saw blade to deliver to Hamilton in prison so that he could escape. The group reconvened and hurried to an abandoned farmhouse to hide. Police, meanwhile, had been tipped off about McBride's relationship to Hamilton and went to her home. She had gone to the prison to see Hamilton, so they decided to wait. Noticing a car circling the block, the police turned off all of the lights in the house. The gang returned, and Clyde approached the front door with a sawed-off shotgun. He noticed the shadow of a policeman in the front window and fired a shot into the house. The police returned fire, and Jones began firing as well. Other officers converged on the front lawn, and Clyde shot one of them at close range, killing him. He made it back to the car, and the group sped away, ending up in Oklahoma. At the end of January, the gang kidnapped and released another police officer.

THE GANG'S NEW MEMBERS

The road gets dimmer and dimmer
Sometimes you can hardly see
But it's fight man to man, and do all you can
For they know they can never be free.

—"The Story of Bonnie and Clyde,"
by Bonnie Parker (Milner, 1996)

In March 1933, Clyde's brother, Buck Barrow, was released from prison after serving time for an auto theft he had committed with Clyde years earlier. He planned to take his wife, Blanche, to visit her parents in Missouri and hoped to settle on their farm. Along the way to Missouri, Buck decided, against his wife's wishes, that he would visit his brother. They met up in Arkansas and drove together to Joplin, Missouri, where they rented a garage apartment. Within a few days, neighbors and police became suspicious of this group with guns and out-of-state license plates. Eventually, police decided to confront them. In April 1933, police pulled up outside the garage, parking their cars in the driveway to block escape routes. Clyde noticed the officers approaching, alerted the group, and grabbed his rifle. Clyde, Jones, and Buck began shooting from the windows. Bonnie started packing, but Blanche was terrified and ran into the street, screaming. The rest of the gang jumped into their car and raced out of the garage, sideswiping a police car on the way. They followed Blanche into the street and pulled her into the car.

In the shootout, two police officers were killed and two others were wounded. When police searched the apartment, they found Buck and Blanche's marriage license as well as the pardon that Buck had received. Two rolls of film that the gang had taken of their exploits were also left behind. The evidence helped police identify the group as the Barrow gang. The pictures immediately made it into the newspapers, and the public had names and smiling, unremorseful faces to go with the stories of their crimes.

In late April 1933, the gang needed a getaway car for a planned robbery. They located a suitable vehicle, and Jones quickly drove away in it. The owner of the car, H. Dillard Darby, and a friend, Sophia Stone, chased after Jones. They came upon Clyde and the rest of the group, who kidnapped the pair, releasing them the next day unharmed and with some money to get home. Buck and Blanche decided to finally go visit her parents in Missouri. In June, they were to meet back up with Bonnie, Clyde, and Jones. On their way to the rendezvous, Clyde was speeding along the highway and did not notice that a bridge had been washed out ahead of them. The car flew into a ravine, flipping twice. Clyde was thrown from the car, and Bonnie was pinned under the wreckage. Clyde pulled Jones out of the car but could not free Bonnie. A farmer who lived nearby arrived to help, and Bonnie was rescued, but not before the car had caught fire and severely burned her legs.

The men carried Bonnie to the farmer's home, where his wife treated the burns. A neighbor had called police, and when they arrived, Clyde and Jones took them hostage. Clyde ordered the two officers into the back of their car and lay Bonnie across their laps. He then drove to meet Buck in Oklahoma. There, they released the two officers, deciding not to kill them since they had been kind to Bonnie. From there, the group drove to Fort Smith, Arkansas, where they rented a tourist cabin. Bonnie's sister, Billie, arrived in Fort Smith to care for her. During their stay in the cabin, Clyde did not leave Bonnie's side. Buck and Jones committed a few robberies to get some cash. In one of those robberies, they shot and killed the town marshal. After that, Clyde knew they would have to move again.

Clyde sent Billie back to Dallas, and the gang drove to the Red Crown Tourist Camp in Platte City, Missouri, committing various robberies along the way. They rented two rooms, and Clyde continued to care for Bonnie and her injuries. The clerk on duty became suspicious of the group with the heavily bandaged woman. He called police, and they realized it was the Barrow gang. Various police agencies pooled their resources and planned their attack. They surrounded the rooms and knocked on the door. Blanche stalled them while the group packed a few belongings and left through a side door into the garage. Police had blocked that exit with an armored car, but Clyde and Jones fired an automatic rifle at it, wounding one of the officers. Meanwhile, Buck fired at the rest of the posse from the cabin window. When they returned fire, he was shot twice in the head. Clyde loaded everyone, including a semiconscious Buck, into their car, and they crashed through the garage, shooting as they went. Police again returned fire, shattering the car windows and sending splinters of glass into Blanche's eyes. They raced out of Platte City.

Clyde drove through that night and the next day, eventually finding a thickly wooded spot near a stream in Iowa. The group rested there and tried to recover from their wounds, but again, local citizens became suspicious. Police in Iowa were alerted and planned an ambush of the group with the help of the Iowa National Guard. Early the next morning, Bonnie noticed the police surrounding their camp. Clyde and Jones grabbed their rifles and began shooting. Bonnie limped to the car, and Blanche struggled to drag Buck in the same direction. On the way, Bonnie was wounded, Buck was shot twice, and Jones was shot in the chest. The group piled into the car but soon realized that they would not be able to avoid the posse's fire. Clyde ordered everyone to hide in the woods. Buck was shot several more times, and Blanche tried to shield him from any more gunfire. Clyde was shot in the arm but carried Bonnie to a nearby farmhouse where they stole a car at gunpoint. Clyde, Bonnie, and Jones escaped, but Buck and Blanche were captured. Several days later, Buck died in the hospital. Blanche was sentenced to 15 years in the Missouri State Prison. Jones eventually left the group but was captured and convicted of murder.

In late November, Bonnie and Clyde began planning a prison break. Raymond Hamilton had been sentenced for the murder of John Bucher, and he was serving his time at Eastham Prison Farm. Hamilton's brother and a former inmate, James Mullin, were also in on the plan to hide two pistols on the grounds of the prison farm. A trusty in the prison retrieved the pistols and passed them to Hamilton and a friend, Joe Palmer. Hamilton and Palmer took the pistols with them the next day when they began work. Clyde and Mullin waited just off prison grounds, and Bonnie stayed in the getaway car. When Hamilton and Palmer drew their pistols, a gunfight erupted between the inmates and guards. Hearing the shooting, Bonnie began honking the horn. Hamilton, Palmer, Henry Methvin, and two other inmates ran toward the sound of the horn and escaped with Bonnie and Clyde. At the prison, one guard had been killed and another wounded.

THE BEGINNING OF THE END

> They don't think they're tough or desperate
> They know the law always wins
> They've been shot at before, but they do not ignore
> That death is the wages of sin.
>
> —"The Story of Bonnie and Clyde,"
> by Bonnie Parker (Milner, 1996)

The prison director at Huntsville, Lee Simmons, swore that he would find and punish those responsible for the death and wounding of the guards at Eastham. Research into the history of the escapees led him to Mullin, who confessed to his part and implicated Bonnie and Clyde. Simmons began formulating his plan. He created a new position, special investigator for the Texas prison system, and selected Frank Hamer, a former Texas Ranger known for his fearlessness, to fill the position. Simmons then convinced Governor Miriam Ferguson to offer a pardon to any associate of the gang who would help in their eventual capture.

After the prison break at Eastham, the gang, now composed of Bonnie and Clyde, Raymond Hamilton, Henry Methvin, and Joe Palmer, continued committing robberies and stealing cars throughout Texas. Hamilton contacted Mary O'Dare, the wife of a former gang member, who agreed to join them as his mistress. Near the end of February 1934, the gang, numbering six, converged on Lancaster, Texas. With Methvin as a lookout, Clyde and Hamilton entered a bank with a sawed-off shotgun and a pistol. Clyde ordered the bank's manager to open the safe. Hamilton collected all of the cash from the safe and from the tellers' drawers, and the two men escaped through a side door. As soon as they were gone, the bank official contacted police, who determined that the descriptions fit Clyde Barrow and Raymond Hamilton.

In this robbery, the gang had pulled off one of their biggest hauls, just over $4,000. The three men joined up with the rest of the gang, and they all drove out of state. On this trip, tempers flared. Clyde observed Hamilton pocketing some of the cash before it had been divided. Bonnie did not like Mary O'Dare or her habit of flirting with all of the men in

BIOGRAPHY OF FRANK HAMER

Frank Hamer was born March 17, 1884, in Fairview, Texas. As a young man, he worked with his father as a blacksmith and as a cowboy on a Texas ranch. During his time as a cowboy, he assisted in capturing a horse thief, impressing the local sheriff, who recommended Hamer to the Texas Rangers. In April 1906, Hamer joined the Rangers, becoming Senior Ranger Captain in 1921. In 1932, at the age of 48, Frank Hamer retired from the Texas Rangers. After Bonnie and Clyde killed one prison guard and wounded another during the Eastham Prison Farm escape, the Texas Prison System, in 1934, appointed Hamer as special investigator with the responsibility of finding the couple. After three months on the job, Hamer and other law enforcement officers ambushed and killed Bonnie and Clyde near Arcadia, Louisiana. His success in this position earned him a great deal of public recognition, and Hamer was honored by the U.S. Congress. He finally retired from the Texas Rangers in 1949 and died in July 1955 in Austin, Texas. Years after his death, Hamer's wife, Gladys, and his son, Frank Jr., sued the producers of the 1967 movie, *Bonnie and Clyde,* arguing that the movie's negative portrayal of Hamer constituted defamation of character. They won an out-of-court settlement.

Source: http://www.texasranger.org/halloffame/HOF.htm

the gang. This conflict reached a breaking point after the Lancaster bank robbery. Clyde and Bonnie left Hamilton and O'Dare in Indiana and returned to Texas with Henry Methvin.

As Easter approached, the couple returned to the Dallas area. On Easter Sunday, April 1934, Bonnie, Clyde, and Methvin napped in their car on a highway near Grapevine, Texas. Police had been assigned to patrol the area for speeders, and three motorcycle officers noticed the parked car. Bonnie woke up and alerted Clyde that the police were approaching. He told Methvin, "Let's take them," implying a kidnapping. Methvin, who had only been with the couple a short time and was not familiar with their habit of kidnapping police, assumed that Clyde meant to begin shooting. He opened fire, killing one officer instantly and severely wounding another, who died on his way to the hospital. The three sped away from the scene, avoiding capture, but this incident further aroused law enforcement.

After the death of the two officers near Grapevine, the captain of the highway patrol also swore that he would find and punish those responsible. He had heard rumors about Hamer's new job and contacted him. He tried to persuade Hamer to include one of his men in the plan. Though he preferred to work alone, Hamer eventually agreed, and highway patrol officer Manny Gault, also a former Texas Ranger, joined up. Hamer and Gault recognized the circular traveling pattern that Bonnie and Clyde favored, from Dallas north through Oklahoma and Kansas, east into Missouri, south to northern Louisiana, and back to Dallas. They concluded that they would have to stop the couple somewhere along that circle.

The tracking party expanded to four when Simmons recognized that Hamer and Gault would not be able to identify Bonnie and Clyde on sight. He contacted Dallas police for assistance, and they assigned two officers, Bob Alcorn, who knew Bonnie and Clyde, and Ted Hinton, who was familiar with the Barrow family. The four men discussed the possibility of gaining help from a gang member in exchange for clemency. They settled on the family of Henry Methvin, who lived in the town of Arcadia in northeastern Louisiana, a spot on the Barrow gang's traveling circle. They contacted the local sheriff, who set up a meeting between Hamer and Henry Methvin's father.

Hamer offered Methvin's father a deal. In exchange for information about where the couple would be at a certain time, the governor would write a letter giving Methvin a full pardon. Over the next few days, the gang was spotted in various towns in Texas and Oklahoma. It had been raining for several days, and outside of Commerce, Oklahoma, the gang's car became stuck in the mud. Unable to wave down a passing car, the group was still struggling to free the car when Chief of Police Percy Boyd and a constable, Cal Campbell, arrived. A gun battle ensued. The officers' shots narrowly missed Clyde, but the gang's gunfire did not miss. Both Boyd and Campbell were seriously wounded, and Campbell died at the scene. Luckily for the gang, a local trucker, Charles Dobson, had heard the shooting and drove toward the scene. Another motorist, Jack Boydston, also appeared. At gunpoint, Clyde ordered the two to use the truck to haul their car out of the mud. Clyde and Methvin forced Chief Boyd, who had suffered a severe head wound, into their car, and they sped away. Boydston and Dobson alerted local police, who determined that the killers were Bonnie and Clyde and began a search involving both police cars and a plane. However, law enforcement lost their trail.

During the chase, Bonnie and Methvin bandaged Chief Boyd's head wound, and Boyd tried to have a friendly conversation with his kidnappers. Clyde claimed that they had had nothing to do with the murders of the two highway patrolmen near Grapevine, and Bonnie asked Boyd to tell the world that she did not smoke cigars. She blamed reporters for spreading that lie about her after the joke pictures of the gang had been discovered in Joplin. Eventually, the gang arrived in Fort Scott, Kansas. Outside of town, the gang released Boyd, who walked back to Fort Scott and told his story to local police and reporters.

THE AMBUSH

> *Someday they'll go down together*
> *And they'll bury them side by side*
> *To few it'll be grief, to the law a relief*
> *But it's death for Bonnie and Clyde.*

—"The Story of Bonnie and Clyde,"
by Bonnie Parker (Milner, 1996)

Throughout April, Bonnie and Clyde eluded police. On April 29, 1934, the gang stole a nearly new, tan-colored Ford V-8 sedan belonging to Jesse and Ruth Warren of Topeka, Kansas. The next day, Bonnie, Clyde, Methvin, and Joe Palmer robbed a Kansas bank and got away with nearly $3,000. Palmer again decided to leave the gang, and Bonnie, Clyde, and Methvin returned to Dallas. They set up a meeting with the Barrow and Parker families. At this meeting, Bonnie requested that her family take her home when she died rather than letting her go to a funeral parlor. She also gave her mother a poem she had written called "The Story of Bonnie and Clyde," in which she foretold Clyde's and her deaths together. This was the last time the families would see the couple alive. Bonnie and Clyde headed toward Louisiana.

On May 19, 1934, Hamer's posse arrived in Shreveport, Louisiana, with heavy firepower. Coincidentally, Bonnie, Clyde, and Henry Methvin were also in town. They had been staying at a cabin with Methvin's father and had gone into town for lunch. While Bonnie and Clyde waited in the car, Methvin went in to place their orders. As they were waiting, Clyde noticed a police car making a routine patrol and sped away, leaving Methvin inside the café. Having planned a rendezvous point in case they got separated, Methvin left the café and hitchhiked back to his father's home. He

Figure 7.2   The bullet-riddled automobile in which Clyde Barrow and Bonnie Parker were shot to death by Texas Rangers. Courtesy of the Library of Congress.

told his father about the meeting, and his father passed the information along to the police, upholding his part of the deal. The next morning, Hamer and his group heard about the strange behavior of the café customers. The waitress identified Methvin as her customer. Hamer also got word that the elder Methvin had passed along important information about a meeting between his son and Bonnie and Clyde that would take place near Arcadia, Louisiana. The four men packed and drove to Arcadia to set up the ambush.

When Hamer's group arrived in Arcadia, they were joined by the sheriff, Henderson Jordan, and his deputy, Prentiss Oakley. The six men drove to the meeting point and staked out their positions overnight. The next morning, May 23, 1934, Methvin's father arrived, parking his truck on the side of the road. He removed the front tire and left the spare lying on the road to make it appear as if he needed assistance. Then, he joined Hamer's group in the trees. Bob Alcorn spotted the tan Ford approaching and identified the couple. Clyde recognized Methvin's truck and slowed. He then saw the officers aiming their rifles and reached for his gun. Hamer's group opened fire. As the car was riddled with bullets, Clyde's foot slid off the brake, and the car rolled off the road. The posse continued to fire until Hamer signaled the men to stop. They approached the car cautiously and observed the slumped, bloodied bodies of Bonnie and Clyde.

After ensuring that his son was not in the car with the couple, Ivan Methvin fixed his truck and left. Hamer instructed members of the posse to arrange for a tow truck and the coroner to respond to the scene. Hinton, another member of the posse, filmed the scene with a 16-millimeter movie camera. Hamer began an inventory of the car's contents and found 15 sets of license plates, three Browning automatic rifles, a shotgun, 11 pistols, a revolver, and more than 2,000 rounds of ammunition (Roth, 1997).

The public heard about the deaths quickly. Local farmers who had heard the gunfire arrived at the scene. In nearby Arcadia, a member of the posse found the coroner, Dr. James L. Wade, and asked him to return to the scene to rule on the cause of death. Dr. Wade called his wife to let her know he would be late for lunch, and the operator, who had stayed on the line and overheard the news, quickly spread the word throughout town. People immediately drove out to the scene. The operator also called the local newspaper, which sent the story out to the rest of the nation. As the word spread, a reporter called Bonnie's mother, asking if she had heard that police had killed Bonnie and Clyde in Louisiana. Other reporters told Clyde's family the news, while still others contacted everyone who had been involved in the crime spree. Some talked with former gang members W.D. Jones and Raymond Hamilton. Others found Bonnie's husband, Roy Thornton. Reporters in Oklahoma talked with Chief Boyd, who had been kidnapped by the gang only weeks earlier.

At the scene, local townspeople began collecting souvenirs, including shell casings, pieces of glass from the car, pieces of bloody clothing, and locks of hair. One man even attempted to cut off Clyde's left ear. The number of people at the scene made Dr. Wade's work extremely difficult. Eventually, the tow truck arrived, and the sedan was towed into town in a procession that included police cars and onlookers. On its way, the caravan passed a high school, and students poured into the streets to look into the sedan.

Eventually, the parade pulled in front of Conger's Furniture Store and Funeral Parlor in Arcadia. The bodies were carried in amid the gaping crowd and taken to a small corner that was the mortuary. Local police wanted to put the bodies on display to give the large and increasingly aggressive crowd what it wanted, and Dr. Wade was hurried through his work. Carroll Rich (1970) published Dr. Wade's autopsy notes, in which he noted three tattoos on Clyde's body and the missing toes on his left foot. Bonnie's autopsy was performed second and was more rushed. He noted Bonnie's tattoo of the name *Roy* and a wedding ring as well as the extensive scars on her legs that had resulted from the car crash a year earlier. Dr. Wade concluded that both Bonnie and Clyde had died as a result of multiple gunshot wounds. A local photographer took pictures of the bodies, selling them to the public for $5 each and to newspaper reporters for $50. After a hurried cleaning and embalming, the couple was covered to the neck with white sheets and rolled into the furniture store for public viewing. A line of people filed by the bodies for nearly six hours.

Clyde's father arrived that afternoon with an ambulance to take his son's body back to Dallas. The hearse to transport Bonnie's body arrived later. In Dallas, neither of Bonnie's last wishes, spoken to her mother and immortalized in her poem, was fulfilled. Their bodies were taken to different funeral homes, where thousands lined up to see their caskets, not home as she had asked. The couple was also not buried together. Bonnie's mother said that Clyde had had her in life, but she would have Bonnie now. They were buried in separate services in separate cemeteries, and Clyde was buried beside his brother Buck. At Clyde's funeral, an airplane dropped a wreath of flowers on his grave. In the four days between the ambush and their burial, newspapers flew off the shelves.

THE FOLKLORE OF BONNIE AND CLYDE

> They're young...they're in love...and they kill people.
> —Ad for *Bonnie and Clyde,* 1967 (Hoberman, 1998)

Throughout Bonnie and Clyde's crime spree, the media faithfully reported on their activities, occasionally aided by the writings and poems that Bonnie sent to newspapers for publication. Some refer to Bonnie and Clyde as the world's most-photographed gangsters. After the ambush at Joplin, Missouri, the police found a roll of pictures taken of the gang. These photos soon appeared in the newspapers. The most famous of these photographs includes a picture of Bonnie in a long, dark-colored dress and beret with one foot perched on the bumper of their car, clutching a pistol and smoking a cigar. From this picture, Bonnie was referred to repeatedly in newspaper accounts as Clyde's "cigar-smoking gun moll" (Treherne, 1985, p. 120). Bonnie disliked this reference. She, in fact, hated cigars and only smoked cigarettes. In another picture, Bonnie holds a shotgun on Clyde. In both of these, Bonnie holds weapons, and this contributes to the image of her as an active participant in the murderous activities. However, members of the Barrow gang interviewed after the deaths of Bonnie and Clyde said that Bonnie never liked guns or fired one.

Cartoonists of the time also weighed in on the events. A cartoon in the April 9, 1934, edition of the *Dallas Journal* depicted law enforcement as a confused sheriff holding a gun and baton, head reeling as he tries to catch Bonnie and Clyde's car jumping in and out of holes in the ground (Treherne, 1985, p. 187). The image clearly demonstrated the gang's knack for escaping very close calls and law enforcement's frustration with trying to capture them. In the May 16, 1934, edition of the *Dallas Journal,* a cartoon appeared foreshadowing a violent end for the couple. The cartoon includes a drawing of an electric chair with a "Reserved" sign hanging on the wall behind it and the inscription "Clyde and Bonnie" (Treherne, 1985, p. 198). Only a week later, the couple would die at the hands of law enforcement.

After the couple's death, the government, particularly the Bureau of Investigation (later the Federal Bureau of Investigation), was determined to portray the pair negatively. A book on gangster crime published in 1936 with a foreword by J. Edgar Hoover stated: "not a kind word may truthfully be said of Bonnie Parker or her mate, Clyde Barrow. They were physically unclean. The woman boasted that she never took a bath" (Treherne, 1985, p. 229). Meanwhile, the Barrow and Parker families were equally as determined to tell their side of the story. Published in 1934, a book based on the stories of Bonnie's mother and Clyde's sister describes two attractive and charming individuals driven to a life of crime by the harassment and unfair treatment they received from the law.

Soon, however, public attention turned to more pressing matters: recovery from the Depression, the rise of Hitler, and an impending world war. As Robertson (2002) points out, the couple languished in the "dusty backroom of the national memory." However, some media attention still focused on the story of Bonnie and Clyde. In 1939, the movie *Persons in Hiding,* based on a book written in collaboration with J. Edgar Hoover, was released. The goal was to dispel the public's sympathetic view of 1930s gangsters. The book and the movie are loosely based on the exploits of Bonnie and Clyde, portraying an attractive woman who longs for a glamorous life. She meets and marries a small-time criminal and turns him into a serious gangster. The movie was only moderately successful, and the government's propaganda did little to dispel the romantic image of Bonnie and Clyde.

Gun Crazy, released in 1950, tells the story of two people, Annie and Bart, who are obsessed with guns. They meet and begin their courtship as sharpshooting acts in a fair sideshow. Then, because of Annie's need for excitement and material possessions, the couple turns to a life of crime, committing bank robberies and murders. The film portrays Annie as dominating the relationship, taking sensual pleasure in shooting and killing, and forcing Bart to participate. This story is among the early versions to link sex and violence, especially in the story of Bonnie and Clyde. The phallic symbolism of the gun and its attractiveness to the female member (Bonnie) appeared in other stories as well. Additionally, the distorted image of Bonnie as the dominant member of the couple continued.

In 1958, *The Bonnie Parker Story* was the first movie to specifically depict the lives of Bonnie and Clyde (called Guy Darrow in the film). Bonnie's story begins as Guy/Clyde shows her his machine gun. She is seduced and excited by their criminal adventures. The couple is joined by Guy/Clyde's brother, Chuck/Buck, and his girlfriend, who are shot by police. After this incident, Bonnie takes charge, organizing a prison break and taking up with a number of different men, including a handsome architect (Paul) who gives Bonnie a glimpse of the life she could have had. In the final scene, Bonnie and Guy/Clyde are killed in an ambush by police. This film further embellishes the image of Bonnie as the dominant partner and Clyde as a nearly impotent sidekick.

The story of Bonnie and Clyde was popularized most by the 1967 movie *Bonnie and Clyde,* directed by Arthur Penn and starring Faye Dunaway and Warren Beatty. Originally criticized as tasteless and grisly, the movie received enormous publicity and became a box office hit, receiving ten Oscar nominations. Hoberman (1998) notes that this movie represented a new style for Hollywood. In 1930, the Motion Picture Association of America's Production Code was revised to eliminate realistic violence in movies, stating that there could be no on-screen bleeding and that a gun and its victim could not appear in the same shot. The major concern of the industry was that viewers should not be seduced into siding with the criminals, so stories should not be told from the criminal's point of view. In 1966, this self-regulation was dismantled, and *Bonnie and Clyde* was among the first movies to take advantage of the change to a rating system.

In the Dunaway-Beatty movie, the title couple was portrayed sympathetically as both victims and offenders, which infuriated critics even as the movie fostered an emotional attachment among audiences to the charming, laughing pair. At the same time, the movie offered a negative depiction of law enforcement, appealing to a strong antiauthoritarian theme in the youth culture of the 1960s. Clyde and Bonnie were portrayed as Robin Hood and Maid Marian, beginning their bank-robbing career after meeting a poor farmer who had lost his farm to the bank. The image in the movie was that of Bonnie and Clyde as champions of the little people who were trapped into a series of violent confrontations. Critics noted that the danger of the movie lay in its claim to historical accuracy. In reality, there are notable inaccuracies in the movie version, from their first meeting to the rumor of Clyde's impotence to the crimes that they committed. However, through the enormous publicity and public support, critics were forced to recant their negative reviews.

Director Arthur Penn commented that the problem with most movies about violence was that they were not violent enough. He viewed the movie as a cautionary tale (Hoberman, 1998). Violence and sexuality are also intimately linked in the movie from the first view of Bonnie, naked in her bedroom, to her first meeting with Clyde, in which she caresses the barrel of his gun and recognizes the thrill and sexual excitement that he offers. Other themes in the movie, including changing positions of women and rebellious youth, also resonated with 1960s moviegoers. After its initial release, and the rerelease in 1968, the movie inspired fashion trends around the world, including calf-length skirts and berets for women, and fedoras and wide ties for men.

Since the smash hit of the 1967 movie *Bonnie and Clyde,* the story has continued to inspire musical and theatrical works, further cementing the couple's place in American history. "Foggy Mountain Breakdown," the theme song from the 1967 movie, reached the top ten on the music charts. Musicians from Merle Haggard to Mel Tormé have told the story of Bonnie and Clyde in a variety of genres, including country, rock, and rap. British singer Georgie Fame used machine-gun fire as a backdrop to his song "The Ballad of Bonnie and Clyde," which was banned in Norway and France (Hoberman, 1998). Today's musicians, including Tori Amos, Travis Tritt, and Eminem continue to invoke the story of Bonnie and Clyde in modern-day versions. Additional movies influenced by the story include *Thelma and Louise, Natural Born Killers, Drugstore Cowboy,* and *Teenage Bonnie and Klepto Clyde.*

An unusual development in the legend is a musical version of the story (*Bonnie and Clyde: The Musical*). The musical premiered July 1, 2003, at the Guildhall School of Music and Drama in London. In addition, after touring the country as a carnival attraction, the Bonnie and Clyde death car and the shirt Clyde was wearing when he died remain on display at the Primm Valley Resort near Las Vegas. Over the years, the couple's names have been loaned to various attractions, including the Bonnie and Clyde Trade Days, a monthly flea market held near Arcadia, Louisiana. Gibsland, Louisiana, also holds the annual Bonnie and Clyde Festival, which includes an appearance by the car used in the 1967 movie and reenactments of a bank robbery and the ambush resulting in the couple's death.

Clyde was just an ordinary criminal, and his crimes were mostly ignored until he met up with Bonnie. She was the unique feature at a time when violent crime was becoming more common, and the combination captured the public's imagination. Throughout their crime spree and in the nearly 70 years since, public perception of the Barrow gang and their crimes has been shaped by the media coverage. Part of the allure of the story of Bonnie and Clyde is the image of the couple as star-crossed lovers. They were the Romeo and Juliet of the 1930s. Their deaths together and Bonnie's self-composed eulogy put a romantic spin on their violence. Later, Hollywood productions went even further and linked their violence to sexuality.

Movies and stories of Bonnie and Clyde imply that, like other outlaws, they were fighting a battle for the little people, robbing the banks that had contributed to the Great Depression and murdering law enforcement officers, symbols of the government. In reality, Bonnie and Clyde's crimes were committed primarily against ordinary citizens, such as John Bucher, a store owner; Howard Hall, a meat market manager; and Doyle Johnson, a man in the wrong place at the wrong time. Of the hundreds of robberies committed by the gang, only a few targeted banks. The story of Bonnie and Clyde has become larger than life, due in part to newspaper coverage at the time and in even larger part to Hollywood exaggerations.

SUGGESTIONS FOR FURTHER READING

Frost, H. G. (1968). *I'm Frank Hamer: The life of a Texas peace officer.* Austin, TX: Jenkins Publishing Company.

Milner, E. R. (1996). *The lives and times of Bonnie and Clyde.* Carbondale, IL: Southern Illinois University Press.

Steele, P. W., and Scoma, M. (2000). *The family story of Bonnie and Clyde.* Gretna, LA: Pelican Publishing Company.

Treherne, J. E. (1985). *The strange history of Bonnie and Clyde.* New York: Stein and Day Publishers.

REFERENCES

Cartwright, G. (2001, February). The whole shootin' match. *Texas Monthly,* 74–79, 119–124.

Hoberman, J. (1998). "A test for the individual viewer": Bonnie and Clyde's violent reception. In J. H. Goldstein (Ed.), *Why we watch: The attractions of violent entertainment* (pp. 116–43). New York: Oxford University Press.

Kirchner, L.R. (2000). *Robbing banks: An American history, 1831–1999.* Rockville Centre, NY: Sarpedon.

Knight, J.R. (1997). Incident at Alma: The Barrow gang in northwest Arkansas. *Arkansas Historical Quarterly, 56,* 399–426.

Milner, E.R. (1996). *The lives and times of Bonnie and Clyde.* Carbondale, IL: Southern Illinois University Press.

Phillips, J.N. (2000, October). The raid on Eastham. *American History,* 54–64.

Rich, C.Y. (1970). The autopsy of Bonnie and Clyde. *Western Folklore, 29,* 27–33.

Robertson, T. (2002). Bonnie and Clyde. In *St. James encyclopedia of popular culture.* Retrieved July 14, 2003, from http://www.findarticles.com/cf_0/g1epc/tov/2419100158/print.jhtml

Roth, M. (1997). Bonnie and Clyde in Texas: The end of the Texas outlaw tradition. *East Texas Historical Journal, 35,* 30–38.

Simpson, W.M. (2000). A Bienville parish saga: The ambush and killing of Bonnie and Clyde. *Louisiana History, 41,* 5–21.

Steele, P.W., and Scoma, M. (2000). *The family story of Bonnie and Clyde.* Gretna, LA: Pelican Publishing Company.

Treherne, J.E. (1985). *The strange history of Bonnie and Clyde.* New York: Stein and Day Publishers.

8

The Scottsboro Boys Trials: Black Men as "Racial Scapegoats"

JAMES R. ACKER, ELIZABETH K. BROWN, AND
CHRISTINE M. ENGLEBRECHT

Scottsboro. The very name of this northern Alabama town evokes images of the racial, regional, and ideological conflicts that smoldered during the Great Depression and then exploded in the trials of nine black youths charged with raping two white women. The trials exposed glaring fault lines in the administration of Alabama justice and represented an indictment against courtrooms and cultural norms throughout the South. The youths' convictions and death sentences produced two landmark U.S. Supreme Court decisions, rulings that were especially noteworthy because of the justices' willingness to measure the fairness of state criminal trials against the demands of the federal Constitution. Through widespread and enduring news and mass media attention, the Scottsboro cases most conspicuously signified the bitter legacy of institutionalized racism and class oppression, and shattered the myth that a nation's entire people could fully participate in the American Dream.

THE ALLEGED CRIMES

In 1931, as the country reeled in the economic crisis ushered in two years earlier by the collapse of the stock market, it was not uncommon for itinerants in search of work to hop the trains that crisscrossed America. A Southern Railroad train left Chattanooga, Tennessee, on March 25 of that year, headed west for Memphis on a route that snaked through northern Alabama. Scottsboro, a town of 3,500 people and the Jackson County seat, lay on the rail line, nearly equidistant from Stevenson to the east and Paint Rock to the west. Four traveling companions, all young Negroes,[1] had boarded the train in Chattanooga, hoping to find jobs in Memphis: Haywood Patterson, 18; Eugene Williams, 13; Andy Wright, 19; and Andy's younger brother, Roy Wright, 13. Many others had hitched rides on the 42-car train as it headed west through Alabama, including five other black youths who lived in scattered parts of Georgia: Olen Montgomery, 17; Clarence Norris, 18; Ozie Powell, 16; Willie Roberson, 17; and Charles Weems, 19. The Georgia teenagers did not know one another, nor did they know the four Chattanooga youths (Carter, 1969, pp. 3–6; Geis and Bienen, 1998, p. 49; Goodman, 1994, pp. 4–5; Linder, 2004a). The nine would soon be irretrievably linked and thereafter identified collectively as the Scottsboro Boys.

Two young white women, 21-year-old Victoria Price and 17-year-old Ruby Bates, had sneaked into a boxcar on the same train. Both women were returning to their homes in Huntsville, Alabama, from Chattanooga, where they had unsuccessfully searched for work. By the time the train pulled out of Stevenson, Alabama, at least some of the black youths crossed paths with several young white men who were also on board. A fight broke out and all of the white youths except one were thrown or jumped from the train. The jet-tisoned youths made their way by foot to Stevenson and complained to the stationmaster. By this time, the train already had passed through Scottsboro and was approaching Paint Rock, some 40 miles west of Stevenson. The Stevenson stationmaster forwarded word that a gang of blacks had assaulted the young white men. A posse of white men were quickly deputized, armed themselves, flagged down the train at Paint Rock, and arrested all of the blacks they could find. The nine Scottsboro Boys were handcuffed, tied together with a rope, and transported in a flatbed truck to the Scottsboro jail.

Not until arriving in Scottsboro did the nine young men learn that Victoria Price and Ruby Bates had accused them of rape. The origins of the charge were somewhat obscure. After the two women were removed from the train in Paint Rock, Price either volunteered that she and Bates had been sexually assaulted by the Negroes or she assented to a deputy sheriff's inquiry that had made that assumption. Price elaborated that six of the young men had raped her at knifepoint, and that another half-dozen black youths had assaulted Bates. The women were whisked away for a medical examination performed by two local physicians. A frightened Roy Wright accused the other young men of committing the crimes while insisting that he, his brother, and his Chattanooga friends were innocent (Carter, 1969, p. 16). The other arrested youths either maintained silence or denied the charges, which brought immediate retribution from their captors (Norris and Washington, 1979, p. 21). At least some of the Scottsboro Boys were unlikely participants in either a fight or a sexual

Figure 8.1   Miss Juanita E. Jackson visiting the Scottsboro boys, January 1937. Courtesy of the Library of Congress.

assault. Olen Montgomery, who claimed to be traveling alone on the train, was blind in one eye and had extremely poor vision in the other. Willie Roberson suffered from both syphilis and gonorrhea, which resulted in swelling and painful lesions about his genitals and caused him to hobble with the aid of a cane (Carter, 1969, p. 6).

As news of the outrageous crimes spread, a threatening mob gathered outside of the Scottsboro jail. Fearing a lynching, Jackson County Sheriff M. L. Wann placed an urgent call to the governor's office. Governor Benjamin Meeks Miller responded by dispatching armed troops to Scottsboro from the nearest National Guard post (Carter, 1969, pp. 7–10). The Alabama Supreme Court later summarized the events of March 25, 1931:

> If the two girls, Victoria Price and Ruby Bates, are to be believed, the defendants were guilty of a most foul and revolting crime, the atrocity of which was only equaled by the boldness with which it was perpetrated.... [I]n many respects [the details are] too revolting, shocking, to admit of being here repeated. (*Powell v. State*, 1932, p. 204)

VICTORIA PRICE (1911–1982)

Victoria Price was born in 1911 in Huntsville, Alabama. Price went to work at a Huntsville cotton mill at the age of 10. She soon became the sole provider for herself and her mother, who had suffered an injury while working. Price was twice married during her adolescent years, and was reported to have turned to prostitution to supplement her income. In 1931, at the height of the Depression, Victoria and her friend Ruby Bates were riding the rails along with many others on a freight train bound for Huntsville from Chattanooga, Tennessee. In the trials that followed her accusations that nine black youths had raped her and Bates, Price presented a vivid description of the alleged attack. She became the subject of unsympathetic characterizations by the defense, who called into question her integrity and virtue. In 1937, having stuck to her story of the alleged rapes through numerous trials, Price faded from public view. Price returned to the public spotlight in 1976 when she filed a lawsuit against the National Broadcasting Corporation (NBC) for airing a made-for-TV movie, *Judge Horton and the Scottsboro Boys,* which she felt misrepresented her character. In the course of that lawsuit, Price reiterated on the witness stand her version of the events of March 25, 1931. Ms. Price was seeking $6 million for libel and invasion of privacy; her case ultimately was settled for an undisclosed amount.

Source: PBS Web site. Accessed November 10, 2006, from http://www.pbs.org/wgbh/amex/scottsboro/peopleevents/p_price.html

IN THE COURTS: THE LEGAL SAGA

The Jackson County grand jury quickly convened. Indictments returned on March 31 charged each of the boys with rape, a crime punishable by ten years' imprisonment to death, at the discretion of the trial jury. The nine defendants appeared in court that same day for arraignment. Acting pursuant to Alabama law, which required the appointment of counsel for indigents accused of capital crimes, Judge Alfred E. Hawkins announced that he was assigning all seven licensed attorneys in Scottsboro to represent the boys (Carter, 1969, p. 17; *Powell v. Alabama*, 1932, p. 49). Not guilty pleas were entered on the boys' behalves, and their trials were scheduled to begin the following week, on April 6. As the trial date approached, however, three of the originally assigned lawyers were assisting in the prosecution of the cases, while others had withdrawn their services.

Stephen Roddy, a Chattanooga attorney hired by concerned citizens from that city, appeared in court on April 6, but insisted that he was unfamiliar with Alabama law, that he had not officially been retained for the case, and that he was unprepared to represent the boys. A Scottsboro lawyer, Milo Moody, volunteered to represent the defendants in conjunction with Roddy. Neither lawyer had investigated the charges, and they had met with the boys for barely half an hour before the trial. Roddy had a drinking problem and already smelled of alcohol when the trial commenced. Moody was approaching 70 years of age and was notoriously forgetful (Carter, 1969, pp. 17–23; Geis and Bienen, 1998, p. 50; Norris and Washington, 1979, p. 22). Judge Hawkins authorized them to proceed on the boys' behalves, "[a]nd in this casual fashion the matter of counsel in a capital case was disposed of" (*Powell v. Alabama*, 1932, p. 56).

The trials progressed in lightning fashion, with predictably disastrous consequences for the defendants. Although Roddy and Moody did not object to the boys' being tried jointly, prosecutors elected to go forward in four separate trials, proceeding first against Clarence Norris and Charles Weems. Victoria Price, the principal prosecution witness, described the fight that had broken out between the black and white youths on the train, culminating with the white boys being thrown from the train. She identified Norris and Weems as among the six Negroes who had raped her in a gondola car filled nearly to the top with chert, or crushed gravel. The two physicians who had examined Price and Bates on their arrival in Scottsboro, shortly after the alleged assault, confirmed the presence of semen in their vaginas.

After the prosecution rested, Weems took the witness stand and admitted participating in the fight with the white boys, but denied seeing any women on the train, let alone having anything to do with Price or Bates. Norris then shocked defense counsel by testifying that Roy Wright had held a knife on the young women while the other Negroes, including Weems, took turns raping them. Norris maintained that he alone did not assault the women. Following the prosecution's closing argument and demand for the death penalty, the defense counsel elected to waive final arguments before the jury. The 12 white men serving as jurors then retired to deliberate on a verdict as jury selection began for the second trial (Carter, 1969, pp. 24–35).

The remaining trials unfolded with minor variations. All concluded by the end of the day on April 9. The verdicts were reported with chilling regularity as one trial gave way to the next. Eight of the Scottsboro boys were convicted of rape and sentenced to death. Because of his youthful appearance, Roy Wright had been prosecuted separately, in the last of the trials, and the solicitor had asked only for a sentence of life imprisonment. The 13-year-old Wright was convicted, but notwithstanding the solicitor's call for mercy, seven members of the jury insisted on sentencing him to death. The resulting lack of unanimity caused a mistrial to be declared in his case. The executions of the remaining defendants were scheduled for July 10, 1931 (Carter, 1969, pp. 35–48).

Shortly after being returned to jail at the conclusion of their trials, the boys were visited by lawyers from the International Labor Defense (ILD), the legal arm of the American Communist Party. Party leaders had seized on the Scottsboro trials as a cause that would help unite black and white workers in the communists' worldwide struggle to achieve political, economic, and social equality. "By publicizing the plight of the boys and defending them in court, the Party saw the chance to educate, add to its ranks, and encourage the mass protest necessary not only to free the boys but also to bring about revolution" (Goodman, 1994, p. 27). Discerning the potential significance of the case too late, the National Association for the Advancement of Colored People (NAACP) engaged in an awkward and eventually losing tug of war with the ILD over the boys' legal representation. To the dismay of the NAACP's leaders, the ILD funded and assumed control over the appeal of the rape convictions (Carter, 1969, pp. 51–102; Goodman, 1994, pp. 32–38; Van West, 1981, pp. 40–43). The scheduled executions were postponed while the eight death-sentenced boys were dispatched to Alabama's death row in Kilby Prison to await the outcome of their appeals (Norris and Washington, 1979, p. 47).

The Alabama Supreme Court wasted little time in affirming the convictions and death sentences (*Patterson v. State,* 1932; *Powell v. State,* 1932; *Weems v. State,* 1932). Only Eugene Williams's conviction was overturned by the state's high court, on the ground that he had not yet turned 16 at the time of the offense and thus fell within the exclusive jurisdiction of the juvenile court unless formally transferred for criminal trial (*Powell v. State,* 1932, pp. 211–213). Chief Justice John C. Anderson dissented from the decisions upholding the other defendants' convictions. He argued that community passions had been stirred to a "fever heat" by the crimes, which, he opined, were "of such a revolting character as to arouse any Caucasian county or community" (*Powell v. State,* 1932, p. 214). This atmosphere, combined with the "rather pro forma" representation provided by appointed counsel, led the chief justice to conclude that the defendants had not been given a fair trial (*Powell v. State,* 1932, pp. 214–215).

CLARENCE NORRIS (1912–1989)

Clarence Norris was born in 1912 in Georgia. With only a second-grade education, Norris worked various jobs before boarding a train the morning of March 25, 1931, in Chattanooga, Tennessee, that was bound for Memphis, where he hoped to find better work. When the Scottsboro Boys were accused of raping two white girls, Norris originally testified that while he was innocent, his fellow defendants had, in fact, committed rape. Norris later recanted those statements and reported that he had been intimidated and threatened before the trial in offering such testimony. While Norris was initially found guilty of rape, his conviction was later overturned. Norris was again convicted of rape in subsequent trials, but his sentence of death was commuted to life in prison. After several tumultuous years in prison (Norris was known to get into fights while incarcerated), he was paroled and, in violation of his parole conditions, moved to New York. He spent two more years in prison for the parole violation before being paroled again. After regaining his freedom, Norris again violated parole by moving to Cleveland and then to New York City. Former defense attorney Samuel Leibowitz helped Norris find a job in New York City in the mid-1950s, despite the fact that he was still a fugitive because of his parole violation. During the 1960s, with the help of the NAACP, Norris began seeking a pardon from the State of Alabama. His quest was finally successful in 1976, when Governor George Wallace officially recognized his innocence by issuing a pardon. Before he died, Norris published a book about his life and legal ordeals. The book, co-authored by Sybil D. Washington, is entitled *The Last of the Scottsboro Boys*.

Source: The Trials of the Scottsboro Boys Web site. Accessed November 28, 2006, from http:// www.law.umkc.edu/faculty/projects/FTrials/scottsboro/scottsb.htm. See also *New York Times* Obituary, 1989.

At the Supreme Court

The ILD retained Walter Pollak, a prominent expert in constitutional law, to pursue the cases in the U.S. Supreme Court. The conservative majority of the nation's high court was known during this era for its unwillingness to approve of President Roosevelt's New Deal reforms, and was almost equally reluctant to become involved in matters traditionally reserved for state law. The justices nevertheless were unable to condone the boys' treatment in the Alabama courts. In a seven to two ruling, the Court reversed the convictions and vacated the death sentences in the seven cases joined for decision in *Powell v. Alabama* (1932).

Justice George Sutherland's majority opinion concluded that the late resolution of appointment of counsel, and the consequent deficiencies in investigation and representation in these capital cases, denied the defendants fundamental fairness as guaranteed by the due process clause of the 14th Amendment. *Powell v. Alabama* had ramifications far beyond reprieving the seven condemned Scottsboro boys. The Court's decision emphatically signaled that the U.S. Constitution imposed limits on how state criminal trial courts would be allowed to conduct business. Powell laid the foundation for the Court's landmark ruling three decades later in *Gideon v. Wainwright* (1963), that the Sixth Amendment entitles indigent defendants charged in state courts with serious crimes to representation by court-appointed counsel (Heller, 1951, pp. 121–125; Lewis, 1964; Mello and Perkins, 2003, pp. 348–355).

Retrial

In preparation for the boys' retrial, the ILD contacted Samuel Leibowitz, a New York City attorney widely regarded as the best criminal defense lawyer of his day. Leibowitz agreed to take on the cases, but wary about the Communist Party using the trials for ideological purposes, refused payment for his services and insisted that he be allowed to work independently of the ILD. After a change of venue was secured to Decatur, 50 miles west of Scottsboro in Morgan County, the new trials were slated to begin March 27, 1933. Leibowitz immediately moved to quash the rape indictments returned by the Jackson County grand jury, and also challenged the Morgan County jury venire. Both motions were based on the systematic exclusion of blacks from the respective jury pools, which Leibowitz attempted to demonstrate through detailed presentation of evidence. Judge James E. Horton, Jr., denied the motions, and the prosecution elected to proceed against Haywood Patterson in the initial trial (Carter, 1969, pp. 181–202).

As if to affirm the Supreme Court's insistence in *Powell v. Alabama* about the importance of competent trial counsel in safeguarding defendants' rights, Leibowitz's entry into the case shed dramatic new light on the rape allegations. During his pounding cross-examination of Victoria Price, Leibowitz introduced records of her prior convictions for adultery and fornication. He portrayed Price as a prostitute who frequented hobo camps and had engaged in sexual relations with a companion, Jack Tiller, shortly before her alleged rape on the train. Following up with one of the Scottsboro doctors who had examined Price just an hour and a half after she was removed from the train, Leibowitz established that Price had appeared calm and had experienced no vaginal bleeding or tearing. She had only a few superficial cuts and small bruises on her arms and back, surprising in light of her story that she had been repeatedly assaulted while lying on top of jagged gravel. The doctor also had detected only a small amount of semen in her vagina—consistent with her having had intercourse with Tiller the previous day, and extraordinary in the face of her claim that she had been raped just a few hours before by six men. Moreover, the sperm in the semen sample were immotile, which the doctor testified was unusual because sperm typically remained alive 12 hours to two days following intercourse (Carter, 1969, pp. 204–210).

When the defense opened its case, Leibowitz aggressively attempted to establish Patterson's innocence. Several of Patterson's traveling companions testified that they had neither seen nor had any interactions with Price on the train. Contrary statements that some of the boys had made during the earlier trials were attributed to fear inspired by their predicament and threats leveled by the authorities. Patterson testified and maintained his innocence. Leibowitz then examined Lester Carter, who described how he and Ruby Bates had engaged in sexual intercourse in a hobo camp on March 23, 1931, while Jack Tiller and Victoria Price had similarly had sexual relations. But the defense's most important witness was Ruby Bates, who made a surprise appearance at the trial. In response to Leibowitz's questioning, Bates recanted her story of being raped. She confirmed Carter's account that the two of them had had sexual intercourse on March 23,

SAMUEL S. LEIBOWITZ (1893–1978)

Samuel Leibowitz, whose original family name was Lebeau, settled in New York City at age 3 when his parents emigrated from their native Romania to escape growing anti-Semitism. As a child he developed a passion for baseball and developed a penchant for debate, acting, and singing with a voice that matured into a rich baritone—talents that would serve him well throughout his legal career. He graduated from Cornell Law School in 1915, achieved the highest score among the more than 600 law school graduates who sat that summer for the New York Bar Exam, and quickly distinguished himself as New York City's top criminal defense attorney. Over time, his reputation rivaled that of Clarence Darrow, and his clients included the infamous gangster Al Capone among many other notables. In the 78 murder cases in which he appeared as defense counsel, Leibowitz compiled a remarkable record of 77 not guilty verdicts and one hung jury. He was asked by the International Labor Defense to represent the Scottsboro Boys in January 1933 and agreed shortly thereafter to take on their defense. The Scottsboro cases demanded Leibowitz's attention for parts of the ensuing four and one-half years, and he remained in touch with several of his clients for decades thereafter. Leibowitz ended his private law practice in 1941, when he was appointed as a trial judge in Brooklyn. Ironically, as a judge Leibowitz was an ardent supporter of the death penalty and was known for his law-and-order disposition. He remained on the bench until 1969. He died nine years later at age 84.

SOURCES

http://www.law.umkc.edu/faculty/projects/FTrials/Scottsboro/SB_bLieb.html
Leibowitz, R. (1981). *The Defender: The Life and Career of Samuel S. Leibowitz 1893–1933.* Englewood Cliffs, NJ: Prentice-Hall, Inc.
Reynolds, Q. (1950). *Courtroom: The Story of Samuel S. Leibowitz.* New York: Farrar, Straus & Co.
Time Magazine. (1978, January 23). http://www.time.com/time/magazine/printout/0,8816,919327,00.html

as did Price and Tiller. Bates then underwent a grueling cross-examination that called attention to her fine clothes and suggested that both her clothes and her testimony had been bought while she had taken refuge in New York City (Carter, 1969, pp. 219–234; Linder, 2004b).

When the attorneys delivered summations to the jury, Morgan County Solicitor Wade Wright vigorously defended the prosecution's case and ripped into Leibowitz's attempt to discredit Victoria Price and her testimony. Solicitor Wright challenged the 12 white jurors from his community: "Show them, show them that Alabama justice cannot be bought and sold with Jew money from New York" (Carter, 1969, p. 235). Leibowitz's furious motion for a mistrial was denied. The jury began its deliberations at one o'clock on a Saturday afternoon. It returned to the courtroom at ten o'clock Sunday morning with a verdict: Haywood Patterson was guilty of rape. His punishment was death.

The verdict was greeted by large demonstrations in New York and other northern cities (Carter, 1969, pp. 243–245). Unable to contain his contempt, Leibowitz explained the trial's outcome to the New York press. Referring to the jurors, he exclaimed, "If you ever saw those creatures, those bigots whose mouths are slits in their faces, whose eyes popped out at you like frogs, whose chins dripped tobacco juice, bewhiskered and filthy, you would not ask how they could do it" (Goodman, 1994, p. 148, quoting the New York Daily News, April 10, 1933). In retrospect, Leibowitz's frontal assault on Victoria Price during Patterson's trial appeared to have backfired. "Too late the chief defense attorney realized that Mrs. Price had become a symbol of white Southern womanhood" (Carter, 1969, p. 210). Southern newspapers excoriated Leibowitz for the "brutal manner" in which he had questioned Price (Carter, 1969, p. 210, quoting Sylacauga, Alabama, News, April 7, 1933).

Conceivably, a local defense without the triple disadvantage of being radical, Jewish, and "northern" could have gained a compromise such as life imprisonment, but the jury's loyalty to its white caste could only be proved unequivocally by a guilty verdict. Whether Haywood Patterson was guilty or innocent was, at most, a peripheral question (Carter, 1969, p. 242).

Judge Horton ordered a delay in the remaining trials to allow the clamor surrounding Haywood Patterson's conviction and sentence to subside and to consider Leibowitz's motion to set aside the verdict. Meanwhile, thousands of marchers supporting the Scottsboro Boys descended on Washington, DC. The NAACP and ILD reached an uneasy truce and agreed to work cooperatively to defend the boys; and even southern papers, including Alabama's Birmingham Post, began questioning the charges (Carter, 1969, pp. 243–254). On June 22, 1933, more than two months after the conclusion of Patterson's retrial, Judge Horton stunned prosecutors and defense counsel alike by announcing in a carefully detailed ruling that the evidence failed to support the jury's verdict. He ordered that Patterson be granted a new trial (Norris and Washington, 1979, pp. 63–78; Street v. National Broadcasting Co., 1981, pp. 1237–1246 [reprinting Judge Horton's order]). Hailed by some as a hero in the Scottsboro saga (Van West, 1981, pp. 44–46) but reviled by others, Judge Horton lost his bid for reelection the following year (Carter, 1969, p. 273). Much later, while reflecting on the Scottsboro cases, Horton recited a Latin phrase to explain his decision: fiat justicia ruat colelum—"let justice be done though the heavens may fall" (Linder, 2004c).

The next round of trials began November 20, 1933, in Decatur before a new judge, William Washington Callahan. Callahan repeatedly clashed with Leibowitz, interrupted

JUDGE JAMES E. HORTON, JR.
(1878–1973)

James E. Horton, Jr., presided over the initial retrial in the Scottsboro Boys case. He set aside Haywood Patterson's conviction and death sentence, ruling that they were not supported by the evidence. Horton was the son of a judge; his father also was a former slave owner and member of the Confederate Army. He was born and raised in Limestone County (Athens), Alabama, which bordered Morgan County, the site of Patterson's and all subsequent retrials. Abandoning his original aspiration to become a physician, Horton earned a law degree from Tennessee's Cumberland University in 1899. After spending several years in private law practice, he was elected to the Alabama Legislature, and in 1922 won election as Circuit Court Judge. He was in the fifth year of his second six-year term as judge in 1933 when he presided over Patterson's trial. He stood a lanky 6'2" and was frequently described as "a Lincolnesque figure," because of his striking resemblance to the former president. He had determined not to seek a third judicial term following the uproar over his decision to grant Patterson a new trial, but reconsidered when presented with a petition signed by all members of the Athens bar urging him to run. He was defeated handily in the 1934 election, on the same day that Thomas Knight, Jr., the state Attorney General who led the prosecution of the Scottsboro Boys, was elected Lieutenant Governor of Alabama. Horton subsequently resumed practicing law and tended to his substantial farm. He remained robust and without regret or reservations about his courageous but personally costly decision to award Patterson a new trial until the time of his death, at age 95. Following his death, county officials installed a plaque in the Athens courthouse, inscribed with portions of Judge Horton's jury instructions in the case that would mark his place in history. "[T]he law," said the judge, "knows neither native nor alien, Jew nor Gentile, black nor white....We have only to do our duty without fear or favor."

SOURCES

Carter, D.T. (1997–1998). "'Let Justice Be Done': Public Passion and Judicial Courage in Modern Alabama," *Cumberland Law Review, 28,* 553–573.

http://www.law.umkc.edu/faculty/projects/FTrials/Scottsboro/SB_BHort.html

Linder, D.O. (2000). "Without Fear or Favor: Judge James Edwin Horton and the Trial of the 'Scottsboro Boys,'" *University of Missouri at Kansas City Law Review, 68,* 549–583.

his questioning of witnesses, hurried the cases along, and indicated in his rulings and demeanor his antagonism to the defense efforts. He denied Leibowitz's renewed motions to quash the Jackson County indictments and the Morgan County jury venire. The judge rejected the former motion after inspecting the Jackson County grand juror rolls and disputing Leibowitz's contention, supported by the testimony of a handwriting expert, that the names of several Negroes had fraudulently been entered after the fact to make it appear as if they had been considered by the jury commissioners. Judge Callahan also refused to allow Leibowitz to interrogate Victoria Price about her sexual activity prior to the alleged rapes—which was crucial to support the defense theory regarding the source of the semen detected during her medical examination—or to introduce Lester Carter's related testimony (Carter, 1969, pp. 274–293). Following the presentation of evidence, the judge's instruction to the jurors included the admonition that "[w]here the woman charged to have been raped, as in this case[,] is a white woman there is a very strong presumption under the law that she would not and did not yield voluntarily to intercourse with the defendant, a Negro" (Carter, 1969, p. 297). The validity of this premise notwithstanding, the defense, of course, had not built its case on consent, but rather disputed that any of the defendants had engaged in sexual relations with Price at all.

The trials of Haywood Patterson and, thereafter, Clarence Norris were conducted before Judge Callahan in this fashion. Following brief deliberations, the separate juries returned guilty verdicts and sentenced each defendant to death. Leibowitz secured a postponement of the remaining defendants' trials to allow the appellate courts to review Patterson's and Norris's convictions and resolve issues that were likely to recur in the ensuing cases. National protests erupted in the wake of these most recent verdicts, while the *Birmingham Post* and many other newspapers assailed Judge Callahan's handling of the trials (Carter, 1969, pp. 300–305).

The Alabama Supreme Court upheld the new convictions and death sentences on appeal. In doing so, it dismissed the argument that blacks had systematically been excluded from the grand jury and jury lists, concluding with dubious logic that their absence "would not, however, show discrimination, but selection only, and the exercise by the [jury] commissioners of their discretion" (*Norris v. State*, 1934, p. 563). The court dismissed Patterson's appeal without even reaching his claims of error, ruling that a filing deadline had been missed in the case (*Patterson v. State*, 1934). The U.S. Supreme Court once again agreed to review the state court holdings. During Liebowitz's oral argument, the justices took the extraordinary step of visually inspecting the juror lists that allegedly had been altered (*Norris v. Alabama*, 1935, p. 593, n. 1) and were visibly dismayed by what they saw (Goodman, 1994, p. 243; Kennedy, 1997, p. 176). In a second important ruling stemming from the Scottsboro proceedings, the justices overturned Norris's conviction because of Alabama's discriminatory jury selection procedures (*Norris v. Alabama*, 1935). The Court also vacated Patterson's conviction and remanded his case with the strong suggestion that the Alabama courts take corrective action notwithstanding the asserted missed filing deadline (*Patterson v. Alabama*, 1935).

Leibowitz continued to represent the boys, although his relations with the ILD had grown increasingly strained, especially after two ILD attorneys were caught offering to bribe Victoria Price to change her testimony (Carter, 1969, pp. 310–318). Following protracted negotiations, the ILD ceded control over the cases to a newly formed coalition, the Scottsboro Defense Committee, while the boys' cases returned to Judge Callahan's courtroom for retrial. A newly formed grand jury in Jackson County, which included a single black member, had returned new indictments against all nine of the Scottsboro Boys in November 1935.

Acknowledging the animosity that many of the locals harbored against him, Leibowitz took a backseat to Alabama attorney Clarence Watts when Haywood Patterson's fourth trial commenced on January 20, 1936. Judge Callahan quickly resumed hectoring the defense and again excluded evidence that the defense lawyers considered essential to cast doubt on Victoria Price's testimony. The new Morgan County solicitor, Melvin Hutson, pointedly reminded the trial jurors that they would have to go home and face their neighbors following their verdict. He requested the death penalty for Patterson as he emphasized that Price "fights for the rights of the womanhood of Alabama" (Carter, 1969, p. 344). The jury once again consisted of 12 white men, as the dozen black venire members called under Morgan County's revised selection procedures either opted out of service or were challenged peremptorily by the prosecutor. The jurors' deliberations lasted the better part of a day. They returned to announce their verdict just as jury selection was being completed for Clarence Norris's trial. To no one's surprise, the jury foreman announced that Patterson had been found guilty. He then shocked the courtroom with the further announcement that the jury had fixed punishment at 75 years in prison, sparing Patterson the death penalty (Carter, 1969, pp. 346–347).

Although the conviction hardly represented a victory for the defense, the sentence was another matter. The *Birmingham Age-Herald* speculated that Patterson's case was "probably the first time in the history of the South that a Negro has been convicted of a charge of rape upon a white woman and has been given less than a death sentence" (Carter, 1969, p. 347, quoting *Birmingham Age-Herald*, January 24, 1936). As Norris's trial loomed, Judge Callahan announced an indefinite recess owing to the illness of the physician who had examined Victoria Price the day of the alleged crimes. Norris, Roy Wright, and Ozie Powell were handcuffed together and placed in the backseat of a sheriff's department vehicle to be transported back to the Birmingham jail. An altercation broke out during the drive. The sheriff characterized the affray as an escape attempt (Goodman, 1994, pp. 259–260), while Norris recounted that it had begun with an exchange of words and a deputy slapping Powell in the face (Norris and Washington, 1979, pp. 162–163). It was undisputed, however, that Powell stabbed the deputy in the neck with a knife that he had secreted on his person. In response, the sheriff, who was driving the car, shot Powell in the head. The bullet lodged in Powell's brain. Although he survived following emergency surgery, Powell "was never the same" (Norris and Washington, 1979, p. 166) following the shooting.

The Alabama Supreme Court affirmed Patterson's most recent conviction in June 1937 (*Patterson v. State*, 1937), barely a month before the remaining trials were to resume before Judge Callahan. Clarence Norris's trial began on July 15, with Clarence Watts again serving as primary defense counsel and Leibowitz playing a supporting role. Pursuant to Callahan's hurry-up procedures, the trial concluded the following afternoon, and the all-white jury returned a guilty verdict and fixed punishment of death. A devastated Watts was unable to continue, so Leibowitz took command as Andy Wright's trial commenced. Declaring that they were satisfied that Patterson and Norris had been the "ringleaders" in the rape, prosecutors conceded that they would not seek the death penalty against Wright. The trial resulted in another swift conviction, and Wright was sentenced to 99 years in prison. The prosecution similarly declined to pursue a capital sentence against Weems, whose trial an angry Leibowitz derided as a "travesty of justice." He railed to the jury that "It isn't Charley Weems on trial in this case, it's a Jew lawyer and New York State put on trial here by the [prosecutor's] inflammatory remarks" (Carter, 1969, p. 374). Weems's conviction followed, and the jury fixed his sentence at 75 years in prison.

Then, in rapid succession, the cases against the remaining defendants were resolved. Ozie Powell pled guilty to assaulting the deputy whom he had knifed; Judge Callahan imposed a 20-year prison sentence. He then dismissed the rape charge against Powell. The prosecution thereupon announced that it was dismissing the rape charges against Olen Montgomery, Willie Roberson, Eugene Williams, and Roy Wright. The lead prosecutor explained that the state was convinced that Roberson, crippled by venereal disease,

DID YOU KNOW?

The events described in Harper Lee's Pulitzer Prize winning book *To Kill a Mockingbird* were loosely based on the Scottsboro trials. While Ms. Lee was only a young girl at the time of the initial trials, aspects of the cases clearly affected the choices she made in her 1960 novel. The fictional trial of Tom Robinson in Ms. Lee's book focused on a similar crime, an alleged rape of a white woman by a black man, and was set during the same historical era (early 1930s) and place (Alabama) as the Scottsboro trials. Additional parallels can be drawn between the events of the Scottsboro trials and the fictional case in *To Kill a Mockingbird*. For example, Atticus Finch, Tom Robinson's lawyer in the book, was modeled after James Horton, who presided over the first of the retrials of the Scottsboro Boys. The motivations, economic circumstances, and social class of the defendant and accuser in the book also mirror those of the principals of the real trials. Ms. Lee's book and the Academy Award winning film that was based on it have helped perpetuate in popular culture the themes of race, class and justice that are the legacy of the Scottsboro trials.

Source: Johnson, C.D. (1994). *Understanding* To Kill a Mockingbird: *A Student Casebook to Issues, Sources, and Historic Documents.* Westport, CT: Greenwood Press.

and the nearly blind Montgomery had not been involved in the assault. Moreover, Williams and Roy Wright were juveniles and each already had served well over six years in prison (Carter, 1969, pp. 375–377). Various newspapers interpreted the dismissals as evidence that all nine of the Scottsboro Boys were innocent, a conclusion disputed by Alabama officials (Carter, 1969, pp. 377–379). Alabama Governor Bibb Graves commuted Clarence Norris's death sentence to life imprisonment in July 1938, just six weeks before Norris's scheduled execution (Norris and Washington, 1979, p. 173).

The Scottsboro Defense Committee then stepped up efforts to secure the release of the five boys who remained incarcerated. Governor Graves appeared to be primed to commute the outstanding prison sentences in November 1938, secure in the belief that Alabama newspapers would support such action. Those plans disintegrated after a disastrous encounter between the governor and the boys, during which Patterson was found in possession of a knife and Norris threatened Patterson's life (Carter, 1969, pp. 386–394; Goodman, 1994, pp. 352–355).[2] The intensity of news media coverage of the Scottsboro Boys' cases subsided shortly thereafter.

WHAT BECAME OF THE PRINCIPALS

The Scottsboro defendants met various fates. With periods of incarceration ranging from six and a half to 19 years, the nine young men in combination spent more than 100 years behind bars following their arrests for rape. Haywood Patterson remained in prison until 1948, when he escaped and made his way to Detroit. The governor of Michigan refused to honor Alabama's extradition request after the FBI discovered Patterson's whereabouts. Patterson killed a man in a Detroit bar in 1950, received a 15-to-20-year prison sentence for manslaughter, and died of cancer two years later while still incarcerated, at age 39 (Carter, 1969, p. 415; Linder, 2004a). Returning from a lengthy stay at sea while employed with the merchant marine in 1959, Roy Wright accused his wife of being unfaithful and then killed her before taking his own life (Carter, 1969, pp. 414–415; Linder, 2004a). Roy's brother Andy was originally paroled in 1944, only to be reincarcerated for a parole violation. He finally was released from the Alabama prison system in 1950, the last of the group to gain his freedom (Goodman, 1994, pp. 370–375; Linder, 2004a).

Most of the remaining Scottsboro Boys "returned to obscurity" (Carter, 1969, p. 415). In the 1970s, however, news media including the *Washington Post,* the *Atlanta Constitution,* and the *New York Times* brought Clarence Norris, the last surviving Scottsboro Boy, back into the spotlight through their coverage of his efforts to obtain a pardon (Van West, 1981, p. 46; Goodman, 1994, pp. 384–388). Norris, who was released from prison in 1946 and then absconded to New York in violation of his parole, enlisted the assistance of the NAACP to campaign for an official pardon (Linder, 2004a). The Alabama Board of Pardons and Paroles finally issued Norris the sought-after pardon in November 1976. Governor George Wallace congratulated Norris personally in his Montgomery office and made the pardon official (Norris and Washington, 1979, pp. 229–247, 271–283). When Norris died in 1989, his obituary was widely printed in major national and international papers (Clarence Norris, Obituary, 1989; Krebs, 1989, p. 21; Associated Press, 1989).

AN ANALYSIS OF THE NEWS MEDIA PORTRAYAL OF SCOTTSBORO

The Scottsboro Boys case exemplifies a "super primary" news story, one that receives sustained coverage not just for weeks or months, but for decades; a story that influences public opinion, politics, and has a lasting impact on the fabric of society (Chermak, 1995). Indeed, the story of the Scottsboro Boys could not accurately be told without acknowledging the important role played by the media. Contemporary newspaper accounts, for example, decisively helped shape public perceptions of the boys and directly affected both prosecution and defense efforts to mobilize support. Beyond the immediate news attention ignited on March 25, 1931, the mass media, including literature, film, and the visual arts, have continued to reaffirm and redefine the social and political significance of the Scottsboro Boys case (Murray, 1977).

When the Memphis-bound freight train carrying its ill-fated passengers pulled into Paint Rock, Alabama, on March 25, 1931, a news story of dramatic proportions was in the making. By that evening, the two local weekly papers, the *Jackson County Sentinel* and the *Progressive Age,* had printed stories detailing the gruesome, violent rapes of two young white women by nine black boys. The *Chattanooga Times* initially depicted the boys as common criminals, although none had police records at the time (Maher, 1997, pp. 103–104). While only a handful of national papers covered the case within the initial days of the boys' arrest, the Associated Press released a story focusing on how the National Guard was called out to maintain order in Scottsboro (Pfaff, 1974, p. 73). The local news coverage sparked an enormous uproar that eventually captured the attention of the nation and the world, and in the process significantly shaped the issues at stake as the boys went on trial for their lives.

Racial issues inevitably permeated and helped frame news media depictions of the case over the years. In addition, during the years immediately following the arrest and conviction of the nine young men, the news media tended to depict the case as a struggle pitting the North against the South, and a Jewish New York lawyer against the Alabama attorney general. The story was also framed as a struggle between the ILD and the NAACP, as both organizations sought to represent the boys, motivated in part by the importance of securing publicity to help gain supporters for their causes. Emphasis shifted again when

DID YOU KNOW?

Powell v. Alabama (1932) was a United States Supreme Court decision stemming from the Scottsboro Boys trials. This court decision concluded that impoverished, uneducated, and otherwise disadvantaged defendants in capital cases were entitled to the assistance of court-appointed counsel. With the exception of Roy Wright, all of the Scottsboro Boys were sentenced to death in a series of one-day trials. The defendants met with their defense counsel only immediately prior to trial, raising serious questions about due process of law. The *Powell* ruling was later expanded by the Supreme Court in *Gideon v. Wainwright* (1963) to include the right to court-appointed counsel for all felony defendants unable to afford their own attorneys.

historical accounts of the case, such as *Scottsboro: A Tragedy of the American South* (Carter, 1969), criticized both the ILD and the NAACP for their handling of the case. The made-for-television movie *Judge Horton and the Scottsboro Boys* later reframed the saga to focus on the actions of Judge Horton (Van West, 1981, p. 45). While racial prejudice was at the heart of the events surrounding the arrest and prosecution of the Scottsboro Boys, the news media helped to create and convey the shifting symbolic and socially important themes related to sectional division and political ideology.

Race and Gender

The Scottsboro case involved the presumption of a crime considered to represent the most egregious breach of Southern cultural boundaries in 1931: the raping of white women by black men. The story of the nine boys and their accusers served as a lightning rod for sentiments about interracial affairs and helped focus attention on issues of racism in the criminal justice system (Bailey and Green, 1999, p. 112; Brownmiller, 1975, p. 210). Rape tended to receive relatively modest coverage in the news media at that time, and the few cases inspiring media attention typically involved blacks accused of raping whites (Brownmiller, 1975, p. 213). The media largely ignored accusations of intraracial sex crimes, particularly those involving blacks (Benedict, 1992, p. 26). News coverage thus delineated the crimes meriting public attention and had the effect of putting white women on a pedestal, elevating them to a "separate and unequal sphere" (Lawson, Colburn, and Paulson, 1986, p. 6), while the plight of black women often was overlooked.

The news media have often been criticized for disproportionately portraying blacks as the perpetrators of crimes (Barlow, Barlow, and Chiricos, 1995). Such portrayals have contributed to and helped perpetuate the image of the dangerous black man, tapping into people's fear about crime generally, and black criminality specifically (Russell, 1998, p. 71; Boser, 2002). "The case of the Scottsboro Boys is perhaps the best known example of Black men being used as racial scapegoats" (Russell, 1998, p. 79; see also Kennedy, 1997, p. 100). Historically, the most notorious false accusation against a black man has been the claim of rape made by a white woman, and in this respect the Scottsboro Boys cases resonate with an intensity similar to the trial in Harper Lee's *To Kill a Mockingbird.* During the era of the Scottsboro trials, capital punishment for rape was confined almost exclusively to the South. Moreover, nearly 90 percent (405 of 455) of the executions for this crime between 1930 and the 1964 involved black defendants, a large proportion of whom had been convicted of raping white women (Wolfgang and Riedel, 1973). The Scottsboro Boys came perilously close to being added to those rolls, with the media coverage of their cases alternatively fanning and attempting to quell the flames of racial prejudice.

Regionalism

By the start of the first trial on April 6, 1931, local townspeople and media had converged on the Scottsboro Courthouse, with only a smattering of national media sources represented (Ross, 1999, p. 50). Soon after the trials concluded and the ILD assumed representation of the boys, however, the northern news media descended en masse on Alabama, where they were not warmly received (Van West, 1981, p. 38). Alabama newspapers, including the *Huntsville Daily Times,* the *Birmingham Age-Herald,* and the local Scottsboro papers, recoiled at what they considered to be a gross imposition by northern papers such as the *Daily Worker,* the *New York Times,* and the *Nation.* The published rhetoric of the *Daily Worker,* for example, was often vehemently refuted and criticized in the southern press. The southern news media perceived northern news sources to be latching onto the case to demonize the South and play savior to the boys, actions which, some charged, would compromise justice. On the other hand, many among the northern news media were moved to assume a protective role by calling attention to the plight of the nine defendants and urging the correction of perceived injustices (Van West, 1981; Ross, 1999, p. 53).

The regional media divide remained strong until March 1932, when the Alabama Supreme Court upheld the boys' original convictions. Then, although the *Montgomery Advertiser,* a prominent Alabama newspaper, supported the state court decision, the *Birmingham Age-Herald* and the *Birmingham Post* began to express doubts about the case (Maher, 1997, p. 109). The softening stance of select southern papers may have been linked to broader national and international campaigns in support of the boys. Red Aid, the international arm of the Communist Party, mobilized support for the boys with the help of individuals including Ada Wright (the mother of Roy and Andy Wright), thus focusing international attention on the case (Miller, Pennybacker, and Rosenhaft, 2001).

The temporary lull in regional media antagonism did not endure, however, for upon losing the retrial in March 1933, defense attorney Leibowitz lashed out at southerners through the *New York Herald Tribune,* claiming that Alabamans were bigoted, dirty, and unintelligent (Maher, 1997, p. 110). Leibowitz's intemperate remarks ignited angry responses from the southern press. In similar fashion, when Ruby Bates spoke out in support of the boys in Washington, DC, Alabama's *Huntsville Times* assailed her character. Likewise, several Alabama newspapers criticized Judge Horton when he publicly expressed doubts about Victoria Price's character. It was the turn of the *New York Times* to criticize the judging in the case after Horton was replaced by the conservative Judge Callahan (Maher, 1997, pp. 110–111).

Ideology

In addition to the regional divide observed in news media coverage of the Scottsboro case, the ILD and NAACP battled for control over the legal defense of the Scottsboro Boys. These two ideologically disparate groups claimed that they were best suited to protect the boys from what they both perceived as a biased justice system. The Communist Party, relying on outlets including the *Southern Worker,* the *Daily Worker,* and international media, portrayed the case as an example of political subjugation of young blacks by the white, capitalist justice system (Maher, 1997, p. 106). The NAACP decried what that organization perceived as racially motivated injustices in the Scottsboro Boys' prosecution.

It has been argued that both groups saw the case as an opportunity to further their own goals, to promote their ideological messages, and add supporters to their rosters, with the effect of dividing what otherwise might have been unified support for the boys (Maher, 1997, p. 108). Whatever their motivations, both the ILD and NAACP utilized the news media to garner attention and mobilize action surrounding the Scottsboro Boys (Miller et al., 2001). Although the NAACP was somewhat overshadowed by the rhetoric of the ILD in the early years of the case, NAACP leaders continued to work on behalf of the boys throughout the resolution of their cases and, thereafter, to protect their legacies.

Popular Culture

The social and cultural impact of Scottsboro also endures through the visual arts, film, music, and literature. The case has influenced and inspired the creation of a vast body of artistic work, much of which conveys powerful social commentary. Though varied in their interpretations, the bulk of the artistic works that draw on the Scottsboro case are sympathetic to and supportive of the boys. These works include paintings, lithographs, and block prints that focused on the newly invigorated antilynching movement (Park, 1993, p. 311). For example, *Christ in Alabama,* a Scottsboro-inspired lithograph, depicts the lynching mentality in the South (Park, 1993, p. 334). Another lithograph shows a young white girl sitting on the lap of an older white man. Underneath the image are the words "Alabama Code—Our Girls Don't Sleep with Niggers (1933)" (Park, 1993, p. 337). A visual history of African American experience is portrayed in *Scottsboro: A Story in Block Prints* (originally called *Scottsboro: A Story in Linoleum Cuts*). The book traces experiences of African Americans, including slavery and subjugation to Jim Crow laws. It features an artistic interpretation of the Scottsboro case in which the Scottsboro Boys were framed and coerced by the white authorities (Williams, 2000, p. 53).

The significance and drama of the Scottsboro case also have been captured in plays and poetry. Originally produced in 1934, John Wexley's *They Shall Not Die* portrayed aspects of the case on the stage. Wexley's production, which depicted lynchings as a sort of "southern holiday," included dialogue from the actual court transcripts, adding to the realism of the piece (Duffy, 2000, p. 31; Williams, 2000, p. 53). *They Shall Not Die* created controversy and stirred antiblack, anticommunist, and anti-Semitic sentiments, as blacks and whites mingled on stage to support the boys and to oppose the Southern oppression of blacks (Hilliard, 2001).

Intermingling themes of both economic and racial oppression, Langston Hughes wrote extensively about the Scottsboro Boys (Duffy, 2000, p. 24). His short poem "Christ in Alabama," which originally was published in a student magazine at the University of North Carolina, encapsulates the racial, social, sexual, and regional conflicts of the case. Hughes voiced frustration during the Scottsboro trials at prominent black leaders, including college administrators, for their silence about the boys' treatment. In an essay titled "Cowards from the Colleges," he blasted southern schools and their leaders for their lack of commitment to the black struggle and, specifically, the injustices associated with the Scottsboro case. Hughes's commitment to the Scottsboro case was evidenced in other work and in his philanthropy. With the help of Carl Van Vechten and Prentiss Taylor, Hughes published a pamphlet, *Scottsboro Limited,* which included a play by the same title, as well as short poems and lithographs (Thurston, 1995). The play attempted to unite the causes of economic and racial justice, evoking references to the "Red Voices" and the

TIMELINE FOR THE SCOTTSBORO BOYS CASES

March 25, 1931	Victoria Price and Ruby Bates allegedly are raped while on a freight train headed from Chattanooga, TN, to their home in Huntsville, AL; the nine youths soon to be known as the Scottsboro Boys are arrested in Paint Rock and taken to the Scottsboro jail.
March 31, 1931	The nine Scottsboro Boys are indicted for rape.
April 6–9, 1931	In a series of four trials, eight of the nine defendants are convicted and sentenced to death; 13-year-old Roy Wright's case ends in a mistrial when the jury cannot reach agreement about his sentence.
November 7, 1932	The U.S. Supreme Court overturns the convictions, ruling in *Powell v. Alabama* that the defendants' due process rights were violated when they effectively were denied the assistance of counsel.
April 9, 1933	Haywood Patterson is convicted following his retrial in Decatur and once again sentenced to death. Presiding Judge James E. Horton, Jr., later grants a continuance of the trials of the remaining defendants following newspaper reports of defense lawyer Samuel Leibowitz's derogatory comments about Decatur jurors.
June 22, 1933	Judge Horton sets aside Patterson's conviction, ruling that it was against the weight of the evidence.
November 20–December 6, 1933	In separate trials before Judge William Callahan, Haywood Patterson and Clarence Norris are convicted and sentenced to death; Judge Callahan continues the other trials to allow issues raised in the completed trials to be resolved on appeal.
April 1, 1935	The U.S. Supreme Court rules in *Norris v. Alabama* that blacks were improperly excluded from jury service, thereby overturning the convictions in Patterson's and Norris's cases and requiring wholesale reforms in jury selection procedures in several southern states.
January 23, 1936	Haywood Patterson is convicted of rape for the fourth time, following another trial in Decatur before Judge Callahan. The jury shocks the courtroom by sentencing Patterson to 75 years imprisonment instead of death.
January 24, 1936	Ozie Powell slashes the throat of a Sheriff's Deputy while being transported back to jail and is shot in the head by another officer. The trials of the remaining defendants are indefinitely postponed.
June 14, 1937	The Alabama Supreme Court affirms Patterson's conviction.
July 12–24, 1937	In Decatur, Clarence Norris is convicted for the third time and sentenced to death; Andy Wright and Charlie Weems are convicted and sentenced to lengthy terms of imprisonment; rape charges against Ozie Powell are dropped after he pleads guilty to assaulting the deputy whose throat he slashed, and Powell is sentenced to 20 years in prison.

July 24, 1937	The prosecution drops all charges against Olen Montgomery, Willie Roberson, Eugene Williams, and Roy Wright, and the four young men are freed after being incarcerated since their arrest in 1931.
July 5, 1938	Alabama Governor Bibb Graves commutes Clarence Norris's death sentence to life imprisonment.
November 15, 1938	Governor Graves declines to pardon the five convicted defendants.
1938–1950	Charlie Weems, Andy Wright, Clarence Norris, and Ozie Powell are paroled, although in several instances their parole is revoked and they are returned to prison before securing their final release. Haywood Patterson escapes from prison in 1948 and makes his way to Michigan; the Governor of Michigan declines to authorize his return to Alabama on extradition.
October 25, 1976	Alabama Governor George Wallace issues a pardon to Clarence Norris, the last known living defendant in the Scottsboro cases.
January 23, 1989	Clarence Norris dies.

"Red Negro." Proceeds from the pamphlet's sales were donated to the ILD fund (Duffy, 2000, p. 29; Thurston, 1995).

The stories of the nine Scottsboro youths can also be seen in films and heard in the lyrics of songs. The Scottsboro case inspired several films, including the 1976 television movie *Judge Horton and the Scottsboro Boys,* which was nominated for Emmy awards for writing and directing. In 1998, a second film, *Crime Stories: The Scottsboro Boys,* was aired on television. Most recently, a 2001 documentary titled *Scottsboro: An American Tragedy* was released to critical acclaim (Internet Movie Database, n.d.).

Many songs were written in response to the boys' struggle. For example, a song entitled "The Scottsboro Boys Shall Not Die" was inspired by the words of Samuel Leibowitz, and was composed to help in the effort to free the nine boys (Williams, 2000, p. 52). Additional songs followed, including "Song for the Scottsboro Boys," "Scottsboro Blues," and simply "Scottsboro Boys." Some of the songs dramatically portrayed southern whites as animals, while the boys were lamented as victims of a racist society and justice system (Williams, p. 59).

THE LEGACY: MEDIA INTERPRETATIONS AND JUDICIAL CHANGE

A large memorial plaque was installed in Scottsboro on January 25, 2004, to commemorate the lives of the nine Scottsboro Boys, more than 70 years after the beginning of their plight. The memorial resides on the lawn of the Jackson County courthouse, the site of the original trial. It represents the town's first official acknowledgment of the Scottsboro case. Scottsboro Mayor Ron Bailey expressed hope that the plaque would help promote the healing process. "Otherwise, [the case] will be a stumbling block to the future," he said (Associated Press, 2004). Ann Chambliss, past president of the Jackson County Historical Association, declared, "we cannot change the course of human events that began on March 25, 1931, but we can unite to heal the long-standing wounds" (Aldrich, 2004). Similar sentiments were expressed by Reverend R.L. Shanklin, president of the Alabama Conference of the NAACP, who stated at the memorial's dedication that "today is the beginning of the healing process" (Aldrich, 2004, p. 1).

Although no memorial can repair the lives shattered in the Scottsboro Boys case, the trials and their aftermath spawned several profoundly significant living legacies. The two major Supreme Court decisions having roots in Scottsboro embody vital principles of American justice, including the right of poor people to the services of competent legal counsel, and the participation on juries of all qualified citizens, free from invidious racial discrimination. The Scottsboro trials harbingered and undoubtedly helped precipitate the civil rights struggles of the ensuing generation that subsumed yet spilled far beyond correcting inequities in criminal justice. The case threatened to cleave the country along many divides and yet, if the contemporary townspeople are correct, perhaps the healing process has begun. However viewed, the enduring significance of the Scottsboro Boys case, and its multiple symbolic dimensions, is the direct outgrowth of the media interpretations and representations of this epic historical event.

SUGGESTIONS FOR FURTHER READING

Acker, J.R. (forthcoming). *Scottsboro and its legacy: Law, justice, and American culture*. New York: Praeger.

Carter, D.T. (1969). *Scottsboro: A tragedy of the American South*. Baton Rouge, LA: Louisiana State University Press.

Goodman, J. (1994). *Stories of Scottsboro*. New York: Pantheon Books.

Heller, F.H. (1951). *The Sixth Amendment to the United States Constitution: A study in constitutional development*. Lawrence, KS: University of Kansas Press.

Norris, C., and Washington, S.D. (1979). *The last of the Scottsboro Boys*. New York: G.P. Putnam's Sons.

NOTES

1. We use the term *Negroes* because this word was commonly employed in media and other reports when the Scottsboro Boys case arose in the 1930s. The term is intended to be used interchangeably with *blacks*, as frequently occurs elsewhere in this chapter.
2. The meeting between the boys and Governor Graves was arranged in anticipation of the governor issuing a pardon before his term of office expired; before acting, Graves wanted to interview the boys and satisfy himself that it would be appropriate to release them from prison.

REFERENCES

Aldrich, M. (2004, January 27). A sign of change, a chance to heal. *Scottsboro Daily Sentinel*. Retrieved February 10, 2004, from http://www.thedailysentinel.com/story.lasso?wcd=323

Associated Press. (1989, January 26). Clarence Norris, falsely accused in key case. *Toronto Star*. Retrieved February 12, 2004, from LexisNexis Academic Database Guided News Search.

Associated Press. (2004, January 13). Marker is planned for landmark case. *New York Times*. Retrieved February 11, 2004, from LexisNexis Academic Database Guided News Search.

Bailey, F.Y., and Green, A.P. (1999). *"Law never here": A social history of African-American responses to issues of crime and justice*. Westport, CT: Praeger.

Barlow, M.H., Barlow, D.E., and Chiricos, T.G. (1995). Economic conditions and ideologies of crime in the media. *Crime and Delinquency, 41,* 3–19.

Benedict, H. (1992). *Virgin or vamp: How the press covers sex crimes.* New York: Oxford University Press.

Boser, U. (2002, August 26–September 2). The black man's burden. *U.S. News and World Report, 133*(8).

Brownmiller, S. (1975). *Against our will: Men, women, and rape.* New York: Simon and Schuster.

Carter, D.T. (1969). *Scottsboro: A tragedy of the American South.* Baton Rouge, LA: Louisiana State University Press.

Chermak, S. (1995). *Victims in the news: Crime and the American news media.* Boulder, CO: Westview Press.

Clarence Norris [Obituary]. (1989, January 27). *London Times.* Retrieved February 12, 2004, from LexisNexis Academic Database Guided News Search.

Duffy, S. (2000). *The political play of Langston Hughes.* Carbondale, IL: Southern Illinois University Press.

Geis, G., and Bienen, L.B. (1998). *Crimes of the century: From Leopold and Loeb to O.J. Simpson.* Boston: Northeastern University Press.

Gideon v. Wainwright. (1963). 372 U.S. 335.

Goodman, J. (1994). *Stories of Scottsboro.* New York: Pantheon Books.

Heller, F.H. (1951). *The Sixth Amendment to the United States Constitution: A study in constitutional development.* Lawrence, KS: University of Kansas Press.

Hilliard, R.L. (2001). When theatre courage counted. *Theatre History Studies, 21,* 5–9.

Internet Movie Database. (n.d.). Retrieved February 16, 2004, from http://www.imdb.com/find?tt=on;nm=on;mx=20;q=Scottsboro

Kennedy, R. (1997). *Race, crime, and the law.* New York: Vintage Books.

Krebs, A. (1989). Clarence Norris, the last survivor of "Scottsboro Boys," dies at 76. *New York Times,* p. 21. Retrieved February 11, 2004, from http://web.lexis-nexis.com/universe/document?_m=c205eb845c74f8bb3a90835c9659

Lawson, S.F., Colburn, D.R., and Paulson, D. (1986). Groveland: Florida's little Scottsboro. *Florida Historical Quarterly, 65*(1), 1–26.

Lewis, A. (1964). *Gideon's trumpet.* New York: Random House.

Linder, D.O. (2004a). Biographies of key figures in "The Scottsboro Boys" trials. Retrieved February 6, 2004, from http://www.law.umkc.edu/faculty/projects/FTrials/scottsboro/SB_biog.html

Linder, D.O. (2004b). Excerpts from the trial of *Alabama v. Patterson,* March–April, 1933. Retrieved February 6, 2004, from http://www.law.umkc.edu/faculty/projects/FTrials/scottsboro/SB_tri33tml.html

Linder, D.O. (2004c). Judge James E. Horton. Retrieved February 6, 2004, from http://www.law.umkc.edu/faculty/projects/FTrials/scottsboro/SB_BHort.html

Maher, M. (1997). The case of the Scottsboro Boys (1931). In L. Chiasson, Jr. (Ed.), *The press on trial: Crimes trials as media events* (pp. 103–116). Westport, CT: Greenwood Press.

Mello, M., and Perkins, P.J. (2003). Closing the circle: The illusion of lawyers for people litigating for their lives at the fin de siecle. In J.R. Acker, R.M. Bohm, and C.S. Lanier (Eds.), *America's experiment with capital punishment: Reflections on the past, present, and future of the ultimate penal sanction* (2nd ed., pp. 347–384). Durham, NC: Carolina Academic Press.

Miller, J.A., Pennybacker, S.D., and Rosenhaft, E. (2001). Mother Ada Wright and the international campaign to free the Scottsboro Boys. *American Historical Review, 106*(2), 387–430.

Murray, H.T., Jr. (1977). Changing America and the changing image of Scottsboro. *Phylon, 38*(1), 82–92.

Norris, C., and Washington, S.D. (1979). *The last of the Scottsboro Boys.* New York: G.P. Putnam's Sons.

Norris v. Alabama. (1935). 294 U.S. 587.

Norris v. State. (1934). 156 So. 556 (Ala., 1934). Reversed in *Norris v. Alabama*. (1935). 294 U.S. 587.

Park, M. (1993). Lynching and antilynching: Art and politics in the 1930s. In Jack Salzman (Ed.), *Prospects: An annual of American cultural studies* (pp. 311–365). New York: Cambridge University Press.

Patterson v. Alabama. (1935). 294 U.S. 600.

Patterson v. State. (1932). 141 So. 195 (Ala., 1932). Reversed in *Powell v. Alabama*. (1932). 287 U.S. 45.

Patterson v. State. (1934). 159 So. 567 (Ala., 1934). Vacated and remanded, *Patterson v. Alabama*. (1935). 294 U.S. 600.

Patterson v. State. (1937). 175 So. 371 (Ala., 1937). Cert. denied, 302 U.S. 733 (1937).

Pfaff, D.W. (1974). The press and the Scottsboro rape cases, 1931–1932. *Journalism History, 1*(3), 72–76.

Powell v. Alabama. (1932). 287 U.S. 45.

Powell v. State. (1932). 141 So. 201 (Ala., 1932). Reversed in *Powell v. Alabama*. (1932). 287 U.S. 45.

Ross, F.G.J. (1999). Mobilizing the masses: The *Cleveland Call* and *Post* and the Scottsboro incident. *Journal of Negro History, 84*(1), 48–60.

Russell, K.K. (1998). *The color of crime: Racial hoaxes, white fear, black protectionism, police harassment, and other macroaggressions.* New York: New York University Press.

Street v. National Broadcasting Co. (1981). 645 F.2d 1227 (6th Cir. 1981). Cert. granted, 454 U.S. 815 (1981). Cert. dismissed, 454 U.S. 1095 (1981).

Thurston, M. (1995). Black Christ, red flag: Langston Hughes on Scottsboro. *College Literature, 22* (3), 30–49.

Van West, C. (1981). Perpetuating the myth of America: Scottsboro and its interpreters. *The South Atlantic Quarterly, 80*(1), 36–48.

Weems v. State. (1932). 141 So. 215 (Ala., 1932). Reversed, *Powell v. Alabama*. (1932). 287 U.S. 45.

Williams, L.B. (2000). Images of Scottsboro. *Southern Cultures, 6*(1), 50–67.

Wolfgang, M.E., and Riedel, M. (1973). Race, judicial discretion, and the death penalty. *The Annals of the American Academy of Political and Social Science, 407*, 119–133.

9

The Lindbergh Baby Murder Case: A Crime of the Century

KELLY WOLF

Charles Augustus Lindbergh was an international hero. In May 1927, he became the first person ever to fly across the Atlantic Ocean alone—3,610 miles in a single-engine plane named *The Spirit of St. Louis*. His fame and popularity with the public were enormous. He met and married Ann Morrow, daughter of Dwight D. Morrow, a U.S. ambassador and extremely wealthy man, in May 1929. Their first baby arrived on June 22, 1930. He was named Charles Augustus Lindbergh, Jr., after his father, and also became known as the "Eaglet." The birth of the baby was a national sensation. The media allowed the Lindberghs little privacy; pictures of the new family were everywhere, as were pictures of their newly built house, the Hopewell Estate in New Jersey. The house was not yet finished, so the family would only spend weekends there, leaving on Mondays for the Morrow Estate where Ann's mother resided.

THE CRIME

One particular weekend in March, the 20-month-old baby became ill, and Ann and Charles decided to spend an extra night at the Hopewell Estate. They phoned the baby's nursemaid, Betty Gow, at the Morrow Estate and informed her that she would be driven to Hopewell to help tend to the child. Gow then phoned her boyfriend, Red Johnson, and canceled her date with him, telling him about the sick child. The butler drove her to Hopewell.

On Monday, March 1, 1932, Gow began getting young Charles ready for bed. Since he had a cold, she gave him some milk of magnesia, which the baby spit out, soiling his pajamas. Gow decided that, since there was a chill in the air, she would make the child a flannel shirt to wear underneath his pajamas. Gow rubbed some Vicks VapoRub on the child and dressed him, once again, for bed. She attached his thumb guards to prevent the baby from sucking his thumb, and put him into the crib. Pulling the blankets tightly around the Eaglet, she put two safety pins, one on each side, into the mattress to secure the blanket. The nursemaid sat in the dark with the baby until 8 p.m., when she could hear him

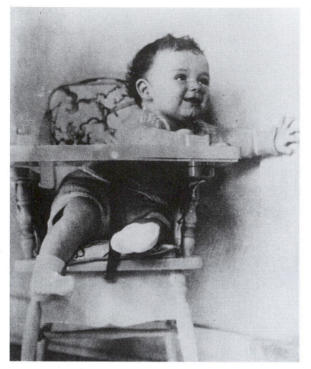

Figure 9.1 Baby Charles Lindbergh, Jr., 1932. Courtesy of the Library of Congress.

breathing evenly. All of the shutters were closed and locked except for the one on the southeast side of the nursery: it was warped and could not be locked. Gow went downstairs to have dinner with the other Lindbergh staff.

Lindbergh had returned home at around 9 p.m. and was having dinner with Ann when he heard a cracking sound that he later identified as slats of an orange crate falling off a chair. At the time, he dismissed it as an accident in the kitchen. Lindbergh and Ann sat in the living room reading the paper and talking for a few minutes. Lindbergh then went upstairs to draw himself a bath. After his bath he went back to the den to do some more reading. Ann decided it was her turn for a bath. While getting cleaned up, she discovered that she had run out of tooth powder. She entered the nursery, which was connected to the Lindbergh's bathroom, and went straight to the dresser. Not noticing that the baby was missing, she took the powder and returned to the bathroom.

At 10 p.m., Gow returned to the nursery for her final check on the baby before turning in. She discovered that he was gone and quickly ran to Ann's bedroom, asking if she had the child. Ann replied no, and they both went downstairs to see whether Lindbergh had the boy. Lindbergh said that he did not and rushed up the stairs, two at a time, to the nursery. He quickly scanned the room and went directly to his closet to grab his Springfield rifle. He looked at his wife and said, "Ann, they've stolen our baby" (Waller, 1961; Fisher, 1987; Behn, 1994, p. 46; Berg, 1998, p. 254; Hixson, 2001). Lindbergh called his personal friend and attorney Colonel Henry Breckinridge, and ordered the butler, Oliver Whately, to call the police.

THE INVESTIGATION

While scanning the nursery, Lindbergh discovered a white envelope lying beneath the open window, which appeared to have been the kidnapper's escape route. He waited for the police to arrive before he opened it. The officer read the ransom letter out loud as the Lindberghs listened intently.

Dear Sir!
    Have 50,000$ redy 2500$ in 20$ bills 1 5000$ in 10$ bills and 10000$ in 5$bills. After 2–4 days we will inform you were to deliver the Mony.
    We warn you for making anyding public or for the polise the child is in gut care.
    Indication for all letters are singnature and 3 holes. (Waller, 1961; Fisher, 1987; Behn, 1994)

There was a symbol at the bottom of the letter. It consisted of two interlocking circles outlined in blue, with a solid red circle where the two other circles connected. There were three holes punched into the paper horizontally, one in the middle of the red circle and the other two in line with the outside two circles. The note was free of fingerprints. In fact, the entire nursery was free of any prints whatsoever—not even Ann's, Lindbergh's, or the nursemaid's prints were found. It was almost as though somebody had wiped down the entire nursery before the police arrived.

Outside, underneath the nursery window, a chisel and a wooden dowel pin were found lying in the mud. It was theorized that the chisel was brought along to pry open the window shutters. When the kidnapper realized that he did not need it, he tossed it to the ground. Footprints were also present; however, police failed to make a mold of the imprints or to take any measurements of their size. A second, smaller print was found near the scene; it was dismissed as being from Ann's earlier walk on the grounds. Fourteen feet away were remnants of a handmade ladder. The ladder could be folded into three parts for easy transportation. It weighed about 30 pounds and could be extended up to 18 and 1/2 feet. There was a split in the side rails; the position where the ladder would have split sat about five feet from the ground. Later tests with a replication ladder also proved that the ladder was able to hold the weight of the kidnapper on the way up, but unable to support both the kidnapper and the baby upon descent.

By midnight, the entire nation knew of the Lindbergh kidnapping. Radio stations broadcast the story over all the airwaves, and newspaper reporters printed special editions of the story. People began flocking to Hopewell to see the crime scene. Police, reporters, and curious onlookers were unrestrained and most likely destroyed crucial evidence. The footprints and tire impressions had been trampled, and so many people had handled the ladder that the kidnapper's fingerprints could not be singled out, if they had been present at all. The head of the New Jersey state police, Colonel H. Norman Schwarzkopf, was unable to control the mob. Schwarzkopf would be a key figure throughout the investigation and trial, and would be criticized for the investigation in the years to come.

With all of the police and media attention, Lindbergh became concerned that the kidnappers would cut off contact. After all, they had specifically told him not to contact the authorities. Lindbergh made sure the police knew that he was in charge and requested that they not interfere in his dealings with the kidnappers. Lindbergh would maintain control throughout the investigation. He set up a communications center in his garage. Five telephone lines ran from nearby Princeton University to the Hopewell Estate. It was through

TIMELINE

May 21, 1927	Lindbergh is the first person to fly across the Atlantic Ocean alone.
May 27, 1927	Lindbergh marries Anne Morrow.
June 22, 1930	Charles A. Lindbergh, Jr., is born.
March 1, 1932	The Eaglet is kidnapped from the Hopewell Estate.
May 12, 1932	The remains of Charles, Jr., are found.
September 19, 1934	Richard Hauptmann is arrested for the murder.
January 2, 1935	The trial begins.
Feb 14, 1935	Hauptmann is convicted and sentenced to death.
April 3, 1936	Hauptmann is executed.

Figure 9.2 Police examining the window from which Charles A. Lindbergh's baby was kidnapped, Hopewell, New Jersey, 1932. Courtesy of the Library of Congress.

this setup that he was able to control what information was released to police as well as the media.

Schwarzkopf, Lindbergh, and most of the detectives were under the impression that the kidnapping was the job of an underworld organization. Upon hearing of the kidnapping, mob leader Al Capone, then serving a prison sentence for tax evasion, offered his assistance in return for his freedom. His offer was refused. Against the advice of Breckinridge, Lindbergh hired a respected figure of the underworld, Morris "Mickey" Rosner. Rosner was given a copy of the ransom letter, which he showed several underworld criminals and forgers, in search of information on the kidnappers. Lindbergh also identified two other underworld agents, Salvatore Spitale and Irving Bitz, as go-betweens for the kidnappers. The use of go-betweens was a common practice at a time when mobsters would kidnap the children of wealthy citizens in order to collect large cash sums from them. For the kidnappers, the purpose was to have an intermediary who would later be unable or unwilling to identify them. The use of newspapers to communicate with kidnappers was also common, and this was another strategy the Lindberghs employed to reach the person who took their baby.

Three days had passed with no word from the kidnappers. Lindbergh was prepared to fully cooperate with everything they demanded. He publicly pledged to keep their identities a secret. This promise upset the authorities, who came out with a statement that reminded the public that Lindbergh did not have the power to grant immunity and that the kidnappers would be prosecuted for their crime. Finally, on March 4, another ransom note, with the designated symbol, arrived:

> Dear Sir. We have warned you note to make anything public also notify the police now you have to take consequences—means we will have to hold the baby until everything is quite. We can note make any appointment just now. We know very well what it means to us. It is realy necessary to make a world affair out of this, or to get your baby back as soon as possible to settle those affair in a quick way will be better for both—don't by afraid about the baby—keeping care of us day and night. We also will feed him according to the diet.
>
> We are interested to send him back in gut health. And ransom was made aus for 50000 $ but now we have to take another person to it and probably have to keep the baby for a longer time as we expected. So the amount will be 70000 20000 in 50$ bills 25000 $ in 20$ bills 15000 $ in 10$ bills and 20000 in 5$ bills Don't mark any bills or take them from one serial nomer. We will form you latter were to deliver the money. But we will note do so until the Police is out of the cace and the pappers are qute. The kidnaping we prepared in years so we are prepared for everyding. (Waller, 1961; Fisher, 1987; Behn, 1994, pp. 87–88)

The letter comforted the Lindberghs that the baby was being taken care of. Ann had published a menu of what the baby ate, hoping that the kidnappers would read it and feed the child accordingly. It appeared that all the kidnappers wanted was money, and they had no intention of hurting the child. They made no threats against the child's life in any of the 13 ransom notes.

A retired schoolteacher from the Bronx took it upon himself to submit a plea in the *Bronx Home News* to the kidnappers offering his life savings of $1,000 in addition to the ransom for the safe return of the child. He also offered himself as intermediary for all ransom dealings. The following day, this man, named John F. Condon, received a letter from the kidnappers. It contained the secret signature.

> dear Sir: If you are willing to act as go-between in the Lindbergh case please follow strictly instruction. Handel incloced letter personaly to Mr. Lindbergh. It will explain everything. don't tell anyone about it as soon we find out the press or Police is notified everything are cancell and it will be a further delay. After you get the money from Mr. Lindbergh put these 3 works in the New-York American
>
> Mony is redy After notise we will give you further instruction. don't be affraid we are not out for your 1000$ keep it. Only act stricly. Be at home every night between 6–12 by this time you will hear from us. (Waller, 1961; Fisher, 1987; Behn, 1994, pp. 96–97)

Condon immediately phoned Lindbergh, who was unimpressed until he heard about the strange symbol. Lindbergh requested that Condon come to the house immediately. When he reached the house, Lindbergh and Breckinridge were waiting. It was decided that they would put the "Mony is redy [sic]" message in the newspaper that following day. They would use Condon's initials, J.F.C., or "Jafsie," as a name by which the kidnappers could identify Condon without alerting the public and press.

Condon received the promised phone call from the kidnappers. He was told to be at home between 6 and 12 o'clock the next evening and he would receive a note giving him further instructions. Toward the end of the phone call, Condon heard a voice in the background yell "Statti citto!" which is Italian for "Shut up!" The caller abruptly hung up. This strange incident served to further encourage the theory that the kidnapper was a part of the underworld and not working alone.

The next evening Condon received a letter from a taxicab driver. In it were directions to a hot dog stand. He was to come alone and bring the ransom money. On reaching the stand, he found a note hidden under a rock. The note told him to cross the street to Woodlawn Cemetery. Condon went to the cemetery as directed by the kidnappers; however, the ransom money was not yet ready. He had hoped to meet the kidnapper in person and speak with him about his terms. Condon wanted proof that the child was still alive. The man in the cemetery identified himself as John and told Condon that he was one of six people involved in the kidnapping. Condon took note of John's face, which he saw only briefly. It was triangular in shape, with deep-set eyes and a small mouth. He appeared to be about 35 years old, five feet ten inches and around 160 pounds. The two talked briefly about John's involvement in the kidnapping. John insisted that his only job was to collect the ransom money, and that he had nothing to do with the actual crime. At one point in the conversation, John became nervous and asked Condon, "What if the baby is dead? Would I burn if the baby is dead?" (Waller, 1961; Fisher, 1987; Behn, 1994, p. 122; Berg, 1998, p. 275; Hixson, 2001). Condon was shocked; what was the point of these negotiations if the child was dead? John quickly recovered and told Condon that the baby was in good health and that there was no need to worry. Condon requested to see the baby before delivering the money. John refused, saying it was too dangerous. He would send proof that the baby was alive. He would send the child's sleeping suit.

On March 16, a package was placed in Condon's mailbox. It contained the Eaglet's sleeping suit and another letter from the kidnappers:

> Dear Sir: ouer man faill to collect the mony. There are no more confidential conference after we meeting from March 12. those arrangemts to hazardous for us. We will note allow ouer man to confer in a way like befor. circumstance will note allow us to make transfare like you wish. It is impossibly for us. wy shuld we move the baby and face danger. to take another person to the place is entirely out of question. It seems you are afraid if we are the right party and if the boy is allright. Well you have ouer singnature. It is always the same as the first one specialy them 3 holes.
>
> Now we will send you the sleepingsuit from the baby besides it means 3 $ extra expenses because we have to pay another one. please tell Mrs. Lindbergh note to worry the baby is well. we only have to give him more food as the diet says.
>
> You are willing to pay the 70000 note 50000 $ without seeing the baby first or note. let us know about that in the New York-American. We can't do it other ways because we don't like to give up ouer safty plase or to move the baby. If you are willing to accept this deal put these in paper.
>
> I accept mony is redy
>
> Ouer program is:
>
> After 8 houers we have the mony received we will notify you where to find the baby. If there is any trapp, you will be Responsible what will follows. (Waller, 1961; Fisher, 1987; Behn, 1994, p. 130)

Lindbergh wondered aloud why the child's garment appeared to have been laundered. Dismissing this oddity, Lindbergh and Breckinridge began their preparation of the ransom package. The kidnapper had specified what type of box to place the money in and even gave specific measurements. When it came time to pack the money into the box, only

$50,000 of it fit. The rest was wrapped in a sack that would later be easily identifiable to authorities.

Although many wealthy members of society generously offered to put up the ransom for Lindbergh, he insisted on coming up with the money himself. In the midst of the Great Depression, Lindbergh was forced to sell over $350,000 worth of stock to raise the $70,000 ransom. J.P. Morgan and Company delivered $50,000 to the Fordham branch of the Corn Exchange Bank; Condon had access to the special vault in which the money was placed. Against Lindbergh's wishes, the serial number from each ransom bill was recorded. Not a single bill was in sequential order. Most of the ransom bills were gold notes, meaning that they contained a round yellow seal. This was helpful in later identifying the ransom bills, as the United States was going off the gold standard. In a few months, it would be illegal to possess a gold note.

That Saturday, Condon received a letter giving him directions to a greenhouse. On the table outside, under a rock, was another set of instructions. Condon was to go to St. Raymond's Cemetery and bring the money with him. Condon got out of Al Reich's Ford Coupe and walked around the area specified by the kidnappers. Lindbergh waited in the car. He was armed. After a few minutes of waiting, Condon walked back to the truck to see what Lindbergh wanted him to do, as the kidnapper was nowhere in sight. Suddenly, they both heard a heavily accented voice call out, "Hey Doctor! Here Doctor! Over here! Over here!" (Waller, 1961; Fisher, 1987; Behn, 1994, p. 146; Berg, 1998, p. 281). Condon approached the man who had spoken, whom he recognized as John. A few minutes later, the ransom was turned over. Condon had talked John out of $20,000, stating that Lindbergh was suffering from hard times because of the Depression and could not afford to pay such an extra amount. John agreed to settle for the original $50,000, which turned out to be a mistake on Condon's part. What Condon failed to realize was that the $20,000 bag contained several large bills in gold notes that would be very easy to identify when they were spent. John gave Condon an envelope with directions on where he could find the baby. The stipulation was that they had to wait eight hours to open it.

Condon managed to talk Lindbergh into opening the letter as soon as they reached a private property owned by Condon. Breckinridge was also present. The letter told them that the baby could be found on a "boad" named *Nelly*, off the Elizabeth Islands. Lindbergh waited the demanded eight hours and began to search the waters of the Elizabeth Islands in an amphibious aircraft. He dreamed of holding his son in his arms; that moment never came. They searched for two days and did not find anything fitting the description John gave of the boat *Nelly*. They realized that they had been scammed.

Lindbergh, refusing to give up hope, contacted another possible lead. Months earlier, a man named John Hughes Curtis had said that he was in contact with the kidnap gang. He said he knew a man named Sam who had directed him to form a committee of prominent Norfolk, Virginia, citizens to act as intermediaries for the kidnappers. The ransom would be deposited in a bank in Norfolk and would be delivered to the kidnappers only upon the return of the child. Initially, Lindbergh agreed to give merit to the story if Curtis could prove that Sam actually had the child. But now, with limited options, Lindbergh followed Curtis's lead. He spent many days at sea with Curtis, searching various areas of the Elizabeth Islands, but to no avail. It was on one of these boats that Lindbergh was told of the discovery of his child's body somewhere else. He had been the victim of a cruel hoax. There was no Sam or kidnap gang. Curtis had made up the entire story.

THE DISCOVERY

On May 12, truck driver Orville Wilson and his partner, William Allen, were delivering lumber to Hopewell when Allen needed to stop on the side of the road to relieve himself. As he stepped into the brush, he discovered a small, decomposing body. Allen went back to the truck to get Wilson. They both agreed that it was the body of a child. They quickly notified the police.

The baby was found face down in a hollow in the ground. It appeared to have been covered with leaves and branches to make it less noticeable. Although the body was badly decomposed, the baby's face, which had not been exposed to air, had been fairly well preserved and was still recognizable. The signature dimple in the baby's chin and the child's overlapping toes on his left foot were key identifiers of the corpse. The child was missing his right leg from the knee down, and both hands were gone. It appeared that wild animals had been at the body. Some of the child's clothes were intact and could be identified as those that the child was wearing the night he was stolen. In the area surrounding the body, the police found tufts of blonde, curly hair, a burlap sack, a toenail, and six human bones. Then they realized that, only a few feet away, lay the cable from Princeton that Lindbergh had used to set up his communication center.

The cause of death was determined to be a blow to the head. Death was instant or within a few minutes of delivery of this blow. Gow, the nursemaid, was asked to identify the clothing that had been taken from the corpse. She said that they were indeed the same articles she had dressed the baby in the night he was kidnapped. She also went to the morgue and positively identified the body. Ann was notified immediately, and a wire was sent to Lindbergh. By 6:30 p.m., the nation had heard of the death of the Eaglet. Once again the airwaves filled with news of the Lindbergh baby. The nation was stunned. How could anyone do such a thing to a national hero?

Lindbergh had decided to view the body so no doubt was left in his mind that this actually was his baby. After only three minutes, Lindbergh remarked, "I am satisfied that this is my child" (Waller, 1961; Behn, 1994, p. 174; Berg, 1998, p. 290; Hixson, 2001). The Lindberghs planned to have the body cremated in order to avoid scavengers and souvenir hunters who might decide to dig up the grave. Before cremation, two unknown reporters gained access to the morgue and took photographs of the Eaglet's remains. They later sold the photographs for $5 apiece.

THE SEARCH

Since the baby had been found murdered, the public was angry and wanted those responsible to be punished. The police had been kept in the dark when it came to the dealings with John, and they had no other leads. It was time to turn to the ransom bills for clues. The previous month, a 57-page pamphlet containing the serial number of each bill had been released to banks across the country. Police now encouraged tellers to keep an eye out for the ransom bills and offered $5 for each bill coming to the authorities' attention.

On June 22, Congress passed the Cochran Bill, nicknamed the Lindbergh Law, making penalties for kidnapping harsher and allowing the Federal Bureau of Investigation (FBI) jurisdiction if the person who had been abducted was transported across state lines. This law made kidnapping a federal offense, punishable by death. However, this law was not retroactive and, therefore, would not apply to the Lindbergh child's killer.

Gold ransom bills began showing up in various places around the Bronx area, including a movie theater and several banks. A $10 gold bill had been passed at a gas station. Fearing he would get in trouble for possessing a gold certificate, the attendant wrote down the license plate number of the man who gave him the bill. Once the bill reached the bank, it was discovered as a ransom bill. The police looked up the license plate number and found that the car belonged to a Bruno Richard Hauptmann.

In the United States illegally, Hauptmann had been born in Germany in 1899. He had served in the German infantry as a teenager and later studied carpentry and machinery in trade school. He was later arrested for the burglary of three homes and robbing two women pushing young children in carriages on the street. He took their food coupons. He was convicted and served four years of his five-year sentence. He was arrested on another stealing charge, but escaped from prison and fled to the United States. His history would follow him throughout the trial and convict him in the minds of many.

The police found Hauptmann's address and began to stake out his residence. He appeared on the morning of Wednesday, September 19, 1934, and went into his heavily secured garage. He got into his 1930 Dodge sedan and drove away, presumably to report to work. The authorities followed Hauptmann onto a busy street. When they thought they might lose him, he was pulled over and searched. In his possession was a $20 gold ransom bill. Hauptmann fit Condon's description of the kidnapper and spoke with a heavy German accent. The initial search of Hauptmann's house turned up nothing. The garage was heavily padlocked, and there was even a switch that could be flipped from the bedroom that would illuminate the entire structure. Upon searching the garage, the police made a shocking discovery: they found large sums of ransom money hidden behind some loosely placed boards. It totaled $11,930. Other evidence later found inside the house included notebooks with sketches of a ladder similar to the one found at the Hopewell Estate; Condon's phone number and address written inside a closet; and Hauptmann's tool chest, missing a chisel the same size as the one found below the Lindbergh nursery (Fisher, 1987; Behn, 1994; Berg, 1998; Hixson, 2001).

The police took Bruno to the station to be questioned. Not understanding what he was being arrested for, he simply thought that the police believed he had stolen the money they had found in his garage. Hauptmann told police that a close friend, Isador Fitch, had given him a box of money to keep until he returned from a trip overseas. Fitch

Figure 9.3 Bruno Richard Hauptmann, after being questioned in connection with the Lindbergh baby kidnapping. Courtesy of the Library of Congress.

died while abroad, and Hauptmann decided to spend some of the money. Hauptmann was interrogated for 32 hours and denied food, sleep, and legal counsel. He accused authorities of tying him to a chair and severely beating him. A prison doctor confirmed that he had been struck repeatedly with a blunt object.

Eyewitnesses including Condon, the taxi driver, the gas station attendant, and the woman who sold a movie ticket to someone who paid with a ransom bill gathered for a lineup. Hauptmann, disheveled and unshaven after his interrogation, was placed in the lineup with 13 well-dressed, clean-cut police officers who were over six feet tall. Every eyewitness identified Hauptmann as the kidnapper, except for Condon. Condon asked all the men in the lineup to repeat certain phrases and to hold out their hands so he could look at them. He made a big show of this and his expertise as an eyewitness. He then refused to identify anyone in the lineup as John, stating, "I have to be sure; a man's life is at stake" (Fisher, 1987; Behn, 1994, p. 221; Hixson, 2001). Condon later received much public criticism and scrutiny for this.

Some accounts say that the police showed the eyewitnesses photographs of Hauptmann before exposing them to the lineup, telling them he was a prime suspect. At one point in his interrogation, Hauptmann was asked to repeat the phrase "Hey Doctor! Here Doctor! Over here! Over here!" from several angles in the room. Unbeknownst to him, Lindbergh was sitting in the room in a disguise. He positively identified Hauptmann as the voice he had heard in the cemetery, on the night the ransom was paid, over two years before.

THE TRIAL

In New York, Hauptmann was found guilty on the count of extortion and was extradited back to New Jersey to stand trial for the murder of Charles Augustus Lindbergh, Jr. James M. Fawcett was appointed Hauptmann's lawyer. In his first criminal trial, David T. Wilentz would act as prosecutor for the case. The trial was set to begin on January 2, 1935.

At the last minute, Mrs. Hauptmann agreed to let the *New Jersey Journal* pay for Hauptmann's defense in exchange for her exclusive story of the events occurring before and during the trial. The *New Jersey Journal* decided to hire the famous Edward J. Reilly to replace Fawcett. Reilly had been known as "Death House" Reilly because he had defended a large number of murder suspects. He had begun drinking, and his career had started to waver.

On the first day of the trial and thereafter, Flemington, New Jersey, was inundated with reporters and sightseers. Everyone seemed to take advantage of the opportunity to make money. Vendors sold food, miniature replicas of the famous kidnap ladder, and fake locks of the baby's golden blonde hair. The town was packed. People were paying huge sums of money to stay in hotels and local residents' homes. No cost was too high.

The jury consisted of eight men and four women. The 78-year-old Thomas W. Trenchard, with 28 years' experience on the bench, presided over the trial. Ann Lindbergh took the stand on one of the first days. She described the events of the evening, identified the child's clothing, and was able to provide a picture of the child to the jury. She was not cross-examined by the defense; they felt she had been through enough already. Charles Lindbergh took the stand and remained poised throughout questioning. He had carried his gun every day of the trial, except for when he took the stand. He knew Reilly would ask him whether he was armed. Rumor had it that Lindbergh would shoot Reilly if the questioning went too far. Betty Gow summoned jurors' sympathy when she described how happy the baby had been the day of the kidnapping. She also described the garment she had sewn for the child the night of his disappearance. She told of how she was able to identify the child at the morgue and described the phone call to her boyfriend, Red Johnson. The questioning had been such a strain on her that she fainted on the way back to her seat. The testimonies of Ann, Charles, and Gow did not add much to the case against Hauptmann, but the prosecution knew that they would be able to stir up the emotions of the jury.

The prosecution's case was well prepared. Prosecution witnesses were poised and appeared credible. They remained calm during cross-examination and told their stories with confidence. Wilentz presented overwhelming evidence and spent thousands of dollars on handwriting experts, wood experts, eyewitness testimony, and autopsy reports. He was organized, well spoken, and polite. In contrast, Reilly was flamboyant, overly dramatic, and disorganized. Instead of attacking holes in the prosecution's case, Reilly came up with far-fetched theories and scenarios of what he thought might have happened that

TRIAL PARTICIPANTS

THE TRIAL OF RICHARD "BRUNO" HAUPTMANN
HELD IN FLEMINGTON, NEW JERSEY
JANUARY 2–FEBRUARY 14, 1935

Presiding:
Thomas W. Trenchard
Prosecution Team:
Edward J. Reilly
Frederick Pope
Egbert Rosecrans
C. Lloyd Fisher
Defense Team:
David T. Wilentz
Anthony Hauck, Jr.
Joseph Lanigan
George K. Large
Prosecution Witnesses:
Anne Lindbergh, Charles Lindbergh, Betty Gow, Joseph Wolfe, Frank Kelly, Amandus Hochmuth, John Condon, Norman Schwarzkopf, John Tyrell, Dr. Charles Mitchell, Arthur Koehler
Defense Witnesses:
John Trendley, Sam Streppone, Peter Somner, Richard Hauptmann
Jurors:
Charles Walton, Rosie Pill, Verna Snyder, Charles Snyder, Ethel Stockton, Elmer Smith, Robert Cravatt, Philip Hockenbury, George Voorhees, May Brelsford

night. He often came back from lunch with alcohol on his breath and appeared to be using the case to gain publicity for himself and his career. Reilly told the press that he believed his client was guilty, and he spent only 36 minutes conferring with Hauptmann throughout the entire trial. Reilly's witnesses and experts were subpar at best. Most of them had inconsistent testimonies, as well as criminal records. He offered money to anyone who would testify on behalf of Hauptmann, and many perjured themselves on the stand in order to make a buck and be a part of the most famous trial of the time. His so-called wood experts were nothing more than lumberyard workers, and his barrage of handwriting experts backed out at the last minute, stating that their testimony would hurt the defense. His cross-examinations often led nowhere and only increased the jury's dislike for the defense. Hauptmann, from another country, did not understand the American legal system but took the stand at the advice of his attorney. It did more harm than good.

The fact that Hauptmann showed very little emotion (and when he did, it was in the form of angry outbursts) did not sit well with the jury. To get some sympathy for the defense, Hauptmann's wife and small child, Manfred, sat in plain view of the jury. However, the fact that the public and media had already tried and convicted Hauptmann may have made the jurors feel that they would be ostracized, if not in danger, if they did not come to the same conclusion.

THE VERDICT

The jury was sent for deliberations at 11:21 a.m., and, although the prosecution's case was based entirely on circumstantial evidence, the jury reached a verdict by 10:28 p.m. On February 13, 1935, the 32nd day of the trial, Bruno Richard Hauptmann was found guilty of first-degree murder. The sentence for murdering the Lindbergh baby was death by electrocution. Hauptmann did not show any emotion when the verdict was read, but upon returning to his cell he broke down, sobbing throughout the night. Hauptmann was transferred to the New Jersey State Prison in Trenton. He was placed in a cell only a few feet from the electric chair. The state of New Jersey had spent a total of $600,000 on the case, the most expensive trial of the time.

All of Hauptmann's appeals were rejected, even his plea for a new trial on the basis of inadequate counsel, which was clearly the case. However, the governor of New Jersey, Harold G. Hoffman, had suspicions that Hauptmann was innocent or at the very least had not received a fair trial. He felt that key evidence had been tampered with or destroyed, and upon reviewing the case he firmly believed that there had to be more than one kidnapper. Knowing very well that his involvement in the case would likely ruin his career, 30 hours before Hauptmann was scheduled to be executed, Hoffman granted him a 30-day reprieve so that further investigation could be conducted.

Among Hoffman's attempts to find evidence that would cast doubt on Hauptmann's guilt was his request to have him take a lie detector test. Hauptmann eagerly agreed to this, but the judge denied the motion. All attempts to enter evidence that would have possibly proved Hauptmann's innocence were blocked by judges as being inadmissible. Hoffman decided to take another approach to save Hauptmann's life. Prosecuting attorney Wilentz and Hoffman visited Hauptmann in prison and urged him to confess, even if he was innocent, and they would commute his sentence to life in prison instead of the death penalty. Hauptmann refused to confess, and would deny all involvement in the kidnapping and murder of the Eaglet for the rest of his short life.

Four years after the kidnapping and murder of Charles Augustus Lindbergh, Jr., Bruno Richard Hauptmann was executed for the crime. On Friday, April 3, at 8:47 p.m., after receiving 2,000 volts of electricity, Hauptmann was pronounced dead. The execution lasted three minutes, and 57 people were present. A quiet ceremony was held for Hauptmann on April 6, in Queens, with 30 people in attendance. He was later cremated.

ALTERNATIVE THEORIES OF THE CRIME

Many people still believe that the wrong man was convicted of the murder of the Lindbergh baby. Several theories have been offered since the kidnap-murder occurred. One theory is that Elisabeth Morrow, Ann's sister, was the murderer. According to this theory, the public believed that Elisabeth would be the one to marry Lindbergh. She became insanely jealous when he chose Ann. One day she went over the edge, lost control, and killed the child. Fearing bad publicity and as a service to the Morrow family, Lindbergh agreed to cover up for Elisabeth; he did so by keeping the police and media at bay during the investigation. Lindbergh counted on the greed of extortionists to direct attention away from family members and toward the underworld. Hauptmann's possession of so much of the ransom money was just a coincidental stroke of luck. As it happened, Elisabeth died of heart disease before Hauptmann's trial began (Behn, 1994).

Another theory is that Lindbergh accidentally killed the child himself while playing one of his infamous practical jokes. He often played jokes on his family and domestic staff. Sometimes they were not so funny. There were reports that he had pretended his son had been kidnapped on a previous occasion after hiding the baby in the closet. Lindbergh might have unintentionally killed his son during one of these games (Behn, 1994; Ahlgren and Monier, 1993).

One popular, but unlikely, theory is that the Lindbergh child was never killed. The child was kidnapped, raised by his abductors, and is still alive today. The body found in the woods was that of a child from an orphanage near the Lindbergh Estate. Many people have come forward claiming to be the Lindbergh heir (Behn, 1994).

THE MEDIA: A CARNIVAL ATMOSPHERE

From the night of the kidnapping to the execution of Bruno Richard Hauptmann, and even thereafter, the media were ever-present in the Lindbergh baby kidnapping case. In many ways, the press hindered the investigation more than it helped. Reporters had arrived at the crime scene shortly after police and tramped through the estate, possibly destroying vital evidence.

However, Lindbergh had a talent for using the media to his advantage. He released only those details of the case that he wanted the press to know. In this way, he had total control of the information that reached the public. The media were also an important element in the correspondence between Lindbergh and the kidnappers, via the newspapers.

The media and the "carnival" atmosphere they produced were most evident during Hauptmann's trial. New Jersey was inundated with nearly 700 reporters, not to mention curious tourists who hoped to get a spot in the courtroom. Spectators were allowed a seat on a first-come, first-served basis, and every available space was filled. As many as 600 people were reported to have crammed into the tiny courtroom. Even though cameras were not allowed inside, Judge Trenchard ignored the feeble attempt made by newsreel companies to hide them, one inside a clock and another in a box on the balcony. It was quietly agreed upon that the cameras could stay as long as the footage was kept secret until the trial's end (Cohn and Dow, 2002). These clips were played in movie theaters in New York and New Jersey.

Outside the courtroom, the town of Flemington bustled with vendors and tourists. Local restaurants got in on the action by touting food specials named after important figures in the case: Lamb Chops Jafsie; Baked Beans Wilentz; and "Lindys," which were nothing more than ice cream sundaes (Berg, 1998). Crowds on the street could be heard inside the courtroom shouting their beliefs that Hauptmann was guilty and deserved the death penalty.

After news of Hauptmann's conviction and his sentence to the electric chair, the media coverage died down significantly. People slowly filed out of Flemington and returned to their normal lives. Very few people gathered outside the prison on the night Hauptmann was executed.

THE AFTERMATH OF THE MAJOR PLAYERS

The case did not end with the execution of Bruno Richard Hauptmann. The lives of the key players would be affected by the case as long as they lived. Hauptmann's wife, Anna, filed a civil suit against the New Jersey officials involved in the case. She sued for $10 million, claiming that they had framed her husband. The case was dismissed, and the U.S. Supreme Court refused to review it.

Defense attorney Edward Reilly checked himself into a mental hospital following his diagnosis of paresis as a result of syphilis. Fourteen months later at 56, he returned to a meager law practice until his death in 1940. In contrast, prosecuting attorney David Wilentz's practice flourished. He died a successful lawyer in 1988, at the age of 93.

Harold Hoffman's political career was ruined following the Hauptmann trial. He had hoped to run for the presidency, but he did not receive support from his party. He was hired as the administrator of the Division of Employment Security (DES), but then allegations of money laundering during his term as governor were made public. Authorities found that Hoffman had mismanaged funds to the tune of $450,000 and had sold political favors while in office. He was forced to step down from his position in the DES. Hoffman was found dead in his apartment on June 4, 1954, apparently from a heart attack. However, rumors spread that Hoffman had committed suicide. Attendance at his funeral was reported to be 10,000.

In 1942, during World War II, H. Norman Schwarzkopf spent five years in Iran heading a mission. He continued his military involvement for several years and then returned to work for the state of New Jersey until his death in 1958. His son, General H. Norman Schwarzkopf, Jr., following in his father's footsteps, was a war hero in Desert Storm in 1991.

The Lindberghs had enough of all the publicity following the trial and decided to flee to England, saying that they were concerned for the safety of their second son, Jon. After lying low for a while, Lindbergh would soon be back in the limelight. He and Ann flew to Germany in response to an invitation sent by Hermann Goering, a high-ranking officer in Adolf Hitler's regime. Not long after, Lindbergh made his affection for Hitler and Germany's Third Reich publicly known. Nazi leaders told Lindbergh of their vast aeronautical machinery and gave him inflated numbers of the German air force and production rates. Lindbergh reported this back to the chief of the United States Army Air Force, insinuating that Germany was invincible and it would be better that the United States stayed out of the war. As a reward for his allegiance, Lindbergh was presented with the highest honor bestowed on a civilian, the Service Cross of the German Eagle. Ann urged Charles to give it back, but Lindbergh refused. It would be a decision he would later regret. Lindbergh continued to speak publicly about keeping America out of the war, swearing that he was not pro-Nazi, just antiwar. His popularity with American citizens plummeted; they felt he had turned on them.

As time went on, Lindbergh regained some of his lost favor with the American public. His autobiography, released in 1953, immediately became a best seller. He was appointed to the Air Force Scientific Advisory Board and became an avid animal activist. He was diagnosed with lymphatic cancer in 1974 and died on August 26 of that year.

"THE CRIME OF THE CENTURY"

It is clear that the Lindbergh kidnapping had a tremendous impact on Americans. The baby of a national hero had been stolen from his crib. The public was shocked and wanted justice. The passing of the "Lindbergh Law" increased the penalties for kidnapping and made it a federal offense, allowing for capital punishment. Meanwhile, newspapers sold out and citizens were glued to their radios. With the massive media coverage, the entire affair turned into a three-ring circus. However, when the trial and execution were over and the dust had settled, many Americans believed they had seen justice done in the case that was described as "the crime of the century."

SUGGESTIONS FOR FURTHER READING

Ahlgren, G., and Monier, S.R. (1993). *Crime of the century: The Lindbergh kidnapping hoax.* Boston, MA: Branden Publishing Company.

Berg, S.A. (1998). *Lindbergh.* New York: G.P. Putnam's Sons.

Waller, G. (1961). *Kidnap: The story of the Lindbergh case.* New York: The Dial Press.

REFERENCES

Ahlgren, G., and Monier, S.R. (1993). *Crime of the century: The Lindbergh kidnapping hoax.* Boston, MA: Branden Publishing Company.

Behn, N. (1994). *Lindbergh: The crime.* New York: Atlantic Monthly Press.

Berg, S.A. (1998). *Lindbergh.* New York: G.P. Putnam's Sons.

Cohn, M., and Dow, D. (2002). *Cameras in the courtroom: Television and the pursuit of justice.* Lanham, MD: Rowman and Littlefield.

Fass, P.S. (1997). Kidnapped: Child abduction in America. In *The nation's child...is dead* (pp. 95–131). Oxford, NY: Oxford University Press.

Fisher, J. (1987). *The Lindbergh case.* New Brunswick, NJ: Rutgers University Press.

Hixson, W.L. (2001). Murder, culture, and injustice: Four sensational cases in American history. In *Vengeance: Bruno Richard Hauptmann and the Lindbergh baby kidnapping* (pp. 67–128). Akron, OH: The University of Akron Press.

Waller, G. (1961). *Kidnap: The story of the Lindbergh case.* New York: The Dial Press.

10

Alger Hiss: No Certain Verdict

MATTHEW PATE

Alger Hiss began his career with enviable credentials. He held degrees from Johns Hopkins University and Harvard Law School. At Harvard he was the protégé of future Supreme Court Justice Felix Frankfurter. From Harvard Hiss went on to clerk for Supreme Court Justice Oliver Wendell Holmes. He experienced what might be termed as the proverbial meteoric rise in the administration of President Franklin Roosevelt. Under Roosevelt, he held numerous government positions including service as general counsel to the Nye Commission and the Agricultural Adjustment Administration. Hiss served as the director of the Office of Special Political Affairs and as the executive secretary of the Dumbarton Oaks Conference, a body pivotal in the formation of the United Nations. Perhaps the most notable, and ultimately the most ironic of positions held by Hiss, was his membership in the U.S. delegation to the Yalta Conference.[1] In 1946, Hiss left government service to assume the presidency of the Carnegie Endowment for International Peace. Hiss remained in that office until May 1949. By the time Hiss was forced out of the Carnegie Endowment, his impressive record of public service would matter much less than the scandal that consumed the rest of his life. In a drama with all the zealous players and plot twists that mid-century anticommunist furor could muster, Alger Hiss, rising statesman, became Alger Hiss, Soviet spy.

Many argue the rush to brand Alger Hiss a spy is a zealous overstatement of the facts (i.e., Cook, 1958; Smith, 1976): Facts, upon which they contend there is little consensus. Facts, that continue to grow as governments slowly release relevant documents. Facts, that increasingly cloud as the motivations and linkages of supporting players come to light. For others (Wienstein, 1997) time and revelation have only solidified the case against Hiss. Regardless of one's conclusion on the matter, the evidence against Alger

Figure 10.1 Undated photo of Alger Hiss. Courtesy of the Library of Congress.

Hiss, the central "facts" of the case, largely begin and end with one man, Whittaker Chambers.

THE GOVERNMENT'S STAR WITNESS

Whittaker Chambers was the first person to publicly implicate Alger Hiss in pro-Soviet espionage. Chamber's motives, reliability, and veracity in the matter are the subject of considerable debate. Where Hiss projected the cool patrician detachment of a career diplomat, Chambers has been described as, "disturbed, idealistic, dysfunctional" (Olmsted, 2002, pp. 28–29). Notably, though, Olmsted adds one other adjective to her depiction of Chambers, "brilliant."

Born Vivian Jay Chambers, the man who would later adopt the more cosmopolitan sounding "Whittaker" had a difficult childhood. Chambers himself described feelings of separation and the negative influence of mentally ill relatives (Tanenhaus, 1998). Despite the troubled start, Chambers was accepted to Columbia University where his writing was recognized for its superior quality and decried for its controversial content. This later aspect coalesced into a small uprising over Chamber's dramatic work "A Play for Puppets." Zeligs (1967) describes the work as, "a disrespectful treatment of an incident in the life of Christ." Disenchanted with the public outcry, Chambers left the university in 1923. Soon thereafter, Chambers found the path that would eventually lead him to Alger Hiss.

Looking a bit like famed character actor, Sydney Greenstreet, Chambers was a plump figure with narrow eyes and bad teeth. Not unlike the Greenstreet portrayal of self-interested and inherently suspect Signor Ferrari in the film *Casasblanca* (1942) Whittaker Chamber's shifting alliances went straight to his credibility. According to Tanenhaus (1998) Chambers was profoundly influenced by Vladimir Lenin's *Soviets at Work.* So moved was Chambers that he joined the Communist Party of the United States (CPUSA) in 1925. While a member of the CPUSA, Chambers used his literary talent to write articles and short stories for party periodicals. As a curious aside, among Chamber's more notable nonpolitical publications was the translation of Felix Stalton's classic children's book, *Bambi, a Life in the Woods.*

By 1932, Chambers involvement in Communist politics gained dimension. He was instructed to begin work as a courier, assisting Soviet agents in the transportation of documents. According to Chamber's (1952) memoir, *Witness,* he worked as part of a group supporting Soviet GRU (*Glavnoe Razvedyvatel'noe Upravlenie* [sic], Main Intelligence Directorate) operations under the command of Alexander Ulrich (aka Ulanovsky). One of the individuals Chambers encountered in this capacity was Harold Ware. Ware was the founder of the so-called Ware Group, an organization of United States government employees who belonged to the CPUSA. Among the members of the Ware Group (later identified by Chambers) were brothers Alger and Donald Hiss.

While the idealized philosophy of Lenin was highly attractive to Chambers, the machinations of late 1930s Stalinist politics were wholly another matter. Worried by the looming threat of Stalinist purges, Chambers began to distance himself from his ideological compatriots. Fearing that other CPUSA associates (e.g., Juliet Poyntz) had been lured back to Moscow, only to be "purged," Chambers refused several requests that he go to the Soviet Union (Tanenhaus, 1998, pp. 131–133). As Chamber's paranoia mounted, he began to secretly collect documents that he would later use to protect himself and his family should his fears be realized. Chamber's disillusionment came to a head with the 1939 signing of the Hitler-Stalin (Molotov-Ribbentrop) Non-Aggression Pact. In an ironic twist of loyalties, Chambers became fearful that information he had funneled to the Soviets would be given to the Nazis. He discussed this with Issac Levine, a Russian-born journalist and anticommunist. In September 1939, Levine arranged a meeting between Chambers and Adolf Berle, an Assistant Secretary of State to President Franklin Roosevelt. With the encouragement of Berle and an assurance of immunity from prosecution, Chambers began to name names (Weinstein, 1997, p. 292). While most of the individuals implicated were of little consequence, others resonated more deeply. Among this later category were State Department officials, Donald and Alger Hiss.

THE HOUSE UN-AMERICAN ACTIVITIES COMMITTEE

The Congressional committee ultimately responsible for the fall of Alger Hiss began in 1934 as the McCormack-Dickstein Committee. Formally organized as the Special Committee on Un-American Activities Authorized to Investigate Nazi Propaganda and Certain Other Propaganda Activities, the most notable investigation of McCormack-Dickstein concerned the "Business Plot," a foiled attempt to stage a military coup for the overthrow of Franklin Roosevelt's presidency.

In 1938 under Representative Martin Dies, the reformed House Committee on Un-American Activities (1938–1944) held superficial investigations on the Ku Klux Klan and of west coast Japanese internment camps, but ultimately focused on anticommunist activities.

In 1946 the House Committee on Un-American Activities was made a permanent house committee under Public Law 601. The primary mandate of this body was the investigation of individuals and organizations suspected of holding communist sympathies. In 1947, the committee investigated the federal Theater Project and began extensive hearings that would ultimately lead to the "blacklisting" of over 300 individuals connected to the motion picture industry. In 1948, the Committee undertook investigations of the federal government that brought Alger Hiss into their sights.

With its investigation of self-proclaimed "Yippies" Abbie Hoffman and Jerry Rubin, HUAC lost credibility. The pair openly mocked HUAC hearings with Hoffman appearing in a Santa Claus suit and Rubin blowing large bubble gum bubbles while their supporters gave committee members Nazi salutes.

Ironically, within days of Richard Nixon's assumption of the presidency, Congress voted to rename HUAC the "House Committee on Internal Security." In the wake of the reformation, Committee chairman, Representative Richard Ichord, clarified the intent of the new committee, "The present mandate is admittedly ambiguous. It gives rise to the thought that the Committee is concerned with political ideas. I am not interested in any witch hunt...or pillorying anybody for unorthodox thoughts" (Geoghegan, 1969).

Figure 10.2 Miss Elizabeth Bentley seated at a table during a House Un-American Activities Committee meeting; to the right are attorney William Marbury and his client Alger Hiss, 1948. Courtesy of the Library of Congress.

Preferring to hold his trump card for a later time, Chambers did not produce his cache of incriminating documents at this meeting. As a consequence, when Assistant Secretary Berle reported the meeting to the president, Roosevelt took no action (Tanenhaus, 1998, p. 163). Roosevelt's hesitance notwithstanding, Berle referred the matter to the Federal Bureau of Investigation (FBI). While the FBI chose to interview Chambers on at least three occasions, it was not until November 1945 that his information drew full government attention. Two notable defections changed Chambers's value to the government: that of Walter Krivitsky, a former GRU agent; and Elizabeth Bentley, a former Soviet agent whose identification of over 80 American spies may have fueled much of the McCarthy era zealousness. With Bentley's testimony in front of the House Un-American Activities Committee (HUAC), the government needed the corroboration that Chambers could supply.

HOUSE UN-AMERICAN ACTIVITIES COMMITTEE

Interestingly, Chambers's fortunes had changed dramatically in the six years since he met with Adolf Berle. He had garnered a position with *Time* magazine and had managed promotion to the level of senior editor. As Dorothy Sterling (1984), a former *Time* co-worker asserts, Chambers's reversal grew into an ironic anticommunist militancy:

Reporting from China, Theodore H. White saw his criticisms of Chiang Kai-shek's autocratic regime replaced with encomiums of Chiang as a defender of democratic principles. When researchers in Time's New York office protested the inaccuracy of the foreign news stories, Chambers habitually replied, "Truth doesn't matter." The facts had to be altered to fit his anti-Communist crusade.

Whether Chambers's apparent about-face on the matter of communist ideology can be regarded as genuine, members of HUAC made clear their resolve. The most notable member of HUAC was a freshman congressional representative from California's 12th district, Richard Nixon. By the time Representative Nixon was appointed to HUAC, he was well practiced in the game of communist baiting. Many attribute Nixon's 1946 success in unseating Democratic rival, incumbent Jerry Voorhis, to a smear campaign that alleged Voorhis's collaboration with "communist-controlled" labor unions.

On August 3, 1948, Chambers appeared before HUAC. In his testimony Chambers admitted his affiliation with and ultimate defection from CPUSA, but more importantly, he gave the names of Ware Group members including Hiss.

Upon learning of Chambers's testimony, Hiss sent a telegram to HUAC chairman, J. Parnell Thomas, emphatically denying the charges and requesting an opportunity to speak for himself:

> I do not know Mr. Chambers and, so far as I am aware, have never laid eyes on him. There is no basis for the statements about me made to your committee. I would further appreciate the opportunity of appearing before your committee.

Hiss appeared before HUAC a day later on August 5. In a calm and straightforward manner, Hiss stated, "I am not and never have been a member of the Communist Party." He repeated the text from his telegram asserting he had "never laid eyes on [Chambers]" adding "I would like to have the opportunity to do so."

Much of the August 5 exchange between HUAC members and Hiss was rather benign on its face. Committee members probed various aspects of Hiss's education and professional background. The questioning then turned to Hiss's knowledge of Chambers and individuals named by him as Ware Group members. Points in the hearing that otherwise augured crucial information became the site of a peculiar levity:

Mr. Stripling (the Committee's chief investigator): You say you have never seen Mr. Chambers?

Mr. Hiss: The name means absolutely nothing to me, Mr. Stripling.

Mr. Stripling: I have here, Mr. Chairman, a picture which was made last Monday by the Associated Press...Mr. Hiss, and ask you if you have ever known an individual who resembles this picture.

Mr. Hiss: I would much rather see the individual. I have looked at all the pictures I was able to get hold of in, I think it was, yesterday's paper which had the pictures. If this is a picture of Mr. Chambers, he is not particularly unusual looking. He looks like a lot of people. I might even mistake him for the chairman of this committee [Laughter] (HUAC, 1948).

The glib response aside, Hiss appeared to have largely disarmed the Committee. President Truman dubbed the matter, "a red herring." Popular accounts generally hold that the membership was ready to dismiss the matter, save for Nixon. Inasmuch as the HUAC circus featured one contest of ideals: the communists versus democracy, its subplot was equally compelling. Apart from the obvious contrast between Hiss and Chambers there was a more substantive contest at issue. In one corner stood the handsome, if slightly effete Hiss, vetted by the liberal Eastern establishment. In the other loomed the brooding figure of Nixon, the conservative working-class boy, spurned by the Ivy League, bitter and offended at the foppish diplomat. Undaunted by the will of the Committee, Nixon pressed and was made chairman of a subcommittee to determine whether Chambers or Hiss was telling the truth.

On August 7, the Nixon subcommittee met in the Federal Courthouse in New York City. At this hearing, Nixon, Representative John McDowell, Representative Edward Herbert, and investigators for HUAC interviewed Chambers. The questions varied across many topics, each designed to probe the depth of Chambers's personal knowledge of the Hiss family. Over the course of approximately three hours, Chambers provided detailed descriptions of the Hiss family home, their dog, and nicknames for one another. Chambers recounted having stayed in the Hiss home for several nights. Numerous otherwise innocuous details of Hiss family life were discussed, but on the matter of their hobbies, an important event was uncovered. According to Chambers, Alger Hiss and his wife, Priscilla, held a mutual passion for bird watching:

Mr. Mandel: Did Mr. Hiss have any hobbies?

Mr. Chambers: Yes, he did. They both had the same hobby, amateur ornithologists, bird observers. They used to get up early in the morning and go to Glen Echo, out the canal, to observe birds. I recall once they saw, to their great excitement, a prothonotary warbler.

Mr. McDowell: A very rare specimen?

Mr. Chambers: I never saw one. I am also fond of birds. (HUAC, 1948)

Approximately ten days later, Hiss was interviewed by the Nixon subcommittee, this time convened in Washington, DC. Over half of the committee's time was spent in an exchange relating as to whether Hiss could make either an identification of Chambers from a photograph or whether Hiss could recall if the person in said photograph had spent a week with the Hiss family approximately 15 years earlier.

At one point, Hiss introduces the name "George Crosley." Crosley, according to Hiss, was a writer that he met while at the State Department. In the course of their acquaintance, Hiss rented Crosley an apartment and allowed him to stay with the Hiss family a

THE PROTHONOTARY WARBLER

Protonotaria citrea

This bird takes its name from the yellow cloaks of the Roman Catholic *protonotarii apostolicii,* a class of papal official. The Prothonotary Warbler is a small insect-eating songbird with bright golden-yellow plumage. On average these birds weigh about half an ounce, measure 5.5'' in length, and fly on wings spanning 8.75''. Prothonotary Warblers can be found in wooded swamps, river bottoms, mangroves, and wet forests at low elevation. They tend to nest in hollowed tree trunk cavities left by woodpeckers (Dunn and Garrett, 1997; Petit, 1999).

few days until furniture could be delivered (Hiss, 1957, p. 20). In a detail that became a source of further legal rumination, Hiss also told the committee that he gave Crosley a long disused Model A Ford. The Committee made much of this "gift," but Hiss explained that the car was so old and forgotten that he had trouble remembering where he had parked it.

After a brief continuation on the subject of the relationship between Hiss, Crosley, and the Model A, Nixon turned the questioning to other matters. The committee discussed seemingly mundane details of the Hiss family's daily life: their apartments, their maid, the family dog. Then, in what was a defining moment for the committee, Hiss was asked about his hobbies:

Mr. Nixon: What hobby, if any, do you have, Mr. Hiss?

Mr. Hiss: Tennis and amateur ornithology.

Mr. Nixon: Is your wife interested in ornithology?

Mr. Hiss: I also like to swim and also like to sail. My wife is interested in ornithology, as I am, through my interest. Maybe I am using too big a word to say an ornithologist because I am pretty amateur, but I have been interested in it since I was in Boston. I think anybody who knows me would know that.

Mr. McDowell: Did you ever see a prothonotary warbler?

Mr. Hiss: I have right here on the Potomac. Do you know that place?

The Chairman: What is that?

Mr. Nixon: Have you ever seen one?

Mr. Hiss: Did you see it in the same place?

Mr. McDowell: I saw one in Arlington.

Mr. Hiss: They come back and nest in those swamps. Beautiful yellow head, a gorgeous bird. (HUAC, 1948)

For members of the committee, this detail confirmed that Chambers knew Hiss. In his memoir, Hiss dismisses the value of the evidence, "The prothonotary was to become... the prime alleged proof of a close relationship between Chambers and me—as if an enthusiast boasts of his finds only to intimate friends" (Hiss, 1957, p. 50).

Perhaps more damning than anything said by Chambers was the testimony of other individuals previously interviewed by HUAC. Several close associates and former Hiss co-workers found themselves in equally tenuous positions. Henry Collins, former Agricultural Adjustment Administration (AAA) employee, was discussed first. Committee investigator Stripling got right to his point, "...I happen to know pretty conclusively that not only is Mr. Collins a Communist but he has been a Communist for many years. In fact, when he used to work in the AAA he was notorious, notorious for sitting around talking about communism" (HUAC, 1948). John Abt and Lee Pressmen were given the same treatment. Hiss denied knowledge of their communist sympathies. Stripling then made the accusation more directly:

> You are an intelligent person and not naive enough that you wouldn't know a Communist if you saw one. Furthermore, I read a lot of Government files from time to time—and I don't say this disparagingly—but I have seen your name for years in Government files as a person

suspected of Communist activity. Now, there has to be some basis for the thing. Why would Charles Kramer refuse to say whether he knew you on the ground of self-incrimination? Why would Henry Collins answer that way? Why would all these people say that? (HUAC, 1948)

In fashion typical of his notably oblique tact toward the committee, Hiss responded, "Do you think those are relevant questions to this inquiry?" It was a lawyerly response, a technical response, perhaps even accurate, but it failed to satisfy those who wanted a categorical denial from Hiss.

In the remaining minutes of the meeting, the committee decided to give Hiss an opportunity to directly confront his accuser in an open forum. Accordingly, the next round of hearings were scheduled for August 25. Before the scheduled meeting could take place, two important things took place. The first of these was a secret meeting between Nixon and Chambers at Chambers's farm. Several sources state that Nixon was given "secret evidence" that fueled his drive to get Hiss. The second intervention was of a more fateful nature. Harry Dexter White, a former Assistant Secretary of State under Roosevelt (also named by Chambers and Elizabeth Bentley) died of a heart attack several days after being questioned by HUAC. Fearing a backlash in the press, Nixon and others decided to accelerate the proceedings.

As Hiss (1957, pp. 80–81) states, he received a telephone call from a member of the HUAC administrative staff on the morning of the 17th. The staffer asked Hiss to meet committee member, Representative John McDowell later that day. At approximately 5:30 that afternoon, Hiss received a call directly from McDowell. The congressman asked Hiss to meet him at the Commodore Hotel, a few blocks from Hiss's office. According to Hiss, McDowell added that "Nixon and one other" would be with him.

Upon arriving at the hotel, Hiss realized that he had been summoned, not to an informal discussion, but to a speedily contrived meeting of the Nixon subcommittee. He was greeted with the presence of not only Nixon and McDowell, but a cadre of staffers, a stenographer, and, perhaps the coup de grace, notification of Chambers's imminent arrival (Hiss, 1957, pp. 82).

Chambers's version of events was not unlike that of Hiss. He had been plucked up by staffers in Washington and quietly whisked to New York. Chambers describes the scene,

When I entered the room, Alger Hiss did not turn to look at me. When I sat down, he did not glance at me....Until we faced each other...I had been testifying about the man as a memory and a name. Now I saw again the man himself...it was shocking. (Chambers, 1952; 602)

Several key things took place at the Commodore Hotel hearing. Hiss identified Chambers as the previously discussed "George Crosley." Chambers denied having used the alias. The committee again returned to specifics of the apartment rental, debts between the men, and the closeness of their association. Nixon, however, got to the heart of the matter, "Mr. Hiss, another point that I want to be clear on, Mr. Chambers said he was a Communist and that you were a Communist" (HUAC, 1948). In trademark fashion, the reply given by Hiss was indirect, "I heard him."

During the exchanges that followed, Hiss inadvertently set in motion events that would culminate in his own prosecution. Representative McDowell turned to Chambers for explicit confirmation of the charges:

Mr. McDowell: Mr. Chambers, is this the man, Alger Hiss, who was also a member of the Communist Party at whose home you stayed?

Mr. Nixon: According to your testimony.

Mr. McDowell: You make the identification positive?

Mr. Chambers: Positive identification.
   (At this point, Mr. Hiss arose and walked in the direction of Mr. Chambers).

Mr. Hiss: May I say for the record at this point, that I would like to invite Mr. Whittaker Chambers to make those same statements out of the presence of this committee without their being privileged for suit for libel. I challenge you to do it, and I hope you will do it damned quickly.... (HUAC, 1948)

On August 25, both Hiss and Chambers appeared before the previously scheduled HUAC session. This meeting was significant for a number of reasons, not the least of which is its status as the first ever televised Congressional hearing. Much of what transpired was predictable. HUAC members armed with lease agreements and various documents tried to impeach Hiss's credibility. Hiss remained defiant and aloof. In what has become a somewhat famous quotation, Chambers characterized Hiss as, "...a devoted and at that time a rather romantic Communist" (HUAC, 1948). More crucial to subsequent events, this hearing (and to a lesser degree, those preceding it) helped establish a timeline for the

Figure 10.3   Whittaker Chambers (right), *Time* **magazine editor, takes the stand before the House Un-American Activities Committee, reiterating his testimony that Alger Hiss was a secret communist, as Alger Hiss (center) looks on. Courtesy of the Library of Congress.**

association between Hiss and Chambers. According to the version given by Hiss, he last saw Chambers in 1935. Hiss discontinued the relationship after Chambers failed to pay rent for the subleased apartment. In contrast, Chambers stated that he last saw Hiss "around the end of 1938." According to Chambers's version, the association was dissolved after an unsuccessful attempt to break Hiss away from the Communist Party.

Within days of the televised hearing, HUAC published an interim report in which Hiss (1957, p. 204) was characterized as "vague and evasive." In response, Hiss (1957) published a 14-page reproach of HUAC for "using the great powers and prestige of the United States Congress to help sworn traitors to besmirch any American they may pick upon."

THE CIVIL SUIT

In an apparent answer to Hiss's challenge, on August 27, Chambers appeared on the radio program *Meet the Press* moderated by Lawrence Spivak. Chambers knew he would be asked to restate his charge that Hiss was a communist, "He [Hiss] would then be free to sue me. I did not want to be sued...Nor did I believe that Hiss would want a suit" (Chambers, 1952, p. 705). Following Chambers's appearance on the program, Hiss filed suit on October 8, 1949.

As part of discovery for the suit, Hiss's attorneys asked Chambers to produce, "...any correspondence, either typewritten or in handwriting from any member of the Hiss family" (Hiss, 1957, p. 159). Shortly thereafter, Chamber went to the Brooklyn home of his wife's nephew, Nathan Levine. From Levine's home, the pair went to Levine's mother's home. They went to a second floor bathroom, "where, over the tub a small window opened into dumbwaiter shaft that had long been out of use. Inside the shaft was some kind of small shelf or ledge. There Levine had laid 'My Things'" (Chambers, 1952, p. 736).

The large envelope Levine exhumed from the dumbwaiter contained a number of items: four notes handwritten by Alger Hiss; 65 typewritten documents (copies of State Department documents, each dated between January and April 1938); and five strips of 35mm film (Hiss, 1957, p. 160). On November 17, the papers were delivered to the defense, but Chambers chose to secretly withhold the film. The papers, soon thereafter known as the "Baltimore Papers" were a disaster for Hiss. If genuine, the Baltimore Papers showed that not only had Hiss known Chambers after 1936, but that Hiss had engaged in espionage.

When William Marbury, Hiss's attorney, continued to take a formal statement from Chambers, he was confronted by evidence that not only obviated the slander suit, but placed Hiss in direct danger of criminal indictment. Not surprisingly, the HUAC took quick notice of the new evidence.

Chambers explained his hesitance in producing the documents as an effort to protect Hiss (who he purportedly regarded as an old friend) from needless tragedy. During the course of the civil suit investigation, however, Chambers became convinced that "Hiss was determined to destroy me—and my wife if possible." It is reasonable to infer that Chambers knew a loss in the civil trial would probably result in his own Justice Department prosecution. Moreover, it is likely that Chambers knew Marbury and the Hiss legal team were attempting to assemble evidence of his reputed homosexual encounters, as well as his family's history of mental illness and suicide.

While Chambers had turned over the paper documents, he still had possession of the film. Chambers placed the film into a hollowed-out pumpkin, and returned the pumpkin to the pumpkin patch on his Maryland farm. In his memoir, Chambers is philosophical about the choice to hide (and ultimately reveal) the microfilm:

> No act of mine was more effective in forcing open the Hiss Case than my act of dividing the documentary evidence against Hiss...It was my decisive act in the Case. For when the second part of the divided evidence, the microfilm, fell into the hands of the Committee, it became impossible to suppress the Hiss Case...That is the meaning of the pumpkin—a meaning that has been widely missed, I feel, in laughter at the pumpkin itself. (Chambers, 1952, p. 742)

On the evening of December 2, 1948, Chambers accompanied two HUAC investigators to his farm whereupon he led them to the hollowed-out pumpkin. Upon inspection, the film was found to include photographs of State and Navy Department documents. During the following months of the scandal, members of the press (amused by the opportunity for cheeky alliteration) came to call the entire set of documents and microfilm "The Pumpkin Papers."

Immediately following the "discovery" of the new evidence, the Hiss legal team published a statement promising, "full cooperation to the Department of Justice and to the grand jury in a further investigation of this matter." In an instant, the controversy was redefined. No longer was it a matter of the erstwhile diplomat defending his reputation against the slander of a godless, homosexual communist. From that point forward, it was whether Alger Hiss, former State Department official had been a Soviet agent. In an extremely small saving grace for Hiss, the statute of limitations for espionage was five years, and the incriminating evidence concerned possible acts at least a decade old.

The bombshell of Chambers's Pumpkin Papers resulted in his summons by the grand jury then empaneled for the Southern District of New York. The grand jury was investigating possible violation of espionage laws. Not coincidentally, Hiss also appeared before the grand jury. Hiss testified on numerous occasions between December 7 and December 15, 1948. On the last day of the jury's term, the panel indicted Hiss for perjury. While Hiss had managed to dodge the bullet of an espionage charge, the statute of limitations for perjury in his testimony to HUAC had yet to expire.

THE FIRST TRIAL

The first Hiss perjury trial began on May 31, 1949, at the Manhattan Federal Courthouse in New York City. Hiss was charged with two counts of perjury, both of which stemmed from his testimony before a federal grand jury the previous December. Hiss was charged with lying in his testimony that he never gave documents to Whittaker Chambers, as well as when he stated he had not seen Chambers since 1937.

Predictably, Whittaker Chambers was the prosecution's primary witness. Chambers told the court that he had begun passing State Department documents with Hiss in 1937. He stated that he and Hiss followed Soviet agent Colonel Boris Bykov's directives for espionage. Included in these directives was the instruction that documents should be carried home and retyped. Chamber identified the documents he had earlier provided and stated that they had been given to him by Hiss at Hiss's home.

Whatever misgivings Chambers may have held with regard to potential character assassination were fully realized at the hands of defense attorney, Lloyd Paul Stryker. In his cross-examination of Chambers, Stryker probed many unsavory and bizarre areas of Chambers's past. He recounted Chambers's play written while at Columbia, and deemed

NIXON'S KODAK MOMENT

One of the primary pieces of evidence against Alger Hiss were the strips of 35mm film Whittaker Chambers secreted away inside a hollowed-out pumpkin. Establishing the date of manufacture for the film would in some measure corroborate Chambers's story. Accordingly, HUAC member, Richard Nixon, sent the film to Eastman Kodak for verification. Chambers stated that he took the pictures in 1938, but results from Kodak indicated the film was made in 1945.

Nixon went "into complete shock." The case that he intended to use as a springboard to national acclaim would instead forever bury him. Nixon and fellow HUAC members called a press conference. They were steeling themselves for a deep public humiliation. Nixon stated that they were going to confess, "we were sold a bill of goods . . . we were all wet."

The phone rang again. It was Kodak, "an error had been made." According to company records, the lot code used for film stock made in 1945 was also used for a previous run in 1938. The HUAC members were spared, but in all the excitement Nixon nearly forgot to tell Chambers—who in the desperation of the moment, had purchased cyanide with which to commit suicide (Powers, 1998, p. 224; Chambers, 1952, pp. 768–771).

it "an offensive treatment of Christ." Stryker asked whether Chambers had ever lived with a New Orleans prostitute called "One-eyed Annie." He got to the heart of Chambers's politics by asking whether he had been, "for some fourteen years an enemy and traitor of the United States of America?"

Chambers had little choice but to acknowledge most of the defense counsel's claims, refuting only his alleged cohabitation with the prostitute. Stryker's final press concerned Chambers's timing and whether he might be more motivated by hopes of helping Republicans portray Harry Truman as soft on communism than any abstract feelings of patriotism.

Esther Chambers, Whittaker's wife, was the next prosecution witness. In testimony generally rebuked in Hiss's (1957) memoir, she provides numerous details of the relationship between her family and the Hisses. Her primary value was her assertion that the relationship extended well beyond January 1937.

After the Chamberses' testimony, there was a parade of witnesses tying Hiss to the typewritten State Department papers supplied by the star witness. Nathan Levine described his trip into the dumbwaiter. HUAC investigator Donald Appel recounted his journey to the Chamberses' pumpkin patch. Walter Anderson, a records expert from the State Department, outlined the importance of each typewritten page and of the handwritten notes. Hiss's own secretary, Eunice Lincoln, was brought in to testify that Hiss often took work home with him.

Where the testimony of both Chambers and the other prosecution witnesses set the stage, Ramos C. Feehan of the FBI laboratory provided substance for the state's case. Feehan explained laboratory comparisons made between documents known to have been typed by Priscilla Hiss[2] circa 1936–1937 (sic. "the Hiss Standards") and the 65 pages retrieved from the Levine's dumbwaiter. Feehan concluded that the two sets of documents had been typed on the same Woodstock brand typewriter. Feehan stated that he "reached the conclusion that the same machine was used to type Baltimore Exhibits 5 through 9 and 11 through 47 that was used to type the four known Standards which were submitted to [him] for comparison with the questioned documents" (Kisseloff, 2006). Feehan based his conclusions in part on comparisons of individual letters. This testimony, along with innumerable murky details regarding ownership, location, and condition of the typewriter would give Hiss and his supporters fodder for decades of appeals and speculation about government conspiracy. Interestingly, however, Feehan was not cross-examined at either Hiss trial.

In its presentation, the defense tried to convince the jury on three points: (a) Alger Hiss was a man of such reputation and achievement that his involvement in espionage would have been absurd; (b) The state's main witness, Whittaker Chambers, was a mentally unstable traitor with a past so suspect as to nullify anything he said; (c) The Woodstock typewriter allegedly used to prepare the Baltimore Papers was given to a former Hiss family maid sometime before the documents' 1938 date, thus rendering it impossible for either of the Hisses to have been the typist.

As to the first goal, the Hiss legal team paraded a cast of legal and diplomatic luminaries of immense public status and credibility. Supreme Court Justices Stanley Reed and Felix Frankfurter portrayed Hiss as a man of "excellent" character. Former Democratic presidential candidate John W. Davis as well as future candidate Adlai Stevenson made similar appraisals. If the matter were merely one of establishing credentials and references the contest was hardly close.

Defense attorney Stryker's cross-examination of Whittaker Chambers bordered on a roasting. The list of character witnesses was beyond challenge. All that remained was to

THE WOODSTOCK 5N: SERIAL NUMBER N230099

The controversy surrounding the Hiss family's Woodstock typewriter was a harbinger of the forensic detective work so prominent in modern criminal investigations. Both sides of the Hiss case raised complex technical issues that required numerous expert witnesses. Does each typewriter have a unique "fingerprint"? Can two different typists using the same machine produce identical typed pages? Can one typewriter be altered to produce results identical to another? These issues along with questions of manufacturing process, wear profiles, and repair techniques were all explored during the Hiss trials and subsequent appeals. While typewriters are seldom the focus of modern forensic investigations, the same kind of issues raised in the Hiss case continue to be hotly debated.

Gil Green (1984), a prominent CPUSA figure, cites a 1959 correspondence between FBI director J. Edgar Hoover and a New York Special Agent in Charge, "To alter a typewriter to match a known model would require a large amount of typewriter specimens and weeks of laboratory work. It is not felt that this technique of altering a typewriter should be considered in this connection..." Adding fuel to the Hiss controversy, this exchange indicates that the FBI had at least considered the possibility of "forgery by typewriter."

defeat the state's case regarding the Woodstock typewriter. This last challenge proved the most difficult.

According to Hiss's testimony, the old Woodstock typewriter had been given to their former maid, Claudie Catlett, sometime in 1936. Catlett's testimony corroborated Hiss (Cook, 1958). Moreover, Catlett also recalled having seen a Hiss family visitor named "Crosby" around the time at issue. Catlett also stated that "Crosby" had visited on several occasions when the Hisses were not home.

Raymond "Mike" Catlett and Perry "Pat" Catlett, Claudia Catlett's sons, likewise remembered being given the typewriter. In fact, it was Mike Catlett who had approached Donald Hiss when the typewriter's whereabouts and provenance became an issue (Hiss, 1957, p. 271). All three of the Catletts gave testimony. Ultimately, their testimony was of mixed value to the Hiss cause (Kisseloff, 2006). The Catletts had been repeatedly visited and interviewed by the FBI and HUAC investigators and in the process appeared to lose certainty on exact dates. This was important as the defense's case hinged on Hiss not seeing Chambers after the end of 1937. The fact that Catlett family (and related) testimony only narrowed the time window to "about three months" around the middle of January 1938 did little to help Hiss (Hiss, 1957, p. 273).

In its refutation of the charges, the defense offered an alternative theory of the purported espionage (Tanenhaus, 1998). During the same period Hiss was at the State Department, economist Julian Wadleigh was a staff member under Dean Acheson in the Trade Agreements Division. Wadleigh, like Chambers, would later admit to his CPUSA membership and, more importantly, to his theft and transmission of State Department documents. According to Wadleigh, he would take documents from the State Department and turn them over to an agent he knew as "Carl" (an alias used by Chambers). Carl would copy the documents and return them to Wadleigh for replacement. Chambers had previously testified to HUAC that Wadleigh might have passed some of the documents contained in the Baltimore Papers. Wadleigh denied that he was the source of the Baltimore documents. In an apparent change of recollection, Chambers's later testimony supported the idea that Wadleigh had not been the source of any Baltimore Papers. Nonetheless, the defense put forth the theory that Wadleigh, through his State Department access could have sneaked into Hiss' office and stolen documents while Hiss was not there.

Alger Hiss took the stand on June 23. Hiss admitted to writing the handwritten notes, but vehemently denied knowledge of either the microfilm or the typewritten State Department documents. Hiss also restated his grand jury testimony regarding the last time he saw Chambers. Echoing the testimony of the Catlett family, Hiss stated that he had given them the typewriter "in the fall of 1937."

Hiss was then subject to cross-examination by prosecutor Thomas Murphy. Murphy focused on discrepancies between Hiss's current and previous testimony. Murphy's tactics during the two trials would later become part of the appeals filed by Hiss.

Priscilla Hiss was the last defense witness in the first trial. Ironically, her testimony was more damaging to her husband's defense. Her seeming inconsistency and role as typist were treated in detail. In particular, she denied and then was forced to admit membership in the Socialist Party. Moreover, she was made to reconcile the fact that she told a grand jury that the typewriter might have been given to the Catletts as late as 1943.

The summations given by Stryker and Murphy were as impassioned and dramatic as one might expect in such a public trial. Chambers (1952, p. 791) describes defense attorney Lloyd Stryker as "spinning and flailing about like a dervish." In perspective, Stryker called Chambers "an enemy of the Republic, a blasphemer of Christ, a disbeliever in God, with no respect for matrimony or motherhood." This is in marked contrast to the defendant, who he characterized as "an honest...and falsely accused gentleman."

Prosecutor Murphy outlined a different path for the jury, "[The evidence left] only one inference...that the defendant, that smart, intelligent, American-born man gave [passed State Department secrets] to Chambers." As Murphy had stated in his opening, "If you don't believe Chambers, then we have no case..." (Zeligs, 1967, p. 366).

The case was given to the jury on July 6, 1949. After more than a day of deliberation, the jury notified the trial judge, Samuel Kaufman, that they were unable to reach a verdict. Kaufman urged the jury to try again. Within a few hours, the jury reported it was hopelessly deadlocked: eight for conviction; four for acquittal. Having no choice, Kaufman declared a mistrial. In later interviews, members of the jury revealed that the four voting for acquittal did so because they felt someone other than Alger or Priscilla Hiss had typed the documents on the Hiss family Woodstock.

THE SECOND TRIAL

The second perjury trial began November 17, 1949. Many changes in personnel ensured this would be a very different proceeding. Nixon and other conservatives were highly dissatisfied with Judge Samuel Kaufman's performance in the first trial. There were discussions of his possible impeachment. The ire directed at Kaufman centered on his refusal to allow the testimony of Hede Massing, a self-confessed Soviet agent. Massing was prepared to (and did eventually) testify to Hiss's involvement in espionage. Taking what might be considered a very strict view of the matter, Kaufman ruled that Massing's information was irrelevant to the trial. Kaufman was replaced by Judge Henry W. Goddard.

The defense team also made a major change. Lead defense attorney, Lloyd Stryker, was replaced by Claude Cross. The defense made a motion for a change of venue to Vermont. Thinking that Cross's more subdued style would play better in Vermont, he was brought on to head the defense effort. The defense was wrong in both instances. Their petition for a change of venue was denied; and Claude Cross's bookish style failed to connect with the jury.

As if the internal events were not sufficiently damaging, the external political climate was equally bad. In the months between the first and second trials, transforming world events had taken place. The Soviets detonated their first atomic bomb. Both the People's Republic of China and the German Democratic Republic were founded. For individuals looking to validate fears of communist domination, the timing for Hiss could not have been worse.

Returning prosecutor Murphy made one major change in his strategy: the inclusion of the aforementioned Hede Messing. Messing (1987) testified that she had met with Hiss at the home of another State Department official, Noel Field. Massing stated she told Hiss, "I understand that you are trying to get Noel Field away from my organization into yours." According to Massing, Hiss replied, "So you are this famous girl that is trying to get Noel Field away from me." While Massing could not remember who said it, she stated that one of them said to the other, "Whoever is going to win, we are working for the same boss."

Julian Wadleigh also reprised his role from the first trial. This time, he had to withstand a much more rigorous cross-examination by Cross. The defense suggested that it was

Wadleigh, not Hiss, who gave Chambers the documents. This was a substantial accusation, but it was logistically complex. In order for Wadleigh to have acted as the defense suggested, it would have required multiple thefts and multiple unnoticed returns. In the end, Wadleigh conceded that he did supply some documents to Chambers, but the defense could not prove he was the sole source.

What could have been a deft use of expert testimony for the defense degenerated into a wholesale evisceration prosecutor by Murphy. The defense called Dr. Carl A. Binger, a practicing Cornell psychiatrist, to provide an analysis of Whittaker Chambers's testimony. On direct testimony Binger categorized Chambers as a "psychopathic personality" and a "pathological liar."

In the cross-examination that followed Murphy suggested that Binger's assessments were little more than hollow psychobabble. Binger's conclusions were quickly turned back upon him. Binger suggested that Chambers's habit of repeatedly looking up at the ceiling was a sign of psychosis. When Murphy pointed out that Binger had himself looked at the ceiling over 50 times in an hour, it was clear that the witness's testimony was rapidly unraveling. Similar farcical turns took place over discussion of Chambers's "untidiness," whereupon the doctor was asked to reconcile the notably untidy Albert Einstein and Thomas Edison. Furthering the doctor's losses were questions surrounding Chambers's numerous equivocations during testimony. The doctor was asked what conclusions should be drawn from the 158 equivocations in the defendant's own testimony. Perhaps most comically, Murphy attacked Binger's assertion that the act of hiding the film in the pumpkin was a symptom of a psychopathic personality. Murphy facetiously asked what conclusions could be drawn from other famous hidings, such as the secreting of the baby "Moses in the bulrushes."

In his memoir, Hiss notes his displeasure with the latitude Judge Goddard granted Murphy:

> [He] was lenient with prosecution witnesses and brusque with defense witnesses. And though he found no occasion to restrain Murphy's attitude toward defense witnesses, Chambers received his protection when Mr. Cross was questioning him. (1957, p. 346)

Hiss's objections aside, the second trial dragged three weeks longer than the first. In his summation, Cross resorted to rather lawyerly technical points. Points that likely resonated with a methodical intellect like Hiss, but missed with less linear thinkers on the jury. An instance of this is Cross's concession that the Baltimore Papers had been typed on the Hiss typewriter. As Cross put it, "it is not the question of what typewriter was used, but who the typist was." Cross suggested that Chambers, in an effort to frame Hiss, may have secretly gotten use of the typewriter after the Hisses discarded it.

Murphy took a more emotive route in his summation. He described the evidence "immutable." Murphy concluded that the friendship between Hiss and Chambers as well as the stolen documents proved Hiss, "[is] a traitor...in love with their philosophy, not ours."

On January 20, 1950, the jury returned its verdict, "We find the defendant guilty on the first count and guilty on the second." Five days later Alger Hiss would be given the maximum sentence. Before Judge Goddard pronounced his fate, Hiss made a statement concluding, "...in the future the full facts of how Whittaker Chambers was able to carry out forgery by typewriter will be disclosed."

THE APPEALS AND AFTERWARD

Later the same year on December 7, the Second Circuit Court of Appeals affirmed Hiss's conviction. Three months later, the U.S. Supreme Court refused to hear Hiss's case. The vote was four to two. Justices Hugo Black and William Douglas voted to grant the review. Justices Frankfurter, Reed, and Tom Clark all voted to disqualify themselves, based on connections either to Hiss or to the case. Hiss reported to Lewisburg Federal Penitentiary on March 3, 1951. He served 44 months of his five-year sentence before being released for good behavior on November 27, 1954.[3]

For others involved in the Hiss trials, mixed blessings were in store. Whittaker Chambers published a memoir, *Witness*, in 1952. It was a widely acclaimed best seller. Arthur Schlesinger, Jr., called it, "one of the greatest of all American autobiographies." Chambers enjoyed financial success as a consequence of the book's reception. On July 9, 1961, Chambers died as a result of a heart attack.

Future President Ronald Reagan credited Chambers's influence in his abandonment of the Democratic Party. In 1984, President Reagan posthumously awarded Chambers the Medal of Freedom. In 1988, Whittaker Chambers's farm, site of the Pumpkin Patch was granted status as a National Landmark by the Department of the Interior. Even today, many conservatives regard Chambers as something of a national hero.

HUAC member Richard Nixon was elected as the 36th vice president of the United States under Dwight Eisenhower. The pair were reelected in 1956. Nixon lost his bid for the presidency to John F. Kennedy. In 1968, Nixon won the election against Democrat Hubert Humphrey to become the 37th president. In the wake of the Watergate Crisis Nixon resigned from office on August 9, 1974.

Nixon never seemed to forget Hiss, remarking on the matter at several occasions. Two particularly intriguing anecdotes demonstrate Nixon's perspective: In July 1972, Nixon admonished White House aide John Ehrlichman, "If you cover up, you're going to get caught. And if you lie you're going to be guilty of perjury. Now basically that was the whole story of the Hiss case. It is not the issue that will harm you; it is the *cover-up* that is damaging." Later, in 1973, Nixon told aides H.R. Haldeman and Charles Colson, "...You know the great thing about...I got to say for Hiss. He never ratted on anybody else. Never. He never ratted" (Kisseloff, 2006).

As for the final curtain on Alger Hiss, he managed to outlive nearly everyone else connected to the case. In 1957, he released a memoir, *In the Court of Public Opinion*, and in it he comments extensively on Chambers's memoir, *Witness*. Throughout his life, Hiss maintained his innocence. In 1972 the "Hiss Act" was repealed as unconstitutional. The act was passed by Congress for the sole purpose of depriving Hiss of his government pension. In 1975, Hiss was readmitted to the Massachusetts Bar. In 1978, with the assistance of the National Emergency Civil Liberties Committee, Hiss filed a petition in federal court for a writ of *coram nobis* to overturn the guilty verdict on the reason of prosecutorial misconduct. Hiss alleged this misconduct was revealed in FBI files obtained through the Freedom of Information Act (Kisseloff, 2006). Through successive appeals the petition was denied. On November 14, 1996, four days after his 92nd birthday, Hiss died in New York City.

THE VERONA POSTSCRIPT

As with any good mystery, the controversy surrounding the Hiss case did not die with Hiss. Where advances in technology and the lens of historical perspective give closure to many scandals, the legacy of Alger Hiss remains clouded. As Roazen (2003, p. 35) states, "The [Hiss] cases has haunted American liberalism for over fifty years now...the contours of the controversy would seem to have expanded as the years have passed."

Numerous details have emerged, but little has been settled. In October 1999, after 51 years, grand jury transcripts in the Hiss case were unsealed by court order. Many contend that these records show misconduct by the government, by Representative Nixon, in particular. In a similarly evocative turn, former Soviet KGB officials have come forward with news that they have no proof Hiss was a Soviet agent.

Arguably the most provocative new evidence in the Hiss case has come from declassified intelligence materials. At the height of the Cold War, U.S. security agencies intercepted and decoded several thousand Soviet intelligence transmissions. These transmissions have since become known as the Verona cables. The English translations of these cables were made public in the mid-1990s. One of these transmissions in particular, "Venona Washington to Moscow No. 1822, a March 30, 1945," includes discussion of an agent code-named "ALES." Many believe that this was a reference to Hiss. The ensuing debate was nothing less than an academic firestorm. On one side there are scholars, such as Alexander Vassiliev and Allen Weinstein (2000), who contend Hiss was guilty. On the other side are Hiss defenders such as John Lowenthal (2000) and Victor Navasky (2005). These four Hiss researchers represent some of the most heated exchanges.

On a certain level, one might wonder why it matters. What does it change whether Hiss was a spy? To leave the question framed in terms of one man is to miss the larger point. While most of the original actors in this drama have passed into eternity, a new generation has taken up the case as a kind of litmus test. As posthumous honors by Ronald Reagan imply, Chambers versus Hiss is less a referendum on the guilt of one man than it is on a matter of political philosophy. Where one stands on Hiss reflects where one fits along the conservative-liberal continuum.

SUGGESTIONS FOR FURTHER READING

Chambers, W. (1952). *Witness.* New York: Random House.
Hiss, A. (1957). *In the court of public opinion.* New York: Alfred A. Knopf.
Smith, J.C. (1976). *Alger Hiss: The true story.* New York: Holt, Rinehart and Winston.
Weinstein, A. (1997). *Perjury: The Hiss-Chambers case.* New York: Random House [(1978) New York: Alfred A. Knopf].

NOTES

1. The Yalta Conference was a 1945 meeting between the leaders of the United States, the United Kingdom, and the Soviet Union to specify the terms of German surrender, the division of postwar Europe, and the formation of the United Nations.
2. Assuming Alger's guilt, many sources appear to concur on speculation that Priscilla Hiss would have likely been the typist for the Baltimore papers as Alger was known to be a "hunt-and-peck" typist. The "Hiss Standards" was a term of convenience used to describe documents known to have been typed by Priscilla Hiss that were used as a baseline for comparison.
3. From prison, Hiss wrote almost 500 letters. In 2000, Hiss's son Tony published the letters in a volume entitled *The View from Alger's Window: A Son's Memoir.*

REFERENCES

Chambers, W. (1952). *Witness.* New York: Random House.

Cook, F. (1958). *The unfinished story of Alger Hiss.* New York: William Morrow.

Dunn, J.L., and Garrett, K.L. (1997). *A field guide to warblers of North America.* New York: Houghton Mifflin Company.

Geoghegan, T. (1969). By any other name. *Harvard Crimson.* Retrieved March 7, 2007, from http://www.thecrimson.com/printerfriendly.aspx?ref=494601

Green, G. (1984, November 10). Forgery by typewriter. *The Nation.*

Hiss, A. (1957). *In the court of public opinion.* New York: Alfred A. Knopf.

House Committee on Un-American Activities. (1948, July 31–December 14). *Hearings Regarding Communist Espionage in the United States Government,* 80th Congress, 2nd session.

Kisseloff, J. (2006). *The Alger Hiss story: Search for the truth.* Retrieved November 11, 2006, from http://homepages.nyu.edu/~th15/home.html

Lowenthal, J. (2000, Autumn). Verona and Alger Hiss. *Intelligence and National Security, 15*(3), 98–130. London: Frank Cass.

Massing, H. (1987). *The deception.* New York: Ballantine Books.

Navasky, V. (2005). *A matter of opinion.* New York: Farrar, Straus and Giroux.

Olmsted, K.S. (2002). *Red spy queen: A biography of Elizabeth Bentley.* Chapel Hill: The University of North Carolina Press.

Petit, L.J. (1999). Prothonotary Warbler (*Protonotaria citrea*). In A. Poole and F. Gill (Eds.), *The birds of North America* (No. 408). Philadelphia, PA: The Birds of North America, Inc.

Powers, R.G. (1998). *Not without honor: The history of American anticommunism.* New Haven: Yale University Press.

Roazen, P. (2003). *Cultural foundations of political psychology.* Somerset, NJ: Transaction Publishers.

Smith, J.C. (1976). *Alger Hiss: The true story.* New York: Holt, Rinehart and Winston.

Sterling, D. (1984, February 28). Whittaker Chambers: Odd choice for the Medal of Freedom [Letter to the editor]. *New York Times.*

Tanenhaus, S. (1998). *Whittaker Chambers: A biography.* New York: Modern Library.

Vassiliev, A., and Weinstein, A. (2000). *The haunted wood: Soviet espionage in America—the Stalin era.* New York: Modern Library.

Weinstein, A. (1997). *Perjury: The Hiss-Chambers case.* New York: Random House [(1978) New York: Alfred A. Knopf].

Zeligs, M.A. (1967). *Friendship and fratricide: An analysis of Whittaker Chambers and Alger Hiss.* New York: Viking Press.

11

Worse than Murder: The Rosenberg-Sobell Atom Spy Affair

ERNEST L. NICKELS

The defeat of Nazi Germany in the spring of 1945 brought a close to the European theater of the Second World War (WWII). In the Pacific, Japanese forces receded against a series of key Allied victories, events that had cost both sides dearly. Plans for a November invasion of mainland Japan forecast American military casualties in the tens of thousands as the Japanese braced for total war if necessary to repel an occupation. That scenario never came to pass. On August 6, the United States Air Force bomber *Enola Gay* released its payload—an atomic bomb dubbed "Little Boy"—over the city of Hiroshima, decimating its civilian population. Three days later, a second bomb, "Fat Man," fell over Nagasaki to similar effect. Japan surrendered within the week.

The atomic weapon program of the United States, the Manhattan Project, was one of many undertaken by the WWII powers, including Japan. As the first to realize nuclear capability, the United States emerged as the original superpower of the postwar era. This monopoly was short-lived. A shade past four years after the Hiroshima bombing, the Soviet Union staged its first successful test of a nuclear weapon, the RDS-1. Operation "First Lightening" (codenamed "Joe One" in U.S. intelligence) caught the West by surprise, arriving years in advance of predictions for what had been thought to be a fledgling research program.

Mere days after the Nagasaki bombing, the U.S. government had publicly released the Smyth Report. This document declassified and described in limited detail the administrative history of the Manhattan Project as well as the elementary principles of nuclear physics involved in atomic bombs. The report did not discuss the actual methods for constructing such weapons nor did it make any mention of design differences between the Little Boy and Fat Man technologies. The unique construction of Fat Man, particularly the distinct implosive mechanism for activating its plutonium core, would not become public knowledge until 1951 when revealed over the course of the Rosenberg-Sobell trial. From the design of the RDS-1, resembling Fat Man down to its (also classified) case construction, it was clear that Manhattan Project secrets had been passed to the Soviets.

189

DUCK AND COVER

First in an instructional booklet and later in film with an entirely surreal, bubbly jingle, Bert the Turtle taught American schoolchildren across the country what to do in case of nuclear attack. In school, at the sight of a bright flash (indicating detonation of an atomic bomb), students were to duck beneath their desks or crouch against the nearest wall away from windows and cover themselves as best they could. At the time this informational campaign was designed, nuclear physics was still poorly understood. It was believed that the primary danger posed by atomic bombs was the severe concussive force and extreme heat generated by the blast. Initial skepticism about the "duck and cover" was validated a few years later when nuclear testing somewhat inadvertently stumbled upon the concept of radioactive fallout.

With Soviet achievement of nuclear weaponry, the emergent Cold War solidified as the definitive force shaping international relations and American political culture for the remainder of the century. By the close of the Rosenberg-Sobell trial, American forces had fought North Korean and Chinese forces to a virtual standstill on the 38th parallel in South Korea. U.S. support operations had begun in French-occupied Vietnam to contain the spread of communism. McCarthy had made himself a household name and "loyalty" the watchword of the day. Nations raced toward the next generation of nuclear weapons, the exponentially more powerful hydrogen bomb. Schoolchildren were drilled to "duck and cover" in the case of nuclear attack. Bert the Turtle, the Civil Defense Administration's cartoon spokesman for this (surely useless) safety measure, awaited his film debut to the American public.

The sentence Judge Irving Kaufman delivered to Julius and Ethel Rosenberg at the end of March 1951 swept past mere legal condemnation to admonish them in the face of history. Responsibility for what had passed in the wake of Joe One, as well as what must surely await the United States and the world, was laid squarely at their feet:

> I consider your crime worse than murder. Plain deliberate contemplated murder is dwarfed in magnitude by comparison with the crime you have committed. In committing the act of murder, the criminal kills only his victim. The immediate family is brought to grief and when justice is meted out the chapter is closed. But in your case, I believe your conduct in putting into the hands of the Russians the A-bomb years before our best scientists predicted Russia would perfect the bomb has already caused, in my opinion, the Communist aggression in Korea, with the resultant casualties exceeding 50,000 and who knows but that millions more of innocent people may pay the price of your treason. Indeed, by your betrayal you undoubtedly have altered the course of history to the disadvantage of our country. (Rosenberg-Sobell, 1952, pp. 1614–1615)

The couple was electrocuted in 1953, a day after their 14th wedding anniversary.

THE ATOM SPIES

Within a year of Joe One, investigation into Soviet espionage in the American atomic program yielded its first major break. In February 1950, the British scientist Klaus Fuchs was arrested in England. Fuchs, a German-born theoretical physicist and communist, had fled Nazi persecution before the war and worked in the British atomic program before collaborating with American researchers on the Manhattan Project. During and after the war, Fuchs had operated as a Soviet agent and had passed nuclear research information

Figure 11.1   Rally to save Julius and Ethel Rosenberg from execution, in the center of Paris, ca. 1953. Huge portraits of the atom spies are mounted behind the speaker's platform. Courtesy of the Library of Congress.

to the USSR. Between 1947 and 1949, Fuchs admitted to having handed over plans for the hydrogen bomb to his contact, Alexandre Feklisov, a case officer with the Soviet intelligence agency, the NKGB. Following his conviction in 1950, Fuchs received 14 years in prison.

Fuchs's confession served to implicate, among others, the American chemist Harry Gold. Under investigation in the United States, Gold admitted to having served as a courier for Manhattan Project secrets passed to the Soviets between 1944 and 1945. Like Fuchs, Gold named names. Among the identified collaborators were the Soviet General Consul Anatoli Yakovlev, an intelligence case officer with the NKVD, and David Greenglass, a machinist and sergeant in the U.S. Army stationed at the Los Alamos project site during the war. At war's end, Yakovlev had returned to the Soviet Union and was therefore beyond the reach of U.S. authorities. The Federal Bureau of Investigations (FBI) arrested Greenglass in June 1950. In custody, Greenglass claimed he had agreed to spy for the Soviets when his wife, Ruth, approached him on behalf of his sister, Ethel Rosenberg, and her husband, Julius.

Julius, born in 1918 to Jewish Polish immigrants, was raised in New York's Lower East Side and later attended the City College of New York (CCNY). There, he pursued a degree in electrical engineering alongside Morton Sobell, an acquaintance through their mutual involvement in the Young Communist League, and Max Elitcher, Sobell's friend and former high school classmate. After graduation, Sobell and Elitcher went to work for the Navy Bureau of Ordnance. Sobell left this position in 1941, but remained in contact with Elitcher as well as with Julius. Several years later, Sobell and Elitcher would reunite as co-workers at the Reeves Instrument Company in Queens, New York.

Ethel was three years Julius's senior, born into more modest circumstances on the East Side of Manhattan. Graduating high school at 15, Ethel found work as a clerk in a shipping company. Four years later, she was fired for helping organize a strike protesting labor conditions of the women workers. Like Julius, Ethel joined the Young Communist League in her youth. The two met during a New Year's Eve union benefit. Soon after Julius's college graduation in 1939, they married and Ethel later bore two sons, Michael and Robert. In 1940, Julius took a position with the U.S. Army Signal Corps as a civilian engineer. Julius and Ethel joined the Communist Party but were no longer active members by 1943. Nonetheless, when Julius's former affiliation with the party was uncovered in early 1945, he was fired from the Signal Corps. Afterward, he briefly worked for the Emerson Radio Corporation before forming the G & R Engineering Company with his brothers-in-law Isadore Goldstein and David Greenglass in 1946.

Julius was arrested in July 1950. Fuchs, Gold, and Greenglass had each chosen to answer accusations of espionage with confessions and information implicating others in order to secure leniency. This pattern emerged as typical in the Cold War hunt for communist spies and sympathizers. Julius, however, clung steadfastly to an unqualified claim of innocence. When Ethel was arrested in August, primarily (or solely) to leverage Julius toward a plea agreement, she followed suit. Although originally denying their direct involvement initially, David Greenglass agreed to testify against both Rosenbergs in exchange for his wife's immunity from prosecution.

At the time of the Rosenbergs' arrest, Morton Sobell was residing in Mexico along with his wife and children. Abducted from his residence under false pretenses by an otherwise unidentified group of Mexican men, Sobell was turned over to FBI custody at the American border and charged as a coconspirator in the atom spy ring. Sobell, like Julius and Ethel, maintained his innocence. Elitcher, like Greenglass, had agreed to turn states' evidence, testifying against both Sobell and Julius Rosenberg.

THE ATOM SPY CONSPIRACY

Investigation into the possible transfer of atomic secrets to the Soviet Union generated a considerable volume of testimony, the result of a sequence of confessions and allegations that served to tie the many supposed co-conspirators together. As it emerged from this web of implications, the government's case against the Rosenbergs and Sobell framed the accused as the key to this conspiracy—and their prosecution as the culmination of its unmasking. From the existing record at the time of the trial, the structure of the alleged conspiracy can be traced through the chain of testimonies most immediately leading up to the involvement of the Rosenbergs and Sobell in charges of atomic espionage (see also, Sharp 1956, p. xv, for a graphical summary). Upon arrest, Fuchs gave up the names of Feklisov and Gold. Gold, in turn, implicated Yakovlev and David Greenglass. The Greenglasses then testified against the Rosenbergs, as did Elitcher. Elitcher additionally spoke to Sobell's involvement, claiming to have witnessed Sobell delivering presumably sensitive materials in a film canister to Julius. A direct connection between Feklisov, Yakovlev, the Rosenbergs, and Sobell could not be established for lack of corroborating testimony on their part. With the Rosenbergs and Sobell alone to answer the allegations against them with a claim of innocence, the final piece of the puzzle fell into place. The portrait of the conspiracy, in whatever its proportions of fact and fiction, appeared complete.

Figure 11.2 Morton Sobell (left), entering Federal Court with Deputy Marshal Eugene Fitzgerald, 1953. Courtesy of the Library of Congess.

THE ROSENBERG-SOBELL TRIAL

The trial in the case of the United States versus Julius Rosenberg, Ethel Rosenberg, and Morton Sobell opened on the morning of March 6, 1951. Accused of conspiracy to commit espionage in time of war under the Espionage Act of 1917,[1] each faced up to 30 years in prison or death. Anatoli Yakovlev and David Greenglass were named as codefendants, but were each granted a severance of trial. Coconspirators Ruth Greenglass and Harry Gold were not charged and instead appeared as state witnesses rather than defendants. U.S. Attorney Irving Saypol headed the prosecution, assisted by Myles Lane, Roy Cohn, John Foley, James Kilsheimer III, and James Branigan. Emanuel Bloch represented Julius Rosenberg; Bloch's father, Alexander, represented Ethel. Harold Phillips and Edward Kuntz represented Sobell. Judge Irving R. Kaufman presided.

Proceedings began with jury selection. The clerk read a list of the state's intended witnesses, over a hundred in all including Gold, the Greenglasses, and renowned figures such as General Leslie R. Groves and Dr. J. Robert Oppenheimer—the director and lead scientist of the Manhattan Project, respectively. Elizabeth Bentley was also named, the so-called "red spy queen" who gained celebrity testifying against many supposed former cooperative Soviet spies. The grand jury indictment was presented detailing the nature of the charge, specified in 11 overt acts. Potential jurors were presented with long lists of (mainly socialist and communist) organizations and publications and asked about the

193

associations they might have with any. After a careful vetting by both prosecution and defense, and questioning about political leanings, whereabouts during the war, and travels overseas, 11 men and one woman were empaneled.

With the jury excused, Judge Kaufman agreed to hear motions. Emanuel Bloch called for an immediate dismissal of the Rosenbergs' indictment. Despite the Court's firm assurance that defense briefs on the matter had been already considered and found unpersuasive, Bloch nevertheless pressed on. The argument comprised three specific challenges. The first two disputed the constitutionality of the Espionage Act itself as violating the First Amendment in failing to establish a definite basis for findings of guilt and, by extension, Fifth Amendment due process protections in denying the accused a fair statement of the charges accused. In prohibiting the transmission of information relating to the "national defense," Bloch reasoned, the Act failed to define that term. Neither lay nor legal dictionaries define "national defense," nor was the phrase an established term of art. This ambiguity effectively granted the military broad license to establish its meaning and thereby the limits of free speech—an effect plainly unintended by the legislature and, in any case, a power that cannot be delegated away. The Supreme Court had considered and rejected this same argument in *United States v. Goren*. However, that challenge was brought on Fifth and Sixth Amendment grounds. Bloch argued that when understood as a question of free speech, the language of the statute could no longer be understood as sufficiently clear as stricter standards are necessarily invoked in First Amendment cases. Bloch noted that the Atomic Energy Act of 1950 was drawn up at the urging of the scientific community in part to address these very concerns—particularly with respect to nuclear research. The failure to amend or repeal the relevant portions of the Espionage Act in light of this legislation, Bloch argued, was clearly an oversight. The third argument to dismiss more narrowly addressed the substance of the indictment, which failed to allege that the information the accused purportedly conspired to transmit to a foreign power fell under the provisions of the statute. Not all national defense information, if revealed, constitutes a crime. The indictment failed to specify that the information in question was so protected.

Judge Kaufman was unmoved. Addressing the final point first, the Court found that the alleged intention of the accused to give "advantage" to a foreign government necessarily implies the information is confidential. The meaning of "national defense" was not found to be vague. Finally, as defense secrets are not protected speech, a challenge on First Amendment grounds failed and, with it, any Fifth Amendment objection. Kaufman did allow the defense to enter their brief into the record, conceding the argument may prove persuasive on appeal.

Kaufman then allowed the prosecution and defense each a brief opening statement to the jury. Attorney Saypol spoke first. Early into this presentation, the caustic tone, impassioned rhetoric, and sharp bickering that came to characterize this trial took shape.

Opening Statements[2]—"A Fair Shake in the American Way"

"The evidence," Saypol claimed, "will show that the loyalty and allegiance of the Rosenbergs and Sobell were not to our country, but that it was to Communism, Communism in this country and Communism throughout the world."

Emanuel Bloch rose to protest—the first of many, progressively outraged, objections to the prosecution's references to the defendants' past ties to communism. Bloch asked Kaufman to direct Saypol to desist from any such remarks since, "communism is not on trial here. These defendants are charged with espionage." Saypol protested this interruption. "I beg your pardon, Mr. Saypol," Bloch replied directly, in breach of courtroom etiquette, "but I am forced to do it."

Kaufman quickly, if impatiently, quieted the skirmish. "Will somebody permit me to make a ruling here?" Chastising Bloch, he complained, "Mr. Saypol objects to your objection and you answer his objection and I can't make a ruling." The jury was directed to observe "the charge in question is espionage, not political affiliation," but Kaufman noted he would allow the prosecution to address the defendants' ties to communism for the purpose of establishing a motive for their crime.

Saypol resumed his opening, elaborating the nature and gravity of the alleged crime. The evidence, he promised, would show that the Rosenbergs, operating at the behest of Soviet agents, had enticed David Greenglass into the role of "a modern Benedict Arnold." Collectively, they had delivered the secret of the atomic bomb—"the most important weapon ever known to mankind"—to the Soviet Union. This spy ring had actively pursued the recruitment of other Americans into espionage and, when discovered, arranged to flee behind the Iron Curtain.

Bloch now demanded a mistrial, describing the prosecution's statement as "inflammatory in character" and as having introduced an element entirely irrelevant to the case at hand, "to wit, Communism." When this motion was also denied, Phillips launched himself into the fray.

Allegations of attempting to flee the country were "quite beside the point, entirely improper, not relevant." Phillips did not pause at the judge's attempt to interject, accusing the prosecution of raising the specter merely to prejudice the jurors.

"I suggest that if you will examine the law books, Mr. Phillips," Kaufman growled, "you will find that it is quite relevant in a criminal case to introduce evidence of flight on the question of guilt."

"After the proof of the act itself has been advanced," Philips conceded, but not before. Asked for his motion, Philips requested that the Court either instruct the jury to disregard these remarks or declare a mistrial. Motion denied. Now Bloch charged the bench's blind spot, rising to reserve his objection to incrimination by association. Judge Kaufman stopped him short: "I wish each and every one of you gentlemen would immediately arise. Invariably, as I get ready to make a ruling, somebody else jumps up." The reserve was noted, and Kaufman once more directed jurors that the charge was conspiracy to commit espionage, "in that matters vital to the national defense were transmitted to Russia for the purpose of giving Russia an advantage, with intention of giving Russia an advantage. That is the charge..."

"This is not the charge," Phillips argued. "Nowhere in the indictment is it stated that information was actually transmitted. The indictment charges that a plan was laid to transmit information."

The Court conceded, but Bloch pushed the point further, complaining before the jury that the indictment was not clear on what specifically was alleged and that he was only now learning what he must defend against.

"This is a very grave crime that these defendants are charged with," Bloch pleaded to the jury. "Very grave. And this trial arises in a rather tense international atmosphere. And I think all of us delude ourselves that we believe that we are completely free from all of those pressures and influences that every minute of the day are upon us." All that he asked of the jurors on behalf of the accused "is a fair shake in the American way." The defendants stood accused of conspiracy to commit espionage, he reminded them, and this was what the government must prove—"not that they believed in one ism or another ism." Bloch enjoined jurors to be skeptical of the witnesses they would hear and to guard themselves from any sympathies, passions, or prejudices they might harbor.

Alexander Bloch spoke next in the defense of Mrs. Rosenberg, casting her as "basically a housewife, and nothing more," who should not be condemned because her brother and sister-in-law have confessed treason. They had plainly been enticed with leniency to implicate others and thus their testimonies were less than credible.

Phillips's presentation raised the more esoteric point that conspiring to transmit national defense secrets could not be considered worse if directed to the Soviet Union than to the United Kingdom, as the statute draws no distinction. Whatever the present relations with the Soviets, the prosecution's references to it could only be read as intending to "inflame your heart." Phillips cautioned he was not "trying to minimize the fact that it is a criminal offense, but for heaven sakes, why maximum it?" Of the 11 acts specified in the indictment, none mentioned Sobell by name. "We will wait and have to wait," he complained, "sit here like so many children, listening, waiting…How is the Government going to connect Sobell by truthful testimony? Untruthful testimony there may be a great deal of; I don't know anything about that." Finally, he observed that Gold, the crux of the prosecution's case, "never had anything to do with Communists and was no Communist. So where is the motive of Communism? So let that at once fly out of your minds."

By the close of the defense's opening statements, the day had expired. Jurors were warned that they would be together for weeks to come. On the next day of the trial, the parade of witnesses began.

The Prosecution

The prosecution's theory slowly unfolded during examination of the state witnesses. Each testimony added another facet to an increasingly intricate tale of subversion and subterfuge, reported back to the nation as so many serial chapters of some generic spy fiction. This story was developed primarily through the testimonies of Elitcher and David Greenglass and then fleshed out in greater detail by Gold and Ruth Greenglass.[3]

It begins shortly after Julius Rosenberg, Sobell, and Elitcher graduated from college in 1938. Working for the Navy, Sobell and Elitcher lived together and were active Communist Party members. They parted ways in 1941 when Sobell returned to school, but kept in touch on occasion. In 1944, Julius Rosenberg, who Elitcher had not seen in six years, came calling.

Julius sought to supply the Soviet Union with U.S. military secrets and was already working in cooperation with Sobell. Now, Julius hoped to enlist Elitcher as well. Initially, Elitcher abstained but later confirmed this conspiracy with Sobell while on vacation three months later. Rosenberg approached Elitcher again the following year. In 1946, Elitcher spoke to Sobell about his military work developing a gunnery control system, telling him of an unfinished pamphlet on the system and was referred back to Julius. Elitcher made contact in late 1946, but Julius had grown suspicious of a leak in the spy ring and put off discussion of the matter. Meanwhile, Sobell began to mine Elitcher for the names of any "progressive" engineering students whom he might recruit for espionage. Elitcher offered none, and decided to quit the Navy in 1948. Sobell and Rosenberg attempted to dissuade him, but without success.

Late in 1948, on a family vacation to stay at the Sobells' home, Elitcher informed his host upon arriving that he had been followed from Washington to New York. Sobell seemed panicked and impressed upon Elitcher the need to be rid of something valuable but dangerous in his home, which had to be delivered to Julius immediately. Sobell retrieved what looked to Elitcher to be a 35-millimeter film can, and the two left for the Rosenbergs' home. Upon arriving, Elitcher waited in the car as Sobell made his visit. Returning to the vehicle, Sobell mentioned Julius's association with Elizabeth Bentley. In the same year, while working together at Reeves, Sobell approached Elitcher again for names of possibly sympathetic engineering students. Elitcher again declined.

Over the same period, the Rosenbergs actively developed this conspiracy in conjunction with their in-laws, the Greenglasses. In 1944, David was assigned to the Manhattan District and was eventually sent off to a secret project at Los Alamos where he machined components for research on high explosives and served as assistant foreman of his workshop. A technical sergeant, David's security clearance denied him knowledge of a project's purpose. While on leave in late 1944, he learned of the true nature of the project from his wife who had been told, in turn, by Julius. Ethel Rosenberg informed Ruth of Julius's activities in the service of the Soviet Union, and the Rosenbergs asked Ruth to pressure David to assist them in gathering information from Los Alamos. Ruth reluctantly agreed, and eventually succeeded in recruiting her husband.

David provided the Rosenbergs with the names of some of the scientists working at Los Alamos (including Oppenheimer and Niels Bohr), the physical layout of the project, and personnel figures. In early 1945, Julius and David discussed the latter's work on high explosive lens molds. Julius asked David to write down any information he had on these parts and the experiments they were used in. David compiled some rough sketches along with some written description, a list of scientists, and the names of possible communist sympathizers in the project and turned this over to Julius. During that exchange, Julius noted that Ethel would type out David's report before sending it on.

Shortly thereafter, the Greenglasses met with the Rosenbergs and a woman named Ann Sidorovich. In that meeting, it was planned that Ruth would move to Albuquerque and serve as a courier between David and Sidorovich. Bomb secrets would be passed through an exchanging of purses with Sidorovich or another agent in a Denver movie theater (later, a Safeway in Albuquerque). The side of a Jello box was snipped into two irregular halves, like pieces of a jigsaw puzzle. Ruth would retain one side, and friendly agents would be identifiable by possessing the other. Meanwhile, David was to meet an operative to discuss the lens molds. Julius introduced the two a few days later.

Upon David's return to Los Alamos, Ruth moved to Albuquerque and David visited on weekends. Though they never saw Sidorovich again, in 1945 the man now identified as Harry Gold came to visit. Claiming Julius had sent him, Gold produced his half of the Jello box. David produced the other, but did not have the requested information ready for Gold. At a second meeting, Gold received some sketches of the lens mold experiments and a list of possible recruits, and the Greenglasses received $500 in cash.

The bomb described to David by Julius was ultimately realized as Little Boy. During his time at Los Alamos, David learned of another weapon in development—the Fat Man design. David sketched the plans and wrote up a description for the implosive device used in this bomb and provided them (along with $200) to Julius at his home. The Rosenbergs proofread the report, and Ethel typed it up. Julius also disclosed to David that he had managed to steal a proximity fuse for the bomb while working at Emerson Radio.

As business partners, Julius spoke to David about bankrolling students attending college. He offered David money to attend MIT or the University of Chicago to gain the education necessary to network with those working in nuclear physics. Julius also spoke of information he had gathered on "a sky platform project" and nuclear powered aircraft, detailed his techniques for passing secrets, and mentioned items he had received from the Soviets. These included a citation, a watch, and a console table modified to microfilm and conceal photographs. After Fuchs's arrest in 1950, David learned from Julius that Gold had been one of his contacts and that they too would likely be arrested soon. Julius insisted David leave the country, by way of Mexico. David received $1,000 from Julius to cover his debts and traveling expenses. David was to take his family to Mexico City to await trans-Atlantic passage. The Greenglasses obtained passport photos; one copy was turned over to the FBI upon arrest. Julius gave David $4,000 more, which he gave to a brother-in-law to keep, but ultimately refused to leave. The Greenglasses and Rosenbergs were arrested shortly thereafter.

The Defense

The material evidence against the defendants consisted primarily of one document from the Albuquerque Hilton Hotel showing Gold had stayed there on the date he was supposed to have met with the Greenglasses and one bank record showing Ruth had deposited $400 shortly after their meetings. The prosecution had also entered as evidence the Greenglasses' passport photos and a paper bag that supposedly once held the $4,000 Julius had given to David. Nothing supported charges that Sobell or the Rosenbergs were directly involved in espionage. The state's other exhibits were simply demonstrative, such as replications of the Jello box codex, the sketches of the lens mold, and a cross section of the bomb that David Greenglass recreated.

From a legal perspective, a case based almost exclusively upon oral evidence is the weakest of accusations against a defendant. Nonetheless, it can also be the hardest to defend against. How does one *prove* they did *not* commit a murder, much less a "crime worse than murder"? Logically, it is impossible to prove a negative.[4] Yet, a successful defense against such grand accusations would seem to require equally grand amounts of disproof.[5] A defense is left to simply and firmly deny the accusations and to attempt to undermine the credibility of the prosecution's theory.

Cross-examining the state's witnesses, the defense scored some minor blows against the prosecution's case but also suffered several miscues that weakened their own position. Elitcher baldly admitted no secrets ever actually passed between either Rosenberg or Sobell and himself. Neither could he say what the supposed film canister contained. Elitcher divulged he had perjured himself in 1947 when he denied belonging to the Communist Party while taking a federal loyalty oath, and that fear of prosecution motivated his choice to testify for the state. David Greenglass, often smirking as he testified, likewise confessed he had never actually seen any of the gifts the Rosenbergs supposedly received from the Soviets. David also revealed a history of serious financial disputes with Julius related to their business venture. Ruth's near verbatim repetition of some of her original testimony under cross-examination suggested coaching by the prosecution.

The state had called expert witnesses to testify to the technical accuracy of the sketches David Greenglass recreated and claimed to have originally passed to the Rosenbergs. In cross-examination, Bloch attempted to demonstrate that these sketches would not have revealed any substantial secret of the atomic bomb. This line of questioning generally failed and muddled the defense's argument that the state simply failed to prove the defendants had either solicited or transferred such information to the Soviets. More egregiously, with the jury present, Emanuel Bloch moved to have David's cross-sectional sketch of the Fat Man design impounded. It was one of few defense motions granted, but it in effect conceded the prosecution's claim that this information did, in fact, constitute the secret of the bomb. Harry Gold was not cross-examined.

The defense called few witnesses of their own, relying primarily upon the Rosenbergs' testimony. Sobell elected not to testify. On the stand, Julius flatly and repeatedly denied all aspects of the prosecution story as recounted by Emanuel Bloch. Julius spoke candidly to his views of communism as compared with capitalism when prompted by Kaufman, admitting he perceived advantages in each system and professed belief that a nation should be free to select its form of government. Julius batted away elements of the Greenglasses' testimony. The Rosenbergs' humble means were highlighted to dispute allegations of access to near-limitless funds from the Soviets. Julius laughed off the suggestion that he would have suggested David attend MIT or the University of Chicago as David would never have been accepted to such prestigious institutions. In fact, Julius had pressured David to quit his part-time schooling and attend more closely to their business. Julius acknowledged owning a console table, but claimed to have purchased it from Macy's. He had made contact with Elitcher during the war years, but for purely social reasons and later in the course of challenging his firing from the Signal Corps. Julius had not seen Sobell during the entirety of the war, only reestablishing their friendship after 1946. Likewise, Ethel dismissed the prosecution's allegations. She supported Julius's testimony that the console table was a Macy's purchase. While owning a typewriter, she used it only to assist Julius with school reports, union activities, his business, and his attempt to be reinstated in his government job. She felt bad being unable to help her brother and his wife with their financial problems, but reported that when the legal troubles began Ruth had told her that she and David were innocent and intended to fight the case.

Julius portrayed a troubled relationship with David, one mired in financial disputes surrounding their failed business and David's ambitions for wealth. Julius claimed Ruth had been the one to ask him to visit the Greenglasses' apartment initially while David was in Los Alamos. There, she had revealed to him that David was scheming to make money by stealing things from the Army and that she was concerned he would be caught. After taking possession of David's share of their failing business as well as that of another co-owner in the spring of 1950, David confronted Julius a couple months later asking for $2,000. Julius, now in debt to their former co-owner, refused. David then asked Julius to help him secure a smallpox vaccination certificate and find out what other vaccinations were necessary to travel to Mexico. David seemed "disturbed" and "agitated," but refused to tell Julius what was the matter. Earlier in the year, David mentioned to Julius the FBI had questioned him about uranium. Julius inferred that David may have followed through with his moneymaking scheme, had been found out, and was now looking to flee the country.

Julius contacted his physician to ask about a certificate for David, but to no avail. David said he would handle the matter himself. In June, David called upon Julius again and now admitted to being in serious trouble and again requested $2,000. Julius again could not comply. David threatened that Julius would be "sorry" if he did not give him the money. At that point, Julius cut the conversation short and sent David home. Believing the matter had blown over, Julius volunteered to answer questions at the FBI office after David's arrest only to discover David had implicated him as a Soviet agent. Julius denied the charge and hired Emanuel Bloch as his defense attorney.

Prosecution Cross-Examination and Rebuttal

Cross-examining the Rosenbergs, Saypol devoted little energy to deconstructing their version of events. He did suggest it was "a little fantastic" that David Greenglass would need $2,000 for a smallpox certificate, and quibbled that the console table sold at Macy's at the time cost much more than what Julius reported spending. Saypol instead emphasized prior associations with communism, returning to Julius's political activities during college. Julius invoked the Fifth Amendment, refusing to discuss involvement with Young Communist League or the Communist Party. When Saypol brought up his termination from the Signal Corps in 1945, Julius conceded there were allegations of communist ties but had denied them at the time and refused any further questions in court. Julius again spoke freely on his views of the Soviet Union, admitting that, as a Jewish American, he appreciated the role they had played in defeating Nazi Germany. He went so far as to admit he believed that as wartime allies of the United States, the Soviets deserved to be privy to the same secrets shared with the United Kingdom. Julius conceded past membership in the Joint Anti-Fascist Refugee Committee, an organization officially considered "subversive," Saypol noted, as well as to holding insurance through the International Workers Order. Saypol introduced a petition from 1939 with Ethel's name in support of a Communist Party candidate running for local office in New York City. Primarily, however, the prosecution sought to discredit Ethel by highlighting her liberal invocation of the Fifth Amendment during her grand jury testimony—questions that she willingly answered at trial. The defense agitated for a mistrial, but fruitlessly. Kaufman ruled the jury might consider the matter in evaluating the credibility of Ethel's testimony. Ethel merely noted she and Julius were under arrest at the time and had reason to believe David might have falsely implicated them.

The prosecution called additional witnesses during its rebuttal, among them a former servant for the Rosenbergs during the war. She testified that Ethel had claimed the console table had been a gift from a friend of her husband's and that it was normally stored in a large closet. Emanuel Bloch's cross-examination revealed she believed the table was purely ornamental and apparently never used for any purpose whatsoever. A surprise witness, revealed to the defense only the day before, was also called—a local photographer who claimed the Rosenbergs had purchased passport photos in 1950, purportedly for a trip to France. In cross-examination, however, he admitted he did not possess the photo negatives nor did he have any record of the transaction.

Summations and Verdict: "The Enormity of the Thing"

Emanuel Bloch delivered the first of the summations. Listing off state's exhibits, Bloch noted that for all the FBI's investigative efforts, they had not managed to locate any evidence concretely tying the Rosenbergs to the alleged conspiracy. The "repulsive" David Greenglass—one who "comes around to bury his own sister and smiles"—and his "evil" wife had fooled the government with their false implications. Already holding ill will against his brother-in-law, David had capitalized on the circumstances surrounding Julius's firing from the Signal Corps and offered up the Rosenbergs in trade for leniency for himself and Ruth. Gold offered no testimony directly implicating the Rosenbergs. Elitcher, also motivated to avoid prosecution, likewise had incentive to testify to this fabrication. The prosecution story, Bloch argued, simply did not make sense. Elizabeth Bentley had testified that she spoke over the phone with an agent named Julius, but why would Julius use his real name? Would not the Rosenbergs' maid have noticed the modifications to the console table? If David's escape plan was so expertly arranged, why was Sobell easily apprehended in Mexico City? Surely, Bloch argued, there was at least reasonable doubt of the Rosenbergs' guilt.

Kuntz summarized Sobell's defense. Echoing Bloch, Kuntz also noted the dearth of evidence the FBI turned up investigating Sobell. Elitcher, a "miserable liar," offered the only testimony implicating Sobell, but his story strained imagination. For such a monumental crime, it would have been recklessly cavalier for Rosenberg to so casually approach Elitcher for assistance. How could Elitcher let a full three months pass before finding it worthwhile to mention the affair to Sobell? Even if Sobell had delivered a canister to Julius, Elitcher himself admitted ignorance of its contents. As for Sobell's supposed "flight" from the country, supposedly proof of a "guilty mind," why would he travel and rent an apartment there under his own name?

Saypol summarized for the prosecution. Confessing a sense of inadequacy in his ability to "express...in words the enormity of the thing," the prosecutor admitted that much of the conspiracy was still unknown to authorities. Nevertheless, it was certain "that these conspirators stole the most important scientific secrets ever known to mankind from this country and delivered them to the Soviet Union." The Rosenbergs' guilt was clear. The Greenglasses' testimony was corroborated by Harry Gold—who was already sentenced and therefore without any obvious motivation to lie—as well as by the documentary evidence including the Albuquerque hotel registration card and Ruth's deposit receipt for $400. Saypol reviewed the evidence of an effort to flee the country and again called into question the idea that the Rosenbergs could have purchased the much-discussed console table during the war years (when furniture was scarce) for the price they had quoted. He further noted it would seem strange for a couple to tell conflicting stories of its origin to their housekeeper and place their finest possession away in a closet. Saypol once more traced the impetus for this crime to Julius and Sobell's communist associations in college. Sobell's participation, he argued, was clear in the testimonies presented by the state witnesses as well as evidence suggesting Sobell used at least five aliases while in Mexico. There have been no defendants who "ever stood before the bar of American

Figure 11.3 **Julius and Ethel Rosenberg, separated by heavy wire screen, as they leave the U.S. Courthouse after being found guilty. Courtesy of the Library of Congress.**

justice less deserving of sympathy than these three" (*Rosenberg-Sobell*, 1952, p. 1535), Saypol argued.

With that, arguments closed and the jury retired to deliberate the case. The trial had lasted only three weeks. In less than 24 hours, the defendants had their verdict—guilty. Kaufman openly approved the finding. Saypol once more trumpeted the importance of the case, characterizing the defendants as "the sharpest secret eyes of our enemies" whose crime involved "implications so wide...[as to]...involve the very question of whether or when the devastation of atomic war may fall upon this world" (*Rosenberg-Sobell*, 1952, p. 1582).

Sentencing and Aftermath

One week after the verdict, the defendants were sentenced. The Rosenbergs were called first. The Court neither formally solicited nor received recommendation from the prosecution with regard to sentencing, but Saypol indicated his preference in referencing the sacrifices of U.S. servicemen in Korea, after which he pointedly asked, "is there room for compassion or mercy?" (*Rosenberg-Sobell*, 1952, p. 1603). Emanuel Bloch maintained the Rosenbergs' innocence, but further noted that at the time the conspiracy supposedly took place the nations were allies and quoted expert opinion suggesting the information in question would have been a minor contribution to the Soviet program at best. When Kaufman delivered his condemnation of the Rosenbergs, it was not without concern for its moral implications. "I am just as human as are the people who have given me the power to impose sentence," he observed. "I have searched the records—I have searched my conscience—to find some reason for mercy—for it is only human to be merciful." However, he concluded, it would be a breach of public trust to show any leniency toward the Rosenbergs. "It is not in my power, Julius and Ethel Rosenberg, to forgive you. Only the Lord can find mercy for what you have done" (*Rosenberg-Sobell*, 1952, p. 1616). The couple was sentenced to death.

Sobell's attorney, Phillips, raised a motion for an arrest of judgment while Sobell contested his deportation from Mexico. The motion was denied, and Phillips pled for leniency as the prosecution had failed to implicate Sobell in any act relating to the transmission of atomic secrets. In addressing Sobell, Kaufman conceded the defendant had played a lesser role in the conspiracy. Sobell received a maximum sentence of 30 years. David Greenglass, the last to be sentenced, received 15 years.

The Rosenbergs and Sobell appealed their convictions over the subsequent two years. Concerned that Kaufman had failed to properly direct the jury in interpreting Ethel's exercise of her Fifth Amendment rights and by sentences that seemed unduly harsh, the U.S. Circuit Court of Appeals nonetheless found no reversible error in the proceedings. Repeatedly, the Supreme Court denied the case a hearing. The defense motioned for a retrial based upon new evidence—most critically that the Greenglasses had committed perjury during the trial, in full knowledge of the prosecution—but this likewise failed. Presidents Truman and Eisenhower were both petitioned for clemency, also unsuccessfully. In 1953, the Rosenbergs' execution date was set.

The government had been confident Ethel's indictment would leverage Julius into co-operation. When that failed, it was perceived to be certain that the threat of death would do the trick. When the Rosenbergs again failed to fall into line, one last offer was extended to the couple via a Justice Department report leaked to the media—if they would confess and provide information of their illicit activities, they would be spared their lives (Neville,

1995, p. 121). From prison, the Rosenbergs publicly delivered their answer, vowing they would, "not be coerced, even under pain of death, to bear false witness…Our respect for truth, conscience and human dignity is not for sale. Justice is not some bauble to be sold to the highest bidder" (quoted in Schneir and Schneir, 1965, p. 195).

After one final delay, the execution was carried out on June 19 just before sundown, the start of the Jewish Sabbath. Julius, whose cell was nearer the death chamber, went first to avoid having his wife pass by his cell on the way to her death. When his body was removed, Ethel followed. Neither spoke any final protest or apology, nor resisted in any way their deaths ("Husband," 1953). In a foster home, their eldest son, Michael, now ten years old, learned of his parents' fate from a brief interruption to the Yankee-Tiger game on television. When younger brother Robert, six at the time, entered the room speaking excitedly about Father's Day that coming Sunday, Michael merely winked to their caretaker who looked on—he would not let on what had happened ("Son," 1953, p. 14).

ATOMIC BOMBS AND NUCLEAR FAMILIES

With the Cold War setting in against the Soviet Union, and a hot war underway in Korea, Sobell and the Rosenbergs stood little chance of a fair hearing in the mainstream press. When a nation mobilizes in the cause of defense, even a free news media tends to err on the side of patriotism. Probative investigation and skepticism of official sources tend to assume lesser priority. During this time, the major daily and weekly periodicals served as an echo chamber to a torrent of governmental revelations regarding the nature and dimensions of the communist menace. When Sobell and the Rosenbergs were swept up into this story as perpetrators of atomic espionage, they were represented to the American public as merely one more datum in the body of evidence suggestive of an impossibly large and seamless conspiracy. The prosecution exploited this atmosphere, for example, in announcing the arrest of the suspected spy William Perl (a former classmate of Sobell and Julius in college) for perjury in denying before a grand jury any acquaintance with the defendants in the middle of the trial. In essence, this allowed Saypol to promote the government's theory of the alleged atomic conspiracy ring in the press (readily available to the unsequestered jury) without having to produce or defend any additional evidence in court (see also Neville, 1995, pp. 14, 41).

Throughout the appellate process and after the executions, their lawyers and defense committees would blast the media for underreporting their side of the story, for uncritically regurgitating inflammatory statements by the prosecution and its supporters, and for blacking out coverage of the clemency movement both in the United States and abroad. However, they were well aware that the question of guilt was already well settled in the minds of most. In pursuing support from the American public and prominent cultural and political figures, issues of fairness in the trial process and the justness of the sentences were narrowly emphasized. Allegations circulating in smaller, leftist publications and the foreign press (particularly France) that Sobell and the Rosenbergs were victims of a governmental "frame-up" or bald anti-Semitism were not openly entertained domestically. In this respect, the Rosenbergs' cause at least managed modest success in stirring an appreciable mainstream movement in their favor—in spite of this wartime journalism, the fear and loathing it voiced and fomented.

Did mere *conspiracy* to commit espionage warrant a death penalty? Even if just, what wisdom was there in permanently silencing potential informants? What American interests would be furthered in letting the Rosenbergs martyr themselves for the communist cause?[6] Many celebrated trials fade quickly from the public consciousness after their initial resolution. The Rosenberg-Sobell affair, however, persisted even over the course of a long and complicated appellate process. Media coverage lightened during this time, peaking again on the verge of the execution, but it also sobered and at length began to entertain framing of the case that did not neatly align with the government's story of a cut-and-dried case of treason for which there was a consensus on the appropriateness of the death penalty. As debate grew at home and abroad, both in size and in volume, the press increasingly conceded its existence. The State Department's propaganda efforts in Europe to counter protests on behalf of the Rosenbergs were related back to the American public (Neville, 1995, p. 96). Public campaigns for Sobell and the Rosenbergs in the United States, initially orchestrated by leftist organizations and dismissed by leading newspapers as communist agitation and propaganda, progressively attracted respectable interests from legal, academic, and religious communities and could no longer be so easily painted as such. At the forefront were a growing number of protestant congregants and clerics—early, vocal critics of "McCarthyism" in all its forms.[7] Large demonstrations outside the White House and in New York City's Union Square in the days leading up to the execution, each with more than 5,000 in attendance, were admixtures of picketings and prayer vigils. Pickets spotted these crowds asking the government to "Show the World America is Merciful" and warning "The Electric Chair Can't Kill the Doubts in the Rosenberg Case." Top physicists likewise called for clemency. Albert Einstein wrote privately to Kaufman asking as much. Kaufman promptly turned the letter over to the FBI, who maintained a file on Einstein as a subversive. When options for relief in the courts were all but exhausted, Pope Pius XII communicated to President Eisenhower concerns with the Rosenbergs' case.

In historical perspective, there are no simple answers to whether or to what extent the defendants had, in fact, been atomic spies. In 1995, the U.S. government declassified a counterintelligence program that has offered some insight. In WWII, the Army began intercepting Soviet intelligence communications. The United States and the United Kingdom worked together decrypting these materials until 1980 when the program, then named Venona, was finally canceled. Most successful decryptions were achieved early on with messages passed between 1943 and 1944. Since its declassification, many have read the Venona documents as clearly implicating Julius Rosenberg and perhaps Ethel in espionage.[8] Additionally, in 1990 the posthumous memoirs of former Soviet leader Nikita Khrushchev praised the Rosenbergs for their critical role in advancing the Soviet Union toward nuclear capability. In 1997, the NKGB officer Alexandre Feklisov also publicly stated Julius had collaborated with him in espionage.

Though damning at first blush, these revelations at best provide an incomplete and often problematic corroboration of the government's case. Of the 19 messages thought to implicate the Rosenbergs, reference is made only to an agent alternately codenamed "Antenna" and "Liberal," which translators footnote as being Julius. When and how this determination was made is not clear, and while this agent is clearly involved in some form of cooperation with the Soviets these messages do not support the specific charges alleged of the Rosenbergs. There is no evidence to suggest Ethel participated or even received a codename. Feklisov has identified Julius as an operative, but only to purportedly set the record straight—that the Rosenbergs had turned over military secrets, but hardly the "secret" to the atomic bomb—during a time when it was fashionable and profitable for former KGB agents (real or not) to offer such confessionals. Julius had passed a lens mold sketch, but Feklisov described it as nothing more than a "child-ish scribble." As to Khrushchev's praise of the Rosenbergs, Feklisov merely described him as "a silly man" without understanding. Feklisov further claimed Ethel had not been involved, though she may have known of Julius's activities ("KGB Agent," 1997).

The Rosenbergs' convictions primarily resulted from the Greenglasses' testimony. In 2001, David admitted to perjury, to lying about his sister's involvement. Ethel's conviction and sentence hinged upon her supposed collaboration in typing up reports for the Soviets. David denied any recollection of this, and claims the assistant prosecutor Roy Cohn com-pelled that testimony.[9] Far from remorseful for sending his sister to her death, David claims he did what he needed to do to keep his family safe and blames the Rosenbergs for refusing to cooperate with authorities ("The Traitor," 2001).

Whatever the facts of the matter, scholars tend to agree the state's case against the defendants was quite weak and the trial botched. The defendants were charged with *con-spiracy* to commit espionage quite simply because the state knew it lacked the evidence to prove actual espionage. Prosecutorial zeal (if not outright misconduct), Kaufman's lack of impartiality and failure to suppress prejudicial statements, an unwise (perhaps incom-petent) defense, and the profoundly anticommunist sentiments of the time all contributed to a process that in retrospect seems substantially less than ideal. Most agree that the death penalty was unjustifiably harsh, particularly in Ethel's case. Even presuming the prosecu-tion's theory was entirely correct, the Rosenbergs' contribution to the Soviet weapon pro-gram simply paled in comparison to that of other, more knowledgeable spies such as Fuchs. Yet, they alone received the death penalty. While technically their espionage tran-spired during wartime, a requirement for capital punishment in Espionage Act cases, the spirit of that Act arguably did not apply to the passage of secrets to wartime allies. The Rosenbergs were, in effect, retrospectively punished for aiding a nation that had since become an enemy. Minus any rigorous evidence, they were convicted and sentenced on little more than implication, innuendo, and association. Whatever the conclusion regard-ing the defendants' relative guilt or innocence, the Rosenberg-Sobell trial remains a prime example of one of the most notorious witch-hunts of modern American history[10]—the second Red Scare.

Witch-hunts tend to occur during periods of serious social upheaval as organized efforts to identify, isolate, exclude, or destroy persons seen as dangerous to conventional society—dangerous not merely for what they do, but also what they stand for.[11] While moderns no longer fear witches, witch-hunting behaviors nevertheless persist and yield many of the celebrated trials in history. The Red Scares are exemplary of this dynamic. In each, "un-Americans," those deemed irreligious in the American spirit and wayward in radical devotions, were purged from respectable society and forced to renounce their heresies, to implicate their fellowship, and to suffer for their sacrilege.

While always premised upon a return to traditional values, witch-hunts tend to serve a progressive function, transitioning a culture from one historical period to another (see Schoeneman, 1975). When the worldview of a people is disrupted by social change, new and dissonant perspectives proliferate. The witch-hunt emerges to police ideological boundaries to reconstitute the cultural order. Although couched in the language of con-servation, witch-hunts, in fact, pursue radical ideals. While usually effective in redefining consensus values in the short term, over time the witch-hunt reliably implodes as a social force when its very operation comes to be viewed as anathema to common ideals.[12] As such, the Red Scare derailed precisely when the purge of "un-Americans" itself came to be viewed as profoundly un-American.

The World Wars had accelerated a number of changes in American society, including residential and occupational patterns, educational achievement, and the composition of households. For a variety of reasons, in postwar America the nuclear family (a husband, wife, and their children residing exclusively in a single home) became an important normative ideal. One powerful influence was the emergence of the evangelical movement in the Protestant churches at the time. Eschewing the social pessimism and apocalyptic yearnings of the now marginalized fundamentalist movement, evangelicalism found cultural currency and popular sway in speaking to more universal concerns about cultivating a rewarding, meaningful family life in the nuclear unit (Watt, 1991). While the reality of family life in the 1950s did not mirror the *Leave It to Beaver* formula propagated by popular media and cultural institutions of the time, that model was nevertheless perceived to be representative of middle-class households and a meaningful element of the American dream as understood by many at the time. Whatever their crimes, guilty or not, to execute a husband and wife—as such—and to orphan two minor children precisely when family life was taking a more central place in the American and Christian identity simply proved unpalatable to many.

Unfortunately for the Rosenbergs, news coverage only began to introduce framings of the case as a story about family—Julius, Ethel, and their sons—in the course of the lead-up to the execution (Neville, 1995, p. 125). In some cases, the dominant patriotic frameworks for narrating the story were neutralized altogether by taking the perspective of the Rosenbergs' children, which set aside the matter of guilt altogether to relate the ordeal in terms that would be entirely sympathetic regardless of one's position on the case as a matter of law. Had this narrative been directed into the public mainstream earlier or more often, if the execution had been delayed another year, it is unclear how their case might have ultimately resolved. However, as the Red Scare slowly ebbed, and U.S.-Soviet relations stabilized, the Rosenbergs' tale emerged as something more than simply one more casualty report from the Cold War.

Sobell has long since been forgotten as a minor, perhaps irrelevant, supporting role. Popular and scholarly consensus on the Rosenbergs' actual guilt or innocence, which has shifted several times over the half-century since their deaths, is driven at least as much by the political and cultural climate of the day as by the facts of the case. The Rosenbergs themselves were nothing exceptional. They lacked the zeal and profundity one would esteem in a visionary and are simply not credible as monsters. The cultural meaning of the Rosenbergs' affair seems to be sought instead in their suffering, in qualities of tragedy as the ancient Greeks understood the form but keenly tuned to the contemporary ear. Sophocles's classic tale, *Antigone,* about a woman who defies a king in order to obey the gods and honor her brother, taking her own life while awaiting an execution that the king concludes (too late) would be a mistake, offers a number of thematic comparisons. Most critically, however, here too one finds no heroes or villains—at least as the terms are understood today. Rather, one is presented with flawed human beings in a contest of wills who pay dearly for questionable principles nonetheless held dear. As generation after generation finds the family unit more fragile and autonomous, there is something compelling in the story of the Rosenbergs. Betrayed by kin, persecuted by the state, and condemned by popular society, this divided family remained faithful to the end. Julius and Ethel faced their deaths unflinchingly, defiantly but in quiet dignity. Even amidst favorable coverage

HUNTING THE UN-AMERICAN

The first scare occurred roughly between 1917 and 1921; the second, between approximately 1948 and 1954. In the first, the "red menace" was popularly understood as a pool of mainly Eastern and Southern European immigrants importing anarchist-communist orthodoxies that resisted assimilation to American values. Infusing these ideas to the organization of labor, this population was thought to have grown to the verge of a critical mass capable of triggering outright insurrection against the established order. In the second scare, the demonology of the Red had changed somewhat, reimagined as the interloper rather than the alien—the wolf in sheep's clothing, the enemy among us. This Red, the Soviet sympathizer, was thought to resemble the "true" American in every aspect of his (or her) outward appearance while nevertheless secretly working to collapse society from within from key positions in government, military, and education.

Bridging these two events was a smaller, and less studied, antifascist movement in the 1930s and 1940s. Targets included sympathizers of German Nazism and Italian Fascism who agitated for militarism, imperialism, and ethnic nationalism in the United States. This hunt drew upon the inquisitorial language, methods, and formal organization of the first Red Scare and contributed an evolution of these tactics to the second (see Ribuffo, 1994). Collectively, these three purges constitute a larger hunt for the "un-American," on fringes of both the left and right, which largely ended when McCarthyism collapsed.

The beginning of the end is generally recognized to be Joseph McCarthy's televised inquisitions and his unwise allegations that the U.S. Army itself was harboring communists, as relayed to a nation of recent war veterans and their families and condemned by such respected figures as the journalist Edward R. Murrow. Anti-McCarthyism, however, won perhaps its earliest victory in securing the dismissal of Joseph Matthews, a zealous anticommunist, from McCarthy's senate committee who led the communist purge. Matthews, in the immediate aftermath of the Rosenbergs' execution, had published an essay in the conservative periodical, *The American Mercury,* claiming that the single largest front for communism in the United States was the Protestant clergy —an allegation inspired by the untimely public activities of this group in resisting McCarthyism, including campaigning on behalf of Sobell and the Rosenbergs' defense. Popular as McCarthy and anticommunist sentiment was at the time, this accusation outraged much of the nation and many fellow senators.

of the execution, reporters present for the event could not help but intone their own sense of awe at the composure of the condemned (see also Neville, 1995, p. 133). With the Soviet Union now a fading memory, the Rosenberg children's adult efforts to humanize and domesticate their ordeal has helped crystallize this tragic reading—a story now as much high drama as pulp (worse-than) murder mystery.

SUGGESTIONS FOR FURTHER READING

Coover, R. (1977). *The public burning.* New York: Viking Press.
Doctorow, E.L. (1971). *The book of Daniel.* New York: Random House.

Meerepol, M. (Ed.) (1994). *The Rosenberg letters: A complete edition of the prison correspondence of Julius and Ethel Rosenberg.* New York: Garland.

Neville, J.F. (1995). *The press, the Rosenbergs, and the Cold War.* Westport, CT: Praeger.

Radosh, R., & Milton, J. (1983). *The Rosenberg file.* New York: Holt, Rinehart, and Winston.

Schneir, W., and Schneir, M. (1965). *Invitation to an inquest.* Garden City, New York: Doubleday & Company, Inc.

Schrank, B. (2002). Reading the Rosenbergs after Venona. *Labour/Le Travail, 49,* 189–210.

NOTES

1. Originally 50 US Code 32. Today, the Act remains in 18 US Code 793, 794.
2. The exchange below can be found in *Rosenberg-Sobell* (1952), pp. 180–198.
3. The transcript for this trial is epic, spanning nearly 2,600 pages. Schneir and Schneir (1965) provide a more detailed and highly faithful synopsis of the testimonies.
4. For this reason, in criminal cases it is the state that is required to prove their case beyond reasonable doubt—not the defense, which need not argue a case at all. Silent defenses are rare, however, because common sense suggests silence indicates concession.
5. This dynamic is common to witch-hunts. The "satanic panic" of the 1980s and 1990s (Victor, 1993) is also exemplary, as in the McMartin Preschool trial.
6. Then and now, portraits of the accused as martyrs to the communist cause, as in Sacco and Vanzetti's executions in the 1920s, were never very persuasive, at least in the United States. Julius's public ambivalence toward communism rendered this framework largely unworkable. So, this concern was often raised but rarely attracted serious consideration or rebuttal.
7. Fundamentalist Christianity, largely banished from the national political scene after the 1920s, reemerged to cooperate with McCarthyism in hopes of driving out "modernists" from the Church (see Wilcox, 1988). Liberal and evangelical Protestants banded together in self-defense. This association eventually served to increase the influence of the evangelical movement and, in turn, initially dampened its political ambitions. Jewish interests also came to the defense of the Rosenbergs, but primarily in response to perceptions of anti-Semitism in their treatment rather than as an anti-anti-communist cause.
8. Venona intelligence was not lent to prosecutions of accused spies, which instead primarily relied on confessions and implications to secure convictions. Legally, the Venona evidence is problematic. Minus the (unlikely) supporting testimony of a party to this communication, it would possibly be ruled hearsay. Even if granted exception, the extent of declassification necessary to overcome even a rudimentary defense would have rendered the program inoperable. The project was so secret, even Presidents F.D. Roosevelt and Truman were not aware of it.
9. Cohn, who pushed Saypol and Kaufman (a family friend) for the death penalty for the Rosenbergs, would later serve as counsel to Senator Joseph McCarthy on J. Edgar Hoover's recommendation.
10. There is a tendency to either understate or overstate Soviet activity in the United States in order to fit or unfit the Red Scare to the witch-hunt analogy. Either impulse misses the point, from a scientific view. "Proportional response" is a moral rather than empirical concept.
11. Literally or metaphorically, for the gods or devils they regularly commerce with. Policing regulates behavior; witch-hunts persecute impurities of the soul.
12. For this reason, witch-hunts are almost invariably movements that society subsequently looks back upon with chagrin, bewilderment, or disgust.

REFERENCES

Husband, wife go to the chair without show of emotion. (1953, June 20). *The Washington Post,* p. 1.

KGB agent says Rosenbergs were executed unjustly. (1997, March 16). CNN Interactive. Retrieved August 28, 2007, from http://www.cnn.com/US/9703/16/rosenbergs/

McKerns, J. (1997). The case of Alger Hiss and the Rosenbergs. In L. Chiasson, Jr. (Ed.), *The press on trial: Crimes and trials as media events* (pp. 131–146). Westport, CT: Greenwood Press.

Neville, J.F. (1995). *The press, the Rosenbergs, and the Cold War.* Westport, CT: Praeger.

Ribuffo, L.P. (1994). United States v. McWilliams: The Roosevelt administration and the far right. In M.R. Belknap (Ed.), *American political trials* (pp. 201–232). London: Greenwood Press.

Rosenberg, E., and Rosenberg, J. (1953). *Death house letters of Ethel and Julius Rosenberg.* New York: Jero Publishing Company.

Schneir, W., and Schneir, M. (1965). *Invitation to an inquest.* Garden City, NY: Doubleday & Company, Inc.

Schoeneman, T.J. (1975). The witch hunt as a culture change phenomenon. *Ethos 3*(4), 529–554.

Sharp, Malcolm P. (1956). *Was justice done? The Rosenberg-Sobell case.* New York: Monthly Review Press.

Son hears TV foretell doom of his parents. (1953, July 19). *Chicago Daily Tribune*, p. 14.

The Rosenberg-Sobell trial: Transcript of the trial of Julius Rosenberg, Ethel Rosenberg, and Morton Sobell in the U.S. Supreme Court, 1951. (1952). New York: Committee to Secure Justice for Morton Sobell.

The traitor. (2001, December 5). *60 Minutes II.*

Victor, J.S. (1993). *Satanic panic: The creation of a contemporary legend.* Chicago: Open Court.

Watt, D.H. (1991). The private hopes of American fundamentalists and evangelicals. *Religion and American Culture, 1*(2), 155–175.

Wilcox, C. (1988). The Christian Right in twentieth century America: Continuity and change. *The Review of Politics, 50*(4), 659–681.

12

The Sam Sheppard Case: Do Three Trials Equal Justice?

KATHY WARNES

My God, Spen, get over here quick! I think they've killed Marilyn!

(Neff, 2001, p. 7)

In the early morning hours of Sunday, July 4, 1954, someone stole into the bedroom of Marilyn Reese Sheppard, the pregnant wife of Dr. Samuel Holmes Sheppard, and beat her to death in her bed. In their lakeside home in Bay Village, a wealthy suburb of Cleveland, Ohio, her seven-year-old son, Sam Reese Sheppard, slept soundly in his bedroom next door, and her husband, Sam, slept on a couch in the living room. Dr. Sheppard wove together the events of the evening and early morning for the officials who answered his frantic call for help. He and his wife, Marilyn, had entertained their friends Don and Nancy Ahern at their home the previous evening. After dinner they watched television in the living room. Later that night, Dr. Sheppard fell asleep on the couch in the living room. For the next 16 years, he told his story of what happened when he woke up countless times, never substantially changing it.

According to Dr. Samuel Sheppard, this is what happened on the morning of July 4, 1954: he was sleeping soundly on the couch when a noise on the second floor awakened him. He was not certain how much time had elapsed from the time he dozed off until he heard the noises upstairs, but he awoke when he heard Marilyn screaming and calling for him to help her, then loud moans and noises. He thought that Marilyn might be having the same painful convulsions that she had experienced during her first pregnancy.

Still half asleep, Sheppard jumped off the couch and rushed upstairs. All the lights were out except a 40-watt bulb in the upstairs dressing room, but as he entered the bedroom he saw a "white form" standing next to the bed where his wife slept. He could not tell whether the shadowy figure was a man or woman, and he did not know how many people were in the room. He started to wrestle with the form, but suddenly someone hit him from behind on the back of his neck and skull and he lost consciousness. He did not know how long he was unconscious.

Dr. Sheppard woke up on the floor beside Marilyn's bed, injured and groggy. He inched himself into a sitting position facing the bedroom door. He saw his wife lying in a pool of blood on her twin bed, beaten and battered on the head and face. She had no pulse and showed no signs of life when he examined her. The doctor ran into their son's bedroom next door and assured himself that his son was sound asleep and unharmed. Then he heard a noise on the first floor and ran down the stairs. He chased what he described as "a large, powerfully built man with a good sized head and bushy hair" through the screen door and down the 36 steps to the beach. He attacked the man, but the man caught him in a stranglehold and choked, hit, and knocked him unconscious for a second time, again for an uncertain amount of time.

The next thing Sam Sheppard remembered was regaining consciousness at the water's edge, his head on the shore, legs in the water, and his body swaying back and forth in the waves. Staggering back to the house, he went upstairs to re-examine the body of his murdered wife. In his dazed state he thought that this might be some horrible nightmare. Then he went downstairs and called his neighbor and friend, Bay Village Mayor Spencer Houk. He shouted, "My God, Spen get over here quick. I think they've killed Marilyn!" (Neff, 2001, p. 7).

Mayor Houk and his wife, Esther, found Dr. Sheppard hunched in an easy chair in the first floor den. He implored them to do something for Marilyn. Esther Houk went upstairs to the northwest bedroom where she discovered the battered body of Marilyn Sheppard. Marilyn lay face up on the bed, her legs hanging over the foot of the bed, bent at the knees, and her feet dangling a few inches above the rug. Blood outlined her body, and blood from her head darkened the quilt, the sheets, and the pillow. Blotches of blood sprinkled the wall, and drops of blood trailed across the carpet and out the door. Her face was turned slightly toward the door and was coated with stringy, clotting blood. About two dozen deep, crescent-shaped gashes scoured her face, forehead, and scalp.

Someone had pushed up Marilyn's three-button pajama top to her neck, leaving her breasts bare. A blanket covered her middle. Her thin pajama bottoms had been removed from one leg and were bunched below the knee of her other leg, exposing her lower body. Esther Houk checked Marilyn's pulse. She did not feel one.

Mayor Houk called the Bay Village police, Sheppard's brother, Dr. Richard Sheppard, and Don and Nancy Ahern. The local police, including Bay Village patrolman Fred Dren-khan, arrived at the Sheppard home. Police officers, relatives, the press, and neighbors trooped through the house. Local police notified Cuyahoga County Coroner Dr. Samuel Gerber and the Cleveland police. Then, Dr. Richard Sheppard arrived, examined Marilyn, and declared that she was dead. He assessed his brother's injuries and took him to Bay View Hospital, which was operated by his family of osteopathic doctors. Conflicting medical reports about Dr. Samuel Sheppard's injuries exacerbated the tensions between osteopathic and medical doctors that existed in the 1950s. Dr. Samuel Gerber and other medical doctors were incensed that osteopaths like the Sheppards performed surgery, prescribed drugs, and competed with allopathic, or traditional, physicians. Gerber felt that osteopaths were bone twisters, a species of inferior doctors, a position that the powerful American Medical Association echoed. The American Medical Association under its bylaws refused to let its member doctors teach at osteopathic medical schools, consult for an osteopath on a patient's care, or even share a common waiting room, and as a result the two branches of medicine did not trust each other. Dr. Gerber mistrusted the Sheppards, their osteopathic training, and their osteopathic hospital; but at this point, Dr. Richard Sheppard managed to care for his injured brother. He also drove his nephew, seven-year-old Sam Reese Sheppard, to his house.

Sam Reese Sheppard remembered that morning. "It's kind of a frozen moment in time. I remember being kind of pushed awake by Uncle Richard, and I was told I didn't have time to get dressed—I was in my pajamas" (Taylor, 1996). A policeman blocked his view into his parents' bedroom. Around him swarmed police officers, coroner's deputies, and jittery relatives. Reporters shouted questions and flashbulbs popped. Sam Reese Sheppard said, "I walked out the back door and down toward the road. There was a clutch of curiosity-seekers and also the press. The flashbulbs started going off in my face. I remember it to this day—the curious murmur of the crowd" (Taylor, 1996).

The crowd still milled around the Sheppard house as Coroner Gerber, the Cleveland police, and other officials arrived. They thoroughly searched the house and surrounding area, taking note of the ransacked living room, the empty medical bag with contents strewn over the floor, and the open desk drawers. They photographed the rooms of the house and interrogated several people, including the Houks and the Aherns. The police sealed the Sheppard home and closed it off to Dr. Sheppard and his family.

From the first moment the police answered the call to the Sheppard home, they suspected Dr. Sam Sheppard of being the murderer. They investigated the case on the theory that Dr. Sheppard had bludgeoned his wife to death, washed the blood off his clothing in the lake, faked his injuries, staged a burglary attempt to deflect suspicion from himself, and delayed calling the authorities to gain time to conceal the evidence. As far as they were concerned, Dr. Sheppard's story of fighting with a bushy-haired intruder was an attempt to cover his guilt. This was the official theory that the Cleveland authorities leaked to the press and the official version of the crime that the state presented at the trial. The authorities did not produce any concrete proof to support this theory.

On the morning of the murder, after searching the Sheppard house and premises, the coroner, Dr. Sam Gerber, is reported to have told his men, "Well, it is evident the doctor did this, so let's go get the confession out of him." The coroner never denied saying this to his staff. Dr. Gerber questioned and examined Sam Sheppard while he was under sedation in his hospital room. During the interrogation, the police gave Coroner Gerber the clothes that Sheppard wore the night of the murder, including the personal items found in them (Pollack, 1972, p. 11).

Dr. E.H. Hexter, a Bay Village medical doctor, examined Sam Sheppard that evening at the hospital. Dr. Hexter reported that Sheppard had missing reflexes on his left side, but did not give his finding much weight. He told Dr. Gerber and the detectives that "the only outward injury" he could find was "swelling around the right eye and cheek." The police used his diagnosis to discount Sheppard's story of a "bushy haired intruder." The police also had Dr. Charles Elkins, a noted neurologist, examine Dr. Sheppard. Dr. Elkins found "serious damage to the spinal cord in the neck region, bruises on the right side of his face and lacerations to the mouth." The extent of his injuries and whether or not they could have been self-inflicted were to play an important part in Dr. Sheppard's trial (Pollack, 1972, p. 28).

On July 7, 1954, Marilyn Sheppard was buried in a private ceremony at the Saxton Funeral Home in the suburb of Lakewood. About 250 of Sam and Marilyn Sheppard's friends and family attended the service. The doctor came in a wheelchair, his neck wrapped in a stiff orthopedic collar. He walked in, wearing a suit with no tie, his eyes shaded with dark sunglasses. Their son, Sam Reese, or Chip, did not attend the funeral because of extensive media coverage, but he had picked some pansies for his mother. Weeping, Dr. Sheppard placed the pansies inside the casket.

The police searched the Sheppard house again during the funeral. Bay View Mayor Spencer Houk had officially turned the investigation over to Coroner Gerber and the county sheriff, and detectives had found some additional pieces of physical evidence during this search of the Sheppard house. Near Marilyn Sheppard's bed they found a small piece of leather and a chip of red paint or enamel. The front pages of the newspapers shouted, "Search Murder Home Again" and "Dr. Sheppard Weeps Beside Coffin of Wife" (*Cleveland News,* July 16, 1954).

A July 7 story in another newspaper featured assistant Cuyahoga County attorney John Mahon sharply criticizing the Sheppard family's refusal to permit the doctor's immediate questioning. From the day of Marilyn Sheppard's funeral on, headline stories, especially in the *Cleveland Press,* repeatedly hammered Sheppard's lack of cooperation with the police and other officials. The newspapers also played up Sheppard's refusal to take a lie detector test and decried "the protective ring" thrown up by his family. Front-page newspaper headlines announced that "Doctor Balks at Lie Test; Retells Story" (*Cleveland Press,* August 1, 1954).

On July 20, 1954, the "editorial front" of the campaign against Dr. Sam Sheppard fired its first salvo with the front-page charge that somebody was "getting away with murder." The editorial charged that the investigation into Marilyn Sheppard's death had been inept because of "friendships, relationships, hired lawyers, a husband who ought to have been subjected instantly to the same third degree to which any other person under similar circumstances is subjected." On July 21, another page one editorial demanded, "Why No Inquest? Do It Now, Dr. Gerber" (*Cleveland Press,* 1954).

The coroner announced on that same day that an inquest would be convened and subpoenaed Dr. Sheppard. The inquest was held the next day in a school gymnasium with Dr. Gerber presiding, the county prosecutor as his advisor, and two detectives as bailiffs. Reporters, television and radio personnel, and broadcasting equipment occupied a long table in the front of the room. The hearing was broadcast live with microphones at the coroner's seat and the witness stand. Police brought Dr. Sheppard into the room and searched him in full view of several hundred people. His counsel was present during the three-day inquest, but was not permitted to participate. When Dr. Sheppard's chief counsel tried to put some documents in the record, the coroner threw him out of the room to the accompaniment of cheers, hugs, and kisses from ladies in the audience. Various officials questioned Dr. Sheppard for five and a half hours about his actions on the night of the murder, his married life, and an affair with a laboratory technician, Susan Hayes.

The newspapers continued to stress the evidence that incriminated Dr. Sheppard and touted discrepancies in his statements to authorities. During the inquest on July 26, a large-type headline in the *Cleveland Press* blared: "Kerr [Captain of the Cleveland Police] Urges Sheppard's Arrest." The story said that Detective James McArthur "disclosed that scientific tests at the Sheppard home have definitely established that the killer washed off a trail of blood from the murder bedroom to the downstairs section," a circumstance casting doubt on Sheppard's accounts of the murder. This evidence was not presented at the trial (*Cleveland Press,* July 25, 1954).

The *Cleveland Press* and the *Cleveland Plain Dealer* also spotlighted Dr. Sheppard's personal life, citing his extramarital affairs as a motive for killing his wife. A July 28 editorial in the *Cleveland Press* asked, "Why Don't Police Quiz Top Suspect?" and demanded that Dr. Sheppard be taken to police headquarters. It described Dr. Sheppard in this way:

> Now proved under oath to be a liar, still free to go about his business, shielded by his family, protected by a smart lawyer who has made monkeys of the police and authorities, carrying a gun part of the time, left free to do whatever he pleases. (*Cleveland Press*, 1954)

On July 30, 1954, a front-page editorial wondered "Why Isn't Sam Sheppard in Jail?" After calling Dr. Sheppard "the most unusual murder suspect ever seen around these parts," the editorial said that "except for some superficial questioning during Coroner Sam Gerber's inquest he has been scot-free of any official grilling." It concluded by charging that Dr. Sheppard was surrounded "by an iron curtain of protection and concealment" (*Cleveland Press*, 1954).

On the night of July 30, 1954, the Cleveland police arrested Dr. Sam Sheppard at his father's home and charged him with murder. They took him to the Bay Village City Hall where hundreds of people, newscasters, photographers, and reporters awaited his arrival. They immediately arraigned him and bound him over to the grand jury.

Publicity continued to escalate until Dr. Sheppard's indictment on August 17, 1954. Typical headlines during this period included "Dr. Sam: I Wish There Was Something I Could Get off My Chest—But There Isn't," "Corrigan Tactics Stall Quizzing," "Sheppard 'Gay Set' Is Revealed by Houk," "Blood Is Found in Garage," "New Murder Evidence Is Found, Police Claim," and "Dr. Sam Faces Quiz at Jail on Marilyn's Fear of Him." There are five volumes filled with similar clippings from each of the three Cleveland newspapers, the *Cleveland Press*, the *Cleveland Plain Dealer,* and the *Cleveland News,* covering the period from the murder until Dr. Sheppard's conviction in December 1954 ("Findings of U.S. Supreme Court," 1996).

One of the few stories favorable to Dr. Sheppard appeared on August 18 under the headline "Dr. Sam Writes His Own Story." A portion of the typed statement signed by Dr. Sheppard was reproduced across the entire front page. It read in part, "I am not guilty of the murder of my wife, Marilyn. How could I, who have been trained to help people and devoted my life to saving life, commit such a terrible and revolting crime?" (*Cleveland Press,* 1954).

It seemed that most local law enforcement officials and many ordinary citizens felt that Dr. Sheppard could commit "such a terrible and revolting crime," because on August 17, 1954, he was indicted for murder. He would not enjoy another day of freedom for nearly ten years.

THE FIRST TRIAL

From August 17, 1954, the day of his indictment, to October 28, 1954, the first day of his trial, the print and broadcast media of Cleveland tried and convicted Dr. Sam Sheppard many times over. On October 9, 1954, a newspaper editorial criticized defense counsel William Joseph Corrigan's poll of the public to show local bias for a change of venue motion.

Twenty-five days before the trial began, 75 people were called as prospective jurors. Jury selection began on October 18, 1954. All three Cleveland newspapers published the names and addresses of the prospective jurors, and many of them received anonymous letters and telephone calls about the prosecution of Dr. Sheppard. Jurors were not sequestered during the trial, and the newspapers printed their names and photos more than 40 times. Jurors were not queried about the media accounts they had heard, and trial transcripts were printed regularly. Police, prosecutors, witnesses, and the families of the judge and jurors gave interviews and appeared on camera.

The news media had constant access to the jurors. Every juror except one admitted to reading about the case in the Cleveland papers or having heard broadcasts about it. Seven of the 12 jurors rendering the verdict had one or more Cleveland papers delivered to their homes.

A radio debate broadcast live over WHK on October 19 featured reporters accusing Dr. Sheppard of trying to block the prosecution and asserting that he conceded his guilt by hiring a prominent criminal lawyer. Dr. Sheppard's counsel objected to this broadcast and requested a continuance, but the judge denied the motion. When counsel asked the court to give some protection from such happenings, Judge Edward Blythin replied, "WHK doesn't have much coverage. After all, we are not trying this case by radio or in newspapers or any other means. We confine ourselves seriously to it in this courtroom and do the very best we can" ("Findings of U.S. Supreme Court," 1966).

A newspaper headline on October 23, 1954, plaintively asked, "But Who Will Speak for Marilyn?" and called for "Justice to Sam Sheppard." The front-page story focused on the family of the accused. The two brothers of Dr. Sheppard were described as "prosperous and poised." His two sisters-in-law were characterized as smart, chic, and well groomed; his elderly father as courtly and reserved. The newspaper report then noted that Marilyn Sheppard's mother had died when she was very young and that her father had no interest in her murder case. Through quotes from Detective Chief James McArthur, the reporter assured readers that the exhibits of the prosecution would speak for Marilyn. McArthur stated, "[H]er story will come into this courtroom through our witnesses." The story concludes, "Then you realize how what and who is missing from the perfect setting will be supplied. How in the Big Case justice will be done. Justice to Sam Sheppard. And to Marilyn Sheppard" (*Cleveland Press*, 1954).

The intense publicity surrounding the Sheppard case continued into the trial. The trial of Dr. Samuel Holmes Sheppard began on October 28, 1954. Assistant County Prosecutor John Mahon sat on one side of the trial table, along with his assistants Saul Danaceau and Thomas Parrino. Assistant Prosecutor Mahon faced an election for a judgeship in three weeks. His two assistants later would use their public renown from the trial to win their own judgeships. The defense side of the table included Fred Garmone; Arthur Petersilge, the Sheppard family lawyer; and William J. Corrigan, Jr. Judge Edward J. Blythin had a reputation as a cautious and patient judge, but he, too, faced voters for reelection in three weeks.

On this first day of the trial, the jury visited the Sheppard home. Hundreds of reporters, cameramen, and onlookers went along with them. The time of the jury's visit was revealed so far in advance that one of the newspapers had time to rent a helicopter and fly over the house, taking pictures of the jury tour.

The newspapers had access to a daily record of the court proceedings, and the testimony of each witness was printed verbatim in the local editions of the newspapers, along with objections of counsel and rulings by the judge. Pictures of Dr. Sheppard, Judge

Blythin, counsel, pertinent witnesses, and the jury accompanied the newspaper and television accounts.

Trial testimony proved to be as damaging and controversial to the Sheppard case as the media coverage. Deputy Coroner Lester Adelson described Marilyn Sheppard's autopsy and showed pictures of her death scene and battered face. Defense Attorney Corrigan forced Adelson to admit that he had not analyzed her stomach contents, had made no microscopic study of the wounds, and did not test for possible rape.

Don and Nancy Ahern, and Spencer and Esther Houk, testified that the Sheppards had been having marital difficulties. Dr. Lester Hoverston, a college classmate of Sam and Marilyn who had been their houseguest in early July but was in Akron the night of the murder, testified that Dr. Sheppard had told him that he was considering divorcing Marilyn.

Appearing as an uncontested expert, Cuyahoga County Coroner Dr. Sam Gerber decried what he termed the Sheppard family's lack of cooperation, and described the bloody pillowcase from the murder bed in graphic detail. Dr. Gerber said that he could make out the impression of a surgical instrument in the bloodstain. He did not go into detail about the type of surgical instrument or produce it, but he insisted that the murder weapon could only be a surgical instrument.

Detective Michael Grabowski of the Scientific Investigation Unit and Mary Cowan, the coroner's chief medical technologist, testified about the physical evidence, describing their scientific tests in detail. The prosecution did not dwell on the fact that Mary Cowan testified that she had found seven human blood spots in the downstairs and basement of the Sheppard house but could not type them as Sam or Marilyn's blood. The prosecution argued that the seven spots were Dr. Sheppard's blood trail.

Mary Cowan conceded that her findings of the blood types on the wristwatches of Sam and Marilyn were not definitive. On Marilyn's wristwatch she had found Marilyn and Sam's blood and also a third, unidentified blood factor. The card recording these findings mysteriously disappeared during the trial and did not surface until the Ohio Supreme Court reviewed the case a year later. She also admitted that the bloodstains on Sam Sheppard's trousers were inconclusive. The entire body of blood evidence seemed to confuse everyone involved in the trial, including the judge, jury, prosecution, and defense.

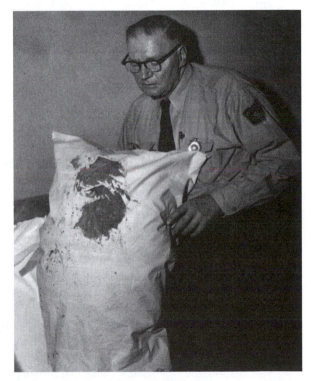

Figure 12.1 Coroner S.R. Gerber testifies that the lower bloodstain on this pillow bore the imprint of a surgical instrument, 1953. The pillow was on Marilyn Sheppard's bed when her battered body was found, he said. © AP Photo.

But laboratory technician Susan Hayes, not blood evidence or Coroner Gerber, turned out to be the star witness at the trial. Ms. Hayes testified that she and Dr. Sam Sheppard had engaged in a long-term affair, directly contradicting his denials of their relationship and seriously undermining his credibility.

Outside of the courtroom, the media onslaught continued. On November 21, 1954, in a radio broadcast on station WHK in Cleveland, nationally known commentator Robert Considine labeled Dr. Sam Sheppard a perjurer. Dr. Sheppard's defense counsel asked Judge Blythin to question the jury to find out how many of them may have heard the broadcast, but Judge Blythin did not do so. He also overruled the motion for continuance based on the same ground, saying, "We are not going to harass the jury every morning. . . . I have confidence in this jury" ("Findings of U.S. Supreme Court," 1996).

On November 24, 1954, a Cleveland Press newspaper headline announced, "Sam Called a 'Jekyll-Hyde' by Marilyn, Cousin to Testify." The story said that Marilyn Sheppard had recently told friends that Sheppard was a "Dr. Jekyll and Mr. Hyde" character and the prosecution had a witness in the wings to testify to Dr. Sheppard's fiery temper, countering the defense claim that the defendant was a gentle physician with an even disposition. William Joseph Corrigan, the defense counsel, made motions for change of venue, continuance, and mistrial, but they were denied. Judge Blythin took no action, and no such testimony was ever presented.

In November 1954, when the trial was in its seventh week, Walter Winchell, a national broadcaster, reported over WXEL television and WJW radio that a woman named Carole Beasley, who was under arrest in New York City for robbery, claimed that she was Dr. Sheppard's mistress and had an illegitimate child by him. Two jurors admitted that they had heard the broadcast, but Judge Blythin took no action.

On December 9, 1954, Dr. Sam Sheppard testified that Cleveland detectives had mistreated him after his arrest. Although he was not at the trial, Captain David Kerr of the homicide bureau issued a press statement denying Sheppard's charges. The statement appeared under a headline calling Dr. Sheppard a "barefaced liar" ("Findings of U.S. Supreme Court," 1996).

Testimony at the trial ended on December 16, 1954, and the jury was sequestered for the first time on December 17. The jury deliberated from December 17 to 21, for five days and four nights. On December 21, the jury returned with a verdict of murder in the second degree. After the verdict was announced, defense counsel William J. Corrigan discovered that the jurors had been allowed to make telephone calls to their homes every day while they were sequestered in their hotel rooms. The judge had not instructed the bailiffs to prevent such calls. Defense counsel Corrigan moved that this ground alone warranted a new trial, but the judge overruled the motion and took no evidence on the question. Although Corrigan objected, Judge Blythin passed immediate sentence upon Dr. Sam Sheppard: life in prison.

The local and national media had obviously overstepped any bounds of objectivity and tried and convicted Dr. Sheppard before the jury did. Law enforcement officials contributed much to this conviction by contaminating the crime scene and handling the evidence incompetently. Many of the people who believed Dr. Samuel Holmes Sheppard guilty of murdering his wife Marilyn considered him a spoiled rich kid and a womanizer. He had conducted at least one adulterous affair with a laboratory technician at Bay View Hospital and slept with her at the home of a colleague, as the prosecution proved without a doubt at his trial. A few witnesses had come forward suggesting that Marilyn Sheppard, in her

turn, had at least one affair and that an outraged wife had murdered her. But the officials pressing for Dr. Sheppard's conviction
prevailed.

As the U.S. Supreme Court was to point
out a decade later, the prosecution errors
were glaringly obvious, but the defense also
made some serious mistakes that helped
convict Dr. Sheppard. One of the most serious defense errors was not obtaining its own
expert to examine the Sheppard house. Even
though Sheppard family members charged
that the police refused to turn over the keys,
the defense never asked to conduct an
examination. The defense also did not vigorously challenge Dr. Sam Gerber's claim that
the bloody imprint on Marilyn's pillow
came from a surgical instrument, and the
defense could have denounced the trial as a
circus, as the U.S. Supreme Court would
later do, and advised Dr. Sheppard to claim
his Fifth Amendment right to be silent.

Figure 12.2 Dr. Sam Sheppard returns to his jail cell after
a jury found him guilty of killing his wife, Marilyn, 1954.
© AP Photo.

Dr. Stephen Sheppard kept his brother from the press and alienated reporters, making
the theory of a Sheppard family conspiracy to get away with murder appear plausible. The
defense did not use the media in its favor as F. Lee Bailey, the lawyer who would ultimately
free Sam Sheppard, did.

But Dr. Sam Sheppard delivered the most damaging blow to his defense himself. He
lied at the inquest, denying his affair with Susan Hayes. One newspaperman accurately
summarized the trial when he said that Dr. Sheppard was tried for murder and convicted
by adultery.

INTERLUDE AND THE SECOND TRIAL

The next 12 years brought great tragedy, great hope, and, finally, freedom to Dr. Sam
Sheppard. After he spent Christmas of 1954 in the county jail, he got the news that on
January 7, 1955, his mother, Ethel Sheppard, had committed suicide. Eleven days later,
Dr. Richard Sheppard, his father, died of a hemorrhaging ulcer and stomach cancer. In
the meantime, William Corrigan presented a brief petition for a new trial, the first in a
dozen unsuccessful tries to overturn the Sheppard conviction.

In March 1955, in preparation for the appeal, the defense hired Dr. Paul Leland Kirk, a
criminalist. He visited the Sheppard home and submitted a 56-page report to William
Corrigan in which he demonstrated that the blood evidence at the scene of Marilyn Sheppard's murder proved the presence of a third person at the scene, and the pattern of blood
spatters proved that Dr. Sheppard could not have been the murderer because he was right-
handed and a left-handed person had killed Marilyn.

On July 13, 1955, the state court of appeals rejected Dr. Sheppard's appeal, and that
summer he was moved from jail in Cleveland to a maximum-security prison near

Columbus, Ohio. William Corrigan continued to file appeals, including one to the Ohio Supreme Court in 1956. In November 1956, the U.S. Supreme Court refused to hear the Sheppard case. William Corrigan continued to appeal the case unsuccessfully.

In the meantime, books about the Sheppard case began to appear. In 1956, Louis B. Seltzer, editor of the *Cleveland Press,* published his autobiography, *The Years Were Good.* In his book, he devoted chapter 26 to discussing the Sheppard murder case and why he wrote a series of front-page editorials alleging that the Sheppard family was engaged in a conspiracy to get away with murder. Seltzer wrote,

> I was convinced that a conspiracy existed to defeat the ends of justice, and that it would affect adversely the whole law-enforcement machinery of the county if it were permitted to succeed. Because I did not want anyone else on the press staff to take the risk, I wrote the editorial myself. (Seltzer, 1956)

In 1961, Paul Holmes, a reporter and lawyer who had covered the trial for the *Chicago Tribune,* wrote the pioneer book about the case, *The Sheppard Murder Case.* In the first two-thirds of the book, he wrote a balanced account of the trial; and in the last third, he theorized what had really happened the morning of July 4, 1954. After covering the trial and after reading Dr. Kirk's report, Paul Holmes concluded that Dr. Sheppard did not and could not have killed his wife, but was the victim of a propaganda war. He theorized that a man and a woman were the perpetrators and said, "I think the whole business robbed luster from American jurisprudence, and is, in its more literal and reverent sense, a God-damned shame" (Holmes, 1961, p. 78).

Dr. Stephen Sheppard wrote his account of the ordeal in 1964 with the help of Paul Holmes. He called his book *My Brother's Keeper* and included a three-page epilogue about Judge Carl Weinman's district court ruling. In 1966, Paul Holmes wrote a sequel to *The Sheppard Murder Case,* which he called *Retrial: Murder and Dr. Sam Sheppard.* The sequel was rushed into print within weeks of the verdict, and only 88 of the 240 pages were devoted to the second trial. At least 50 pages were the transcripts of testimony by Mary Cowan and Dr. Kirk.

The name of a possible suspect in the murder surfaced in November 1959, when a window washer named Richard Eberling was arrested for stealing from customers. The stolen items he had in his possession included Marilyn Sheppard's ring. He had stolen the ring from Marilyn's sister-in-law, who had received it after her death. When police questioned him, Eberling told them that he had washed Sam and Marilyn Sheppard's windows days before the murder. While he did this, he had cut his finger and dripped blood down the stairs to the basement, where he washed the cut.

The Bay Village police took his statement to John T. Corrigan, the county prosecutor (no relation to William J. Corrigan, the defense lawyer), but John Corrigan displayed little interest in the information. The police relayed the information to Cuyahoga County Coroner Sam Gerber, who said he would have Richard Eberling take a lie detector test, but then he changed his mind. The information lay dormant for 30 years.

Deaths of some of the key players in the Sheppard murder case continued throughout the years that Sam Sheppard spent in prison. In 1958, Judge Edward Blythin died; and on February 13, 1963, Thomas Reese, father of Marilyn Sheppard, committed suicide. In July 1961, William Corrigan, the original defense attorney for Dr. Sheppard, died, paving the way for F. Lee Bailey to take over the defense. On April 13, 1963, F. Lee Bailey filed a new *habeas corpus* petition in U.S. district court. On July 16, 1964, federal district court

THE SUSPECTS

MAJOR JAMES CALL

Two former FBI agents wrote books about the Sheppard murder case, writing from opposite viewpoints about the guilt of Dr. Samuel Sheppard. In April 2002, Bernard F. Conners, a former FBI agent, published a book called *Tailspin: The Strange Case of Major Call.* In 1954 Major Call, an Air Force pilot, deserted and went on a burglary spree across the country. Saying that he would kill anybody who got in his way, Call made good his threat and killed a policeman who surprised him during a burglary in New York. Agent Conners writes that about the time of the Sheppard murder, Call visited his sister in Mantua, Ohio, which is about 30 miles from downtown Cleveland. A woman from Mantua called the police the day after Marilyn Sheppard was murdered to report that she had seen a man with "bushy hair" catching a bus out of town.

According to Agent Connors, the Sheppard murder fit into Call's pattern. He carried a crowbar, which could have been the murder weapon, and he also carried a Luger, which could have left the bloody imprint on Marilyn Sheppard's pillowcase. Fingerprints that had been taken after his arrest for the murder in New York revealed a recent injury to his forefinger that resembled a bite mark. He was also limping in the way that Dr. Sam Sheppard had described "the bushy haired intruder" as doing and he did not have an alibi for the July 3–4 time frame. Connors also turned up a witness, Dr. Gervase Flick, who had picked up a hitchhiker heading east from Ashtabula, Ohio. The hitchhiker had blood on his shoes and seemed unnaturally interested in newscasts about the murder. In 1997 Flick picked out a photo of Call, identifying him as the hitchhiker.

Despite another set of witnesses who identified Call as the bushy haired man that they had seen on Lake Road before the murder of Marilyn Sheppard, Conners could not find any direct evidence connecting Call to the crime. Call was killed in an automobile accident in 1970.

RICHARD EBERLING

Despite the finding of the civil jury in Cleveland, Richard Eberling is still a suspect. The jury did not hear about his conviction for the brutal 1984 murder of Ethel Durkin and the circumstantial evidence that linked him to the suspicious deaths of her two sisters. He was familiar with the Sheppard house and had left a trail of blood there before the murder of Marilyn Sheppard. In 1959, he volunteered the information to the police that he had dripped blood in the house.

In 2001, James Neff published a book called *The Wrong Man: The Final Verdict on the Dr. Sam Sheppard Murder Case,* in which he concluded that Eberling had killed Marilyn Sheppard. He based his opinion on forensic evidence uncovered by Dr. Paul Kirk and an interview that he had conducted with a dying Richard Eberling. Neff described Eberling snapping to alertness and imagining himself back in the blood-soaked bedroom of Marilyn and Sam Sheppard. According to Eberling blood was spattered everywhere and he was horrified. "My God, I had never seen anything like it," he said. "I got out of there."

Then catching himself, Eberling clammed up and would not talk about the scene any longer. Richard Eberling died before James Neff could return for another interview.

The opposite side of Neff's theory is that Eberling was known as a pathological liar and had previously confessed to the murder of Marilyn Sheppard. In another version he confessed, implicating Dr. Sheppard and at other times asserting his innocence.

Even after another DNA expert, Dr. Mohammad Tahir, asserted that his analysis of blood evidence implicated Richard Eberling, Bailey remained unconvinced. He thought that Eberling could have been the killer, but he still believed Esther Houk a more likely suspect.

J. SPENCER AND ESTHER HOUK

The gossip around Bay Village in 1954 seemed to reinforce F. Lee Bailey's suspicions. A tooth chip that did not belong to Marilyn or Sam Sheppard was discovered in their bedroom where the murder had taken place. Rumor had it that a certain Bay Village resident had teeth extracted immediately after the murder. In 1966, the police brought former part-time Bay Village Mayor J. Spencer Houk to the Central Police Station for questioning because Dr. Stephen Sheppard had given them certain information. F. Lee Bailey suspected the Houks, and before the second trial in 1966, he hinted to reporters that the killer was a left-handed woman as opposed to Eberling who was a right-handed male. During cross-examination at the 1966 trial, Bailey established that the Houks were familiar with the Sheppard house. He also established that the Houks could travel between their house and the Sheppard house using the beach and that they had set a fire in their fireplace on a July night with a low temperature of 64 degrees. Bailey had planned to call a bakery driver who swore that he had seen Mayor Houk kissing Marilyn, but he was not allowed to do so.

After the acquittal of Dr. Sam Sheppard, Bailey persuaded Bay Village police to investigate the evidence against the Houks. The Grand Jury heard witnesses, but doubted that Mayor Houk, who walked with a limp, was the man who had run from Sheppard. Why would Sheppard have run from a neighbor that he knew well and called a friend, and why would Houk have been the first person that Sheppard called when he discovered the murder of his wife? The Grand Jury took no action.

At one point in the investigation, Samuel Reese Sheppard had acquired a tape of an interview with Spencer Houk shortly before his death in 1980 that seemed to implicate him in the murder. Sheppard took the tape seriously enough to devise two scenarios, one with Spencer Houk as the killer and the second featuring Esther. As the evidence against Eberling began to mount, Sheppard stopped following the threads of evidence implicating the Houks, but F. Lee Bailey always believed that one or both of them had murdered Marilyn Sheppard.

In his 1966 book, *The Sheppard Murder Case,* Paul Holmes maintains an objective tone devoid of speculation. However, at the end of the book he lays out a "hypothesis" that features Marilyn Sheppard being killed with a flashlight by a woman whose husband fakes a burglary to cover up for her. They accidentally set up Dr. Sheppard as a suspect, and the setup succeeds. As Holmes put it, "No one will ever look for ashes in their grate or examine their car for bloodstains."

In 1972 Jack Harrison Pollack published a book, *Dr. Sam: An American Tragedy,* and he entitled his final chapter ''The Guilty.'' In that chapter he reported that before he died, a private detective who had worked for the Sheppards had planned to write a book about the ''explosive new findings'' he had discovered. The detective, Harold Bretnall, had written in his notes, ''Marilyn Sheppard was murdered by someone who was a frequent visitor to the Sheppard home. After carefully ruling out all other possibilities, Bretnall concluded that Marilyn's killers were a woman and a bushy-haired man living in bondage with their awful secret.''

Bretnall's findings impressed Pollack and matched Pollack's conclusions. Pollack also believed that the murderers were a couple—a woman and a man.

DR. SAMUEL HOLMES SHEPPARD

No direct evidence connecting Dr. Sam Sheppard with the murder of his wife has even been found despite his conviction for murder in the winter of 1954 and nearly one decade in prison. In 1966, a jury found Dr. Sheppard not guilty ''beyond a reasonable doubt.'' Local opinion proved to be not as charitable. The 2000 jury ruling on the same evidence found him ''not innocent.''

It seems that Dr. Sam Sheppard was his own worst witness. His story of what happened in the early morning hours of July 4, 1954, did not ring true to many local and later national sensibilities. How could an intruder attack his wife while he slept downstairs without waking his son in the next room? How could a shadowy form knock him out twice? Why the long delay in calling the police? Where was the missing T-shirt? Why did he answer ''I don't know,'' to the many questions that his family, friends, and the police asked him?

At the first trial, Dr. Sheppard made some serious errors. He denied having an affair with Susan Hayes, whom the prosecution flew in from California to prove that they did indeed have an affair. She testified that he had spoken of divorcing his wife and marrying her.

Coroner Dr. Samuel Gerber's description of the murder weapon as being similar to a surgical instrument and no expert testimony to counter his evidence also eroded his creditability with the first jury. The prosecution also charged in the first trial that he had faked the injuries that he had received in his encounters with the ''bushy haired'' man.

The prosecutors requested doctors to examine him in jail, and they concluded that his injuries were genuine, but they were not called to testify at the first trial. Prosecutors did not challenge his injuries in the second trial, and Dr. Robert White, who testified for the state in the third trial, had not examined Dr. Sheppard.

Prosecutors at the second trial did not call Susan Hayes or bring in any evidence of other women in his life or attempt to introduce testimony that the Sheppards had considered divorce. As some observers said, in the first trial Sheppard had been tried for murder and found guilty of adultery. Evidence of Dr. Sheppard's extramarital activities was missing from the second trial, leaving the jurors to puzzle over Dr. Sheppard's motive for killing his wife.

For years, even his best friends had struggled with disbelief over his story about what had happened on the night of July 3 and 4, 1954. Another former FBI agent,

Gregg O. McCrary, had analyzed crime scenes and created criminal profiles. After a study of Sheppard crime photographs, police reports, and other records, he concluded that the murder was "a staged domestic homicide committed by Dr. Samuel Sheppard." His former FBI supervisor, John E. Douglas, studied the same materials and arrived at a radically different conclusion. Douglas said that the Sheppard murder was a sexual and not a domestic homicide.

Judge Carl Weinman ruled that Dr. Sheppard had been denied a fair trial, and he was released from prison. In May 1965, an appeals court voted two to one to reverse Judge Weinman's decision, but on June 6, 1966, the U.S. Supreme Court agreed with Judge Weinman, ruling that the Sheppard trial had been a "carnival" and that Sheppard was denied a fair trial because the judge failed to control the courtroom atmosphere and prevent jury bias from excessive media coverage.

Dr. Sam Sheppard's second trial began on October 24, 1966, and the new judge immediately sequestered the jury. He also severely limited media access to the courtroom. F. Lee Bailey had intended to introduce evidence to support his belief that Dr. Sheppard's neighbors, Spencer and Esther Houk, were the real murderers, but his attempts to introduce this evidence were suppressed. But, Bailey proved to be an effective cross-examiner. He got Coroner Gerber to admit that he could not describe which "surgical instrument" had made a blood imprint on Marilyn Sheppard's pillowcase. He also forced Coroner Gerber to acknowledge that he had never found the surgical instrument. This admission negated the effect of his impressive testimony during the first trial. Some of the mistakes that the police had made during the original investigation came out in this trial, including missing evidence. A cigarette butt found on the scene had disappeared, and there had been no exam for evidence of rape. The defense rested without calling Sam Sheppard to testify on his own behalf. All the prosecution could do was make the rest of its case against Dr. Sheppard by the strength of its closing arguments. The strategy did not work.

VERDICT AND AFTERMATH

On November 16, 1966, the jury found Dr. Sheppard not guilty "beyond a reasonable doubt." After spending ten years in prison and two years undergoing a second trial, Dr. Sam Sheppard attempted to pick up the strands of his life and forge ahead, but the ghosts of the past haunted him for the rest of his life. He married Ariane Tebbenjohanns in July 1964, when he was released from prison, but they divorced in December 1968. He drank heavily, and his attempts to resume his medical career resulted in malpractice suits. In 1969, after trying to return to medicine, Sheppard took up team wrestling and married Colleen Strickland. Four years after being declared not guilty in his second malpractice trial, Sam Sheppard died on April 6, 1970, of liver failure at the age of 46.

Two more books about the Sheppard murder case appeared in the 1970s. F. Lee Bailey published *The Defense Never Rests* in 1971, in which he admitted that he had not allowed Dr. Sheppard to testify during his second trial because the doctor was often incoherent from alcohol and drugs. Jack Harrison Pollack published *Dr. Sam: An American Tragedy* in 1972. Pollack became interested in the Sheppard case after he wrote a sympathetic article about Dr. Sheppard before he was freed. His book is a straightforward, objective account of the story, with 16 pages of photographs and an index.

The 1980s marked the deaths of four more principals in the Sheppard murder case. Spencer and Esther Houk, who were divorced in 1962, died in 1981 and 1982, respectively; and Dr. Sam Gerber, Cuyahoga County coroner, died in 1987.

In 1989, Richard Eberling was convicted of aggravated murder in the death of Ethel May Durkin, an elderly widow, who died on January 3, 1984, after being hospitalized six weeks from a fall in her home. In October 1989, Sam Reese Sheppard began his attempts to solve the murder of his mother, Marilyn Sheppard, and to speak out publicly about his family's ordeal. Not content to have his father declared merely "not guilty," he wanted him to be declared innocent, a legal distinction in Ohio that would forever clear his father's name and possibly open the way for Sam Reese to sue the state of Ohio for damages.

THIRD TRIAL

"I had one night with Dad, after he was arrested. It was in August 1954. I think they were trying to see if he would confess to me. Anyway, I was brought back from summer camp for questioning by the coroner.

"He was let out of jail for one night and allowed to go to my uncle's house. He and I talked. He said a huge mistake had been made, but this was the United States and they couldn't convict the wrong person. Mom was in heaven, and soon they would find the right person, the one who did it. Then I woke up and he was gone."

Samuel Reese Sheppard has spent his adult life attempting to deal with the destruction of his family when he was just seven years old. For years he tried covering up his painful past, but later he decided to try to clear his father's name. In 1999, Samuel Reese Sheppard, with the help of his attorney, Terry Gilbert, sued the State of Ohio in the Cuyahoga County Court of Common Pleas for the wrongful imprisonment of his father.

Attorney Gilbert explained the motives of Samuel Reese Sheppard:

In 1995, we initiated a legal action which seeks a declaration of innocence from the trial court. We must prove by a preponderance of the evidence that Dr. Sheppard did not commit the murder. After obtaining that declaration, we would be able to get reparations from the state for the ten years of wrongful imprisonment. The acquittal at the fair trial did not eliminate the prejudiced mindset of the people of Cleveland and elsewhere that Dr. Sheppard was guilty and simply got off because of the slick tactics of a young lawyer named F. Lee Bailey. So we need to get the legal system to go beyond the original acquittal in 1966 and to affirmatively proclaim his innocence and that he was wrongfully imprisoned.

Cuyahoga County prosecutor William D. Mason headed the trial team of the State of Ohio and assistant prosecutor Steve Dever and Dean M. Boland rounded out his team. They argued that Dr. Sheppard was still the most logical suspect in the murder of his wife, and they introduced expert testimony suggesting that her murder represented a case of textbook domestic homicide. The court ordered the exhumation of Marilyn Sheppard's body, partially to determine if Dr. Sheppard had been the father of the baby she was carrying when she died and to obtain samples of DNA and reexamine her wounds. Samuel Reese Sheppard's attorney, Terry Gilbert, suggested that the coroner's office under Dr. Samuel Gerber had possibly concealed evidence.

Samuel Reese Sheppard, his father's former attorney F. Lee Bailey, and his present day attorney Terry Gilbert, had differing theories about who had really murdered Marilyn Sheppard. Attorney Terry Gilbert pointed the finger at Richard Eberling, as the most likely person who had murdered Marilyn Sheppard. Eberling, an occasional handyman and window washer at the Sheppard home, had been caught with one of her rings after a burglary investigation. Eberling died in prison in Ohio in 1998, while serving a life sentence for the 1984 murder of Ethel May Durkin, an elderly wealthy widow from Lakewood, Ohio. DNA testing of Richard Eberling's blood to see if it matched the blood found at the murder scene proved to be inconclusive.

F. Lee Bailey testified that he believed that Eberling could not have been the killer. Instead, he suggested that Esther Houk, wife of Bay Village mayor Spencer Houk, had killed Marilyn in a jealous rage after discovering that Marilyn and Mayor Houk had engaged in an affair.

The trial lasted for ten weeks and featured 76 witnesses and hundreds of exhibits. The case went before an eight person civil jury that deliberated just three hours. On April 12, 2000, it announced its unanimous verdict that Sam Reese Sheppard did not prove that his father had been wrongfully imprisoned. It ruled that Dr. Samuel Sheppard was "not innocent" of the murder of his wife Marilyn.

Attorney Gilbert appealed the verdict to the Eighth District Court of Appeals, and on February 22, 2002, the Court ruled unanimously that the case should not have gone to the jury because only the person actually imprisoned could make a wrongful imprisonment claim. A family member, even a son, could not bring such a claim. The Court of Appeals ruled that the legal standing to bring such a claim had died with the person who had been imprisoned, Dr. Samuel Holmes Sheppard. In August 2002, the Supreme Court of Ohio affirmed the appeals court's decision.

WHO KILLED MARILYN SHEPPARD?

Books continued to be published about the Sheppard murder case as Sam Reese fought to clear his father's name. In 1995, Cynthia L. Cooper and Sam published *Mockery of Justice: The True Story of the Sheppard Murder Case.* It is written from the family's viewpoint, but comprehensively summarizes the case, with 328 pages of text, 21 illustrations, 40 pages of endnotes, and a 15-page index. In 1996, *Endure and Conquer: My 12-Year Fight for Vindication,* by Dr. Sam Sheppard, was published. Dr. Sam Sheppard's story was written, according to his son, by a ghostwriter with the doctor's notes. It narrated his prison experiences, but did not include endnotes or an index. In April 2000, Bernard F. Conners published *Tailspin: The Strange Case of Major Call,* in which he pinned the Sheppard murder on James Call, an Air Force pilot who in 1954 deserted and launched a nationwide burglary spree. Conners suggested that Call could have murdered Marilyn Sheppard while he was visiting his sister in Ohio.

In 2001, James Neff published his book about the Sheppard case, called *The Wrong Man: The Final Verdict on the Dr. Sam Sheppard Murder Case.* A former *Plain Dealer* reporter, Neff worked on the book for years. In it he pointed out the weaknesses in the case against Sheppard, dismissed the Houks as suspects, and suggested that Eberling was the killer. Neff also identified the key thread in all three trials when he said,

[S]ome of the most compelling evidence in the Sheppard case—DNA test results on blood and semen from the crime scene—had not registered with the jury. Dr. Tahir's lab work

THE FORENSICS OF BLOOD

Two experts in the science of blood analysis applied their expertise to the Sheppard murder case. In 1955, Dr. Sam Sheppard's attorney, William Corrigan, telephoned Dr. Paul Kirk, a famous criminalist who taught at the University of California at Berkeley and performed crime scene analysis for police departments and prosecutors, free of charge. By the time Corrigan had contacted Dr. Kirk, he had helped solve over 630 criminal cases. He cautioned Corrigan that he followed his scientific findings and that he might end up building a case against Dr. Sheppard.

Dr. Kirk flew to Cleveland and visited the crime scene at the Sheppard home in Bay Village. Then he visited the Cuyahoga County prosecutor's office to view the physical evidence in the case. Dr. Kirk had arrived in Cleveland feeling that Dr. Sheppard probably was guilty of the murder of his wife. He returned to Berkeley convinced that the prosecution had gotten most of its case wrong. He sent William Corrigan his report in late April 1955. Dr. Kirk's report consisted of scientific testing and reasoned scenarios that built a strong case that someone besides Dr. Sheppard had killed his wife. He argued that the killer had swung a weapon, probably a flashlight and certainly not a surgical instrument, with a level, left-handed swing. Blood had certainly misted the killer's pants and shirt, and the blood trail in the Sheppard home came from a flowing wound, possibly a bite from Marilyn Sheppard.

One of the more telling tests that Kirk made was of the large, one inch blood spot on the closet door in the murder room. The blood spot reacted so differently from Marilyn and Sam Sheppard's blood that Dr. Kirk concluded that it came from a third person— likely the killer. Kirk believed that the Marilyn Sheppard murder was a sex crime and that it was "completely out of character for a husband bent on murdering his wife."

William Corrigan filed a motion for a new trial, citing new evidence that Dr. Kirk had discovered, emphasizing that the blood of a third person had been discovered at the crime scene. Coroner Dr. Sam Gerber knew that he had to destroy Dr. Kirk's credibility to maintain his standing in national forensic circles. Behind the scenes, Dr. Gerber blackballed Dr. Kirk. In the summer of 1955, the Ohio Appeals Court, a panel of three elected judges, denied the motion for a new trial, arguing that Kirk's blood typing and other interpretations were "highly speculative and fallacious."

Reporters called Dr. Kirk in California for his reaction and he said, "I'm just as positive as I am of my own name that Dr. Sam didn't do it."

Over four decades later, in the summer of 1996, Dr. Mohammad Tahir, a respected DNA scientist in Indianapolis and the director of the DNA and serology laboratories at the Indianapolis–Marion County Forensic Services Agency, began the painstaking process of attempting to extract DNA from the bits of blood and hair collected from the 1954 murder scene. They had been discovered in a vault at the Cuyahoga County coroner's office. Dr. Tahir focused on what he felt might be the key pieces of evidence: a drop of blood lifted from a basement step, the large bloodstain on the knee of Dr. Sam's trousers, and the bloodstain from the wood floor of the back porch.

Like Dr. Kirk, Dr. Tahir was working without a fee, and, also like Dr. Kirk, he told Terry Gilbert that he was taking a gamble as a lawyer because the results of his tests might incriminate Dr. Sam Sheppard. He said that the Sheppard team would have to live with the results of his tests, and Attorney Gilbert said that he understood.

Dr. Tahir conducted exhaustive tests and produced intriguing findings. He found the presence of sperm from a vaginal swab taken from Marilyn Sheppard's body at her autopsy that did not belong to Dr. Sam Sheppard, which supported the theory that Marilyn Sheppard's murder was a sexual and not a domestic homicide. He discovered that the bloodstain on Dr. Sheppard's trousers did not contain his DNA nor did it contain any DNA from Marilyn Sheppard, indicating that the killer probably put the stain there when he ripped a ring of keys from Dr. Sheppard's belt loop. A drop of blood from one of the stairs contained no DNA from Sam or Marilyn Sheppard, casting doubt on the state's theory that Marilyn's blood dropped from a murder weapon as the killer carried it out of the house.

showed that sperm from a man other than Dr. Sheppard was in his wife's vagina when she died. But Tahir's heavily accented testimony was "hard to follow," as Judge Suster put it. Furthermore, Terry Gilbert's direct examination of Tahir failed to give the jurors a solid understanding of how DNA worked, said Assistant prosecutor Steve Dever, who was grateful. (p. 281)

Just as in the first trial, confusion and misunderstanding about blood and semen evidence worked in favor of the prosecution, and Dever dismissed Tahir's results as junk science. His position revealed a great irony, since he, as a criminal prosecutor, routinely used DNA test results produced by coroner's office technicians trained by Dr. Tahir to get convictions. The jury in this trial simply dismissed the DNA evidence. Just as in the first trial, the jury ignored forensic evidence that could possibly exonerate Dr. Sheppard.

Eliminating Dr. Sam Sheppard and James Call as possibilities, the writers and scholars of the Sheppard murder case have suggested three strong suspects in Marilyn Sheppard's murder. Despite the civil jury's finding, Richard Eberling remains a strong suspect because of the long string of suspicious deaths connected to him and his conviction for the 1984 murder of Ethel May Durkin. Eberling knew the Sheppard house well, including the basement entrance, which often was left unlocked. The trail of blood down the steps is almost certainly Eberling's. He stole repeatedly over decades and may also have burglarized homes that he knew.

On the other hand, there is no evidence to place Eberling in the house on the morning of the murder, although he did fit the general description of the "bushy haired intruder" that Dr. Sheppard wrestled. There is no evidence that Eberling was ever involved in a sex crime, and he was believed to be homosexual. Dr. Leland Kirk in his extensive analysis of the blood evidence said that the killer was left-handed, while Eberling was right-handed.

James Neff, in his book *The Wrong Man*, concluded that Eberling was the killer. He based his opinion on the same evidence that Pollack uses in *Dr. Sam: An American Tragedy* and on a final interview with a dying and possibly delirious Eberling.

F. Lee Bailey favored the theory that Spencer and Esther Houk separately or together killed their neighbor Marilyn Sheppard, although on superficial examination it seems far-fetched. But suspicion of Mayor Houk goes back to August 1966 when police unceremoniously brought him to the central police station for questioning as a result of a lead that Dr. Steve Sheppard had given the police. Before the second trial, F. Lee Bailey had hinted to reporters that the killer was a left-handed woman and the Houks were his suspects at the second trial. During cross-examination, Bailey brought out that the Houks were familiar with the Sheppard home and could get between their house and the Sheppard's house by walking on the beach. He brought out that they had set a fire in their fireplace on a July night when the overnight low was 64 degrees. If he had been allowed, Bailey would have called a bakery driver who had seen Houk kissing Marilyn Sheppard to testify.

After Dr. Sheppard's acquittal, Bailey convinced Bay Village police to investigate the evidence against the Houks, but after hearing the evidence the grand jury did not act. Grand jurors doubted that Houk, who walked with a limp, could have been the man who ran from Dr. Sheppard.

In 1982, the owners of the property that had formerly belonged to the Houks found a pair of fireplace tongs buried four to five inches under their back yard. The tongs were nearly two feet long and weighed one and three-quarters pounds. They appeared to match some but not all of the wounds in Marilyn's head, but a metallurgist said that the absence of corrosion indicated that they could not have been buried for 28 years.

Sam Reese Sheppard said that he had a tape of an interview with Spencer Houk made shortly before he died in 1980 that appeared incriminating. He took the accusations seriously enough to lay out two scenarios, one in which Spencer Houk was the killer and one in which it was Esther. He stopped his inquiry into the Houks only when the evidence against Eberling began to mount.

Paul Holmes avoided speculation through most of *The Sheppard Murder Case,* but in the end he suggested a "hypothesis" in which Marilyn was killed with a flashlight by a woman whose husband faked a burglary to cover up for her and inadvertently set up Dr. Sheppard as a suspect. Holmes wrote that no one ever checked their car for bloodstains or tested the ashes in their grate.

Jack Harrison Pollack titled the final chapter of his 1972 book, *Dr. Sam: An American Tragedy,* "The Guilty." In this chapter, he reported that Harold Bretnall, a private detective who worked for the Sheppards, had planned before he died to write a book about the Sheppard murder. In his notes, Bretnall had written, "Marilyn Sheppard was murdered by someone who was a frequent visitor to the Sheppard home." Pollack said, "After carefully ruling out all other possibilities, Bretnall concluded that Marilyn's killers were a woman and a bushy-haired man living in bondage with their awful secret" (Pollack, 1972, pp. 225–235).

Pollack was impressed with Bretnall's findings, and he also concluded that the finger of suspicion still pointed most stubbornly to a couple, a woman and a man. According to Pollack, the gossip of Bay Village seemed to support this theory, especially the word that a tooth chip belonging to neither Marilyn nor Sam was found in the bedroom after the murder and the tooth of one Bay Village resident was reportedly extracted immediately after the crime. Pollack did not document or give a source to these statements.

When the accusations resurfaced in the 1990s, the Houks were both dead, but their grandchildren insisted that their grandparents could never have committed such a horrible crime. They said that Esther was not left-handed as had been often reported, and they said that as Esther lay dying in 1982, she called her daughter to her bedside and asked her to defend her if they accused her of the Sheppard murder (McGunagle, *Crime Library*).

Marilyn Sheppard was the first victim in this 50-year-old murder case, but her murder irrevocably changed and claimed other lives as well. Other victims included her husband, her mother- and father-in-law, her father, and her son. But perhaps the most tragic victim of all is the belief of ordinary citizens in the impartiality of the American judicial system.

SUGGESTIONS FOR FURTHER READING

Bailey, F.L., with Aronson, H. (1971). *The defense never rests.* New York: Stein and Day.

Cooper, C.L., & Sheppard, S.R. (1995). *Mockery of justice: The true story of the Sheppard murder case.*

DeSario, J.P., and Mason, W.D. (2003). *Dr. Sam Sheppard on trial: The prosecutors and the Marilyn Sheppard murder.* Kent, OH: Kent State University Press.

Evans, C. (2003). *A question of evidence: The casebook of great forensic controversies from Napoleon to O.J.* Hoboken, NJ: John Wiley & Sons, Inc.

Holmes, P. (1961). *The Sheppard murder case.* New York: McKay.

Holmes, P. (1966). *Retrial: Murder and Dr. Sam Sheppard.* New York: Bantam Books.

Kilgallen, D. (1967). *Murder one.* New York: Random House.

Neff, J. (2001). *The wrong man: The final verdict on the Dr. Sam Sheppard murder case.* New York: Random House.

Pollack, J.H. (1972). *Dr. Sam: An American tragedy.* Chicago: Henry Regnery Co.

Seltzer, L.B. (1956). *The years were good* (chapter 26). Cleveland, OH: The World Publishing Co.

Sheppard, Dr. S. (1996). *Endure and conquer: My 12-Year fight for vindication.* Cleveland: World Publishing Co.

Sheppard, S. (1964). *My brother's keeper.* New York: David McKay Co.

REFERENCES

Cleveland News. (1954, July 7; 1954, July 16). Sheppard case.

Cleveland Press. (1954, July 20, 21, 24, 25, 26, 28, 29, 30; August 1, 18; October 9, 23).

Findings of the U.S. Supreme Court: *Sheppard v. Maxwell.* Retrieved from http://www.samreesesheppard.org/shepvsmax.html [The transcript is also available at FindLaw as *Sheppard v. Maxwell* 384 U.S. 333 (1966)].

Holmes, P. (1961). *The Sheppard murder case.* New York: McKay.

McGunagle, F. Dr. Sam Sheppard. *Court TV's Crime Library.* Retrieved May 15, 2007, from http://www.crimelibrary.com/notorious_murders/famous/sheppard/marilyn_18.html?sect=1

Neff, J. (2001). *The wrong man: The final verdict on the Dr. Sam Sheppard murder case.* New York: Random House.

Pollack, J.H. (1972). *Dr. Sam: An American tragedy.* Chicago: Henry Regnery Co.

Seltzer, L.B. (1956). *The years were good.* Cleveland, OH: The World Publishing Co.

Sheppard, S. (1964). *My brother's keeper.* New York: David McKay Co.

Taylor, M. (1996, April 7). *San Francisco Chronicle.*

13

The Emmett Till Murder: The Civil Rights Movement Begins

MARCELLA GLODEK BUSH

In the early hours of a Saturday morning in August 1955, two men kidnapped 14-year-old Emmett Till from his great-uncle's house near Money, Mississippi. Three days later, Till's tortured, swollen, and decomposing body was found snagged on some tree branches in the Tallahatchie River—one eye gouged out, one side of his forehead crushed, a bullet in his skull, and a 75-pound cotton gin fan tied around his neck. His body was so badly bloated and disfigured that his great-uncle Mose Wright could only identify Till by the initial ring, once his father's, that he wore.

Till was a black adolescent from Chicago, Illinois, the only son of Louis Till and Mamie Carthan. He had suffered from nonparalytic polio since age three, and the effects of the disease left him with a slight stutter. His mother taught him to whistle to aid his fluency. His speech impediment did not make him shy, however. His family and friends described him as an outgoing boy who liked to tell jokes. Till's father was killed while serving in the army in World War II. When the army returned his father's personal effects, the ring bearing the initials LT was included. Emmett Till's mother later married, and divorced, Gene Bradley.

Mrs. Mamie Till Bradley, Till's mother, was born in Mississippi but moved to Chicago with her parents when she was two years old. Many aunts and uncles still lived in Mississippi, and Emmett and his cousin Curtis Jones planned to visit relatives for two weeks in August 1955. The boys would stay with their great-uncle, Wright, a preacher and a sharecropper who grew cotton. Till was looking forward to seeing his Mississippi cousins again, and his mother was happy that her son could enjoy the countryside after a hot city summer.

On August 20, Mrs. Till took her son to the 63rd Street railroad station in Chicago. Knowing that her son was unskilled in the differences between segregation in the North and segregation in the South, and aware of his impulsive nature and penchant for jokes, she warned him about his behavior while in the South. She advised him not to speak to white people or risk trouble with them, and to be humble if necessary.

MONEY, MISSISSIPPI

In 1955, only 55 residents lived in Money, Mississippi, a cotton gin town with a gas station and three stores. On the evening of August 24, Jones and Till drove with several cousins to Bryant's Grocery and Meat Market, which was owned by Roy and Carolyn Bryant. The Bryants had two small sons and eked out their living selling basic necessities to poor black sharecroppers. Poor themselves, the Bryants lived in a room behind the store. The Bryant-Milam family owned a chain of such stores in the Mississippi delta (Huie, 1956).

Till and Jones joined several other black youths who were listening to music and talking on the front porch of Bryant's store. While Jones played checkers with an elderly black man, Till boasted about life in the North, particularly his friendships with white people. When he showed the others a photograph of a white girl that he kept in his wallet, and bragged that she was his girlfriend, the Mississippi youths dared Till to go into the store and flirt with Mrs. Bryant. Till took the dare. Accounts differ about what Till did after he entered the store. After Mrs. Bryant testified at the trial, various newspapers reported that Till said, "Bye baby," "What's the matter baby? Can't you take it?" "You needn't be afraid of me," and "I've been with white women before" (Metress, 2002). Some mentioned that he gave a "wolf whistle" as he was leaving the store, but that was not mentioned in Mrs. Bryant's testimony. If he did whistle, however, he may have been using the whistle to overcome his stuttering. Till's actions shocked the crowd outside the store. The old man playing checkers warned Till about the consequences of his actions and urged him to leave the area. When Mrs. Bryant came outside to get a gun from her brother-in-law's car, Jones, Till, and the cousins jumped into the truck and fled the scene.

Bryant was not alone in the store that evening. When her husband was out of town, her sister-in-law Juanita Milam came to the store with her children in the afternoon and stayed until closing: 9 p.m. on weekdays and 11 p.m. on Saturdays. Milam then drove Bryant and her children to the Milam home. In the morning, either Milam or his wife would drive Mrs. Bryant back to the store. Bryant's husband carried a .38 Colt automatic, and Milam kept a .45—a souvenir from World War II. Mississippi law permitted its citizens to carry guns whenever they thought they were in imminent danger. Mrs. Bryant was afraid that evening. She knew that Till was not from the area, and she claimed later that she thought he was a man. Till was five feet, five inches in height and weighed about 160 pounds. Bryant was 21 years old and stood five feet tall and weighed 103 pounds.

REPRISAL

Initially, the adolescents kept the incident secret from their great-uncle, but news of Till's actions quickly spread throughout the black community. Till wanted to go back to Chicago and his cousin, Jones, agreed, but the Wright family thought that if he stayed away from Bryant's store, he would be safe. No one in Wright's family thought that Mr. Bryant would come looking for Till—he was only a boy and he was from the North. Three days later, however, when Mr. Bryant returned from a trucking job in Texas delivering shrimp, he heard about Till's action from the black community. He could not ignore the situation or he would be labeled a fool. He asked his half-brother Milam to meet him early Sunday morning.

In his *Look* magazine article, Huie (1956) detailed the events of Till's kidnapping. Bryant and Milam drove out to Wright's cabin sometime after midnight, demanding to see the boy from Chicago. Wright tried to bargain with the two men in an effort to minimize their anger, and Wright's wife Elizabeth offered to pay them for any trouble that her nephew caused. Wright begged them to just give Till a whipping and pleaded that they not take Till with them. The two men, however, ordered Till to dress and to get into the back of their pickup truck. They ordered Wright not to cause any trouble, and they drove off. Associated Press correspondent Sam Johnson and Global News Network editor Olive Arnold Adams (1956) both state that Wright testified to this kidnapping sequence of events at the trial (Metress, 2002, p. 222).

THE ARRESTS

Wright did not call the police, but Jones informed Leflore County Sheriff George Smith the next morning that Till was missing. The sheriff questioned Milam and Bryant, who both admitted abducting the adolescent, but reported that they had turned him loose, unharmed, that same night. They were arrested and charged with kidnapping. When Till's body was found three days later, the indictment changed to murder. Because the body was found in Tallahatchie County, that county was ascribed jurisdiction. The two defendants remained, however, in Sheriff Smith's custody until the grand jury convened the following Monday, September 5.

TIMELINE	
May 17, 1954	Supreme Court orders public schools desegregated.
1955	Black activists Lee and Smith killed in Mississippi.
August 21, 1955	Till in Mississippi.
August 24, 1955	Incident at Bryant's Grocery.
August 28, 1955	Till kidnapped and murdered.
August 28, 1955	Bryant and Milam arrested.
August 31, 1955	Till's body found.
September 3, 1955	Till's body viewed in Chicago.
September 6, 1955	Till's funeral/trial date.
September 15, 1955	*Jet* magazine publishes corpse photograph.
September 19–23, 1955	Bryant and Milam acquitted.
November 9, 1955	Jury refuses to indict for kidnapping.
December 1, 1955	Rosa Parks incident in Montgomery, Alabama.
January 24, 1956	*Look* magazine publishes Milam's confession.
1980	Milam dies of cancer in Mississippi.
1990	Bryant dies of cancer in Mississippi.
January 6, 2003	Till's mother Mamie Till Mobley dies.
May 10, 2004	The U.S. Department of Justice reopens Till's case.
May 31, 2005	Till's body exhumed and reburied.
August 26, 2005	Body positively identified; federal investigation closed.

The sheriff wanted to bury the body immediately, stating that because the body was so badly decomposed, identification could not be made. Jones called Mrs. Till to tell her about her son's death and his forthcoming burial in Mississippi. Till's mother wanted her son's body and insisted that it be shipped back to Chicago. The sheriff directed the mortician in Mississippi, however, to sign an order for the coffin to remain unopened.

Initially, no local lawyers agreed to defend Milam and Bryant. Therefore, the state appointed a special prosecutor but gave him no budget or personnel to conduct a probe. The sheriff did not investigate the murder, nor did he help the prosecution prepare its case.

THE MEDIA

When Milam and Bryant were arrested, several Mississippi newspapers reported the story, but when Till's mother insisted on an open-casket funeral, she brought national attention to her son's murder. During the four days of the viewing at the Rainer Funeral Home in Chicago, thousands of people saw Till's body. Till's photograph gained national attention in newspapers and magazines and mobilized the National Association for the

BIOGRAPHICAL DESCRIPTIONS

Bradley, Mamie Carthan Till (1921–2003), Emmett Till's mother

Breland, J.J., lead defense attorney

Bryant, Carolyn Holloway (1934–), Roy Bryant's wife; present during the incident in the family's grocery store

Bryant, Roy (1931–1994), accused killer of Emmett Till

Chatham, Gerald, lead prosecutor

Collins, Levy "Too Tight," tied to Till's murder by various witnesses

Cothran, John Ed, deputy sheriff of Leflore County; arrested J.W. Milam on kidnapping charges

Hodges, Robert, discovered Emmett Till's body

Hubbard, Joe Willie, alleged accomplice of J.W. Milam and Roy Bryant in Till's murder

Huie, William Bradford, *Look* magazine reporter

Loggins, Henry Lee, alleged accomplice to Milam and Bryant

Milam, John William "J.W." (1919–1980), Roy Bryant's half-brother; alleged murderer of Emmett Till

Milam, Juanita Thompson, J.W.'s wife; present in Bryant's Grocery during incident

Mobley, Gene (1923–2000), married Mamie Till Bradley two years after Till's death

Reed, Willie, testified that he heard the beating in the tool shed on Milam's plantation

Strider, Henry Clarence "H.C.," sheriff of Tallahatchie County; witness for the defense

Swango, Curtis M., presiding judge

Till, Emmett (1941–1955), son of Mamie Charthan and Louis Till

Till, Louis (1921–1945), father of Emmett Till; he died during WWII

Wright, Moses (1892–1977), sharecropper, preacher, and Till's great-uncle; identified J.W. Milam and Roy Bryant in court as the men who kidnapped Emmett Till

Advancement of Colored People (NAACP). According to media reports, the photograph inflamed both northern and southern audiences, who subsequently denounced the barbarity of segregation in the South and demanded justice in Mississippi in the Till case. When the case became a national event, five prominent Mississippi delta attorneys signed on to the case; they raised $10,000 for the defense fund. *Jet* magazine published an unedited photograph in its September 15 issue of Emmett as he lay in his coffin.

MOUNTING THE TRIAL

In Mississippi, the severe censure from northern press editorials and civil rights groups solidified white public opinion in defense of their society. Influential African American weeklies such as the *Chicago Defender,* the *Baltimore Afro-American,* the *New York Amsterdam News,* and the *Cleveland Call and Post* denounced southern injustice and promised reprisal if Mississippi failed to provide a fair trial. The National Association of Colored People labeled the crime a "lynching" and, in doing so, received recrimination from southern newspapers. Tom Ethridge, a writer for the *Jackson Daily News,* explained that "lynching" was defined by militant Negro zealots as "any killing involving a colored victim and a white killer" (Metress, 2002). Mississippi Governor Hugh White and others stated that the crime was not a "lynching" but a murder. More than 70 newspapers and magazines sent reporters—including the black press—to the trial. Medgar Evers, the first field secretary for the NAACP, was also present.

Indicted for murder by the grand jury on September 6, Bryant and Milam were taken to Tallahatchie County for arraignment; the sheriff's office held no inquest prior to the trial. Again the accused admitted to kidnapping Till, but insisted that they released Till unharmed. At the time of the trial, Mississippi preserved transcripts of appealed cases only; consequently, no transcript exists of the Bryant and Milam trial. Information, therefore, about court proceedings depends on newspaper and other media accounts as well as personal recollections and interviews.

Circuit Judge Curtis M. Swango presided over the trial and determined that the case would be tried in open court; he ruled that no photographs, sketches, recordings, or broadcasts would be allowed in the courtroom. District Attorney Gerald Chatham served as the prosecuting attorney and was assisted by former FBI Agent Robert B. Smith; five defense attorneys included senior defense attorney J.J. Breland, C. Sidney Carlton, J.W. Kellum, John C. Whitten, and Harvey Henderson. All officers of the court were white.

JURY SELECTION

Jury selection began on September 19, and it took a day and a half to appoint an all-male, all-white jury from the defendants' county. According to an article published in the African American newspaper the *Chicago Defender,* prospective jurors were dismissed if they had contributed to the defense fund of the defendants, if they were related to the attorneys or defendants, if they had formed any definite opinions about the defendants' guilt or innocence, or if they lived in the county where the killing took place (Metress, 2002).

Accounts differ about court attendees, but men outnumbered women and whites outnumbered blacks; the courtroom was segregated with blacks sitting in a corner in the back of the hot, crowded courtroom, and the white press near the judge and jury. The press included local, national, and foreign representatives, and the three existing national television networks also covered the trial, but did not broadcast from the courtroom. The defendants faced the judge with their wives and children (four boys, ages two to four years) next to them each day. Till's mother arrived on the second day of the trial with her father, a cousin from Chicago, and Congressman Charles Diggs from Michigan; both Mrs. Till and Diggs sat at the black press table. Sheriff Strider placed the two defendants under guard and called out the National Guard to support city police because he had received anonymous letters and telephone calls that threatened mob violence. In coverage by the *Jackson Daily News* on September 5, 1955, Strider is quoted as reporting that most of the letters were postmarked from Chicago.

TESTIMONY

The state based its case on identification: the jury would find that both defendants could be identified as Till's assailants, and the identification of the body pulled from the river could be identified as Till's *beyond a reasonable doubt*. The state called six witnesses: Wright; Till's mother; Mrs. Bryant; Chester Miller the undertaker; Levy ("Two Tight") Collins (a black who allegedly accompanied Bryant and Milam in the kidnapping and murder); Sheriff Strider (who stated that a bullet caused the hole in the deceased's head); and Robert Hodges, the boy who found the body. Mrs. Till testified that she positively identified her son's body and her late husband's ring, and had warned her son about his behavior with white people while visiting his Mississippi relatives. When defense counselor J.J. Breland began questioning her about the newspapers that she read in Chicago, Prosecutor Smith objected to that line of questioning, fearing that the photo of Till might be introduced. Judge Swango removed the jury to determine whether the defense's line of questioning was relevant or diversionary. He subsequently deemed it not relevant to the case, excluded every question, and allowed no references to the questions. As a result of the ruling, the defense had to drop Till's mother as a witness.

Prosecutor Chatham's opening statement promised to put the defendants together with Till and in the area where Till's body was found. The NAACP undertook the responsibility to provide a safe place for the trial witnesses that Chatham had ferreted out from their hiding places. Chatham well understood how dangerous it was for blacks to testify against whites in a court of law in Mississippi.

Chatham opened with the prosecution's first witness: Mose Wright, who testified that Milam and Bryant were the two men who had taken his nephew Emmett that night. Chatham's other witnesses, also blacks, testified that they had seen Bryant and Milam at a plantation and had heard screams and cries coming from a shed in the back. They testified also that they unloaded a tarpaulin from that shed and then cleaned the truck used to transport the tarpaulin. After their testimonies, the NAACP secured hiding places for them outside Mississippi.

Cross-Examination

On cross-examination, Defense Attorney Carlton challenged Wright's identification of Bryant and Milam as the two men who came to his house in the early morning hour of August 28. Wright insisted that he could identify the two accused even though the only light available was a flashlight allegedly held by Milam. Then the judge ruled out Smith's testimony about a conversation with Bryant that placed Bryant at Wright's home and later with Till at his store; the jury was out of the room, however, for that testimony. According

Figure 13.1   Roy Bryant and J.W. Milam, charged with murdering Emmett Till, sitting in a courtroom with their attorney, 1955. Courtesy of the Library of Congress.

to Associated Press correspondent Sam Johnson, the judge ruled that the state must first prove that Till was murdered before an identification of the murderers could be allowed.

The defense next raised the issue about the identification of the body. Leflore County Deputy Sheriff Cothran's testimony suggested that the cotton gin fan might have caused the damage to the body's head. Sheriff Strider testified that the decomposition of the body was more like that of a body that had been in the river ten days, not three, and a Greenwood physician concurred. Strider also testified that a photograph of Till did not match that of the body pulled from the river. Neither defendant took the stand in the trial.

Closing Remarks and the Verdict

The defense attorneys argued that there was no motive for the crime, no positive identification, no reasonable theory, no identification by Bryant of Till, and no positive identification of the body from the river. Defense attorney Kellum appealed to the jury that because they were white men, they should not convict other white men in a black man's killing (Gado, 2003). Defense attorney Carlton argued that the theory of the crime offered by the prosecution was unreasonable: if the men who came to Wright's house planned to murder Till, why would they identify themselves?

The prosecution appealed to moral and legal issues. District attorney Chatham—a southerner—argued that a whipping, not a killing, would have been the moral thing to do if Till had insulted Bryant. He stressed that Wright, Willie Reed—a black field hand whose testimony placed J.W. Milam and Till together on the morning after the kidnapping—and the others were telling the truth, and he urged the jury to consider the case

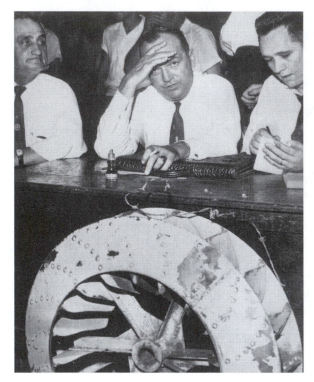

Figure 13.2 District Attorney Gerald Chatham sitting at the prosecution's table during the trial of Roy Bryant and J.W. Milam for the murder of Emmett Till; the cotton gin wheel tied to Till's body stands in front of the table. Courtesy of the Library of Congress.

on its merits—Till's mother identified the body as her son's; several people on the river scene identified the body as a black male.

On the fifth day of the trial, in 67 minutes, the jury returned a verdict of not guilty. One jury member later told a reporter, "It would have been even shorter, but we stopped to drink some pop" (Huie, 1956). Bryant and Milam were free men who, under double jeopardy, could not be tried again for the murder.

THE OUTCOME OF THE TRIAL

The outcome of the trial caused controversy in the media. In the months following the trial, northern white daily newspapers and black weeklies condemned Mississippi for its inability to bring justice in a particularly brutal murder of a youth; some called for federal intervention (Metress, 2002). Others raised questions about what truly happened in the case. Few, if any, focused on the effects that the murder and its subsequent trial had on citizens in the hamlet of Money, Mississippi. Most white southern newspapers tempered their censure of Mississippi and focused blame on the sheriff's lack of investigation in the case, and on the prosecutors who went to trial with flimsy evidence (Metress, 2002). Mississippi media blamed organizations like the NAACP for agitating the situation or decried it as a communist plot to destroy the South's way of life and to display America's racial inequality to the world. Individuals expressed their opinions in letters to newspaper editors, and radio announcers stated their views in on-the-air editorials and on-the-spot coverage of the trial (Metress, 2002; Smith, 2003). Some northerners expressed moral outrage about the verdict as a miscarriage of justice, while others wrote about equal justice out of religious convictions; still others demanded equality for blacks. Some southerners defended southern mores, insisting that white women deserved protection from black men in the South. Individual expressions of feelings included impotence, frustration, revenge, and retaliation. Black commentators expressed anger, but not surprise about the verdict (Metress, 2002).

LOOK MAGAZINE INTERVIEW

In the months following the trial, theories of conspiracy surfaced in the press. In 1956, the two defendants told their story to William Bradford Huie, a *Look* magazine journalist and author, and were paid $4,000[1]—not for their interview, but for a release for their movie rights. Other sources report different amounts paid to Milam and Bryant. During the interview, Milam confessed to the killing and rationalized his reasons for doing so. Milam revealed that at first they planned to scare Till. When they failed, Milam rationalized that "as long as I live and I can do anything about it, niggers are going to stay in their place...and when a nigger even gets close to mentioning sex with a white woman, he's tired of livin'" (Metress, 2002). Milam interpreted Till's bra-

vado as arrogance. Till was a trouble-maker. He came from the North with money to spend and nicer clothing than his cousins living in the South. He gave blacks in the South ideas about racial equality. Milam decided to make an example of Till (Gado, 2003). He and Bryant and two black men drove for several hours trying to find a cliff that Milam had discovered when he was duck hunting the year before—a bluff with an impressive 100-foot drop to a canyon below. Milam intended to scare Till by pistol-whipping him, during which he would then shine a flashlight into the canyon with the implication that he would push Till over the cliff. After Milam's failure to locate the cliff in the dark, Milam took him to a shed in back of his house. There, Milam pistol-whipped the boy, and when Emmett still would not humble himself to Bryant and Milam, they wrapped him in a tarpaulin, put him back in the truck, and drove to the Tal-lahatchie River. At the river, Milam

TRIAL PARTICIPANTS

STATE OF MISSISSIPPI VS J.W. MILAM AND ROY BRYANT

Held in Sumner, Tallahatchie County, Mississippi September 19–23, 1955
Presiding:
Judge Curtis M. Swango
Prosecution Team:
Gerald Chatham
Robert B. Smith, III
James Hamilton Caldwell, Jr.
Defense Team:
Jesse Josiah Breland
C. Sidney Carlton
Robert Harvey Henderson
Joseph W. Kellum
John W. Whitten
Prosecution Witnesses:
Mary Amanda Bradley, Mamie Till Bradley, John Ed Cothran, Robert Hodges, Chester Miller, Benjamin L. Mims, Charles Nelson, Add Reed, Willie Reed, George Smith, C.A. Strickland, Moses Wright
Defense Witnesses:
Lee Russell Allison, L.W. Boyce, Carolyn Bryant, Grover Duke, Pete McGaa, Harry D. Malone, Juanita Milam, Luther B. Otkens, Harold Perry, James Sanders, Franklin Smith, Henry Clarence Strider
Jurors:
Howard Armstrong, Ed Devaney, George Holland, Bishop Matthews, Davis Newton, Jim Pennington, Lee L. Price, Gus Ramsey, James Shaw, Jr., Travis Thomas, James Toole, Ray Tribble
Alternate:
Willie D. Haven

gave Till one last chance to humble himself. When Till did not, Milam ordered him to remove his clothes, made him carry the 75-pound cotton gin fan to the river's edge, and shot Till in the head with his .45 Colt revolver.

Milam and Bryant felt that they had nothing to hide when telling their story. They never thought that they were in legal jeopardy. They assumed that the white community knew what they did and later sanctioned their act by contributing money to their defense fund. In the rural South in 1955, the plantation system still existed. Because blacks were not well educated in the South, they were tied to low-paying jobs, and most were sharecroppers. Milam rented Negro-driven mechanical cotton pickers to plantation owners. He was considered a bully who kept blacks working hard and in their place. In an interview with Milam and Bryant's defense attorney, John C. Whitten, Huie quotes Whitten as saying "that Milam was the killer and Bryant a coat-holder. Milam is older; he won a battlefield commission; he looks like the family leader....He's the overseer type; he works Negroes, lives among them" (Metress, 2002).

The blacks who helped Milam and Bryant on the night of Till's murder did so because their lives and livelihood depended on their support. Neither Milam nor Bryant regretted killing Till, but they understood why the black community shunned them after the trial. They could not understand, though, why the white community shunned them. Journalist Huie wrote in his *Look* magazine article that a Tallahatchie citizen explained the situation to him: "[Y]ou know there's just one thing wrong with encouraging one o' these peckerwoods to kill a nigger. He don't know when to stop—and the rascal may wind up killing you" (Metress, 2002).

AFTER THE TRIAL

The NAACP's field secretary Medgar Evers attended the Till trial and continued to investigate the murder after the trial to ferret out issues not raised at the trial. Other black organizations staged major rallies in the northern cities and in the Midwest. They promoted black marches both to protest the verdict in the Till case and to engender their cause for equality. Looking ahead to an indictment and trial of Bryant and Milam for kidnapping, and the need for black witnesses to testify, black organizations requested defense funds for these witnesses' safety. Bryant and Milam were never indicted on charges of kidnapping, however, even though they had publicly confessed. The state of Mississippi never explained why.

In fear for their lives, Wright's family left Money after the night Bryant and Milam appeared at their home; Wright returned for the trial, but his wife did not. Other blacks who testified include Willie Reed, who placed Bryant and Milam at the plantation shed, and Amanda Bradley, who testified to the beating in the shed. They, too, needed and received assistance to relocate away from Mississippi and the South.

Wright and his family moved to Chicago and never returned to Mississippi. Blacks boycotted Bryant's store, it closed, and the family moved to Texas. Eventually, all the stores that the Bryant-Milam family owned closed also. The Bryants divorced in 1979. Milam tried farming, but blacks refused to work for him, and whites demanded a salary that he could not afford to pay. Eventually, he, too, moved to Texas. Both brothers died of cancer.

Emmett Till's mother became a teacher in Chicago. Sponsored by the NAACP, she lectured throughout the United States about segregation and her son's death. She retired in 1978 and died in 2002 at the age of 81. Her death once again brought Emmett's memory to the public forum. Nearly complete at the time of her death, Mamie Till Bradley's memoir *Death of Innocence: The Story of the Hate Crime That Changed America* (written with Christopher Benson) has been subsequently published by Random House. Public Broadcasting Service (PBS) aired *The Murder of Emmett Till* on January 20, 2003.

On May 10, 2004, the U.S. Justice Department and the Mississippi District Attorney's office for the 4th District reopened the case after learning about new witnesses discovered by Keith Beauchamp when he created his documentary, *The Untold Story of Emmett Louis*

Till. Beauchamp does not name the witnesses in his film, but believes at least ten people were involved. Witnesses claim that Henry Lee Loggins—a black man, who worked for Milam—was in the truck with Till, when Till was abducted. Mose Wright also testified that there was a black man on the porch that night. Wright also reported hearing a woman's voice—believed to be Carolyn Bryant—from the truck.

An FBI report states that a warrant was issued for Mrs. Bryant, now Carolyn Donham, but she was never arrested or charged. Federal investigators exhumed Till's body on June 1, 2005, because defense attorneys had argued that the body found in the Tallahatchie River was not Till's. DNA tests, however, confirmed Till's identity. He was reburied on June 4. The FBI also found a copy of the trial transcript that would allow them to compare testimony given then to testimony in a new trial. Although the five-year statute of limitations expired, Carolyn Bryant Donham was brought before a grand jury in Leflore County, Mississippi, but on February 23, 2007, a grand jury issued a "no bill," a term that indicates insufficient evidence to support criminal prosecution. Donham is probably the only living person who could possibly be associated with the murder. Till's death continues to raise issues about racial inequality in America.

SOCIAL, POLITICAL, AND LEGAL ISSUES

The U.S. Supreme Court's school decision in *Brown v. Board of Education* on May 17, 1954, opened to the world the social fabric of the southern way of life—a society in which racial segregation permeated all spheres of life. In response to the court ruling, southern states each began a movement of resistance. Mississippi formed the Mississippi Sovereign Commission to prevent federal and judicial interference in the powers of the state government. A new group, the Citizen's Council, formed to control blacks economically by threatening their jobs, credit, and mortgage renewal if they participated in desegregation.

Public Remarks about Segregation in Mississippi

Mississippi Senator James Eastland advised his constituency that "[o]n May 17, 1954, the Constitution of the United States was destroyed because of the Supreme Court's decision" in *Brown v. Board of Education* and admonished them to "not be obliged to obey the decisions of any court which are plainly fraudulent [and based on] sociological considerations" (Williams, 1987, p. 38). Lew Sadler, a white Mississippi radio announcer covering the trial, defended the South's way of life and stressed that blacks and whites mingled daily without ramifications in Mississippi. He said, "the only line we draw is at the door of our schools" (Metress, 2002).

Election Year Efforts for Voting Registration

In contrast, while blacks in the North also faced discrimination and segregation, they had access to the voting ballot and entry-level jobs in the city government. In the summer of 1955, the executive secretary of the NAACP, Roy Wilkins, addressed an audience on the city of Chicago's "Salute to Negroes in Government" day. In the North, blacks were moving against the apartheid of American history.

The South feared and subdued any efforts to mobilize the black vote—by lynching if necessary. Just prior to Till's arrival, two black men were killed in Mississippi: Lamar Smith, an NAACP activist, and the Reverend George W. Lee, both solicitors of black voting registration. In Tallahatchie County in 1955, more than half of the residents were blacks, but none were registered voters. Therefore, none of them could serve on the Bryant-Milam trial jury. Milam, in his interview with Huie, asserted, "Niggers ain't gonna vote where I live! If they did, they'd control the government" (Metress, 2002).

Political and Social Overtones at the Trial

The media crush that descended on Tallahatchie County soon recognized the political and social scene of the South. Sheriff Strider had segregated black and white reporters and photographers, and audibly announced to the assembled courtroom audience, "We haven't mixed so far down here and we don't intend to" (Metress, 2002). He acknowledged black reporters by saying, "Hello, niggers" (Metress, 2002). Another deputy sheriff also audibly expressed his opinion in the courtroom about the political position of Charles C. Diggs, a U.S. congressman, when Diggs requested seating in the courtroom. "What?" he asked. "A nigger Congressman?" (Williams, 2002, p. 51).

In his closing remarks, District Attorney Smith moved for a justice that protected the rights of both blacks and whites. He stated that "Emmett Till down here in Mississippi was a citizen of the United States; he was entitled to his life and his liberty" (Metress, 2002). Defense attorney Kellum, however, used his summation to continue prevailing southern tradition. He declared, "I want you to tell me where under God's shining sun, is the land of the free and the home of the brave if you don't turn these boys loose; your forefathers will absolutely turn over in their graves" (Williams, 2002, p. 52).

National-Level Observations

Both Mississippi writer William Faulkner and former first lady Eleanor Roosevelt mirrored Smith's concern for justice, especially since, as a nation, American democracy must uphold justice. But President Eisenhower made no official statement about the Till murder and subsequent trial outcome. In a letter to Attorney General Herbert Brownell and FBI Director J. Edgar Hoover, James L. Hicks drew a blueprint for justice in the Till case. Hicks, an investigative reporter, had the credentials to warrant their interest. He served as bureau chief for the NAACP and, in 1955, became the executive director of the *New York Amsterdam News*. He was the first black member of the state department's correspondence association and the first black reporter to cover the United Nations. Newspapers throughout the United States ran his coverage of the trial.

In the letter to Brownell and Hoover, Hicks appealed for a federal investigation of the trial based on his charge of witness tampering. In minute detail, Hicks described how the sheriff's office prevented witnesses from testifying, named witnesses who knew details of the case not brought out at trial, and named accomplices to the murder, along with their locations. Neither the attorney general nor the FBI offices responded.

Social Effects of the Trial in Mississippi

A small group of Mississippi citizens pulled Emmett Till's body from the Tallahatchie River and tried to bury it, both literally and figuratively, in Mississippi's consciousness and soil. Till's mother, however, determined that the world would be witness to the fate that her only son, 14 years old, endured in a South that alienated, segregated, and discriminated against blacks. While the world saw the injustice of the South, the black citizens of the delta saw black witnesses testifying against white citizens—the beginning of the mobilization of the black response to their lack of basic legal, social, and political rights. The civil rights movement, sparked by the death of Till, would bring political, legal, and social upheaval in a time of unprecedented economic prosperity in America. Television would be the new medium to bring these events into the American living room.

Although television shows in the 1950s emphasized traditional white family roles and society's conformity, young people were becoming aware of the increasing integration of black and white cultures in America, especially in music. While conformity and complacency defined Americans in the 1950s, Americans were socially challenged by a rebellious youth culture, the Beat Generation, and the decisive civil rights struggle.

THE TRIAL IN LEGAL AND POPULAR CULTURE

The train traveling to Mississippi on August 20 conveyed Till and Jones to a society that had developed a Jim Crow legal system after the Civil War —a system that treated blacks as inferior to whites. Jim Crow laws violated blacks' civil rights despite the

EMMETT TILL FACTOIDS

- December 1, 1955: Rosa Parks recalled the photo of Till's corpse when she refused to give up her seat to a white man on an Alabama bus.
- July 1, 2005: Two U.S. Senators introduced *The Unsolved Civil Rights Crimes Act* (The Till Bill) to prosecute civil rights–era murder cases.
- February 24, 2006: Emmett Till's elementary school in Chicago became the Emmett Till Math & Science Academy on February 24, 2006.
- Civil Rights Activist Medgar Evers was field secretary for the Mississippi chapter of the NAACP at the time of Till's murder. He was gunned down in his driveway on June 12, 1963.
- Ruby Hurley, who disguised herself as a field worker to procure witnesses for the prosecution in the Milam-Bryant murder trial, was the first professional civil rights worker in the South.
- David Jackson, photographer for *Ebony* and *Jet* magazines, took the photograph of Emmett Till in his coffin that shocked the nation; the photograph appeared in *Jet* magazine.

1868 constitution of Mississippi, which guaranteed in its bill of rights that "[a]ll persons resident in this State, citizens of the United States, are hereby declared citizens of the State of Mississippi" (Johnson, 1955). Under the U.S. Supreme Court ruling of the 1896 *Plessy v. Ferguson* "separate but equal" doctrine, blacks could be legally segregated as long as equal accommodations were provided for them; thus, blacks were segregated from public parks, buildings, and classrooms. Blacks could vote but had to pass a literacy test in order to do so. Most could not pass the literacy test because they were segregated from the white school system. Blacks were also fixed to a limited economic position that reduced them to segregated, inferior public accommodations and low-quality housing. Blacks drank from separate water fountains and could not use public toilets. They could not enter a white person's house through the front door, and they had to step aside when a white person passed them on the street. A black man had to remove his hat and bow his head when spoken to by a white person. Businesses and restaurants refused to serve blacks or provided separate counters away from white customers. Blacks could not rent or purchase homes in white neighborhoods. Whites in Mississippi, therefore, did not fear public opinion or punishment when white supremacists felt it necessary to punish black transgressions, because white supremacists controlled the court system and legislature.

Till violated the most sacrosanct category of black behavior toward whites: he did not show respect to a white woman. In the *Look* magazine interview, Milam claimed that he and Bryant only wanted to scare Till, but Till refused to acknowledge his transgression against Bryant's wife, and he would not even beg for mercy. Operating within a supremacist mind-set, the men felt that they had no other choice but to kill Till. An all-male, all-white-supremacist court of law justified their action when they voiced the words *not guilty*.

Southern Violence, National Involvement

Emmett Till returned to Chicago by train—not as the young man returning home from a visit to relatives in the South—but as a body in a wooden casket bearing an order to remain sealed. His mother's insistence to open that casket at the railroad station in Chicago sparked the civil rights movement, and when *Jet* magazine released the photograph of Till's body, it spotlighted the violence that blacks in the South suffered. Till's death focused national attention on American racial inequality that ultimately led to the passage of the Civil Rights Act in 1964 and the Voting Rights Act in 1965 (Crowe, 2003). The civil rights movement also elevated black consciousness and racial pride.

Popular Culture

Till's murder inspired numerous songs, poems, essays, and novels by both famous artists and amateurs, who submitted their entries to local newspapers. Popular songwriters Bob Dylan and Pete Seeger, poet Langston Hughes, authors Toni Morrison and Lewis Nordan, and actors and producers Ossie Davis and Ruby Dee are among the famous artists who memorialized Emmett Till. Chris Crowe's (2002) book *Mississippi Trial, 1955* blends history and fiction, in which his protagonist determinedly tries to solve the murder. Amateur writers and poets submitted their works primarily to local newspapers. The realities of the case may have been misconstrued in some works, but their primary focus portrays injustice. We do not know exactly what Till said or exactly how he reacted to Milam and Bryant during his ordeal, but the literary response was "bravery," and his bravery helped raise black consciousness. Some contend that Till was a murder victim and should not be called the sacrificial lamb of the civil rights movement. Till's mother, however, made the nation look at her son and face how he was killed. The media's coverage of Till's murder increased civil rights organizations' membership, and the civil rights movement attracted young people who began to peacefully boycott buses and march for equality. According to Christopher Metress (2002), editor of *The Lynching of Emmett Till*, the proliferation of materials about Till enables the reader to appreciate how people grappled with the issues of the murder and trial in 1955, and allows us to continue the process today.

SUGGESTIONS FOR FURTHER READING

FBI press release. (2004, May 24). *FBI asks community for information on historic case.* http://jackson.fbi.gov/pressrel/2004/till052404.htm

Huie, W.B. (1956, January 24). The shocking story of approved killing in Mississippi. *Look.* http://www.mindfully.org/Reform/Emmett-Till-Look24jan56.htm

Huie, W.B. (1956, January). Killers' confession. *Look.* Retrieved September 10, 2003, from http://www.pbs.org/wgbh/amex/till/sfeature/sf_look.html

Metress, C. (Ed.). (2002). *The lynching of Emmett Till: A documentary narrative.* Charlottesville, VA: University of Virginia Press

Primary Sources—Letters to Chicago from Emmett and his Aunt Elizabeth to Mamie Till Mobley: http://www.pbs.org/wgbh/amex/till/filmmore/ps_letters.html

Reactions in writing of the murder: http://www.pbs.org/wgbh/amex/till/filmmore/ps_reactions.html

Telegrams, letters, memorandum, and documents relating to the case: http://www.eisenhower. archives.gov/dl/Civil_Rights_Emmett_Till_Case/EmmettTillCase.html

2004 U.S. Justice Department's Investigation Decision: http://www.usdoj.gov/opa/pr/2004/May/ 04_crt_311.htm

Williams, J. (1987). *Eyes on the prize: America's civil rights years, 1954–1965.* New York: Viking.

NOTE

1. $3,000 for Milam and Bryant; $1,000 to Defense Attorney J.J. Breland's law firm according to Randy Sparkman. (2005, June 21). *Slate Magazine.* Retrieved July 28, 2007, from http:// www.slate.com/id/212078$3,500 to Milam and Bryant according to CourtTV.com. Retrieved July 28, 2007, from http://www.courttv.com/onair/shows/specials/emmett_till/key_players.html $3,150 to Milam and Bryant; $1,260 to Defense Attorney J.J. Breland's law firm according to Steve Duin. (2006, December 9). William Bradford Huie and Emmett Till. *The Oregonian.* Retrieved July 28, 2007, from http://steveduin.blogs.oregonlive.com/default.asp?item=379248

REFERENCES

Crowe, C. (2003, Summer). The lynching of Emmett Till. *The History of Jim Crow.* Retrieved September 3, 2003, from http://www.jimcrowhistory.org/resources/lessonplans/hs_es_ emmett_till.htm

Crowe, C. (2002). *Mississippi trial, 1955.* New York: Phyllis Fogelman Books.

Gado, M. (2003). Mississippi madness: The story of Emmett Till. *Court TV's Crime Library.* Retrieved September 10, 2003, from http://www.crimelibrary.com/notorious_murders/ famous/emmett_till/index.html?sect=7

Huie, W.B. (1956, January). The shocking story of approved killing in Mississippi. *Look.* Retrieved September 10, 2003, from http://www.pbs.org/wgbh/amex/till/sfeature/sf_look.html

Johnson, S. (1955, September 21). Wright's testimony. Greenwood Commonwealth. 1868 constitution of the state of Mississippi. (2002–2003). *Mississippi History Now.* Retrieved September 3, 2003, from http://mshistory.k12.ms.us/features/feature8/1868_state_ constitution.html

Metress, C. (Ed.). (2002). *The lynching of Emmett Till: A documentary narrative.* Charlottesville, VA: University of Virginia Press. Retrieved September 10, 2003, from http://archipelago.org/ vol6-1/hicks.htm

Nelson, M. (2005). *A wreath for Emmett Till.* Boston: Houghton Mifflin.

Smith, M.A. (2003). The murder of Emmett Till: The film and more. WGBH Foundation: Public Broadcasting Service. Retrieved September 3, 2003, from http://www.pbs.org/wgbh/ amex/till/sfeature/sf_look_letters.html

TeachingBooks.net. (2005). Author Program In-depth Interview. Insights into *A wreath for Emmett Till.* Retrieved July 27, 2007, from http://www.Teachingbooks.net/content/Nelson_qu.pdf

Tuttle, K. (2003). Jim Crow. *Encarta Africana.* Retrieved September 3, 2003, from http:// www.africana.com/research/encarta/tt_026.asp

Williams, J. (1987). *Eyes on the prize: America's civil rights years, 1954–1965.* New York: Viking.

14
Mississippi Burning

SHANI P. GRAY

The 1960s were turbulent times for the entire South as many Blacks, collectively, began to demand and pursue equal rights. During the Civil Rights Era, Mississippi became known as one of the most racist and violent states in the country (Bell, 1973; Kennedy, 1997). Since 1955, when 14-year-old Emmett Louis Till was beaten, killed, and weighed down by a gin fan in the Tallahatchie River, in Money, Mississippi, for whistling at a White woman, Mississippi had been under the watchful eye of the nation (Benson, 2006). Mississippi was again thrust into the national spotlight when on the evening of June 13, 1963, Medgar Evers, Mississippi's most prominent Black leader, was assassinated. He was shot by Byron De La Beckwith while entering his house after returning home from work (Johnson, Jr., 2000; Smith, 2002). In the wake of the Till and Evers deaths the founding meeting of the White Knights of the Ku Klux Klan of Mississippi was held on February 15, 1964, and, to inform the nation of their existence and unity, on April 24, 1964, the KKK burned 61 crosses at separate locations across Mississippi (Linder, 2006d).

In the summer of 1964 the Student Nonviolent Coordination Committee had decided to send 600 student volunteers into every corner of the state of Mississippi to assist Blacks in registering to vote. This project, known as the Mississippi Summer Project, had been established under the premise that if segregation could be cracked in Mississippi, it could be cracked anywhere (Linder, 2002). Mississippi's 1890 constitution supported the state-enforced segregation policy, which facilitated the prohibition of Blacks' participation in many activities (e.g., attending state universities and registering to vote) (Burns, 2003; *U.S. v. State of Mississippi*, 1964).

In spite of the violence that had been perpetrated as a symbol of the extent to which the segregationist ideal would be defended in Mississippi, some churches had agreed to allow student civil rights workers to conduct voter registration schools on-site. In Longdale,

---

A special thanks to Chuck Brown for his assistance in researching this project.

Mississippi (Neshoba County), Mt. Zion Methodist Church had agreed to house a voting registration school at their facility. Civil rights workers were aware that Neshoba County was a high risk area for violent attacks from people who were against the provision of civil rights to Blacks, and that the sheriff, Lawrence Rainey, and the deputy sheriff, Cecil Price, had a reputation of being tough on Blacks and were also suspected of being Klansmen. Michael Schwerner and James Chaney, two civil rights workers associated with the Mississippi Summer Project, spoke to the congregation of Mt. Zion Methodist Church on Memorial Day 1964. On June 16, 1964, armed KKK members, looking for Schwerner, assaulted leaders of Mt. Zion Church, and on June 17, 1964, the Klan burned Mt. Zion Church to the ground. It is believed that the church was intentionally burned to lure Schwerner back to Mississippi. Mt. Zion church became one of the 20 Black churches in Mississippi that were firebombed in the summer of 1964. The FBI's investigation of the church bombing was codenamed "MIBURN," for "Mississippi burning," a name that would be used to encapsulate not only the church bombing of Mt. Zion Methodist Church but all the tragic events that ensued (Linder, 2006d).

MURDER IN NESHOBA COUNTY

At the time of the church burning Chaney and Schwerner were in Ohio attending training for the Mississippi Summer Project. While there they recruited Andrew Goodman to assist them in their efforts in Neshoba County. On June 21, 1964, Schwerner, Chaney, and Goodman drove to Mt. Zion Methodist Church to investigate the church burning. They also spoke with church leaders to hear their account of what happened. Later in the afternoon the three began their return to the Congress of Racial Equality (CORE) headquarters in Meridian, Mississippi. They never made it. On their way back to Meridian, they were arrested by Deputy Sheriff Cecil Price allegedly for suspicion of their involvement in the church arson. They were taken to the county jail in Philadelphia, Mississippi. While Chaney, Goodman, and Schwerner were held in jail, Price and other local Klan members (e.g., Edgar Ray Killen) conspired to murder the three civil rights workers. At approximately 10 p.m. someone paid Chaney's bail and the three were released from jail. As Chaney, Goodman, and Schwerner drove back to Meridian, the blue CORE station wagon was overtaken on a rural road by Price and other Klansmen (e.g., Killen, Wayne Roberts, Sam Bowers, and James Jordan). They were removed from the car, placed in Deputy Sheriff Price's patrol car and taken to a remote site, on Rock Cut Road. The three civil rights workers were removed from the patrol car and were shot and killed by Wayne Roberts as other Klansmen watched. James Jordan would later tell FBI agents that Doyle Barnette also fired two shots at Chaney. Forensic evidence suggests that they were beaten before they were killed; however, Klan members deny beating the three civil rights workers. The three bodies were transported to the Old Jolly Farm owned by Olen Burrage and buried in a dam (Federal Bureau of Investigation, 1964; Linder, 2002, 2006a, 2006d).

THE MISSISSIPPI BURNING INVESTIGATION

On June 22, 1964, the FBI, authorized by John Doar—the U.S. Assistant Attorney General for Civil Rights, began its investigation into the disappearance of Chaney, Goodman, and Schwerner. Joseph Sullivan, the FBI's major case inspector headed the investigation and worked closely with Meridian-based FBI agent John Proctor (Linder, 2006a, 2006d).

Figure 14.1 The burned automobile in which civil rights workers James Chaney, Michael Schwerner, and Andrew Goodman were riding when they disappeared. Courtesy of the Library of Congress.

Many Southerners were well aware of Hoover's reluctance to get involved in civil rights matters. There were reports of FBI agents watching idly as many Blacks and their supporters were assaulted. While Hoover may have personally gone to Mississippi to check on the progress of the investigation and for the first time poured endless resources and manpower into the MIBURN investigation to give the impression to the North that the government cared, Sullivan and Proctor were determined and dedicated to the discovery of what happened to the three civil rights workers and bringing those involved to justice (Bell, 1973; Kennedy, 1997; Linder, 2006a; Rossman, 2005).

While looking for the three civil rights workers in the Mississippi River, Navy divers found parts of two bodies that were later identified as Charles Moore and Henry Dee. One body only had a torso and the other was headless. They had been weighed down with bricks and an engine block so that they would not be found. Moore had just been expelled from college for participating in a student demonstration. He and Dee were looking for jobs when Klansmen found them and thought they were Black Muslims trying to organize an uprising. After this discovery it became clear to both Sullivan and Proctor that unless they received local cooperation they would never know what happened to the three civil rights workers (Benson, 2006; Linder, 2002, 2006a, 2006b).

Therefore from June to July 1964, the FBI interviewed about 1,000 Mississippians, at least half of whom were believed to be Klansmen. Proctor used his rapport with the community to gather information from informants in and around Philadelphia, Mississippi.

TIMELINE*

May 25, 1964 (Memorial Day)	Michael Schwerner and James Chaney speak at Mt. Zion Methodist Church in Neshoba County and urge its all-Black congregation to register to vote.
June 14, 1964	Student volunteers attend training session for Summer Project volunteers in Oxford, Ohio. Andrew Goodman and CORE members Schwerner and Chaney are among the attendees.
June 16, 1964	Armed KKK members assault leaders of Mt. Zion Methodist Church.
June 17, 1964	Mt. Zion Methodist Church is burned to the ground by Klan members. FBI begins its investigation into church bombings in Mississippi codenamed "MIBURN," for "Mississippi burning."
June 20, 1964	Schwerner, Chaney, and Goodman drive from Ohio to the CORE office in Meridian, Mississippi.
June 21, 1964	Schwerner, Chaney, and Goodman drive to site of burned church in Neshoba County. On their way back to Meridian, they are arrested by Deputy Sheriff Cecil Price and taken to the county jail in Philadelphia, Mississippi. Price releases the three from jail at 10 p.m., and shortly thereafter the three civil rights workers' station wagon is stopped on a rural road by Price and other Klan conspirators, the three are beaten and shot, their bodies buried in an earthen dam, and their car burned.
June 22, 1964	The FBI begins its investigation into the disappearance of the three civil rights workers. Joseph Sullivan is appointed to head the investigation.
July 2, 1964	President Lyndon B. Johnson signs the Civil Rights Act of 1964 into law.
August 4, 1964	The bodies of Schwerner, Chaney, and Goodman are discovered.
December 4, 1964	Nineteen members of the conspiracy are arrested and charged with violating the civil rights of Schwerner, Chaney, and Goodman.
December 10, 1964	A U.S. Commissioner dismisses charges against the 19.
January 1965	A federal grand jury in Jackson reindicts the 19.
February 24, 1965	Judge William Cox dismisses the indictments (except against Price and Rainey) on grounds that the conspirators were not "acting under color of state law."
March 1966	The United States Supreme Court reinstates the original indictments, overruling Judge Cox.
February 28, 1967	A new grand jury indicts the 19 conspirators.
October 7, 1967	The trial of the Neshoba County conspirators begins.
October 20, 1967	The jury returns verdicts of guilty against seven conspirators, nine are acquitted, and the jury is unable to reach a verdict on three of the men charged.
December 29, 1967	The conspirators found guilty are sentenced to prison terms ranging from three to ten years.

*Information obtained from Linder, 2006d.

After two months of investigation and offering a $30,000 reward for information, on July 31, 1964, the FBI was informed, through a third party, of the probable location of the bodies. A search warrant was obtained on August 3, 1954, to search for the bodies of the three civil rights workers in the dam at the Old Jolly Farm. Later that day the bodies of Chaney, Goodman, and Schwerner were discovered. Local law enforcement, including Deputy Sheriff Cecil Price, were on-site to assist in the recovery of the bodies (Federal Bureau of Investigation, 1964; Linder, 2002, 2006a).

By this time, Sullivan and Proctor had begun to suspect that local law enforcement agents were involved with the KKK and that they had assisted with the murder of the three civil rights workers. Over the next few months Proctor worked relentlessly to obtain confessions from local Klansmen. On October 13, 1964, with a promise of $3,500 and a staged arrest, James Jordan confessed his involvement in the conspiracy to murder the three civil rights workers and agreed to testify for the prosecution. Klan member Horace Barnette also admitted his involvement in the conspiracy and provided an account of the actual shootings; however, he reneged on his agreement to testify for the prosecution at the trial. In spite of Barnette's refusal to testify, Proctor and Sullivan had collected enough evidence to obtain warrants for the conspirators' arrests. Proctor and Sullivan's theory about needing local involvement to crack the case had been correct. Ironically, all the key informants obtained during the MIBURN investigation were members of the Lauderdale County chapter (klavern) of the KKK, which is in Meridian. They were unable to develop key informants in Philadelphia, which is in Neshoba County where the murders took place. Had Sullivan and Proctor continued spinning their wheels in Neshoba County or had the Neshoba County chapter of the KKK carried out the murders on their own, the bodies of the three civil rights workers and the details of the killings may have never been discovered (Federal Bureau of Investigation, 1964; Linder, 2002, 2006a).

On December 4, 1964, the FBI arrested 19 members of the conspiracy and charged them with conspiring to violate the civil rights of Schwerner, Chaney, and Goodman under the code of law and for conspiring to defraud the national government (U.S. Code, Title 18, Chapter 13, 2004; U.S. Code, Title 18, Chapter 19, 2004). Six days later the charges were dismissed on grounds that the confession used to obtain the arrests was hearsay evidence. In January 1965 John Doar and other U.S. Department of Justice

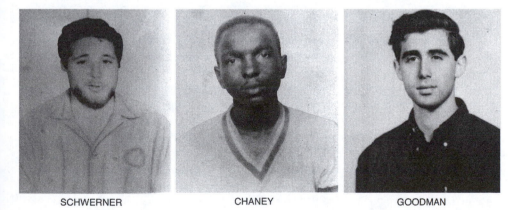

SCHWERNER   CHANEY   GOODMAN

Figure 14.2 The FBI distributed these pictures of civil rights workers, from left, Michael Schwerner, James Chaney, and Andrew Goodman, who disappeared in 1964. © AP Photo/FBI.

KEY FIGURES IN THE MISSISSIPPI BURNING TRIAL*

VICTIMS

James Chaney: CORE chief aid, native of Meridian, Mississippi, eldest son of five children, first affiliated with CORE in October 1963, duties ranged from working in the office to traveling to rural counties to set up meetings, plasterer by trade, killed June 21, 1964, at the age of 21, Black male.

Andrew Goodman: Mississippi Summer Project volunteer, native of New York, second son of affluent parents, active in integration protests in high school, spent only one day in Mississippi, killed June 21, 1964, at the age of 20, White male.

Michael Schwerner: also known as "Mickey," Meridian, Mississippi, office, CORE director, native of New York, youngest of two sons, while obtaining his sociology degree successfully campaigned for his fraternity to admit a Black member, dropped out of graduate school to work as a social worker in an impoverished area of New York, very active in civil rights issues, first White civil rights worker permanently based outside of Jackson, Mississippi, despised by the KKK for his efforts to register Blacks to vote and his success in getting a local hardware store to hire a Black employee, referred to as "Goatee" or "Jew boy" by the Klan, death ordered by Imperial Wizard Sam Bowers in May 1964, killed June 21, 1964, at age 24, White male.

CONSPIRATORS

Cecil Price: deputy sheriff of Neshoba County, known for terrorizing Blacks in the county, key conspirator in the murders of Schwerner, Goodman, and Chaney, stopped the blue Ford CORE station wagon on June 21, 1964, arrested and jailed the three civil rights workers in the Neshoba County Jail, released the three civil rights workers at 10:30 p.m. sending them into a trap, found guilty at trial and sentenced to six years in prison, which he served in Minnesota, returned to Philadelphia upon release and worked in the community, died on May 6, 2001, at the age of 64, from injuries sustained from falling from a lift in an equipment rental store in a hardware store three days prior.

Lawrence Rainey: elected sheriff of Neshoba County in 1963, native of Neshoba county, known for being tough on Blacks through the shooting of a Black from Chicago and his involvement in the naked whipping of a Black man, not present during the murders of Chaney, Goodman, and Schwerner, one of 19 arrested in December 1964 on conspiracy charges to deprive the three civil rights workers of their civil rights, acquitted in the 1967 trial, became a folk hero to local Whites, term as sheriff ended in November 1967, never able to work in law enforcement again, died from throat and tongue cancer on November 8, 2002, at the age of 79.

Wayne Roberts: known for his temper and drunkenness, involved in the Mt. Zion Methodist church beatings, wanted Schwerner dead, shot and killed Schwerner, Goodman, and Chaney on Rock Cut Road on June 21, 1964, kicked a CBS cameraman in the groin and hit him in the head after a 1965 hearing, found guilty of conspiracy to deny the civil rights workers their civil rights in the 1967 trial, sentenced to ten years in prison, served his sentence in Kansas, returned to Meridian and worked in a car dealership in Meridian.

Edgar Ray Killen: ordained Baptist minister, lead conspirator in the murders of the three civil rights workers in Mississippi on June 21, 1964, ''kleagle,'' or klavern recruiter and organizer, for the Neshoba and Lauderdale County Klan, organized the Mt. Zion Church arson, notified by Price that the civil rights workers were jailed, organized the murders of Chaney, Goodman, and Schwerner down to the minute detail including telling participating Klan members to get rubber gloves, one of the 19 men arrested on December 4, 1964, acquitted in the 1967 trial, retried on state charges in June 2005, convicted of manslaughter of Chaney, Goodman, and Schwerner, sentenced to three 20-year terms.

Sam Bowers: known as a proponent of White supremacy who did not support the views held by the Supreme Court and loved guns and swastikas, Navy veteran, manager of Sambo Amusements in Laurel, Mississippi, established the White Knights of the Klu Klux Klan in 1963 that had a well structured organization, which included a rank-ordered chain of command, chapters in several counties, and armed tactical squads, became the imperial wizard of the KKK of Mississippi in 1964, which had approximately 10,000 members, authorized Schwerner's ''elimination,'' found guilty of conspiracy in the 1967 Mississippi Burning trial, for overseeing the ''elimination'' of Chaney, Goodman, and Schwerner, sentenced to ten years, imprisoned in Washington State, upon his release resumed management of Sambo Amusements, in August 1998, at the age of 74, sentenced to life in prison for the 1966 murder of Vernon Dahmer, a civil rights activist who was killed in a firebombing of his house after he allowed Blacks to pay the $2 poll tax to register to vote in his store.

CONSPIRATORS AND PROSECUTORIAL WITNESSES

James Jordan: in 1964 he was a newcomer to Meridian, worked in a motel and operated an illegal speakeasy outside of Meridian, recruited Meridian Klansmen to participate in the June 21 conspiracy, suspected of having shot Chaney in the abdomen, claims he was a lookout at the turnoff onto Rock Cut Road and was not near Deputy Sheriff Price's car until after Roberts had shot Chaney, Goodman, and Schwerner, prosecution's only witness to the June 21, 1964, shootings of Chaney, Goodman, and Schwerner, was paid $3,500 for his full testimony, brought into custody through a staged arrest after which his family was moved to Georgia, testimony was given on October 12, 1967, under heavy guard and after suffering from hyperventilation and one fainting spell, tried in Atlanta for his role in the Mississippi Burning murders, pled guilty, sentenced to four years in prison.

Delmar Dennis: Methodist minister and Klan member, at the age of 24 joined the Lauderdale County Klan and became the chaplain (klavern's kludd), claimed that he was tricked into joining the Klan, refused to purchase a gun, declined to attend or participate in the Mt. Zion Methodist church burning, encouraged by Wallace Miller, the first Klan informant to the FBI, to assist in the investigation, a vital witness for the government in the Mississippi Burning trial, met FBI agents in secret at Meridian cemeteries and the naval air station, was paid $15,000 over three years for his testimony, agents compiled 40 pages of notes on the conspiracy from his testimony, described the June 16 Klan meeting in which the plan to murder Schwerner was discussed, described and explained a coded letter from Sam Bowers instructing Klan members to say nothing about the murders during the FBI investigation, contributed to Bower's conviction by quoting him as saying of the murders of the three civil rights workers: ''It was the first time that Christians had planned and carried out the execution of a Jew.''

CRIMINAL JUSTICE AGENTS

Joseph Sullivan: became FBI's Major Case Inspector in 1963, directed FBI's nine month MIBURN investigation, began working for the FBI in 1941, joined the FBI's Domestic Intelligence division in the early 1950s, known for his thoroughness and efficiency, realized conducting an investigation and not a search was the only way to discover what had happened to the three civil rights workers, developed key informants that were all members of the Lauderdale County chapter (klavern) of the KKK, which is in Meridian, but was unable to develop key informants in Philadelphia, which is in Neshoba County where the murders took place.

John Proctor: born in 1926 in Reform, Alabama, FBI agent based in Meridian, in 1952 began working for the FBI, in 1962 became a resident agent in Meridian working under the supervision of the FBI's New Orleans office, duties included investigating alleged violations of civil rights laws, to assist in performing his duty he cultivated friendships with all types of people (e.g., bootleggers, Klansmen, local law enforcement officials, Black leaders, and civil rights workers), very knowledgeable about the people in Neshoba county and their ways, on June 22, 1964, began investigation of the disappearance of the three civil rights workers and initially concluded that no federal laws had been violated, on June 23, 1964, ten additional FBI agents and Sullivan joined him in Meridian to conduct the investigation, received the tip that disclosed the whereabouts of the burned CORE station wagon, on August 4, 1964, took photos of Chaney's, Goodman's, and Schwerner's bodies that would later be used in the 1967 trial, broke open the Mississippi Burning case by obtaining James Jordan's confession and convincing him to turn state's evidence, persuaded Sheriff Rainey to not cause problems during Martin Luther King, Jr.'s visit to Philadelphia, retired from the FBI in 1978 and opened his own detective agency in Meridian.

John Doar: born 1921 in Minneapolis, Minnesota, in 1960 began working for the Justice Department in the Civil Rights Division, in June 1963 prevented a riot in downtown Jackson, Mississippi, after the assassination of civil rights leader Medgar Evers, in 1962 assisted James Meredith in becoming the first Black student to register for class and attend classes at the University of Mississippi, in 1964 was the Assistant Attorney General for Civil Rights, instrumental in the passing of the Voting Rights Acts in August 1965, first federal official notified of the disappearance of Chaney, Goodman, and Schwerner, authorized the FBI to investigate the case, lead prosecutor in the 1967 Mississippi Burning Trial, in 1967 left government service to begin his private practice in New York, returned briefly to government service in 1974 as counsel to the House Judiciary Committee during the Nixon impeachment crisis.

William Cox: federal district judge, known segregationist, appointed to the federal bench by President Kennedy in exchange for Senator James Eastland's support of

Thurgood Marshall's placement in the Second Circuit Court of Appeals, constantly frustrated the Justice Department's integration initiatives, rulings were consistently overruled on appeal, almost impeached in 1964 for calling a group of Black witnesses "a bunch of chimpanzees," threw out the indictments against most Neshoba County conspirators in February 1965, which was overruled by the Supreme Court in 1966 and the indictments were reinstated, presided over the October 1967 Mississippi Burning trial, endorsed the guilty verdict reached by the jury.

*Information obtained from Linder, 2002, 2006b.

attorneys convinced a federal grand jury in Jackson, Mississippi, to reindict all 19 conspirators, but on February 24, 1965, Judge William Cox dismissed the indictments brought against the 17 private citizens accused of conspiracy on grounds that the conspirators were not "acting under color of state law." However, in March 1966 the U.S. Supreme Court reinstated the original indictments, reversing and remanding Judge Cox's ruling. Consequently, on February 28, 1967, a new grand jury, again at the prodding of Doar and his team of attorneys, indicted 19 conspirators (*U.S. v. Price et al.,* 1966). Included in the final list of indicted conspirators were Sheriff Lawrence Rainey, Deputy Sheriff Cecil Price, Imperial Wizard Sam Bowers, Wayne Roberts, Jimmy Snowden, Billy Wayne Posey, Horace Barnett, Olen Burrage, Frank Herndon, and Edgar Ray Killen (Federal Bureau of Investigation, 1964; Linder, 2002, 2006a).

MISSISSIPPI BURNING HEADLINES

The difficulties the FBI encountered in trying to obtain information related to the case are mirrored in the articles published in the *New York Times* and *Washington Post* from June 23, 1964, to October 21, 1967. Many of the articles documented the problems FBI agents encountered when searching for the three civil rights workers. However, many of the articles primarily focused on the federal government's commitment to finding the missing civil rights workers. Articles detailed increases in FBI manpower, the arrival of 200 sailors to assist in the investigation, and Hoover's visit and inspection of the progress of the MIBURN investigation. The continued reported failure of the federal government to make much progress in the investigation was dotted with successes such as the discovery of the car, the discovery of the corpses of other civil rights workers, and eventually the discovery of the bodies of Chaney, Goodman, and Schwerner ("Rest of mutilated bodies," 1964; Sitton, 1964a, 1964b).

In the midst of the reports of the federal government's involvement in Mississippi, another story line weaved its way through the headlines and newspaper articles. Initially, it was presented in the form of shock as local officials suggested the three men were hiding to build publicity for their voting registration campaigns. During the investigation, it could be found in the officials' supposed inability to provide information surrounding the three civil rights workers' disappearances and the numerous statements made to the media expressing their frustration about not being informed of the FBI's progress in the case. Finally, it was evident when Sheriff Rainey refused to talk to FBI agents without a warrant on August 11, 1964; the officials in Neshoba County, Mississippi, were hiding something, and if left up to them it would never be revealed to outsiders, especially not ones from the North. Neither the media from the North nor local sources would overtly say it, but little had changed in Mississippi in spite of the MIBURN investigation. Racism was still rampant and death was highly likely for anyone who challenged the segregationist establishment (Rossman, 2005).

However, once the trial began, the successes and failures of the U.S. Department of Justice were chronicled as well as the overtly racist actions of Neshoba County citizens and members of the Mississippi legal system. Most articles simply reported the facts with very little commentary. Occasionally a journalist would question the absurdity of withholding information that the state of Mississippi claimed did not contain incriminating evidence or point out the number of violent acts against Blacks that had gone unpunished in the South. However, for the most part the media allowed the facts of the case to speak for themselves: three civil rights workers were murdered, and the perpetrators of the offense were charged by the federal government, not the state of Mississippi, for conspiracy to violate the civil rights of the civil rights workers, not murder, when they planned and executed their killing ("7 Klan convictions," 1969; Bigart, 1965; Corrigan, 1964; Herbers, 1964, 1965a, 1965b; "Judge in Mississippi," 1967; "Murder in Mississippi," 1964; Rossman, 2005).

In the late 1980s the media began to cover the Mississippi Burning case differently. This was especially true of southern papers such as the *Clarion-Ledger,* which is based in Jackson, Mississippi. Investigative reporters began to dig up information that had been covered up, inaccessible, or unintentionally overlooked during the 1964 investigation and 1967 trial. No person (e.g., Edgar Ray Killen) or entity (e.g., southern newspapers) found to be involved in said miscarriages of justice were exempt from investigation and critique by various media sources.

For example, Mississippi-based papers such as the *Clarion-Ledger* and the *Jackson Daily News* participated in the segregationist tradition for many years. Without asking any questions or conducting their own investigations, both papers often published information that had been secretly spoon-fed to them by segregationist organizations like the Mississippi Sovereignty Commission, which was a state-run spy agency. Once Jerry Mitchell, a news reporter for the *Clarion-Ledger,* discovered this during his investigation of the Mississippi Sovereignty Commission, he was able to successfully convince the *Clarion-Ledger* management to let him run a story admitting both papers' involvement in assisting the commission by printing racial propaganda. The running of this story signified a new era in Southern media, where media were being used as advocates against discrimination that were willing to identify all perpetrators of injustice even if it involved pointing a finger at themselves (Smith, 2002). Eventually, Mitchell's investigation of a statement made by Sam Bowers, imperial wizard of the KKK in Mississippi in 1964, during an interview was instrumental in getting the Mississippi Burning case reopened. Bowers said of the 1967 trial that he was glad to be indicted because it in essence allowed the person who orchestrated the murders of the three civil rights workers to go free. Mitchell was able to identify Edgar Ray Killen as the orchestrater Bowers referred to, which eventually aided in reopening the Mississippi Burning case (Montagne, 2005).

This was a stark contrast from how the events surrounding the case were covered in the 1960s as segments of the media were now willing to become involved in covering all aspects of a case and openly scrutinize their sources and findings. This new strategy used to cover cases, and a new generation of district attorneys and legislators in Mississippi dedicated to punishing past injustices that were tried as civil rights violations during the state's segregation era, would lead to the first manslaughter conviction in the Mississippi

Burning case and open the door for the potential of additional arrests in the future (Alberts, 2005; "Brother recalls," 2005; "Civil rights," 2005; "Defense opens," 2005; "Ex-Klansman sentenced," 2005; "Ex-Klansmen to testify," 2005; "Former Klansman," 2005; "Man claims innocence," 2005; "Mississippi burning," n.d.; "'Mississippi burning' trial begins," 2005; "'Mississippi burning' trial set to start, 2005; Montagne, 2005; Smith, 2002).

THE MISSISSIPPI BURNING TRIAL

After two dismissals of the indictments, the Mississippi Burning trial, which included 19 defendants, began on October 7, 1967 (*U.S. v. Price et al.*, 1967). Judge William Cox presided over the trial and John Doar was the lead prosecutor for the United States. The case was tried in front of an all White jury composed of a panel of five men and seven women who ranged from 34 to 67 years of age. During jury selection Judge Cox denied a challenge for cause of a White male, who admitted being an ex-member of the KKK. It was clear early on that Judge Cox's segregationist viewpoints would influence his ruling in this trial as it had in his dismissal of the previous indictments brought against the conspirators. During cross-examination, defense council Laurel Weir asked whether Reverend Johnson, the prosecutor's witness, and Schwerner had attempted to get young Negro males to sign a pledge to rape one White woman a week during the summer of 1964. Surprisingly, Judge Cox demanded to know who asked the question and reprimanded the defense council for his inappropriateness. Edgar Ray Killen, a defendant, was identified as the author of the question. Thus, it was also clear that Judge Cox intended to run a tight courtroom and, while his segregationist views may have affected some of his ruling, those views were not going to cause him to allow the defense to skate through the trial. If they wanted their clients to walk as free men, they would have to present a sound case (Linder, 2002, 2006a).

The government's case was built around the testimony of three witnesses and co-defendants to the conspiracy: Wallace Miller, Delmar Dennis, and James Jordan. Miller's testimony detailed the organization of the Lauderdale chapter of the KKK and the plans made on June 21, 1964, by Frank Herndon and Edgar Ray Killen. Dennis's testimony sealed the fate of Sam Bowers, the Imperial Wizard of the White Knights of the KKK in Mississippi. Dennis told of Bowers's comment that Schwerner had been the first Jew killed by Christians. Dennis also deciphered a letter from Bowers that warned Klan members that the FBI investigators were getting close and that they should continue to remain silent. Jordan's testimony was the most vital to the case as he was the only witness who could provide an account of the actual shootings of Chaney, Goodman, and Schwerner. Jordan's testimony was highly anticipated, and there was a grave concern that the Klan might attempt an assassination. Even Jordan was nervous as he had a hyperventilation incident and a fainting spell that delayed his testimony by one day. Thus, Jordan was escorted into the courtroom by five agents with their guns drawn. His testimony described the events surrounding the killings, from the time the Klan members gathered in Meridian on June 21, 1964, to the burying of the bodies in the dam at Old Jolly Farm (Linder, 2002, 2006a).

The defense's case was composed solely of alibi and character witnesses who testified about the integrity of the accused and their alleged whereabouts on June 21, 1964, during the time of the murders. On October 18, 1967, closing arguments were presented and the jury began its deliberations. On October 19, 1967, the jury reported being deadlocked, and they were charged by Judge Cox to reach a verdict (Linder, 2002, 2006a; Rugaber, 1967).

GUILTY IN MISSISSIPPI

The jury returned its verdict on October 20, 1967, just two days after it had begun its deliberation and one day after it had reported being deadlocked. Deputy Sheriff Cecil Ray Price, Jimmy Arledge, Sam Bowers, Wayne Roberts, Jimmy Snowden, Billy Wayne Posey, and Horace Doyle Barnette were found guilty. Bernard Akin, Sheriff Lawrence Rainey, Olen Burrage, Frank Herndon, Richard Willis, Herman Tucker, and James Harris were acquitted. The jury was unable to reach a verdict for three of the conspirators: Edgar Ray (Preacher) Killen, Jerry McGrew Sharpe, and Ethel Glen "Hop" Barnett (Linder, 2002, 2006a; "7 Klan convictions," 1969).

On December 29, 1967, Judge Cox sentenced Roberts and Bowers to ten years in prison, Posey and Price to six years in prison, and Arledge, Barnette, and Snowden to three years in prison. They did not begin serving their sentences until March 19, 1970, after they had exhausted all their appeals (Linder, 2002, 2006a; "Ex-Klansman sentenced," 2005; "Ex-Klansmen to testify," 2005; "'Mississippi burning' trial begins," 2005; "'Mississippi burning' trial set to start," 2005).

Noticeably missing from the list of conspirators that were convicted was Edgar Ray Killen's name. Many, including John Doar, believed Killen played an integral role in the conspiracy to murder Chaney, Goodman, and Schwerner. There were speculations that Killen escaped conviction because much of the evidence tying him to the case was more circumstantial than the evidence used to convict the other conspirators, and that the one juror who caused the 11-1 deadlock during deliberations over Killen's guilt stated that he refused to convict a preacher ("Defense opens," 2005; Linder, 2006a; "Ex-Klansman sentenced," 2005; "Ex-Klansmen to testify," 2005; "'Mississippi burning' trial begins," 2005; "'Mississippi burning' trial set to start," 2005).

In 1999, thirty-five years after the murders of the three civil rights workers, the state of Mississippi reopened the case. Since the state did not do any investigations in 1964, the FBI turned over 40,000 MIBURN files to assist them in their investigation. One of the many problems that the state faced during the investigation is that many of the key witnesses for the case were dead as were many of the potential defendants. To have a successful case, they would either need to find new witnesses who were still alive or convince some of the living coconspirators to testify for the prosecution. Time was the enemy as many of the coconspirators were also dead or would end up dying during the investigation, such as Cecil Price who died on May 6, 2001, three days after falling from a lift in an equipment rental store ("Brother recalls," 2005; Byrd, 2006; Linder, 2006a; "'Mississippi burning' trial begins," 2005; "'Mississippi burning' trial set to start," 2005).

Regardless of the state's concerns about the strength of their case, the citizens of Mississippi demanded action. "On October 6, 2004 approximately 500 people marched in support of state prosecution of former Klan preacher Edgar Ray Killen for the murder of James Chaney, Andrew Goodman, and Michael Schwerner" (Linder, 2006a, p. 7 of 9, ¶3). Thus, despite the death of Cecil Price, who could have been either one of the state's key witnesses or a primary defendant in the reopened case, on January 6, 2005, the state of Mississippi charged 79-year-old Edgar Ray Killen, another of its key defendants in the reopened MIBURN case, with the murder of Chaney, Goodman, and Schwerner. In his arraignment on January 7, 2005, Killen pleaded not guilty to all three murder charges ("Brother recalls," 2005; "Man claims innocence," 2005).

Killen's case is significant as it was the first time that the state of Mississippi brought charges against anyone in the 1964 MIBURN case. There were mixed feelings about Killen's arrest and indictment. Billy Wayne Posey, one of the original seven coconspirators convicted and sentenced in 1967, expressed outrage that Killen was being prosecuted after 40 years. However, Carolyn Goodman, Andrew Goodman's mother, was excited about the news. Even at age 89 she was still hopeful that her son's killers would eventually be imprisoned ("Brother recalls," 2005; Linder, 2006a).

Jury selection began in the Killen murder trial on June 13, 2005. Killen, who had broken his legs in March in a tree-cutting accident, watched the proceedings from a wheelchair. While family members of the victims (e.g., Ben Chaney—brother of James Chaney) were encouraged by the prosecution, other civil rights advocates were not satisfied as they wanted to see other surviving conspirators prosecuted together with Killen. As of June 19, 2006, nine of the 19 coconspirators originally indicted on federal charges were still alive (e.g., Olen Burrage—owner of the dam site where the bodies of the three civil rights workers were buried) ("Brother recalls," 2005; Byrd, 2006; Linder, 2006a; "'Mississippi burning' trial begins," 2005; "'Mississippi burning' trial set to start," 2005).

Opening statements in the Killen murder trial began on June 15, 2005 ("Ex-Klansmen to testify at," 2005). The trial was recessed indefinitely on June 16, 2005, as Killen was taken from the courtroom on a stretcher. Killen's failing health would be a concern throughout the trial ("Edgar Ray Killen," 2006). Two days after Killen was taken from the courtroom to the hospital, the defense presented its opening arguments and the prosecution presented Judge Marcus Gordon with a motion requesting that the jury be allowed to consider the lesser charger of felony manslaughter in addition to the original murder charge ("Defense opens," 2005). The motion was granted by Judge Gordon—a decision that may have prevented a mistrial or a not guilty verdict.

On June 21, 2005, Judge Gordon sentenced 80-year-old Edgar Ray Killen to 60 years in prison. He was ordered to serve three, 20-year consecutive terms, one for each manslaughter conviction in connection with the deaths of Chaney, Goodman, and Schwerner. Killen was not convicted of murder because the jury was not certain that Killen intended for the Klansmen to kill the three civil rights workers. Ironically, Killen's conviction was handed down exactly 41 years after the murders of Chaney, Goodman, and Schwerner ("Ex-Klansman sentenced," 2005; "Former Klansman," 2005; Linder, 2006a; "Miss. Supreme Court," 2006).

Killen has been serving his 60-year sentence at the Central Mississippi Correctional Facility in Pearl, Mississippi, which is in Rankin County ("Killen released," 2006; "Miss. Supreme Court," 2006). Killen has been at the correctional facility since he was sentenced in June 2005, aside from a brief release on a $600,000 bond in August 2005 due to concerns about Killen's failing health. The bond was revoked after several witnesses notified Judge Gordon that they had seen Killen driving and walking around at a gas station ("Edgar Ray Killen," 2006).

Killen is appealing his three manslaughter convictions. Judge Gordon's decision to grant the prosecution's motion to allow the jury to consider the lesser charge of felony manslaughter after the trail had already begun, the prosecution's timing in pursuing the case—intentionally waiting for better political climate, and his denial of due process by not receiving a speedy trial have become the basis for Killen's appeal ("Defense opens,"

2005; Elliot, 2006; "Ex-Klansman sentenced," 2005). Killen will have to continue to await the outcome of his appeal in prison as he was denied bond on July 14, 2006 (Times Wire Reports, 2006). On December 8, 2006, the Mississippi Supreme Court notified Killen's attorneys that oral arguments would not be heard in the case. The attorneys will be allowed to present their arguments in briefs, which the justices will use to assist them in making their decision (Elliot, 2006; "Miss. Supreme Court," 2006).

SOCIAL, POLITICAL, AND LEGAL ISSUES

The Mississippi Burning case shed light on several social, political, and legal issues that were either being abused or ignored prior to the 1964 murders and 1967 trial. The precedent had been set by the Supreme Court that states had sovereignty over addressing legal issues. The absence of checks and balances from the federal government fueled the abuse of power, especially among law enforcement and the judiciary. This is the legal system that was in place on June 21, 1964, when Deputy Sheriff Cecil Price assisted in planning and executing the murders of Chaney, Goodman, and Schwerner and used his marked sheriff's patrol car to stop them, transport them to the murder scene, and transport his coconspirators to and from the murder scene.

Race relations had become increasingly strained in the 1960s because of the national efforts of Blacks to obtain equal rights. There was significant mistrust of Whites among Blacks. This was especially true of members of the law enforcement, since some were known to be and others were suspected of being members of the KKK. It was no secret that Hoover, the FBI Director, did not support the civil rights movement and that some FBI agents were often just as racist as local law enforcement, often turning a blind eye to the abuse perpetrated on Blacks. The amount of time and money put into prosecuting the Mississippi Burning trial suggested the federal government, including the FBI, seemed willing and capable to avenge the injustices associated with the violation of civil rights, but in the 1960s it was not clear if they were willing and capable of proactively protecting civil rights activists (Kennedy, 1997; Rossman, 2005).

While the guilty verdicts in the Mississippi Burning trial took a large step toward ensuring the government would protect Blacks as they pursued their civil rights, the fact that the conspirators were charged only with a violation of the civil rights act and interfering with a federal investigation, in lieu of murder, sent society the message that Blacks' and other minorities' lives were devalued. Many civil rights activists argue that the fact that to date, over 42 years later, only one of the 19 conspirators has been tried for murder and convicted of manslaughter symbolizes to society that minorities' lives are devalued (Rossman, 2005; Saigo, 1989). In addition, many civil rights activists also argue that this symbolic devaluation of minority life transcends race lines. Within the Black race, this negative stigma (devaluation) has been attached primarily to lower class Blacks. In an effort to escape the negative stigma and feel valued, middle class Blacks move to more affluent areas and in so doing remove themselves as middle class role models in the Black community. In time middle class Blacks also begin to see lower class Blacks as the other, inferior, of lesser value, in effect taking part in the actual devaluation of lower class Blacks. This phenomenon has resulted in a wider gap between Blacks who have and Blacks who have not (a deepening of the poor situation), as well as a divided Black race and the absence of a unified Black community (Fishman, 2002; Walker, 2000).

INVESTIGATIVE REPORTER: JERRY MITCHELL*

Jerry Mitchell is an investigative reporter for *The Clarion-Ledger* in Jackson, Mississippi. He has been employed at the *Clarion-Ledger* for the past 14 years. He was born in 1959 in the South, received his education in the Midwest (The Ohio State University), and now lives in Jackson, Mississippi, with his wife and their two children. Mitchell is most known for his investigative stories that helped put some of the most notorious civil rights murderers behind bars:

- Imperial Wizard Sam Bowers for the 1966 murder of NAACP leader Vernon Dahmer.
- Former Klansman and minister Edgar Ray Killen for helping orchestrate the June 21, 1964, killings of Michael Schwerner, James Chaney, and Andrew Goodman.
- Klansman Byron De La Beckwith for the 1963 murder of NAACP leader Medgar Evers.
- Former Klansman Bobby Cherry for the 1963 bombing of a Birmingham church that killed four girls.

Using the information he gathered from his investigation of Killen, Mitchell authored *The Preacher and the Klansman* (1998). This book is used with special curricula as a supplemental text in many classrooms in the United States. His worked has earned him 14 national awards. Mitchell's exploits were documented in the movie *Ghosts of Mississippi,* and he has been featured on ABC's *20/20,* in *Civil Rights Martyrs,* a Learning Channel documentary, in the "First Person" segment of *ABC Evening News,* and in *Newsweek* as one of "America's Best" in 2005.

Mitchell is also recognized as an expert in his field and as a result has often appeared on CNN, the *Lehrer News Hour,* and other programs. In spite of all his notoriety, Mitchell is known as a very humble man who shies away from the spotlight. He is a man who is motivated by the pursuit of truth and justice, his love for the South, and his desire to see the South do what is right regardless of how much time has passed.

*Information obtained from "Investigative Reporter," 2006; "Jerry Mitchell," n.d.; Johnson, Jr., 2000.

IMPACT ON LEGAL CULTURE

The Mississippi burning case has had a tremendous impact on justice in the United States. The FBI agents of 1964 demonstrated that law enforcement can protect and serve all people regardless of race, religion, or sex (Linder, 2002, 2006a). The jury of the 1967 case demonstrated that the use of jury nullification as a legal strategy to keep Whites from being punished for violence against Blacks was no longer a viable strategy for avoiding conviction. The federal government also expressed its intolerance of the jury nullification strategy by adding Section 245 to the U.S. criminal code, giving the federal government the jurisdiction to prosecute perpetrators for violating "federally protected activities" (Kennedy, 1997; U.S. Code, Title 18, Chapter 13). Prosecutor John Doar set the precedence for the extent to which the federal government will respectfully interfere in local government when the rights of citizens, including minorities, are violated. In addition, Doar jump-started the practice of U.S. Justice Department attorneys' leaving Washington and going to the scene of the crime to prepare for a case (Linder, 2002).

Despite Doar's effort to use his office as the voice of the victims of civil rights violations, the law and legal processes were and are still seen by many minorities as the "means by which the generalized racism in the society was made particular and converted into standards and policies of social control" (Burns, 2003, p. 158). The Supreme Court's 1966 ruling set the precedent for demanding that conspiracy and civil rights charges be looked at seriously by the court, and that said violators are prosecuted to the full extent of the law. This precedent gave some hope as it suggested that even the sheriffs in the Deep South were not out of the reach of the "long arms of justice." The MIBURN case helped dispel the ruling of *Stanford v. Scott,* which found that Blacks did not have the same rights as Whites nor could they obtain them as Blacks had been treated as inferior to Whites for years. Every civil rights case won by the U.S. Department of Justice in conjunction with the MIBURN cases added value to the Black life and supported the notion that Blacks and Whites are equal and should be treated as such. In essence, law was the tool used "to effect positive social change," at least in theory (Burns, 2003, p. 161).

IMPACT ON POPULAR CULTURE

Forty-two years later, popular culture is still affected in a variety of ways by the Mississippi Burning trial. A fear of the Deep South and its dirt roads, rivers, lakes, streams, and dams, whether it is real or perceived, still permeates the minds of many minorities. Still others look on the South with disgust. Some southerners and many northerners, still have a view of southerners as uncultured, rural, and barbaric. Last, the younger generations see the South as a boring place and are not inclined to visit and spend many tourist dollars because of the previously mentioned assumptions that many people still hold about the South (Bell, 1973; Jansson, 2005; Kennedy, 1997; Salvaggio, 1991).

One of the clearest ways to see the impact of the Mississippi Burning trial on popular culture is in film. *Mississippi Burning* is an Orion Pictures film directed by Alan Parker. It appeared in the cinema in 1988 and cast notable actors such as Gene Hackman and Willem Dafoe in lead roles. They play two FBI agents who are sent down to Jessup County to investigate the disappearance of three civil rights workers. Alan Ward (Dafoe) is the chief investigator who goes by the book. His partner, Rupert Anderson (Hackman), is the direct opposite of Ward and uses the aggressive tactics he learned growing up and serving as a sheriff in Mississippi to collect evidence in the investigation. Both characters are based loosely on the two key FBI investigators in the 1964 MIBURN case. Anderson's character is based loosely on FBI agent John Proctor, and Ward's character is based loosely on FBI agent Joseph Sullivan. There were other characters in the film who were loosely based on real participants associated with the MIBURN case. In the film Geoffrey Nuffts plays Goatee, a nickname the Klan had given to Michael Schwerner. Deputy Sheriff Clinton Pell's character played by Brad Dourif represented Deputy Sheriff Cecil Price, and Sheriff Ray Stuckey's character played by Gailard Sartain represented Sheriff Lawrence Rainey's involvement in the case.

Reviews of the film were mixed as many film viewers and some critiques such as Vincent Canby called the film "first-rate" and Roger Ebert gave the film four stars, calling it "the best American film of 1988" (Canby, 1988, p. C12; Ebert, 1988, p. 3 of 4, ¶2; Emerson, n.d.; Linder, 2006c). Most critics, while acknowledging that the film was indeed dramatic and provocative, argued that *Mississippi Burning* did more to overemphasize the zeal of the FBI in solving the MIBURN case, paint southern Blacks as passivists, and depict southern Whites as Klansmen than it promoted positive dialogue about how to address current racial issues that were carry-overs from or mimicked the racial issues of the nation's past. It was argued that the filmmakers were more concerned with selling out the box office than promoting social change, which critiques argued was evident in the limited number of facts about the case and the large amount of Hollywood drama that appeared in the film (Emerson, n.d.; Linder, 2006c; "Mississippi burning," n.d.).

Brinson (1995) argued that the underlying themes in the story attempt to communicate the old myth of White supremacy. In so doing the film "symbolically and rhetorically asserts the solutions provided in *Mississippi Burning* are the same answers for current problems" (p. 211). Brinson sees the film as an attempt by White elites to demonstrate how they have lost power (sociocultural, political, and economic). This perspective stands in sharp contrast to the film critiques that acclaimed the film as the best of 1988 and heralded the film for its use of fiction to historically account the events surrounding the 1964 deaths of the three civil rights workers and bring to light many of the discrimination issues that still needed to be addressed 24 years later (Brinson, 1995; Canby, 1988; Ebert, 1988; Emerson, n.d.; Linder, 2006c).

Jansson (2005) argued that there is an American national identity born out of the view of the South as a region that is fundamentally different from the rest of the United States. It is a place where racism, violence, poverty, and other negative characteristics dominate the culture. In contrast to the tyrannical South, "America" stands in opposition and is the proponent of tolerance, justice, and peace. The film is said to contribute to the construction of such a national identity.

Emerson (n.d.) echoed Jansson's assertion and offered a critique that examined the *Mississippi Burning* film from all angles—capturing both the film's flaws and value. Emerson argued that Parker did a terrible job accurately portraying history. For example, the FBI is represented by two White agents who use the Klan's tactics of violence to solve the case (e.g., using a Black FBI agent to get a confession from the mayor by threatening to castrate him). In many ways the FBI is portrayed as the hero that rescues the passive Blacks of the South and conquers the violent Whites of the South, when in actuality it was a combined effort of both Blacks and Whites dedicated to the peaceful strategies, advocated by Dr. Martin Luther King, Jr., and the advancement of the civil rights movement as well as a $30,000 bribe paid to a Klan informant that lead to the cracking of the case. Hoover, the director of the FBI during the MIBURN investigation, was known for his dislike of Blacks and their leaders, especially Dr. King. Hoover had agents constantly looking for dirt on Dr. King, especially related to his sex life. In addition, most of the FBI agents involved in the case had no desire to work the case and shared Hoover's dislike of Blacks. The MIBURN case is an important event; it was a turning point in the civil rights movement during the 1960s. Thus, many critiques argue that to distort the facts surrounding that event, in any way, especially in the way Parker did in the film *Mississippi Burning*, whether intentional or not, denigrates the contributions made by so many Blacks and Whites during that era (e.g., James Chaney, Andrew Goodman, Michael Schwerner, Dr. Martin Luther King, Jr., Medgar Evers, Robert Kennedy, and John Doar).

Emerson also argued that Parker did an excellent job accomplishing his goal of shocking the senses of film viewers. Parker used music, actors, scenery, and other cinematic tools to draw the viewer in.

> The movie leaves no room for considerations of history, ethics, justice, or morality—things you'd think would be vitally important to this story. Instead, like the exploitation picture it is, it sacrifices all such matters to the throat-grabbing thrill of the "powerful" moment.

You're too busy flinching to experience anything deeper than an autonomic response. (Emerson, n.d., p. 3 of 5, ¶4)

In many ways the film *Mississippi Burning* did not condemn the racial violence of the 1960s as much as it showcased it (Emerson, n.d.; "Mississippi burning," n.d.). Many critics agree that this is Parker's way of reaching the audience (Canby, 1988; Ebert, 1988; Emerson, n.d.). He uses tension, gut-wrenching scenes, and dramatic moments to shake up the audience, provoking them to think about the key issues portrayed in the film (e.g., racism and excessive violence). While Parker's strategy may be somewhat over the top resulting in a film with fewer facts about the case than originally advertised, Emerson and other critiques argue that this in and of itself does not make *Mississippi Burning* a bad film (Emerson n.d., "Mississippi burning," n.d.).

> Even so, although you can certainly take issue with the many bizarre choices Parker has made, lots of movies—even great ones—have distorted history. Just because *Intolerance* or *Citizen Kane* or *Gone With the Wind* or *Chinatown* take liberties with historical fact, that alone doesn't diminish them as brilliant movies—any more than it would make sense to condemn Stanley Kubrick's vision of the future in *2001* if it doesn't turn out to be exactly accurate. The best movies create their own worlds; they're timeless. (Emerson, n.d., p. 2 of 5, ¶6)

Ultimately, what seems to turn many critics against the film *Mississippi Burning* is the polish, attention to detail, and aesthetic appeal of the film that used "cinema as a sledge hammer to pound knee-jerk reactions out of audiences, compelling them to kneel, mindlessly and helplessly, before the altar of 'powerful' moviemaking," instead of facing the facts surrounding the MIBURN case, acknowledging how the facts affect current events, dialoguing about positive solutions, and moving toward them (Emerson, n.d., p. 5 of 5, ¶2).

The effect of the MIBURN case on popular culture can also be seen in the declining support of the Ku Klux Klan. The Klan whose membership has always been secretive in the South used to receive public support of their philosophies and activities. The Klan, in the South, no longer enjoys that public support, as it is no longer politically correct to support KKK activities or adhere to such ideals. What has not changed is the difficulty in solving race crimes. Crimes that are racially motivated are still clandestine and difficult to prove. There is still a strong sense of camaraderie or deep-seated loyalty that keeps anyone from talking (Linder, 2002, 2006a; Rossman, 2005). Consequently, race relations are still strained as there is still an unspoken mistrust of Whites by Blacks and of law enforcement by minorities. (Bell, 1973; Jansson, 2005; Kennedy, 1997; Salvaggio, 1991).

Finally, the Mississippi Burning case and other civil rights cases have led to the development of and the idolizing of the investigative reporter who is part detective and part reporter. The investigative reporter is someone who pursues the "missed or ignored facts of the case" and ends up cracking the case and actively assisting the prosecution in obtaining convictions. It is unclear whether the relentless coverage of racially motivated crimes, whether confirmed or suspected, by the national media and the continued extensive coverage of any follow-up to said cases is creating an overemphasis on the issue, which could be fueling either an oversensitivity or desensitization to the issue ("Investigative Reporter," 2006; Jerry Mitchell, n.d.; Johnson, Jr., 2000). Recent discoveries in civil rights crimes of the 1960s have prompted the legislature to consider bills (e.g., "The Unsolved Civil Rights Crime Act" or "The Till Bill") that would allow for the reopening of unsolved civil rights cases so that known perpetrators could be brought to justice (Benson, 2006). It is probable that the Mississippi Burning case will continue to influence popular culture for years to come as this case has come to signify the United States' value of Black life and an absence of tolerance for the savagery Blacks have experienced and in many covert forms are still experiencing.

SUGGESTIONS FOR FURTHER READING

An extensive collection of information on this case can be found on the bibliography page of
the Mississippi Burning trial Web site: http://www.law.umkc.edu/faculty/projects/ftrials/
price&bowers/bibliography.html

In addition to reviewing the material posted on the aforementioned Web site the following materials
should also be consulted:

Bailey, F.Y., & Green, A.P. (1999). *"Law never here": A social history of African-American responses to issues of crime and justice*. Westport, CT: Praeger.

Blaustein, A.P. (1968). *Civil rights and the American Negro: A documentary history*. New York: Trident Press.

Huie, W.B. (2000, June). *Three lives for Mississippi*. Jackson, MS: University Press of Mississippi.

Kennedy, R. (1997). *Race, crime, and the law*. New York, NY: Vintage Books.

Mitchell, J. (1998). *The preacher and the Klansman*. Jackson, MS: Clarion-Ledger.

Nossiter, A. (2002). *Of long memory*. Cambridge, MA: Addison-Wesley, Da Capo Press.

Reiner, R. (Director). (1996). *Ghosts of Mississippi* [Motion picture]. United States: Castle Rock Entertainment, Columbia Pictures Corp.

Vollers, M. (1995). *Ghosts of Mississippi: the murder of Medgar Evers, the trials of Byron de la Beckwith, and the haunting of the new South*. Boston, MA: Little, Brown.

Walker, S., Spohn, C., & DeLone, M. (1996, 2000). *The color of justice: Race, ethnicity, and crime in America*. Belmont, CA: Wadsworth.

REFERENCES

7 Klan convictions in killings upheld. (1969, July 18). *The New York Times*. Retrieved August 24, 2006, from http://proquest.umi.com/login?

Alberts, S. (2005, June 13). Mississippi reporter keeps racists on the run: Stories helped lead to several convictions. *The Calgary Herald*. Retrieved August 24, 2006, from http://web.lexis-nexis.com

Bell, D.A. (1973). *Race, racism, and American law*. Boston, MA: Little, Brown.

Benson, C. (2006, October 8). Civil rights murders: The Till bill would create two cold case squads to reopen and solve dozens of murders—if Congress can pay attention long enough to make it law. *The Chicago Sun-Times*. Retrieved November 28, 2006, from http://web.lexis-nexis.com

Bigart, H. (1965, January 13). Jury hears the final witnesses in Mississippi rights slayings. *New York Times*. Retrieved August 24, 2006, from http://proquest.umi.com/login?

Brinson, S.L. (1995, Spring). The myth of white superiority in *Mississippi burning*. *The Southern Communication Journal 60*(3), 211–221.

Brother recalls horrible summer of '64: Family waited 44 days for news of James Chaney's fate. (2005, January 7). *CNN.com*. Retrieved November 26, 2006, from http://www.cnn.com/2005/LAW/06/13/miss.killings

Burns, W.H. (2003). Law and race in early America. In C.E. Reasons, D.J. Conley, & J. Debro (Eds.), *Race, class, gender, and justice in the United States* (pp. 158–161). Boston, MA: Allyn and Bacon.

Byrd, S.B. (2006, June 19). Annual observance takes on new meaning after Killen conviction. The *Associated Press State & Local Wire*. Retrieved November 28, 2006, from http://web.lexis-nexis.com

Canby, V. (1988, December 9). Retracting Mississippi's agony, 1964. *The New York Times*. Retrieved January 27, 2007, from http://proquest.umi.com/login?

Civil rights murder defendant goes to hospital. (2005, June 16). *CNN.com*. Retrieved November 26, 2006, from http://www.cnn.com/2005/LAW/06/13/miss.killings

Corrigan, R. (1964, August 30). FBI tries to weld case in triple slaying. *The Washington Post, Times Herald*. Retrieved August 24, 2006, from http://proquest.umi.com/login?

Defense opens in civil rights era murder trial: Prosecutor seeks lesser manslaughter charge. (2005, June 18). *CNN.com*. Retrieved November 26, 2006, from http://www.cnn.com/2005/LAW/06/13/miss.killings

Ebert, R. (1988, December 9). *Mississippi burning*. Retrieved January 27, 2007, from http://rogerebert.suntimes.com/apps/pbcs.dll/article?AID=/19881209/REVIEWS/812090301/1023

Edgar Ray Killen taken from prison to Jackson hospital. (2006, March 29). *The Associated Press State & Local Wire*. Retrieved November 28, 2006, from http://web.lexis-nexis.com

Elliot, J., Jr. (2006, December 8). Killen: Miss. prosecutors waited for better political climate to indict him. *The Associated Press State & Local Wire*. Retrieved November 28, 2006, from http://web.lexis-nexis.com

Emerson, J. (n.d.). *Mississippi burning (1988)*. Retrieved May 25, 2006, from http://cinepad.com/reviews/mississippi.htm

Ex-Klansman sentenced to 60 years: Killen convicted in 1964 slayings of civil rights workers. (2005, June 23). *CNN.com*. Retrieved November 26, 2006, from http://www.cnn.com/2005/LAW/06/13/miss.killings

Ex-Klansmen to testify at "Mississippi burning" trial: Man accused in killings of three civil rights workers in 1964. (2005, June 15). *CNN.com*. Retrieved November 26, 2006, from http://www.cnn.com/2005/LAW/06/13/miss.killings

Federal Bureau of Investigation. (1964). MIBURN. Retrieved May 25, 2006, from http://foia.fbi.gov/foiaindex/miburn.htm

Fishman, L.T. (2002). Images of crime and punishment: The black bogeyman and white self-righteousness. In C.R. Mann & M.S. Zatz (Eds.), *Images of color, images of crime* (2nd ed., pp. 109–129). Los Angeles: Roxbury.

Former Klansman found guilty of manslaughter: Conviction coincides with 41st anniversary of civil rights killings. (2005, June 22). *CNN.com*. Retrieved November 26, 2006, from http://www.cnn.com/2005/LAW/06/13/miss.killings

Herbers, J. (1964, October 1). Mississippi jury critical of F.B.I.: Says data were withheld in rights murder study. *New York Times*. Retrieved August 24, 2006, from http://proquest.umi.com/login?

Herbers, J. (1965a, January 28). Sheriff and 16 plead not guilty in Mississippi rights slaying. *New York Times*. Retrieved August 24, 2006, from http://proquest.umi.com/login?

Herbers, J. (1965b, February 26). U.S. judge voids a major charge in rights deaths: Rules out conspiracy count for 17 in Mississippi—lesser accusation stands. *New York Times*. Retrieved August 24, 2006, from http://proquest.umi.com/login?

Investigative reporter Jerry Mitchell to speak at ACU. (2006, January 25). Retrieved November 26, 2006, from Abilene Christian University, News Archives Web site: http://www.acu.edu/events/news/archives2006/060125_jerry_mitchell.html

Jansson, D.R. (2005, September). "A geography of racism": Internal orientalism and the construction of American national identity in the film Mississippi burning. *National Identities, 7*(3), 265–285.

Jerry Mitchell. (n.d.). Retrieved November 26, 2006, from http://www.clarionledger.com/crimes/jerrybio.html

Johnson, R.H., Jr. (2000, Fall). Jerry Mitchell: Crusading for justice long overdue. *Human Rights, 27* (4), 18–20. Retrieved November 26, 2006, from http://www.abanet.org/irr/hr/fall00/johnson.html

Judge in Mississippi to convene a new inquiry in rights deaths. (1967, February 2). *The New York Times*. Retrieved August 24, 2006, from http://proquest.umi.com/login?

Kennedy R. (1997). *Race, crime, and the law*. New York, NY: Vintage Books.

Killen released from Jackson hospital. (2006, April 10). *The Associated Press State & Local Wire*. Retrieved November 28, 2006, from http://web.lexis-nexis.com

Linder, D.O. (2002, Winter). Bending toward justice: John Doar and the "Mississippi burning" trial. *Mississippi Law Journal, 72*. Retrieved May 25, 2006, from http://web.lexis-nexis.com

Linder, D.O. (2006a). *A trial account: The Mississippi burning trial (U.S. vs. Price et al.)*. Retrieved May 25, 2006, from University of Missouri-Kansas City, School of Law Web site: http://www.law.umkc.edu/faculty/projects/ftrials/price&bowers/Account.html

Linder, D.O. (2006b). *Key figures in the "Mississippi burning" trial*. Retrieved May 25, 2006, from University of Missouri-Kansas City, School of Law Web site: http://www.law.umkc.edu/faculty/projects/ftrials/price&bowers/Price_BIOG.html

Linder, D.O. (2006c). *"Mississippi burning": The movie*. Retrieved May 25, 2006, from University of Missouri-Kansas City, School of Law Web site: http://www.law.umkc.edu/faculty/projects/ftrials/price&bowers/movie.html

Linder, D.O. (2006d). *The Mississippi burning trial: A chronology*. Retrieved May 25, 2006, from University of Missouri-Kansas City, School of Law Web site: http://www.law.umkc.edu/faculty/projects/ftrials/price&bowers/miss_chrono.html

Man claims innocence in 1964 civil rights murders. (2005, January 11). *CNN.com*. Retrieved November 26, 2006, from http://www.cnn.com/2005/LAW/06/13/miss.killings

Mississippi burning. (n.d.). Retrieved May 25, 2006, from http://www.spartacus.schoolnet.co.uk/USAburning.htm

"Mississippi burning" trial begins: Jury selection under way in 1964 murder case. (2005, June 14). *CNN.com*. Retrieved November 26, 2006, from http://www.cnn.com/2005/LAW/06/13/miss.killings

"Mississippi burning" trial set to start: Jury selection begins Monday in 41-year-old civil rights case. (2005, June 13). *CNN.com*. Retrieved November 26, 2006, from http://www.cnn.com/2005/LAW/06/13/miss.killings

Miss. Supreme Court says oral arguments not needed in Killen case. (2006, December 6). *The Associated Press State & Local Wire*. Retrieved November 28, 2006, from http://web.lexis-nexis.com

Montagne, R. (2005, January 7). *Morning edition*. Washington, DC: National Public Radio. Retrieved August 24, 2006, from http://web.lexis-nexis.com

Murder in Mississippi. (1964, August 6). *The New York Times*. Retrieved August 24, 2006, from http://proquest.umi.com/login?

Rest of mutilated bodies hunted in Mississippi. (1964, July 15). *The Washington Post, Times Herald*. Retrieved August 24, 2006, from http://proquest.umi.com/login?

Rossman, V. (2005, July/August). The war at home: Forgotten events in the civil rights movement. *Humanist, 65*(4), 43–45.

Rugaber, W. (1967, October 20). Deadlocked Jury Is Ordered to Continue Deliberations in Mississippi Slayings of 3 Rights Workers. *New York Times*. Retrieved November 28, 2006, from http://proquest.umi.com/login?

Saigo, R.H. (1989, November/December). The barriers of racism. *Change, 21*(6), 8–10, 69.

Salvaggio, D.W. (1991, Summer). Mississippi travelin' a teacher's portrait of the south with continued racism. *Education, 111*(4), 568–572.

Sitton, C. (1964a, June 24). Tip leads to auto: Wreckage raises new fears over fate of the missing men. *New York Times*. Retrieved August 24, 2006, from http://proquest.umi.com/login?

Sitton, C. (1964b, August 5). Graves at a dam: Discovery is made in new earth mound in Mississippi. *New York Times*. Retrieved August 24, 2006, from http://proquest.umi.com/login?

Smith, T. (Host). (2002, April 18). A NewsHours with Jim Lehrer Transcript Online Focus: Jerry Mitchell. Arlington, VA: Public Broadcasting Service. Retrieved November 28, 2006, from http://www.pbs.org/newshour/media/clarion/mitchell.html

Times Wire Reports. (2006, July 15). The nation; In brief/Mississippi; Ex-Klan leader denied release during appeal. *Los Angeles Times*. Retrieved November 28, 2006, from http://web.lexis-nexis.com

U.S. Code, Title 18, Chapter 13. (2004, January 19). Retrieved November 26, 2006, from http://caselaw.lp.findlaw.com/casecode/uscodes/18/parts/i/chapters/13/toc.html

U.S. Code, Title 18, Chapter 19. (2004, January 19). Retrieved November 26, 2006, from http://caselaw.lp.findlaw.com/casecode/uscodes/18/parts/i/chapters/19/toc.html

U.S. v. Price et al., 383 U.S. 787 (1966).

U. S. v. Price et al., Civ. A. No. 5291 (S.D. MS, 1967).

U.S. v State of Mississippi, 229 F. Supp. 925 (S.D. MS, 1964).

U.S. v. Williams, 341 U.S. 70 (1951).

Walker, S., Spohn, C., & DeLone, M. (2000). *The color of justice: Race, ethnicity, and crime in America* (2nd ed.). Belmont, CA: Wadsworth.

15

The Bombing of the Sixteenth Street Baptist Church: The Turning Point of the Civil Rights Movement

MARCELLA GLODEK BUSH

By the fall of 1963, Birmingham, Alabama, had a history of racially motivated bombings—so many that the city earned the nickname "Bombingham" (Sikora, 2005). But none of the bombings against blacks had happened in daylight, nor killed anyone, until September 15, 1963, when a dynamite bomb exploded in the Sixteenth Street Baptist Church basement killing four girls and injuring more than 20 other adults and children. The four girls murdered were Addie Mae Collins, 14; Denise McNair, 11; Carole Robertson, 14; and Cynthia Wesley, 14. Their bodies were found together within minutes after the explosion. Denise McNair was the first to be pulled from the wreckage; a chunk of cement was embedded in her skull. All were badly burned and mangled, and Cynthia Wesley suffered decapitation. The basement clock captured the moment when the bomb exploded: 10:22 a.m.

September 15th was the inaugural Youth Day at the Sixteenth Street Baptist Church. The Reverend John Cross hoped to enliven his conventional congregation by adding a monthly Youth Day. By 9:00 a.m., the 80 teenage girls, who were members of Mrs. Ella Demand's Sunday school class, were gathered in the basement, while several hundred adults attended formal Sunday service on the first floor. Mrs. Demand's focus of instruction that morning was "the love that forgives."

The girls usually went to a nearby drugstore to wait for the adult services to end, but today they were going to sing and act as ushers during the 11:00 a.m. service. Denise, Addie, her sister Sarah, Carole, and Cynthia went to the basement restroom to primp. After a while, Mrs. Demand sent Bernadine Mathews to admonish the girls to return to the classroom. Cynthia said that she needed more time to fix her hair, causing Bernadine to comment, "Cynthia, children who don't obey the Lord live only half as long"

(McWhorter, 2001). Earlier that morning, as Cynthia and her father were about to go to church, Cynthia's mother admonished her to fix her slip. Her mother frequently told Cynthia to "Always put your clothes on right, 'cause you don't know how you might be coming back" (McWhorter, 2001).

As Sarah Collins washed her hands at the sink in the women's restroom, she remembered seeing her sister Addie tying the sash on Denise McNair's dress. She awakened in the darkened rubble.

THE CRIME SCENE

The bomb—a bundle of dynamite that exploded under the girls' restroom—collapsed the Sixteenth Street wall and left a crater five-and-one-half feet wide and two-and-one-fourth feet deep; demolished the foundation; and decimated the staircase that connected the door to the sidewalk. All the stained glass windows on the upper floor shattered. Pieces of mortar had crushed the basement ceiling and filled the basement with debris and dust from the upper floor. The bomb had created a seven-feet-by-seven-feet hole in the women's restroom wall. Amazingly, the stained glass window, whose sill was about four feet above the lounge floor, remained intact; only the face of Jesus was gone. Broken glass littered the sidewalks outside. Nearby cars were overturned and crushed, windows smashed. The blast also blew out the windows of neighboring shops. One man claimed that he was blown out of his car; another from a telephone booth. People in the neighborhood houses felt the blast and people as far as 30 blocks away reported hearing the noise. Another bomb had struck Birmingham.

VICTIMS AND SURVIVORS

Dazed survivors began emerging from the church, covered in dust, some bleeding profusely from glass shrapnel from the stained glass windows. Reverend Cross found his daughter and assessed her injuries as minor. He next searched the classroom and guided children outside to find their parents. He returned to the church with several deacons and civil defense workers to excavate the basement rubble looking for more survivors. Various accounts describe finding the bodies in the restroom rubble. One reported that the girls flew through the air like rag dolls; another stated that the girls were stacked up like firewood. Still another stated that their clothes had torn off their bodies, they were burned, and they looked like old women. The man who had found Cynthia Wesley's skull could not describe it as human.

Deacon Pippen recognized his granddaughter Denise by her shoes. Samuel Rutledge found Sarah Collins alive, but initially unrecognizable because glass shards and blood covered her face. She called again and again for her sister Addie and hoped that because Addie did not answer it meant that she had escaped.

THE SCENE OUTSIDE THE CHURCH

A large crowd gathered quickly after the explosion and soon became unruly. City police, unable to protect the crowd scene because of rescue efforts, fired their weapons over the heads of people, who were throwing bricks and bottles at them (Hansen & Archibald, 1997). Reverend Cross and Reverend Billups used bullhorns to urge the crowd to return home and to forgive as Jesus did.

TIMELINE

September 15, 1963	A dynamite bomb explodes at Sixteenth Street Baptist Church, killing Denise McNair, Cynthia Wesley, Carole Robertson, and Addie Mae Collins, and injuring 20 others.
1965	FBI agents recommend charging four suspects with the bombing.
1968	FBI closes its investigation with no charges filed.
1971	Alabama Attorney General Bill Baxley reopens the bombing investigation.
September 1977	A grand jury indicts Robert Chambliss for the murder of Denise McNair.
November 18, 1977	A grand jury convicts Robert "Dynamite Bob" Chambliss of first degree murder in the death of Denise McNair and sentenced to life in prison.
1980	Jefferson County, Alabama's District Attorney reopens the case after a U.S. Department report states that FBI Director J. Edgar Hoover blocked evidence in 1965. No additional charges were filed.
1985	Robert Chambliss died in prison at age 81.
October 1988	Federal and State prosecutors reopen the investigation after Gary A. Tucker confessed that he helped set the bomb. No new charges were filed.
July 10, 1997	The FBI reopens the investigation after a secret, yearlong review.
May 17, 2000	Thomas Blanton, Jr., and Bobby Frank Cherry surrender to Jefferson County, Alabama, authorities after a grand jury indicts the men of first degree murder charges in connection with the 1963 Sixteenth Street Baptist Church bombing.
April 2, 2000	A judge rejects a request to move Blanton's and Cherry's trial to another county because of pretrial publicity.
May 4, 2000	Bobby Frank Cherry rejected a deal in which he would have received probation if he pleaded guilty to transporting explosives over state lines. Cherry continued to deny that he was involved in the bombing.

Jim Lay and Hosea Hudson, Jr., used the same bullhorns to clear the streets as fire trucks, police cruisers, and ambulances (from black funeral homes) arrived. Medical workers came and began caring for the injured and transporting them to the hospital. Sarah called for her sister and prayed to Jesus while in transport. She complained that she could not see. She had lost one eye and her sister.

OTHER VICTIMS

After throwing rocks at the police, 16-year-old James Robinson fled the scene. A police officer shot him in the back and killed him in an alley near the church. Later in the day, the driver of a moped decorated with a Confederate flag shot and killed 13-year-old Virgil Ware, who was riding on the handlebars of his brother's bike. Approximately 50 fires were set throughout the day.

TWO FUNERALS

The hospital had set up a makeshift morgue. There Claude Wesley identified his daughter Cynthia by her class ring and black patent leather shoes. Chris McNair also identified his daughter Denise by her shoes. Carole Robertson was wearing her first pair of strapless pumps with medium heels.

Carole Robertson's parents chose to hold her funeral separately on Tuesday, September 17, at St. John's A.M.E. Church rather than with Addie, Denise, and Cynthia's mass funeral held on Wednesday, September 18, at the John Porter's Sixth Avenue Baptist Church. Carole's mother, Alpha Robertson, took offense at a remark Dr. Martin Luther King, Jr., made. When interviewed by reporters, King said, "What murdered these four girls? The apathy and complacency of many Negroes who will sit down on their stools and do nothing and not engage in creative protest to get rid of this evil" (McWhorter, 2001, p. 533). Mrs. Robertson countered, "Carole lost her life because of the movement" (McWhorter, 2001, p. 533). King delivered the eulogy at the three girls' funeral. More than 8,000 mourners, including 800 clergymen, black and white, attended the service, but no city officials turned out. The funerals marked the first time whites attended a predominantly black event in Birmingham. Nearly $23,000 was donated to rebuild the church and help the bereaved families.

Figure 15.1   The casket with the body of 14-year-old Carole Robertson carried out of the church, 1963. Courtesy of the Library of Congress.

BIOGRAPHICAL DESCRIPTIONS

Baxley, Bill	As Alabama Attorney General, he prosecuted Robert Edward Chambliss for the four murders
Blanton, Thomas, Jr.	A Ku Klux Klan member, who was convicted in May 2001 of the 1963 murder of four girls
Cash, Herman Frank	A suspect in the 1963 bombing, who died in 1994 before charges could be brought against him
Chambliss, Robert Edward	A Ku Klux Klan member nicknamed ''Dynamite Bob,'' he was convicted in 1977 for the murders of the four girls killed in the bombing; he died in prison in 1985
Cherry, Bobby Frank	Convicted in 2002 of the four murders, he died in prison on November 18, 2004
Cobbs, Elizabeth	Star witness for the prosecution; she testified against her uncle Robert Chambliss
Collins, Addie Mae	Bombing victim, 14 years old, one of seven children of Oscar and Alice Collins
Collins, Sarah	Bombing victim Addie Mae Collins's sister, who lost an eye in the bombing
Connor, Theophilus Eugene	Nicknamed ''Bull,'' he served as an Alabama police official during the Civil Rights Movement; he was a staunch racial segregation advocate
Cross, Reverend John	Pastor of the Sixteenth Street Baptist Church at the time of the bombing in 1963
Hoover, J. Edgar	Director of the Federal Bureau of Investigation
Jones, Doug	U.S. Attorney for the northern district of Alabama and prosecutor in the Robert Chambliss trial
McNair, Carol Denise	Bombing victim, 11 years old, the first child of Chris and Maxine McNair
Posey, Robert	Assistant U.S. Attorney and prosecutor in the Robert Chambliss trial
Robbins, John	Defense attorney in the Robert Chambliss trial
Robertson, Carole	Bombing victim, 14 years old, the third child of Alpha and Alvin Robertson
Rowe, Gary T.	FBI informant within the Ku Klux Klan
Wallace, George	Governor of Alabama in 1963
Wesley, Cynthia	Bombing victim, 14 years old, the first adopted daughter of Claude and Gertrude Wesley

Thirty-five years later, a new headstone on the grave of Addie Mae Collins prompted her sister Janie Gaines to visit the Greenwood Cemetery. She was distressed at the neglected condition of the cemetery and decided to move the body. When a crew excavated the grave they found no body there.

THE INVESTIGATION OF THE CASE

The Federal Bureau of Investigation (FBI) Director J. Edgar Hoover opened the investigation—codename BAPBOP—of the Sixteenth Street Baptist Church bombing with a team of 11 agents, an addition to those already on staff to investigate previous bombings in Birmingham (McWhorter, 2001). Special Agents followed leads, gossip, suspects, and alibis; planted informants in the Ku Klux Klan (KKK); and conducted interviews with individuals in the church's neighborhood, in the church congregation, KKK members, and members of the States Rights party. When U.S. Attorney General Robert Kennedy learned of the bombing, he informed President John F. Kennedy that he was sending his civil rights negotiator Burke Marshall to Birmingham and ordered 25 additional FBI agents including bomb experts to work with Hoover's team.

The Birmingham City police combined their efforts with the Birmingham State police. Experienced homicide detective Maurice House served as the lead detective for the local police department. Conversable in the black community, House had earlier been assigned to the city's civil rights detail created a week before the 1963 Easter protests. To prevent a reprisal from the black community, police restricted blacks to their neighborhoods, and Governor George Wallace ordered 300 state troopers to the city. Local police armed with shotguns guarded the crime scene. By Sunday evening, the Alabama National Guard joined them. Birmingham initially offered a reward of $52,000 to find the suspects, and Governor Wallace contributed $5,000; the city's fund quickly grew to $75,000 and subsequently topped at $80,000.

Witnesses and Suspects

Civil rights activists blamed Alabama Governor George Wallace for the killings. One week prior to the bombing, Wallace, in an interview for *The New York Times,* stated that Alabama needed a "few first-class funerals" (McWhorter, 2001, p. 503) to stop integration in his state. Locals blamed "outsiders" and professional bombers from Georgia, Tennessee, and Virginia. On Monday, September 16, local police took the Sixteenth Street church's janitor Willie Green in custody. He had been seen walking down the church's side steps moments before the explosion. Rumors had also circulated that the girls were smoking in the bathroom. Early suspicion, however, soon centered on the Cahaba Boys —Robert Edward Chambliss, Bobby Frank Cherry, Herman Frank Cash, and Thomas Blanton, Jr.—who were members of the KKK's Eastview 13 Klavern. Several sources identified Tommy Blanton as the driver of his turquoise-and-white Chevrolet in the neighborhood of the church around 2:00 a.m. on Sunday, September 15. Neighborhood witnesses agreed that a white man emerged from that car and had planted the bomb. Another neighbor, however, identified Cherry as the man who placed a package of dynamite in a window well or under the steps outside the church; another identified Chambliss. Others stated that two of the four men in the car wore police uniforms.

Given his nickname "Dynamite Bob" and his participation in terrorizing black neighborhoods, Chambliss, 59 years old, was a likely suspect. He had learned to use dynamite as a quarryman for the Lone Star Cement Company and in the mines during the Depression. He had been active in the KKK since the 1940s, and served as Exalted Cyclops until 1951. When police discovered that Chambliss purchased a case of dynamite on September 4, 1963, they arrested him and two other Klansmen, Charles Cagle and John Wesley Hall, on charges of possession of dynamite without a permit. They were fined $1,000 each and received a six-month jail term that was suspended. Hall later failed a polygraph test, indicating that he knew something about the case, but it was not enough to get an indictment.

Figure 15.2   The four girls killed in the Sixteenth Street Baptist Church bombing (from left to right): Denise McNair, Carole Robertson, Addie Mae Collins, and Cynthia Wesley. © AP Photo.

Bobby Frank Cherry, age 32, drove a truck for Baggett Transportation—a local company that hauled dynamite and dynamite caps for local coal companies and that transported munitions for commercial shippers. Cherry gained demolition expertise in the Marine Corps and the nickname "Cherry Bomb."

The extremism of the States' Rights Party (SRP) had attracted 38-year-old Thomas Blanton, Jr., away from the Eastview 13 Kavern. When he and his 85-year-old father "Pops" Blanton had begun picketing with the neo-Nazis, and when they would not sever their ties with the SRP, the Klan formerly expelled them. Tommy's conversations were filled with racial prejudice and hatred of Catholics (Hansen & Archibald, 1997). Although a high school graduate, his associates described him as motivated by alcohol, not intelligent enough to make a bomb, but dumb enough to place it.

The fourth suspect, Herman Frank Cash, was a 45-year-old truck driver for the Dixie-Ohio Truck Company described by his associates as a hard-drinking segregationist and so easily frightened that they nicknamed him "Fearless" and "Old Blood and Guts" (Archibald & Hansen, 1997).

Hoover Closes the Case

On May 13, 1965, local agents in Birmingham wrote a memorandum to FBI Director J. Edgar Hoover: "The bombing was the handiwork of former Klansmen Robert R. Chambliss, Bobby Frank Cherry, Herman Frank Cash and Thomas F. Blanton, Jr." (McWhorter, 2001). Hoover, however, did not approve an arrest; he stated that "the chance of a prosecution in state or federal court is very remote" (Gado, 2007) and closed the case in 1968. Almost four decades would pass before three of the men were convicted for the murders of the four girls: Robert E. Chambliss in 1977; Thomas Blanton, Jr., in 2001; and Bobby Frank Cherry in 2002. Herman Frank Cash died in 1997 without being charged in the case.

The Media

Both the press and television coverage of the Civil Rights Movement broadened the nation's increasing awareness of racial tension. Initially, the media outside Alabama covered Birmingham's racial conflicts before the state and local media did. Publicly, *The*

275

Birmingham News advised photographers from other states that, as an institution, the *News* refrained from publishing photos and stories that would further exacerbate racial tension. White management of the press in Birmingham, however, operated under the belief that if you do not print photographs and stories about desegregation, it will go away. In response, news agents sent reporters to Birmingham by the hundreds.

The New York Times detailed Birmingham's racial problems throughout the 1950s and early 1960s with increasing frequency, giving Birmingham a reputation that angered its citizens. Harrison Salisbury, a reporter with *The New York Times,* wrote an inflammatory article on segregation in Birmingham entitled "Fear and Hatred Grip Birmingham" (published April 12, 1960, in *The Times*). The article resulted in a $6 million libel suit against *The Times* by Birmingham's Commissioner of Public Safety T. Eugene "Bull" Connor and others as a deliberate plan to keep reporters from the *Times* from covering the state until the Alabama Supreme Court reached a decision in the lawsuit. The strategy cost the *Times* coverage of some of the most important events in the Civil Rights Movement, e.g., the Freedom Rides and sit-ins. The Supreme Court ruled in favor of the *Times* in 1964.

Another embarrassment to the city occurred when a photograph of a burning Freedom Riders' bus appeared in a Japanese newspaper when the President of the Birmingham Chamber of Commerce was visiting Japan in 1961.

The Most Segregated City in the South

As more and more mainstream newspapers carried stories about the Civil Rights Movement, the opportunity to shape the media was not lost on American Civil Rights Movement leader the Reverend Martin Luther King, Jr. King chose Birmingham—the largest industrial city in the South—and dubbed it "the most segregated city in the south" to dramatize that racial hatred was no longer manageable there; federal intervention would be required (King, 1990). King hoped to goad Bull Connor, an infamous segregationist, into his usual outrageous reactions to the nonviolent demonstrations that King and his associates planned. Connor was a man who stated in 1948: "Damn the law, we don't give a damn about the law. Down here we make our own law" (McWhorter, 2001, p. 138). Connor did not disappoint. His use of fire hoses and police attack dogs against children participating in protests produced remarkable photographs that captured an international audience by summer 1963. Connor came to represent the fight against integration in Birmingham. When the four girls died in the Sixteenth Street Baptist Church bombing, their faces portrayed the immorality of America's social structure.

Newspapers around the world carried the story of the Sixteenth Street Baptist Church bombing: "Six Dead After Church Bombing Blast Kills Four Children"; "Riots Follow"; "Two Youths Slain"; "State Reinforces Birmingham Police" (United Press International, September 16, 1963); "Angry Police Sift Blast Clues"; "Judge Decries Mockery of Law" (*The Birmingham News,* September 16, 1963); "Racial Tension Mounts in Birmingham After Four Killed in Church Bombing" (Osgood, September 16, 1963). "This really was the seminal moment, it changed the course of the civil rights movement largely because people just did not care that much what was happening to Southern blacks," said Mark Potok, spokesman for the Southern Poverty Law Center, a civil rights organization based in Montgomery, Alabama (Chebium, 2000, paragraph 10). "But they could not stomach the image of these four little girls in white dresses being blown to pieces on a Sunday morning in church. It awoke the conscience of white America, which until that point had been in a long sleep" (Chebium, 2000, paragraph 10).

Black Press

The power of the black press had been diminishing since the 1940s and 1950s, even though black activism pushed for desegregation in society after Truman desegregated the military in 1948. Conservative advertisers pressured black newspaper owners to limit coverage on race issues. Fears of McCarthyism and the integration of black and white reporters in the mainstream press brought closure or decline to the smaller black newspapers. White communities barely knew that black newspapers existed and, if they did, would not have read them. But, newspapers like the *Baltimore Afro-American* and the *Amsterdam News* provided powerful editorials about racial injustice.

Television

In 1962, the CBS television affiliate in Atlanta, Georgia—Martin Luther King, Jr.'s hometown—did not even broadcast the CBS evening news. Two NBC affiliates, offended by John Chancellor's accurate, but described aggressive, reporting of school desegregation in Little Rock, Arkansas, dropped their broadcast of the "Huntley-Brinkley Report," the station's flagship program. At the beginning of the Civil Rights Movement, newscasters focused on the sensational events, but with an indifferent affectation. Television coverage in 1963, however, was revolutionary and compelling. Now, important local news stories could be carried across networks beyond the station's broadcast territory. Riots and violence often shaped the coverage, and both civil rights activists and television news directors took advantage of the expanding networks' news hour. Dr. King's powerful preaching style and presence made him a symbolic prophet for the Civil Rights Movement, and television was his perfect medium.

Racial tension increased during the spring and summer of 1963, as King and activist Fred Shuttlesworth organized sit-in protests and Freedom Rides. The Sixteenth Street Baptist Church was their meeting place. The bomb that took the lives of Denise McNair, Addie Mae Collins, Carole Robertson, and Cynthia Wesley was intended to be a warning —retaliation for the role the church played in the Civil Rights Movement thus far. The Klan's hoped-for response of fear became public outrage instead. Within days, details of the bombing and the bombing victims, and the numerous accounts of violence that followed the bombing, the four girls' funerals, and criticisms of American leadership appeared in national and international newspapers and on television.

The Media's Impact on the Trials

During the 37 years that separated the bombings and justice, the media stressed the importance of the murders of the four girls each time the FBI or the State of Alabama reopened its investigations in 1971, 1977, 1980, 1988, and 1997, and whenever the state obtained an indictment or conviction against the three suspects, Chambliss, Blanton, and Cherry. The deaths of Cash, Chambliss, and Cherry also generated press coverage. The media that became the tool of Civil Rights activists and Southern segregationists became a tool to discuss the role of the FBI, the Federal Government, and the State of Alabama in bringing those responsible for the bombings to justice. The *Birmingham Post-Herald* won several awards for its coverage of Blanton's trial. In 1998, in a centennial edition, the *Birmingham News* commented on its coverage of the Civil Rights Movement:

"The story of the *Birmingham News*' coverage of race relations in the 1960s is one marked at times by mistakes and embarrassment, but, in its larger outlines, by growing sensitivity and change" (Wright, 2006, paragraph 15).

Cameras in the Courtroom

In Alabama, any party to a legal case may veto camera coverage of a trial. In the Thomas Blanton trial, County District Attorney David Barber objected to audiovisual coverage. In response, the Radio-Television News Directors Association (RTNDA) cited the importance of the public's "right to know" and the *Katzman v. Victoria's Secret Catalogue* (923 F. Supp 580, S. D. N. Y.) that states that cameras in the courtroom do not impede justice—they demonstrate the importance of public trials.

Radio

Radio was the most effective communication within the black community (Julian, 2005). Most blacks then could not afford a television and many were illiterate. Gospel songs and coded messages alerted listeners to gather at certain churches to organize a sit-in or demonstration. The stations also provided clues to police roadblocks and other obstacles, as well as ways to avoid discrimination or confront it. Researchers are now realizing the importance of the radio for blacks in the Civil Rights Movement.

THREE TRIALS

In 1971, Alabama Attorney General Bill Baxley reopened the case against the four suspects. Without the cooperation of the FBI, however, he made little progress. In 1976, the *Birmingham Post Herald* reported that the FBI informant Gary Thomas Rowe provided Baxley with a list of suspects (Africanonline, 1976). Baxley reopened the case in 1980 and again in 1988, after Gary A. Tucker confessed that he helped set the bomb. Jefferson County obtained no convictions or filed any new charges, however. In 1993, FBI agents met with black leaders of Birmingham to review the case again. Thomas Blanton, Jr., was still living in Birmingham, but Bobby Cherry had moved to Texas in the 1970s. Reportedly, he had married five times and had fathered 15 children (Sack, 2000). Herman Cash died from cancer in 1994.

The Trial of Robert Edward Chambliss

On September 24, 1997, a grand jury indicted 73-year-old Robert Chambliss to stand trial in Birmingham's Jefferson County Courthouse for the murders of the four girls. On September 26, Judge Wallace Gibson ordered four separate bonds—one for each girl—to total $200,000. Chambliss, unable to meet bail, remained in prison. The judge set the case to begin on Monday, November 14, and Chambliss to be tried for the murder of Denise McNair. Defense Attorneys included Art Hanes, Sr., and Art Hanes, Jr., who argued that the number of years between the murder and the trial denied their client "due process" and a "speedy trial." They also asked that the indictments be quashed because they contained Chambliss's nickname "Dynamite Bob." Hanes, Jr., protested that the nickname would prejudice the jury. Prosecutor George Beck countered that Chambliss was well known in the community by his nickname. The judge overruled to quash the indictments, but deleted the alias as prejudicial.

Witnesses placed Chambliss in his car at the scene of the bombing on Saturday night, September 14, and following the explosion on Sunday, September 15. Several witnesses testified that he had dynamite in his possession. The judge sealed the courtroom for the testimony of Chambliss's niece Elizabeth Cobbs. She entered the courtroom through a gantlet of armed sheriff deputies. Cobbs provided insight into her uncle's state of mind, before and after the bombing. She testified that he said before the bombing, "Just wait until after Sunday morning and they'll beg us to let them segregate!" (McWharton, 2001, p. 559). After the bombing, she overheard him say, "It wasn't meant to hurt anybody; it didn't go off when it was supposed to" (Gado, 2005, "Dynamite Bob" paragraph 4). He also stated that "...he had enough stuff to flatten half of Birmingham" (Gado, 2005, "Dynamite Bob," paragraph 4). In his closing argument, Prosecuting Attorney Baxley asked the jury to "give Denise McNair a birthday present" (McWhorter, 2001, p. 574)—she would have been 26 years old that day. The jury found Chambliss guilty of one count of murder in the death of Denise McNair. And once again, the case went cold.

New Evidence

In spite of the deaths of 130 possible witnesses, the FBI reopened its investigation in 1996, focusing on suspects Thomas Blanton, Jr., and Bobby Frank Cherry. Assigned to the case were William Fleming and Ben Herren. Fleming discovered tape recordings of Blanton's conversations with the initial investigators in the 1960s—enough to convene a grand jury on October 27, 1998. The Grand Jury did not hear the testimony of Chambliss's niece Elizabeth Cobbs because she died in 1998 from cancer. Bobby Cherry's family members, however, testified that he bragged about the murders and was proud of his participation. He bragged about lighting the fuse and about being a Ku Klux Klan leader. The Grand Jury indicted both men on eight counts of first-degree murder.

Blanton and Cherry Arrested

After 37 years, 61-year-old Thomas Blanton, Jr., and 69-year-old Bobby Frank Cherry surrendered to Jefferson County authorities in Alabama on May 17, 2000. Alabama extradited Cherry from Texas where he was serving a prison sentence since 1971 for molestation charges. Cherry's lawyer requested a hearing with Judge James Garrett declaring that his client suffered from dementia and would not be fit to stand trial. The judge declared Cherry incompetent and committed him to the state's mental hospital for a 90-day inpatient evaluation (McWhorter, 2001).

The Thomas Blanton, Jr., Trial

Circuit Court Judge James Garrett rejected a request from Blanton's attorney, David Luker, to have the trial moved from Birmingham. Jury selection began on April 16, 2000. For the jurors' safety, the judge closed the selection process and withheld their names. Jurors, instead, filled out a questionnaire that was not released to the public. Judge Garrett sequestered the jury panel—eight white women, three black women, and one black man; four alternates included two white men and two black men.

The prosecution team—U.S. Attorney Doug Jones, Assistant U.S. Attorney Robert Posey, and Jefferson County Deputy District Attorney Jeff Wallace—called 22 witnesses to testify against Thomas Blanton, Jr. Posey introduced into evidence taped conversations from Blanton's apartment where the FBI had hidden microphones in 1964. One transcript quotes Blanton telling FBI informant Mitchell Burns, "I like to go shooting. I like to go

---

CHAMBLISS TRIAL PARTICIPANTS

STATE OF ALABAMA VS. ROBERT EDWARD CHAMBLISS

Jefferson County Courthouse, Birmingham
November 14–November 18, 1977
Transcript available at http://www.bplonline.org/Archives/collections/alabamatenthjudicialcircuitcourtstatevschambliss.asp#Contents

Presiding:
Circuit Court Judge Wallace E. Gibson

Defense Team:
Art Hanes, Sr., and Art Hanes, Jr.

Prosecution Team:
Alabama Attorney General Bill Baxley
Assistant Attorney General George Beck

Jury:
9 whites and 3 blacks

Prosecution Witnesses:
Reverend John Cross, Elizabeth Cobbs, Kirthus Glenn, Timothy M. Casey, Yvonne Young, E.H. Cantrell, William Jackson, Glenn Norman Collins, Sr., Edward K. Alley, Jack E. LeGrand, Sarah Collins Riley, William E. Berry, Joe Donald, J.O. Butler, Sr., W.L. Allen, Jewel Christopher (Chris) McNair, Thomas H. Cook, Jack Shows, Timothy Michael Casey, Jr., Yvonne Young, Aaron Rosenfeld, John McCormick

Defense Witnesses:
Billy D. Webb, Paul Hurst, Floyd C. Garrett, Raymond Wells, Juanita Winston, Chris E. Poe, Lucian Troulias, Robert Louis Gifford, John W. Lowery, E.L. Caswell, F.J. Feltman, James E. Sparks, Bennie Mae Brown, Edward Thilt Walker, Maurice H. House

---

fishing. I like to go bombing" (Court TV Online, 2001, "Judgement Day," paragraph 3). Also: "I am going to stick to bombing churches" (McWhorter, 2001, p. 594). Jones pointed to Blanton and stated, "That is a confession out of this man's mouth" (CNN.com, 2001, paragraph 25); Defense Attorney John Robbins countered: "You can't judge a conversation in a vacuum" (Court TV Online, 2001, paragraph 26), arguing that the prosecutors failed to play the 26 minutes of previous conversation—the ramblings of drunken Klansmen. He stressed that a man should be convicted for his actions, not for his beliefs. Posey called only two witnesses and argued that the FBI tapes were illegal (Sack, 2001). While he spoke, several large TV screens displayed family photographs of the victims. After six days of testimony, the jurors deliberated just less than two-and-one-half hours, finding Blanton guilty of all counts of murder in the first degree. He was sentenced to life imprisonment.

The Bobby Frank Cherry Trial

When both the court and the defense team's psychiatric evaluation of Bobby Frank Cherry declared him fit for trial, the last of the four suspects went on trail on May 13, 2002, in a drab basement courtroom in Birmingham with Judge James Garrett again

BLANTON TRIAL PARTICIPANTS

STATE OF ALABAMA VS. THOMAS E. BLANTON, JR.

Jefferson County Courthouse, Birmingham

Presiding:
Circuit Court Judge James Garrett

Prosecution Team:
U.S. Attorney for the Northern District of Alabama Doug Jones
Assistant U.S. Attorney Robert Posey
Jefferson County Deputy District Attorney Jeff Wallace

Defense Team:
John C. Robbins
David Luker

Jurors:
Eight white women, three black women, and one black man
Four alternates: two white men and two black men

Prosecution Witnesses:
Waylene Vaughn, Bill Jackson, Reverend John H. Cross, Alpha Robertson, Maxine McNair, Jean Casey Blanton Barnes, Mitchell Burns

Defense Witness:
Mary Cunningham, Eddie Mauldin

presiding (McWhorter, 2001). U.S. Attorney Doug Jones once again led the prosecution team and Attorney Mickey Johnson the defense. The lawyers chose six white women, three white men, and three black men to serve as jurors with three whites and one black alternates. Cherry was charged with four counts of murder and four counts of arson.

U.S. Assistant Attorney General Robert Posey opened for the prosecution declaring that Cherry boasted that he was involved in the bombing and wore his crime like "a badge of honor" (*ABC News Online*, 2002, paragraph 1). The prosecution team took four days to recreate the bombing in the context of the Civil Rights Movement and to present its 11 witnesses: family members of the girls, retired FBI agents, a civil rights leader, an ex-wife, and Cherry's granddaughter. They disproved Cherry's alibi that he was at home with his wife, who was stricken with cancer, at the time of the bombing—his wife was not diagnosed until several years after the church bombing.

During the one-and-a-half days of the defense team's case, defense attorney Mickey Johnson repeatedly stated that the state had produced no credible witnesses and provided no forensic evidence linking his client to the bombing. Defense witnesses testified that the defendant was no longer a racist. Despite being a Klansman in 1963, Johnson beseeched the jury to not convict on guilt by association. The jury returned a guilty verdict on the four counts of murder and arson in less than seven hours.

AFTER THE TRIALS

The alleged suspect Herman Frank Cash died in 1994 without going to trial. Robert Edward Chambliss served eight years for his role in the Sixteenth Street Baptist Church

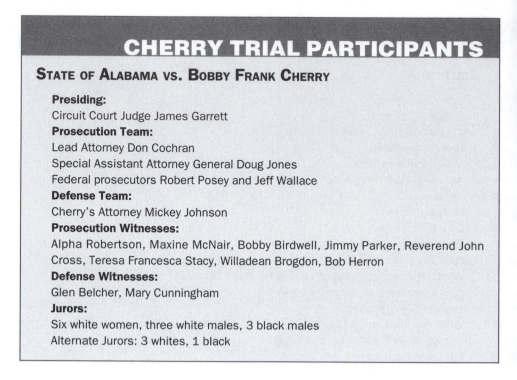

CHERRY TRIAL PARTICIPANTS

STATE OF ALABAMA VS. BOBBY FRANK CHERRY

Presiding:
Circuit Court Judge James Garrett
Prosecution Team:
Lead Attorney Don Cochran
Special Assistant Attorney General Doug Jones
Federal prosecutors Robert Posey and Jeff Wallace
Defense Team:
Cherry's Attorney Mickey Johnson
Prosecution Witnesses:
Alpha Robertson, Maxine McNair, Bobby Birdwell, Jimmy Parker, Reverend John Cross, Teresa Francesca Stacy, Willadean Brogdon, Bob Herron
Defense Witnesses:
Glen Belcher, Mary Cunningham
Jurors:
Six white women, three white males, 3 black males
Alternate Jurors: 3 whites, 1 black

bombing. He died in prison at age 81 of natural causes on October 29, 1985. He never admitted guilt publicly. Bobby Frank Cherry died from cancer in the Kirby Correctional Facility in Montgomery, Alabama, at age 74. He had served only two years of his sentence. Cherry's lawyers had appealed his conviction arguing that he was not given a "speedy trial" and, therefore, after 37 years, favorable witnesses were dead or could not be located, and the considerable media coverage impaired him from getting an objective trial. The Alabama Court of Criminal Appeals denied the appeal stating that the pretrial news coverage was factual and did not prejudice the jury. Cherry's lawyers also explored the possibility of parole based on 1940 laws that were operative in 1963 when the crime was committed. Thomas E. Blanton, Jr., also lost his appeal to the Alabama Court of Criminal Appeals because the court ruled that the delay was not intentional. Cherry is currently serving his prison sentence. His lawyer plans to take his case to the Supreme Court.

A Remaining Question

When Jerry Jazz Musician interviewed author Diane McWhorter, he asked if she thought that the bomb went off on schedule. McWhorter believes that it did not because the bombers were not sophisticated enough to build a bomb with a timing device. Most bombs were thrown out of a car window at a house or a church. Mabel Shorter—the woman filling in for the church secretary on the day of the bombing—reported that the telephone rang often that Sunday morning and the caller hung up when she answered (McWhorter, 2001). After the bombing, she reflected that someone might have been checking to determine if anyone was there, an oddity on a Sunday morning when people would naturally be there for services and religion classes. The higher-ranking Klansmen met after the bombing, and their discussion indicated that the bomb was supposed to detonate when the building was unoccupied. Once placed, however, the outcome the bombers allowed was the possibility of death and violence. The Reverend Abraham Woods, who urged the FBI to reopen their case against Chambliss, Blanton, and Cherry, considered their guilty verdicts as a "...statement on how far we've come" (Court TV Online, 2001, paragraph 8).

LEGAL AND SOCIAL ISSUES OF THE CASE

Birmingham, Alabama, was a city built on social injustice. The founding of Birmingham as an industrial hub in 1871 attracted blacks with an opportunity to escape sharecropping on white-owned farms. Harsh conditions in Birmingham factories and mines, however, continued the blacks' social, political, and economic discrimination. Segregation and Jim Crow laws limited blacks' access to education, respectable living conditions, medical care, and public transportation. After World War II, black veterans began pressing the city government for permission to establish middle class neighborhoods for blacks. These neighborhoods created business opportunities for blacks: funeral homes, ambulance services, barbershops and beauty salons, movie theaters, and insurance agencies. Despite economic gains, however, political and social gains were nil. One transitional neighborhood was bombed so often that it earned the nickname "Dynamite Hill" (McWhorter, 2001).

Full equality was not the plan of Governor George Wallace, who stated in his 1963 inaugural address that "...I say segregation now, segregation tomorrow, and segregation forever." In June 1963, Wallace appointed himself the temporary university registrar and stood in the doorway at the University of Alabama to block the admission of two black students, who were legally enrolled there; national television stations aired the event. In response, President John F. Kennedy federalized the Alabama National Guard to escort the students to the campus.

THE CHURCH AND ITS ROLE IN THE AMERICAN CIVIL RIGHTS MOVEMENT

The Cahaba River insurgents targeted the elegant, socially elite, yet conservative Sixteenth Street Baptist Church for its role in Martin Luther King, Jr.'s civil rights activities in Birmingham in 1963 (Wilson, 2003). The bombing became the galvanizing event for the American Civil Rights Movement and exposed the depths of racial hatred. Ultimately, the bombing encouraged moderates to speak out against racial violence and broadened the support for the American Civil Rights Movement.

MARTIN LUTHER KING, JR.'S EULOGY FOR THE BOMBING VICTIMS

In his eulogy for the three bombing victims, Collins, McNair, and Wesley, King challenged the consciences of ministers, politicians, political parties, the government, racists, blacks, and whites to no longer remain silent or cautious about the system in America that produces hatred and racism. He highlighted that the passive silence of moderates was a bigger tragedy than the bombings and murders that took place in Birmingham.

TERRORISM

In his closing arguments in the trial of Bobby Frank Cherry, prosecuting attorney Doug Jones called Cherry, Chambliss, Cash, and Blanton "the forefathers of terrorism." Author McWhorter (2002) compares the Birmingham Civil Rights District to the Ground Zero

FACTOIDS

- BAPBOMB was the FBI code name for the Sixteenth Street Baptist Church bombing. "BAPBOMB" is also the title of a play by Hubert Grissom to honor Dr. Martin Luther King, Jr. The play advances the idea that inaction in the face of injustice is the worst enemy.

- "Birmingham Sunday": A song, composed by Richard Farina and recorded by Joan Baez, chronicled the events and the aftermath of the bombing.

- Sonya Jones renamed her youth center the *Addie Mae Collins Youth Center* as a memorial to an aunt she never knew.

- Chicago residents established the *Carole Robertson Center* for Learning in 1976. Named after Carole, the social service agency is dedicated to the memory of all four girls.

- *The Alabama National Guard* that protected the Sixteenth Street Baptist Church crime scene was also the air strategists for the Bay of Pigs invasion.

area of New York, the site of the September 11, 2001 terrorists' attack. Bobby Frank Cherry earned a new nickname: Osama Bin Cherry. Birmingham's Civil Rights District was established in 1992 as a symbol of the struggle for human rights. The district includes the Sixteenth Street Baptist Church, Kelly Ingram Park—where police unleashed dogs on protestors and fireman attacked them with fire hoses, the Birmingham Civil Rights Institute, the Fourth Street Business District (the city's black retail center), and other black cultural and social institutions.

GOVERNOR GEORGE WALLACE'S LEGACY

Despite the 1964 Civil Rights Act, there was no easy solution to racial tension. In the Wallace years, Alabama lost important economic ground. While Atlanta was peacefully desegregating and beginning three decades of vibrant white-collar growth, Birmingham was violently resisting the Civil Rights Movement, only to see the shrinkage of its once substantial blue-collar base—the steel industry—and an outflow of talented people of all races. The state's economy, regarded as progressive when manufacturing was the leading edge of growth, seemed backward at the end of the Wallace era.

THE LEGACY OF THE SIXTEENTH STREET BAPTIST CHURCH BOMBING

On June 11, 1963, President Kennedy recognized and stated the need for civil rights. He was the first president to do so. The Birmingham protests of 1963 led to the Civil Rights Act of 1964, the most important antidiscrimination law since the 14th Amendment, legislation that would shape America's social and political development.

Black businessmen, professionals, and religious leaders had slowly pushed forward their economic success in Birmingham. But, the demonstrations in the summer of 1963 inspired poorer blacks to demand equality, not only in Birmingham, but nationally. They wanted access to better jobs, better housing, education, and legal rights. The bombing of the Sixteenth Street Baptist Church acknowledged that racism was out of control in Birmingham. The chaos induced President Kennedy to propose a sweeping civil rights bill. He was unable to advance the bill before he was assassinated on November 22, 1963, but his successor Lyndon B. Johnson championed the cause as reflected in his vision of "A

Great Society." A Southerner by birth, he knew that his efforts might cost him his Democratic party's support from the Southern states. He reportedly commented to an aid after he signed the 1964 Civil Rights Act that "We have lost the south for a generation" (Wikiquote, Attributed, item 11). Johnson addressed the nation and urged the passage of the civil rights bill as a monument to Kennedy's ideals.

The 1964 Civil Rights Act

The House of Representatives passed the measure (with a 290–130 vote) on February 10, 1964. After the Senate passed the measure, President Johnson signed it into law on July 2, 1964. Although the Supreme Court had declared civil rights measures beyond the scope of congressional power in 1883, the Court unanimously upheld the Congress' capacity under the 14th Amendment to protect black Americans' civil rights. The act requires that employers provide equal employment opportunities and secures uniform voting standards. Racial discrimination is illegal, and federal funding will be eliminated if evidence of discrimination based on color, race, or national origin is found. Discrimination in public places is also illegal. Statutes enacted prevent discrimination based on a person's sex, age, religion, previous condition of servitude, physical limitations, and in some cases sexual preference.

Popular Culture

Literature, film, and song celebrate the success of the civil rights struggle in Birmingham and commemorate the lives of the four girls who died in the church bombing on September 15, 1963. Toni Morrison's character Guitar in the *Song of Solomon* reflects on the bombing of the church and portrays how racism can alienate and isolate human beings. Nina Simone responded to the bombing by writing "Mississippi Goddam," as did Richard Farina with "Birmingham Sunday," recorded by Joan Baez. Spike Lee's film *4 Little Girls* focuses on the political and personal ramifications of the bombing and earned him an Academy Award nomination. Historians agree that the four girls put "the face" on the American Civil Rights Movement, and Lee, by foregoing voice-over, allowed the parents of Denise McNair and the mother of Carole Robertson, as well as various aunts, uncles, neighbors, and teachers, to help the audience to know these girls.

Pulitzer Prize winner Diane McWhorter's book *Carry Me Home* details Birmingham's history and its role in the civil rights era that includes the church bombing. The same age as the girls, she does not remember the event. She relates that in her mother's diary that day's entry mentions that their community theater production was canceled: the *trouble downtown* might rile up the *outside agitators* to riot. *Until Justice Rolls Down* by Frank Sikora, a longtime journalist with the *Birmingham News*, takes the reader through the events of the tragedy, examines the social and psychological effects of racial hatred, and, finally, relays the account of the legal efforts to find and convict those responsible for the bombings. Baltimore youth reflect on the girls' lives in *The Children of Birmingham*, an animated film that illustrates the role Birmingham's youth had in changing segregation laws.

Memorials

Parents and community residents formed the Carole Robertson Center in 1976 in memory of all four girls. The center has since evolved into a comprehensive family development agency. Sonya Jones named her center the Addie Mae Collins Youth Center as a

DEFINITIONS

DEMONSTRATION

A demonstration is a form of activism that expresses the common opinion of a group of people. Demonstrations against social injustice usually take the form of a physical gathering of people—the more people that participate, the more successful the demonstration. A protest is a similar action that attempts to influence public opinion or government policy.

DUE PROCESS

Due process of the law, in the context of the United States, refers to how and why laws are enforced and applies to all persons, citizen or alien, and to corporations. In the Fifth Amendment of the Constitution, the reference applies only to the federal government and its courts and agencies; in the 14th Amendment, the reference extends protection to all state governments, agencies, and courts.

FREEDOM RIDERS

Freedom Riders of different ethnicities and backgrounds and trained in nonviolence protesting boarded buses, trains, and planes that were headed to the South to challenge Jim Crow laws and the South's noncompliance with a Supreme Court decision that prohibited segregation in all interstate public transportation facilities.

A GREAT SOCIETY

Lyndon B. Johnson (1963–1969) proposed or enacted a set of domestic programs that included social reforms to eliminate poverty and racial injustice.

KU KLUX KLAN

Also called the KKK or the Klan, members of this white secret society wear white robes and hoods and burn crosses at their outdoor meetings in order to frighten non-members. (See http://www.spartacus.schoolnet.co.uk/USAkkk.htm) They oppose the advancement of blacks, Jews, Catholics, and other minorities. A *klavern* is a subset of a main or state Ku Klux Klan. The *Eastview Klavern 13* was the most violent subset of the Ku Klux Klan in Alabama. The *Cahaba River Group* or *Cahaba Boys* was a Ku Klux Klan splinter group formed by Bobby Cherry and Tommy Blanton and included Robert Chambliss and Herman Cash. They met beneath the Cahaba River Bridge on U.S. 280 in Birmingham, Alabama. *Exalted Cyclops* is the title of the leader of a local klavern of the Ku Klux Klan; Robert Chambliss served as Exalted Cyclops of the Eastview Klavern 13.

NATIONAL ASSOCIATION FOR THE ADVANCEMENT OF COLORED PEOPLE (NAACP)

Founded in 1909, the organization, dedicated to full political power and civil rights for African Americans, was the largest and most influential civil rights organization in the United States when Martin Luther King, Jr., was born. His father headed the Atlanta NAACP. King was a lifelong member, but chose nonviolent, direct-action tactics rather than litigation and lobbying tactics of the NAACP.

RACE RIOT

A race riot or racial riot is an outbreak of violent civil unrest with race as the key factor. Before the Civil Rights Act of 1964, blacks resisted oppression in the South by three basic means: retaliatory violence, organized nonviolent protest, and northward migration.

SOUTHERN CHRISTIAN LEADERSHIP CONFERENCE

This is a civil rights initiative founded by Dr. Martin Luther King, Jr., and his Birmingham colleague and Baptist Preacher Fred Lee Shuttlesworth. Invited to Birmingham by Shuttlesworth to boost the faltering initiative, King violated a court injunction against marching and was subsequently jailed in the Birmingham jail, where he wrote his famous ''Letter from Birmingham Jail''; see http://coursesa.matrix.msu.edu/%7Ehst306/documents/letter.html

This organization was an umbrella organization of affiliates and coordinated the activities of local organizations.

SIT-IN

A sit-in is a form of civil disobedience in which demonstrators occupy seats and refuse to move.

SPEEDY TRIAL

The Sixth Amendment of the United States Constitution ensures that defendants are not subjected to lengthy incarceration prior to a trial. Violations may be a cause for dismissal of a criminal case; state statutes determine the length of time.

STATES' RIGHTS PARTY

A far right group founded in Tennessee in 1958, it expanded to Birmingham in 1960. Based on anti-Semitism and segregation, an FBI investigation deemed them harmless. This is not to be confused with the National States' Rights Party (NSRP, also known as the Dixiecrat Party; this group split from the Democratic Party and sponsored its own presidential candidates in the 1948 election).

memorial to the aunt she never knew. The children in her center learn how to deal with tragedy and overcome adversity. Artist John H. Waddel created four, life-size bronze sculptures entitled, *That Which Might Have Been, Birmingham 1963.* They are displayed in the Sculpture Garden of the George Washington Carver Museum and Cultural Center in Phoenix, Arizona. A number of Internet sites, some interactive, have also been created to memorialize the girls. Another memorial to the girls, four broken columns, stands in nearby Kelly Ingram Park, where marchers gathered to protest and held sit-in demonstrations. In 1996, the Jack and Jill of America Foundation honored Carole Robertson (once a member) with the Carole Robertson Memorial Award (Davis, 1993).

The Sixteenth Street Baptist Church as a Memorial

The Sixteenth Street Baptist Church still has an active congregation of about 200 members, yet about 200,000 visitors tour the church annually as it is part of Birmingham's Civil Rights District. The National Register of Historic Buildings included the church in 1980 and on February 20, 2006, the United States Department of the Interior officially dedicated the church as a National Historic Landmark. A prominent plaque inside honors the four girls: "Denise McNair, Cynthia Wesley, Addie Mae Collins, Carole Robertson. Their lives were taken by unknown parties on September 15, 1963, when the Sixteenth Street Baptist Church was bombed. May men learn to replace bitterness and violence with love and understanding." A small nook in the basement marks the spot where the girls died. "When the bomb went off the clock stopped and time for Birmingham stood still" (Sack, *The New York Times,* April 25, 2001, paragraph 21).

SUGGESTIONS FOR FURTHER READING

Cobbs, E.H., & Smith, P. (1994). *Long time coming.* Birmingham, AL: Crane Press.
King, Dr. M.L., Jr. (1992). In J.M. Washington (Ed.), *I have a dream.* New York City: Harper Collins Publishers.
Lee, S. (1998). *4 little girls.* 1 videocassette. New York: Home Box Office.
McWhorter, D. (2001). *Carry me home.* A Touchtone Book. New York: Simon & Schuster.
Sikora, F. (1991) *Until justice rolls down.* Tuscaloosa, AL: The University of Alabama Press.

CIVIL RIGHTS DOCUMENTS

Historic Places of the Civil Rights Movement, A National Register of Historic Places Travel Itinerary by the National Park Service. Retrieved on the World Wide Web on October 2, 2006, from http://www.cr.nps.gov/nr/travel/civilrights/index.htm
Inaugural speech of George Wallace. Retrieved on the World Wide Web on October 2, 2006, from http://www.archives.state.al.us/govs_list/g_wallac.html
Janet Reno's speech on January 15, 1997. Retrieved on the World Wide Web on October 2, 2006, from http://www.4littlegirls.com/renospch.html
Martin Luther King's Eulogy for the funeral service of Addie Mae Collins, Denise McNair, and Cynthia Wesley. Retrieved on the World Wide Web on October 2, 2006, from http://www.stanford.edu/group/King/speeches/pub/Eulogy_for_the_martyred_children.html
"Martin Luther King's 'Letter from Birmingham Jail.'" Retrieved on the World Wide Web on October 2, 2006, from http://coursesa.matrix.msu.edu/%7Ehst306/documents/letter.html
Photograph collection of Civil Rights Movement. Retrieved on the World Wide Web on October 2, 2006, from http://faculty.smu.edu/dsimon/Change-Civ%20Rts.html

REFERENCES

ABC News Online. (2002, May 15). Retrieved from the World Wide Web on December 6, 2006, from http://72.14.209.104/search?q=cache:f85K-JYpGoYJ:www.abc.net.au/news/newsitems/200205/s556462.htm+cherry+posey+badge+of+honor&hl=en&gl=us&ct=clnk&cd=1

Africaonline. Civil Rights. (1976, February 19). Baxley Reopens Probe of Birmingham Bombing. *Montgomery Advertiser*. Found on July 28, 2007, at http://www.africanaonline.com/1977 trial.htm

Archibald, J., & Hansen, J. (1997, September 7). Death spares scrutiny of cash in bomb probe. *The Birmingham News*.

Archibald, J., & Hansen, J. (1997, September 21). KKK used terror with political power. *The Birmingham News*.

Ayres, B.D., Jr. (1977, November 21). Amens at church in Birmingham are loud after bombing verdict. *The New York Times*.

Baxley, B. (2001, May 3). Why did the FBI hold back evidence? *The New York Times*.

Bragg, R. (1997, July 11). FBI reopens investigation into landmark crime of the Civil Rights Era. *The New York Times*.

Casey, R. (1977, November 19). Chambliss jury was stuck at 11-1 till finally: Guilty. *The Birmingham News*.

Chebium, R. (2000, May 17). Suspects in Civil Rights Era bombing charged with murder. Retrieved from the World Wide Web on October 2, 2006, from http://archives.cnn.com/2000/LAW/05/17/church.bombing.03/

CNN.com./LAW CENTER. (2001, May 1). Retrieved from the World Wide Web on December 6, 2006, from http://72.14.209.104/search?q=cache:p_MWU7XJRaUJ:www.cnn.com/2001/LAW/05/01/church.bombing.05/index.html+thomas+blanton+burns&hl=en&-gl=us&ct=clnk&cd=3

Cobbs, E.H.,& Smith, P. (1994). *Long time coming*. Birmingham, AL: Crane Press.

Court TV Online. (May 1, 2001). Retrieved from the World Wide Web on December 6, 2006, from http://72.14.209.104/search?q=cache:jbPem0c1qWcJ:www.useekufind.com/peace/trial.htm+robert+chambliss+trial&hl=en&gl=us&ct=clnk&cd=1

Davis, A.Y. (1993). Remembering Carole, Cynthia, Addie Mae & Denise. *Essence 24*,(5).

Gado, M. (2005). Birmingham church bombing. *Court TV Time Library*. Retrieved from the World Wide Web on December 6, 2006, from http://216.239.51.104/search?q=cache:aGFm R-gmlG4J:www.crimelibrary.com/terrorists_spies/terrorists/birmingham_church/7.html +hoover+chances+of+a+prosecution+in+state+or+federal+court+is+very+remote&h-l=en&gl=us&ct=clnk&cd=1

Gado, M. (2007). CourtTV Crime Library. Found on July 28, 2007, at http://www.crimelibrary.com/terrorists_spies/terrorists/birmingham_church/index.html

Hansen, J., & Archibald, J. (1997, August 31). Klansman still on suspect list. *The Birmingham News*.

Hansen, J., & Archibald, J. (1997, September 15). Church bomb felt like world shaking. *The Birmingham News*.

Hansen, J., & Archibald, J. (1997, September 7). Death spares scrutiny of cash in bomb probe. *The Birmingham News*.

Hansen, J., & Archibald, J. (2001, April 15). Change blowing in wind during '63. *The Birmingham News*.

Huie, W.B. (1964, March 24). Death of an innocent: What kind of mind could have planted the bomb that killed four children in Birmingham? *Look*, 23–25.

Jenkins, R. (1977, September 28). 3 Reportedly indicted in bombings in Birmingham. Witness in church-bombing trial links dynamite to the defendant. *The New York Times*.

Jerry Jazz Musician. (2002, July 25). Retrieved from the World Wide Web on December 6, 2006, from http://www.jerryjazzmusician.com/

Judge decries mockery of law. (1963, September 16). *The Birmingham News.*

King, M.L., Jr. (1990). In J.M. Washington (Ed.), *A Testament of Hope: The Essential Writings and Speeches of Martin Luther King, Jr.* New York: HarperOne.

King, Dr. M.L., Jr. (1992). In J.E. Washington (Ed.), *I have a dream.* New York City: Harper Collins Publishers.

McWhorter, D. (2001). *Carry me home.* A Touchstone Book. New York: Simon & Schuster.

Osgood, A. (1963, September 16). Racial tension mounts in Birmingham after four killed in church bombing. *The Montgomery Advisor.* Retrieved from the World Wide Web on August 29, 2007, http://www.useekufind.com/peace/a_1963_church_bombing.htm#RACIAL%20TENSION

Padgett, T., & Sikora, F. (2003, September 22). The legacy of Virgil Ware. *Time.*

Poe, J. (2002, May 23). Birmingham bombing victims: Church bomber guilty at last. *The Atlanta Journal Constitution.*

Raines, H. (1978). Inquiries link informer for FBI to major Klan terrorism in 60's. *The New York Times.*

Raines, H. (1980, February 17). FBI cover-up seen in 60s Klan attacks. *The New York Times.*

Raines, H. (1980, February 18). Federal report says Hoover barred trial for Klansman in '63 Bombing. *The New York Times.*

Raines, H. (1983, July 24). The Birmingham bombing. *The New York Times.*

Reeves, J. (2002, May 22). Ex-Klansman convicted in '63 bombing. *Associated Press.* Retrieved from the World Wide Web on December 6, 2006, from http://216.239.51.104/search?q=cache:bm5asYD0jCAJ:www.crimelibrary.com/terrorists_spies/terrorists/birmingham_church/14.html+Reeves,+J.+associated+press+Ex-Klansman+Convicted+in+%2763+Bombing.+Associated+Press.&hl=en&gl=us&ct=clnk&cd=1

Sack, K. (2000, May 20). Suspects in 1963 Birmingham church bombing lead hardscrabble lives. Retrieved from the World Wide Web on December 6, 2006, from http://select.nytimes.com/gst/abstract.html?res=FA0713FE3B5E0C738ED-DAC0894D8404482&n=Top%2fReference%2fTimes%20Topics%2fPeople%2fC%2fCherry%2c%20Bobby%20Frank

Sack, K. (2001, April 13). A bitter Alabama cry: Slow justice is no justice witnesses testify defendant displayed hatred of blacks. *The New York Times.* Retrieved from the World Wide Web on December 6, 2006, from http://select.nytimes.com/gst/abstract.html?res=F20915F73E550C708DDDAD0894D9404482&n=Top%2fReference%2fTimes%20Topics%2fPeople%2fC%2fCherry%2c%20Bobby%20Frank

Sack, K. (2001, April 25). As church bombing trial begins in Birmingham, the city's past is very much present. *The New York Times.* Retrieved from the Wide World Web on December 7, 2006, from http://query.nytimes.com/gst/fullpage.html?sec=health&res=9E0-CE6DB1739F936A15757C0A9679C8B63

Sack, K. (2001, April 27). Ex-Klansman is found guilty in '63 bombing. *The New York Times.* Retrieved from the World Wide Web on December 7, 2006, from http://query.nytimes.com/gst/fullpage.html?sec=health&res=9E0CE6DB1739F936A15757-C0A9679C8B63

Sikora, F. (1991). *Until justice rolls down.* Tuscaloosa, AL: The University of Alabama Press.

The Birmingham News. (1977, November 16). Retrieved from the World Wide Web on December 6, 2006, from http://72.14.209.104/search?q=cache:jbPem0c1qWcJ:www.useekufind.com/peace/trial.htm+robert+chambliss+trial&hl=en&gl=us&ct=clnk&cd=1

Thomas, W.G., III. (2004, November 3). Television news and the Civil Rights struggle: The views in Virginia and Missussppi. *Southern Spaces.* http://www.southernspaces.org/contents/2004/thomas/4d.htm

United Press International. (1963, September 16). Six dead after church bombing. Washington Post.com. Retrieved from the World Wide Web on August 29, 2007, http://www.washingtonpost.com/wp-srv/national/longterm/churches/archives1.ht

White, J. (2000, May 20). Former Klansmen indicted for murder in 1963 bombing of Birmingham, Alabama church. *World Socialist Website.*

Williams, J. (2005, May). Black radio and Civil Rights, Birmingham 1956–1963. *Journal of Radio Studies.* Retrieved from the World Wide Web on October 2, 2006, from http://www.leaonline.com/doi/pdf/10.1207/s15506843jrs1201_5#search=%22julian%20williams%20%20black%20radio%22

Wikiquote. Retrieved from the World Wide Web on December 6, 2006, from http://en.wikiquote.org/wiki/Lyndon_B._Johnson.

Wilson, C., Dr. (2003, September 16). Four girls killed in Birmingham church bombing. *Birmingham Times.*

Wright, B. (2006, February 26). From negatives to positives. *Birmingham News.* Retrieved from the World Wide Web on December 6, 2006, from http://www.al.com/unseen/stories/index.ssf?story.html

16

Charles Manson and the Tate-LaBianca Murders: A Family Portrait

MARIE BALFOUR

The summer of 1969 was a remarkable period in American history that defined a generation and rocked the nation. Over the span of a month and a half, the nation was riveted to the news, beginning with the coverage of Senator Edward Kennedy and the Chappaquiddick incident and ending with the Woodstock music festival. The summer of 1969 has become famous for other reasons as well. On July 20, Buzz Aldrin and Neil Armstrong became the first men to walk on the moon. Yet, it was the disturbing events of August 9 and 10 that would remain in the headlines for years to come.

THE MANSON MURDERS

Late in the evening on August 8, 1969, four members of the Manson Family arrived at 10050 Cielo Drive in Los Angeles County, California. After parking the car and cutting the telephone wires, Manson Family members Charles Watson, Susan Atkins, Patricia Krenwinkel, and Linda Kasabian entered the property armed with some rope, three knives, and a gun. After ordering the girls to hide, Watson murdered 18-year-old Steven Parent, who was in his car getting ready to leave. Leaving Kasabian to stand watch, Watson, Atkins, and Krenwinkel entered the house where they proceeded to attack and brutally murder the people inside. Sharon Marie Tate-Polanski, the 26-year-old wife of movie producer Roman Polanski, was found on the floor of the living room tied by a rope around her neck to international hair stylist, 35-year-old Jay Sebring. Tate was eight months pregnant. The body of Roman Polanski's friend, 32-year-old Voytek (Wojciech) Frykowski, was found near the porch; and the body of Abigail Anne Folger, the 25-year-old heiress to the Folger coffee fortune, was found in the grass. Before leaving, one of the killers printed the word "PIG" on the porch door in Sharon Tate's blood. The killers returned to the rest of the Manson Family at Spahn Ranch in the Simi Hills; they learned the names of their victims the following day during a television broadcast.

ROMAN POLANSKI

Roman Polanski, husband of murdered actress Sharon Tate, has not been back to the United States since 1978, when he fled the country while awaiting sentencing for his conviction of drugging and raping a 13-year-old girl at the Los Angeles home of actor Jack Nicholson. Polanski has been living in France since his escape, but has continued to direct a number of films, including the 2002 Oscar-winning movie *The Pianist*.

SOURCES

Benmussa, R. (Producer), & Polanski, R. (Director). (2002). *The Pianist* [Motion picture]. France: R.P. Productions.

Polanski remains fugitive from U.S. law. (2003, February 11). *CNN.com*. Retrieved November 19, 2006, from http://www.cnn.com

Vachss, A. (2006). *Roman Polanski media reports archive*. Retrieved November 19, 2006, from http://www.vachss.com/mission/roman_polanski.html

On the morning of August 9, 1969, when housekeeper Winifred Chapman arrived for work, she discovered the house in disarray and the living room spattered in blood. The first body Chapman saw was Parent, who was lying in his car; she ran down the driveway to alert the neighbors and call the police. When the Los Angeles Police Department (LAPD) arrived soon after, they found the bodies of five victims. The murder scene was gruesome: Tate had been stabbed 16 times, and the coroner would later determine from the autopsy that she had been hanged for a short period of time; Sebring had been stabbed seven times and shot once; Folger had been stabbed 28 times; Frykowski had been stabbed 51 times, bludgeoned 13 times, and shot twice; and Parent, who was on the premises visiting the caretaker, had been shot four times and had a defensive slash wound on his wrist.

Despite the horrific brutality of the crimes, there was little time for the Los Angeles community to absorb the shock, for a similar murder occurred on the following evening.

Frustrated by the "messy" way in which the Tate murders had happened, Charles Manson decided to join his Family on the evening of August 9, 1969. According to Kasabian's testimony at the trial, Manson ordered her to drive through Los Angeles, and he repeatedly ordered her to stop so that he could scout out a house with occupants to murder. On this particular night, Manson was accompanied by Watson, Krenwinkel, Leslie van Houten, Susan Atkins, Linda Kasabian, and Steve Grogan. After selecting a house on Waverly Drive, Manson entered the house first, tying up Leno and Rosemary LaBianca. When Manson returned to the car, he told Watson, van Houten, and Krenwinkel to hitchhike back to Spahn Ranch. Atkins would later add that Manson had told the three to "paint a picture more gruesome than anybody had ever seen" (Bugliosi and Gentry, 1974, p. 247). When Leno and Rosemary LaBianca's bodies were discovered the next day, Leno was found with his hands tied behind his back with a leather thong, a pillowcase over his head, and the electrical cord of a large lamp around his neck. When the pillowcase was removed, a small kitchen knife was found lodged in Leno's throat. A two-tined carving fork was sticking out of his stomach, and the word "WAR" had been carved into his skin. He had been stabbed 12 times, and there were 14 additional wounds from the carving fork. Rosemary LaBianca was found on the floor of the bedroom, also with a pillowcase and electrical cord around her neck. She had been stabbed 41 times. Again, words had been written in the victims' blood: "Death to Pigs" was found on the living room wall, "Rise" was near the front door, and "Healter Skelter" was found on the refrigerator door.

Within hours after beginning the search at the Tate residence, the LAPD had what they thought was a plausible motive: drugs. Friends of both Folger and Frykowski admitted to police that they had been steady users, along with Sebring. Frykowski was known for using cocaine, mescaline, marijuana, and LSD; Folger, along with Frykowski, were both found to have had methylenedioxyamphetamine (MDA), today commonly known as ecstasy, in their bloodstreams at the time of their death. In searching the premises, police found cocaine and marijuana in Sebring's car. Expecting to find a drug deal gone wrong as the motive, police began checking all known drug connections generated from Frykowski and Sebring's habits. Police also interrogated William Garretson, the caretaker at the Tate residence, and they had Garretson take a polygraph. Garretson repeatedly stated that he had heard nothing throughout the night; he was released from custody after passing the polygraph test.

Another team of LAPD officers worked on the LaBianca murders. Cooperation between the two groups was limited despite the similarities of the two cases. For their part, the LaBianca detectives were also attempting to find some motive for the killings. With the exception of Rosemary's wallet and wristwatch, nothing was found to be missing from the house. The LaBianca detectives attempted to find leads; they looked into neighborhood activities and investigated Leno's financial records. Although they uncovered information relating to a huge debt run up over racehorse betting, nothing relating to Mafia connections could be established. The LaBianca detectives concentrated their efforts on a former neighbor with previous arrests, including one for attempted murder.

At the time of the first progress reports, the Tate detectives were still concentrating on the possibility of a drug motive. In the LaBianca report, there was a mention of the Beatles album *SWBO 101*, better known as the *White Album*, on which there were songs entitled "Helter Skelter," "Piggies," and "Blackbird," which included the lyrics "arise, arise" (Bugliosi and Gentry, 1974, p. 101). Unbeknownst to them, the LaBianca detectives had hit upon an important piece of information that would later become useful in explaining Manson's conspiracy theory. However, pursuing numerous leads, neither the Tate nor LaBianca detectives were any closer to finding the murderers than they had been at the beginning of their respective investigations.

THE MAN BEHIND THE MURDERS

Born "no-name Maddox" on November 12, 1934, Manson spent the majority of his youth being shuffled between relatives, neighbors, and juvenile detention centers. His mother, Kathleen Maddox, a teenage prostitute, was both incapable of caring for a child and unwilling to do so. She was married for a short time to William Manson, who gave her son his name. "No-name Maddox" was now Charles Milles Manson. After Kathleen finished serving a sentence for armed robbery, Manson lived with his mother until he was 12, when she had him sent to the Gibault School for Boys. Manson spent his teenage years in a number of institutions, and he committed his first federal offense in 1951 after escaping from a boys' school in Indiana. Arrested for driving a stolen car across a state line, Manson was remanded to a federal training school for boys in Washington, DC, until he came of age. Because of his numerous disciplinary infractions while in detention, Manson's sentence was extended. He was 19 years old when he was eventually paroled on May 8, 1954.

On the outside again and now an adult, Manson met and married a waitress named Rosalie. Less than a year later, Manson was back in federal court in California, this time with his pregnant wife in tow. The presence of a pregnant wife must have been reassuring to the court. In part because of Rosalie's condition, and combined with a court-appointed psychiatrist's favorable recommendation, Manson was given five years probation. However, unable to stay in one place for long, Manson skipped town and headed east. He was eventually caught in Indianapolis and returned to Los Angeles in March 1956. Initially sentenced to three years, Manson attempted to escape one month before his parole hearing after learning that his wife was living with another man. Manson's escape attempt was unsuccessful, and he was ultimately sentenced to another five years' time; his wife filed for divorce and retained custody of their son.

Manson spent the majority of his twenties either breaking the law or residing in jail. Pimping, check forgery, and grand theft auto had Manson back in prison for ten years. While awaiting federal prosecution on the forgery charges, Manson married a woman named Leona who had told his parole officer she was carrying Manson's child. The parole officer had initially managed to get Manson a suspended prison term, but after Manson returned to pimping and violated his probation, he was sent to the U.S. Penitentiary in Washington State during July 1961. Divorce came soon after, but not before Charles Luther Manson was born.

While incarcerated in Washington, Manson became interested in Scientology, which he would later combine with his own ideas into the philosophy that became the Manson Family. Prison records state that besides his interest in Scientology, Manson's only other permanent interest was music. Manson taught himself to play the guitar and drums, and he wrote some 80 or 90 songs while in prison. Manson's obsession with the Beatles was sparked while incarcerated in Washington. "It didn't necessarily follow that he was a fan ....He told numerous people that, given the chance, he could be much bigger than the Beatles" (Bugliosi and Gentry, 1974, p. 202). Manson also learned how to play the steel guitar from fellow inmate Alvin Karpis, a former member of the Ma Barker gang. Paroled on March 21, 1967, Manson is reported to have asked to stay in prison; he seemed to prefer institutional life to that on the outside.

Following his parole, Manson was granted permission to go to San Francisco, and during the coming months in the Haight-Ashbury section of San Francisco, Manson began collecting his Family members.

MANSON'S CONTROL

Manson wandered through San Francisco following his 1967 release from prison; he used music, drugs, and love to gain a following among the hippies who lived there. Describing her first encounter with Manson, Lynette (Squeaky) Fromme said of Manson, "'Up in the Haight...I'm called the gardener,' he said. 'I tend to all the flower children' ...He had the most delicate, quick motion, like magic as if glided along by air, and a smile that went from warm daddy to twinkely devil" ("The girl," 1975). During his time in Haight, Manson received a grand piano from an "admirer." He traded the piano for a beaten up bus, which would eventually serve to take Manson and his followers out of Haight. By the time he left, Manson had an entourage that comprised the core of the Family, including Susan Atkins and Patricia Krenwinkel. Surviving on what they could scrounge from "garbage runs" and credit cards donated by Krenwinkel, the Family eventually settled at Spahn Ranch outside Los Angeles, where their numbers continued to grow.

Spahn Ranch was run-down, but was frequently used as a movie set. Given permission to stay on the property by the elderly and blind owner, George Spahn, the Family helped with ranch chores. While cooking and cleaning for Spahn, the Manson girls also served as his eyes and ears. Lynette Fromme grew especially close to Spahn. Although not a direct participant in the Manson murders of 1969, Fromme would eventually attempt to assassinate President Gerald Ford in Sacramento in 1975. "One of Manson's shrewdest, toughest, and most slavishly obedient followers," Fromme was assigned to tend to Spahn in the hope that she would eventually inherit the ranch upon his death ("The girl," 1975). It was from Spahn Ranch that Manson sent his Family out to commit the Tate-LaBianca murders of 1969.

Manson's control over the Family stemmed from a combination of charisma, intelligence, and an ability to "work the system." Manson was able to see and understand what his Family needed: security, faith, a father figure, and a leader. Dr. David Smith, who worked in a free clinic in San Francisco's Haight-Ashbury district, had the following to say about Manson and the Family:

> A new girl in Charlie's Family would bring with her a certain middle-class morality. The first thing that Charlie did was to see that all this was torn down. The major way he broke through was sex...If they had hang-ups about it, then they should feel guilty. That way he was able to eliminate the controls that normally govern our lives. (O'Neil, 1969, p. 26)

The way in which Manson exerted his control was evasive and difficult to pinpoint. Rarely giving directions, Manson would "suggest" something, and it would be done. Some of the Family members believed Manson could read their thoughts, and others thought he was the second coming of Jesus Christ. Arrested during the Barker Ranch raid, Manson listed his aliases as "Jesus Christ" and "God" (Bugliosi and Gentry, 1974, p. 180). During her grand jury testimony, Atkins said of Manson, "Charles Manson changes from second to second. He can be anybody he wants to be. He can put on any face he wants to put on at any given moment" (Bugliosi and Gentry, 1974, p. 246). Manson's adaptability and his ability to proselytize his sermons and philosophies to the Family gave him immense power over their actions. The heavy use of LSD among the Family members, a drug that is known to lower inhibitions and make the user more susceptible to suggestion, also indicates another manner in which Manson reached his target audience. Manson attempted to break down the existing moral conscience of his Family by encouraging "creepy-crawls." Manson would send out Family members dressed in dark clothing to enter occupied houses at night with the instructions to rearrange items, steal small trinkets, and play mind games on "the establishment."

THE MANSON FAMILY

Invariably, the young men and women who composed the Manson Family were searching for something. Mostly middle-class youth, who had run away from home or broken with the establishment, they found alternately a father figure, a brother, a leader, and a Christ-like quality in Charles Manson. Manson's prison records have noted that he could get something from everyone, and that he had a remarkable talent for adapting himself to all situations. Using these talents along with his music, drugs, and sex,

Manson's Family grew. Safe in the knowledge that Manson was, indeed, a "Christ-like fig-ure," his Family members became capable of murder.

Before falling in with the Manson crowd, Charles Denton Watson had been an aca-demically talented high-school athlete. Although active in his Methodist church, Watson became involved in drugs after moving away to college. Dropping out of North Texas State University while in his third year, Watson fell in with the Manson Family while they were living with Dennis Wilson. Although he initially moved away from the Family to sell dope with a girlfriend, Watson rejoined the Family in time to participate in the Tate-LaBianca murders. After participating in the murder of a worker at Spahn Ranch, Watson fled back to Texas in October 1969, and it was from there that Watson fought extradition to California.

Patricia Krenwinkel's change from a quiet, normal girl to one of a member of the Man-son Family was quite abrupt. Originally from the Los Angeles area, Krenwinkel's parents separated during her teens. After half a year of college in Alabama, she moved to Los Angeles and got a job at an insurance agency. "She abandoned her car in a Manhattan Beach parking lot in September 1967, quit her job without picking up her paycheck, and went off with Charlie Manson" (O'Neil, 1969, p. 26). Put in charge of the Manson Fam-ily's garbage runs, Krenwinkel would go through grocery store trash bins to find food for the Family. Although Krenwinkel never provided a handwriting sample before the trial, scribbles on her legal pad showed the words "Healter Skelter," misspelled in the same way as had been found at the scene of the LaBianca murders.

Susan Atkins, who had a strained relationship with her family, was a particularly important piece of the puzzle surrounding the initial inquiry into the Tate-LaBianca mur-ders. Her father had left home to look for work, and her mother had died when she was 15 years old. When Atkins was getting into trouble with the police, "her father com-plained that the courts were 'too lenient' because they let her out of jail" in the first place (Roberts, 1970, p. 40). Dropping out of school, Atkins sold magazine subscriptions and waited tables. After serving a short jail sentence and probation for armed robbery, Atkins moved back to San Francisco where she began working as a topless dancer. One of Man-son's most loyal devotees, Atkins would become the driving source of information that would return a grand jury indictment on the Manson Family members for the Tate-LaBianca murders.

Linda Drouin Kasabian was born and raised in Biddeford, Maine. She dropped out of high school in her sophomore year and was married and divorced within a year. Marrying again, this time to Bob Kasabian, Linda had her first child in 1968. Trouble in the mar-riage sent Linda back to the East Coast, but Bob convinced her to join him in Los Angeles. Moving to be with Bob Kasabian, Linda met a Manson Family member through a friend, and she left her husband to join the Family. At the Family's urging, she returned the next day to steal money from her friend, which she then turned over to Manson. Kasabian's participation in the Tate-LaBianca murders was limited, having been chosen to come along because she was the only Manson Family member with a valid driver's license.

Leslie van Houten, although charged only with the LaBianca murders, was tried with Manson, Krenwinkel, and Atkins. Although she was initially convicted with the other Manson Family members, van Houten was granted a second trial because her defense law-yer disappeared during the main trial. When the second trial ended in a deadlocked jury, she was given a third trial, which ended in a conviction, and she was sentenced to life imprisonment.

Van Houten came from the same broken family atmosphere as the other Manson girls. Her parents divorced when she was in her early teens, and she grew up in the Los Angeles area where she eventually discovered the drug scene. She met Manson Family members Catherine Share and Robert Beausoleil in 1968; she was introduced to Manson and the Family soon after, and she never left.

Beausoleil was born in Santa Barbara, California, in 1947. Originally a musician, Beausoleil was also called "Cupid" for his good looks and the ease with which he attracted women. Before meeting Manson, Beausoleil had starred in a Kenneth Anger film called *Lucifer Rising* (1973), also writing the music for the short cult film. Beausoleil also sang backup on Frank Zappa's first album *Freak Out* (1966). Beausoleil met Manson while he was living with Gary Hinman—the same man Beausoleil would later be convicted of killing.

THE INVESTIGATION

While the autopsies were being done on the Tate murder victims, LAPD detective Sergeant Jess Buckles was approached by two detectives from the Los Angeles Sheriff's Office (LASO), Sergeant Paul Whiteley and Sergeant Charles Guenther. They were investigating the homicide of 34-year-old music teacher Gary Hinman in Topanga Canyon. Whiteley and Guenther thought the LAPD would be interested in their investigation for several reasons. First, Hinman had been violently stabbed to death, and the words "political piggy" had been written on the wall in his blood. Although the body had been discovered on July 31, the LASO officers believed the victim had been murdered several days earlier. LASO had arrested a young hippie by the name of Robert Beausoleil driving Hinman's car, and a knife was found in the wheel well. Although Beausoleil had been in custody at the time of the Tate murders, it was possible he was not the only one responsible for the Hinman murder. "Beausoleil had been living at Spahn's Ranch, an old movie ranch near the Los Angeles suburb of Chatsworth, with a bunch of other hippies. It was an odd group, their leader, a guy named Charlie, apparently having convinced them that he was Jesus Christ" (Bugliosi and Gentry, 1974, p. 62). However, LAPD Detective Buckles, firmly convinced that the Tate murders had a drug connection, disregarded the information from the LASO detectives.

As part of their investigation into the Hinman murder and a string of car thefts, the LASO raided Spahn Ranch in the middle of August and arrested close to 40 members of the Manson Family. However, problems with the warrant resulted in their release. When another raid in mid-October netted the same individuals in Inyo County at the Barker Ranch, this time for car thefts and arson, LASO officers finally got a break. During the three-day search of the Barker Ranch, Inyo County officers found two girls who were fleeing the Family. One was a young woman, Kitty Lutesinger, who was pregnant with Robert Beausoleil's child. Knowing she was connected to Beausoleil, the LASO officers drove to interview her in Inyo County, where she provided information that connected Susan Atkins and the Manson Family not only to the Hinman murder but also to the Tate murders (Bugliosi and Gentry, 1974, p. 114). Lutesinger also provided the names of other Family associates who had been involved with the Family during the recent months.

Working from information provided in Lutesinger's interview, the LaBianca detectives began looking for a Straight Satan motorcycle gang member. According to Lutesinger, Manson had tried to recruit members of the Straight Satan gang to join the Family to be personal bodyguards for Manson. Only one had taken the bait, and the rest of the Straight Satan members had not been impressed by the idea. Danny DeCarlo had lived with the Family on and off for several months. DeCarlo was able to link Manson, Beausoleil, Atkins, and several other Family members to the Hinman murder. He also provided information about the supposed murder of a Black Panther Party member named Bernard Crowe, who had been shot by Manson after threatening retaliation against the Family. Manson had shot Crowe, and his friends dumped the body in Griffith Park near the LaBianca residence. Although DeCarlo and Family members were convinced that Manson had killed Crowe, what they did not know was that Crowe had lived. Crowe, who did not even belong to the Black Panther Party, later testified during the guilt phase of Manson's trial.

Once Atkins had been implicated in the Hinman murder through Lutesinger's interview, she was moved to the Sybil Brand Institute where she told fellow inmates about her participation in the Hinman and Tate murders. Atkins provided enough detail to her dormitory mates Virginia Graham and Ronnie Howard to convince them that she was truly involved. As the LAPD was gathering the story behind the Tate-LaBianca murders from DeCarlo, Graham, who had been transferred to another jail, and Howard, were both attempting to tell the authorities what they knew about Atkins's involvement. By the time Howard was able to get her message to the LAPD, they already knew what she wanted to tell them, having learned of the connection between the Family and the Tate-LaBianca killings through Lutesinger and DeCarlo.

The information provided by Atkins and Lutesinger was enough for the police to begin putting together a sketch of the events surrounding the Tate-LaBianca murders. Arrest

Figure 16.1 Susan Atkins, Patricia Krenwinkel, and Leslie van Houten, left to right, are shown en route to court, 1970. The three women, displaying the symbol "X" on their foreheads as followers of the Manson cult family, are on trial for killings that included actress Sharon Tate. © AP Photo.

warrants were issued for Charles Watson, Patricia Krenwinkel, and Linda Kasabian. Manson and Atkins were already in custody. Watson fought extradition from Texas, and although Kasabian waived extradition proceedings and was immediately returned to California from where she surrendered in New Hampshire, Krenwinkel also fought extradition from Alabama (Bugliosi and Gentry, 1974, p. 220). As part of a deal to spare her from a death sentence, Atkins testified before the grand jury. Convinced by her first defense lawyer that it was in her best interest to cooperate, the grand jury indictment was, to a large extent, the direct result of Atkins's testimony. With the combination of information garnered from Lutesinger, DeCarlo, and Atkins's first-person narratives, indictments were returned on Manson, Watson, Krenwinkel, Kasabian, and Atkins on seven counts of first-degree murder and one count of conspiracy. Leslie van Houten was also indicted on two counts of first-degree murder and one count of conspiracy. However, the prosecution suffered a serious setback when, following a meeting with Manson, Atkins recanted her grand jury testimony, fired her lawyer, and refused all further cooperation with the authorities.

Having lost Atkins's cooperation, the prosecution's star witness became Linda Kasabian. Kasabian had professed her desire to testify since the beginning, and she was considered a better witness than Atkins since she had not physically killed anyone, although she had been present at the Tate murders and had driven the car on the evening of the LaBianca murders. In return for her testimony, Kasabian was granted full immunity and was not charged in any of the Manson murders.

"THE DEFENSE RESTS"

By the time the Manson trial was over, the jury had been sequestered for almost nine months, and the defense team for Manson, Atkins, Krenwinkel, and van Houten had changed composition numerous times. Throughout the trial, Manson kept demanding that he be allowed to represent himself, and although each time his request was denied, Manson was undoubtedly the driving force behind the defense strategy.

Out of a multitude of lawyers willing and eager to represent him, Manson finally chose Irving Kanarek, "whom he regarded as the most obstructionist and time-consuming lawyer in Los Angeles, in hopes of badgering the judge into allowing him to defend himself" ("Manson's shattered defense," 1970, p. 45). The Manson girls went through a multitude of lawyers during

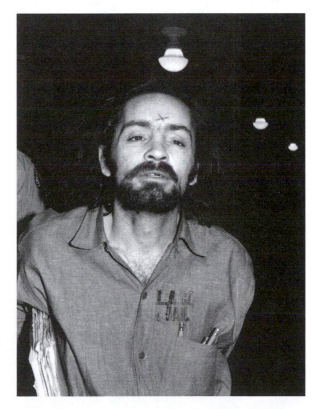

Figure 16.2 Unsuccessful in his attempts to obtain a mistrial, Charles Manson heads for court to listen to further cross-examination of the state's star witness, Linda Kasabian, in his trial for murder in the slayings of actress Sharon Tate and six others, 1970. © AP Photo.

301

the trial. Whenever a lawyer would try to separate his client from the rest of the Family, by way of requesting a psychiatric examination or by utilizing a defense tactic not approved by Manson, within days the Family member would request a new lawyer.

After the prosecution rested in the case, the defense immediately rested without attempting to call any witnesses or present any evidence. Their failure to present a case was due to the fact that the lawyers of the three Manson girls had heard that their clients intended to take the stand, to "confess" to the murders, and to absolve Manson of all responsibility. When the girls were given a chance to take the stand out of the presence of the jury, they refused. Only Manson took the stand to "rap" about his philosophies, but he ultimately refused to repeat his testimony in front of the jury.

During the trial, van Houten's lawyer disappeared. Ronald Hughes, who had been one of the first lawyers to visit Manson in jail, had been van Houten's counsel since the start of proceedings. Hughes had the dubious distinction of having never tried a case before being selected as part of the Manson defense. When Hughes failed to show up in court after a weekend break at the beginning of December 1970, new counsel was appointed for van Houten. Hughes's body was found months later in a creek bed near where he was known to go camping. Although the body was too badly decomposed to determine the cause of death, there is significant speculation regarding the nature of Hughes's death and the possibility of the Family's involvement. Because of Hughes's disappearance, van Houten would eventually be granted a retrial.

The Manson case was prosecuted by Vincent Bugliosi of the Los Angeles District Attorney's office. Bugliosi wrote the most comprehensive narrative regarding the Manson murders, *Helter Skelter: The True Story of the Manson Murders* (1974). Although preliminary hearings were done before a separate judge, the trial itself was heard before Judge Charles H. Older. Older, in refusing Manson's repeated requests to represent himself, became Manson's target inside the courtroom on several occasions. The defendants were repeatedly removed from the courtroom for causing disturbances, and, on one occasion, Manson leaped over the defense table toward Older with a pencil in hand, screaming, "In the name of Christian justice, someone should cut your head off!" (Bugliosi and Gentry, 1974, p. 286).

THE FINAL TALLY

The Tate murders were committed by Charles Watson, Patricia Krenwinkel, Susan Atkins, and Linda Kasabian on Manson's orders. For the LaBianca murders, Watson and Krenwinkel were accompanied by Leslie van Houten for the actual killings, while Manson participated long enough to tie up the LaBiancas. Also along in the car that night were Atkins, Kasabian, and Steve Grogan. Of the participants, Manson, Krenwinkel, Atkins, and van Houten had a joint trial, which resulted in their convictions on seven counts of first-degree murder and one count of conspiracy to commit murder for Manson, Krenwinkel, and Atkins. van Houten was convicted of one count of conspiracy to commit murder and two counts of first-degree murder in the deaths of Leno and Rosemary LaBianca. During the Manson trial, Watson was fighting extradition from Texas, which, in effect, guaranteed that he would have a separate trial from Manson and the girls. Although his ploy worked and Watson arrived in California too late to be tried with Manson and the girls, he was convicted during a separate trial of seven counts of first-degree murder and one count of conspiracy. Kasabian was granted immunity in return for her testimony at the Manson trial.

Although the Manson Family members were all given death sentences for their 1971 convictions, they have not been executed. Under California law, death sentence cases must be automatically appealed. If no technical errors are found at the end of the appeal process, the conviction and death sentences are allowed to stand. However, in early 1972, the California State Supreme Court ruled that the death penalty was unconstitutional under the state's constitution, which prohibits "cruel and unusual punishment." This ruling, which predated the federal case *Furman v. Georgia* (1972) by only a few months, automatically invalidated the death sentences given to the Manson Family members, and replaced their sentences with life imprisonment with the possibility of parole. Although California has since reinstated the death penalty, it is not a retroactive statute. The Manson Family members remain in prison, even though they have each come up for parole multiple times.

MANSON'S MUSIC AND MOTIVE

One of Manson's goals after leaving prison in 1967 was to produce an album of his songs and guitar music. Believing he could be bigger than the Beatles, Manson used his connections in San Francisco to mingle with people in the movie and music industries. One man he befriended was talent scout Gregg Jakobson, whom Manson met through Dennis Wilson of the Beach Boys. After twice picking up the same two women hitchhiking in the spring of 1968, Dennis Wilson returned home one evening to find the girls, Manson, and other Family members in his house. Wilson was intrigued by Manson for a few months, but eventually severed the relationship. Before he did, however, he introduced Manson to Gregg Jakobson. Jakobson was intrigued by Manson's Family but not enough to join. In an effort to promote what he saw as Manson's musical talent, Jakobson introduced Manson to Terry Melcher who was in the music production business. At the time, Melcher was living at 10050 Cielo Drive, the house that would eventually gain infamy as the site of the Tate murders.

Although Jakobson encouraged Melcher to record Manson's songs, Melcher was not interested. It was discovered during the pretrial investigation that during Manson's time with Dennis Wilson, Manson had actually gone with Wilson to drop Melcher at his house on at least one occasion. This was particularly important information because it showed that Manson had previously been to the scene of the Tate murders. Melcher, unimpressed, had this to say about Manson's music:

> There were forty or fifty of them; . . . they were everywhere, mostly young women, and they all seemed to be part of the same group, they all sang together with Charlie Manson. He played a guitar, and it seems to me some of the girls were playing tambourines. . . . The type of music they were doing and the whole setting itself was rather peculiar to the pop music business, to say the least. (Gilmore and Kenner, 2000, p. 78)

Melcher decided not to pursue things, and Manson's music career never got off the ground. Manson's obsession with music did not fade, however. Throughout the course of the trial, numerous witnesses would testify to Manson's obsession with the Beatles and his peculiar interpretation of the Bible chapter Revelation 9. To Manson, the release of the 1968 *White Album* by the Beatles was proof that Manson and the Beatles were connected. Reinterpreting the lyrics of songs, Manson felt that the Beatles were calling to him

303

MANSON FAMILY PAROLE HEARINGS

If their current history of parole denials is any indication of future events, the Manson Family members currently behind bars will most likely never see the outside of a prison again. Charles Manson was denied parole for the 10th time in 2002; Leslie van Houten was denied parole in 2006 for the 16th time; Susan Atkins was denied parole in 2005 for the 11th time; Patricia Krenwinkel was denied parole in 2004 for the 11th time. Bruce Davis, who was convicted of Gary Hinman's murder, is awaiting the results of his 23rd parole hearing at the present time. Although Manson Family member Lynette Fromme did not participate in the Tate-LaBianca murders, she did attempt to assassinate President Gerald Ford in 1975. Sentenced to life in prison, Fromme had her first parole hearing in July 2005, but is still serving time in a federal penitentiary in Fort Worth, Texas.

SOURCES

Charles Manson denied 10th parole bid. (2002, April 25). *CBS News*. Retrieved November 19, 2006, from http://www.cbsnews.com

Charles Manson follower denied parole for 11th time. (2004, July 7). *North County Times: The Californian*. Retrieved November 19, 2006, from http://www.nctimes.com

Former Charles Manson disciple denied parole. (2006, September 6). *International Herald Tribune*. Retrieved November 19, 2006, from http://www.iht.com/articles/ap/2006/09/08/america/NA_GEN_US_Manson_Follower.php

Former Manson follower Susan Atkins denied parole. (2005, June 2). *The Associated Press State & Local Wire*. Retrieved November 19, 2006, from LexisNexis database.

Mclaren, J. (2005, June 27). Would-be Ford assassin up for parole. *The Lexington Herald Leader*. Retrieved November 19, 2006, from http://www.kentucky.com/mld/kentucky/

Thompson, D. (2006, October 17). Parole debated for Manson follower Bruce Davis. *The Mercury News*. Retrieved November 19, 2006, from http://mercurynews.com

across the Atlantic Ocean, telling him to get ready for the revolution. Manson's reply was to be in the form of an album: the album that Terry Melcher would not produce.

Chapter 9 from the book of Revelation was an integral part of Manson's interpretation of the Beatles' *White Album* and their call to him.

> Then the fifth angel blew his trumpet, and I saw a star that had fallen from the sky to the earth. It was given the key for the passage to the abyss. It opened the passage to the abyss, and smoke came up out of the passage like smoke from a huge furnace. The sun and the air were darkened by the smoke from the passage. Locusts came out of the smoke onto the land, and they were given the same power as scorpions of the earth. They were told not to harm the grass of the earth or any plant or any tree, but only those people who did not have the seal of God on their foreheads. (*The New American Bible*, 1987, 9:1–4)

In Manson's interpretation, the locusts were "beetles," and the abyss was a hole in the desert where Manson would lead his Family when the war came upon them. The passage continues on to describe the locusts, which were said to have "chests like iron breastplates," which Manson took to be the Beatles' guitars. According to various witnesses,

Manson believed that he was the fifth member of the Beatles and that they were calling to him through the *White Album* to tell him to make ready for the war that was coming.

In a twisted explanation of the Beatles' music, Manson believed that the *White Album* foretold the coming of a race war. Whereas the police initially believed the Tate murders to be drug related, the motive presented at trial was completely different. The Manson trial motive was one of "Helter Skelter." Not only were the words "Helter Skelter" found written on a door at the Spahn Ranch, they were also written and misspelled as "Healter Skelter" in Leno LaBianca's blood on the wall of the LaBianca home.

> Among the circumstances implicating Manson in the Tate-LaBianca murders are his frequently proclaimed prophesies of Helter Skelter. Predicting a war started by blacks "ripping off" white families in their homes, Manson stated that "Blackie" (the blacks) would revolt against and kill the "Pigs" (the white establishment). From 1968 through the summer of 1969 Manson told various people about Helter Skelter....He said Helter Skelter "was coming down fast" and that he "would like to show the Blacks how to do it." (*People v. Manson,* 1976)

Believing that blacks were taking too long in starting the race war, Manson believed that he could initiate the war that he thought was coming. Manson spoke of a cave beneath Death Valley, to which only he knew the entrance. There, the Manson Family would hide while "Helter Skelter" came down. The following excerpt from the trial testimony of former Family member Paul Watkins describes Manson's ideas:

> As we are making the music and it is drawing all the young love to the desert, the Family increases in ranks, and at the same time this sets off Helter Skelter. So then the Family finds the hole in the meantime and gets down in the hole and lives there until the whole thing comes down. (Testimony of Paul Watkins, 2003)

To facilitate the start of these race wars, after Manson tied up the LaBiancas and took Rosemary LaBianca's wallet, he had Kasabian hide the wallet in a bathroom at a gas station in a black neighborhood. Manson had hoped that a black person would find the wallet, use the credit cards, and thus the murders would be pinned on the black community. Unfortunately for Manson, when Kasabian hid the wallet in the bathroom on the evening of August 10, 1969, it went unnoticed and undiscovered for months until being recovered on December 10, 1969, by an attendant cleaning the toilet. However, the particular gas station where the wallet was hidden was not even in a black neighborhood, as pointed out by one of the defense attorneys at the trial. Yet, the prosecution was able to prove that the gas station was in the vicinity of Pacoima, which is a black ghetto in the San Fernando Valley (Bugliosi and Gentry, 1974, p. 494).

Although other motives have been offered, "Helter Skelter" was the motive used in court to prove the link between Manson, his Family, and the murders. Prosecutor Bugliosi's cocounsel at the beginning of the trial, Aaron Stovitz, encouraged the use of another motive during the trial, before he was pulled off the case due to time constraints. In Stovitz's opinion, "Manson ordered the killings to convince police the Hinman's murderer was still loose on the streets and that it was not Beausoleil. That's why it was important for Susan Atkins to write 'pig' in blood at the Tate home" (Keys, 1976, p. A14). At the Hinman murder scene, "political piggy" had been written on the wall. The connection had to be clearly visible if the police were to realize that the killer was still on the loose.

LAPD did tie the Hinman murder to the Tate-LaBianca murders but not in a manner that exonerated Beausoleil.

MEDIA COVERAGE OF THE MURDERS AND TRIAL

The Tate-LaBianca murders sparked immediate and intense media coverage. From the discovery of the bodies through the end of the trial, the media played a large part in what has since become known as one of the most convoluted and mystifying trials in American history. On August 10, 1969, the *Los Angeles Times* headlines read, "'Ritualistic Slayings' Sharon Tate, Four Others Murdered"; and the *New York Times* headlines read, "Actress Is Among 5 Slain at Home in Beverly Hills." The following day, as Tate's husband Polanski returned to the United States from London, new headlines reported the discovery of the LaBiancas. The *Los Angeles Times* connected the Tate and LaBianca murders at a time when even the LAPD was disavowing any connection with "2 Ritual Slayings Follow Killing of 5," "New Murders in Silverlake; Fresh Tate Clue."

Throughout the investigation, the media, with even less evidence than the police, misrepresented details of the crime and reported satanic overtones. The towel used to write "Pig" on the door at the Tate residence, when thrown back into the living room by Atkins, landed on Sebring's head. The towel became a "hood" in the media, leading *Newsweek* magazine to report dealings with black magic and voodoo. Speculation by friends indicated "that the murders resulted from a ritual mock execution that got out of hand in the glare of hallucinogens" ("Crime: The Tate Set," 1969). In the LaBianca case, the *Los Angeles Times* stated that "XXX" had also been carved into Leno's skin, when in reality only the word "WAR" was found (Torgerson and Thackrey, Jr., 1969). However, because of the amount of evidence released to the media, the police had difficulty retaining even a minimum of information to use during polygraph examinations. Eventually the police were forbidden to discuss the cases outside of work.

Whereas Sharon Tate had achieved only minor stardom during her lifetime, she was critically acclaimed in death. Studios rereleased some of her earlier movies, including *Valley of the Dolls* (1967) and *The Fearless Vampire Killers* (1967). The Hollywood jet set worried about the murders due to the proximity and the identity of the victims. The presence of drugs at the scene led to mass disposal of paraphernalia throughout the area. Quoted in *Life*, a film figure stated, "Toilets are flushing all over Beverly Hills; the entire Los Angeles sewer system is stoned" (Bugliosi and Gentry, 1974, p. 45).

As time went on and the trial began, the media coverage picked up again. The media played off of the American public's view of the trial and the defendants. Three young women and an older man were on trial for these brutal murders. As the information behind the identities of the defendants grew, the public recoiled at the truth: drugs, sex, violence, and the mind control of an older charismatic ex-convict. Articles were written about a band of hippies, known as the "Manson Family," living in Death Valley. Police were first told about the Family's possible connection to the Tate-LaBianca murders while interviewing a Family member involved in yet another murder case from Topanga Canyon, California.

Once all of the suspects were in custody, the state began building its case. Jury selection began on June 15, 1970, approximately ten months after the murders. Immediately sequestered following selection, the jury members were allowed only limited access to media sources in an attempt to guarantee the Manson Family members a fair and impartial trial. Jury members were allowed to read newspapers only after all articles and headlines pertaining to the Manson Family and the trial had been removed. When the trial finally began, the defendant's antics in the courtroom, as well as the actions of the Family members holding their vigil outside the court building, attracted continuous media attention. After Manson's lawyer initially requested and was denied a change of venue for the trial, the judge issued a "gag order" to limit the amount of press that would be associated with the trial. With the gag order in place, no one associated with the trial was allowed to discuss it. This occurred too late to stop the publication of Susan Atkins's tell-all "confession" interview. First a newspaper exclusive and eventually a book, the deal went through the evening before the "gag order" was issued (Bugliosi and Gentry, 1974, p. 262). For the general population, however, all they had to do was turn on the television or the radio to hear about the trial.

With the publication of Atkins's story, the media actually made a significant contribution to the prosecution's case. Atkins provided details about leaving the scene of the Tate murders after which the murderers changed clothes in the car and then stopped and tossed the bloody clothing over the side of a canyon road. Using the Atkins's story as a guide, a Los Angeles television crew from KABC-TV retraced the killers' route. "They found three sets of clothing: one pair of black trousers, two pairs of blue denim pants, two black T-shirts, one dark velour turtleneck, and one white T-shirt which was spotted with some substance that looked like dried blood" (Bugliosi and Gentry, 1974, p. 267). The clothing would later be identified as having come out of the Family's communal clothing pile in Manson's bus.

Even President Richard Nixon commented on the Manson trial. Standing in the federal building in Denver, Colorado, and complaining that the press had made Manson a glamorous hero, Nixon said, "Here was a man who was guilty, directly or indirectly, of eight murders without reason" ("Justice: A bad week," 1970, p. 7). Although he immediately issued a retraction, the damage was done. Newspaper headlines claiming, "Manson

CHARLES MANSON IN PRISON

Charles Manson is one of the most frequently communicated with prisoners in the entire Federal Bureau of Prisons. His past communiqués have not only helped university professors lead classes, but have also landed him interviews with CNN, BBC, and NBC's *Today Show* (Bugliosi, 1994, p. 651). Manson's current address is listed here (verified with Corcoran Prison's Mailroom, in November 2006):

Charles Manson
B – 33920
4A 4R-52L
PO Box 3476
Corcoran, CA 93212-3476

SOURCE

Charles Manson offers his help in teaching political science course. (1999, March 16). *Kansas News*. Retrieved February 25, 2004, from http://cjonline.com/stories/030299/kan_manson.shtml

Guilty, Nixon Declares," appeared across the country. Manson himself managed to gain access to a newspaper in the courtroom and displayed it to the jury before a bailiff pulled it away. The motion for a mistrial was denied, and the trial continued.

Outside the courthouse, the circus continued. Clustered on the street corner outside the courthouse were some of the Manson Family girls. Following the lead of the defendants inside, they carved Xs into their foreheads, and shaved their heads, yet again demonstrating the hold of Manson over his Family. The girls even vowed to set themselves on fire if Manson was sentenced to death ("Jury votes death," 1971).

MANSON IN THE MEDIA TODAY

More than 30 years have passed since the Tate-LaBianca murders and the sentencing of their killers. But Manson and the Family have stayed in the headlines. An Internet search will yield millions of Web sites listing Manson, his music, and the Family. Manson admirers can order T-shirts with his face on them, join his fan club, and even correspond with him. Incarcerated in California's Corcoran Prison, Manson still receives a great deal of fan mail from people wanting to join the Family. In 1999, Manson was contacted by Kansas political science professor Robert Beattie to help in his Newman University class. Manson provided Beattie with a 45 minute interview that the students used to hold a mock trial ("Charles Manson offers," 1999).

Numerous tell-all books by the defendants, other Family members, jurors, and the prosecutor, Vincent Bugliosi, have set out varying renditions of the motives, the facts, and the teachings of Manson. A CBS television movie *Helter Skelter,* which was initially released in 1976 and starred Steve Railsback as Charles Manson, has been authorized for a remake. "CBS's first adaptation of *Helter Skelter* was the highest-rated telecast of the 1975–1976 television season" (de Moraes, 2003). The 2004 version stars Jeremy Davies as Manson, and is described by the executive producer as focusing "on who Manson is, why he did what he did, and how he got people to kill for him" (Andreeva, 2003). Manson's music, drawings, and writings are also highly sought after. Music groups, including Guns 'N' Roses and the Beach Boys, have recorded Manson's lyrics. The group Nine Inch Nails purchased the infamous Tate mansion and turned it into a recording studio called "Le Pig." Marilyn Manson recorded parts of the album *Portrait of an American Family* (1994) at the Nine Inch Nails's studio.

Though he dislikes being labeled a "hippie," Manson's image throughout the trial was exactly that. During the age of American free love, the notions of peace, flower power, and a flourishing drug culture were permanently warped by the actions of Manson's Family. Particularly disturbing to the American psyche was the realization that one charismatic individual could warp the minds of average middle-class youth, and murder without guilt became possible. The strength of the American collective revulsion is evenly balanced by the allure of what Manson preached against and by the twisted meaning that free love came to embody. The Tate-LaBianca murders instilled fear into the establishment. Yet, the fear that remains etched on the American consciousness even today is not so much a result of the murders themselves, but rather revulsion at the nature of Charles Manson and the seemingly carefree manner in which the Manson Family murdered.

SUGGESTIONS FOR FURTHER READING

Bugliosi, V., and Gentry, C. (1974). *Helter skelter: The true story of the Manson murders.* New York: W.W. Norton and Company.

Emerson, B. (2004). Cielo Drive. Retrieved February 1, 2004, from http://www.cielodrive.com/
Linder, D. (2002). *Famous trials: The trial of Charles Manson 1970–71.* Retrieved November 19, 2006, from the University of Missouri-Kansas City School of Law Famous Trials Web site: http://www.law.umkc.edu/faculty/projects/ftrials/manson/manson.html

REFERENCES

Andreeva, N. (2003, August 4). CBS focusing on Manson for "Skelter" redo. *Hollywood Reporter, 379,* 1(2).
Anger, K. (Producer/Director). (1973). *Lucifer rising* [Motion Picture]. United States: Mystic Fire.
Atkins, S., & Slosser, B. (1977). *Child of Satan, child of God.* Plainfield, NJ: Logos International.
Bardsley, M. (2005). *Charles Manson and the Manson family.* Retrieved November 19, 2006, from Court TV: The Crime Library Web site: http://www.crimelibrary.com/serial_killers/notorious/manson/murder_1.html
Beausoleil, R. (n.d.). *Welcome to BeauSoleil.* Retrieved November 19, 2006, from http://www.beausoleil.net/
Benmussa, R. (Producer), & Polanski, R. (Director). (2002). *The pianist* [Motion picture]. France: R.P. Productions.
Bravin, Jess. (1997). *Squeaky: The life and times of Lynnette Alice Fromme.* New York: St. Martin's Press.
Bugliosi, V., & Gentry, C. (1974). *Helter skelter: The true story of the Manson murders.* New York: W. W. Norton and Company.
Bugliosi, V., & Gentry, C. (1994). Afterword by V. Bugliosi. *Helter skelter: The true story of the Manson murders* (2nd ed., pp. 637–70). New York: W.W. Norton and Company.
Charles Manson denied 10th parole bid. (2002, April 25). *CBS News.* Retrieved November 19, 2006, from http://www.cbsnews.com
Charles Manson follower denied parole for 11th time. (2004, July 7). *North County Times: The Californian.* Retrieved November 19, 2006, from http://www.nctimes.com
Charles Manson offers his help in teaching political science course. (1999, March 16). *Kansas News.* Retrieved February 25, 2004, from http://cjonline.com/stories/030299/kan_manson.shtml
Crime: The Tate set. (1969, August 25). *Newsweek,* p. 24.
de Moraes, L. (2003, August 5). With "Helter Skelter" remake, CBS again gives evil the eye. *Washington Post,* p. C7.
Emerson, B. (2004). Cielo Drive. Retrieved February 1, 2004, from http://www.cielodrive.com/
Faith, K. (2001). *The long prison journey of Leslie van Houten: Life beyond the cult.* Boston: Northeastern University Press.
Federal Bureau of Prisons. (n.d.). *Federal Bureau of Prisons Website.* Retrieved November 19, 2006, from http://www.bop.gov/index.jsp
Former Charles Manson disciple denied parole. (2006, September 6). *International Herald Tribune.* Retrieved November 19, 2006, from http://www.iht.com/articles/ap/2006/09/08/america/NA_GEN_US_Manson_Follower.php
Former Manson follower Susan Atkins denied parole. (2005, June 2). *The Associated Press State & Local Wire.* Retrieved November 19, 2006, from LexisNexis database.
Furman v. Georgia. (1972). 408 U.S. 238.
Gilmore, J., and Kenner, R. (2000). *Manson: The unholy trail of Charlie and the family.* Los Angeles: Amok.
Good, S. (2000). *Air, Trees, Water, Animals.* Retrieved November 19, 2006, from http://web.archive.org/web/20010514150113/http://www.atwa.com/
Jury votes death for Manson, girls. (1971, March 30). *Sacramento Union News,* pp. A1, A9.
Justice: A bad week for the good guys. (1970, August 17). *Time, 96*(14), 6–8.
Keys, L. (1976, June 13). "Helter Skelter" lawyer sees movie role as wry disguise. *(Pasadena) Star News,* p. A14.

King, G. (2000). *Sharon Tate and the Manson murders*. New York: Barricade Books.

Linder, D. (2002). *Famous trials: The trial of Charles Manson 1970–71*. Retrieved November 19, 2006, from the University of Missouri-Kansas City School of Law Famous Trials Web site: http://www.law.umkc.edu/faculty/projects/ftrials/manson/manson.html

Manson, C. (1986). *Manson in his own words*. New York: Grove Press Inc.

Manson, C. (1993, December 15). *Lie: The love and terror cult* [Audio CD]. Kendall Park, NY: Aware One Records.

Manson, M. (1994, July 19). *Portrait of an American family* [CD]. United States: Interscope Records.

Manson's shattered defense. (1970, November 30). *Time, 96*(22), p. 45.

Mclaren, J. (2005, June 27). Would-be Ford assassin up for parole. *The Lexington Herald Leader*. Retrieved November 19, 2006, from http://www.kentucky.com/mld/kentucky/

O'Neil, P. (1969, December 19). The wreck of a monstrous "Family." *Life, 67*(25), 20–31.

People v. Manson. (1976). 61 Cal. App. 3d 102.

Polanski remains fugitive from U.S. law. (2003, February 11). CNN.com. Retrieved November 19, 2006, from http://www.cnn.com

Polanski, R. (Producer). (1967). *The fearless vampire killers* [Motion Picture]. United States: Warner Home Video.

Polanski, Roman. (n.d.). *Roman Polanski*. Retrieved November 19, 2006, from the Internet Movie Database Web site: http://www.imdb.com/name/nm0000591/

Roberts, S.V. (1969, August 10). Actress is among 5 slain at home in Beverly Hills. *New York Times*. pp. 1, 63.

Roberts, S.V. (1970, January 7). Manson cult: Broken-family product. *Chicago Today*, p. 40.

Robson, M. (Producer), and Weisbart, D. (Writer). (1967). *Valley of the dolls* [Motion Picture]. United States: Twentieth Century Fox.

Testimony of Paul Watkins in the Charles Manson trial. (2003). Retrieved February 25, 2004, from http://www.law.umkc.edu/faculty/projects/ftrials/manson/mansontestimony-w.html

The Beatles. (1968, November 22). *White album* [Record]. U.K.: Capitol Records

The girl who almost killed Ford. (1975, September 15). *Time, 106*(11), pp. 8–12, 17–19.

The new American bible. (1987). Grand Rapids, MI: Catholic World Press.

Thompson, D. (2006, October 17). Parole debated for Manson follower Bruce Davis. *The Mercury News*. Retrieved November 19, 2006, from http://mercurynews.com

Torgerson, D. (1969, August 10). "Ritualistic slayings" Sharon Tate, four others murdered. *Los Angeles Times*, pp. A1, A18, A19.

Torgerson, D., and Thackrey Jr., T. (1969, August 11). 2 ritual slayings follow killing of 5. *Los Angeles Times*, pp. A1, A3.

Turner, M. (2004). *Charlie Manson.Com*. Retrieved February, 1, 2004, from http://www.charliemanson.com/home.htm

Turner, M. (2006). *CharlieManson.com*. Retrieved November 19, 2006, from http://www.charliemanson.com/

Vachss, A. (2006). *Roman Polanski media reports archive*. Retrieved November 19, 2006, from http://www.vachss.com/mission/roman_polanski.html

Watson, C.D. (2005). *A prisoner outreach with abounding love*. Retrieved November 19, 2006, from http://www.aboundinglove.org/

Whitehouse, J. (2005). *Susan Atkins-Whitehouse*. Retrieved November 19, 2006, from http://www.susanatkins.org/

Zappa, F. (1966). *Freak out: Mothers of invention* [Record]. United States: Rykodisc, Massachusetts.

17

The Ageless Anguish of Kent State

KATHY WARNES

One of the tragic legacies of the May 4, 1970, events at Kent State University is that the acrimonious debate and painful perspectives are still as fresh and real as if the confrontation had happened yesterday instead of nearly four decades ago. Historians, writers, and people from all walks of life discuss Kent State in different languages. Some history textbooks call the Kent State incident "the Kent State riot," while others, especially the survivors and their families, consider it "murder." Some Kent, Ohio, natives still feel that the students "got what they deserved," while others, like Dean Kahler who was wounded and paralyzed for life at Kent State, struggle daily with its impact. Elaine Holstein, the mother of Jeffrey Miller, one of the students killed, notes that she thinks about her son and Kent State daily and that the tragedy transformed her into a different person (Kelner and Munves, 1980, p. 26) People, both privately and publicly, have dispensed blame across a wide spectrum including the administration of Kent State University at the time, the Kent State professors, the Nixon Administration, Kent townspeople, parents, and the victims themselves. The Kent State confrontation between Americans can be considered one of the unhealed wounds of the Vietnam War era. Perhaps the fact that the events at Kent State are still being hotly debated is a positive indicator that free speech still exists in America in the midst of another controversial, divisive war.

The facts of the Kent State tragedy are that on Monday, May 4, 1970, Ohio National Guardsmen fired a 13 second fusillade of at least 67 shots into a crowd of Kent State University demonstrators, killing four and wounding nine Kent State students.

The circumstances leading up to the clash between the Ohio National Guardsmen and the students, many of them of the same generation, are reflections of the bitterness and divisiveness that the Vietnam War and the cultural conflicts of the 1960s had caused in America. American involvement in the Vietnam War continually escalated during the 1960s and in late April 1970, President Richard M. Nixon expanded the war by launching the invasion of Cambodia. He announced his decision on national television and radio on April 30, 1970, and stated that the invasion of Cambodia would enable the United States to attack Viet Cong headquarters, which used Cambodian territory as a sanctuary. College

311

Figure 17.1   A Kent State University student lies on the ground after National Guardsmen fired into a crowd of demonstrators in Ohio, 1970. © AP Photo.

students across the country angrily protested these actions, while many of their parents, many of the World War II generation that had sacrificed much, were torn between honest questioning and dismay at the behavior of the younger generation, which they felt was unpatriotic and did not know the meaning of sacrifice.

Kent State University students were among those who had strong feelings about the Vietnam War. The events leading up to the Kent State tragedy began on *Friday, May 1, 1970,* when students met to organize a protest demonstration against the Nixon Administration's invasion of Cambodia. They buried a copy of the American Constitution to emphasize that they felt that it had been "murdered," and called a second meeting for Monday, May 4, 1970, at noon. May had brought warm weather to Kent, and student indignation over the invasion of Cambodia rose with the temperatures. On Friday evening, drinking and excited debates produced a crowd that moved toward the center of Kent. Students broke some windows, and police were called and scattered the crowd at the intersection of Main and Water Streets. Leroy Satrom, the mayor of Kent, appraised the situation and, spurred on by rumors of a radical plot, declared a state of emergency and called Ohio Governor James Rhodes for help. The governor sent out a National Guard officer, and local authorities immediately closed the bars. Police in riot gear herded

Figure 17.2 **Ohio National Guardsmen throw tear gas at students during an anti–Vietnam War demonstration at Kent State University, 1970. The Guard killed four students and wounded nine.** © AP Photo.

the hundreds of people in the streets toward campus with tear gas. By 2:30 a.m., a deceptive peace settled over the town of Kent, Ohio.

The next day, *Saturday, May 2, 1970,* Kent students came back to help with the downtown cleanup. Kent merchants received them nervously because they had heard widespread rumors of radical activities and threats to their businesses. University officials increased tensions by securing a court injunction prohibiting the students from damaging buildings on campus. The Office of Student Affairs publicized the injunction by distributing leaflets. The National Guard entered the campus for the first time and set up camp directly on the university grounds.

Shortly after 8:00 that Saturday evening, 1,000 or more people surrounded the barracks that housed the Army Reserve Officer Training Corps on campus. A few people set the building on fire. Firemen tried to extinguish the blaze, but had to give up after someone punctured and cut open the fire hoses. Mayor Satrom requested Governor Rhodes to send the Ohio National Guard to Kent, because he feared that local forces were inadequate to stop disturbances. The Ohio National Guard, already on duty in Northeast Ohio, mobilized quickly and arrived in Kent about 10:00 p.m. Confrontations between Guardsmen and demonstrators, tear gas, and arrests punctured the night. The Guardsmen cleared the campus, herding students and nonstudents alike into dormitories. Many of them spent the night there.

KENT STATE AND KENT CITY

Kent State University had been founded as a normal school (a school that trains teachers) in 1910, and by the 1950s enrollment stood at 5,500 students. By 1970 it had grown to 21,000, and the population of the adjacent city of Kent kept the pace by expanding from a population of 4,500 in 1910 to 27,600 by 1970.

Even though Kent State and the city of Kent grew together, the university had not gained national renown. It attracted about 85 percent of its students from Ohio, and the typical Kent State student lived within driving distance of the University. For the most part, Kent State students were the sons and daughters of middle class people who had worked hard to give their children the college education that they never had experienced themselves.

As both the city and the college grew, their relationship changed. Once the university and municipal community had enjoyed mutual respect and admiration for each other, but time and a changing political climate in America turned the relationship suspicious and adversarial. Once Kent citizens had rented rooms and apartments to Kent State students, but eventually high rise dormitories replaced the housing provided by Kent residents. Families who lived in Kent were economically dependent on the industries located in the Kent-Akron area, and Kent residents expected students to fit in with the local economical and cultural expectations. Many of them did, but some students became radicalized and involved in the Students for a Democratic Society (SDS) and student antiwar demonstrations. Many Kent citizens believed that all students were radicals, refused to listen to their parents, dressed like "hippies," and did not appreciate America or the educational opportunities they were enjoying.

The makeup of the average college student had changed at Kent State and throughout the country. The evidence indicates that radical students did not make up a majority of the student population at Kent State. During the 1950s, panty raids had been the most radical events on campus along with the traditional mud fights that accompanied the yearly coming of spring.

The political and social upheavals of the 1960s brought unrest to the campus but did not radicalize it. In the fall of 1968, the SDS held its initial meeting at Kent State and both Bernadine Dohrn, the national SDS interorganizational secretary, and Mark Rudd, Columbia University SDS chairman, visited the campus. When Rudd concluded his speech in the University Auditorium, only 20 people applauded him. Even at the height of its popularity, the SDS membership figures totaled only one percent of the student body and many Kent State students opposed the organization and its goals.

In November 1968, the SDS again appeared on the campus calendar. The SDS and the Black United Students (BUS) sponsored a sit-in to protest the Oakland, California, Police Department's "vendetta" against the Black Panther party and what they saw as university administration oppressing radical groups and disrupting the recruiting of possible candidates by the Oakland Department. The Kent State administration threatened to bring charges of disorderly conduct against the sit-in participants. Six hundred Black students walked off the campus to protest the university action, and the administration admitted that it did not have enough evidence to press charges. The SDS interpreted the university admission as a weakening of its power and a student victory, but the BUS leaders dissolved their pact with SDS, because they saw the SDS leadership as being caught up in a fantasy revolution with victory and publicity attaining equal status.

In the spring of 1969, the Students for a Democratic Society again confronted the Kent State administration. Approximately 250 SDS members presented a list of their demands, including the abolition of the campus ROTC, and attempted to introduce the list at a meeting of the Kent State University's Board of Trustees held on campus in April.

The university police and a large crowd of about 700 anti-SDS students met the SDS members, and the two groups battled each other. The university suspended two SDS leaders and revoked the SDS charter as an official campus organization.

In April 1969, the university administration held a suspension hearing for an SDS member charged for his involvement in the clash between the SDS and the non-SDS students. SDS leaders slipped into the Music and Speech building during the hearing, and hundreds of anti-SDS students and university police confronted them in a demonstration. Eventually, the university called the Ohio State Patrol and 58 people were arrested and two SDS leaders were charged with inciting to riot and assault and battery.

Students revealed conflicting opinions in a referendum about the Music and Speech building demonstration. By nearly two to one margins, the students favored the suspensions, did not favor reinstating the SDS charter, but voted against the university bringing criminal charges against the people involved. Obviously, Kent State students did not support the SDS and its actions, and equally revealing was the fact that fewer than half of the student body cast ballots in the referendum. Even at the height of its popularity, the SDS membership figures totaled only one percent of the student body.

By the fall of 1969, Kent State University administrators were still on edge about the possibilities of further violence on campus, but the student body remained calm. Many Kent State students took part in the National Moratorium Day against the war in Vietnam, while others focused their attention away from politics and to the World Series and its outcome. Another "radical" sector of students had sponsored a "No Bra Day."

Relative calm still prevailed on campus for the spring quarter of 1970. Students did not turn out in droves for Earth Day, and fewer than one percent of the student body participated in an antiwar march. In April, Jerry Rubin, associated with the radical movement, visited Kent State and drew a crowd of about 1,000 students. The most controversial statements that Rubin made included a part where he advised students to buy guns and kill their parents. This frightened many citizens of Kent, but according to the editor of the campus newspaper, *The Kent Stater,* most of the students did not take Rubin seriously. Later in the month, nearly 300 Kent State students participated in the annual mud fight.

A survey taken in the spring of 1970 revealed these Kent State student body opinions:

78% favored retaining ROTC

63% opposed President Nixon's Cambodia decision

47% favored immediate and complete withdrawal from Vietnam

54% supported increased Vietnamization and gradual withdrawal

(The Ohio Council for Social Studies Review, 1998)

These statistics indicate that Kent State did not have a radical student body advocating total revolution against the government in 1970. Many students believed in working within the system to bring about change, and some were more concerned about a poor grade than the events in Southeast Asia. Other Kent State students were becoming increasingly dissatisfied with social and political conditions in America. Some students vigorously opposed the Vietnam War and others considered the citizens of Kent as part of the "silent majority" that Richard Nixon touted.

Then on April 30, 1970, in a televised address, President Richard Nixon told Americans of his decision to send American troops into Cambodia. On May 4, 1970, Ohio National Guard Troops fired into a crowd of students on the campus of Kent State University.

By *Sunday, May 3, 1970*, the Ohio National Guard, nearly 1,000 strong, occupied the campus of Kent State University and the town of Kent. Meetings between various factions produced conflicting perceptions and misunderstandings between state, local, and university officials. Governor Rhodes held a press conference that day, and his remarks underscored the "get tough" policy against demonstrators that the Federal Government sometimes expressed. He said that dissident groups using violence were going to be countered with:

> every part of the law enforcement agency of Ohio to drive them out of Kent. We are going to eradicate the problem. We're not going to treat the symptoms. And these people just move from one campus to the other and terrorize the community. They're worse than the Brown Shirts in the communist element and also the Night Riders and the vigilantes. They're the worst type of people that we harbor in America. . . . And I want to say that they're not going to take over a campus. (Gordon, 1990, p. 53)

Governor Rhodes vowed that he would keep the National Guard at Kent State University until he got rid of the dissenters. He implied that he would seek a court order declaring a state of emergency, something unprecedented. Both National Guard and university officials assumed that he was, in effect, declaring a state of martial law, which meant that the Guard controlled the campus instead of university leaders.

Curiosity seekers swelling the ranks of the crowd added to the confusion. As dusk fell, a crowd gathered on the Commons, a large, grassy area in the middle of campus, at the Victory Bell, which in calmer times was rung after winning games. The crowd would not disperse and at 9:00 p.m., the Ohio Riot Act[1] was read and tear gas fired.

The crowd scattered and demonstrators reassembled at the intersection of East Main and Lincoln Streets in Kent, blocking traffic. They anticipated that officials would appear and address their concerns, but no one came. This caused the crowd to turn hostile, and at 11:00 p.m. the Riot Act was read again and more tear gas fired. In the melee, both Guardsmen and demonstrators were injured, and on both sides there was bitter resentment.

Classes resumed on the Kent State Campus on *Monday, May 4, 1970,* but demonstrators were determined to hold the rally at noon, even if they were forbidden to do so. For its part, the National Guard vowed to disperse any illegal assembly. Throughout that

May morning, people continued to gather, and by noon, 2,000 people filled the commons and vicinity. Many of them knew that they were not supposed to be there. Others, especially the commuters, did not know about the ban on gathering. The National Guard ordered the crowd to disperse. Some of the crowd chanted, cursed, and threw rocks in answer. Shortly after noon, the Guard fired tear gas canisters, but the wind blew strongly so the gas had little effect. Next, the approximately 70 National Guardsmen moved forward with fixed bayonets, forcing the demonstrators to retreat. The Guard reached the crest of the hill by Taylor Hall, and forced the demonstrators over to a nearby athletic practice field, which was fenced in on three sides. The crowd had not scattered and the Guardsmen and the demonstrators traded more rocks, tear gas, and taunts. Witnesses reported that they saw the National Guardsmen go into a "huddle" on the practice football field.

Then the Guardsmen turned and retracted their steps, some demonstrators following as close as 20 yards but most between 60 and 75 yards behind the Guardsmen. Suddenly, the Guardsmen turned near the crest of Blanket Hill. In 13 seconds, 28 of the Guardsmen fired between 61 and 67 shots toward the parking lot.

Ironically, the scene resembled a Civil War battlefield. Four people were dying and nine were wounded. Jeffrey Miller, Allison Krause, William Schroeder, and Sandra Scheuer were killed. Jeffrey Miller was shot in the mouth while he stood in an access road leading into the Prentice Hall parking lot, approximately 270 feet from the Guardsmen. Allison Krause, shot in the left side of her body, stood in the Prentice Hall parking lot about 330 feet from the Guardsmen. William Schroeder stood about 390 feet from the Guardsmen in the Prentice Hall parking lot when a bullet struck him in the left side of his back. Sandra Scheuer stood about 390 feet from the Guardsmen in the Prentice Hall parking lot when a bullet pierced the left front side of her neck. Joseph Lewis, John Cleary, Thomas Grace, Alan Canfora, Dean Kahler, Douglas Wrentmore, James Russell, Robert Stamps, and Donald MacKenzie were wounded. All 13 were Kent State University students.

Among the demonstrators, stunned disbelief, fear, and fumbling attempts at first aid turned to flaming anger. Quickly, a group of 200 to 300 demonstrators gathered on a nearby slope. The National Guard ordered them to move. The situation teetered on the brink of additional carnage, but Kent State faculty members convinced the group to disperse. The Guardsmen, many who later said that they shot because they were fearful for their lives, were indeed in danger at this point in the confrontation. Many demonstrators in the large and intensely angry crowd were willing to risk their lives if the nervous and terrified Guardsmen again opened fire.

When the demonstrations had flared up days earlier, a group of Kent State University faculty had appointed marshals to monitor the situation. Professor Glenn Frank led other faculty members in imploring the National Guard leaders to allow them to talk to the demonstrators. The Kent State faculty begged the students not to risk their lives in another confrontation with the Guardsmen. After pleading with the students for about 20 minutes, the faculty marshals convinced them to leave the Commons.

A Kent State University ambulance rolled slowly through the campus announcing over the public address system that "By order of President White, the University is closed. Students should pack their things and leave the campus as quickly as possible" (Taylor et al., 1971, p. 10). Later that afternoon, the county prosecutor, Ronald Kane, secured an injunction from Common Pleas Judge Albert Caris that closed Kent State University. The Kent State campus stayed closed for six weeks. Classes did not resume until the summer of

1970, but faculty members worked through mail and off campus meetings to enable Kent State students to finish the semester.

RESPONSES TO THE SHOOTINGS

Combined with the nationwide student anger about the Vietnam War and general student unrest and rebellion against what many considered oppressive authority, the shootings ignited protests on college campuses across the United States, and many colleges closed because of violent and nonviolent demonstrations. Five days after the shootings, 100,000 people demonstrated against the Vietnam War in Washington, DC.

Commissions were created immediately after the killings. Kent State President Robert White created the first commission, which he titled "Commission on KSU Violence." The FBI made an 8,000 page long report on the shootings. The Ohio Bureau of Criminal Investigation made a report. The Knight newspaper chain made a 30,000 word report on the Kent State shootings. The most cited report is the Report of the President's Commission on Campus Unrest, which contains an investigation into what happened at Kent State, a report on the killings of two black students two weeks later at Jackson State College, and a report on campus unrest in general.

The President's Commission on Campus Unrest and the 1970 FBI report underscored and perpetuated the controversy surrounding the shootings at Kent State. The FBI report contains some troubling statements, including the assertion that some Guardsmen had to be physically restrained from continuing to fire their weapons, and that of the 13 students shot, none, "so far as we know, were associated with either the disruption in Kent on May 1, 1970, or the burning of the ROTC building on Saturday, May 2, 1970." Among the conclusions and statements of the Scranton Commission was the opinion that "the indiscriminate firing of rifles into a crowd of students and the deaths that followed were unnecessary, unwarranted, and inexcusable" (The Report of the President's Commission on Campus Unrest, 1970). Most of the reports concluded that the students were disorderly and destructive, but the Ohio National Guardsmen had no rationale to fire upon the students (Hensley, 1981, p. 24)

There are conspiracy theories about Kent State, and there are some indications that the Nixon White House could have been involved to some extent. A government memo dated October 9, 1973, reveals that "undercover federal narcotics agents were present on the Kent State Campus on May 4, 1970. The government's infamous Counter Intelligence Program (COINTELPRO), created within the Federal Bureau of Investigation (FBI) with the purpose of investigating, disrupting, and ultimately crushing antiwar dissent, flourished on May 4. During 1956–1971 the COINTELPRO operations targeted contemporary organizations that the FBI considered to be politically radical such as the Weathermen, the Black Panthers, Ku Klux Klan, American Nazi Party, and even Dr. Martin Luther King, Jr.'s Southern Christian Leadership Conference.

The legal aftermath of the Kent State shootings dragged on through the decade of the 1970s. The legal questions that the court cases addressed focused on the Guardsmen and their answer to the fundamental question: Why did they fire into a crowd of unarmed students? They did so, the Guardsmen said, because they feared for their lives. They felt that the demonstrators were threatening enough to justify firing their weapons in self-defense. If, on the other hand, the demonstrators did not present an immediate threat to the safety of the Guardsmen, the shootings were not justified. Federal, criminal, and civil trials

KEY INDIVIDUALS

THE CASUALTIES

The Dead

William Knox Schroeder and Sandra Scheuer were not protesting the Vietnam War on the day they were killed. Instead, they were trying to get to class despite the demonstrators protesting the War on their campus at Kent State University...

Ironically, William Knox Schroeder had won an ROTC scholarship to attend Kent State University, and had avoided all demonstrations and campus unrest. Most accounts say that he was walking away from the demonstrations when a bullet hit him in the back of the head, killing him.

Born on July 20, 1950, William Schroeder was raised in Lorain, Ohio. He applied for and received the Army Reserve Officer Training Corps Scholarship at age 17. A psychology major at Kent State, Schroeder also received the Academic Achievement award from the Colorado School of Mines and from Kent State. He earned the Association of the United States Army award for excellence in history.

William Schroeder's college roommate, Lou Cusella, is now a communications professor at the University of Dayton. Although Lou is a year older, he and Bill Schroeder grew up a block apart in Lorain, Ohio, and were good friends. He went to the morgue to identify his friend and remembered feeling sick at the sight of the orange corduroy bell-bottoms that Bill had bought during a shopping trip the two young men had taken together. "He was shot with a textbook in his hand. Along with being a great personal tragedy, it was a great national tragedy," Lou said.

Sandra Scheuer, was born August 11, 1949. She was an honors student in speech therapy and did not take part in any of the demonstrations, but had been walking to her class, 400 feet away from the Guardsmen. Her mother, Sarah Scheuer, said, "My daughter was a special person who was not involved in any of the demonstrations, yet in the press she was called a communist. We left Germany to guarantee that our daughters could live in a country with freedom" (Taylor et al., 1971, p. 11).

Mary Vecchio, a Florida runaway, saw a girl being carried into the yard at Prentice Hall, and she ran over with a rag thinking she could help. She realized that the girl was her friend Sandy. "She was so blue and gray. She had been shot in the jugular vein, and I didn't even recognize her" (Taylor et al., 1971, p. 12).

Allison Krause and Jeffrey Miller were more politically active and participated in some of the campus protests. Jeffrey Miller, a 20-year-old junior at Kent State, had graduated from Plainview High School in Long Island, New York, and entered Kent State as a psychology major. Again, Mary Vecchio, the runaway who should not have been at Kent State, but was there making friends, appeared in the center of the action. This time she knelt over the body of Jeffery Miller on the tarmac of the Prentice Hall parking lot, screaming. She told people that she was calling for help because she did not think she could do anything for Jeff Miller. John Filo, a Kent State photography major, stood near the Prentice Hall parking lot when the Guard fired. He saw the bullets hitting the ground, but did not take cover because he thought they were blanks. He stayed to take the picture of Mary Vecchio screaming over the body of Jeff Miller, he submitted it to a local newspaper, and the photograph took on a life of its own. It appeared in newspapers and magazines all over the country and eventually won John Filo the Pulitzer Prize.

The father of Jeffrey Miller said a few days after his son was killed, "This was not a violent kid. He was brilliant. He loved music. Why the devil did the guys have to have bullets in their guns, right in the chamber? It was one set of kids against another" (*New York Times,* May 7, 1970, p. 19).

Allison Beth Krause and her boyfriend Barry Levine also participated in the demonstrations. Allison said to him, "Barry, I'm hit." Levine said that he couldn't believe that she really had been hit. He stroked her cheek and saw a smudge of blood on her cheek. "And it had come from my hand, which was underneath her. I realized at that point she had been shot in the back and she was bleeding. And as it turns out, she was dying" (Taylor et al., 1971, p. 10).

The Wounded

Nine students were wounded in the Kent State shootings. Alan Canfora, age 21, from Barberton, Ohio, was shot in the wrist. John Cleary, age 19, from Scotia, New York, was hit in the upper left chest, and Thomas Mark Grace, age 20, from Syracuse, New York, was wounded in the left ankle. Dean Kahler, age 20, from Canton, Ohio, was shot in the spine and paralyzed for life. Joseph Lewis from Massillon, Ohio, was standing still with his middle finger extended at the Guard when bullets hit him in the right abdomen and left lower leg. Donald MacKenzie, from Summit Station, Pennsylvania, was hit in the neck, and James Dennis Russell, of Teaneck, New York, was struck in the right thigh and the right forehead. Robert Stamps, 19, from South Euclid, Ohio, was wounded in the right buttock, and Douglas Wrentmore, 20, from Northfield, Ohio, was wounded in the right knee.

Alan Canfora was the most active of the survivors of the Kent State shootings. Following the events at Kent State, he spoke throughout the country about the Kent State shootings and fought for other causes that he believed championed the common person. He stated that he believed that there was an extensive conspiracy of local, state, and federal officials to cover up the facts of what happened at Kent State University on May 4, 1970. He said that the criminals who committed murder did not spend one day in jail,

> but our efforts to expose the truth will serve as an example to others who are victims of such injustice. It is clear now that the cover-up went all the way up to the highest office. The secret memo indicates Nixon said to stall the Federal Grand Jury. (Casale and Paskoff, 1971)

Joe Lewis shared Alan Canfora's feeling that the responsibility for the Kent State shootings traveled up the chain of command beyond the National Guard to the state and federal governments. He stated that he believed that the significance of the 1970 Kent State incident to all Americans is that it was

> an enormous violation of Civil rights and the problem has never been answered. The trial in 1979 set a precedent. I don't think law enforcement officers will be as apt to shoot in situations similar to Kent State. (Taylor et al., 1971, p. 44)

THE GUARDSMEN

On May 4, 1980, John Dunphy of the *Akron Beacon-Journal* interviewed Larry Shafer, who had been one of the Guardsmen at Kent State on May 4, 1970. In the interview

Shafer said that he felt that the former General Robert Canterbury who was in charge of the troops did not have control of the situation and that the shootings could have been prevented. At the time of the interview, Shafer was a 34-year-old Ravenna fireman, and he said that city and campus police, the Ohio Highway Patrol, and the Portage County sheriff's office could have handled the situation. He also charged that Ohio Governor James A. Rhodes's decision to send the National Guard to Kent was calculated to aid his unsuccessful 1970 candidacy for the United States Senate.

Shafer contended that a sudden surge of rock throwing, screaming demonstrators convinced him and his fellow Guardsmen that they were in danger. The 1970 FBI investigation countered that the Guardsmen were not surrounded at the time of the shooting and there was not a sudden surge of students. The FBI also said that the Guardsmen fabricated the story that their lives were in danger after the shooting. Shafer argues that there was no conspiracy among the Guardsmen to fire into the crowd of demonstrators. Eventually, the FBI investigation precipitated the convening of a federal grand jury in December 1973. Shafer and eight other Guardsmen were indicted on criminal charges of violating the civil rights of demonstrators, but they were later acquitted. He was also one of the defendants in the civil suit that was settled in 1979, including the statement that the plaintiffs claimed as an apology. Shafer said that the statement was not an apology, but a statement of regret. "The whole thing was totally regrettable," he said (*Akron Beacon-Journal,* May 4, 1980).

Ohio National Guard Chaplain John Simons was also present at Kent State on May 4, 1970. He does not think that any one person is to blame for the 1970 shootings and does not think that his life was in danger. As for the historical significance of Kent State, he says that "it was the first time that middle class white students were shot by middle class young people" (*Akron Beacon-Journal,* May 4, 1980).

Seven members of Ohio National Guard Company G admitted firing their weapons, but claimed that they did not fire at the students. Five interviewed in Company G, the group of Guardsmen closest to Taylor Hall, admitted firing a total of eight shots, "but none of them at a specific student." Sergeant Richard Love of Company C said that he could not believe that the others were shooting in the air and he lowered his weapon (*Akron Beacon-Journal,* May 4, 1980).

The Faculty

The role that the faculty played in the events at Kent State on May 4, 1970, is often overlooked. After the faculty marshals talked the demonstrators into dispersing after the shootings on campus, they continued to advocate for the students. After the administration closed the university, the professors contacted the students with plans for them to finish their courses. One professor said that the university was "in fact never closed" (The Ohio Council, 1998).

Linda Lyke, now an Assistant Professor of Art at Occidental College, taught at Kent State in May 1970. Many students wanted to talk with the townspeople in the weeks after the killings. The students said they wanted to talk, so that it would not happen again. Meetings were held, but few Kent residents participated. She feels that "most of the townspeople have not changed. I don't think there's lots of sympathy in Kent" (*Akron Beacon-Journal,* May 4, 1980).

Glenn Frank, a Professor of Geology at Kent State, played a pivotal role in preventing additional violence. He wrote a letter to an eighth grade student in Ohio ten years after

> the May 4, 1970, tragedy in which he summed up the essence of the Kent State trag-
> edy. He said,
>
> > It is not at all curious that both extremes in this event firmly, and almost reli-
> > giously, believe that they have moral justice and righteous power supporting their
> > particular perceptions. Both extremes appear to delight in confrontation, provid-
> > ing that "their side" wins in court or in the "minds of Man." The extreme will
> > possibly not change their perceptions, and many of us are too emotionally
> > involved to differentiate between fact and perception, but this event is part of his-
> > tory and probably only time and the writers of history will sort out the good and
> > evil. We cannot change the past, but we can affect the future. (*Akron Beacon-
> > Journal,* May 4, 1980)

accepted the position of the Guardsmen that the shootings were justified. In 1974, District
Judge Frank Battisti dismissed a case against eight Guardsmen who had been indicted by a
federal grand jury. He ruled at mid trial that the government's case against the Guardsmen
was so weak that the defense did not have to present its case. In 1975, a longer and more
complex federal civil trial resulted in a jury vote of 9-3 that none of the Guardsmen were
legally responsible for the shootings. The last trial of the decade in 1979 ended with an out
of court settlement for $675,000, and the Guardsmen who fired the shots signed a state-
ment of regret. The State of Ohio, instead of the Guardsmen, paid the money, and the
Ohio National Guard viewed their statement as a declaration of regret instead of an
apology or admission of wrongdoing.

THE CASE IN AMERICAN CULTURE

The story of Kent State has been compiled, analyzed, chronicled, dissected, and interpreted by countless writers and historians with many of the analyses focusing on the guilt
or innocence of the Ohio National Guardsmen. In 1971, James Michener, a Pulitzer Prize
winning author who had written best sellers such as *Tales of the South Pacific* and *Hawaii,*
wrote what is probably the best known book about the shootings, *Kent State: What Happened and Why.* He took the position that the National Guardsmen fired in self-defense.
In 1973, Peter Davies, in *The Truth About Kent State: A Challenge to the American Conscience,* argued that the National Guard conspired to fire upon the students. In 1974,
Edward J. Grant and Michael Hill wrote *"I Was There": What Really Went on at Kent
State.* This is the only book written by members of the Ohio National Guard members.
The two Guardsmen give a retrospective of the hostile environment they were thrust into.

The vast body of literature written about Kent State still does not address some basic
questions about what happened on the campus on that fateful first week in May 1970.
These questions include:

1. Who was responsible for the violence that happened three days before the May 4 shootings? Were there really "outside agitators" as Governor Rhodes charged? Who really did
   set fire to the ROTC building?
2. Did officials including Ohio Governor James Rhodes and Kent State University President
   Robert White overreact? Was it really necessary to call in the National Guard?

JACKSON STATE COLLEGE: TRAGEDY TEN DAYS AFTER KENT STATE

College campuses seethed with unrest in the spring of 1970, a twisted, contorted stream of conflict and change continued from the 1960s. The issues in contention included Vietnam and its escalation, the Nixon Administration's sending of troops to Cambodia, the environment, civil rights, and women's rights. College campuses across America resounded with riots, confrontations, and calls for change.

Students at Jackson State College, a 3,500 student campus, heard about and protested the deaths of four Kent State College students ten days earlier on May 4, 1970. Jackson state students had spent the week before May 14, 1970, demonstrating and clashing with motorists harassing them along Lynch Street. Many of the students were upset because the Jackson Police Department refused to shut down the street.

Jackson State students also dealt with and protested against entrenched racism. Founded as a teacher's college in the late 1800s, Jackson State soon moved from its original location close to an all white area and established a new campus in a black neighborhood. A street called Lynch Street after Mississippi's first black congressman, cut across the Jackson State campus and linked west Jackson, a white suburb to downtown. Jackson State students did not participate in many protests because, as a state school, Jackson could not afford to alienate the all white board of education. Instead, students sometimes threw rocks and bottles at white drivers who shouted racial slurs at them as they drove downtown and back on Lynch Street. Earlier that spring a white motorist struck a female student who was crossing Lynch Street, but students gathered at Lynch Street had not rioted. On May 13, 1970, Mississippi Governor John Bell Williams ordered the Highway Patrol to keep order on the Jackson State campus, and the students did not resist. Governor Williams insisted that the 360 uniformed troopers of the Mississippi highway safety patrol were professional law officers, "not hotheads."

Then on May 14, about 9:30 p.m. Jackson State students heard a devastating rumor. Word had it that Charles Evers, brother of slain Civil Rights activist Medgar Evers, and his wife had been shot and killed in Fayette, Mississippi, where Charles Evers was the mayor. Again students gathered on Lynch Street, and this time they rioted. They set the ROTC building on fire, broke a street light, and built a small bonfire. They overturned a dump truck that had been left on campus at a sewer line construction site. Students threw rocks at passing cars, and the white motorists that they hit called the police. Firemen came to put out the fires, but they had to request police protection because students attacked them as they fought the fires. Police came and blocked off Lynch Street and an area of about 30 blocks surrounding Jackson College.

Mississippi National Guardsmen who were still on duty from rioting the night before massed on the west end of Lynch Street. They carried weapons without ammunition, and some weapons were mounted on armored personnel carriers. At least 75 Jackson City policemen and Mississippi State Highway Patrol officers armed with carbines, submachine guns, shotguns, service revolvers, and other weapons arrived at the Lynch Street side of Stewart Hall, a men's dormitory. Founded in 1939, the Mississippi State

Highway Patrol existed mainly to patrol highways, but then, in 1964, the Civil Rights movement focused on Mississippi. At this point, the state legislature gave patrolmen full power to enforce "all the laws of the state," including the ones supporting segregation. Local police and the state troopers held back the rioting students long enough for firemen to put out the fire and leave. After the firemen left, the police and state troopers, weapons at the ready, marched along Lynch Street toward Alexander Center, a women's dormitory. About 75–100 students stood shoulder to shoulder in front of the officers at a distance of about 100 feet, shouting obscenities at officers and throwing bricks. Someone broke a bottle on the pavement and the noise reverberated like gunfire.

Accounts differ about what happened next. Some students say that police advanced in a line, warned them, and opened fire. Others thought that a campus security officer had controlled the students. At 12:05 a.m. on May 15, Jackson police began shooting and fired for approximately 30 seconds. Students ran for cover, struggling to get inside the Alexander West dormitory. They stampeded at the west end of the door, frantic to get in. Some were trampled and others fell from buckshot pellets and bullets. Others were left on the grass or dragged inside.

When the order to cease fire rang out and the shooting stopped, Phillip Lafayette Gibbs, 21, lay dead 50 feet from the west end entrance to Alexander Hall. He had four gunshot wounds, two in his head, one under his left eye, and one in his left armpit. Gibbs had a wife, an 18-month-old son, and another child on the way. Across the street behind the police line, James Earl Green, 17, lay dead in front of the B.F. Roberts Dining Hall. A senior at Jim Hill High School, Green had been on his way home from work at a grocery store when he stopped to watch the riot. A single buckshot blast had killed him.

Besides the two dead men, casualties included 15 wounded students. One of the wounded had been sitting inside the dormitory lobby. Fonzie Coleman, Redd Wilson, Jr., Leroy Kenter, Vernon Steve Weakley, Gloria Mayhorn, Patricia Ann Sanders, Willie Woodard, Andrea Reese, Stella Spinks, Climmie Johnson, Tuwaine Davis, and Lonzie Thompson were taken to University Hospital for treatment for gunshot wounds, and several others were treated for hysteria and injuries from shattered glass. Gunfire riddled the five-story Alexander West dormitory. Later FBI investigators estimated that over 460 rounds had hit the building, shattering every window facing the street on each floor. There were over 160 bullet holes in the outer walls of the stairwell, and some of them can still be seen.

Shortly after the shooting the police and state troopers left the Jackson State College campus and National Guardsmen replaced them. John Peoples, who was the university president at the time, heard about the shooting from the National Guardsmen who arrived at his house located on campus carrying fixed bayonets. Jackson authorities denied that city police had taken part in the shooting, but never disputed that the highway patrolmen had fired. Later investigations revealed that the troopers did not bring tear gas, but instead, they loaded their shotguns with 00 shot, the largest available.

Police later insisted that someone inside the Alexander West dormitory had fired upon them and that they had spotted a powder flare in the third floor stairwell window. They also said that they had been fired on from the dining hall. Two television news reporters agreed that a student had fired first, but were unsure as to where. A radio reporter believed that a hand holding a pistol had extended from a window in the women's dormitory.

A U.S. Senate probe by Senators Walter Mondale and Birch Bayh later revealed that police did not call ambulances to take the wounded to University Hospital, which was only 20 minutes away, until the officers had picked up their shell casings.

According to other accounts, police also began to remove the shattered glass, but students and some sympathetic whites stood vigil on the lawn to keep them from doing this until investigators arrived.

On June 13, 1970, President Richard Nixon created the Commission on Campus Unrest, and it held public hearings at Jackson, Mississippi; Kent State, Ohio; Washington, DC; and Los Angeles, California. Despite the testimony of Jackson State administration, faculty, staff, and students, no arrests or convictions were made.

A civil trial was held, but none of the officers involved in the shootings were indicted. In 1974, a United States Court of Appeals ruled that the officers had overreacted, but they could not be held liable for the two deaths.

The Jackson City Council voted to close Lynch Street permanently to through traffic, and the Gibbs-Green Plaza, a multilevel brick and concrete structure that lies between Alexander Hall and the University Green, was constructed.

3. Did the Governor's banning of the rally violate the First Amendment rights of the demonstrators? Was this ban the flash point of no return for the demonstrators?

4. Why did the National Guardsmen fire on the unarmed students? Were they justified, and did they conspire to shoot students?

5. Was there one person or group of people ultimately responsible for the Kent State shootings?

The name of Kent State University will always be linked with the events of Monday, May 4, 1970, the only time in American history that federal troops shot United States students. Many people, including historians and the families of the victims, believe that more than any other historical event the shootings at Kent State helped turn public opinion against the Vietnam War. They believe that the United States withdrawal from the Vietnam War saved lives and to them that is the important legacy of Kent State. Writer Erich Segal expressed a sadder view in the *Ladies' Home Journal* when he said, "The meaning of the deaths of Allison, Sandy, Jeffrey and Bill is that they had no meaning. And yet even this is not the real tragedy of Kent State. The real tragedy is that some people thought they deserved to die."

The anguish of Kent State is that it happened in America, between Americans, and could have been avoided. As the Ohio National Guardsmen in their statement of regret said, "Some of the Guardsmen on Blanket Hill, fearful and anxious from prior events, may have believed in their own minds that their lives were in danger. Hindsight suggests that another method would have resolved the confrontation. Better ways must be found to deal with such a confrontation."

SUGGESTIONS FOR FURTHER READING

Caputo, P. (2005). *13 Seconds: A look back at the Kent State shootings* [Book and DVD]. New York: Chamberlain Bros.
Gordon, W.A. (1990). *The fourth of May: Killings and coverups at Kent State.* Buffalo: Prometheus Books
Payne, J.G. (1981). *Mayday: Kent State.* Dubuque: Kendall/Hunt.

NOTE

1. The Kent State University Web site about the tragedy questions the existence of an Ohio Riot Act. It reproduces a page of the General Laws of the One Hundred Eighty General Assembly of the State of Ohio, which gives generalized instructions about dealing with civic disturbances, but does not specifically refer to an "Ohio Riot Act." *Source:* http://speccoll.library.kent.edu/4May70/exhibit/chronology/riotact.html

REFERENCES

Bills, S. (Ed.). (1988). *Kent State/May 4: Echoes through a decade.* Kent: Kent State University Press.
Casale, O.M., & Paskoff, L. (Eds.). (1971). *The Kent affair: Documents and interpretations.* Boston: Houghton Mifflin.
Davies, P. (1973). *Kent State: A challenge to the American conscience.* New York: The Noonday Press.
Esterhas, J., & Roberts, M.D. (1970). *Thirteen seconds: Confrontation at Kent.* New York: Dodd, Mead and Company.
Gordon, W.A. (1990). *The fourth of May: Killings and coverups at Kent State.* Buffalo: Prometheus Books
Gordon, W. (1995). *4 Dead in Ohio: Was there a conspiracy at Kent State?* Laguna Hills: North Ridge.
Grant, E., & Hill, M. (1974). *I was there: What really went on at Kent State.* Lima: C.S.S. Publishing Co., Inc.
Hensley, T.R., & Lewis, J.M. (Eds.). (1978). *Kent State and May 4th: A social science perspective.* Dubuque, IA: Kendall/Hunt Publishing Company.
Hensley, T.R. (1981). *Kent State: Impact of judicial process on public attitudes.* Westport, CT: Greenwood Press.
John Dunphy interview with (former) Sergeant Larry Shafer, in "Guardsman Ends 10-Year Silence on KSU," *Akron Beacon-Journal,* May 4, 1980.
Kelner, J., & Munves, J. (1980). *The Kent State coverup.* New York: Harper and Row.
Michener, J. (1971). *Kent State: What happened and why.* New York: Random House.
The Ohio Council for the Social Studies Review, Summer 1998, Vol. 34, No. 1, pp. 9–21.
The report of the President's commission on campus unrest. (1970). New York: Arno Press.
Segal, Erich, "Death story." *Ladies' Home Journal,* October 1970, pp. 100–101, 148–49.
Taylor, S., Shuntich, R., McGovern, P., & Genthner, R. (1971). *Violence at Kent State May 1 to 4, 1970. The students' perspective.* New York: College Notes and Texts Inc.

18

The Attica Trials: A Thirty-Year Pursuit of Justice

SIDNEY L. HARRING AND GEORGE W. DOWDALL

The uprising at Attica Prison in 1971 and the political trials that followed represented an era of increasing politicization of the American prison. The civil rights movement, the Vietnam War, the student movement, and the law and order politics of the 1960s all had an impact on the men and women in prisons. Not only were politically astute leaders of the black and student movements in and out of prison themselves, but much of the prison population was increasingly politically aware. Eldridge Cleaver's book *Soul on Ice,* Alex Hailey's the *Autobiography of Malcolm X,* and other books had a profound impact on politics both inside and outside of prisons. Recurring political trials such as the trial of the Chicago Seven were on the evening news. Black, Hispanic, Native American, and white political organizations such as the Black Panther Party, the Weathermen, and the American Indian Movement had members both inside and outside of prison, as radical political action came to routinely result in prison time.

The election of President Richard Nixon in 1968 was a victory for the forces of "law and order" that had promised a "crackdown" on crime and led to a "war on drugs" and a "war on crime"—the domestic versions of the Vietnam War. Police tactics became increasingly militarized; legislatures passed new laws such as New York's Rockefeller Drug Laws that provided much longer prison sentences—up to life for possession of drugs. Prisons then, as they are now, were almost entirely filled by minorities, which made prisons a fertile ground for political organizing.

By the end of the 1960s, there was unrest in prisons all over the United States. In California, San Quentin Prison had a major strike in 1970. Also in 1970, three inmates at Soledad Prison in California were shot dead by a guard, an event widely believed by inmates to have been planned in advance.

THE ATTICA UPRISING AND THE RETAKING OF THE PRISON

These political and racial tensions came together in September 1971 in an explosive mix at Attica Correctional Facility in New York; Attica is a maximum security prison about 40 miles east of Buffalo, New York.[1] Attica appeared to observers at the time as a fairly typical maximum security prison that was similar to the other five prisons operating in New York State. Inmates lived in cells that were six feet wide by nine feet long, with all the buildings enclosed by a 30-feet-high wall. Attica held 2,243 inmates; about 20 percent had been convicted of homicide, manslaughter, or murder; and 10 percent were serving life sentences or awaiting execution. Unlike prisoners of the previous generation, many of Attica's inmates grew up on the streets of inner city ghettos, and the inmates often thought of themselves as political prisoners rather than common criminals. Although rehabilitation of these inmates composed part of the official rhetoric of Attica, the reality of everyday life centered on confinement within an institution devoted literally to maximum security. Education or training programs were rarely available for those who wanted them.

"Security" has continued to be the dominant theme: the fantasy of reform legitimatized prisons but the functionalism of custody has perpetuated them....For inmates, "correction" meant daily degradation and humiliation: being locked in a cell for 14 to 16 hours a day; working for wages that averaged 30 cents a day in jobs with little or no vocational value; having to abide by hundreds of petty rules for which they could see no justification. It meant that all their activities were regulated, standardized, and monitored for them by prison authorities and that their opportunity to exercise free choice was practically nonexistent: their incoming and outgoing mail was read, their radio programs were screened in advance, their reading material was restricted, their movements outside their cells were regulated, they were told when to turn lights out and when to wake up, and even essential toilet needs had to be taken care of in view of patrolling officers (New York State Special Commission on Attica, 1972, p. 2).

Medical care was poor. Sick call was held behind a screen but in the cellblock with little privacy. While doctors dispensed pills for simple ailments, long-term care and care for serious illnesses was either inadequate or nonexistent.

Built into daily life was a series of deprivations and humiliations that ranged from inadequate health care, an absence of recreation, bad food, and shabby clothing to the threat of violence, unwelcome sexual advances, menial work paid for at a fraction of regular wages, and despair at ever being paroled. In many ways, Attica approached the perfect definition of a "total institution," providing 24-hour-a-day and seven-day-a-week conformity to an absolute authority and an unwavering mass routine of life (Goffman, 1961). Incarceration in a total institution for years at a time must have had a great impact on a person's sense of self. Any inmate of such an institution might experience daily life as enormously frustrating, but one factor made it almost unendurable: the perception and reality of racism.

Race shaped every facet of daily life. Black inmates came to increasingly resent the degrading racism of white guards. Black prisoners could be routinely "written up" for minor disciplinary infractions and be locked up for weeks in the "hole." As social relations deteriorated, inmates became increasingly organized. A prison, in the best of times, is a difficult social organization and one in which inmates have many forms of organization and control that are invisible to their guards.

Black and Hispanic inmates did not have access to the best prison jobs, and jobs were important sources of power and social gratification in prison. Whites worked the good jobs as clerks, as runners, and in the officers' kitchen. Blacks and Hispanics worked in the shops and factories and cleaned the floors.

There were religious grievances as well. Black Muslims, in particular, were denied the right to practice Islam. The food being prepared in the prison kitchen was beyond their control, and conditions made it impossible to observe dietary requirements. Prison cooks were rumored to secretly put pork in many dishes, forcing devout Muslims to not eat any form of food that they could not clearly identify. Muslims were denied access to members of the clergy; however, these privileges were long granted to Catholic, Protestant, and Jewish prisoners. Muslims were denied leave from their work assignments on Friday afternoon to attend religious services. These adversities forged a strong Muslim culture within the prison: Muslim prisoners were highly disciplined and organized to protest these injustices.

In the fall of 1971 at Attica, the inmates had a sense that they had little to lose. They were serving hopelessly lengthy sentences in a prison with poor and deteriorating conditions. With daily tensions on the rise, the relationships between inmates and guards got worse, as did the interracial tensions among inmates. The heavily black and Hispanic inmate population, many from the New York City area, which was hundreds of miles away, was watched by a staff of 543 white guards from rural or small towns. "In the end, the promise of rehabilitation had become a cruel joke. If anyone was rehabilitated, it was in spite of Attica, not because of it" (New York State Special Commission on Attica, 1972, p. 4).

The Riot

In 1971, there was little evidence of organized planning of a revolt at Attica. Instead, the underlying tension exploded in a series of unplanned events that cumulatively brought about the capture of the prison by its inmates. A police force that was itself poorly organized reacted and took back the prison under circumstances that guaranteed great loss of life.

Events during the late summer of 1971 had led to an atmosphere charged with the threat of violence. Just as in the society outside the prison, organized protests against what were seen as inhumane conditions began to occur more frequently. Increasingly militant prisoners had drawn up a manifesto of demands, many surprisingly moderate, but they found little reason to think that prison authorities would respond to them. Correctional officers thought that their authority was being undermined, and mutual suspicion and fear became widespread.

In such an atmosphere, small events can lead to catastrophic outbursts. A misunderstanding among some inmates had escalated into a confrontation between the inmates and guards, and one guard was struck by a soup can thrown by a prisoner. On the next day, September 9, in A Block, which was one of four major sections of the prison, an altercation led to several prisoners attacking an officer who was trying to get them to return to their cells after breakfast. The prisoners broke free and began running through the cellblock on a violent rampage. Things might have ended there had a locked gate's bad weld not broken under pressure, which had allowed the inmates access to a control area known as "Times Square," which contained keys to other gates. The inmates began opening cellblocks and attacking correctional officers; one officer, William Quinn, was murdered.

TIMELINE

September 9, 1971	Prisoners seize control of Attica Correctional Facility. Corrections officer William Quinn murdered.
September 11, 1971	Prisoners present 28 demands to New York State officials.
September 12, 1971	New York's Governor Nelson Rockefeller refuses to visit Attica.
September 13, 1971	Corrections Commissioner Oswald presents ultimatum to prisoners. Prisoners reject ultimatum. State police forces retake prison; 39 prisoners killed, over 80 wounded.
1972	New York State Special Commission on Attica (McKay Commission) report published.
1973	Trials of Attica Brothers begin in Buffalo, NY. Inmate John Hill convicted of the murder of Officer William Quinn.
1976	The Meyer Commission recommends appointment of new special prosecutor. Governor Hugh Carey ends all Attica criminal prosecutions.
2001	Inmate class action civil suit settled; 502 inmates share $8 million award.

Resistance by the prison's guards was minimal, and within a few hours 1,281 inmates had seized control of much of the prison and had taken over 40 hostages with most congregating in the yard in D Block.

Prison officials were unable to respond quickly enough to quell the uprising; insufficient manpower, an inadequate communication system, and no plan for dealing with a large uprising contributed to the outcome. A later investigation would reveal that this was not a planned rebellion but more of a spontaneous riot. Apparently there had been some talk among prisoners of a sit-down strike, but there was no prior evidence of anyone taking over the prison. Prison officials and, after a time, New York State Commissioner of Corrections Russell Oswald began negotiating with those prisoners who emerged in the yard as leaders. A hastily assembled force of state police, correction officers, and county sheriffs kept watch outside of the prison walls. The media also began to gather outside with press and film crews from all over the world eventually reaching the site.

After a period of disorganization and anarchy, the emerging leaders of the rebellion began to negotiate in earnest. A 50-yard buffer, or no-man's-land (termed the "DMZ," or demilitarized zone), separated inmate spokesmen and state authorities; communication between the two sides initially involved shouting across that space. Commissioner Oswald rushed from Albany to take charge of the scene. Several notable journalists, lawyers, and politicians joined the negotiations as observers. Herman Schwartz, a professor of law, and Arthur O. Eve, an assemblyman, had come from Buffalo, and they were allowed by the commissioner to visit the inmates in D yard; Oswald, Schwartz, and Eve returned together for a second visit, and they were accompanied by reporters and television cameras. The leaders in D yard began to discuss demands and talk with observers who continued to visit them. Tom Wicker, associate editor and columnist for the *New York Times,* joined the team of observers and later wrote one of the most important eyewitness accounts of the uprising and retaking of the prison (Wicker, 1975).

By Saturday afternoon on September 11, the observers had formulated a 28-point list of prisoner demands that were deemed acceptable by Commissioner Oswald; the list included reforms that addressed many of the sources of tensions. Some of the demands

Figure 18.1 Inmates of Attica State Prison raise their hands in clenched fists as they voice their demands during a negotiating session with New York's prison boss, Commissioner Russell Oswald, 1971. The Commissioner subsequently agreed to some of the 21 demands listed by prisoners. © AP Photo.

were unchanged from the language used by the prisoners and observers. For example: "6) Allow all New York State prisoners to be politically active, without intimidation or reprisal"; and "7) Allow true religious freedom" appeared as both the observers' proposal and as a proposal acceptable to Commissioner Oswald. Others were different. For example, the observers stated, "Apply the New York State minimum wage law to all work done by inmates. STOP SLAVE LABOR." The proposal acceptable to Commissioner Oswald stated, "Recommend the application of the New York State minimum wage law standards to all work done by inmates. Every effort will be made to make the records of payments available to inmates." Although Oswald held firm on the issue of criminal amnesty, he agreed that there would be no administrative reprisals or criminal charges that dealt with property damage during the rebellion (New York State Special Commission on Attica, 1972, pp. 250–258).

Retaking the Prison

A few hours later, the "Twenty-Eight Points" that Commissioner Oswald found acceptable were rejected by the prisoners because the list did not include criminal amnesty. Rumors about reprisals circulated among the inmates that made further negotiation almost impossible. Criminal amnesty became the critical issue; many of the prisoners feared that a wave of mass prosecutions would follow the retaking of the prison. A few of the inmates were also worried about their involvement in the murder of Officer William Quinn on the rebellion's first day and in the murders of several prisoners during the following days. On Sunday, September 12, as negotiations failed, the outside observers and eventually Commissioner Oswald requested that Governor Nelson Rockefeller come to the prison. By Sunday evening, Rockefeller declined, instead approving the retaking of the prison by force with as little violence as possible.

At 7:40 a.m. on Monday, September 13, the commissioner's ultimatum was read to the prisoners in D yard. The prisoners' response came about an hour later: eight blindfolded hostages with knives to their throats were paraded across the catwalks. If a slim hope of a peaceful resolution had existed, it was now gone. At 9:30 a.m., the prisoners formally rejected the ultimatum, and 16 minutes later, the assault on the prison began with tear gas being dropped on inmates in D yard by a state police helicopter.

What happened next is best described in the often-cited words of the Special Commission that investigated the events at Attica:

> Forty-three citizens of New York State died at Attica Correctional Facility between September 9 and 13, 1971. Thirty-nine of that number were killed and more than 80 others were wounded by gunfire during the 15 minutes it took the State Police to retake the prison on September 13. With the exception of Indian massacres in the 19th century, the State Police assault which ended the four-day prison uprising was the bloodiest one-day encounter between Americans since the Civil War. (New York State Special Commission on Attica, 1972, p. xi)

Figure 18.2 **Inmates of Attica state prison, right, negotiate with state prisons Commissioner Russell Oswald, lower left, at the facility in Attica, NY, 1971. © AP Photo.**

One correctional officer had been killed on the first day of the uprising, and several prisoners had been murdered by their fellow inmates; the remaining 39 deaths were from police bullets. The conditions under which the prison was retaken virtually guaranteed a very high loss of life, despite specific orders to use minimum force. The police forces that retook the prison used weapons such as shotguns, which were likely to cause numerous casualties. Police and correctional officers had no training in this type of assault, and they did not seek assistance from other forces, including the military, which was trained. Police feared that the inmates were heavily armed, and over 1,400 weapons were confiscated after the retaking of the prison. Correctional officers participated in the takeover, despite orders from the governor to not do so for fear of revenge against prisoners, and these officers were responsible for several deaths. Rumors quickly spread that guards had their throats slit, but no evidence was found to support this charge.

After the resistance ended, the occupying forces secured the prison and forced the prisoners to strip naked before returning to their cells. In the ensuing hours, prisoners were brutally beaten by state employees, and reports of torture were alleged. Medical treatment of the wounded was delayed for four hours by inadequate planning; and although no prisoner died as a result of the delay, many prisoners suffered unnecessarily from excruciating wounds. An inventory of prisoner injuries taken several days after the retaking of the prison found that 45 percent of the prisoners had broken bones as well as other signs of the reprisals against them.

MEDIA COVERAGE OF ATTICA: AN "EXPLOSION OF RHETORIC"

A unique aspect of the events at Attica was the extraordinary media coverage. Television cameras were allowed into the prison when the commissioner and several observers began negotiations. The result was characterized by one observer as "an explosion of rhetoric"; prisoners stated their grievances while state officials attempted to justify their actions.

Media from around the world covered the uprising and retaking of the prison, and much of the retaking was photographed by state police using still and video cameras. These images were published in newspaper and television accounts all over the world, and shaped the public perceptions of Attica. Years later, the images found their way into several powerful documentary films such as *Attica* and *Ghosts of Attica*. Tom Wicker's first-person account of his role as an observer provided the basis for the film *Attica*.

Initial coverage of the prison retaking tended to follow the arguments presented by state officials. On the day immediately following the state police assault on Attica, the *New York Times,* one of America's most influential newspapers published the following: "In this worst of recent American prison riots, several of the hostages—prison guards and civilian workers—died when convicts slashed their throats with knives. Others were stabbed and beaten with clubs and lengths of pipes." The following day, the *Times* commented, "The deaths of [the hostages] reflect a barbarism wholly alien to our civilized society. Prisoners slashed the throats of utterly helpless, unarmed guards whom they had held captive through around-the-clock negotiations, in which the inmates held out for an increasingly revolutionary set of demands." The *New York Daily News* ran a story with the headline, "I saw seven throats cut" (New York State Special Commission on Attica, 1972, pp. 455–456).

IMPORTANT INDIVIDUALS AND GROUPS

Attica Brothers Legal Defense: Legal defense team that represented inmates in criminal trials.

Attica Correctional Facility: Maximum security prison 40 miles east of Buffalo, NY, and site of the 1971 uprising.

Carey, Hugh: Governor of New York who dismissed all criminal prosecutions of Attica inmates.

Clark, Ramsay: Former U.S. Attorney General who led criminal defense efforts.

Eve, Arthur O.: New York State Assemblyman, and observer during uprising.

Fair Jury Project: Part of legal defense that used surveys and research to pick fair juries.

Fink, Elizabeth: Lawyer who pursued civil damages on behalf of Attica inmates.

Hill, John: Only Attica inmate convicted of murder of Officer William Quinn.

Kairys, David: Civil rights lawyer who led criminal defense efforts.

Kuntsler, William: Famous radical lawyer who led criminal defense efforts.

McKay, Robert B.: NYU Law Dean who chaired commission that studied the uprising.

Oswald, Russell: New York State Corrections Commissioner who negotiated for surrender of Attica.

Quinn, William: Corrections officer murdered during first day of uprising.

Rockefeller, Nelson: Governor of New York at the time of the uprising; refused to visit the prison.

Schwartz, Herman: Professor of Law at SUNY Buffalo, and observer during uprising.

Shulman, Jay: Social psychologist who aided legal defense efforts.

Wicker, Tom: *New York Times* reporter, and observer during uprising.

Days later, newspapers would run stories that confirmed that all nine dead hostages had died from bullet wounds as part of the massive assault by state police forces. However, the false media images of revolutionary prisoners slitting hostage throats had already been burned into the public consciousness; those persisting images would shape the ensuing trials.

New York State convened a Special Commission on Attica, also known as the McKay Commission, which was named after New York University's law school dean who was named to chair the commission. The commission interviewed 1,600 inmates, 400 correctional officers, and 270 officers of the New York State Police. The commission also had access to autopsy reports and other physical evidence. The commission's report (New York State Special Commission on Attica, 1972) and books by observers such as *New York Times* journalist Tom Wicker (1975) provide a virtually complete account of the events. What happened in the retaking of the prison is not in doubt, but its political meaning remains controversial to this day.

THE POLITICAL CHARACTER OF THE PROSECUTIONS

Governor Nelson Rockefeller of New York was one of the leading Republican politicians in the United States, and Rockefeller had clear presidential ambitions. His reputation was at stake, and it required vindication. Accordingly, the Attica prosecutions were directed by Assistant Attorney General Anthony Simonetti, who had been appointed special prosecutor along with a large staff of prosecutors handpicked from around New York State and a much larger staff of police investigators. The police investigations were biased from the start. Although state police had fired almost all of the 3,000 shots, state police investigators led the investigation, which was a clear conflict of interest. Moreover, from the start, the investigation was focused on crimes committed by unarmed inmates to the exclusion of the crimes committed by armed state police and prison guards; evidence clearly showed that state police and prison guards had killed dozens of people and tortured hundreds more.

This bias aside, the investigation proceeded in an uneven and incompetent manner. The evidence was in chaos, as thousands of witnesses remembered fluid and complex events in very different ways. The inmates, as well as the officers, were all dressed alike, and individual identifications were uncertain at best. A few inmate "stooges" were promised immediate release if they testified against fellow inmates. Evidence was deliberately distorted in a one-sided way to overemphasize inmate actions and exonerate guard actions.

Three years into the trials, Malcolm Bell, an assistant prosecutor, resigned his position in protest of the political nature of the prosecutions and submitted a lengthy report to Governor Hugh Carey—the new governor of New York who was a Democrat. Bell detailed the bias and misconduct in the special prosecutor's office. Carey appointed a commission, the Meyer Commission, which was named after its chairperson. The Meyer Commission reported some months later that the prosecution was riddled with bias and other problems, and the commission recommended that Carey appoint a new special prosecutor to begin investigation into the state's misconduct as well. Carey reacted by "closing the book" on the Attica case by ending all the criminal prosecution. The case was over. By this time, former Governor Rockefeller was now Vice President of the United States with no political authority left in New York State.

THE ATTICA BROTHERS LEGAL DEFENSE AND THE FAIR JURY PROJECT

A unique aspect of the Attica trials was the organization of the defense efforts—the Attica Brothers Legal Defense (ABLD). The ABLD assembled a legal staff, raised funds to support their efforts, publicized the defense view of the trials and its political agenda, and led demonstrations in support of the defendants in Buffalo and in New York City. The ABLD assumed that the inmates' defense should not be a narrow legal response to the charges against them, but rather a broad effort to promulgate their version of the rebellion and advance their political views about the need for radical change throughout the United States.

The team of lawyers who began to work for ABLD included the famous radical lawyer William Kunstler (defense lawyer for the Chicago Seven and other antiwar radicals of the 1960s), Ramsay Clark (former Attorney General of the United States and a spokesperson for radical social change), and David Kairys (at the beginning of a career as a civil rights and constitutional lawyer). Other attorneys who worked on the trials included Elizabeth

Fink, who for several decades conducted an effort on behalf of civil damages for the inmates of Attica.

ABLD also helped launch an effort that became known as the Fair Jury Project, which was designed to deal with the extraordinary challenges the Attica Brothers faced as criminal defendants. The initial indictments against the defendants were brought in Wyoming County, which is the county in which Attica is located. All the defendants were serving time after convictions for very serious crimes. Most were African Americans and Hispanics from New York City who were about to be tried in a virtually all-white upstate county at a time of high racial tension. Television, radio, and print coverage of the uprising had blanketed western New York with indelible images of violence, and rumors had circulated that the prisoners had tortured hostages and slit their throats. Attica Prison was one of the largest employers in Wyoming County, and many potential jurors had ties to the prison.

The Fair Jury Project conducted a telephone survey of Wyoming County that established empirically that many potential jurors would have a difficult time in providing the defendants with a fair trial. Potential jurors admitted that they could not follow a judge's instructions to ignore the enormous pretrial publicity or presume that the defendants were innocent of the charges until proven guilty. The survey helped support defense arguments for a change of venue, but the court ruled that the trials would be moved to nearby Erie County and not to New York City, as the defense had argued.

A storefront in downtown Buffalo was used as the base of operations for ABLD, and the legal team worked several blocks away out of separate offices. In addition, an office was opened in New York City, both to influence the national media and to provide services for those brothers who came from downstate New York. Other ABLD offices functioned for a time in several other cities, including Detroit, Michigan, and Oakland, California.

The Fair Jury Project studied the jury pool of Erie County and used statistical analysis to show that its composition was skewed toward being disproportionately white, middle-aged men. The composition again posed major difficulties for the defendants' chances of a fair trial by a jury of peers (Levine and Schweber-Koren, 1977). Staff from the jury commissioner's office verified that potential female jurors were being excluded because of improper use of a "women's exemption" allowed at that time under New York law. A series of charts made clear that the Erie County jury pool was anything but a reasonable cross-section of the community from which it was drawn. A motion submitted by the defense led to 97 percent of the existing Erie County jury pool to be thrown out; this was perceived as a major victory for the defense.

A telephone survey of 651 registered voters was conducted by the Fair Jury Project to help defense lawyers assess which individuals might be most likely to set aside their prior opinions about prisoners and the uprising and follow the judge's instructions to presume innocence. The survey results provided a snapshot of contemporary opinion about the trials, indicating widespread bias against the defendants. As one press release from the ABLD summarized, "The results of the study not only show strong and pervasive prejudice against black people, persons who seek change, and persons accused of crime—all leading to the conclusion that most people in Erie County could not function as impartial jurors if called to sit on these cases." The survey found that 69 percent of the potential jurors blamed the prisoners for the killing of 43 persons, and 19 percent still believed the rumors that the hostages had been castrated or had their throats slit. Most people viewed strong protest as unjustified, and about a third would imprison black militants and radicals solely for their beliefs. About 50 percent believed prison conditions to be excellent or satisfactory.

The survey findings were combined with courtroom analysis of potential juror body language and response to voir dire questions in an effort to help select a "fair jury." This part of the project was led by Jay Schulman, a social psychologist who had previously used these techniques in picking a jury for the Harrisburg, Pennsylvania, trial of Catholic anti-war activists (Hunt, 1982; Schulman, Shaver, Colman, Emrich, & Christie, 1973). ABLD staff sat at the defense table during jury selection in an attempt to guide attorneys in their decisions about which potential jurors to challenge "for cause" or which to deselect for other reasons.

THE SIX ATTICA CRIMINAL TRIALS

Sixty-two inmates and one prison guard were indicted by a grand jury in Wyoming County, the rural county where Attica Prison was located, for 1,289 alleged crimes that ranged from assault to murder. Only 8 of the 62 inmates were ultimately convicted. John Hill was the only inmate convicted of murder for the death of Officer William Quinn; Officer Quinn's death occurred during the initial taking of the prison. Joseph Pernasilice, also charged in Quinn's murder, was acquitted, but he was convicted of the lesser crime of attempted assault.

The evidence at this trial reflected the difficulty of these cases. Quinn, a young man, had died tragically with a wife and children left behind. He was the only guard killed, which clearly indicated that the inmates had no plans to kill guards in the uprising. Rather, Quinn had been at the wrong place at the wrong time; he was in a stairwell as hundreds of excited inmates pushed past him. Some of the testimony was that he fell; other testimony was that he was pushed or trampled accidentally. Still, other testimony indicated that Hill and Pernasilice had beaten Quinn with different and inconsistent descriptions of the weapon used. In the end, the jury believed that Hill had beaten Quinn to death.

The special prosecutor's years of investigation and preparation collapsed in poorly presented cases (Light, 1995). One government witness, a prison employee, had positively identified an inmate as holding a flare gun in a tunnel during the riot. A defense lawyer asked the witness if he had ever called inmates "niggers." The prison employee admitted that he had but qualified that he only did so when it was appropriate in the context of their rehabilitation. The lawyer then asked the officer to describe how that word contributed to rehabilitation. The jury acquitted—such testimony could have no credibility.

In one trial, several inmates were charged with the murder of inmate "snitches." The testimony was inconsistent, and inmates had been offered various inducements to testify. The jury did not believe the witnesses and acquitted.

The trials were still proceeding at the time Special Prosecutor Malcolm Bell wrote his memo to Governor Carey. Carey not only ended the trials, but he pardoned the seven Attica Brothers who had been convicted—and commuted the 20-years-to-life sentence of John Hill. If the prison guards and state troopers were not to be punished for firing the 3,000 shots that killed 40 inmates and guards or for torturing Big Black and the hundreds of other inmates, it was not fair to punish John Hill for killing William Quinn. Nothing in these results represented justice from any standpoint.

THE CIVIL CASES

The Attica civil cases, filed by inmates and hostages, are some of the most complex and lengthy civil suits ever filed against New York State (Light, 1995). The most important of the early lawsuits, *Inmates of Attica Correctional Facility v. Rockefeller,* was filed immediately after the retaking of the prison while inmates were being tortured. The United States Court of Appeals for the Second Circuit issued what is still considered a landmark opinion denouncing the use of force by corrections officers:

> The beatings, physical abuse, torture, running of gauntlets, and similar cruelty—was wholly beyond any force needed to maintain order. It far exceeded what our society will tolerate on the part of officers of the law in custody of defenseless prisoners.... [T]he mistreatment of inmates in this case amounted to cruel and unusual punishment in violation of their Eighth Amendment rights. (*Inmates of Attica Correctional Facility v. Rockefeller,* 1971)

Inmates of Attica Correctional Facility v. Rockefeller was part of a wide range of lawsuits filed by prisoners in the 1970s that created a new category of human rights law: the law of prisoners' rights. Prisoners today live under improved prison conditions because of this litigation. It is now clear that a prisoner still maintains substantial rights as a citizen while incarcerated. Hundreds of lawsuits about prisoners' rights—to medical care; safe working conditions; improved "housing" conditions; access to lawyers, courts, reading materials, and the media; religious freedom; and due process rights in prison discipline—were all litigated in the wake of the Attica litigation. Attica prisoners had taken a stand that prisoners needed to be respected as U.S. citizens and as human beings.

Other lawsuits seeking to remove indicted inmates held in segregated housing units and to block prison disciplinary hearings against inmates for their role in the uprising were not successful.

Other cases went through the courts for many years. The 28 hostages and/or their families who were killed or injured in the uprising filed many lawsuits. All except one of these lawsuits were dismissed on a technicality: as state employees they were barred from filing lawsuits for damages if they had accepted workmen's compensation. Most of the state employees had taken such checks—they were working people with no money to live on —without realizing that such acceptance would bar filing lawsuits. The widow and daughter of Herbert Jones were the only officer's family members to prevail; they had not accepted their checks and were awarded $550,000 plus interest. This left the families of the officers feeling bitter: the state denied them the right to sue for their injuries on the technicality of workmen's compensation law.

Fourteen inmates sued in the Court of Claims for injuries sustained in the uprising; nine inmates were awarded about $1.5 million in damages. These cases moved at a proverbial snail's pace. Inmate Peter Tarallo complained in 1983 that his life had been shortened by his injuries in the Attica retaking and that he would not live to see any money. His estate was awarded $164,000 in 1989—18 years after the uprising and after Tarallo was, as he had feared, dead.

In 2001, the inmate class action suit was settled almost 30 years after the retaking of the prison. This complex lawsuit sought damages of $2.8 billion from Governor Rockefeller, Corrections Commissioner Oswald, Attica Warden Vincent Mancusi, Deputy Warden Karl Pfiel, and other state officials for violation of prisoner rights, excessive force, unrestricted firepower that caused death, serious injury, and suffering (Light, 1995). The case had a complicated legal history and was tried in Buffalo in 1991. Ten more years of appeals and negotiations passed before a settlement was agreed to in 2001. The 502 inmates would share $8 million, apportioned by the judge into five categories, depending on the degree of their injuries. More than half fell into the lowest category, receiving what can only be called a token payment of $6,500. The other half received either $10,000, $25,000, or $31,000 for the relatives of inmates who had died. Fifteen inmates received the highest award of $125,000. Elderly men and their families came to court for the settlement. They told stories that many had not told since they left Attica, but all of them agreed that it was important that the case was settled. The world would know that the New York State had committed serious crimes against them at the retaking of Attica prison.

THE LEGACY OF ATTICA

What impact did the Attica trials have? A year after the uprising, the McKay Commission argued,

> Unless the cry to "Avenge Attica" can be turned to reforms that will make repetition impossible, all effort will have been in vain. Change should not be lightly undertaken, but the status quo can no longer be defended. The only way to salvage meaning out of the otherwise senseless killings at Attica is to learn from this experience that our Atticas are failures. The crucial issues remain unresolved; and they will continue unresolved until an aroused public demands something better. (New York State Special Commission on Attica, 1972, p. xxi)

Now, decades later, prison reform appears to be grappling with remarkably similar issues. Racial inequality remains at the heart of the U.S. criminal justice system, and prisons still incarcerate a far larger proportion of minorities than would be expected from population size alone.

One of the legacies of the Attica trials was the impact of the ABLD. Though not the first trials to use expert social science research techniques to challenge potential jury composition or selecting juries, the Attica trials set a new standard for those efforts. At a minimum, the ABLD led a successful effort to change the venue from Wyoming County to Erie County (Buffalo), which probably enabled the defense to mount a more successful political struggle. Several of the Attica Brothers credited the ABLD with helping them win their trials. The ABLD efforts also delayed several of the criminal trials until a new governor took power in Albany and set in motion the eventual dismissal of indictments. Beyond the Attica trials, these jury techniques would be used in other trials, and expert consultation on jury selection would become a significant new part of American courtroom practice.

The United States in the post-Attica period has five times as many people in prison and most of them are still minorities. New York State currently has 74 prisons; in 1971, there were 16. Sentences now are two or three times longer then they were in 1971. Violence in prison is still prevalent, and guards, still mostly white, mistreat inmates (Butterfield, 2003). The war on crime, going strong since 1968, shows no sign of abatement, except that some politicians have noted its high cost. In New York State, there has been significant discussion of the need to repeal the draconian Rockefeller drug laws that played such a major role in the growth of the prison population. But, thus far, there has been no successful effort to repeal the laws, and the prison population remains large and continues to grow.

Attica reminds us of how high the costs of this mass reliance on imprisonment can be, with up to 3 million Americans imprisoned at any given moment. Prison is a difficult type of institution to administer and is a violent social institution. The goal of rehabilitation, established with the first prisons in the United States, is as elusive as ever.

SUGGESTIONS FOR FURTHER READING

Attica Revisited. A Talking History Web site. Accessed November 29, 2006, from http://www.talkinghistory.org/attica/index.html

Kairys, D., Schulman, J., and Harring, S. (1975). *The jury system: New methods for reducing prejudice.* Philadelphia: National Jury Project and National Lawyers Guild.

Light, S.C. (1995). The Attica litigation. *Crime, Law & Social Change, 23,* 215–234.

National Advisory Commission on Civil Disorders. (1968). *Report of the national advisory commission on civil disorders.* New York: Bantam.

New York State Special Commission on Attica. (1972). *Attica: The official report of the New York State special commission on Attica.* New York: Bantam Books.

Schulman, J., Shaver, P., Colman, R., Emrich, B., and Christie, R. (1973, May). Recipe for a jury. *Psychology Today,* 37–84.

Wicker, T. (1975). *A time to die.* New York: Quadrangle.

NOTE

1. The best account of the events at Attica is the New York State Special Commission on Attica in 1972; much of this chapter is based on the commission's findings.

REFERENCES

Butterfield, F. (2003, May 8). Mistreatment of prisoners is called routine in the U.S. *New York Times,* p. A11.

Cleaver, E. (1967). *Soul on ice.* New York: McGraw-Hill.

Goffman, E. (1961). *Asylums.* New York: Anchor.

Hunt, M. (1982, November 28). Putting juries on the couch. *New York Times Magazine,* p. 70ff.

Inmates of Attica Correctional Facility v. Rockefeller. (1971). 453 F.2d 12.

Kairys, D., Schulman, J., and Harring, S. (1975). *The Jury system: New methods for reducing prejudice.* Philadelphia: National Jury Project and National Lawyers Guild.

Levine, A.G., and Schweber-Koren, C. (1977). Jury selection in Erie County: changing a sexist system. *Law & Society Review, 11,* 43–55.

Light, S.C. (1995). The Attica litigation. *Crime, Law & Social Change, 23,* 215–234.

Malcolm X. (1964). *The autobiography of Malcolm X.* New York: Grove Press.

National Advisory Commission on Civil Disorders. (1968). *Report of the national advisory commission on civil disorders.* New York: Bantam.

New York State Special Commission on Attica. (1972). *Attica: The official report of the New York State special commission on Attica.* New York: Bantam Books.

Schulman, J., Shaver, P., Colman, R., Emrich, B., and Christie, R. (1973, May). Recipe for a jury. *Psychology Today,* 37–84.

Wicker, T. (1975). *A time to die.* New York: Quadrangle.